THE BOOK OF WORLD HOROSCOPES

THE BOOK OF WORLD HOROSCOPES

by

Nicholas Campion
President of the Astrological Lodge of London

THE AQUARIAN PRESS

First published 1988

British Library Cataloguing in Publication Data

Campion, Nicholas
The book of world horoscopes
1. Horoscopes
I. Title
133.5'4   BF1728.A2

ISBN 0-85030-527-6

*The Aquarian Press is part of the
Thorsons Publishing Group,
Wellingborough, Northamptonshire, NN8 2RQ, England*

Printed in Great Britain by Biddles Limited,
Guildford, Surrey

1   3   5   7   9   10   8   6   4   2

Dedicated to Michael Baigent
and Charles Harvey.

Et In Urania Ego . . .

CONTENTS

APPENDIX 1: INAUGURATION HOROSCOPES

APPENDIX 2: POLITICAL PARTIES

APPENDIX 3: TOWNS AND CITIES

APPENDIX 4: ECONOMIC ORGANIZATIONS

APPENDIX 5: MILITARY ORGANIZATIONS

APPENDIX 6: THE NUCLEAR ERA

APPENDIX 7: THE ERA OF MANNED FLIGHT AND SPACE TRAVEL

APPENDIX 8: EARTH ZODIACS

APPENDIX 9: WORLD HOROSCOPES

ABOUT THE AUTHOR

Nicholas Campion read History at Queens' College Cambridge, following which he took post-graduate studies in History and Politics at the School of Oriental and African Studies and in International Relations at the London School of Economics. He was awarded his M.A. by London University in 1975 for a study of the formation of the state of Malaysia.

He has studied astrology since 1972, and has worked as a professional astrologer since 1976. His other books include *An Introduction to the History of Astrology, Mundane Astrology* (with Michael Baigent and Charles Harvey) and *The Practical Astrologer*.

Nicholas Campion's work has appeared in various specialist journals including the *Investors Bulletin* and the *Journal of the Institute of Chartered and Technical Analysts*, and he has also worked as a regular contributor to *Today* newspaper. He teaches in adult education and has lectured widely on aspects of astrology and mythology.

He is currently President of the Astrological Lodge of London.

ACKNOWLEDGEMENTS

Deep thanks are owed to all those people who over the last seven years have sent me data from their collections, much of which appears in this book. In particular I would like to thank Derek Appleby, Julian Armistead, Michael Baigent, Olivia Barclay, Didier Basilios, Jenny Bennet, Andrew Bevan, Dymock Brose, Ernesto Cordero, Michael Edwards, Emily Fawcus, David Fisher, K. C. Foong, Dennis Frank, Russell Grant, Michael Harding, Antonio Harries, Charles Harvey, Ron Howland, Robert Hume, Chester Kemp, Nick Kollerstrom, Serafin Lanot, Jo Logan, Maurice McCann, Jeff Meddle, Ray Merriman, David Moncks, Al H. Morrison, Peter Nockolds, Rafal Prinke, James Russell, Derek Seagrief, Nadia Shakshir, N. D. Strachan, Peter Styles, Gregory Vlamis, Stephanie Walker, and all those others too numerous too mention.

Special thanks are also due to Neil Michelson and Astro Computing Services for their patience and professionalism. Without them this book would not have appeared in its present form.

PREFACE

Great advances have been made over the last two decades in the field of astrological data. The work of Françoise and Michel Gauquelin in researching birth times from birth certificates has set a new minimum standard for accuracy, and the published chart collections of Lois Rodden have drawn distinctions between data culled from reliable and that from less reliable sources. Astrologers who wish to study the horoscopes of the great, the famous and the eccentric now have a wealth of material at their disposal.

Yet in mundane astrology the situation is as bleak as ever. There are some half dozen collections of mundane horoscopes on the market, all riddled with elementary faults of the sort that the Gauquelins and Lois Rodden have helped to expunge from natal work. Horoscopes are poorly researched, and are often set for wholly inappropriate events and dates. Rectified charts are interspersed with those based on accurate times. Sources are misread, misquoted and even invented. Frequently no adequate sources are given. The naive astrologer is then left with no alternative but to use such horoscopes, often misled by the packaging which announces itself with such titles as 'Accurate World Horoscopes'.

This volume does not pretent to be an infallible and comprehensive guide to national horoscopes. However, every horoscope is based on a published source, and every source is given as precisely as circumstances allow. The purpose of this accuracy is to allow other astrologers to begin their own research as simply as possible, especially in the case of horoscopes for which there may still be some historical doubt.

This book represents an innovation in that the historical event upon which each chart is based is described, and when there are instances of different possible dates or times, or events of equal significance these are also given. For countries in which there are two or three possible national charts, all the alternatives are given. This is in complete contrast with the previous practice in which either no justification is given for the relevant horoscope, or that given is so brief as to be useless, is misleading, or even completely wrong.

If the day comes when astrologers claim that the date and time for which a horoscope is set are entirely irrelevant, and that a horoscope generated at random is as satisfactory as one cast for the time of an event, then there will be no complaint about such collections of data with all their rectified and spurious charts. There will also be no complaint about the cynical disregard for other astrologers which allows such charts to be dressed up with false claims of historical research. However, in the present climate, in which great importance is ascribed to exact times, the need for this present book is pressing and immediate.

The author and publishers hope that this book will provide a foundation for future work and a benchmark by which to judge all collections of mundane data.

INTRODUCTION

Part One

The Scope of this Book and the Uncertainty of Astrology

Astrology books consist mainly of rules for the interpretation of horoscopes, and the beginner is easily seduced into the belief that, once these rules have been learnt, he will be able to obtain a satisfactory interpretation and even make accurate predictions from any chart. However, problems are soon encountered. It is very soon found that synthesis of all the relevant factors in the chart is the final stage, and that in this, there is no such thing as an absolute rule. So-called rules are nothing more than guides to action, pointers to the astrologer to follow a certain path of interpretation, hoping that this will lead him to the right answer. The horoscope is a map, and astrology is the language that allows the astrologer to read its signs and symbols. Few astrologers ever begin and end in the same place. Many have different destinations, either aiming for a psychological reading, or a spiritual experience, or setting their sights on a prediction of a future event. Those astrologers that do reach the same destination will never agree on how they arrived there. Some will have travelled via a modern technique, some a traditional, some a trine and some a square. Judicial astrology therefore seems to be inherently uncertain in its workings.

Within astrology the mundane art magnifies these problems. The horary astrologer has only a limited range of specifics to consider. The natal astrologer has a person to work with, with a personality and aspirations that are relatively well defined. The mundane astrologer takes the whole world as his field of operations, with all the possibilities that the world contains, political, social, economic, geographical and psychological. The sheer scope of information, both astrological and otherwise, which the mundane astrologer is required to handle, dwarfs that needed by horary or natal astrologers, and the possibilities of interpretation are correspondingly huge.

The Rarity of Mundane Events

Uncertainty for the mundane astrologer is increased by the rarity of the types of events and situations with which it deals. The saturation news coverage of current affairs conveys the impression that we live in a world dominated by wars, violence, conflict, economic disasters and other events of the type that fill our newspapers and TV screens. This impression is highly misleading, and in a world in which there are some three hundred sovereign nations, and millions of industrial companies, wars, revolutions and strikes are exceedingly rare. In the last twenty years there have been only four genuine revolutions in the world — Iran, Kampuchea, Nicaragua and Portugal — an average of one every five years (I am excluding states where there have been been *coups d'état* or in which governments have been overthrown with no real change in the life of the people). Yet every year there may be half a dozen planetary configurations which indicate revolutionary potential, and perhaps thirty or forty countries in which such an event might be expected. The fact is that such alignments may manifest themselves through an enormous variety of different events, and in terms of the current state of the art, even the greatest astrologer is destined to be wrong on many occasions.

Astrology and the Mass

Why are powerful astrological alignments so rarely translated into corresponding events of sufficient magnitude? As far as events of a human nature, such as wars and revolutions, are concerned, the answer is clear. It is exceptionally difficult for groups of people to take decisions, and mundane events may involve many hundreds or even hundreds of millions of people. The consciousness involved is a group consciousness that is gripped by inertia and tends all too easily to be at the mercy of material circumstances. It is often said that mundane events are fated to an extent that the individual life is not, and this is offered as the reason for the tendency of crowds to act in irrational, hysterical or violent ways; the group often sanctions behaviour for which individuals are ostracized. Yet the reverse is also true and many countries in the world are remarkably peaceful precisely because of the dominance of the group mind. England is one notable example — it is now 350 years since the last major outbreak of civil violence, apart from the occasional riot. Indonesia is one state in Asia which has confounded political scientists by refusing to have a revolution in spite of the presence of all the normal socio-economic pressures. Other states are famous for their instability, even though material conditions may be easier than in those countries that do break down.

In other words the mundane astrologer is faced with two problems: the creature with which he is dealing — the collective mind — is far greater than the individual mind, and that much more difficult to comprehend. In addition, the expression of this mind is shaped through material circumstances which require considerably more understanding than those of any individual client an astrologer may encounter.

A good example of the interaction of the group mind with the material world to produce historical events is provided by the case of Nazi Germany, a trauma which unleashed forces so terrible that we are still struggling to understand what happened.

Orthodox historians have shown quite adequately that the rise of the Nazis can be explained by a network of socio-economic changes, such as the industrialization that threw large numbers of skilled artisans out of work, creating resentment against the political system and a readiness to listen to Hitler's dream of a new Germany. Yet while economic difficulties can be reflected in political upheaval, such arguments are entirely inadequate to explain the phenomenon of Nazism. Some historians explain Nazism in terms of the psychological trauma of defeat in the Great War, or the German national character. However, it was up to a psychologist, C. G. Jung, to develop the theory of the collective unconscious and its role in history.[962] Jung's explanation for Nazism was based on the eruption into the German national psyche of the long-suppressed archetype of Wotan, the ancient god of the Teutons.

Jung's theory is neat in that it complements the materialistic approach to history, while expanding the range of concepts open to the astrologer. However, problems remain, and Jung's work did not clear up the original problem of the uncertainty that seems to be inherent in astrology.

The Philosophical Background — Platonism

Jung's theory of the collective unconscious with its archetypes is essentially a restatement of the Platonic belief in the Ideal World of Being containing Ideal Forms, of which all physical things, in the material world of Becoming are a shadow or reflection. Such beliefs can be traced back to the earliest animist religions in which all physical matter was believed to contain the divine, and in which the gods and goddesses were immanent in all material objects, including the stars.

These beliefs are known as Idealist because they elevate consciousness — the realm of ideas — to a position of greater importance than matter. The opposing materialistic beliefs (held by most scientists, Marxists and behavioural psychologists) hold that consciousness and ideas are a bi-product of matter. It would be believed, for example that the mind is purely a product of the brain in combination with material circumstances.

Astrology itself is strongly Idealistic, and Idealism itself posits an inherent uncertainty in all human knowledge. In animist religion the future is uncertain because the gods and goddesses may change their minds and their intentions. In Platonic philosophy all knowledge gained by a study of the material world is uncertain precisely because that world is a mirage, and illusion, and a shadow of another Ideal, real world.

However, there is a paradox within astrology for though idealistic, its statements are derived from a study of the motions of the stars and planets, themselves physical bodies. For this reason, strict Platonic philosophers have, ironically, frequently been antagonistic towards astrology, and the art's most devastating critics have been Platonists. Yet in the West, Platonism has been appropriated as the dominant philosophy of astrology.

The Nature of Astrology

Where does this paradox leave the astrologer? The answer, surprisingly, is in an exceptionally strong position, for astrology's success in surviving for four thousand years is due to its ability, unlike any other art or science, to deal with both the physical and metaphysical understanding of existence. Astrology is at once both oracular and divinatory, magical even, and yet still essential to such physical matters as the movement of the Sun and seasons, the change from night to day or summer to winter. It is the only human study which is capable of uniting the fragmented disciplines of learning under one banner. Some astrologers call astrology an art, some a science, some call it psychology or divination. The truth is that no one explanation, description or definition will do, for it is by its own claims, all-encompassing. In modern terms it requires the use of both the right and left lobes of the brain, the faculties of reason and logic and those of unreason and intuition.

This much was well understood by the tenth-century Muslim

astrologer, Abu Ma'shar, who is credited with having written the *Centiloquium* ascribed to Claudius Ptolemy. The first aphorism of the *Centiloquium* defined the nature of astrological practice:

> Judgment must be regulated by thyself, as well as by the science; for it is not possible that particular forms of events should be declared by any one person, however scientific; since the understanding conceives only a certain general idea of some sensible event, and not its particular form. It is, therefore, necessary for him who practices herein to adopt inference. They only who are inspired by the deity can predict particulars.[963]

Given that the author of the *Centiloquium* overstated his case, for it most certainly *is* possible to make astrological judgements based on science (i.e. strict observance of the rules of astrology) alone, he was right to point to the broader nature of most astrological practice. He made the vital point that science — the rules of astrology — is in the main insufficient and weakened by the inherent uncertainty of astrology which then makes it necessary to 'adopt inference'. In the main it is only possible for those 'who are inspired by the deity' to 'predict particulars'. A modern view is that only those who allow themselves to use some intuitive or clairvoyant faculty (which we all have if we care to use it) can make accurate predictions. Even then

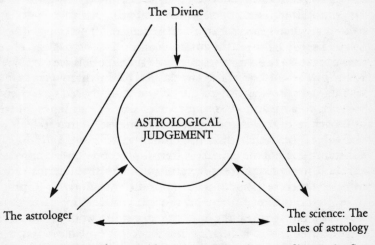

Figure 1. The threefold nature of astrological practice according to the first aphorism of Ptolemy. The complete practice of astrology requires the interaction of the astrologer with the rules of astrology and an additional level of inspiration.

the astrologer must work with common sense — 'Judgment must be regulated by thyself' (see Figure 1).

This book addresses itself solely to the question of astrological science. By the provision of accurate data it is hoped to give astrologers the tools to do their work better than in the past, but it is not pretended that a collection of horoscopes set for accurate times will make the bad astrologer a good astrologer, or compensate for the uncertainty that lies at the very heart of astrology.

It would perhaps not be helpful if this were the case, for it is in uncertainty that our capacity lies to make choices for the future, transforming the demands of Fate into the fulfilment of Destiny. As the author of the *Centiloquium* continues, 'A sagacious mind improves the operation of the heavens, as a skilful farmer, by cultivation, improves nature.'[964]

History, Mythology and Astrology

The analysis of change in the collective unconscious is a matter of subjective personal judgement, and by itself it cannot be measured or quantified. The corresponding evaluation of business, economic, social and political cycles is dependent on the quality and type of data gathered, and the individual inclinations and expectations of social scientists. Any attempt to relate the two is therefore riddled with uncertainty and liable to be easily dismissed. It must therefore be emphasized that models which relate the two are not designed as accurate descriptions of an objective state of affairs but as attempts to shed some light on the human condition, the passage of time and the events of history. In this sense such models are comparable to the myths which were used by classical historians to serve as moral lessons, or to provide insights into a state of affairs that was otherwise reduced to a meaningless sequence of battles and dates. Such an approach to history is known as 'substantialist' in that it deals with the substance, rather than the ephemera of human affairs. This substance cannot be analysed statistically, but only appreciated through myth or philosophy, and until the seventeenth century astrology was considered essential to the substantialist approach.

However, it is incumbent on the substantialist historian to take a reasonable view of the art, otherwise his work all too easily degenerates into an ignorant quest for occult explanations or a glib belief in divine intervention.

The Need for this Book

This collection of horoscopes fills a gap first mentioned by my predecessor as President of the Lodge, Charles Carter, in 1951. Carter discussed the failure of mundane astrology during the Second World War, and what should be done about this:

> During the Second World War there was, as was natural, a considerable amount of interest in Political Astrology, and my attention, as well as that of many others, was attracted to this work as never before.
>
> It soon became apparent that new methods and a vastly more copious and more trustworthy collection of data were needed; but this was more easily perceived than effected. [965]

Others have dealt with the quest for new methods; this book is a major step towards an adequate collection of data. I am not the first to continue Carter's work, and would like to pay tribute to two other former Presidents of the Lodge, Chester Kemp and Derek Appleby.

It may be surprising to the modern astrologer that national horoscopes are a relatively new invention. The first known political horoscope is 2,500 years old, and this is hardly surprising, for astrology's original concerns were political. Yet astrologers at the beginning of this century still rarely used horoscopes for countries. Instead they relied heavily on ingress and lunation charts combined with national astrological rulerships largely derived from Ptolemy's *Tetrabiblos*. Horoscopes were cast for cities, for politicians, for royalty and for events such as coronations and elections, but not for states. I have discussed the possible reasons for this in *Mundane Astrology*, drawing on the fact that the nation state is a fairly recent concept in human history. Even at the beginning of this century there was anxious correspondence in astrological journals concerning the relative merits of zodiacal rulerships for geographical areas, such as Palestine and for peoples, such as the Jews. [966] To combine these two into the chart for the nation state — the artificial institution of political organization in a defined geographical location, did not seem to occur to mundane astrologers.

The earliest example of a national horoscope known to the author seems to be that for the USA published by Ebenezer Sibly in 1787, [957] and Carter's *Political Astrology*, published in 1951, was the first British text to pay serious attention to these charts.

The material produced in this book is therefore almost entirely the product of recent research, and of these Sibley's horoscope for the USA was the only non-British chart published in the UK before this century.

Mundane Astrology and the Individual

Much is said these days about the 'holistic' nature of astrology, yet it must be said that those who proclaim this truth the loudest frequently have but a marginal knowledge of their own subject. They are usually psychological natal astrologers of a 'spiritual' complexion who have no grasp of horary astrology and but a superficial comprehension of mundane astrology. Yet the natal astrologer who has no knowledge of, or competence in, the other branches of astrology is no more a holistic practitioner than the modern doctor who treats symptoms but not causes, or who examines one part of the body and ignores another. Worse, with the restricted experience of astrology that results from an exclusive concentration on natal astrology, comes a limited understanding of astrology as a whole.

For the first two thousand years of its practice astrology dealt solely with the collective, and for a further two thousand it concerned itself with both the collective and the individual. Only in the twentieth century has the term astrology come to mean natal astrology alone. This is tragic, for the individual is still as much a part of the mass as ever, and by pandering to the excessive individualism of this century, astrologers are compounding a problem which is manifested in the alienation of individuals from their environment.

The truth is that just as the individual is contained within the collective, so natal astrology is contained within mundane astrology. By ignoring the collective, people will only surrender their personal ability to influence the directions it takes, and by ignoring mundane astrology, astrologers are distorting the balance of their art.

It is Charles Carter who is credited with formulating the doctrine of subsumption by which the natal chart is subsumed or contained within the group chart, and charts for small groups are subsumed within those of greater groups (see Figure 2):

> At the moment the horoscope of the individual, or nativity, appears to be the principal field of astrological study. But actually the nativity cannot adequately be considered as isolated from the social environment, as represented astrologically by horoscopes of greater amplitude. Could the nativities of the victims at Hiroshima all have indicated the death and ruin that overtook them on that fateful day of August 1945? Perhaps, and yet the horoscope of that city, could it have been studied, would surely have been helpful in judging them. [967]

Almost exactly two thousand years earlier, in about 44 BC, Cicero, a critic of astrology had made a similar point: 'Did all the Romans who fell at Cannae have the same Horoscope? Yet all had one and

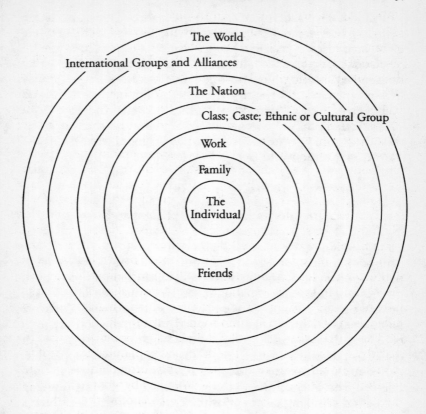

Figure 2.

the same end.'[968] The question has been waiting to be answered for two thousand years. Perhaps Carter was wrong in believing that the answer to his question could be found. But we shall never know until we have tried.

The Doctrine of Subsumption

The doctrine of subsumption draws on the nature of astrology expounded in the Hermetic tradition. As John Addey put it:

> Astrology belongs inherently to that tradition which sees the whole manifested cosmos, and everything in it, as being brought forth by a hierarchy of principles, proceeding from unity into multiplicity by stages in which each superior principle is the parent of a number of effects at a lower level.[969]

This model is not a totally satisfactory means of describing astrology, for event charts for plane crashes, space flights or gas explosions are difficult to place, especially when the degree of human involvement in relation to mechanical failure or success is difficult to assess. Neither does horary astrology fit into this model, unless one sees it as a divinatory short cut, bypassing the spheres of human existence and making straight for the realm of truth. Essentially the doctrine of subsumption refers to horoscopes for humans and their societies, though at some greater level the whole is contained within the horoscope for the world (see Appendix 8).

Part Two

Problems in Historical Research

The Question of the Historical Moment

This book was conceived in the summer of 1980 as a collection of national birth charts, that is, horoscopes for the foundation or birth moments of independent nation states. However, such an approach begged the question of when exactly is a state founded. There are many types of political unit in the world, all with their own systems of self-regulation, and it soon proved difficult to generalize about the birth moment, or to select criteria that were universally applicable.

Around the time that *Mundane Astrology* was in preparation, I agreed with Michael Baigent's hypothesis that 'the beginning of the period of taking of power' is the critical moment for which a national horoscope should be set, a principle which it seemed, could be applied with apparent simplicity to events such as *coups d'état* or revolutions. However, on closer study it became clear that in differing circumstances, the middle or the final culmination of the coup could be as critical. The hypothesis shifted in favour of the critical moment being that at which the balance of power passes irrevocably from the old order to the new.

Each society follows its own mechanisms for transferring power from one person or group to another in a legal, orderly fashion. These mechanisms may include coronation, election, or acclamation, may be ceremonial or bureaucratic and may take place in the full glare of public attention, as in the United States, or behind closed doors, as in the Soviet Union.

Every society in the world has also at some time experienced an illegal transfer of power via revolution, military coup or foreign invasion, although such events are invariably accompanied by legal processes or other means by which they are legitimized in the eyes of popular opinion or of a political or religious establishment.

What is at stake in all these events, legal or illegal, is power and its transference between groups and individuals, and in each country different criteria must be selected to determine when this moment takes place. These criteria must be relevant to the circumstances in the country itself, and must take into account the fact that such occasions always involve a process extending through a number of different events. In the United Kingdom, for example a change in government begins with a general election and culminates when the leader of the largest party is asked by the monarch to form a government. Even in the most violent revolutionary circumstances it is possible to discern series of critical events. The Russian Revolution, for example, broke out in February 1917, a republic was proclaimed in March, the Bolsheviks seized the capital, Petrograd, in November, and, after a long struggle, the Soviet Union came into *de facto* existence in 1922 and *de jure* existence in 1924. After consideration of all the historical issues, I concluded that the culmination of the Bolshevik coup at 2.12 a.m. on 8 November 1917, marked the critical moment at which power in Russia passed to the Communists from the old regime. The brute seizure of power by the Bolsheviks is given symbolic importance by the fact that they had taken over the capital city, not some provincial town, and that this moment was recognized as the crucial time in the revolution by Trotsky, who with Lenin was the main architect of the day's events. Until the final research for this book I had taken the time researched by Michael Baigent at which the Bolsheviks used the Soviets (workers' and soldiers' councils) to legitimize their rule, but, on the basis that this legitimization added little to the actual seizure of power now prefer the former moment.

A contemporary example is provided by the Iranian revolution of 1979. On 16 January 1979 the Shah left the country, leaving the old order intact but dying, his departure depriving that order of its power to resist the coming of the new order. On 1 February the Ayatollah Khomeini arrived in the capital, Tehran, to be welcomed by such massive popular support that the Government could control the institutions of state but not the country as a whole: the old and new orders were balanced. On 11 February the army leaders decided to remain neutral, depriving the Government of its power to control the institutions of the state and handing *de facto* — though not *de jure* — power, to the revolutionaries. Three days later, on 4 February, the socialist Bani-Sadr was sworn in as President, giving the revolutionaries control over the institutions of state and complete *de jure* power. However, the revolution had a further course to run and the new order was not formally created until 1 April when Khomeini proclaimed the inauguration of the Islamic Republic. The obvious question for the astrologer is which of the above dates to select for the horoscope of contemporary Iran.

In the present collection two possible dates have been selected. The first is that for Khomeini's arrival in Tehran, a moment of profound symbolic importance. From this date millions of Iranians looked to him as the legitimate authority inside Iran, and his arrival sealed the doom of the old order. It could also be seen as the inauguration of the Islamic regime in much the same sense as the Easter Rising is seen as the foundation of Eire even though independence was not achieved until six years later.

The second horoscope is set for the proclamation of the Islamic Republic, this being the culmination of the revolutionary process, the moment at which the new Islamic fundamentalism achieved complete legal control over the state.

Historically it is possible to discern a difference between the two events. The former represents, perhaps the personal rule of Khomeini. The second signifies the commencement of the Islamic Republic as a legal entity.

Astrologically the difference between the two may be tested using techniques of transit and progression. The purpose of including both charts here is to avoid a false impression that there is one national chart for Iran, and to encourage the use and investigation of different horoscopes.

This is a precise example involving one stage of transition in a country's life, but for many of the countries covered in this volume two or more possible horoscopes are given. In some cases this is a result of disputed data. In others it is because the state has experienced a number of major transformative points which require astrological study.

One further general principle that arises out of this historical confusion is the difference between charts based on the transfer of power through legal means — *de jure* — and that through revolution or military force — *de facto*. Some horoscopes are based on the former, some on the latter and most on a combination of the two. In cases when it is clearly based on one or the other this has been specified.

These instances are related not merely as examples of the problems of historical research, but as pointers to the author's current attitude. My attitude, based on the experience of researching this book, is that the search for the national birth chart is misleading. The real quest is for politically significant moments in the life of a society. Ultimately it does not matter whether this is a 'beginning' moment, an 'ending' moment, or any other sort of moment, so long as it has sufficient historical significance.

State and Society

The relationship between state and society was discussed simply in *Mundane Astrology*, so there is no need to cover the same ground in the present volume. It is sufficient to recall that national horoscopes are cast for significant moments in the life of the state, usually those at which power in the state changes hands or in which the state significantly reorganizes its constitutional system (which tends also to involve a transfer of power). Such moments are frequently declarations of independence, coronations, elections or revolutions.

The state itself has only an ephemeral existence, being represented by those institutions and systems of social relationship by which a society chooses to organize and regulate individual behaviour.

So, when a horoscope is cast for a state, the astrologer is really erecting the chart for a society at a particular stage in its development as witnessed in a major political event, that is, a moment for the reorganization of the state. The society itself has no beginning or foundation moment but in its current form is usually the cumulative result of thousands of years of historical development, hundreds of thousands of years of prehistoric human evolution and millions of years in the life of the planet.

It is obviously impossible to cast a birth chart for a society, so the political horoscope for the state is the next best thing, and in this sense may be perceived as the window through which the astrologer may see the condition of the society at any one time. It is also, of course, a map of the political life of the society.

It is also clear that the national chart may represent the culmination of a series of processes in the life of the state as much as it represents the beginning of a new order. The search is therefore that for significant moments, and once this is realized the researcher is freed from the narrow quest for elusive beginning moments, the point of foundation which may be lost. Such a practice is entirely consistent with ordinary astrological thought, which, although it makes great play of the need to isolate beginning moments, also insists that existence as embodied in the circular motions of the planets and zodiac has no beginning.

If this book is an attempt to answer the challenge laid down over thirty years ago by Charles Carter in the foreword to *An Introduction to Political Astrology*, when he defined the need for a collection of astrological data for nations and states, then it also represents a modification of Carter's definition of the criteria for that data. In Chapter 4 Carter drew a unifying proposition through all the different species of mundane charts — that they were all inceptions, or birth moments. If this proposition is discarded then the task becomes that much clearer.

This does not mean that such horoscopes should not be used as inceptional charts, having significance for the subsequent state or regime to which they refer, but that in historical research it must be recognized that there are no beginnings, only critical junction points when underlying trends of change manifest in major political moments.

Political Origins and Independence Horoscopes

Many national horoscopes are set for the moment at which states achieve their independence from a colonial master, yet it is entirely false to describe independence as marking the foundation or beginning of the state. Of all those states which achieved independence from the British Empire, only three — Israel, India and Pakistan — did not exist as political and territorial units prior to independence. There was usually an initial date at which the territory to be administered by the state was defined by the colonial rulers. Subsequently political institutions were created to exercise colonial power, themselves gradually accumulating more and more responsibility at the expense of London. Then, usually on a well-defined date, full internal self-government was granted, with local political organizations having legal control over internal administration while the imperial power retained control over military and foreign affairs (and retaining in practice the power to intervene in internal matters). The next step was for the colonial power to grant full sovereignty to the new state, at which point legal control was gained over foreign and defence matters. This is the point known as the granting of independence. However, there was usually a final legal step — the proclamation of a republic, removal of the last vestiges of legal power from London and full separation from the British Crown. Most countries left a decent interval of a few years after independence before making this final step. Burma made it at the same time as independence. Australia has still not made it: even in the 1970s an Australian prime minister was removed by order of the British governor.

The independence moment is therefore the culmination of a series of developments in the state, not its foundation. For example, the horoscope used for Zimbabwe is that for independence from Britain in 1980, yet this state was first defined territorially in 1899. The modern state is the product of that colonial territorial definition in combination with the political aspirations of a black society that has emerged from tribalism to modern political consciousness via a period of rule by Britain.

The concept of independence itself is relative and should not be elevated into some sort of totem. No state is truly independent. Many ex-colonial states remain in a condition of partial dependency either politically, militarily or economically on their former masters, or on the other nations and institutions of the industrialized world. Even the world's great powers lack genuine independence. For example the United Kingdom has voluntarily surrendered partial control of its foreign and defence policy as well as its internal economic and political administration to a series of international organizations, such as the EEC and NATO. At the same time, the country is in an unequal relationship with the USA, which has the power to influence its foreign policy, put pressure on its economy and even enforce its own laws within the UK.

The attaining of independence by a state is therefore not a magical point at which it comes into existence, or if already in existence, achieves some great control over its own destiny, but a point at which power shifts irrevocably from the old to the new order, the surrender of legal rights by the old order having reached a point at which the new order may successfully challenge what power the old order retains.

If this is borne in mind then cases of spurious independence are easy to spot. For example, France after 1945 devised the policy of offering its colonies independence 'within the French Union', a species of political existence in which the colonial power retained full control. Thus Cambodia was given independence by France on a number of occasions, each of which proved unsatisfactory, and a real measure of independence was only gained with the collapse of French military power in 1954.

Such habits were particularly rife until the 1960s, when the European countries finally found it impossible to hold on to their colonial possessions, and they account for a certain amount of confusion in determining the independence horoscopes of some countries.

A vivid example is provided by Egypt, which became effectively independent at the beginning of the nineteenth century while remaining under *de jure* Turkish control. In 1914 the country became a British protectorate, which meant that *de jure* control passed to Britain, which allowed the existing dynasty and political system to remain, but abrogated the power to interfere in any decision with which it disagreed. The presence of British troops provided the means to enforce this intention. 'Full independence' was granted in 1922 when the Protectorate was renounced by the British Government, and the Sultan was elevated to the rank of King.

However, the grant of independence becomes meaningless when the condition of the country before and after 1922 is compared. Before 1922 the country had retained its own ruling dynasty and political apparatus, which had to rule by taking the wishes of the British into account. After 1922 the same internal political structure continued, and the Egyptian Government still had to take British wishes into account, for British troops still garrisoned the country. It is possible to doubt, therefore, whether Egypt truly became independent in 1922.

Confusingly, it is equally possible to doubt whether the country was ever really part of the British Empire. It was never a colony directly administered from London, and was governed under a relationship with Britain, similar, say, to the relationship between Czechoslovakia and the Soviet Union. Then we may ask whether Czechoslovakia is a sovereign independent state. If it is, then so was Egypt before 1922.

The question is not purely academic, but an example of the pitfalls into which the astrologer will fall if universal criteria such as independence moments are accepted for all states.

The significance of the 1922 chart for Egypt is that it represents an irrevocable shift of power so that when, some thirty years later a group of rebellious generals, led by Colonel Nasser, overthrew the King and expelled the British, they were able to succeed. In a sense the horoscope for the Egyptian republic given below is also an independence chart.

So much depends on historical and political evaluation, and the astrologer must take this into account together with a historical analysis of local conditions. For example it must be understood that Egypt between 1914 and 1922 bore fundamentally the same relationship to Britain as Czechoslovakia to the Soviet Union since 1945, but the fact that Czechoslovakia is popularly considered to have been independent while Egypt was not is also significant.

The mundane astrologer must reconcile two disciplines. As he is using historical sources he must be familiar with the presuppositions of the historian and political commentator. But as an astrologer he must also take the assumptions of astrology into account.

An Astrological Perspective

Astrology deals in the symbolic and the significant, and an awareness
of phenomena which fall into this category can help with the quest
for data, and can introduce a new, non-historical criterion by which
data can be evaluated. There is, in my experience, a law in astrology
to the effect that if the time of an event given in a non-astrological
source produces a horoscope that is symbolically appropriate, then
that time is the appropriate time for the event, even if there is reason
to believe that the event occurred at a different time. This rule holds
good until such time as further research produces another quoted
time, at which point careful historical and non-astrological evaluation
must be made.

This law is represented in this book mainly in those charts cast
for *coups d'état*, and in which the time given in the press for the
coup may be set for a variety of different events. It may be for the
time at which the tanks begin to move, or at which the presidential
palace is seized, or at which the old government is arrested, or at
which the new regime is publicly announced, or at which the rebels
have complete control of the capital city or the country. In such cases
it may be impossible to work out historically the moment of the
taking of power, or of the irrevocable transfer of power from the old
to the new regimes, but the press has supplied a time. Working on
the sound principle that in an astrological universe nothing happens
at random, it follows that the selection by the press of such a time
becomes significant. This then becomes the working time from which
the astrologer must produce the national horoscope, if the change
of power is sufficient to warrant this. The horoscopes for the current
regimes in Libya and Iraq are two examples of this principle.

The phenomenon here is one in which historical records and
sources conspire to lead the astrologer to the appropriate time, a
concept which is legitimate within the realms of astrology, but not
in accepted contemporary historical practice. However, in everyday
practice this same phenomenon is quite accepted by many historians
in their own work. Most researchers experience the strange sensation
that arises when they casually walk past a shelf and idly pick up a
book which then happens to fall open at the right page, revealing
new information which shifts a block and presents a new avenue
for study. Such remarkable coincidences cannot be measured or
weighed by scientists but are an accepted part of human experience.
They may not be 'respectable' in the age of rationalism, but they
occur. The astrologer who stumbles across the appropriate time and
the appropriate horoscope is operating in the same dimension.

However, it must be insisted that this experience and understanding of astrology does not justify the deplorable, sloppy and dishonest habit of so many astrologers of passing off ignorantly researched charts as true mundane horoscopes. One might as well spin a roulette wheel and observe where the planets and signs come to rest.

This book is more than a collection of horoscopes. It is part of an attempt to bring a reconciliation between astrological and historical studies based on equal respect for the practices and assumptions and world view of both.

Part Three

The Accuracy of the Charts in this Book

Source Data

All the computer-drawn horoscopes based on precise times have been calculated by Astro Computing Services from data which I have personally checked in non-astrological sources, with the exceptions of the charts for the first powered manned flight, the French Third Republic, and for London Bridge. When historical sources pointed only to approximate times then full reasoning has been given in the text for the time used. When there was only a vague indication that the event in question occurred at night, a solar chart has been cast for 00.00 hrs LT, and when the evidence pointed to the day, a solar chart has been cast for 12.00 hrs noon LT. When there was no indication of any time a solar chart was cast for 00.00 hrs LT.

No rectification has been used and no computer-drawn horoscopes are based on rectified data taken from other sources.

Prior to the calculation of the horoscopes a complete list of data was compiled and sent to Astro Computing Services (ACS). I then checked the list against my own notes, and where possible, double-checked against the original sources. ACS meanwhile checked all the time differences and geographical co-ordinates and produced a computerized data listing. I then personally rechecked every item on this list against the original data listing, returned it to ACS, and subsequently double-checked it before giving authorization to proceed with the calculation of the charts.

The hand-drawn charts in the appendices at the back of the book have been reproduced from astrological sources for historical interest.

Time Changes

All time changes have been calculated either by Neil Michelson at ACS, or by me using, *The International Atlas*, by Thomas G. Shanks, published by ACS in 1985. If the data listing inside the chart wheel indicates that it was calculated in GMT, then the time difference was calculated by me. However, times given in the text are always as taken from the original source, so the accuracy of the calculations may be tested against these. Unless stated all times given in the text are in local time (LT). If there is an apparent discrepancy between the time given in the text and that printed in the centre of the chart wheel, the former is correct.

Some confusion arises over the use of the term 'midnight'. In most sources this means 00.00 hrs, although it can mean 24.00 hrs. For example, in *Keesing's Contemporary Archives*, midnight generally signifies 24.00 hrs although in some cases (such as the report on the independence of Guyana), it can mean 00.00 hrs. When this was unclear in the sources, reports were cross-checked in the daily press.

In this book 'midnight' always means 00.00 hrs.

The situation concerning the use of zone standard time and local mean time in all those states which came into being as a result of the Russian Revolution must be considered uncertain.

Latitude and Longitude

Even reputable atlases and gazeteers are likely to disagree by minutes or even degrees over the latitude and longitude of the same place. In some cases I took co-ordinates from the *Times Atlas of the World* which were corrected by ACS on the basis of the International Atlas. For the sake of consistency, co-ordinates given in the International Atlas were accepted.

Places

In some instances the historical sources were unclear as to the precise location of an event. In these cases the horoscope was set either for the current or the subsequent capital city:

Carpatho-Ukraine: chart set for Khust, the main town.
Chile, 1810 proclamation of independence: chart set for Santiago the subsequent capital.
Costa Rica, independence 1821: chart set for San José, the subsequent capital.

Costa Rica, independence 1848: chart set for San José, the subsequent capital.

Ecuador, independence 1822: chart set for Quito, the modern capital.

France, Vichy Republic: chart set for Paris, the capital.

Greece, revolution 1821: chart set for Athens, the subsequent capital.

Italy, proclamation 1861: chart set for Turin, the capital of Piedmont.

Nicaragua, independence 1821: chart set for Managua, the subsequent capital.

Nicaragua, independence 1839: chart set for Managua, the modern capital.

Switzerland: chart set for Altdorf, the main town of the canton of Uri, the focus of the independence movement.

Turkish Cyprus: chart set for Nicosia, the Cypriot capital.

Yugoslavia, kingdom, 1 December 1918: chart set for Belgrade, capital of Serbia and modern capital of Yugoslavia.

Planetary Accuracy

The accuracy of the planets from the Sun to Pluto has been specially extended by ACS back to 4004 BC to include the earliest charts in the book, and the results are the best that can be obtained with current technology. Chiron's accuracy extends back only to 1770 and this planet should be discarded for all charts prior to this date.

Historical Source Problems

Once an event has occurred it is not possible to repeat it to verify the time at which it took place. All historical records are based on human reporting, and so once the event is past, errors inevitably creep into even official accounts. Such errors then find their way into 'authoritative' works of reference, there to become established truth. Even immediately after an event, different newspapers may give their own accounts with varying times. Reference works compiled after a longer interval frequently contain erroneous and contradictory dates, let alone times. The researcher therefore needs to double-check all sources and to be able to evaluate the information in different sources according to its likely reliability.

An official report is most likely to be accurate, and a newspaper report which quotes verbatim from an official report is more likely to be accurate than one that does not. A detailed blow-by-blow account is also more likely to be accurate than one which carries only a vague report. Other historical accounts must be judged according to whether first-hand sources are being quoted, whether footnotes and references are given, and according to the academic standing of the author.

During the research leading to this book many instances arose of apparently contradictory data from different sources. When this concerned dates it was usually a simple matter to resolve, but when times were involved the issues were more complicated.

One example concerned the independence of the Philippines. According to the official account, independence was achieved when the United States flag was lowered and the Philippines flag was raised at 9.15 a.m., but a report in the *New York Times* specified a time of 10.00 a.m. In this case it was decided to rely on the official report. There are a number of reasons why the press report could have been inaccurate; there could have been a misprint in the paper; there could have been a misunderstanding between the reporter in Manilla and the editor in New York; the journalist in Manilla might have got his sources wrong, might have quoted a time based on an anticipated time for the flag changing, or might not even have been at the ceremony but might have been relying on other sources. A mistake is less likely to arise in an official account, compiled without the pressure and deadlines under which the journalist works.

In other instances a press report may correct an erroneous account in an authoritative reference. For example, the date of the proclamation of independence in Syria is given as 27 September 1941 in the *Statesman's Year Book*, normally regarded as an unimpeachable source. However, this event actually took place on 16 September 1941, and was reported in the *New York Times* on the following day.

The highly respected *Whittaker's Almanack* actually contradicts itself within its own pages. The 1925 edition reported on page 762 that the Hungarian republic was proclaimed on 12 November 1918, but on page 796 gave a completely different date for the same event — 17 November 1918.

The less reputable *Langer's Encyclopaedia of World History* reported on page 974 that the small Balkan state of Montenegro joined Yugoslavia on 1 December 1918, but on page 1021 that this union had already taken place on 26 November.

In such cases it was usually possible to turn to primary sources, chiefly contemporary press accounts, although these also proved inadequate in many cases, especially concerning Eastern and Central Europe.

Limitations on Research
The research for this book was constrained by those sources available

in England and in the English language, although some French
sources were also used. The evidence available to me was therefore
limited by what British and United States academics or newspaper
editors have considered newsworthy or important to study. The result
is that data for two regions tends to be much weaker than that for
the rest of the world. These two regions are Latin America and Eastern
and Central Europe.

Eastern Europe
I am satisfied that the book does contain accurately timed horoscopes
for all the modern countries of Eastern and Central Europe with the
exceptions of Austria, Hungary and Yugoslavia. However, for all the
countries of this region there are two periods of historical change
which require further research. These are the periods of the
disintegration of the Russian, German and Austrian Empires from
1917 to 1918 and that of the creation of the Communist regimes
from 1944 to 1948. The main problem with research in these areas
is caused by the inadequacy of the English language newspapers.
In 1917–18, the press was concerned almost exclusively with the war
on the Western Front, and reports from Eastern Europe, even from
Berlin or Vienna, could take as long as three days to reach London
and were often based on hearsay. The result is that press accounts
of the creation of five new republics — Poland, Czechoslovakia,
Yugoslavia, Austria and Hungary, vary from the non-existent to the
confused, inconsistent and self-contradictory.

In this situation standard histories are also frequently of no use.
These are predominantly concerned with the main trends, their causes
and results, rather than with chronology. It is for example, possible
to read all the accounts in the English language contained in the
British Library on the creation of the Hungarian republic, and still
emerge with only the haziest idea of when this took place. I was lucky
enough to find a full account of the creation of Czechoslovakia which
included a detailed chronology, but this was a very rare occurrence.

The 1944–48 period is also covered in little detail. The English
papers, especially *The Times*, suffered from the belief that anything
that did not concern the British Empire did not matter. *The Times*
still gave precedence to society gossip and cricket scores over
international news. Even the independence of India was given
coverage no more prominent than that for, say, the Henley Regatta.

The papers in general, including the normally excellent *New York
Times*, failed to report events in Eastern Europe in sufficient detail,
perhaps because one more coup in a small European republic was

about as interesting to their readership as a revolution in Peru might be to the average Briton. In other words, the significance of the events was not appreciated at the time. A cabinet change in Czechoslovakia which is now seen as marking the beginning of the Communist regime attracted little attention in 1948 when the country had experienced so many such changes and had, in any case, been under Soviet occupation since 1945.

Latin America

The severest source problems arose when trying to ascertain the dates of independence of the Latin American countries with the exception of Panama and Cuba and, of course, the non-Latin states of Central and South America. These states all achieved independence as a result of war and/or the gradual disintegration of colonial power, and in some cases the independence process lasted over twenty years. The English language sources for the history of Latin America tend not to deal with events that to the historian represent the trivia of political history but to the astrologer are vital parts of the jig-saw. In standard references the dates for events such as the proclamations of independence vary enormously. The classic work on Central America, Hubert Howe Bancroft's multi-volume history, is likewise confused, especially concerning the dates of independence of the Central American states from the Central American Federation.

Countries Not Included

Only two modern states are not included in this collection, Andorra and San Marino. In neither case was it possible to ascertain a horoscope based either on the origins or history of the respective states, or their current constitutional practice. Other twentieth-century states which are no longer independent and which are not included are Tibet, the United Arab States, Kasai, Tanu Tuva, Manchukuo, the Baltic State, Fiume, Katanga, the Moldavian Republic, and the Republic of the Don.

Further Research

In view of source and research problems it is unlikely that a truly comprehensive collection of national horoscopes could ever be compiled and this book does not pretend to be such a work. It is, however, to my knowledge the most comprehensive work to date, and the only one to include detailed sources and footnotes for all data. This is in contrast to some other books which have provided no sources, or have even manufactured sources, and which have therefore contained a high proportion of erroneous charts. The purpose of providing detailed references is so that in those cases where no times have been located, or where data may be disputed, it is possible for other researchers to take up the search.

The obvious areas in need of further research include Latin America and Eastern Europe, although particular countries on which further work is needed include Portugal, and Belgium in Europe and China in Asia.

The only authoritative research for Latin America will have to involve Spanish (or for Brazil, Portuguese) language sources, and may only be possible using the archives of the countries concerned.

Politicians' Data

It was originally hoped to include a section on politicians' horoscopes in this book. However, it was found that existing research was in many respects flawed, and that there was insufficient time to compile a reputable listing of data. This is especially the case with British politicians, and even prime ministers. There is scarcely a British prime minister for whom there is an undisputed and authenticated birth time. That this is so is largely the result of the low standards expected by astrologers in the past, a failure to quote adequate sources when these exist, and a willingness to confuse rectified charts with those based on quoted times. Every existing horoscope for past British prime ministers therefore requires thorough re-checking.

An excellent collection of the data of prime ministers, monarchs and presidents from France, Germany, the United Kingdom, Austria, Belgium, Spain, the United States, Italy, and the Soviet Union, is given in Andre Barbault's *La Prévision de l'avenir par l'astrologie*, published in Paris in 1980 and corrected and updated in 1986 as *La Prévision astrologique*, published by Editions Traditionelles, 11 Quai Saint Michel, Paris V^e.

All Barbault's data is based on stated sources, the majority from birth certificates or other civil documents, and the remainder from biographies, encyclopaedias or dictionaries. However, although the type of source (birth certificate, biography and so on) is included against the relevant data, the individual source is not. This then makes further checking and the resolution of disputed times very difficult, a particular problem in the case of British prime ministers.

Michel and Françoise Gauquelin have compiled an extensive list of birth times of politicians from Germany, France, Italy, Belgium and the Netherlands taken from birth certificates, for which regular updates or corrections are provided in the Françoise Schneider (formerly Françoise Gauquelin) journal, *Astro-Psychological Problems*. This data is as reliable as is possible, given that the only errors that cannot be corrected will result from the original recording of the data. However, the Gauquelins' purpose was to collect large samples of data for statistical research, and there is no emphasis in their lists on those famous and newsworthy politicians who are of special interest to the mundane astrologer. Some important names are therefore missing.

The data is available as 'Birth and Planetary Data Gathered Since 1949, Series A, Volume 5, Actors and Politicians', by Michel and Françoise Gauquelin, from Laboratoire d'Etude des Relations entre Rythmes Cosmiques et Psychophysiologiques, 8 Rue Amyot - 75 - Paris V^e, France.

The Calculation of Historical Charts
It is obviously essential to use computers to calculate horoscopes for those dates for which printed ephemerides are unavailable, which in most cases means all charts set for before 1900. However, the unwary should be aware that most computer programmes become increasingly inaccurate for past centuries. A graphic example of this was revealed recently in my own experience when two different programmes were used to compute the horoscope for the time Napoleon took power in France (see Chart 94). One programme produced results much as in this book while the other calculated the planetary positions for twenty-four hours earlier.

In such circumstances it is essential to use the best programmes and computers available, and in my experience these are operated by Astro Computing Services, who calculated all the computer-drawn horoscopes in this book. ACS have an additional service of special interest to the mundane astrologer; they will provide an ephemeris page, of the same format as in their *American Ephemeris* for one month of any year between 2500 BC and AD 2500, an essential tool if progressions are to be used.

Astro Computing Services are to be found at PO Box 16430, San Diego, California 92116–0430, USA.

NATIONAL HOROSCOPES

AFGHANISTAN

It is not possible to establish a 'birth date' for Afghanistan. For long periods during the last two thousand years there have been independent kingdoms based in the same geographical area as modern Afghanistan, but the region was also frequently under the sway of more powerful neighbours, often forming a part of a succession of empires based in Persia.

Since the mid nineteenth century the state has maintained its independence in the face of global rivalries, initially between Russia and the British Empire and in recent decades between the USSR and the USA.

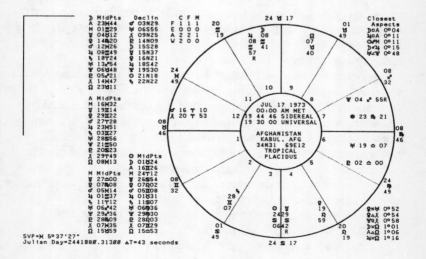

1: Afghanistan, Republic 1973

The current regime in Afghanistan is the third in a series that commenced with the *coup d'état* of 17 July 1973. Pressure for modernization in Afghanistan had resulted in a previous constitutional adjustment on 20 September 1962 when the absolute monarchy accepted constitutional restraints. The abolition of the monarchy in 1973 was essentially a palace coup, but it did pave the way for the current Communist regime.

The 1973 coup was led by General Daoud, the brother-in-law of King Mohammed Zahir Shah. No accurate times are available for the progress of the coup, but it seems that late in the night of 16 July troops from the garrison of Kharqua Sharaf, 30 miles from Kabul, moved into the capital city, surrounding the radio station, government offices and the royal palace.[1] Having secured control of Kabul, General Daoud proclaimed the republic, of which he was to be President, during the morning of 17 July.[2] News of the proclamation was broadcast by Delhi Radio in India at 6.35 a.m. GMT, the proclamation itself therefore having been prior to this time.[3] In the absence of exact records the horoscope for the Afghan Republic (Chart 1) is set for 00.00 hrs LT.

A further horoscope for contemporary Afghanistan could reasonably be set for the first Communist coup of 30 April 1978.

ALBANIA

During the Medieval period Albania enjoyed some periods of autonomy, although it was generally under the domination of its neighbours — Venetians, Serbs and Greeks. Following their conquest of Constantinople in 1453, the Ottoman Turks occupied Albania, retaining control until 1912.

Independence was proclaimed by the first National Assembly meeting at Valona (also known as Valone, Vlore or Vlone) on 28 November 1912.[4] The independence of Albania was promoted by the Austrians and Italians with the aim of preventing the imminent Serbian conquest of the country, backed by France and Russia. It was therefore left to the subsequent great power Conference of London in 1912 to 1913, to secure international recognition for the new state. However, in view of the collapse of Turkish authority, independence was effective from the Declaration of Valona.

In the absence of accurate records the horoscope for independence (Chart 2) is set for 12.00 hrs noon LT.

Albania was occupied by the Italians on 12 April 1939, and Communist control of the country was complete with the liberation of Shkoder, the last German-held town, on 29 November 1944. The

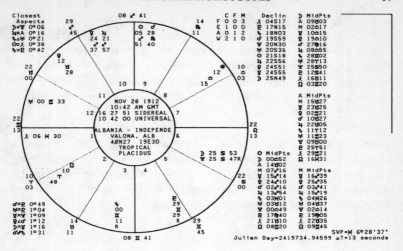

2: Albania, Independence, 1912

first step towards the formation of a legal Communist government was the meeting of the First Congress of the Anti-Fascist Council of National Liberation of Albania in Permet from 24 to 28 May 1944. The provisional Communist-dominated government was recognized

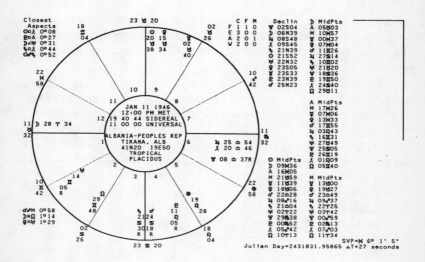

3: Albania, Communist, 1946

by the UK, USA and USSR on 10 November 1945.

The formal proclamation of the Peoples' Republic, marking the full implementation of the Communist constitution and rule, occurred on 11 January 1946 in Tirana. In the absence of any press reports or other accurate records, the horoscope for the Communist regime (Chart 3) is set for 12.00 hrs noon LT on 11 January 1946.[5]

ALGERIA

Following a period under Turkish suzerainty, Algeria was occupied and colonized by France during the nineteenth century. Following a long and bitter rebellion, Algeria was granted independence by France on 3 July 1962. The *New York Herald Tribune* of 4 July carried the most detailed English language report:

> President Charles de Gaulle, acting in the name of the nation, today solemnly renounced France's 132-year-old rule of Algeria.
>
> In a proclamation published at 10:38 a.m. Gen. de Gaulle announced the birth of the new nation.
>
> 'The President of the French Republic', he declared, 'solemnly recognises the independence of Algeria'.
>
> At that moment, in the eyes of France, the North African country she invaded in 1830 officially became an independent and sovereign state.[6]

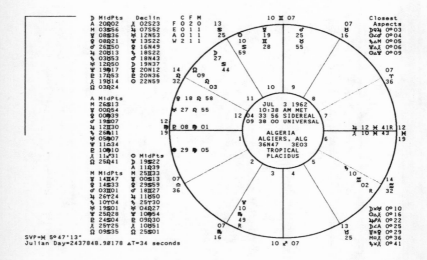

4: Algeria, Independence, 1962

The publication of the proclamation of independence was given in other sources as 10.30 a.m.[7] There are two possible explanations for this confusion. Either publication was scheduled for 10.30 a.m. but delayed to 10.38 a.m., or the *New York Herald Tribune* carried a misprint. On the assumption that the former explanation is correct the horoscope for independence is set for 10.38 a.m., but the question must remain open. A similar problem arises with the time for the independence of the Philippines.

ANGOLA

Angola was granted independence from Portugal at 00.00 hrs on 11 November 1975, following a long rebellion. The independence celebrations began in the capital, Luanda, at the moment of independence, although the new President, Agostino Neto, was sworn in during the late morning.

Neto was the leader of the dominant liberation movement, the left-wing MPLA, but parts of the country were under the control of its South African and CIA-backed rivals, Unita and the FNLA. These two groups held their own independence celebrations, Unita in Huambo (formerly Nova Lisboa) and the FNLA in Carmona Ambriz. Holden Roberto, the leader of the FNLA, was proclaimed President on behalf of the two South African backed groups in Kinshasa, the capital of Zaïre.[8]

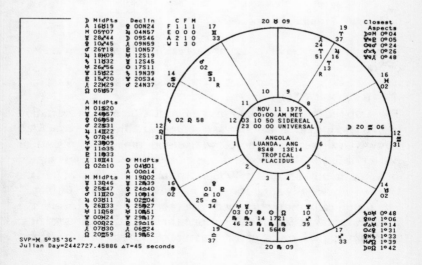

5: Angola, Independence, 1975

The horoscope given here (Chart 5) is that for official independence at 00.00 hrs on 11 November 1975 in Luanda.

ANTIGUA-BARBUDA

The Caribbean island state of Antigua-Barbuda was granted independence by Great Britain at 00.00 hrs on 1 November 1981.

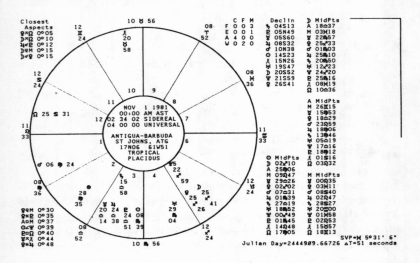

6: Antigua Barbuda, Independence, 1981

It remains a member of the Commonwealth with the Queen as Head of State.[9]

ARAB FEDERATION

The Arab Federation, also known as the Àrab Union, was a federation of Iraq and Jordan. It was seen as a conservative move towards Arab unity as an alternative to the left-wing unions proposed by President Nasser of Egypt. The proclamation creating the union was signed at 7.30 a.m. on 14 February 1958 in Amman, the capital of Jordan, and simultaneously announced in Baghdad, the capital of Iraq.[10] The union came into effect with the proclamation and while the horoscope may reasonably be set for either capital city, it is set here for Amman, the location of the signature of the proclamation (Chart 7).

King Hussein of Jordan and King Feisal of Iraq were second cousins, both being great-grandchildren of Sherif Hussein, the leader of the

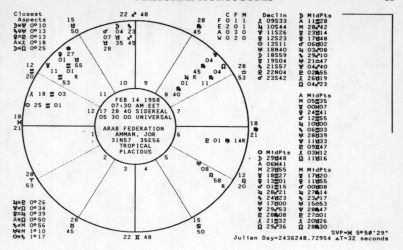

7: Arab Federation, Formation, 1958

Arab revolt against the Turks, and the union was broken up by the *coup d'état* in Iraq on 14 July 1958. Following the murder of King Feisal on the morning of 14 July, King Hussein succeeded him as head of the union at 3.17 p.m. The new Iraqi regime refused to recognize Hussein's action and announced its decision to withdraw from the union at approximately 10.45 p.m. [11]

ARGENTINA

There are two main plausible dates for which Argentinian independence may be set.

Following the proclamation of Joseph Bonaparte, brother of Napoleon, as King of Spain on 6 June 1807, and the collapse of the authority of the Bourbons, the Spanish colonies in Latin America began to move towards self-rule rather than accept the authority of the Bonapartes.

A leader in this movement was the city of Buenos Aires, where a congress of local dignitaries met on 22 May 1810 to decide how to cope with the breakdown of Spanish authority. On 25 May the Spanish Viceroy was deposed and a patriotic junta installed. Formal Spanish authority was still acknowledged, but effective independence was taken, and this was the only Latin American revolution during the Napoleonic wars that was to be successful. Effective Argentinian independence is dated from the revolution of 25 May. [12] In the absence of accurate records the horoscope for this

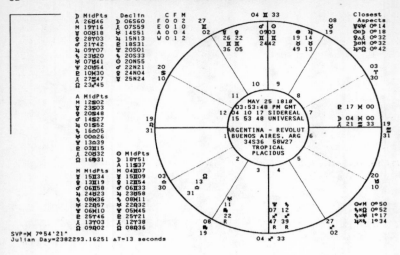

8: Argentina, Revolution, 1810

date is cast for 12.00 hrs noon, LMT (Chart 8).

The formal declaration of independence by the United Provinces
of La Plata, as the state was then known, was issued on 9 July 1816
by the Congress of Tucuman.[13] The time for the declaration has not

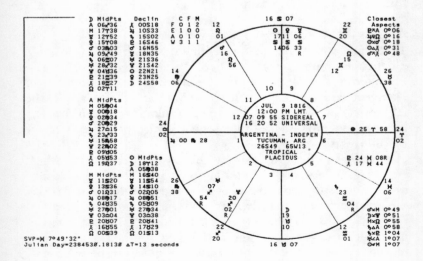

9: Argentina, Independence, 1816

been historically confirmed, although a horoscope set for 2.00 p.m. LMT has been published.[14] Other times are in circulation amongst astrologers, including one for 12.04 p.m. LMT.[15] It is recommended that in these, as in all cases in which adequate sources are not supplied, the times be disregarded.

The horoscope given here is a solar chart set for 12.00 hrs noon LMT in Tucuman (Chart 9).

ARMENIA

Armenia achieved independence for the first time since the medieval era in 1918. Initially the state separated from Russia as part of the anti-Bolshevik and nationalist Transcaucasian Federative Republic. This republic effectively came to an end when Georgia seceded on 26 May 1918, Armenia then becoming an independent state. In the absence of accurate records the horoscope (Chart 10) is set for 12.00 noon in the capital, Eriven, on 26 May 1918.[16]

Other evidence suggests that Armenia did not formally secede from the Transcaucasian Federative Republic until 28 May,[17] although this does not change the date of effective independence. A subsequent declaration of independence, issued in Paris on about 1 December 1918 by the Armenian National Delegation to the great powers meeting at Versailles, would seem to have been aimed at Turkish Armenia.[18] The Turks finally recognized the independence of the

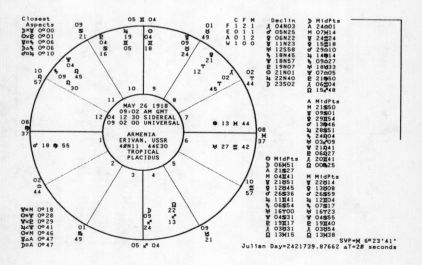

10: Armenia, Independence, 1918

Turkish portions of Armenia at the Treaty of Sevres on 10 August 1920.[19] On 2 December 1920 a Bolshevik regime was set up, to be followed by a second Nationalist regime in February 1921 and a second Bolshevik government on 2 April 1921.

On 12 March 1922 Armenia surrendered its independence by joining the Transcaucasian Soviet Socialist Republic, a Bolshevik revival of the Transcaucasian Federative Republic.[20]

The Turkish portions of Armenia were reconquered by Turkey during the early 1920s.

AUSTRALIA

Australia is an effectively independent member of the Commonwealth, with the British monarch as Head of State. The British authorities retain residual powers, and these were last exercised in the dismissal of the Australian Labour Government by the British Governor in the late 1970s.

Two horoscopes are given here for the Australian Federation. The first is set for 00.00 hrs on 1 January 1901, in Melbourne, the new capital city (Chart 11). This is based on the assumption that the legal implementation of the legislation creating the federation came into effect at this time. In Melbourne the celebrations began at a banquet held on the night of 31 December 1900 to 1 January 1901.[21] The second horoscope (Chart 12) is set for the ceremonial proclamation

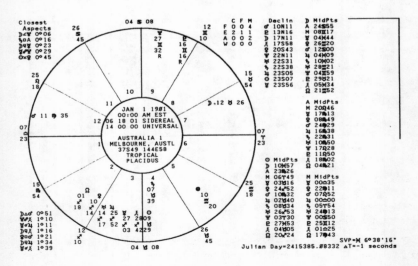

11: Australia, Legal Creation, 1901

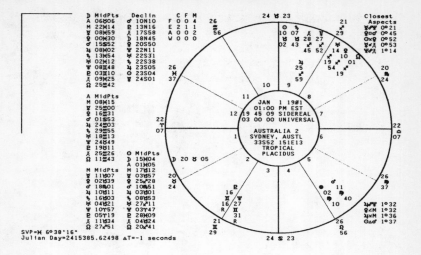

12: Australia, Independence Ceremony, 1901

of the federation at approximately 1.00 p.m. on 1 January in Sydney.[22] It seems that there were two significant moments, one a formal, legal moment, and the other a symbolic and ceremonial one.

Other horoscopes for Australia may be set for the time when Captain Cook landed on Possession Island on 22 August 1770, for the establishment of New South Wales colony on 26 January 1788, the foundation of Tasmania on 3 December 1825, the proclamation of Western Australia on 18 June 1829, of South Australia on 28 December 1836, Victoria colony on the 1 July 1851, and Queensland on 10 December 1859.[23]

AUSTRIA

The name Austria is first found in a document of the Holy Roman Emperor Otto III, issued on 1 November 996, and referring to Ostarrichi. The traditional anniversary of the first use of the name is held on 28 October.[24] Austria began its rise to the status of a great power in the twelfth century. Following the election of its ruler, Rudolf of Hapsburg, as Holy Roman Emperor in 1273, the arch-duchy became the centre of an empire that was to last until 1918.

In the absence of any feudal 'foundation' the most appropriate date for an Austrian horoscope is found in the proclamation of the Republic in 1918. The circumstances surrounding this event are confused.

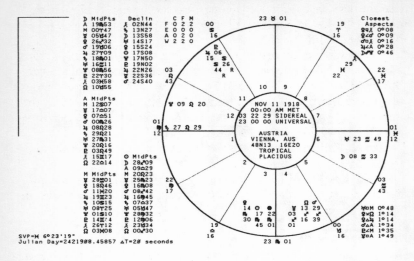

13: Austria, Republic, 1918

During October 1918 the Austro-Hungarian Empire began to disintegrate, and on 21 October the Austrian National Council in Vienna proclaimed the independence of German Austria from the other parts of the Empire.[25] This proclamation seems to have had little effect.

On 30 October an insurrection broke out in Vienna which resulted in the proclamation of a republic by the President of the National Assembly.[26] However, the Emperor continued to exercise authority, and no legal recognition was given to the proclamation.

The crucial event took place 'in the early hours of November 11th 1918' in Vienna, when the Emperor Karl signed 'what was in effect an abdication'.[27] In fact the document was a 'withdrawal' which allowed the Emperor the option of returning at a later date. In spite of the Emperor's reservations, the document was taken as an abdication by Austrian politicians, and later in the day the third sitting of the Provisional National Assembly passed a law establishing German Austria as a democratic republic.[28]

In spite of the importance of the event the historical records are vague and confused. Even though the law proclaiming the Republic was passed in public, and to applause from the public galleries, no time was recorded in the secondary sources and some texts give 12 November for the proclamation of the Republic and 13 November for Charles' abdication.[29] The position is partly confused by the facts that the new Chancellor, Karl Renner, was sworn in on 12 November[30] and by Charles' separate abdication as Emperor of Hungary on 13 November 1918.

The newspaper reports of the time were unclear. The *New York Times* of 13 November carried the following report. 'Copenhagen, Wednesday. Nov. 13 (3.50 a.m.) The abdication of Emperor Charles of Austria is officially announced.'[31] No date was specified in the text and it is not clear whether the date and time in the headline refer to the event or the despatch.

Similar confusion surrounds the creation of all the successor states to the Austrian Empire.

In the absence of historically recorded times, the horoscope for the Austrian Republic is set for 00.00 hrs on 11 November 1918, in Vienna (Chart 13).

AZERBAIJAN

During the disintegration of the Russian Empire in 1917 Azerbaijan became part of the independent nationalist Transcaucasian Federative Republic. The federation disintegrated following the secession of Georgia on 26 May 1918, but formal independence does not seem to have been assumed in Azerbaijan until 28 May. The precise position is confused.[32] In the absence of more detailed records the horoscope is set for 12.00 noon on 28 May 1918 in Baku, the capital

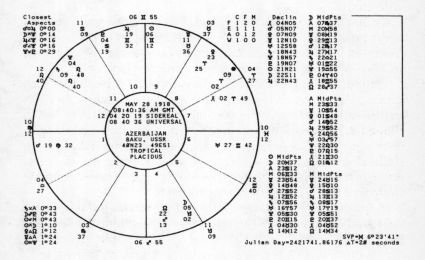

14: Azerbaijan, Independence, 1918

city (Chart 14). From 1918 to 1920 a socialist 'Menshevik' regime controlled the country, being replaced by a Communist administration after the Bolshevik occupation of Baku on 27 to 28 April 1920. Independence was surrendered on 12 March 1922 through union with Armenia and Georgia in the Transcaucasian Soviet Socialist Republic.

BAHAMAS
The Bahamas were granted independence from Great Britain at 00.00 hrs on 10 July 1973.[34] Chart 15 is set for this data.

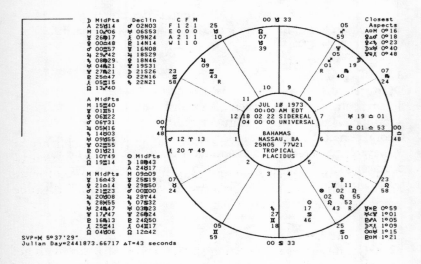

15: Bahamas, Independence, 1973

Formal ceremonies were held at 10.00 a.m., and the British monarch remained Head of State.

BAHRAIN
Bahrain was granted independence from Great Britain on 14 August 1971. It seems that the formal end of British control centred on the termination of various treaty agreements during the day of 14 August, but neither the British Parliamentary Papers nor any English language press report give any indication of the time.

The proclamation of independence was broadcast over the radio during the day by Shaykh Isa Bin Salmon Al Khalifeh, and Iran radio reported that the proclamation was published during the afternoon.

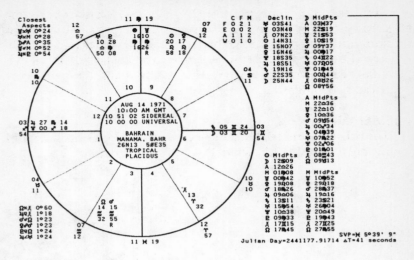

16: Bahrain, Independence, 1971

Kuwait radio broadcast the news of Bahrain's independence at 10.00 a.m. GMT (1.00 p.m. LT).[33] This suggests that the time of independence was at or around midday. In the absence of more accurate times, the horoscope is cast for 10.00 a.m. GMT, the time of the Kuwaiti broadcast (Chart 16).

BANGLADESH

The circumstances surrounding the formation of Bangladesh are highly confused, even though the state came into being as recently as 1971.

The rebellion in the then state of East Pakistan began on 23 March 1971. When the Pakistani authorities declared a curfew at 2.20 a.m. GMT on 26 March, and proclaimed martial law at 4.00 a.m. GMT, the fighting developed into open rebellion.[35] During the evening of 26 March Sheikh Mujibur Rahman, the nationalist leader, proclaimed East Pakistan independent as the Sovereign Independent People's Republic of Bangladesh.[36] This is clearly a vital moment, and the first horoscope is set for 26 March. In the absence of an accurately recorded time the chart is set for 12.00 hrs noon, even though the proclamation took place in the evening (Chart 17). The proclamation was not reported by Dacca radio during its summary of the day's events.[37] The date 26 March is recorded in various secondary sources as the effective proclamation of independence,

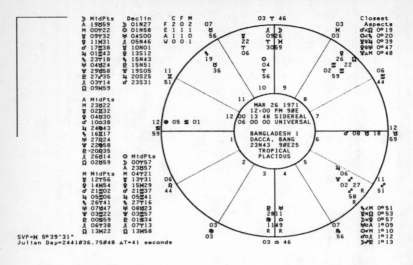

17: Bangladesh, Proclamation, 1971

even though Pakistani forces continued in control.[38]

The second date often considered as the foundation of Bangladesh is 17 April 1971, when a government in exile was formally established at Delhi.[39] A formal flag-raising ceremony took place, but the event

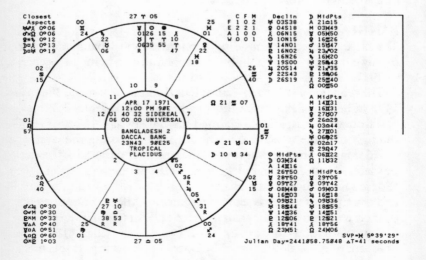

18: Bangladesh, Government in Exile, 1971

attracted little attention; for example it was not reported in *The Times* even though Bangladesh joined the Commonwealth on 18 April (signifying full international recognition). In the absence of accurate recorded times the horoscope for this event is set for noon. The proclamation took place in Delhi, but the horoscope here is set for Dacca, the future capital of the independent state (Chart 18). A chart set for Delhi may yield more accurate results.

Actual independence came to Bangladesh with the surrender of the Pakistani Army in East Bengal. The evidence surrounding this event is also confused. An original ceasefire between Indian and Pakistani forces was scheduled for 2.30 p.m. on 15 December 1971, but this seems to have been ineffective, with air attacks on Dacca continuing until 5.00 p.m.[40]

According to press reports, Pakistani forces in East Bengal — now to be independent Bangladesh — surrendered at 11.01 a.m. GMT (5.01 p.m. LT) on 16 December,[41] while radio reports recorded that the Pakistani Army signed its surrender at 2.45 p.m.[42]

From 16 December, authority in Bangladesh was vested in the Bangladesh government. Given that the discrepancy between press and radio reports cast some uncertainty on the matter, the third chart is cast for 11.01 a.m. GMT on 16 December 1971 in Dacca (Chart 19).

An additional moment of symbolic importance occurred when the new government arrived in Dacca. The acting President of

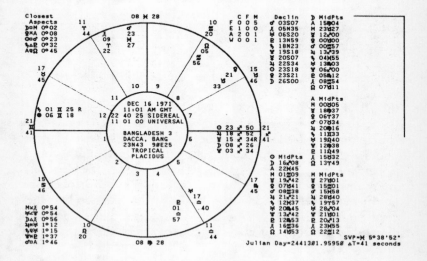

19: Bangladesh, *de facto* Independence, 1971

Bangladesh, Sayed Nasrul Islam, flew into Dacca from Delhi on 22 December 1971. He arrived at the airport and made a speech, the first ceremonial act of the new government, at 11.00 a.m. GMT [43]

BARBADOS

The Caribbean state of Barbados gained independence from Great Britain at 00.00 hrs on 30 November 1966.[44] The state is a member of the Commonwealth with the British monarch as Head of State.

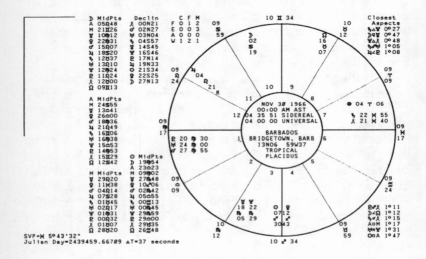

20: Barbados, Independence, 1966

Chart 20 is set for this data, and for the capital, Bridgetown.

BELGIUM

During the fourteenth and fifteenth centuries the area now occupied by Belgium consisted of a series of minor feudal states under the control of the Dukes of Burgundy. At the end of the sixteenth century the lands of the Duchy of Burgundy were inherited by the Hapsburg family and, until the 1790s the area was under the control of first the Austrian, then the Spanish, and finally the Austrian branches of this family. In the 1790s the area was conquered by France, and from 1814 formed part of the Kingdom of the Netherlands, ruled from The Hague.

During 1830 the southern, predominantly Catholic portion of the kingdom rebelled against the northern, predominantly Protestant

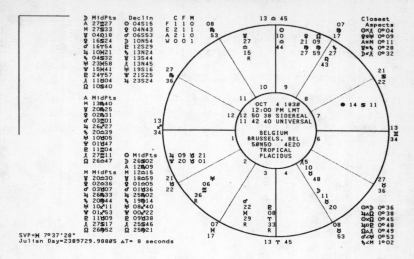

21: Belgium, Independence, 1830

part. A formal proclamation of independence by Belgium was issued
on 4 October 1830. Although this is a vital symbolic event,
contemporary press reports attached little importance to it as the
insurrection against the Netherlands was already under way.[45]
Nevertheless, with hindsight this can be seen to be a crucial date.
In the absence of a recorded time, the horoscope for the proclamation
of independence is set for 12.00 noon.

Belgium achieved *de facto* international recognition under the
Treaty of London on 20 December 1820, and the final signature of
this treaty on 19 April 1839 marked the country's full legal
independence. These events were constitutional developments which
were of little significance in the face of the reality of Belgian self-rule.

BELIZE
Belize gained its independence from Great Britain at 00.00 hrs on
21 September 1981.[46] Chart 22 is set for this data, and for the capital,
Belize City.

BENIN
Benin, formerly known as Dahomey, was granted independence from
France within the French Community on 4 December 1958. However,
the French retained total control and genuine independence was
not granted until 1 August 1960.[47] Although no press reports could

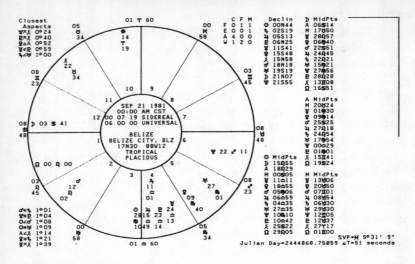

22: Belize, Independence, 1981

be located which mentioned a time for independence, this may be assumed to be 00.00 hrs, the time at which all the other French sub-Saharan territories gained independence. Chart 23 is set for this data, for the capital, Porto Novo.

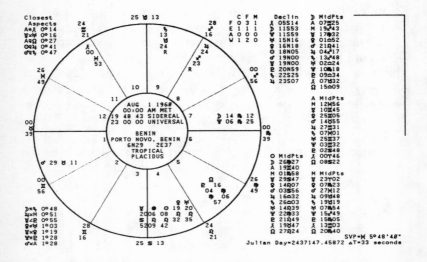

23: Benin, Independence, 1960

On 30 November 1975 it was announced that as from 30 December 1975 Dahomey would be known as Benin.[48] This state is not to be confused with the mid-western state of Nigeria which enjoyed brief independence under the name Benin in the 1960s.[48a]

BHUTAN

Bhutan is a kingdom in the Himalyas whose historical origin is obscure. The current horoscope at any time should be that for the coronation of the reigning monarch, the moment for this being elected by the court astrologers. The present king, Jigme Singye Wangchuk, succeeded his father on 21 July 1972 and was formally enthroned on 24 July 1972.[49] Astrologically however, the crucial moment was the coronation which 'was not held until a year of national mourning had been held and the Buddist clergy had decided on an auspicious astrological conjunction for the ceremony'.[50]

The coronation itself was held on 2 June 1974, the significant moment coming 'just after 9.00 a.m. at the auspicious hour of the serpent'.[51] At this moment the new king was draped with the scarf of five colours worn by the rulers of Bhutan, in a ritual that took form when the Wangchuk dynasty was established in 1904 by Sir Ugyen Wangchuk, the country's first hereditary ruler. Although there is a crown, the King chose not to use it.

No doubt the astrologers also took the King's birth date into

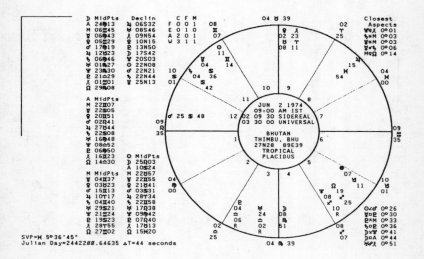

24: Bhutan, Coronation, 1974

account — he was born on 11 November 1955 [52] — although they would have used a system substantially different to contemporary Western astrology.

Chart 24 is set for 9.00 a.m. on 2 June 1974, in Thimbu, the capital of Bhutan.

BIAFRA

Biafra was the former Eastern state of Nigeria which declared independence in May 1967, precipitating a bitter civil war that was not settled until 1970.

The first move towards independence occurred in the evening of 27 May 1967 when the Assembly of Eastern Nigeria voted to declare the province independent. [53] The actual declaration of independence occurred in the early hours of 30 May in the capital, Enugu. The Biafran leader-to-be made an independence speech, which was broadcast live, beginning at 3.00 a.m. and concluding about an hour later with the words 'Long live the Republic of Biafra' and the playing of the national anthem. [54] The independence horoscope is set for 3.00 a.m. the beginning of the speech, although it may also reasonably be set for the conclusion at approximately 4.00 a.m. The horoscope is set for the capital, Enugu (Chart 25).

Biafra formally renounced its independence and rejoined Nigeria at a ceremony in Lagos on 15 January 1970.

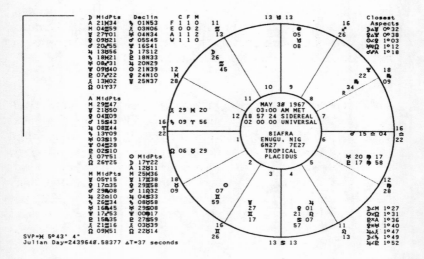

25: Biafra, Independence, 1967

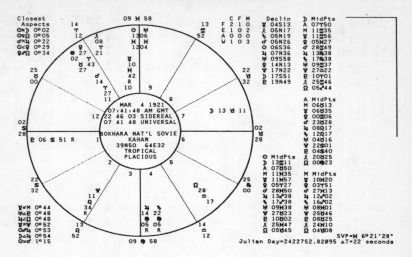

26: Bokhara National Soviet Republic, Independence, 1921

BOKHARA NATIONAL SOVIET REPUBLIC

In the nineteenth century the Emirate of Bokhara was under the suzerainty of the Russian Empire. During the Russian civil war the area became independent. On 4 March 1921 Russia recognized its independence under a local Bolshevik regime, the capital moving from Bokhara to Kahan. The state was still recognized as independent in 1925, though by 1928 had joined the USSR as part of the much larger state of Uzbekistan.[55] In the absence of accurate records the horoscope is set for 12.00 noon LT (Chart 26).

BOLIVIA

The independence movement in Bolivia is considered to have begun on 25 May 1807 with a coup in support of the Spanish king Ferdinand VII, who had been imprisoned by the French.[56] Even though the purpose of the coup was ostensibly to support Spanish authority, this never recovered from the damage inflicted by the French occupation of Spain, and the effect was to shift political responsibility onto the shoulders of local dignitaries away from the representatives of Madrid. However, control was re-established by the authorities in Buenos Aires, acting perhaps as much in their own interests as in those of Spain (see Argentina). A second, more radical, declaration of independence was issued in July 1809, but its supporters were suppressed.

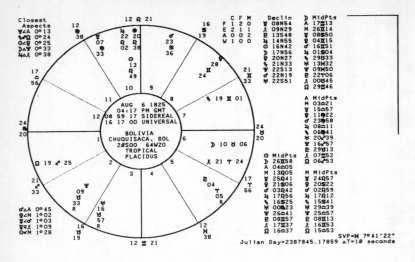

27: Bolivia, Independence, 1825

Over the following decade a rebellion built up under the leadership of Simon Bolivar and José de San Martin. At that time Bolivia formed part of the Provinces of Upper Peru, and San Martin's proclamation of Peruvian independence at Lima on 28 July 1821 has some relevance to the Bolivian situation.[57]

Following the Battle of Ayacucho on 9 December 1824 (see Peru), the region was effectively independent and only isolated pockets of Spanish authority remained.[58] For the next eight months Bolivia was technically under the rule of Peru although there was a constitutional case for Argentian claims.[59] However, separatist tendencies were strong, and on 6 August 1825, following a convention of local dignitaries, a proclamation was issued to the effect that 'the Provinces of Upper Peru, firm and unanimous, declare that their irrevocable will is to be governed by themselves'.[60] This proclamation, issued at Chuquisaca, marks the beginning of Bolivian independence. In the absence of accurate information the horoscope is cast for 12.00 noon (Chart 27).

The name 'Republic of Bolivar' was established amid acclamation on 11 August 1825, a date which also has symbolic importance.[61] The name was amended to Bolivia in October 1825.

A subsequent confederation between Peru and Bolivia, following the Bolivian conquest of Peru in 1835, was dissolved on 6 August 1839.[62]

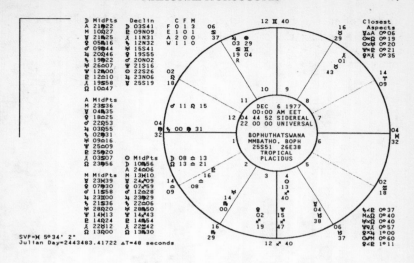

28: Bophuthatswana, Independence, 1977

BOPHUTHATSWANA

Bophuthatswana is one of four African 'homelands' in South Africa declared independent by South Africa, but in fact remaining totally dependent on that country. Independence was declared at 00.00 hrs on 6 December 1977 in the capital, Mmbatho.[63]

BOTSWANA

Botswana is the former British Protectorate of Bechuanaland, given independence at 00.00 hrs on 30 September 1966.[64] The chart is set for the capital, Gabarone (Chart 29).

BRAZIL

A former Portuguese colony, Brazil proclaimed its independence at Iparanga on 7 September 1822. The event, which has gone down in history as the 'cry of Iparanga' took place between 4.00 and 5.00 p.m. LMT.[65] The horoscope shown here is cast for 4.30 p.m. LMT half-way between the two times, although Brazilian astrologers use a chart rectified to 4.43 p.m. (with acknowledgements to Antonio Harries).

BRUNEI

The former British Protected State of Brunei received full

independence at 00.00 hrs on 1 January 1984.[66] Chart 31 is set for
this data and for the capital, Bandar Seri Begawa.

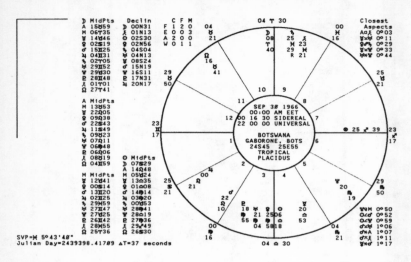

29: Botswana, Independence, 1966

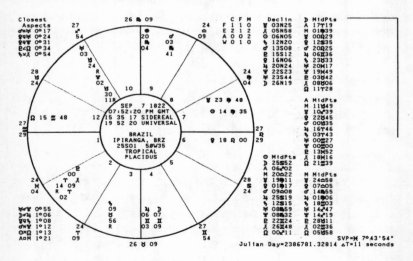

30: Brazil, Independence, 1822

BUGANDA

Buganda was a kingdom which formed part of the British Protectorate of Uganda from 1884, and which declared UDI in 1960. The move towards independence began on 8 October 1960 when the Lukiko

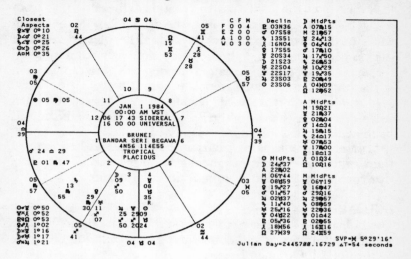

31: Brunei, Independence, 1984

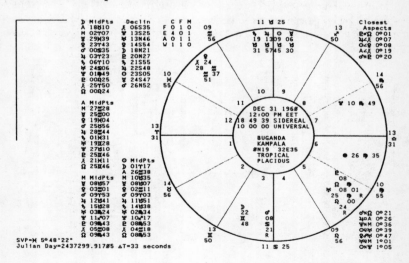

32: Buganda, UDI, 1960

(parliament of Buganda) requested termination of the British protectorate. On 15 December the Lukiko agreed to open negotiations with the British with a view to gaining independence, but their request was rejected by Great Britain on 29 December. On 31 December 1960 the Lukiko passed a motion to the effect that 'from today Buganda is independent. From this declaration HM the Queen will hand over to the Kingdom of Buganda all her possessions which she has been protecting.'[67] In the absence of accurate information the horoscope for the proclamation of independence is cast for noon in the Bugandan capital, Kampala (Chart 32).

Buganda officially rejoined Uganda on 31 October 1961 when an agreement reached with the British on 9 October (and agreed by the Lukiko on 26 October) was signed.[68]

Many of the problems in Uganda since independence have resulted from strife between the Bugandans and other tribes. This chart therefore has more than mere historical significance.

BULGARIA

The Bulgarian kingdom established in the ninth century became a major Balkan power and dominated the area until its conquest by the Turkish Ottoman Empire in 1393.

Moves towards Bulgarian independence began in the mid-nineteenth century and proceeded through a series of gradual steps of which the principal were the granting of autonomy by Turkey in

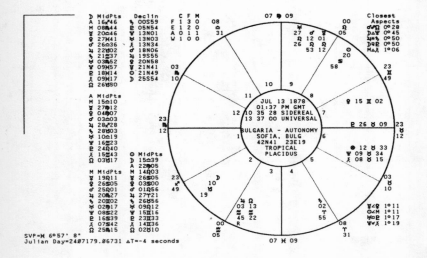

33: Bulgaria, Autonomy, 1878

1878 and the proclamation of independence in 1908.

The 18th of February 1878 is remembered as the day when Bulgaria attained its freedom,[69] although the chart given here is cast for the international recognition of this by the Treaty of Berlin. By the terms of the Treaty, which was signed in Berlin at 2.30 p.m. LMT on 13 July 1878, Turkey agreed to recognize Bulgaria's autonomy.[70] From this moment Bulgaria was effectively independent, any power that Turkey had to intervene in its affairs being offset by that of Russia. The horoscope for this moment is cast for 3.10 p.m. LMT in Sofia (Chart 33).

A second major stage along the route to national freedom is remembered as the unification of Bulgaria with Eastern Rumelia, the southern portion of the country, on 6 September 1885.[71]

Independence was finally proclaimed on 5 October 1908 in the city of Tirnova. Amid great ceremony Prince Ferdinand of Bulgaria arrived at the city by train at 11.00 a.m. He walked through the streets, lined with crowds, and went to the Church of the Forty Martyrs where the proclamation was to take place. As he arrived an anthem was sung, followed by a moment of silence and the reading by Ferdinand of the proclamation.[72] It is a fair assumption that the proclamation took place around 12.00 noon, and this horoscope is set for that time (Chart 34).

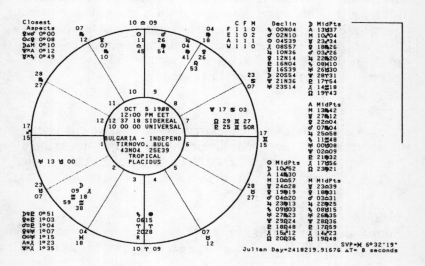

34: Bulgaria, Independence, 1908

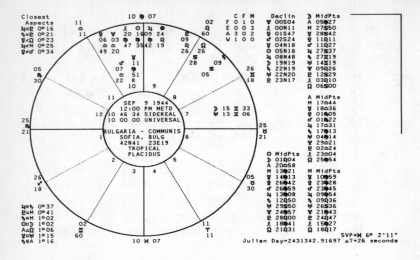

35: Bulgaria, Communist, 1944

The third horoscope for Bulgaria is set for the formation of the Communist government. Following the declaration of war by the USSR on Bulgaria (which was a German ally) on 5 September 1944, there was a general uprising throughout the country. On 9 September 1944 the uprising was successful and a Communist-dominated 'Fatherland Front' government was set up. This is considered to mark the end of bourgeois rule in Bulgaria and the beginning of the socialist era.[73] In the absence of accurate records the horoscope for this moment is set for 12.00 noon LT (Chart 35).

BURKINA

Burkina, commonly known as Burkina-Faso, was formerly known as Upper Volta or the Voltaic Republic. The country was granted full independence by France at 00.00 hrs on 5 August 1960, in the capital, Ouagadougou.[74] Chart 36 is set for this data.

BURMA

Burma was the only part of the Indian Empire to separate itself completely from Great Britain on gaining independence. Full independence was granted at 4.20 a.m. on 4 January 1948, 'the hour having been chosen by Burmese astrologers as auspicious'.[75] The independence ceremonies took place 'before dawn in bright

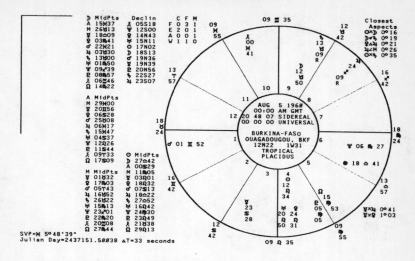

36: Burkina-Faso, Independence, 1960

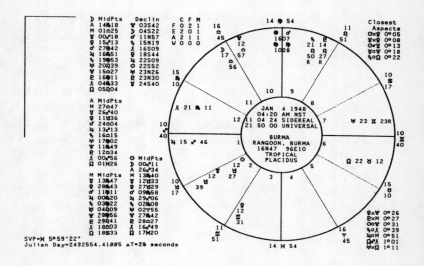

37: Burma, Independence, 1948

moonlight',[76] in the capital, Rangoon. Chart 37 is set for this data.

BURUNDI

The central African state of Burundi, formerly a Belgian Mandate,

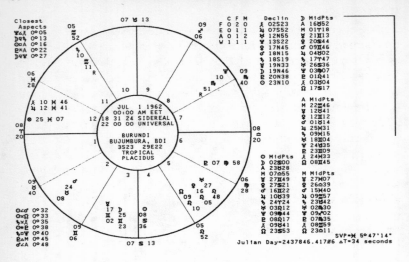

38: Burundi, Independence, 1962

was granted full independence at 00.00 hrs on 1 July 1962 in the capital, Bujumbura (formerly known as Usumburu).[77] Chart 38 is set for this data.

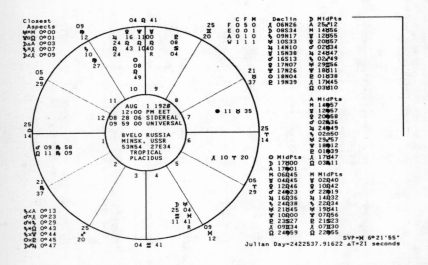

39: Byelorussia, Communist, 1920

BYELORUSSIA

The independence of Byelorussia — or White Russia — was originally proclaimed by a national Assembly in Vilna in January 1918, during the German occupation of that part of the Russian Empire. In February 1918 a separate proclamation of independence was issued by anti-German nationalists in Minsk, and in March 1918 a joint government was formed by the two rivals. This state was essentially a German puppet, although after the collapse of German power in November 1918 the state enjoyed what independence it could in the midst of the Russian civil war. On 1 August 1920 a Bolshevik regime was established and on 30 December 1922 the state agreed to join the USSR.[78] The memory of nationalist aspirations is kept alive in the state's separate flag and seat in the United Nations. This horoscope (Chart 39) is set for the Bolshevik republic and, in the absence of accurate information, is cast for 12.00 noon. The chart is set for the Bolshevik capital, Minsk.

CAMEROON

The former French colony of Cameroon was granted full independence at 00.00 hrs on 1 January 1960, the celebrations taking place in the capital, Yaoundé.[79] Chart 40 is set for this data.

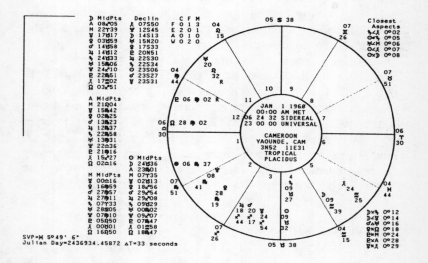

40: Cameroon, Independence, 1960

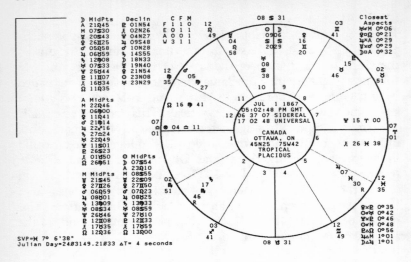

41: Canada, Dominion, 1867

CANADA

The Dominion of Canada came into existence at 00.00 hrs on 1 July 1867, the capital of the new state being Ottowa. The *New York Times* of 2 July reported that 1 July 'has given birth to a new infant, the Dominion of Canada'.[80] The advent of the state was hailed at 00.05 hrs by the ringing of bells and a 101-gun salute, although the legislation would have come into effect five minutes earlier, and the horoscope is set for 00.00 hrs (Chart 41).

A second possible horoscope for Canada is based on the 'Repatriation of the Constitution' at 11.35 a.m. on 17 April 1982 in Ottawa.[81] This was the moment at which Queen Elizabeth signed the legislation transferring sovereignty from Westminster to Ottawa, and represents the time at which Canada attained full independence, even though the British monarch remains Head of State. However, Canada already possessed full effective independence, and historically this chart represents only a minor constitutional adjustment. The chart for the creation of the Dominion in 1867 must remain the major Canadian horoscope.

CAPE VERDE ISLANDS

The Cape Verde islands, which had been ruled by Portugal since the fifteenth century, were granted independence at 12.00 noon on 5 July 1975.[82] Internal self-government had been granted in

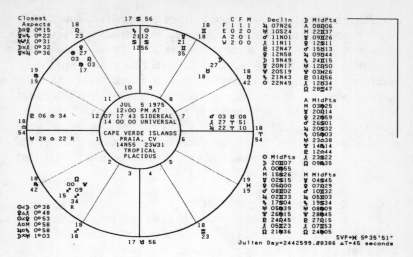

42: Cape Verde Islands, Independence, 1975

December 1974. The independence horoscope is set for the capital, Praia (Chart 42).

CARPATHO-UKRAINE

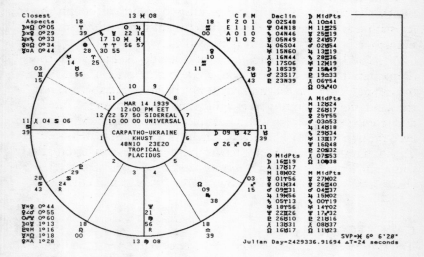

43: Carpatho-Ukraine, Independence, 1939

The Republic of Carpatho-Ukraine must be one of the most short-lived of any independent state. Located in Ruthenia, which until 1939 was controlled by Czechoslovakia, the republic came into existence on 14 March 1939 when the local Hungarian population proclaimed independence. The Czechs were driven out and the state enjoyed one day's independence under the leadership of Augustin Volosin. At 6.00 a.m. on the following day, 15 March, the country was invaded by Hungary. The state was formally annexed by its invaders on 16 March. [83] In the absence of more accurate information the chart is set for 12.00 noon and for the main town, Khust (Chart 43).

CENTRAL AFRICAN REPUBLIC
The Central African Republic was granted full independence by France at 00.00 hrs on 13 August 1960, the proclamation taking place in the capital, Bangui. [84] Spurious 'independence' within the French Community had earlier been granted on 1 December 1958. [85] The French habit of granting such fake independence was designed as a means to maintain the French empire in Africa, and has resulted in a certain amount of confusion over the independence dates of various of the former French colonies.

The Republic was known briefly as the Central African Empire under the rule of the notorious Emperor Bokassa. The Empire was

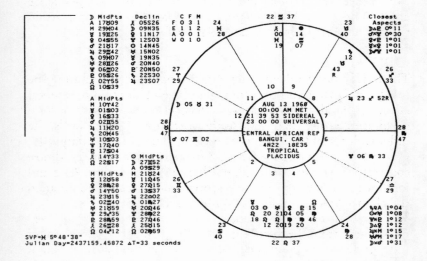

44: Central African Republic, Independence 1960

proclaimed on 4 December 1976[86] and Bokassa was crowned on 4
December 1977.[87]

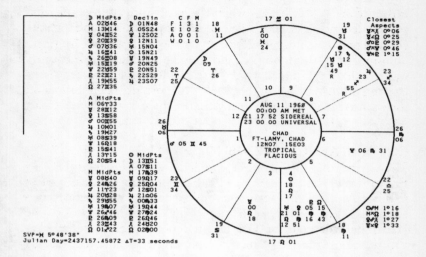

45: Chad, Independence, 1960

CHAD

The former French colony of Chad was granted full independence
at 00.00 hrs on 11 August 1960, the proclamation taking place in
the capital, Fort Lamy.[88] Chart 45 is set for this data.

CHILE

The build-up to Chilean independence began in 1810 during the
collapse of Spanish authority throughout the whole of Latin America.
Although local government was effectively in the hands of local
dignitaries, rather than Royal authorities, from 1810 onwards, the
independence of Chile was not proclaimed until 12 February 1818,
by which time José de San Martin's campaign of liberation was almost
complete.[89] The first horoscope (Chart 46) is set for this date and
for the capital, Santiago. In the absence of more accurate information
the chart is calculated for 12.00 noon LMT.

A royal army, representing the Government in Spain, was
dispatched from Peru to suppress the Chilean declaration of
independence, and met the Chilean forces at the Battle of Maipu
on 5 April 1818. The battle was fought on the plain of Maipu
immediately to the south of Santiago, began at noon and lasted

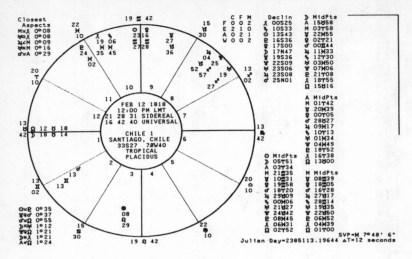

46: Chile, Independence, 1818

approximately two hours. When the battle ended, the royal army was defeated and most of Chile was in the hands of the independent government. As from that moment Chile was effectively completely independent.[90] Chart 47 is cast for the approximate time of the

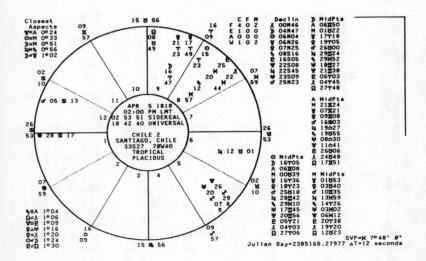

47: Chile, Battle of Maipu, 1818

conclusion of the Battle of Maipu at 2.00 p.m. LMT, and for the co-ordinates of Santiago.

The question of the dates of independence of all the Latin American countries is uncertain. Essentially most states have three plausible foundation dates: the date of the coup which brought local dignitaries to power, replacing the authority of Spain, the date of the proclamation of independence, and the date of the battle which secured complete independence. For Argentina the first and second dates have been used for the horoscopes in this book, but for Chile the second and third dates have been used.

CHINA

The origins of the Chinese state lie in the second millennium BC, and any attempts to establish its 'birth chart' are therefore spurious. The history of modern China is rooted in the revolution of 1911 which overthrew the last Imperial dynasty (the Manchus), even though this was briefly restored in 1917.

The revolution was triggered by a bomb attack on Hankow on 9 October 1911, although the following day saw the beginning of the revolt in the city of Wuchang. This day is regarded as the 'dawn of the Republic'.[91] The revolution gathered momentum and on 30 December 1911 Sun Yat-sen was elected president of the United Provinces of China by a revolutionary provisional assembly at

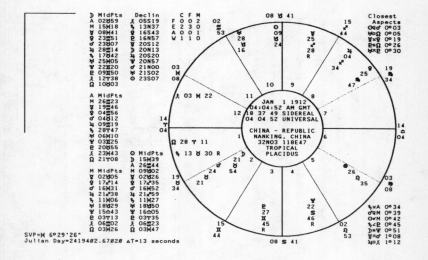

48: China, Republic, 1912

Nanking. The situation, as in all revolutionary conditions, was confused and other sources give 29 December.[92]

On 1 January 1912 Sun Yat-sen was inaugurated in Nanking, and issued an edict proclaiming the Republic. In his autobiography Sun Yet-sen regarded this event as the creation of the Republic[93] and the chart given here is set for his proclamation (Chart 48). In the absence of accurate information the chart is set for 12.00 noon.

The creation of the Republic was recognized nationally six weeks later. On 12 February the Emperor Hsüan T'ung abdicated and on 13 February (some sources give 15 February), Yuan Shih-k'ai became President in place of Sun Yat-sen.[94] Either of these dates could also be used as the basis for a horoscope for the Chinese republic.

The major horoscope for contemporary China must be that for the establishment of the Communist Peoples' Republic in 1949, but no time has been recorded for this event. The foundation of the Peoples' Republic of China was proclaimed at the opening session of the Chinese Peoples' Political Consultative Conference (CPPCC) in Peking on 21 September 1949. The conference was opened by Mao Tse-tung who summarized the history and purpose of the CPPCC, and the history of the revolutionary struggle going back to 1911, and then proclaimed the republic with the following words 'We announce the establishment of the Peoples' Republic of China.'[95]

On the assumption that the CPPCC opened during the morning,

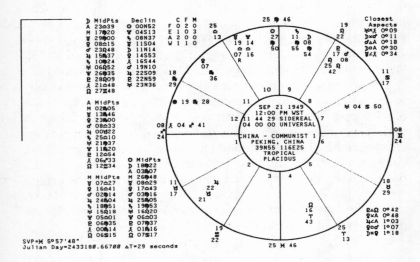

49: China, Communist, 1949 (1)

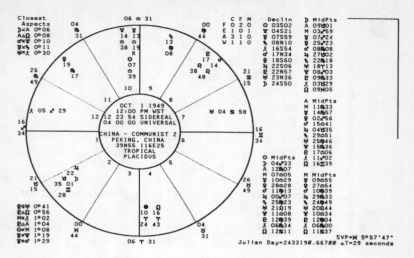

50: China, Communist, 1949 (2)

Mao's proclamation would have taken place perhaps around 9.00 or 10.00 a.m. A broadcast of Mao's speech was heard in San Francisco, but it is not known if this was live and no time is given.[96] Chart 49 for the proclamation of the Peoples' Republic of China is cast for Peking on 21 September 1949, and in the absence of accurate information is set for 12.00 noon.

Over the following week the CPPCC debated and designed a new constitution and system of government for China, and on 30 September elected a government with Mao Tse-tung as Chairman.[97]

The process was completed on 1 October 1949 with a massive rally in Peking. It is often stated that this rally witnessed the inauguration of the Peoples' Republic. In fact it was the scene of the proclamation of the central government of the new republic — which had taken office earlier in the day.[98] It would be reasonable to cast horoscopes either for the time that the Government took office or for the proclamation. Of the two events the proclamation has the greater symbolic importance as, even though the Peoples' Republic had been created ten days earlier, this was the moment at which the Communist regime was publicly announced to China and the world.

Even though the proclamation was broadcast live, and, like that of 21 September, was heard in San Francisco,[99] no historical source has been located to verify the time. The horoscope (Chart 50) is therefore set for 12.00 noon on 1 October in Peking, even though the implication of the BBC summaries is that it took place in the afternoon.

The *New York Times* reported that at 8.00 a.m. on 1 October 1949 all the radio stations in Shanghai played the national anthem.[100] This may be evidence for assuming that the government itself took office at that time.

The accepted time used by astrologers for this proclamation is that given by Charles Carter in *An Introduction to Political Astrology*. Carter gives a time of 3.15 p.m. but does not cite a historically verifiable source.[101] Astrologers have, however, found that a horoscope cast for this time gives suitable results.

CHINA (NATIONALIST)

When the Communists took over mainland China in 1949, the previous 'Nationalist' regime was still in control of substantial areas of the country. By the end of 1949 the bulk of mainland China was in the hands of the Communist government, although nationalist forces continued fighting in the south throughout 1950. The last major campaign of the Chinese civil war concluded on 2 May 1950 when the Communists took complete possession of the island of Hainan. Thereafter the Nationalist regime was confined to the island of Formosa, also known as Taiwan. Establishing an origin for the

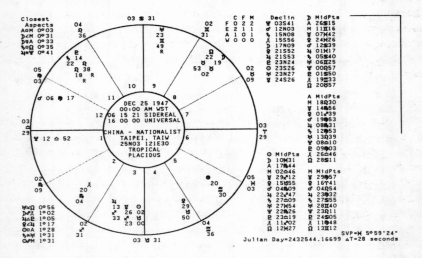

51: China, Nationalist, 1947

current nationalist Chinese state is therefore virtually impossible.

It would be reasonable to use the horoscope for the original foundation of the Chinese Republic on 1 January 1912 (or perhaps on 13 February 1912). It would also be reasonable to cast a horoscope for the proclamation of the Peoples' Republic, either on 21 September 1949 or 1 October 1949, symbolizing the separation of the two Chinas, and set this for Taipei, the capital of Taiwan.

In the face of such uncertainty the horoscope given here (Chart 51) is cast for the last major constitution of the Nationalist regime which came into force on 25 December 1947.[102] In the absence of accurate information the chart is set for 00.00 hrs and, although the nationalist capital at the time was Nanking, it is located in Taipei, the current Nationalist seat of government. To add to the confusion, although the constitution came into legal force on 25 December, none of the appropriate machinery had been set up, and it did not begin to function until some time later.

CISKEI

The African 'homeland' of Ciskei was granted independence by South Africa at 00.00 hrs on 4 December 1981 in the capital, Bisho.[103] In fact the country is totally dependent on, and dominated by South Africa, which is the only state to recognize its independence.

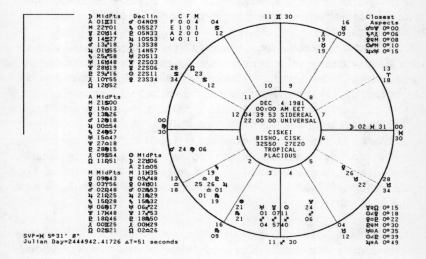

52: Ciskei, Independence, 1981

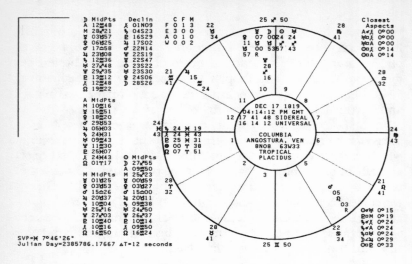

53: Colombia, Independence, 1819

COLOMBIA

The state of Great Colombia was originally proclaimed independent at Caracas on 5 July 1811.[104] The state, consisting of the modern republics of Colombia, Ecuador, Venezuela and Panama, was reconquered by the Spanish in 1812, although, under the leadership of Simon Bolivar the rebels re-grouped and gradually gained the upper hand.

The state of Great Colombia was again proclaimed at the Congress of Angostura on 17 December 1819, consisting of Quito (modern Ecuador), New Granada (modern Colombia), Panama and Venezuela. Following the secession of Ecuador and Venezuela from Great Colombia in 1830, the state took on the name of New Granada. The name Colombia was revived in 1863.

From this confused state of affairs it is clear that there are many likely 'birth dates' for Colombia. The horoscope given here (Chart 53) is set for the declaration of the Congress of Angostura on 17 December 1819, and in the absence of accurate information is set for 12.00 noon.

COMOROS

The Comoros islands declared their independence from France on 6 July 1975 by a vote in the Comoros Islands Chamber of Deputies.[105] Chart 54 is set for this date, and in the absence of accurate

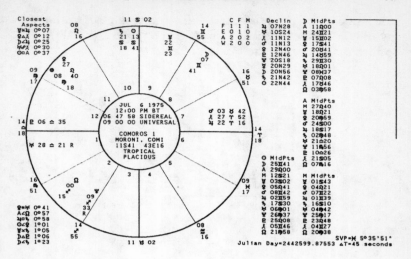

54: Comoros, Independence, 1975 (1)

information, is calculated for 12.00 noon. The French Government refused to recognize the declaration, but were pressurized into passing legislation to accept it. The Comoros achieved full legal independence on 31 December 1975 when the French Government enacted the

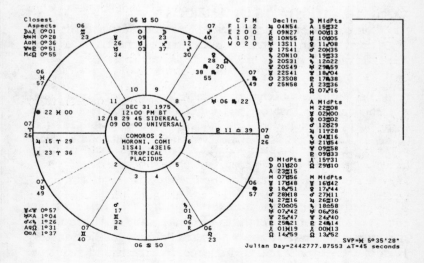

55: Comoros, Independence, 1975 (2)

independence bill.[106] It is believed that this took place during the day and the horoscope for this date (Chart 55) is set for 12.00 noon. Both charts are set for the capital, Moroni.

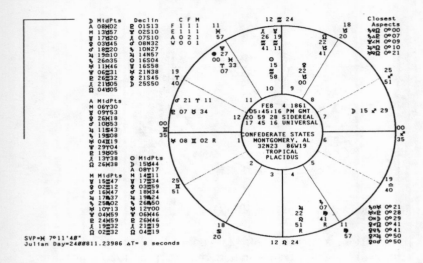

56: Confederate States of America, 1861

CONFEDERATE STATES OF AMERICA

The Confederate States of America began their formal existence at 12.00 noon LMT on 4 February 1861 in Montgomery, Alabama (Chart 56). The official account of the event records that

> on the fourth day of February, in the year of our Lord one thousand, eight hundred and sixty one, and in the Capitol of the State of Alabama, in the city of Montgomery, at the hour of noon, there assembled certain deputies and delegates from the several independent Southern States of North America, to wit: Alabama, Florida, Georgia, Louisiana, Mississippi, and South Carolina.[107]

This meeting marked the formal beginning of the first session of the Provisional Congress of the Confederate States of America. Later in the meeting Howell Cobb was elected President of the Congress. Each of the six states had at that time declared its independence from the USA, and each would therefore have its own separate horoscope beginning with that of South Carolina (on 20 December

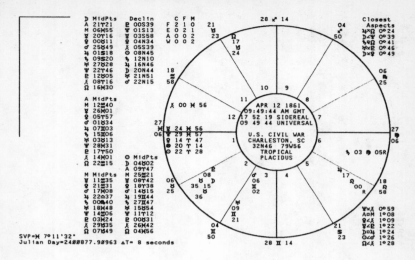

57: US Civil War, 1861

1860) and continuing with the other states during the first weeks
of 1861.[108] Subsequently Texas, Virginia, Arkansas, Tennessee and
North Carolina seceded from the USA to join the Confederacy.

The first shot in the civil war between the Confederacy and the
Union was fired at 4.30 a.m. LMT on 12 April 1861 at Fort Sumner,
Charleston and the war officially began at 2.30 p.m. LMT on 13 April
1861, also at Fort Sumner, when the Union forces in the fort
surrendered.[109]

Chart 57, for the first shot in the Civil War is reproduced both
as an example of a mundane war chart, and as the moment at which
the split between the Confederate and United States of America
became irrevocable.

CONGO

The Congo was granted full independence from France at 00.00 hrs
on 15 August 1960 in the capital of Brazzaville.[110] Chart 58 is set
for this moment. The republic had earlier been granted spurious
independence within the French Community on 28 November
1958.[110'] The Congo is sometimes known as Congo-Brazzaville to
distinguish it from the neighbouring state of the Congo, now known
as Zaïre.

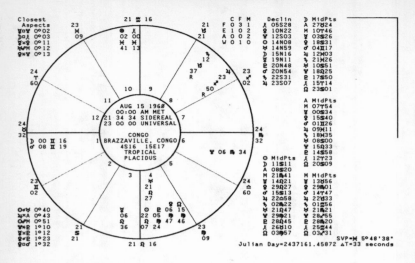

58: Congo, Independence, 1960

COSTA RICA

Formerly part of the Spanish Captain-Generalcy of Guatemala, Costa Rica proclaimed its independence from the newly independent Guatemala on 27 October 1821.[114] In the absence of accurate

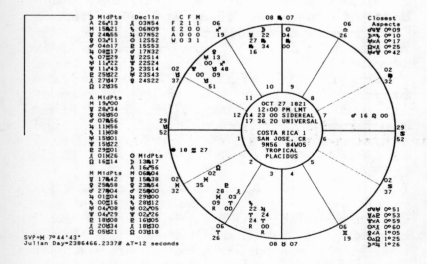

59: Costa Rica, Independence, 1821

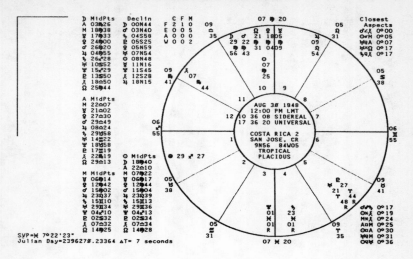

60: Costa Rica, Independence, 1848

information Chart 59 is set for 12.00 noon LMT on the 27 October 1821 in the capital, San José.

The situation throughout Central America was highly unstable until the mid nineteenth century, and none of the former Spanish territories enjoyed long periods of independence. Costa Rica itself was annexed by Mexico in 1822, becoming independent in 1823 as part of the United Provinces of Central America. Thereafter Costa Rica remained either a *de jure* or *de facto* member of a series of Central American federations and confederations, finally proclaiming her complete sovereign independence on 30 August 1848.[115] It is only from this date that Costa Rica has experienced continuous independence and it is reasonable to regard this as the basis for a second independence horoscope (although there may be many others). In the absence of accurate information, Chart 60 is set for 12.00 noon on 30 August 1848, and is calculated for the capital, San José.

CUBA

Cuba was ruled by Spain until 1898. Under the Treaty of Paris, signed in Paris at 8.45 p.m. LMT on 10 December 1898, Spain relinquished sovereignty of Cuba.[116] Chart 61 is set for the equivalent time (3.06 p.m. LMT) in Havana.

However, the aspirations of the Cubans were aborted by the United

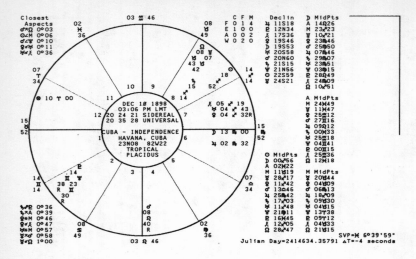

61: Cuba, Treaty of Paris, 1898

States, which occupied the country on the same day. The occupation officialy began at 12.30 p.m. LMT on 10 December 1898 when the Stars and Stripes was unfurled over the City Hall of Marianao in Havana. [117]

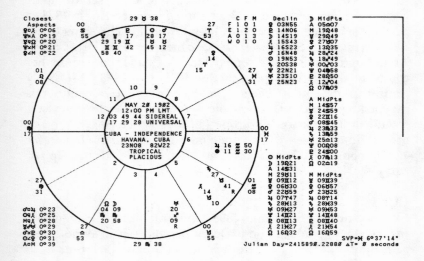

62: Cuba, Independence, 1902

Full independence was granted to Cuba by the USA at 12.00 noon on 20 May 1902. Chart 62, set for this time, should be regarded as the prime horoscope for Cuba, even though some sources quote 10 December 1889 as the date of independence.[119]

The present Communist regime in Cuba traces its origins to 1 January 1959 when the dictator Batista fled Havana in the face of a joint force consisting of Castro's guerrilla army and regular Cuban troops. The regime owes its legal origins to Castro's announcement that Manuel Urrutia had been appointed President (even though Urrutia was not a Communist and subsequently resigned). The announcement was made by Fidel Castro in a public speech (which was also broadcast live) at 1.00 a.m. on 2 January 1959 in Havana.[120] Chart 63 is set for this time.

CYPRUS
Cyprus was occupied by the British on 16 July 1878, replacing the Turks. Full independence was granted at 00.00 hrs on 16 August 1960, in the capital, Nicosia.[121] Chart 64 is set for this data.

CYPRUS (TURKISH)
The formation of the Turkish Republic of North Cyprus, consisting

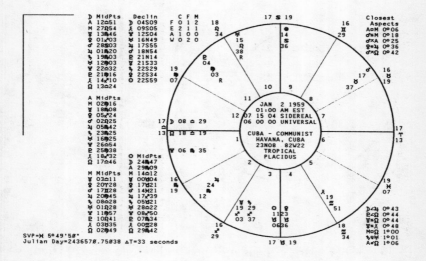

63: Cuba, Communist, 1959

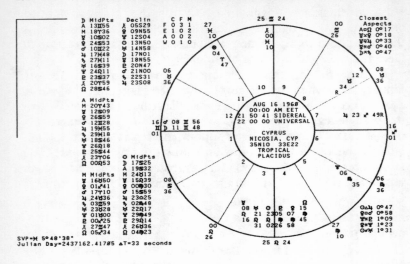

64: Cyprus, Independence, 1960

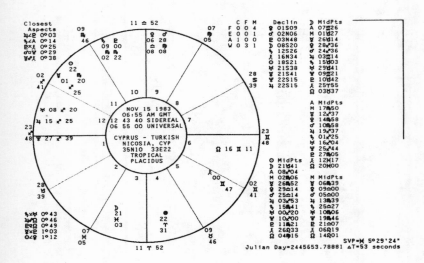

65: Cyprus, Turkish, 1983

of the northern part of the island then under Turkish occupation, was announced at 6.55 a.m. GMT on 15 November 1983 by Radio Bayrack.[122] This announcement was made immediately following the ratification of the independence declaration by the Turkish Cypriot Legislative Assembly. Chart 65 is set for the announcement as the time of the ratification is not known. The chart is set for Nicosia, the Cypriot capital, in the absence of other accurate information. Turkey is the only foreign state to recognize the Republic.

CZECHOSLOVAKIA

The build-up towards the independence of Czechoslovakia, much of which had been ruled by Austria since the seventeenth century, reached its culmination in 1918 with the collapse of the Austro-Hungarian Empire in the First World War.

From September 1918 there were two main political groupings pressing for independence, the Czech National Committee, which was a broad nationalist coalition, and the Socialist Council. An initial attempt by the Socialist Council to proclaim independence in Prague on 14 October was suppressed by a massive show of military force, although statements in favour of independence were made at several provincial centres.[123] The Czech National Committee planned to proclaim independence on 8 November 1918, the anniversary of the great Austrian defeat of the Bohemian forces at the Battle of the White Mountain in 1618, but this plan was overtaken by events.[124]

During October 1918 United States President Wilson attempted

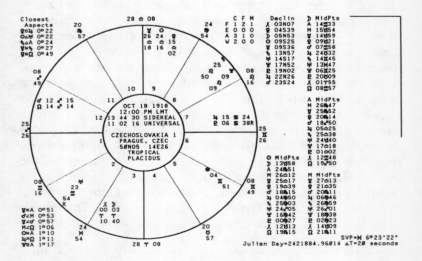

66: Czechoslovakia, Independence, 1918 (1)

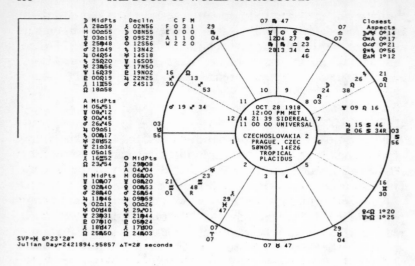

67: Czechoslovakia, Independence, 1918 (2)

to extract concessions from the collapsing Austrian Government on the future status of the various national minorities which populated the Austro-Hungarian Empire. On 18 October the Austrian Government made a reply that could be construed as accepting the principle of independence for the nationalities, including the Czechs. Seizing the opportunity Thomas Masaryk, the President of the National Committee issued a declaration of independence in Washington. [125] On the same day the USA recognized the provisional government of Czechoslovakia, and, even though still under Austrian domination, the various allied states followed by tacitly accepting Czech independence. The 18th of October must therefore be regarded as a symbolic declaration of independence, and Chart 66 is set for this date. It has not been possible to establish the time of the declaration, as Masaryk does not mention it in his autobiography and the newspapers were too preoccupied with the progress of the war. The chart is set for 12.00 noon in Prague, even though, if Masaryk issued his declaration at around noon in Washington this would correspond to around 6.00 p.m. in Prague. A chart could reasonably be set for Washington, the location of the declaration, although the chart here is set for Prague.

The revolution in Czechoslovakia took place on 28 October 1918. On 26 October the Czech National Council had decided that at 9.00 a.m. on the 28th it would take over control of the Corn Institute

in Prague in order to prevent Austrian misuse of Czech food supplies.
The take-over was complete by 9.30 a.m., and all officials were
instructed to obey the Czech National Committee.[126] At 11.00 a.m.
a rumour began to spread that the Austrians had recognized Czech
independence in response to President Wilson's demand, and by
noon Prague was in the grip of celebrating crowds.[127] At 11.30 a.m.
the National Committee called an emergency meeting and resolved
that it would take over all authority, with itself as the representative
of the independent Czech state. The delegates moved off to the office
of the Austrian viceroy, the crucial moment occurring 'a few minutes
after noon' when 'the members of the Presidium of the National
Committee . . . announced to the viceroy's representative, Kosina,
that the National Committee had decided to take charge of the entire
administration'.[128] This is the true moment of Czech independence,
and Chart 67 is set for this time.

That afternoon the leaders of the National Committee issued a
proclamation announcing that 'The Independent Czechoslovak state
has come into being.'[129] The National Committee then began to
behave like a Parliament, passing legislation. By late evening all Czech
troops in the Austrian Army were placed under the command of
the National Committee, which, with Austrian backing, assumed
the power of the Austrian viceroy;[130] full *de jure* independence was
not yet recognized by Austria, although the state had achieved

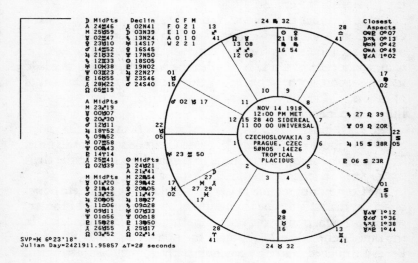

68: Czechoslovakia, Independence, 1918 (3)

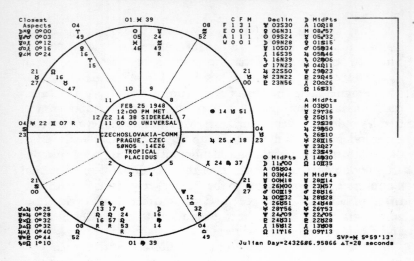

69: Czechoslovakia, Communist, 1948

complete *de facto* independence.

On 29 October the Slovak National Committee assembled and proclaimed the Slovak nation a part of Czechoslovakia [131] (a move that had been assumed by the use of the name Czechoslovakia in the previous day's events).

On 30 October the Prague National Committee summoned a Constituent National Assembly, [132] and on the 31st a proclamation of the Czech representatives in Geneva reaffirmed the declaration of independence. [133] On 12 November the National Committee held its last session, to be replaced in the evening by the Council of Ministers; [134] Czechoslovakia now possessed all the trappings of a fully independent state.

Full legal independence finally came into being at 12.00 noon on 14 November 1918 in Prague, [135] and Chart 68 is set for this time. This horoscope is important, though perhaps less so than the chart for *de facto* independence on 28 October.

The Communist regime in Czechoslovakia took complete power on 25 February 1948. The Communist coup began on 24 February with the resignation of the non-Communist cabinet ministers. In the mid-afternoon of 25 February the non-Communist President Benes was obliged to accept a predominantly Communist government under Klement Gottwald. [136] Over the next few months a brutal purge was conducted climaxing in the election of Gottwald as President on 14 June. In the absence of an exact recorded time in any of the English language press, Chart 69 for the Communist regime is cast for 12.00 noon on 25 February 1948 in Prague.

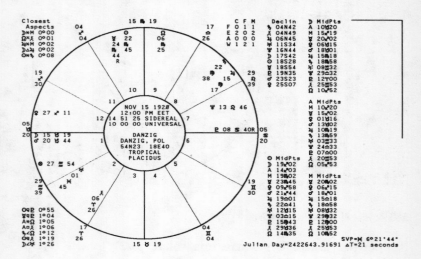

70: Danzig, Independence, 1920

DANZIG

The formal proclamation of the Free City of Danzig took place during the day of 15 November 1920 at a meeting of the city's Constituent Assembly.[137] In the absence of accurate information the horoscope for this moment (Chart 70) is set for 12.00 noon.

DENMARK

It is not possible to establish a date for the beginning of the Danish Kingdom, which made its appearance upon the historical stage during the tenth century, and achieved the status of a great European power with its conquest of England, Norway and Sweden. The current Danish horoscope is usually set for the foundation of the liberal constitution with its constitutional monarchy and parliamentary government on 5 June 1849.[138] In the absence of accurate information the horoscope for this day is set for 12.00 noon LMT (Chart 71). The constitution was signed by King Frederick VII in Copenhagen.

(A traditional horoscope used by Danish astrologers is set for 10.26 a.m., although it has been reported recently that the signing ceremony did not begin until 11.00 a.m., and an 11.15 a.m. chart

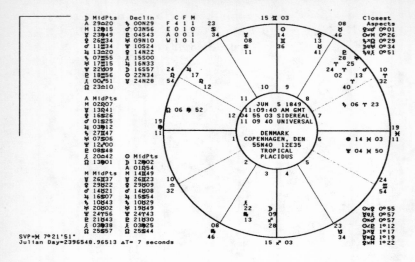

71: Denmark, Constitution, 1849

has been suggested. *Future* magazine, Vol. II, no. 27, June 1893 gives
a time of between 12.30 and 1.00 p.m.)

DJIBOUTI

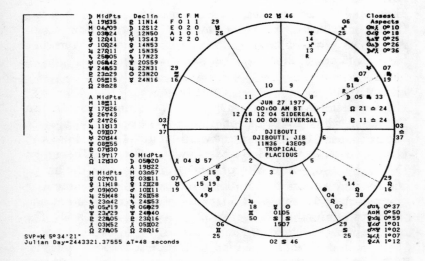

72: Djibouti, Independence, 1977

Djibouti was granted independence by France at 00.00 hrs on 27
June 1977.[139] Chart 72 is set for this data, and for the capital, Djibouti.

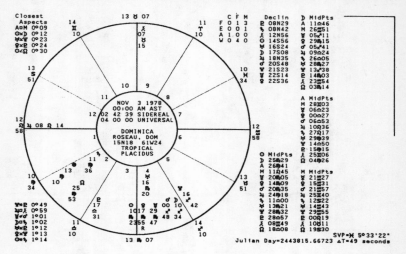

73: Dominica, Independence, 1978

DOMINICA

Dominica was granted independence by Great Britain at 00.00 hrs
on 3 November 1978 in the capital, Roseau.[140] Chart 73 is set for
this data.

DOMINICAN REPUBLIC

The Dominican Republic originally gained independence from
France on 1 December 1821.[141] In the absence of more accurate
information Chart 74 is set for 12.00 noon on 1 December 1821,
in the capital Santo Domingo.

The republic also proclaimed independence on three other
occasions: on 27 February 1844 (following its conquest by Haiti in
1822), on 1 May 1865 (following its annexation by Spain on 18 March
1861), and on 21 October 1922 (following its occupation and
annexation by the USA in 1905–16).[142] Any of these dates could
form the basis for a national horoscope, especially the last, following
which the republic has enjoyed its longest period of continuous
independence.

ECUADOR

The precise date of Ecuador's independence from Spain is difficult

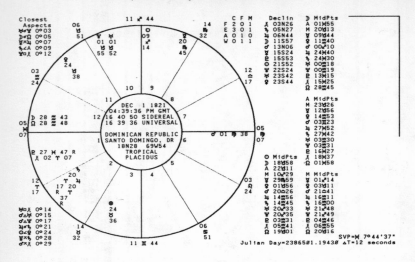

74: Dominican Republic, Independence, 1821

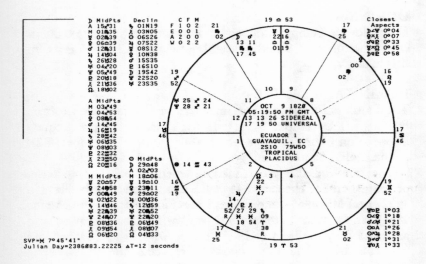

75: Ecuador, Independence, 1820

to define. Technically the area was included in the declaration by Great Colombia on 17 December 1819,[143] although the first revolt in Quito, the leading city, had occurred on 10 August 1809. At the time of the 1819 declaration at Angostura, the region was still under the control of the Spanish, and the final build-up to independence began when the province of Guayaquil was declared independent on 9 October 1820.[144] Both 10 August 1809 and 9 October are regarded as 'national days', but the horoscope given here is for the latter date. In the absence of more accurate historical information, Chart 75 is set for 12.00 noon, and is cast for Guayaquil, where the declaration took place.

The complete liberation of Ecuador was completed immediately following the Battle of Pichina, on 24 May 1822, at which the Spanish Army was decisively defeated, but the country never attained its independence and was absorbed into Great Colombia. A separatist movement developed which culminated in Ecuador's proclamation of independence on 13 May 1830.[145] The situation here is slightly confused, and 27 April is mentioned as a date of Ecuadorian independence.[146] The date of formal independence, however, seems to be 13 May. Chart 76 is set for this date, for the capital, Quito, and, in the absence of accurate information, for 12.00 noon LMT. The question of which horoscope has the greater validity must remain open. The first map obviously represents independence from Spain, but the second embodies the complete fruition of national aspirations.

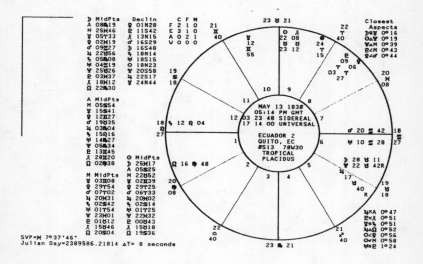

76: Ecuador, Independence, 1830

EGYPT

For most of the last 5,000 years Egypt has had an independent political existence. In fact Egypt may claim to be the oldest political unit in the world. For 600 years the country was controlled by the Romans, but during the period of Arab ascendancy it usually had effective self-rule (even if officially ruled from Baghdad), and during the Turkish period enjoyed a fair measure of automomy. Turkish suzerainty, which had only been nominal since the 1790s, was replaced by British occupation in 1882 and a British protectorate in 1914.

The date often given for Egyptian independence from Britain — 28 February 1922 — is incorrect. In fact it was on this date that the British Prime Minister, Lloyd George, presented to the House of Commons a declaration abolishing the Protectorate.[147] The Government required that the House of Commons approve its policy, which it did in a vote taken at 10.43 p.m. on 14 March 1922[148] As this vote was taken the Protectorate was considered abolished and Egypt became a sovereign independent state.[149] Although the event took place in London, the chart may be set for Cairo, and represents the *de jure* restoration of Egyptian independence. Chart 77 is set for this time.

A second chart may reasonably be based on the official proclamation of Egyptian independence and of the Egyptian

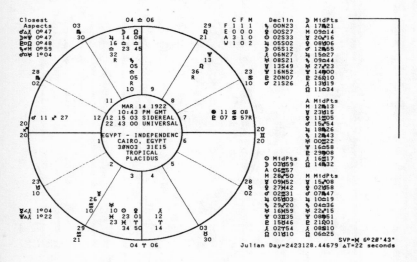

77: Egypt, Independence, 1922

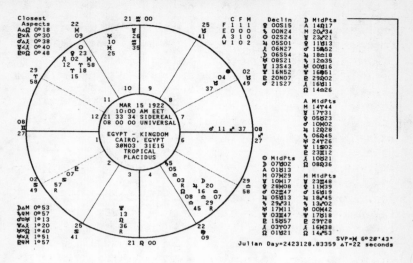

78: Egypt, Kingdom, 1922

kingdom issued by the Sultan at 10.00 a.m. on 15 March in Cairo.[150] Even though the protectorate had come to an end and celebrations had been continuing throughout the day, this is undoubtedly a moment of importance, if only for the future of the royal house. Chart 78 is set for this time.

However, Britain retained considerable power to interfere in Egyptian domestic and foreign affairs, backed up by occupying troops in the Suez Canal zone. It is therefore necessary to consider the horoscope for the proclamation of the Republic by the future President Nasser as not only a map of the current republic regime, but also as that symbolizing the complete *de facto* independence of Egypt (even though British power was only finally dealt with by the Suez crisis of November 1956).

The build-up to the proclamation of the Republic commenced on the night of 22–23 July 1952 when a *coup d'état* by radical army officers resulted in the civil administration of the country becoming dependent on this group, led by Nasser. Different times are given for the beginning of the coup although that given by *The Times* (approximately 11.00 p.m. on the 22nd) seems to fit in with other facts better than that given by the BBC (1.00 a.m. on the 23rd).[151] King Farouk left Egypt at 6.00 p.m. on 26 July, and his abdication was broadcast at 8.55 p.m. GMT. However, the monarchy was maintained, and Farouk's son,

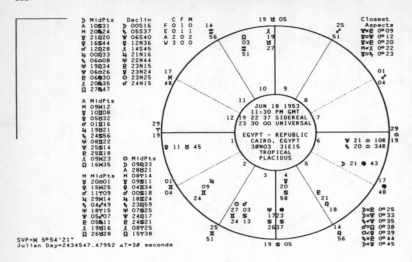

79: Egypt, Republic, 1953

Ahmad Fouad II was proclaimed king at 8.57 p.m. GMT.[152]

Although the events of July 1953 could reasonably form the basis for a horoscope of the Republic, the main events took place almost a year later, in June 1953. Realizing that their time had come, the radical officers engineered a second coup on 18–19 June, the culmination of which was the proclamation of the Republic at 11.30 p.m. GMT on 18 June in Cairo,[153] and Chart 79 is set for this time.

Some confusion has been caused by the *New York Times'* report that the republic was proclaimed 'shortly after 10.00 p.m.' on 18 June,[154] but the BBC, giving transcripts and times of the relevant live broadcasts, confirms 11.30 p.m. GMT. This was the time when the rebels's figurehead, General Neguib, read the proclamation of the Republic over the radio.

Nasser himself was elected President on 23 June 1856.

EIRE

There are three possible charts for Eire — the Republic of Ireland. The first (Chart 80), is that favoured by Irish astrologers, and is set for the proclamation of independence that initiated the 'Easter Rising' in Dublin at 12.00 noon (12.25 p.m. GMT) on 24 April 1916.[155]

The second chart (Chart 81) is set for independence on 6 December 1922. Royal assent was given to the Irish Act, setting up the Irish

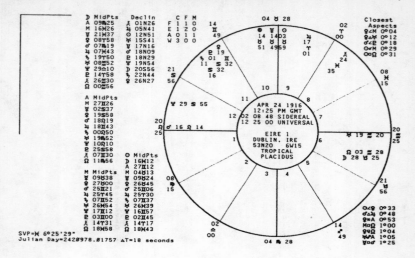

80: Eire, Easter Rising, 1916

Free State, by George V on 5 December 1922. The King signed the proclamation creating the state on 6 December and 'shortly after 5.00 p.m.', the Parliament of the Irish Free State assembled in

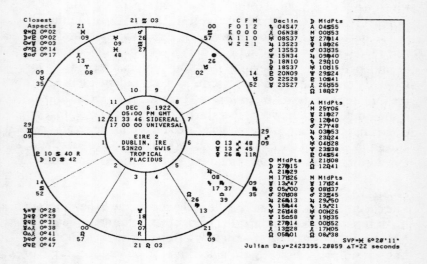

81: Eire, Irish Free State, 1922

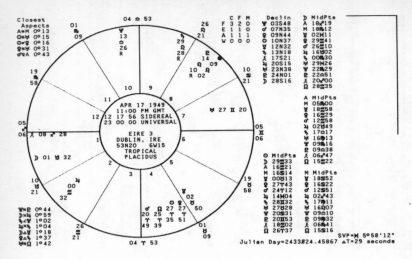

82: Eire, Republic, 1949

Dublin.[156] This chart is set for the assembly of the Parliament, although the time of the signature of the royal proclamation, shortly before, could also reasonably be the basis of a horoscope.[156a]

The third chart (Chart 82) is that for the creation of the Republic, which was the moment of complete and total separation from Great Britain. This took place at 00.00 hrs on 18 April 1949, in Dublin.[155]

The historical distinction between the three charts is simple. The first represented the beginning of the movement that culminated in independence, and symbolizes the national aspiration for independence, the second represents *de facto* independence, and the third represents complete *de jure* separation from Great Britain. It should be noted, however, that the first chart was a proclamation of the independence of the whole of Ireland while the second two are cast for stages in the creation of the Republic of Southern Ireland, the northernmost counties remaining in the United Kingdom.

EL SALVADOR

The circumstances surrounding the independence of El Salvador are as confused as those for the other Central American republics. On 6 November 1811 a creole government was established in an uprising, but was suppressed shortly after. Technical independence came to El Salvador when the Spanish Captain-Generalcy of Guatemala (of which El Salvador was a part) declared independence on 15 September

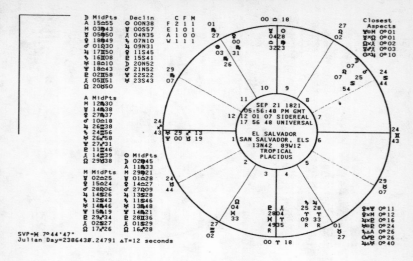

83: El Salvador, Independence, 1821

1821. The independence of El Salvador itself must be dated from its declaration of independence on 21 September 1821, and Chart 83 is set for this date, for the capital, San Salvador, and (in the absence of accurate information), for 12.00 noon LMT.[158]

The position is somewhat confused by the fact that a formal proclamation of independence was issued eight days later and that there was still a recognition of the authority of Guatemala. Independence was short-lived and the country was annexed by Mexico.

Independence was received from Mexico as part of the United Provinces of Central America, a federation which spent most of its existence in a state of disintegration. El Salvador seems to have seceded from the federation on 13 February 1833,[159] but only resumed full sovereign status on 1 February 1841. Thereafter El Salvador was a member of three other Central American states, the first in the 1850s, the United Provinces of Central America (in the 1890s) and the Federation of Central America (in the 1920s).

EQUATORIAL GUINEA

The former Spanish colony of Equatorial Guinea was granted independence on 12 October 1968[160] In the absence of accurate information Chart 84 is cast for 12.00 noon, and for the capital, Malabo (formerly Santa Isabel).

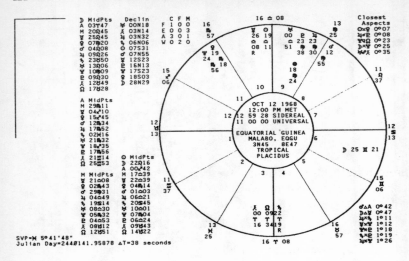

84: Equatorial Guinea, Independence, 1968

ESPERITU SANTO

The island of Esperitu Santo declared its independence from the British-controlled New Hebrides islands on 27 December 1975.[161]

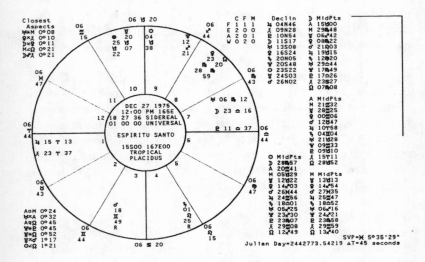

85: Esperitu Santo, UDI, 1975

In the absence of accurate information, Chart 85 is set for 12.00 noon. The declaration of independence was later withdrawn.

ESTONIA

Estonia proclaimed its independence from Russia on 28 November 1917 following the Bolshevik revolution. [162] Chart 86 is set for this date, for the capital, Reval, and, in the absence of accurate information, for 12.00 noon. The Russians attacked the new state, but their advance was blocked by the Germans, and on 24 February a second proclamation of independence was issued under German protection. [163] Russia recognized Estonian independence at the Treaty of Brest Litovsk on 3 March 1918.

The country was invaded by the Soviet Union in 1939, becoming a republic of the USSR. It was again occupied by Germany from 1941 to 1944.

On 22 September 1918 Estonian independence was legally interrupted when it became a part of the Baltic State (in union with Latvia and Livland), under German protection, but this artificial creation survived for a few weeks only, disintegrating in November 1918. [164]

Contradictory evidence has been received concerning the use of zone time or local mean time in Estonia from 1917 to 1918, which may affect the accuracy of this horoscope.

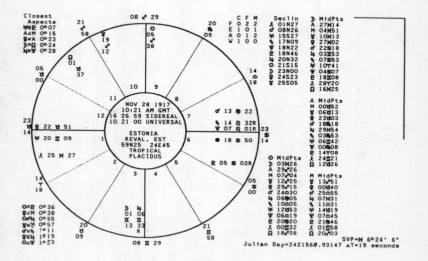

86: Estonia, Independence, 1917

ETHIOPIA

Ethiopia has a long history, and it is impossible to locate a date for independence. Occupation by the Italians in the 1930s was short-lived.

The current horoscope should be set for the revolution of 1974. This was known as the 'creeping revolution' on account of its gradually escalating course. The revolution began with an army mutiny in January 1974, [165] and the first significant army action occurred at 10.00 a.m. on 26 February 1974 when the army seized control of Asmara, the second city. [166] Initially army demands were concerned with pay and conditions, but a radical element quickly came to the fore and army actions developed a broader political dimension, with increasing pressure being put on the Government itself. The revolution culminated with a *coup d'état* on 12 September 1974, which began at approximately 4.30 a.m. in the capital, Addis Ababa, with tanks surrounding the royal palace and other government buildings.

The crucial moment occurred at 10.00 a.m. when the leaders of the Armed Forces Coordinating Committee read out the proclamation deposing the Emperor Hailie Selassie and establishing a provisional military government. [167] This was the moment at which full *de jure* and *de facto* power passed to the new regime, and Chart

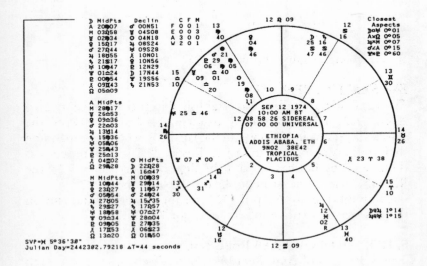

87: Ethiopia, Revolution, 1974

87 is set for this time.

The abolition of the monarchy and the proclamation of the republic took place in a live broadcast on 21 March 1975.[168] However, this was a purely formal move which had no impact on the transfer of power that had taken place on 12 September 1974. The Emperor Merid Azmatch Asfa Wassen, who formally succeeded Hailie Selassie on 12 September 1974 (at 10.00 a.m.), was paralysed from the waist down and had lived in Switzerland since 1967.[169]

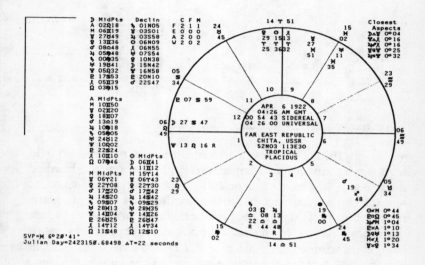

88: Far Eastern Republic, Formation, 1922

FAR EASTERN REPUBLIC

The Far Eastern Republic was established in the city of Chita on 6 April 1922, its purpose being to serve as a buffer between the Bolshevik regime in Moscow and the Japanese, who were expanding their military operations in eastern Russia.[170] The government was dominated by Bolsheviks, and the Republic was annexed by the Russian Soviet Socialist Republic on 19 November 1922.

Chart 88 is set for 6 April 1922, for the capital, Chita, and, in the absence of accurate information, for 12.00 noon LT.

FEDERATION OF ARAB REPUBLICS

The Federation of Arab Republics, otherwise known as the Arab Federation, was a union of Libya, Egypt and Syria created on 1–2

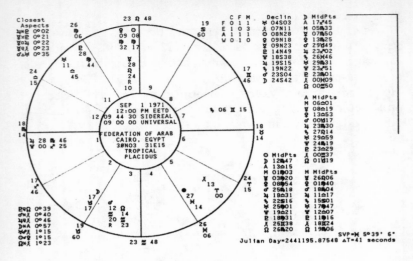

89: Federation of Arab Republics, Formation, 1971

September 1971. The union was confirmed by a referendum held in all three countries on 1 September, polling for which finished in Cairo at 2.30 a.m. on 2 September.[171] Egypt changed its name from the United Arab Republic to the Arab Republic of Egypt, shortly before 9.00 a.m. GMT on 2 September, in order to prepare for the union (the UAR was the name of the now defunct prior union with Syria) and broadcast the voting figures at 9.00 a.m. GMT.[172] This suggests that, as far as Egypt was concerned the Federation came into effect at 9.00 a.m. GMT. However, the Libyans announced that 1 September, the date of the referendum, would be known as the anniversary of the Federation.[173] While there may be reason to cast a chart for 2 September, this horoscope (Chart 89) is cast for 1 September, and in the absence of other information is cast for 12.00 noon. The horoscope is cast for Cairo, on the grounds of Egypt's role as a leader of the Arab union, although horoscopes cast for Tripoli (the capital of Libya) or Damascus (the capital of Syria) should pertain particularly to the role of those countries in the new state. It would also be valid within the accepted practices of astrology to cast a horoscope for the closing of the polls in the referendum, or the opening if this time were known.

Due to national rivalries the Federation never became operative, and was formally scrapped by the Egyptian Parliament on 1 October 1984.[174]

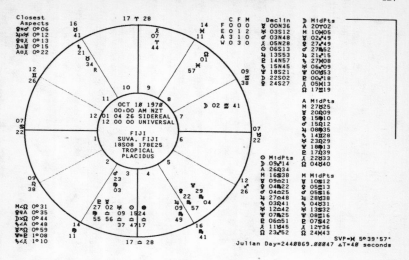

90: Fiji, Independence, 1970

FIJI

Fiji has a long history as a Pacific kingdom, but the present horoscope is based on the date of independence from the British on 10 October 1970. The British flag was lowered for the last time at sunset on 9 October, and the Fijian flag was raised after dawn the following morning, but no English language report could be found which specified the time of independence.[175] It is assumed that this was 00.00 hrs, and Chart 90 is set for this time in the capital, Suva.

FINLAND

Finland was dominated by Sweden from the fourteenth century until its conquest by Russia in 1808.

Independence was gained during the chaos of the Russian revolution in 1917, and the timetable by which this occurred is confused. There seems to have been a declaration of independence a few days prior to 20 June 1917 O/S, although this was not recognized and did not alter the situation in relation to Russia.[176] On 5 July O/S 1917 the Sejm (Finnish parliament) passed a law making itself the supreme political power, although Russian suzerainty was still recognized.[177] However, when the Russian Government ordered the Sejm to dissolve, it backed down and held new elections.[178]

A new government was formed which, on 27 November decided to work towards immediate independence in view of the Bolshevik

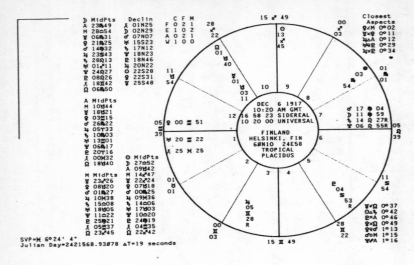

91: Finland, Independence, 1917

seizure of power in Russia. On 4 December a proposal for independence was submitted to Parliament, and on 6 December this was accepted.[179]

All the secondary sources accept without question 6 December 1917 as the date of Finnish independence, and Chart 91 is set for this date for Helsinki, the capital, for 12.00 noon (in the absence of accurate information concerning the time).

The Finnish claim to independence was accepted by the Sovnarkom (Soviet Committee for Nationalities) on 31 December 1917, and became fully legal when the All Russian Central Executive Committee of Soviets confirmed Sovnarkom's acceptance on 4 January 1918.[180]

FRANCE

France owes its origins to the Frankish kingdom established in northern Germany during the sixth century, and which subsequently expanded to northern Italy and much of modern Germany and France. The area approximating to modern France was first distinguished by the Treaty of Verdun in 843, which subdivided the Frankish Empire into three portions. The area which was to become France was then known as Carolingia, and was ruled by Charles the Bald. The birth chart for France should be fixed for the date of this treaty, even though France was not definitely established as a political unit until the reign of Hugh Capet in 987.

Since the French Revolution of 1792 it has been customary to set the French horoscope for the foundation of the current regime — Imperial, Monarchical or Republican. In spite of the fact that France was ruled by three kings and two emperors following the revolution, it may be safely assumed that the horoscope for the original Republic has a validity for modern French affairs. All subsequent French politics have been decisively shaped by the events of 1789 to 1792.

The decisive event which may be taken as the beginning of the French Revolution occurred when the third estate (the commoners) declared themselves to be the National Assembly, the sole representative of France, thus displacing the roles of the other two estates of the States General (equivalent of the Parliament), the nobility and the clergy. This was an act of defiance that set the radical bourgeoisie on a collision course with the old order, and which was proclaimed (probably late) in the morning of 17 June 1789 at Versailles.[180] A subsequent critical moment occurred on 20 June when, by the so-called Tennis Court Oath, the members of the new National Assembly resolved never to separate until they had written a new constitution for France.[181] The storming of the Bastille on 14 July is also undoubtedly a moment of great symbolic importance in the revolution, and is the anniversary on which the revolution itself is commemorated.

The first French Republic was proclaimed at a session of the

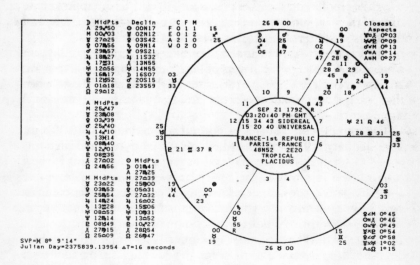

92: France, First Republic, 1792 (1)

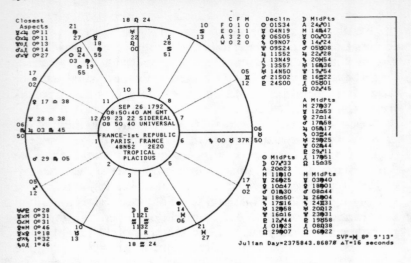

93: France, First Republic, 1792 (2)

National Assembly on 21 September 1792, this date being known subsequently as day 1 of year 1 of the Republic. The proclamation was the third decree of the day, and was passed shortly before the session broke up at 4.00 p.m. LMT.[182] An estimate based on the length of reports and speeches points to 3.30 p.m. as the approximate time of the proclamation, which came into effect immediately, and Chart 92 is set for this time in Paris.

The Republic was proclaimed in public with great ceremony and a procession through the streets of Paris beginning at 9.00 a.m. on 26 September 1792.[183] Chart 93 is set for this time on the grounds that such ceremonial moments are frequently of astrological significance.

The former King Louis XVI himself was executed at 10.20 a.m. on 21 January 1793,[184] a time which must have significance in terms of the fortunes of the French royal house, although it was by now insignificant in terms of the basis of power in the new Republic.

Chart 94 is set for the legal accession to power of Napoleon as one of three members of a triumvirate (with Sieyes and Ducos) which he was to dominate. Napoleon took power during the 'Coup of 18th Brumaire' which began on 9 November 1799 when he was given the military command of Paris, through which he then paraded with 1,500 cavalry, and culminated at approximately 2.00 a.m. on 11 November when he and his two colleagues were formally given

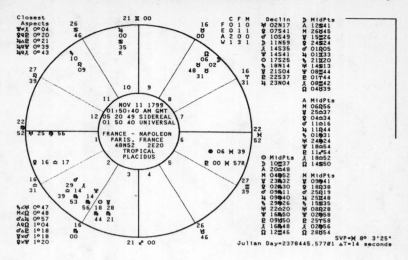

94: France, Napoleon Consul, 1799

executive powers as Consuls of the Republic.[185] This chart (Chart 94) is of historical interest, although in view of Napoleon's vital role in creating the modern French state it also has contemporary relevance.

Napoleon's subsequent proclamation (18 May 1804) and coronation (2 December 1804) as Emperor added nothing to the power he had already acquired.

Following the fall of Napoleon in 1814 the monarchy was restored, to be replaced by the Second Republic in 1848 and the Second Empire in 1852.

The Third Republic, which persisted until 1946, came into being on 4 September 1870 in Paris, being proclaimed as a result of the collapse of the government of Napoleon III and the French defeat by Prussia at Sedan two days earlier.[186] It is likely that this event took place during the afternoon, and horoscopes for this event have been set for various times from 4.00 p.m. to 6.00 p.m. Chart 95, given here, is the speculative variant set for 4.00 p.m. LMT.

The so-called Vichy Republic which was the legal authority in France during the German occupation was a constitutional continuation of the Third Republic, but deserves separate analysis. This regime, so-called because it was based in the town of Vichy, may be timed from the decision to collaborate with the Germans

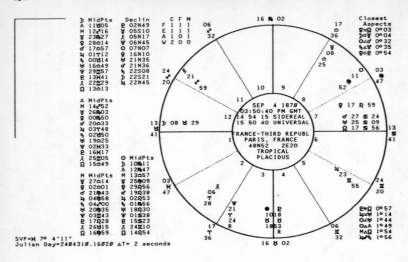

95: France, Third Republic, 1870

at approximately 10.00 p.m. on 16 June 1940, [187] and Chart 96 is set for this time in Paris. The regime adopted a constitution on 10 July 1940.

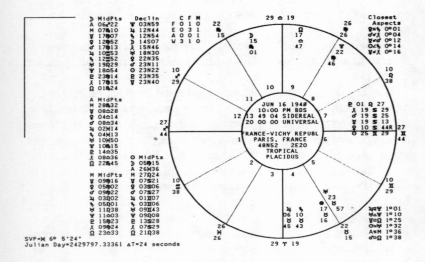

96: France, Vichy Republic, 1940

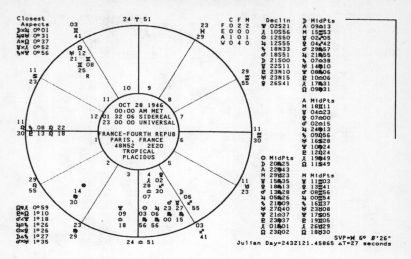

97: France, Fourth Republic, 1946

The Fourth Republic officially came into being with the publication of the constitution of the Republic on 28 October 1946.[188] It is understood that the legislation creating the Republic came into effect at 00.00 hrs and the horoscope (Chart 97) is set for this time in Paris. The Republic came into being through a gradual constitutional process and a number of different dates are quoted for its origin. The constitution was approved by a referendum on 13 October 1946, and this date may be considered to constitute an 'emotional beginning' of the Republic. Subsequent press reports referred to it as a 'provisional beginning'.[189]

The first ceremonial moment of the Republic — when the Great Seal of France was affixed to the constitution on 30 October — would seem to be the basis of the horoscope used by Charles Carter.[190] The 'functional beginning' of the Republic took place on 24 December 1946 with the first meeting of the Council of the Republic.[191]

The current horoscope for France is that of the Fifth Republic, created by General de Gaulle following the failure of the Fourth Republic. The Fifth Republic came into existence with the publication of the new Constitution in the *Journal Officiel* on 5 October 1958, in Paris.[192] It is understood that the legislation creating the Republic came into effect at 00.00 hrs and the horoscope for the Republic (Chart 98) is set for this time.

The first ceremonial moment of the new Republic occurred when

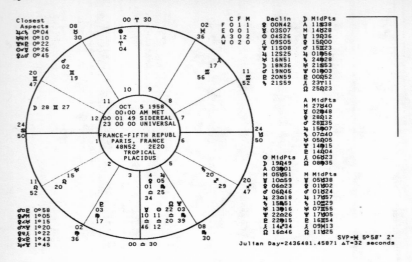

98: France, Fifth Republic, 1958

the State Seal was affixed to the Constitution on 6 October 1958.[193] The Republic became 'functionally operative' when de Gaulle became President (the constitution gave the power for Presidential rule) at 12.20 p.m. on January 1959.[194]

A separate horoscope for the period of de Gaulle's rule in France from 1958 to 1969 may be based on the time he became Prime Minister — between 7.35 and 7.45 p.m. on 1 June 1958 in Paris.[195]

GABON

Gabon was granted autonomy within the French Community on 28 November 1958 and achieved full independence at 00.00 hrs on 17 August 1960.[196] Chart 99 is set for the capital, Libreville.

GAMBIA

The Gambia was granted independence by Great Britain at 00.00 hrs on 18 February 1965.[197] Chart 100 is set for the capital, Bathurst.

GEORGIA

The independence of Georgia was proclaimed by the national Diet (parliament) meeting in the capital, Tbilisi, on 26 May 1918.[198] In the absence of accurate information, the horoscope for Georgian independence (Chart 101) is set for this data and for 12.00 noon LT.

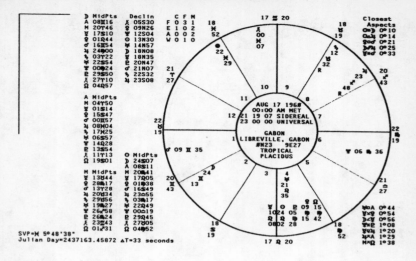

99: Gabon, Independence, 1960

A German protectorate was established, although this came to an end with the collapse of Germany in November 1918, and the country was occupied by the British from 1918 to 7 July 1920. In

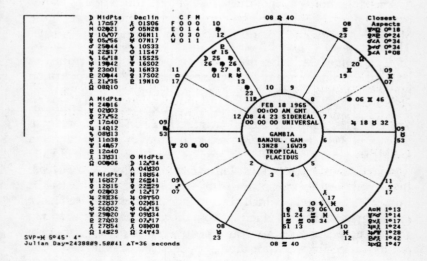

100: Gambia, Independence, 1965

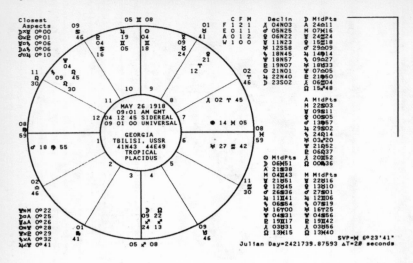

101: Georgia, Independence, 1918

February 1921 a Bolshevik regime replaced the socialist, nationalist government, and on 12 March 1922 Georgia formally surrendered its independence by joining the Transcaucasian Soviet Socialist Republic, which itself agreed to become a part of the USSR on 30 December 1922.[199]

GERMANY

The area now occupied by West Germany was first included in one political unit in the fifth century under the Frankish emperors. The political entity of Germany is sometimes traced back to the coronation of the Frankish monarch Charlemagne as first Holy Roman Emperor in 800. The German (eastern) section of the Frankish dominions was separated from the French (western) section by the Treaty of Verdun in 843, and from this time a kingdom of Germany was in continuous existence until 6 August 1806. In 962 the title of Holy Roman Emperor was revived and the title King of Germany was henceforth tied to that of Emperor (often being the title of the Emperor's heir) and gradually became meaningless. Unlike France and England the forces of feudal power in Germany were so strong that the emperors failed to create a central power, or exert their own authority effectively outside their personal fiefs. Germany — or the Holy Roman Empire — existed as a political unit only in theory, not in practice.

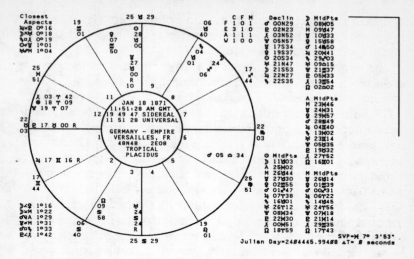

102: Germany, Empire Proclamation, 1871

On 12 July 1806 Napoleon put an end to the Imperial system by reorganizing the many states, kingdoms and principalities of the Holy Roman Empire into the Confederation of the Rhine, under French protection. On 6 August 1806 the title Holy Roman Emperor was formally abandoned, the royal line being henceforth known as the Emperors of Austria.

Following the collapse of the French Empire in 1814 the confederal system was continued in the form of the German Confederation. However, the dominant power in Germany was no longer Austria (the fief of the former Holy Roman Emperors), but Prussia. Since the seventeenth century this state had been gradually expanding its power, transforming itself from the small Electorate of Brandenburg into the Kingdom of Prussia, a military force to be reckoned with.

In 1819 a significant step towards unity was taken with the formation of the Zollverein, a Prussian-dominated customs union which excluded Austrian influence. Throughout the first half of the nineteenth century the debate on national unity continued with liberals pressing for integration between the various states, and conservatives seeking to preserve the sovereignty of the German principalities and kingdoms. However, all attempts at unity failed until backed up by Prussian military force in the 1860s, under the leadership of Bismarck, the 'Iron Chancellor'. By 1866 Prussia was in direct or indirect control of the whole of northern Germany and in October 1870 all the German states except Austria were united under one federal constitution.[200]

The symbolic culmination of this drive for unity was witnessed in the proclamation of the German Empire by Prussian King William I (henceforth Kaiser William I) in the Hall of Mirrors at Versailles on 18 January 1871.[201] Although in retrospect this event is accorded great importance, contemporary reports make it clear that little significance was attached to it at the time.[202] Germany already had one overall government and the Reichstag had discussed the proposed foundation of an empire in December 1870.[203] Nevertheless, the proclamation has vital symbolic importance, and is the basis of Chart 102. The timetable of this event shows that it took place early in the afternoon: 'Soon after noon his Imperial Majesty entered the Hall [of Mirrors].'[204] Once he had entered, a religious ceremony began, psalms were sung, prayers were said, the court preacher gave a short sermon, and a final psalm concluded the service. William then read the text proclaiming the Empire.[205] The standard horoscope for the proclamation is set for 1.00 p.m. LMT, and this time conforms roughly to the historical moment. However, as no press report or secondary source could be found to verify this time, and in view of astrologers' poor record of fabricating data, it has been thought best to follow the pattern set throughout this book and set the horoscope for 12.00 noon, subject to further historical clarification. The horoscope for this date is of obvious historical interest, but in view of its importance as a map for Germany as a whole, still has modern relevance. It is also important to realize that historically the proclamation of the Empire did not create a truly united Germany and that the various minor kingdoms and other states retained their sovereignty.

The Imperial system came to end in the German revolution on 9 November 1918. The revolution itself began with a mutiny by the sailors of the German North Sea fleet at Kiel. The first signs of disobedience were apparent on the night of 29 October 1918, but the revolution proper can be timed from 8.00 a.m. on 30 October, when the crew of one ship refused to put to sea. By evening other crews had seized their ships and over the following days the revolution spread throughout Germany.

The Kaiser, William II, abdicated on the night of 8 November, leaving Prince Max as regent.[206] The Kaiser left Germany at 7.30 a.m. on 10 December 1918, crossing into exile at Eysden, between Liege and Maastricht.[207] However, in order to contain the exploding

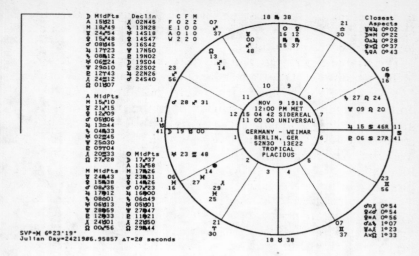

103: Germany Weimar Republic, 1918

revolution the socialist leaders had proclaimed a republic on 9 November in Berlin (Chart 103). In the morning of the 9th a general strike hit Berlin and 'towards midday government buildings were occupied by [mutinous] soldiers and sailors. Then a rally was held outside the Reichstag. This was addressed by Scheidemann (the socialist leader) who announced the abdication and proclaimed the Republic.'[208] The horoscope normally given for this event is set for 1.30 p.m. CET[209] and press reports indicate that this is close to the actual time. However, in view of the current lack of historical corroboration the horoscope for this moment is set for 12.00 noon LT.

Chart 103 is set for the formation of the so-called Weimar Republic, the capital of which was moved to Weimar from Berlin to make a psychological break with the Imperial system. The political system was still federal and Germany was not a centralized unitary state. Considerable power remained with the individual states — Bavaria, Saxony and so on.

Germany only became a unitary centralized state with the advent of the Nazi regime, and under Hitler's rule the country enjoyed the only period (twelve years) of real political unity in its history.

Hitler's personal rule dates from 30 January 1933, when he was appointed the last Chancellor of the Weimar Republic. There are differing reports of the time of this event. Otto Strasser, the leader of the Nazi stormtroopers wrote that 'As the clocks struck twelve the

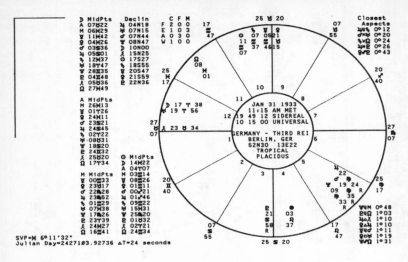

104: Germany, Third Reich, 1933

Bohemian corporal presented himself to Field Marshall von Hindenburg [the President] as Chancellor of the Reich.'[210] This account receives support by inference from at least one major secondary source.[211]

However, Herman Goering, who was present when Hitler was appointed, wrote that 'On Monday the 30th January at 11 o' clock in the morning, Adolf Hitler was appointed Chancellor by the President, and seven minutes later the Cabinet was formed and ministers sworn in.'[212] This time is that used for the standard horoscope for Nazi Germany.[213] Yet it seems that even Goering's account may be inaccurate. According to another eyewitness account Hitler was due to be sworn in at 11.00 a.m., but decided to insist first on a guarantee that fresh elections be held. Hindenburg, who despised Hitler, was not used to being kept waiting, and threatened to cancel the appointment. Hitler gave way at 11.15 a.m., dropped his demand for elections and was immediately sworn in as Chancellor.[214]

Chart 104, for Nazi Germany is set for 11.15 a.m. on 30 January 1933 in Berlin.

Hitler's personal rule was complete when he became President and Chief of the Armed Forces at 12.00 noon on 2 August 1934 in Berlin, following President Hindenburg's death at 9.00 a.m. on the same day.[215] Hitler died at 3.30 p.m. on 30 April 1945, in

Berlin, [216] but the Nazi regime legally came to an end at 10.00 a.m. on 23 May 1945 when British troops at Flensburg arrested his successor, Admiral Donitz, with the rest of the German Government. [217]

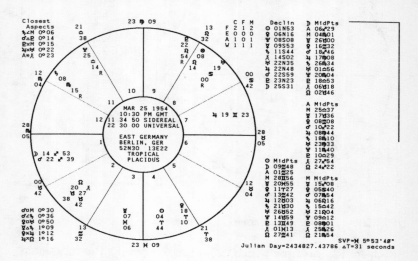

105: Germany, East (GDR), 1954

GERMANY — EAST

East Germany — the communist German Democratic Republic — was proclaimed on 7 October 1949 in Berlin, having been subject to Soviet administration since May 1945. [218] A horoscope for the proclamation of the new state has been set for 30 May 1949, but in fact this was the date on which the Third German Peoples' Congress adopted the proposed constitution for the GDR, and was merely a legal step on the way to proclamation. [219] Chart 105 is set for the time of complete *de jure* East German independence when sovereignty was transferred from the Soviet military authorities to the East German Government. The announcement of this move took place at 10.30 p.m. GMT on 25 March 1954, and the chart is set for this time. [220]

Contemporary reports implied that *de facto* sovereignty was achieved with the announcement, but it is possible that there was another time for the *de jure* event.

GERMANY — WEST

West Germany — the capitalist Federal Republic of Germany —

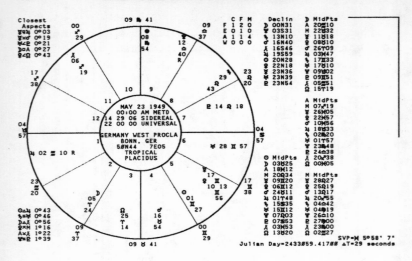

106: Germany, West, Proclamation, 1949

106 is set for this time which, it is clear, represents the functional was proclaimed at 00.00 hrs on 23 May 1949[221] — following four years of British, French and American military administration. Chart

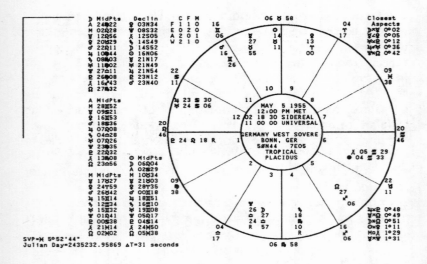

107: Germany, West, Independence, 1955

beginning of the West German state.

However, full independence was only attained when sovereignty was transferred from the allied powers to the West German Government at 12.00 noon on 5 May 1955.[222] Unlike East Germany, which seems to have publicly ignored the equivalent event in its own history, the gaining of full independence by West Germany was an occasion of public celebration, and this, rather than the proclamation of 1949, was regarded as the true beginning of the state's existence. Chart 107 set for 12.00 noon on 5 May in the capital, Bonn, must be regarded as a national horoscope jointly with that of 23 May 1949.

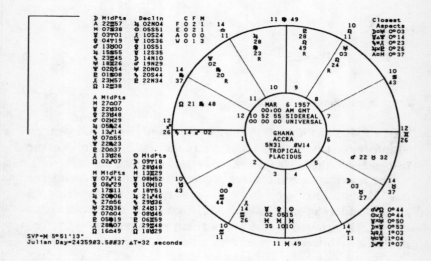

108: Ghana, Independence, 1957

GHANA

The West African state of Ghana was granted full independence by Great Britain at 00.00 hrs on 6 March 1957 in the capital, Accra.[223] Chart 108 is set for this data.

GREECE

The area covered by modern Greece first experienced a legal independent political unity in 307 BC under the kingship of Cassander, one of the generals of Alexander the Great. However, this kingdom did not survive, and the Greek states were annexed by Rome in 146 BC. Thereafter Greece was ruled by the Roman and

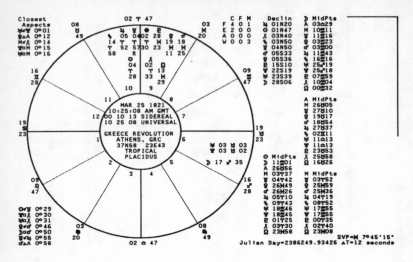

109: Greece, Revolution, 1821

then the Eastern Roman (Byzantine) Empire until 1204. It then disintegrated into smaller states until conquest by the Turks in the fifteenth century.

The revolt against the Turks began in 1821, and independence day (25 March) in Greece is the anniversary of a date when this was already underway. On 25 March 1821 Germanos, the Metropolitan of Old Patras, raised the banner of revolt at his monastery.[224] Also in March 1821 the national leader Ypsilantis invaded Greece, calling for national liberty, and in the ensuing campaign the Turks lost control of the Pelleponese, which became self-governing.[225] The revolt of March 1821 therefore resulted directly in the first *de facto* independent Greek state, and 25 March is accepted as the symbolic date of the revolt. Chart 109 is set for this date, and in the absence of accurate information is cast for 12.00 noon. As the location is uncertain the chart is set for Athens, the future capital. Full legal Greek independence was obtained on 3 February 1830 when Britain and France signed a protocol abolishing Turkish suzerainty and establishing independence.[226] Greece was then able to begin functioning as an internationally recognized state, and on 11 February became a kingdom under Leopold of Saxe-Coburg. Chart 110 is set for 3 February, and, in the absence of accurate information is cast for noon.

Since independence, Greece has experienced several different

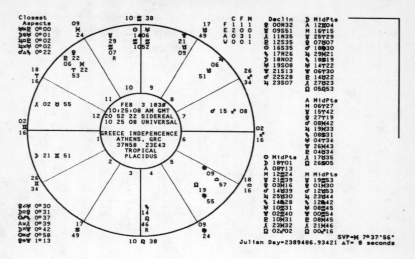

110: Greece, Kingdom, 1830

periods of monarchical and republican government, both
authoritarian and democratic. The current republican parliamentary
democracy dates from 24 July 1974 when, immediately following

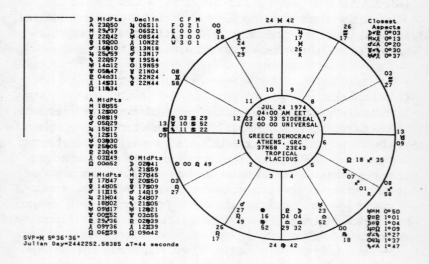

111: Greece, Democracy, 1974

the collapse of the military dictatorship, Constantine Karamanlis
was sworn in as Prime Minister. This event took place at 4.00 a.m.
in Athens, and Chart 111 is set for this time.[227]

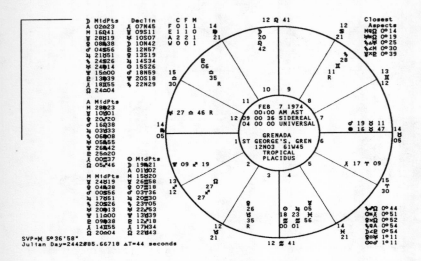

112: Grenada, Independence, 1974

GRENADA

The Caribbean island state of Grenada was granted independence
by Great Britain on 7 February 1974 at 00.00 hrs in the capital, St
George's.[228] Chart 112 is set for this data.

GUATEMALA

The Spanish Captain Generalcy of Guatemala proclaimed
independence on 15 September 1821. The proclamation took place
at a public meeting in Guatemala City, for which the crowds began
assembling at 8.00 a.m. A major debate ensued between the pro-
and anti-independence factions, following which motions in favour
of independence were passed, and the Act of independence was
drawn up, sworn to and signed there and then.[229] In the absence
of accurate information Chart 113 for Guatemalan independence
is set for 12.00 noon.

However, the position was extremely fluid, and the country
voluntarily united with Mexico. Following separation from Mexico,
Guatemala became a part of the United Provinces of Central America,

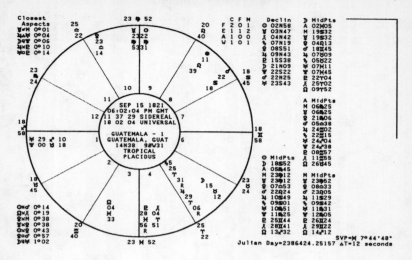

113: Guatemala, Independence, 1821

a state which spent decades disintegrating. Guatemala declared itself independent from this state on 17 April 1839,[230] and Chart 114 is set for this date for Guatemala City and, in the absence of accurate

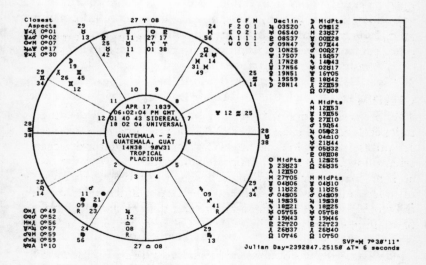

114: Guatemala, Independence, 1839

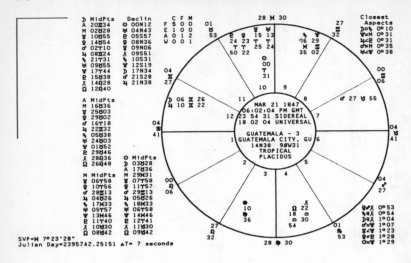

115: Guatemala, Independence, 1847

information, for 12.00 noon.

A further and final declaration of independence was issued on 21 March 1847 (and ratified on 14 September 1848), and this date would seem to represent that on which the state decided definitely on separation rather than union.[231] Chart 115 is set for this date, for Guatemala City and, in the absence of accurate information, for 12.00 noon. Guatemala's last experiment with federation was the Federation of Central America (with El Salvador and Honduras) which lasted from 9 September 1921 to 14 January 1922.

Chart 113 should represent the birth moment of independent Guatemala, although Charts 114 and 115 should also have relevance. The question is open.

GUINEA

The French colony of Guinea achieved its independence at 00.00 hrs on 1 October 1958.[232] Chart 116, for this moment, is set for the capital Conakry. There was no public celebration as the independence was granted in a hurry and with bad grace by France after Guinea declined in a referendum to join the French Community. On the morning of 29 September 1958 the French informed the Guinean Government that the state was 'separated from the territories of French West Africa',[234] a move which led to press reports that 'French

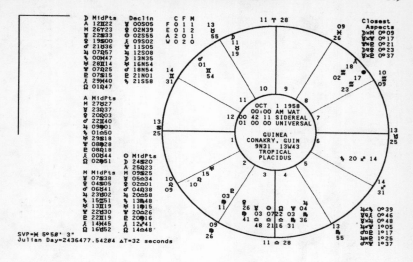

116: Guinea, Independence, 1958

Guinea . . . has today (i.e. 29 September) been informed that she is no longer French Territory'.[235] There are grounds for assuming a *de facto* grant of independence on 29 September, although in either case, the chart given here represents the grant of full *de facto* and *de jure* independence.

However, it was not until 2 October that 'The Territorial Assembly of Guinea formally proclaimed Guinea an Independent Republic following the receipt of the French note of September 29th' which informed the state that it had separated from France.[236]

GUINEA-BISSAU

The Republic of Guinea-Bissau was proclaimed by the nationalist 'African Party for the Independence of Guinea-Bissau and the Cape Verde Islands' at a public assembly on 24 September 1973.[236a] At the time the country was fighting a guerrilla war against the Portuguese, who refused to recognize the proclamation, which took place in one of the country's 'liberated zones'. This date is now regarded as independence day.[236b] and deserves consideration as the basis for the national horoscope.

Legal independence was granted by Portugal on 10 September 1974. A small independence ceremony was conducted during the day.[236c] but the fact that the Portuguese Radio Guinea-Bissau ceased broadcasting at 11.00 p.m. GMT (10.00 p.m. LT) on 9

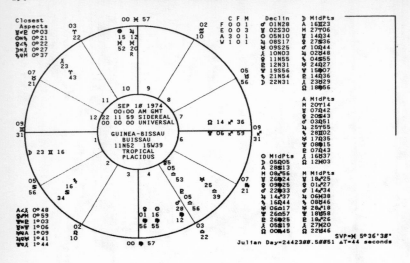

117: Guinea-Bissau, Independence, 1974

September[237] suggests that 00.00 hrs was the legal moment of independence.

On this assumption Chart 117 is set for 00.00 hours on 10 September 1974 in the capital, Bissau.

GUYANA

British Guiana became the independent state of Guyana at 00.00 hrs on 26 May 1966, in the capital, Georgetown.[237] Chart 118 is set for this data.

HAITI

After being colonized by Spain, Haiti was ceded to France in 1697. Pressure for independence first came from escaped slaves, and in 1784 France recognized their independence. However, on the night of 14 August 1791 a slave rebellion began that was to lead to independence for the whole state.[238] In 1801 the state received a constitution giving self-rule, though under French sovereignty.[239] *De facto* independence was gained on 4 December 1803 when the last French troops left Saint Dominique 'marking the colony's first day of true freedom and independence'.[240] It would be reasonable to cast a national chart for this day, although the chart given here is that for full *de jure* independence which was gained on 1 January

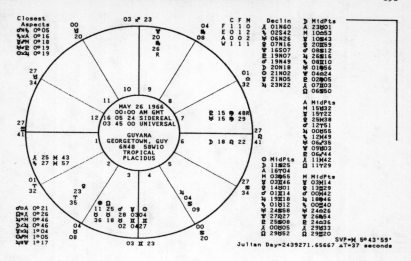

118: Guyana, Independence, 1966

1804 when the Act of Independence was signed at Gonaives.[241] In the absence of accurate information Chart 119 is set for 12.00 noon LMT.

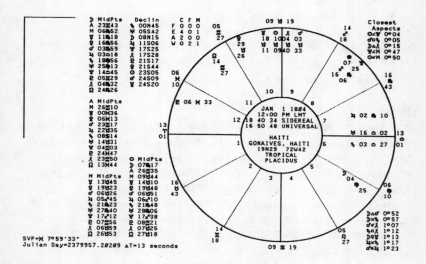

119: Haiti, Independence, 1804

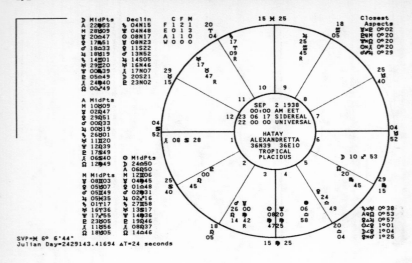

120: Hatay, Independence, 1938

HATAY

The Republic of Hatay was proclaimed on 2 September 1938 in the city of Alexandretta.[242] Chart 120 is set for this date and place, and in the absence of accurate information is cast for 12.00 noon. Alexandretta had been occupied by the French in 1918 after the defeat of Turkey in the First World War, but was separated from French Syria and given autonomy on 4 March 1923. The independent republic was to be short-lived. It was dominated by Turkey, and on 23 June 1939 France (the major regional power), agreed to its outright incorporation into Turkey.

HOLY ROMAN EMPIRE

The Holy Roman Empire was proclaimed on Christmas Day 800 in Rome when Pope Leo III declared the Frankish monarch Charlemagne to be 'Augustus' and 'Emperor'. The proclamation took place at early morning Mass,[243] and although the exact time is unknown, Chart 121, set for 6.00 a.m. is a reasonable approximation.

At the time, the proclamation was intended by the Pope to be a restoration of the Western Roman Empire (which had disappeared in 476) in order to bolster his own position against the Eastern Roman Empire. However, Charlemagne and his successors had different ideas, and the Empire was to be based in Germany rather than Italy. The Holy Roman Empire of Charlemagne and his successors, who held

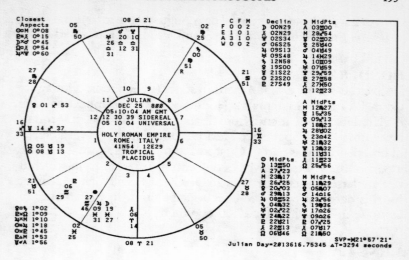

121: Holy Roman Empire, Coronation of Charlemagne, 800

the Imperial title until 905, is always distinguished by historians from the revived Empire founded in 962 by Otto I. The Empire was formally dissolved on 12 July 1806 by Napoleon, and the title Holy

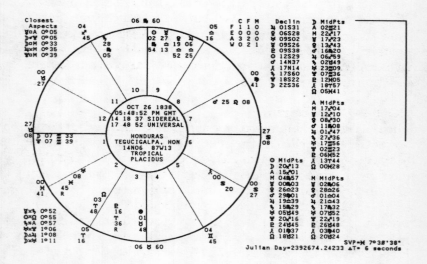

122: Honduras, Independence, 1838

Roman Emperor was abandoned on 6 August 1806: for one thousand years the Empire had played a central role in European affairs.

HONDURAS

Unlike the other Central American states (El Salvador, Nicaragua, Costa Rica and Guatemala), Honduras does not appear to have declared its independence from Spain in 1821. Instead, it seems to have moved from Spanish to Mexican control, perhaps via a period of independence as part of Guatemala. In 1823 Honduras became a part of the United Provinces of Central America, from which it declared itself independent on 26 October 1838.[244] Chart 122 is set for this date, for the capital Tegucigalpa, and, in the absence of accurate information, for 12.00 noon LMT.

HUNGARY

The Duchy of Hungary became the Kingdom of Hungary around the year 1,000, and the country then began a long period as a great Central European power. In 1526 the crown of Hungary passed to the Hapsburg family and thereafter the country was under the domination of the Austrians, a great part of it being occupied by Turkey between 1541 and 1699.

In 1867 nationalist pressure resulted in the country being granted

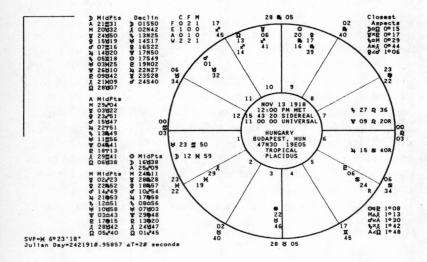

123: Hungary, Republic, 1918

autonomy, and the Austrian Empire was henceforth known as the Austro-Hungarian Empire.

Independence from Austria was achieved in 1918, but the exact sequence of events is unclear. On 15 October the Austrian Government recognized the Hungarian National Council, along with all the other national councils in the Empire, as the representative of its people.[245] This was an attempt to create a federal system under Austrian control, but was disregarded by the Hungarians and on 25 October the National Council proclaimed the independence of Hungary.[246] However, this proclamation appears to have had no effect on the situation, which only began to move after an insurrection in Budapest on 30 October.[247] A press report indicated that nationalist leader Michael Karolyi had set up an independent government by 29 October,[248] although other sources indicate that the National Council didn't ask Karolyi to form a government until 31 October.[249] Another press report indicated that a republic had been proclaimed on 3 November, and that the Austrian Emperor had granted the country independence.[250] The Emperor seems to have abdicated in Hungary on 13 November, the day after his abdication in Austria,[251] and a republic was officially proclaimed by the Hungarian Parliament on 16 November.[252]

Under these confused circumstances the chart for Hungary given here is that for the abdication of the Emperor on 13 November 1918 on the grounds that of all the various dates, this represented the greatest shift in circumstances. Earlier proclamations, either of independence from Austria, or of a republic, had tended to be ineffective, while the proclamation of the republic on 16 November was a recognition of what had already taken place on the 13th. The chart (Chart 123) is set for Budapest on 13 November, but in the absence of accurate information is set for 12.00 noon.

Hungary was ruled by a Communist regime from March to August 1919. In March 1920 the country was proclaimed to be a kingdom, although no monarch was restored. On 1 February 1946 a republic was again proclaimed. Through 1947 and 1948 the Communists concentrated on gaining power via the established political parties, and by the end of 1948 were in effective control of the government. The Communist Peoples' Republic seems to have been proclaimed on 1 February 1949.[253]

HYDERABAD

When India was given independence the princely state of Hyderabad refused to join the new state. It therefore received independence

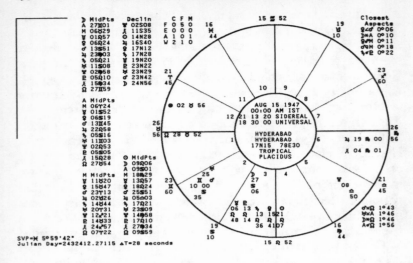

124: Hyderabad, Independence, 1947

from Great Britain at 00.00 hrs on 15 August 1947, at exactly the same moment as India. The chart (Chart 124) is set for Hyderabad. The independent existence of Hyderabad came to an end a year later when India invaded on 13 September 1948. The Indian invasion began at 4.00 a.m. and was launched from Chanda, Sholapur and Bezuada.[254]

ICELAND

Iceland was an independent republic from 930 to 1264, when it passed under the rule of the Norwegians. From 1381 until 1918 it was ruled directly by Denmark.

Two dates are given for the independence of Iceland from Denmark, both of which may be the basis for a national horoscope. Legal sovereign independence was granted on 1 December 1918,[256] although a confederal arrangement was maintained with Denmark and the Danish King remained Head of State. Chart 125 is set for this date, for the capital, Reykyavik and, in the absence of accurate information, for 12.00 noon.

The second date is that for the severance of all links with Denmark and the proclamation of a republic on 17 June 1944 in Reykyavik.

The Danish Icelandic Union Treaty was abrogated on 16 June, leaving the way clear for a republic to be declared.[257] On 17 June

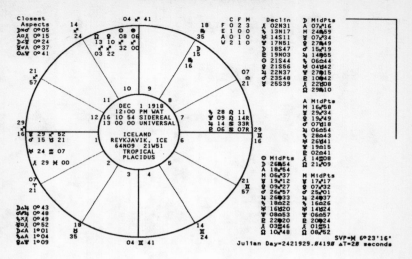

125: Iceland, Independence, 1918

the constitution was announced and the Republic formally
inaugurated at 2.00 p.m. with great ceremony,[258] and Chart 126 is
set for this time.

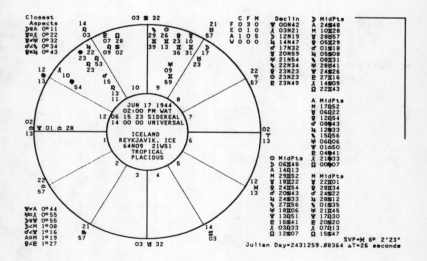

126: Iceland, Independence, 1944

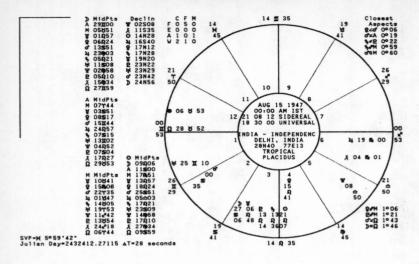

127: India, Independence, 1947

INDIA

The greater part of India experienced political unity for several periods of history, notably during the medieval 'Mogul' Empire. The current

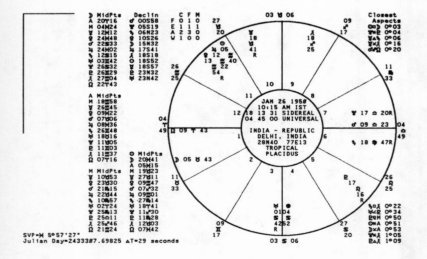

128: India, Republic, Proclamation, 1950

horoscope is based on the time of independence from the British at 00.00 hrs on 15 August 1947, in Delhi.[259] Chart 127 is set for this data.

A second horoscope for India is set for the proclamation of the republic at a time which was very likely elected astrologically. The proclamation of the Republic of India was read in New Delhi at 10.15 a.m. on 26 January 1950, immediately after which the new government was sworn in.[260] Chart 128 is set for this data. The 26th January was chosen as the twentieth anniversary of the call for independence by the Congress in 1930.

INDONESIA

Indonesia attained its independence in a gradual process lasting from 1945 to 1954. As a Dutch colony, it was occupied by Japan during the Second World War. Following the Japanese surrender, the local nationalists under the leadership of Mohammed Hatta proclaimed the independence of the Republic of Indonesia on 17 August 1945.[261] The Dutch refused to recognize the new government and colonial rule was restored by British and Dutch troops. Even though the independence movement was suppressed it would be consistent to take the time for this proclamation (if it were known) as the basis of the national horoscope (as is the case in Eire, where the initial

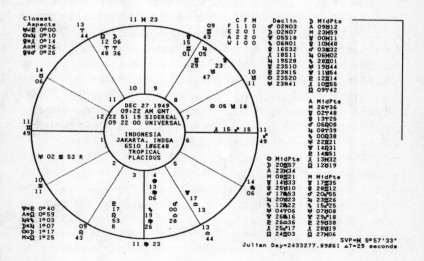

129: Indonesia, Independence, 1949

proclamation of independence was suppressed).

In 1947 the Dutch attempted to set up a state with spurious independence in a similar fashion to that the French were following in their Asian colonies. An 'Indonesian Republic' consisting of Sumatra, Madura and West Java was created on 4 May 1947, the capital being Bandung.[262] The Dutch retained a far greater degree of control than was acceptable to nationalist feeling, and the independence struggle continued. Finally, on 27 December 1949, the Dutch gave independence to the United States of Indonesia, consisting of the Indonesian Republic together with the other islands of the Indonesian archipelago, including Dutch Borneo. The formal transfer of sovereignty from the Netherlands to Indonesia took place at 10.22 a.m. when Queen Juliana signed the act of transfer in Amsterdam.[263] Chart 129 is set for 9.22 a.m. GMT on 27 December 1947, for the new capital, Djakarta.

The last formal connection with the Netherlands occurred during the evening of 11 August 1954 when the Netherlands-Indonesian Union was dissolved.[264]

IRAN

Iran, formerly known as Persia, began its ascent to international power on the accession of King Cyrus in 550 BC. Following the conquest of Babylon in 539 BC the Persian Empire entered its period of greatness. Throughout the classical and medieval periods a succession of empires were based in the Iranian plateau, some ruled by native dynasties, some by foreign, such as the Mongols. From 1520 to 1979 the country was ruled by native dynasties, although from the nineteenth century until the 1940s larger areas of the country were under periodic foreign occupation, mainly by the British or Russians.

The present parliamentary regime in Iran was founded in 1906 following pressure by an alliance of commercial and clerical interests, and in view of this systems's survival of the collapse of the monarchy and foundation of the republic in 1979, its creation may still be considered a 'birth moment' for modern Iran.[265] The Shah agreed to the creation of a parliament (majlis) on 5 August 1906. On 7 October the majlis held its first meeting, and on 30 December the Shah signed a liberal constitution.[266] The 7th October should be considered the critical date.

The Pahlavi dynasty, which was overthrown in 1979, owes its origins to the military coup of 21 February 1921 when a Cossack commander, Reza Khan, marched on the capital, Tehran, and proclaimed himself Minister of War and Commander-in-Chief.[267] The coup appears to

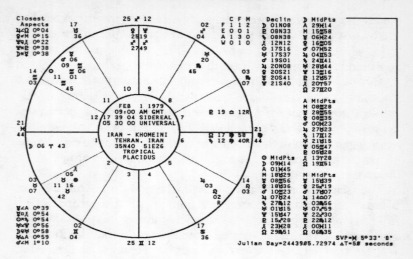

130: Iran, Khomeini, 1979

have begun at 00.40 hrs a.m. LMT in Tehran.[268] Reza Khan became
Prime Minister on 28 October 1923 and was proclaimed Shah by
the majlis on 13 December 1925.[269] Reza Khan's coronation appears
to have taken place at 4.10 p.m. LMT on 25 April 1926.[270]

On 21 March 1935 Reza Khan officially changed the country's
name from Persia to Iran, a symbol of the rapid modernization that
was taking place.[271] It is not suggested that the various horoscopes
for Pahlavi rule should be used as current charts for Iran (unless the
dynasty should ever be restored), but they are of considerable
historical interest in view of the critical role of Iran in world events
following the 1979 revolution.

It is by no means clear which time should be taken as the horoscope
for the contemporary regime in Iran. The revolution began during
1978 and was effectively successful when the Shah left the country
on 16 January 1979. The royal jet left Tehran with the Shah on board
at 1.24 p.m. on 16 January,[272] a date which symbolically marks the
end of the old regime, and which could be taken as the basis for
a national horoscope.

Ostensibly the Shah had left the country only for medical treatment
and it was not until 11 February that the regime officially surrendered
power. The critical moment came at 10.20 a.m. when the army leaders
decided to remain neutral in the struggle between the Government
and the Revolution, a decision that was broadcast at 2.00 p.m., and

which deprived the Government of any ability to govern. [273] The Shah's last prime minister, Bakhtiar, resigned later in the day.

However, the religious leader, Ayatollah Khomeini, had already returned to Tehran from his exile in Paris on 1 February 1979, an event which could be taken as the symbolic foundation of the Islamic Republic. Khomeini landed in Tehran 'shortly after 9.00 a.m. LT' or '12.30 New York time'. [274] Unfortunately, as so often happens, press accounts varied, and a time of 9.50 a.m. LT has been suggested. [275] It is suggested that in the absence of further research the earlier time be taken, and Chart 130 is set for 9.00 a.m. on 1 February 1979, Tehran.

The Islamic Republic itself was proclaimed on 1 April 1979 in a radio broadcast by Ayatollah Khomeini. [276] Unfortunately no English language press reports carried the time of this proclamation. However, a time can be inferred from the report that the Republic was declared 'less than seventeen hours' after voting had ceased in the referendum of 31 March, [277] and that the voting period had been extended by four hours, to finish at 10.00 p.m. [278] This gives a time of approximately 3.00 p.m. on 1 April for the proclamation. Unfortunately the report that the proclamation took place seventeen hours after voting ceased included the information that it took place 'last night'. All other reports, however, agree that the proclamation took place during the day. [279] Chart 131 for the formal founding of

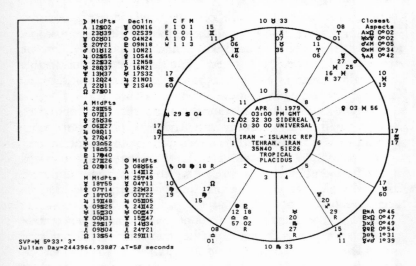

131: Iran, Islamic Republic, 1979

the Islamic Republic is therefore set for 3.00 p.m. on 1 April 1979 in Tehran.

IRAQ

The modern state of Iraq occupies the Tigris-Euphrates valley, the heartland of the ancient Babylonian and Assyrian Empires, dating back to 1800 BC. Following the fall of Babylon in 539 BC the region was dominated by Persia (with brief Greek and Roman intervals) until its conquest by the Arabs in the seventh century AD. Under Arab rule the area regained its political independence, the Caliphate of Baghdad becoming a major international power. From the thirteenth century until 1918 the region was ruled by the Mongols, Persians or Turks. In 1918 the area passed under the rule of the British who, on 23 August 1921 formally created the Kingdom of Iraq.

Even though the British retained control under the League of Nations mandate, the horoscope for this date deserves to be taken as a national chart in view of the fact that an entirely new state was being recognized for the first time. Chart 132 is set for the beginning of the proclamation ceremony at 6.00 a.m. on 23 August 1921 in Baghdad, the capital. [280]

Full *de jure* independence was accorded to the new state when the British Mandate was terminated on 4 October 1932. This event does not seem to have been regarded as particularly important at

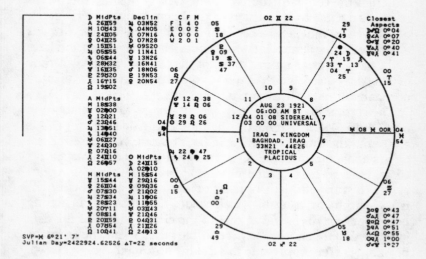

132: Iraq, Kingdom, 1921

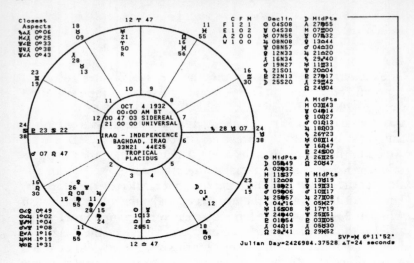

133: Iraq, Independence, 1932

the time, at least not by the British press, perhaps because the state already possessed *de jure* internal self-rule, and because the British intended to continue their domination of Iraqi foreign policy. No mention was made of the end of the Mandate in the British press, although the congratulations of King George V and other heads of state on the Iraqi admission to the League of Nations (a result of full *de jure* independence) was noted.[281] Nevertheless, this was an important legal moment, representing the independence of Iraq, and Chart 133 is set for this date, for the capital Baghdad. A time of 00.00 hrs is used, which would be consistent with the termination of mandates in other countries.

The current Republic of Iraq owes its origins to a military coup on 14 July 1958 in Baghdad. The time normally taken for this is 5.00 a.m., the time when the rebellious officers, having seized the radio station, broadcast the news of the overthrow of the monarchy.[282] Chart 134 is set for this time, date and place. Another press report, giving the time of the first broadcast as 'towards seven o' clock',[283] is too late to be plausible. Please note the difficulty in setting horoscopes for *coups d'état*, due to the erratic nature of the data given in contemporary reports. If possible a chart should be set for the beginning of the coup, but in this case the time for this is not known.

It would also be acceptable to set a chart for the proclamation of the Republic, which in this case seems to have been made over

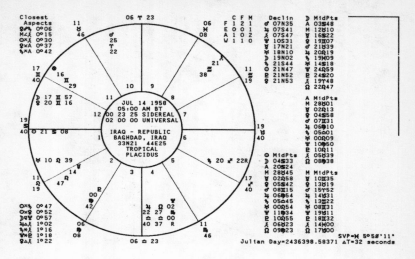

134: Iraq, Republic, 1958

the radio at 9.40 a.m.,[284] although in terms of the day's events this does not seem to have been an important moment. See also Chart 7 for the Arab Federation.

The current Baathist (radical-nationalist) regime in Iraq came into power in a military coup on 8 February 1963. It is difficult to ascertain a time for the moment of the coup,[285] and it is best to use the Republic chart for the current regime.

ISRAEL

From the Roman conquest at the beginning of the Christian era until 1948 the area occupied by modern Israel was consistently under Roman, Arab, or Turkish domination. The crusader kingdom of Jerusalem (1099–1244) extended over an area equivalent to Israel but was dominated by Norman and French barons.

In 1918 Palestine, the name normally applied to the geographical area, was occupied by the British, who received a League of Nations mandate. After decades of international negotiation the concept of a Jewish state of Israel received backing from the United Nations, and in an atmosphere of increasing violence, Britain resolved to give the state independence at 00.00 hrs on 15 May 1948.[286] However, in the atmosphere of crisis, and an invasion by the Arab Legion at dawn on 12 May,[287] the Jewish leaders arranged a meeting to proclaim

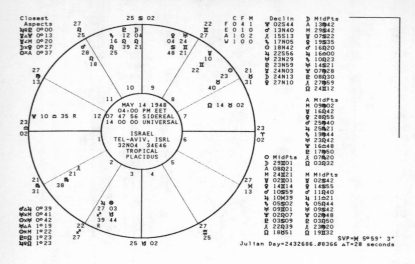

135: Israel, Independence, 1948

independence at 4.00 p.m. on 14 May in the Tel Aviv museum, pre-empting the legal end of British rule by six hours.[288] A Jewish provisional government had been in existence since March.[289]

The meeting began at precisely 4.00 p.m., as arranged, when Ben Gurion, the first prime minister, struck the table with his gavel. The audience then rose spontaneously and burst into the Hatikva, the anthem of the Zionist movement.[290]

Chart 135 is set for the exact moment of *de facto* independence at 4.00 p.m. on 14 May 1948.

De jure independence was observed at 00.00 hrs on 15 May by the British, whose representative, the High Commissioner General Cunningham, waited on board HMS *Euryalus* off the coast of Haifa,[291] a situation to be repeated at the independence of South Yemen in 1967. The chart for this moment could be considered a map for Palestine (see Chart 198).

The horoscope in the book *Mundane Astrology* by Baigent, Campion and Harvey, is given for 4.37 p.m. on 14 May.[292] This is based on the symbolic importance of Ben Gurion's statement after reading the two pages of the independence proclamation that 'The State of Israel has arisen.'[293] However, it is clear that Ben Gurion himself regarded 4.00 p.m. as the critical time, noting in his diary: 'At four the Proclamation of Independence'.[294]

ITALY

The bulk of the area comprising modern Italy formed a political unit under the Roman Republic by 238 BC. By 200 BC Roman possessions extended beyond Italy itself, and thereafter the area was to be the hub of the much greater Roman Empire. From AD 476 until the mid sixth century Italy again became a political unity under first the German patrician Odovacer and then the Ostrogoths. By 554 the country had been reconquered by the Eastern Roman Empire, but following the invasion of the Lombards in 568 the region began the slide into feudal disintegration and division between small competing states and domination by foreign powers that was to last until the mid nineteenth century. During the medieval period the title King of Italy was a meaningless honour attached to the Holy Roman Empire.

Pressure for Italian unification built up following the wave of liberal revolutions across Europe in 1848. During 1859 and 1860 a series of plebiscites in the various independent states resulted in votes in favour of unification, although this would not have been achieved without a military campaign directed from the kingdom of Piedmont. A key symbolic moment was achieved on 12 October 1860 when the northern and southern parts of the country were united.[295]

The Kingdom of Italy formally came into being on 17 March 1861 when the *Official Gazette* (henceforth the *Official Gazette of the*

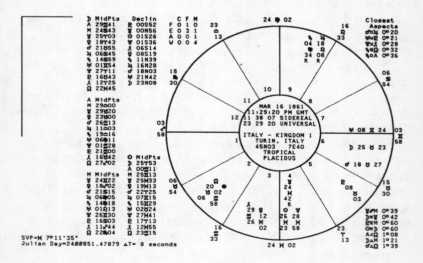

136: Italy, Proclamation, 1861

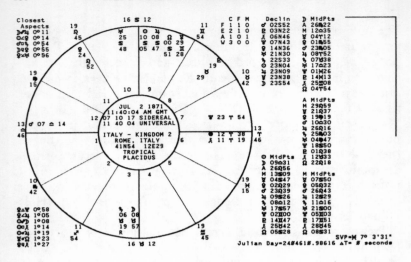

137: Italy, Entry of Victor Emmanuel into Rome, 1871

Kingdom of Italy) published the law by which King Victor Emmanuel II of Piedmont assumed for himself and his successors the title of King of Italy.[296] Chart 136 is set for this date, for Turin, the capital of Piedmont (although a chart for Rome might have symbolic value) and for 00.00 hrs (i.e. 16 March GMT). The time of 00.00 hrs is assumed, but consistent with the general principle that laws published in Official Gazettes come into force at 00.00 hrs.[297]

The Italian horoscope in *Mundane Astrology*[298] is set for the entry of King Victor Emmanuel into Rome, a moment which was greeted with great celebration, and which may be taken as the basis for a national horoscope. The city of Rome, formerly under the rule of the Papacy, had been attacked by Italian troops on 20 September 1871, and fully occupied by the 23rd.[299]

Victor Emmanuel himself did not enter Rome until 2 July 1871, arriving by train at the new capital at 12.30 p.m., to be greeted by a ceremonial ride through cheering crowds, and public banquets and celebrations.[300] If 17 March 1861 was the legal beginning of the Kingdom of Italy, 2 July 1871 was clearly the ceremonial beginning, and Chart 137 is set for this date and for the time of the King's arrival at the railway station. The source for the chart given in *Mundane Astrology*, set for 11.40 a.m., is not known.

The horoscope for the Italian Republic is set for 10 June 1946. King Victor Emmanuel III, who was tainted by his association with

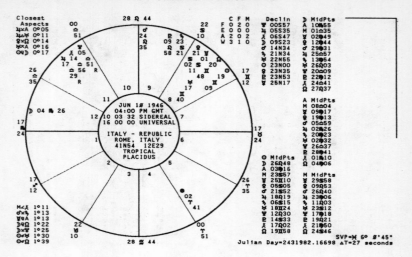

138: Italy, Republic, 1946

Mussolini, abdicated on 9 May 1946 in favour of his son Humbert. On 2 June a referendum was held on the future of the monarchy, which produced a majority in favour of abolition. The announcement of the referendum results by the Government at 6.00 p.m. on 10 June was taken as a *de facto* proclamation of the Republic,[301] and Chart 138 is set for this data. However, Humbert refused to accept the decision and the *de jure* birth of the Republic technically depended on a proclamation by the Court of Cassation. Any proclamation by the Government preceding this was technically illegal. However, Humbert eventually accepted the reality of the situation and went into exile on the afternoon of 13 June, absolving Italians from their oath to the monarchy before leaving.[302] It might be useful to compare this horoscope with that for the earlier proclamation of a Roman Republic under French auspices on 15 February 1797.[303]

IVORY COAST

The Ivory Coast received independence from France at 00.00 hrs on 7 August 1960, in the capital, Abidjan.[304] Chart 139 is set for this data.

JAMAICA

Jamaica received independence from Great Britain at 00.00 hrs on

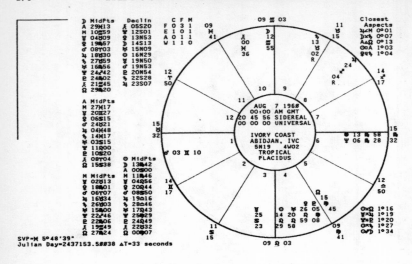

139: Ivory Coast, Independence, 1960

6 August 1962, in the capital, Kingston.[305] The new state remained a member of the Commonwealth with the British monarch as head of state. Chart 140 is set for this data.

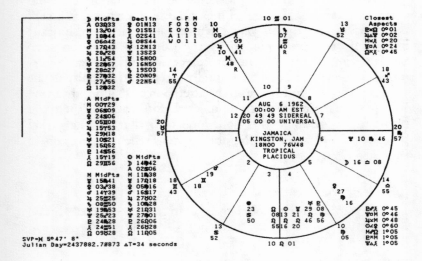

140: Jamaica, Independence, 1962

JAPAN

Japanese historical mythology dates the foundation of the state from the accession of the first emperor, Jimmu, in 660 BC, although it seems likely that real political unity was not achieved until the first centuries of the Christian era. [306]

The history of modern Japan is often dated from the promulgation of the first modern constitution, the so-called Meiji Constitution, on 11 February 1889. The Constitution, which was modelled on that of Germany, came into effect as the Emperor Meiji handed it to the prime minister, Count Kuroda, in a brief ceremony at the royal palace. [307] Even though the constitution did not fulfil the liberal reforms it promised, its promulgation is a highly symbolic moment in Japan's advance to the status of a world power. During the 1890s the country experienced an industrial revolution and by 1906 was able to challenge European military power. The promulgation of the constitution took place during the day, and in the absence of accurate information Chart 141 is set for 12.00 noon LMT, for the capital, Tokyo.

Horoscopes for modern Japan are also set for the revival of the country following its defeat in the Second World War in 1945, and its occupation by the USA. One alternative is set for the coming into effect of the post-war constitution, apparently at 00.00 hrs on 3 May 1947 in Tokyo. [308] The constitution had been promulgated on 3

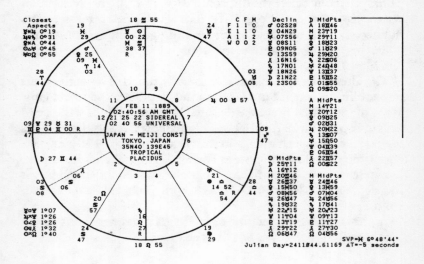

141: Japan, Meiji Constitution, 1889

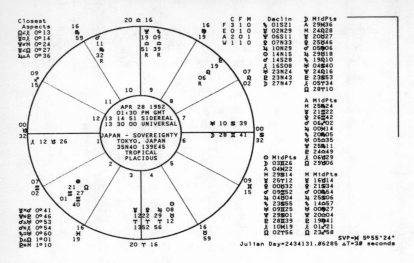

142: Japan, Sovereignty, 1952

November 1946, being formally presented to the Diet (Parliament) by the Emperor in the morning and marked by ceremonies in the afternoon.[309] The day the constitution came into effect, 3 May 1947, was also a day of celebration. The crucial time seems to have been a brief ceremony before the Imperial Palace at which 'the constitution was formally put into effect'.[310] The fact of a daytime ceremony does not necessarily preclude a *de jure* beginning for the constitution at 00.00 hrs (see for example the 1801 horoscope for the United Kingdom).

The alternative given here is accurately timed. This is the chart for the official restoration of Japanese independence and sovereignty, at the moment that peace was declared between Japan and the USA. This took place on 28 April 1952. Different press reports listed times in different forms including 2.30 p.m. British time,[311] 9.30 a.m. New York time,[312] 9.30 a.m. Eastern Daylight Time[313] and 10.30 p.m. Japanese time.[314] Chart 142 for Japanese post-war independence is therefore set for 1.30 p.m. GMT on 28 April 1952, and for the capital, Tokyo.

A press report giving a time of 11.30 GMT was erroneous due to being written three days prior to the event.[315]

JORDAN
The situation surrounding the independence of Jordan is unclear.

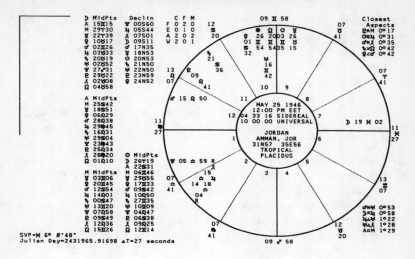

143: Jordan, Independence, 1946

The region had never existed as a political entity before its occupation by the British in 1917. The British mandate was assigned by the League of Nations on 25 April 1920, [316] although it does not seem to have come into force officially until 29 September 1923, [317] four months after the state apparently became autonomous under British sovereignty. [318] A further measure of self-control seems to have been granted on 20 February 1928, although reports that this date represented internal independence seem exaggerated. [319]

A possible horoscope for the beginning of the political entity of Jordan, if not its independent existence, could be based on the appointment of King Abdullah by the British in April 1921, a move which separated Jordan from Palestine, Iraq and Syria, all of which had previously been regarded as potentially parts of the same Arab state. [320]

Full independence was granted by the British in 1946, but there is confusion over the correct date. On 22 March 1946 Emir Abdullah and British Foreign Secretary Ernest Bevin signed an agreement in London, of which Article 1 was a recognition by Britain of Jordanian independence. This was reported at the time as a full recognition of Jordanian independence, the moment of the signing being regarded as that at which Jordan gained sovereign status. [321]

However, the fact that the agreement was to be referred to Parliament suggests that the moment of signature did not bring full independence, and that there were further constitutional procedures to follow. [322]

There are therefore good grounds for taking the second of two 'independence dates' as the true date. This was 25 May 1946. The state was officially inaugurated, the king proclaimed and full independence achieved at a series of ceremonies in the morning of 25 May in the capital, Amman. [323] Chart 143 is set for this date and place, and in the absence of accurate information, for 12.00 noon.

KAMPUCHEA

Kampuchea was formerly known as the Khmer Republic, or more commonly as Cambodia. Throughout the medieval period the Khmer Empire was a regional power in South-East Asia, becoming a French protectorate in 1863. During the Second World War the country was occupied by Japan, following which the French were unable to fully reassert their authority. In March 1945, five months before the Japanese collapse, King Sihanouk had proclaimed Cambodian independence, and a chart for this time could be considered a national horoscope. In October 1945, British and French troops occupied Cambodia with a view to re-imposing French rule. However, under nationalist pressure, France granted autonomy in 1946 and *de jure* independence in 1949. The grant of independence was spurious as France retained control of defence, foreign affairs

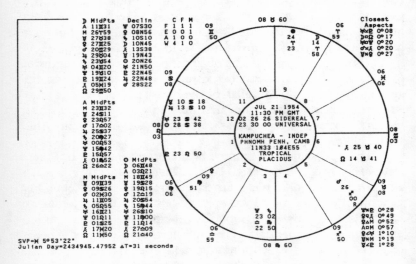

144: Kampuchea, Independence, 1954

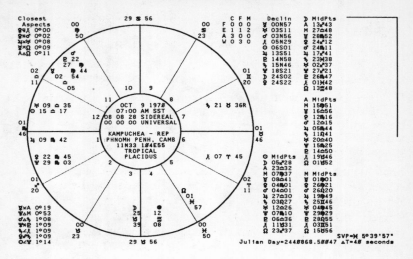

145: Kampuchea, Republic, 1970

and internal security. Subsequent independence agreements were
also spurious. It was not until the signing of the Geneva Accord at
11.30 p.m. GMT on 21 July 1954 that France recognized the complete
independence of Cambodia,[324] and Chart 144 is set for this date
and time, and for the capital Phnomh Penh. This horoscope may
be considered the national chart for Kampuchea.

In 1970 a Republic was proclaimed. The chart for this moment
may have some relevance still, as the country is still a republic, even
though Communist. The chart is, however, of added interest as it
was almost certainly elected astrologically — the new leader, General
Lon Nol, was known to take astrological advice on all political matters.
Prince Sihanouk was officially deprived of the office of Chief of State
at 1.00 p.m. on 18 March 1970,[325] and the Khmer Republic officially
came into existence at 7.00 a.m. on 9 October 1970.[326] Chart 145
is set for this date and time, and for the capital, Phnomh Penh.

The Communist regime in Kampuchea took power on 18 April
1975. The President, Lon Nol, had fled on 2 April (on astrological
advice?), the Americans pulled out on 13 April and on the 15th,
units of the Communist Khmer Rouge guerrilla force entered the
outskirts of Phnomh Penh. At the start of the morning of 18 April
Khmer Rouge units reached the heart of Phnomh Penh at which
point celebrations burst out all over the capital. By 8.00 a.m. sporadic
firing in the outskirts had died down.[327] Chart 146, for the

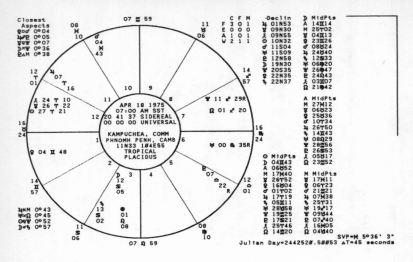

146: Kampuchea, Communist

Communist regime is therefore set for 7.00 a.m., the approximate time of dawn in Phnomh Penh, on 18 April 1975.

The Khmer Rouge regime has since been replaced by the pro-Vietnamese government under the leadership of Heng Samrin (on 8 January 1979) so Chart 146 may be considered to have dubious relevance as far as present developments are concerned. However, as this is the chart for the infamous Pol Pot government, under which one third of the population was exterminated, it has considerable historical importance.

KENYA
Kenya received full independence from Great Britain at 00.00 hrs on 12 December 1963, in the capital, Nairobi.[328] Chart 147 is set for this data.

KHALISTAN
Khalistan is the name for the proposed independent Sikh state of Kashmir, currently part of India. The decision to create a Sikh homeland was taken at an international conference of Sikhs held in Birmingham, England, on 5 May 1984. Chart 148 is set for the beginning of the press conference called on 13 June 1984 to announce the formation of the Khalistan Government in exile. The press

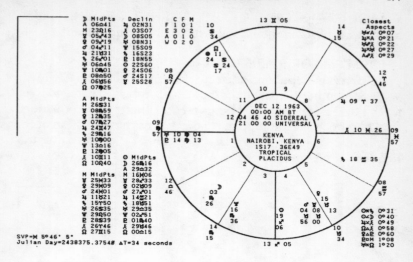

147: Kenya, Independence, 1963

conference commenced at 3.00 p.m. in London,[329] but the chart is set for the Sikh capital, Amritsar. The fact that the Moon, which at 3.42 p.m. was eclipsed, was conjunct the Ascendant to the minute

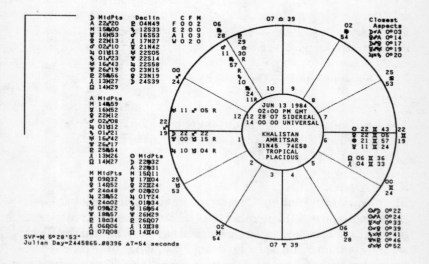

148: Khalistan, Proclamation of Government in Exile, 1984

at Amritsar suggests that the start of the press conference in London may have had some intentional astrological significance.

KHOREZEM SOVIET REPUBLIC

The Khorezem Republic was created during the Russian Civil War on 30 September 1920, with its capital at Khiva. [427] Chart 149 is set for this date and place and, in the absence of accurate information, for 12.00 noon. The Republic is now part of the Soviet Union.

A horoscope such as this may reasonably be used to analyse the trends in contemporary Soviet Asia.

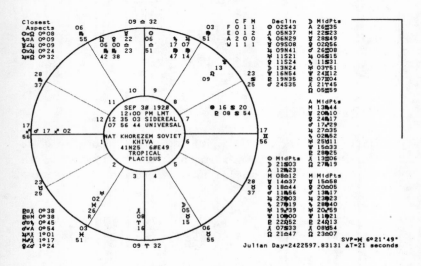

149: Khorezem Republic, Creation, 1920

KIRIBATI

The British-ruled Gilbert Islands were given independence as the state of Kiribati at 00.00 hrs on 12 July 1979, in the capital, Tarawa. [330] Chart 150 is set for this data.

KOREA — NORTH

The Communist Peoples' Democratic Republic of Korea was given independence on 12 September 1948 following three years of Soviet occupation. [331] This event aroused a total lack of interest in the West, and no mention could be found in any English language press report or in the *BBC Summary of World Broadcasts*. The position is complicated by the fact that different dates, such as 9 September,

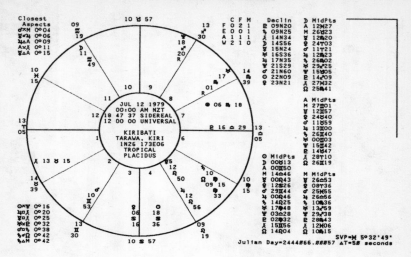

150: Kirabati, Independence, 1979

are given for independence.[332] In the absence of further information Chart 151, for North Korea is set for 12.00 noon on 12 September 1948, for the capital, Pyongyang.

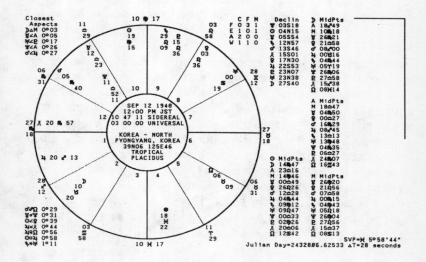

151: Korea, North, Independence, 1948

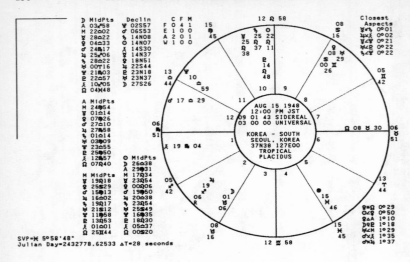

152: Korea, South, Independence, 1948

KOREA — SOUTH

The pro-Western Republic of Korea was given independence on 15
August 1948 following three years of occupation by the USA.[333] The
independence ceremonies seem to have taken place during the day.[334]
In the absence of further information Chart 152 for South Korea
is set for 12.00 noon on 15 August 1948, for the capital, Seoul.

KUWAIT

Kuwait attained full independence on 19 June 1961 when an
exchange of letters between the British Political Resident in Kuwait
and the Arab ruler, terminated the Protectorate which had been
established on 23 January 1899.[335] The wording of the agreement
to the effect that the Protectorate 'shall be regarded as terminated
on this day's date'[336] suggests that independence was granted at 00.00
hrs, yet the exchange of letters took place during the day. In the
absence of more accurate information Chart 153 for the independence
of Kuwait is set for 12.00 noon on 19 June 1961, for the capital, Kuwait.

It was noted at the time that Kuwait had enjoyed *de facto*
independence for about two years, and that this agreement was a
formal recognition of an existing state of affairs.[337]

LAOS

The South-East Asian state of Laos is part of a region with a long

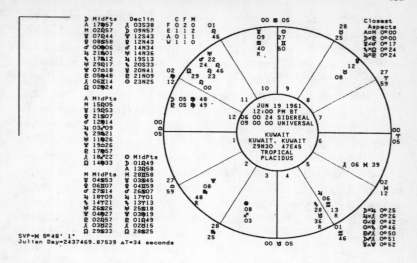

153: Kuwait, Independence, 1961

history, but itself only existed as a unified political entity following the collapse of French colonial rule in the 1950s.

Under Japanese occupation in the Second World War, nationalist

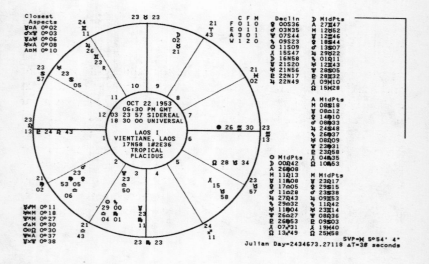

154: Laos, Independence, 1953

aspirations were encouraged and a declaration of independence was made on 15 April 1945. [338] Even though the country was still under Japanese control, the horoscope for this event could be considered to be a national birth chart (as for example with the similar declaration of independence in Cambodia, or the declaration of independence in Poland under German auspices), on the grounds that the chain of events initiated at that time were to result in full independence.

Following the defeat of Japan in August 1945 the country was occupied by the Chinese (on behalf of the French) and then in 1946 by the French themselves. However, a rebel government was operating in alliance with the Communist revolutionaries in Vietnam, and the French sought to diffuse this threat by compromising with conservative nationalist forces (as in Cambodia and Vietnam). On 19 July 1949 the country was granted autonomy as an Associated State within the French Union, which meant in fact that the French retained full control. [339] However, under pressure from the Communist Pathet Lao guerrillas, and facing total defeat in Vietnam, the French subsequently conceded full independence to Laos. Even though Laos remained within the French Union the country does seem to have achieved effective independence, perhaps because of the general collapse of French control in the region. This is in contrast to those African states for whom independence within the French

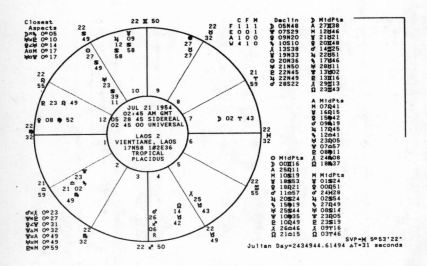

155: Laos, Independence, 1954

Union was a means to guarantee continued French control.

Chart 154 for the independence of Laos is cast for the moment of the signature of the treaty granting independence at 7.30 p.m. on 22 October 1953 in Paris. [340] The chart is set for Vientiane, the Laotian capital.

Full legal independence (free of the constraints of the French Union) was granted to Laos by the signing of the Geneva Accord at 2.45 a.m. GMT on 21 July 1954 in Geneva. [341] Chart 155 is set for this moment, for the Laotian capital, Vientiane. Although this chart is for a historically important moment in the history of Laos, Chart 154 may be considered to have the greater relevance.

The Communist rebels were never satisfied by the grant of independence, and continued a guerrilla war until 1975. The present Communist regime may be dated from 11 May 1975 when the head of state, Prince Souvanna appointed General Khamouan Boupha, a Communist leader, as Minister of Defence and head of the armed forces. This followed the effective Communist military victory on 9 May 1975. [342]

LATVIA

Political organization in Latvia dates back to the rule of the Teutonic Knights in the thirteenth century. Following periods of control by Sweden and Poland the area was conquered by Russia in 1721.

Following occupation by the Germans in 1917, and the Russian Revolution, the Latvian National Council took control on 16 November 1917 [343] and there seems to have been a declaration of independence on 12 January 1918. [344] However, on 22 September 1918 the Germans recognized the independence of the Baltic State, comprising Livland (or Livonia, the geographical region of Latvia) and Estonia. This was to be a Grand Duchy under the hereditary rule of the German Kaiser, but collapsed only three weeks later when Germany suffered total defeat and revolution. [345]

The collapse of both German and Russian authority left a vacuum into which the Latvian nationalists stepped to take control. On 17 November 1918 the various Latvian parties combined to select a President, Vice-President and Prime Minister. On 18 November 1918 the Latvian National Council assembled in the capital, Riga. The first business of the meeting was to formally elect the President, Vice-President and Prime Minister, and the second business was the reading of the declaration of independence. [346]

Chart 156 for Latvian independence is set for this date and place and, in the absence of accurate information, for 12.00 noon.

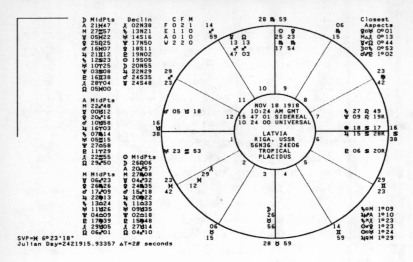

156: Latvia, Independence, 1918

German troops continued to occupy the state with British approval in order to attack the Communist government which was created in January 1919, but withdrew after Russia formally recognized Latvian independence on 11 August 1920.

The country lost its independence on 21 July 1940 when, following Soviet occupation in June, it was incorporated into the Soviet Union.[347] From 1941 to 1944 the country was again occupied by Germany.

LEBANON

The area occupied by modern Lebanon is that of the ancient land of the Phoenicians. From its conquest by the Assyrians in the eighth century BC until independence in the 1940s the region experienced only one brief period of political independence as the crusader-ruled County of Tripoli in the twelfth and thirteenth centuries (under the suzerainty of the Kingdom of Jerusalem).

Occupied by France in 1917 following the defeat of the Turks, Lebanon was granted formal independence on 26 November 1941.[348] At the time France was occupied by the Germans while the Lebanon was under the control of the anti-German Free French leader General Georges Catroux. The declaration of independence, which was accompanied by various public celebrations was a ploy designed to

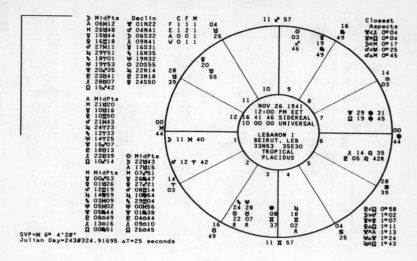

157: Lebanon, Independence, 1941

gain Arab support for the Allied cause. Chart 157 for the independence of the Lebanon is set for 26 November 1941, for the capital, Beirut, and, in the absence of accurate information, for 12.00

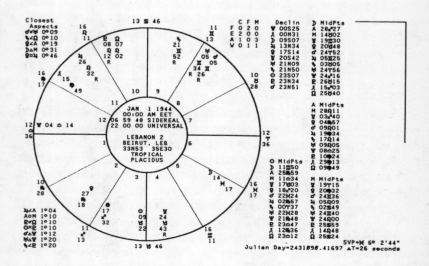

158: Lebanon, Independence, 1944

noon (it is known that the proclamation took place during the day).

However, the French double-crossed the new Lebanese Government, and all power remained in the hands of the Free French authorities. A crisis broke in 1943 when the French decided that the Government was acting as if the Lebanon were truly independent. On 11 November the French declared martial law and imprisoned the Lebanese Government. [349] However, the response of the Arab world, the British and the Americans was so hostile that on 22 November the French were forced to back down and free the Lebanese Government. [350] On 27 December 1943 the French agreed to hand over to the Lebanese authorities all the powers of the mandate that they had retained in defiance of the declaration of independence in 1941. This agreement came into force on 1 January 1944, at which time the country became independent in both law and fact. [351] Chart 158 is set for 1 January 1944, for the capital, Beirut and, in the absence of accurate information, for 00.00 hrs. It would be consistent with other similar agreements if 00.00 hrs were the true time of independence.

LESOTHO

The former British protectorate of Basutoland was given independence as the state of Lesotho at 00.00 hrs on 4 October 1966, in the capital, Maseru. [352] Chart 159 is set for this data.

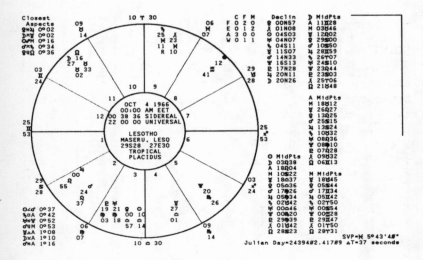

159: Lesotho, Independence, 1966

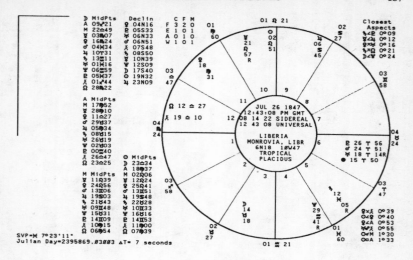

160: Liberia, Independence, 1847

LIBERIA

The West African state of Liberia owes its origins to the American Colonization Society, set up in 1816 to resettle former American slaves in Africa.[353] The state was given independence on 26 July 1847.[354] Chart 160 is set for this date, for the capital, Monrovia, and, in the absence of accurate information, for 12.00 noon.

LIBYA

From 642 to the sixteenth century Libya was a part of the great Muslim Empire, often enjoying political independence and unity, sometimes being linked to Egypt or Tunisia. Turkish domination weakened in the nineteenth century until the Italians took control in 1912. Following the Italian defeat in 1943 the country was occupied by Britain, regaining full independence at 00.00 hrs on 24 December 1951,[355] the formal proclamation being made during the day of the 24th by King Idris. Chart 161 for Libyan independence is set for 00.00 hrs on 24 December 1951, for the capital Tripoli.

The current republican regime in Libya was brought to power in a military coup on 3 September 1969. Rebel troops and tanks converged on Tripoli at 2.00 a.m., reached key positions in the city by 4.00 a.m., and were in complete control by 5.00 a.m.[356] Chart 162 for the Libyan republic is set for 5.00 a.m., the time when the rebels took complete control, for 3 September 1969, and for Tripoli.

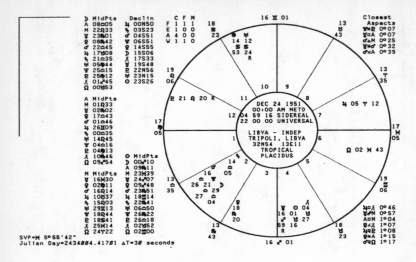

161: Libya, Independence, 1951

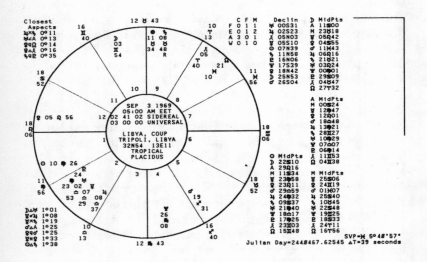

162: Libya, Republic, 1969

LIECHTENSTEIN

The origins of the state of Liechtenstein are impossible to trace and
it is the only one of the hundreds of states of the medieval Holy

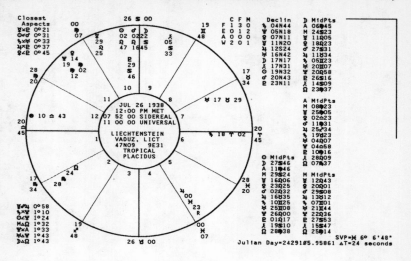

163: Liechtenstein, Franz Joseph II, 1938

Roman Empire to avoid conquest by its larger neighbours. [357] Modern constitutions were adopted in 1869 and 1921, though it is probably best to follow the traditional astrological practice of taking the natal chart, accession or coronation of the ruling monarch as the current horoscope. Chart 163 is therefore set for the accession of the current Duke, Franz Joseph II, on 26 July 1938, and for the capital, Vaduz. [358] In the absence of accurate information the chart is set for 12.00 noon. When the current Duke dies, the national horoscope will be that for the accession of his successor.

LITHUANIA

The Grand Duchy of Lithuania was founded in approximately the year 1240, [359] and by the mid-fourteenth century the country extended over a vast area of Central Europe from the Baltic to the Black Sea. In the fourteenth and fifteenth centuries the country was united with Poland, which gradually became the dominant partner. In 1793 to 1795 Lithuania was occupied by Russia, proclaiming its independence during the Russian Revolution of 1917.

On 13 March 1917 (old style) the Lithuanian National Council demanded autonomy in federation with Russia. [360] By 7 June the General Lithuanian Conference (Sejm) in Petrograd was demanding complete independence for a neutral Lithuania. [361] Independence

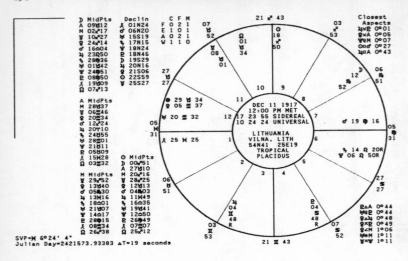

164: Lithuania, Independence, 1917

was finally established on 11 December 1917,[362] even though the country was at the time under German occupation. Chart 164 for Lithuanian independence is set for this date, for the capital, Vilna, and, in the absence of accurate information, for 12.00 noon. A further proclamation or declaration of independence, perhaps a legal completion of the events of 11 December 1917, seems to have taken place on 16 February 1918,[363] a date which was described as the 'foundation of the Lithuanian republic'.[364]

The country was occupied by the Soviet Union in June 1940 and incorporated into the Soviet Union on 21 July 1941.[365]

LUXEMBURG

It is not clear which date should be used for the national horoscope of Luxemburg. From the fifteenth to the eighteenth century Luxemburg formed part of the Austrian or Spanish Netherlands. In the 1790s it was occupied by France, and following the peace settlements of 1815 was separated from the rest of the Netherlands. The event normally taken as the foundation of the modern state is that for the international recognition of the country's independence and neutrality by the Treaty of London in 1867. Dates given for this recognition include 11 May 1867[366] and 31 May 1867.[367] Chart 165 for Luxemburg is set for 9 September 1867, the date of the final

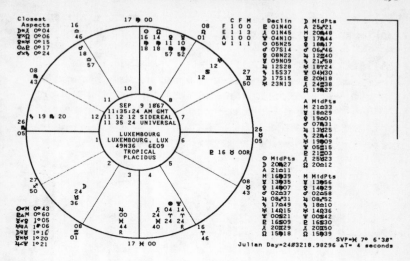

165: Luxemburg, Independence Recognized, 1867

signature of the Treaty,[368] for the capital, Luxemburg and, in the absence of accurate information, for 12.00 noon.

The problem of establishing the correct date is made more difficult

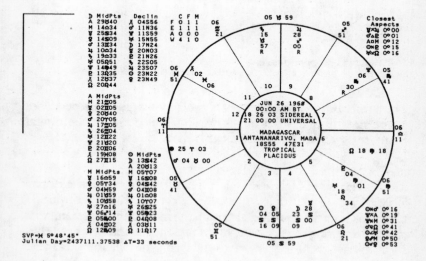

166: Madagascar, Independence, 1960

by the extraordinarily sparse press reporting of the Conference of London and the resulting treaty.

MADAGASCAR

Madagascar received independence from France on 26 June 1960.[369] The independence celebrations took place during the morning of 26 June,[370] although an independence time of 00.00 hrs would be consistent with normal French practice. Chart 166 is cast for 00.00 hrs on 26 June 1960 for the capital, Antananarivo.

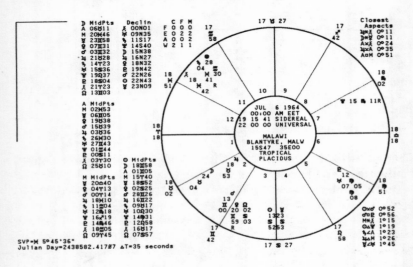

167: Malawi, Independence, 1964

MALAWI

The former British protectorate of Nyasaland was given independence as the state of Malawi at 00.00 hrs on 6 July 1964, in the capital Blantyre.[371] Chart 167 is set for this data.

MALAYA

The federation of Malaya was granted independence by the British at 00.00 hrs on 31 August 1957, in the capital, Kuala Lumpur.[372] Chart 168 is set for this time, although the independence ceremonies took place during the following morning. The ceremonies themselves seem to have included a moment of such symbolic importance as to merit consideration as a second horoscope: at 8.15 a.m. the Duke of Gloucester, the British representative, handed the proclamation

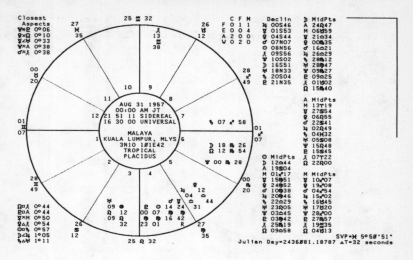

168: Malaya, Independence, 1957

of independence to the Prime Minister, Tengku Abdul Rahman. The Prime Minister then uttered three shouts of 'Merdeka' (independent) into the microphone, a cry which was taken up by the assembled crowds. [373]

Prior to British occupation in the nineteenth century, Malaya consisted of a number of small independent states. In 1963 the country was united with Singapore, Sabah and Sarawak to form the federation of Malaysia, although local Hindu astrologers continue to use the horoscope for the independence of Malaya rather than that for the formation of Malaysia. [374]

MALAYSIA

The federation of Malaysia was formed in 1963 as a union of Malaya with the British-ruled states of Sabah, Sarawak and Singapore. The time originally fixed for the creation of the new state was 00.00 hrs on 31 August 1963, the anniversary of the independence of Malaya, but international problems caused a delay until 16 September 1963. [375] The state came into being at 00.00 hrs. [376] Chart 169 is set for this data.

Each state of the new federation held its own ceremonies in addition to the general celebrations that took place at 00.00 hrs. In Sabah proclamation ceremonies were due to be held in the capital Jesselton at 7.30 a.m. on 16 September. In Sarawak proclamation ceremonies were due to be held in the capital, Kuching, also at 7.30

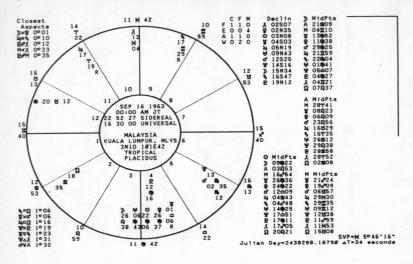

169: Malaysia, Independence, 1963

a.m. In Singapore the proclamation was due to be read from the steps of the City Hall at 5.00 p.m. In Malaya an inaugural ceremony was due to take place in Kuala Lumpur at 8.00 a.m., and the proclamation itself was due to be read on the evening of 17 September.[377] Horoscopes for these events might be relevant in indicating the different situations of the various states of the federation, especially in the light of Singapore's subsequent secession.

Hindu astrologers in Malaya still use the horoscope for Malayan independence rather than that for the creation of Malaysia.[378]

MALDIVE ISLANDS
The Maldive Islands gained independence when the agreement revoking the British protectorate was signed on 26 July 1965.[379] The agreement, referring to the revoking of the protectorate on 26 July, would normally be taken as evidence of an independence time of 00.00 hrs on 26 July.[380] However, the agreement was not signed until the morning of 26 July itself in Colombo.[381] The position is further complicated by the fact that, although standard reference books regard 26 July as independence day[382] and some press comment considered that the time of signature of the agreement constituted the time of independence,[383] other accounts implied that full constitutional independence still lay in the future.[384] A similar confused situation surrounds the granting of independence by the

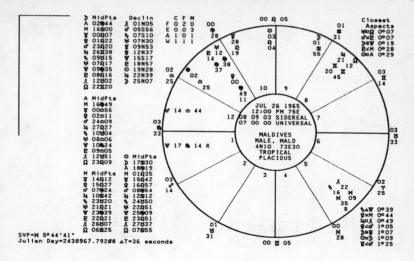

170: Maldive Islands, Independence, 1965

British to Bahrain, Jordan, Kuwait and Qatar.

Chart 170 for the independence of the Maldive Islands is cast for 12.00 noon on 26 July 1965, and for the capital, Malé.

MALI — FEDERATION

The Federation of Mali, not to be confused with the Republic of Mali, was given independence by France on 20 June 1960, in the capital Dakar: 'The independence of Mali was proclaimed by M. Leopold Senghor, President of the Federal Assembly, in the Assembly Building in Dakar, shortly after midnight on June 19–20, after the Assembly had unanimously voted the independence law.'[385] Chart 171 is set for 00.00 hrs on 20 June 1960, for Dakar.

The Federation disintegrated in August and September 1960 (see Mali — Republic and Senegal, Charts 172 and 223).

MALI — REPUBLIC

Mali was formerly the colony of French Sudan, which received independence on 20 June 1960 as part of the Federation of Mali, together with Senegal (see Chart 171). The Republic of Mali, still known as Sudan, became effectively independent from the Federation of Mali at 2.00 a.m. on 20 August 1960 when Senegal seceded from the Federation,[386] a moment which could be taken as the basis for a national horoscope. However, the Sudan did not formally leave

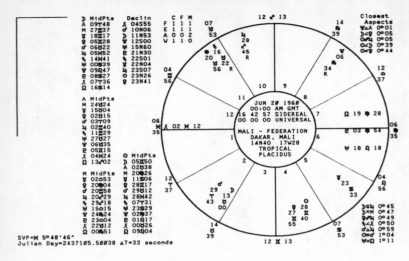

171: Mali, Federation, Independence, 1960

the Federation and rename itself until 22 September 1960: 'On
September 22nd the Sudanese Assembly decided to proclaim Sudan
independent as the Republic of Mali, in confirmation of similar

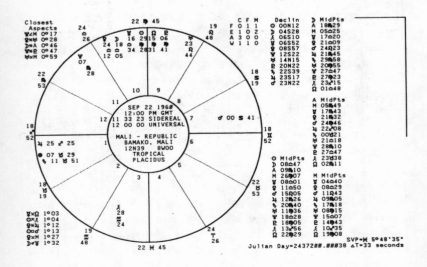

172: Mali, Republic, Independence, 1960

decisions by a special congress of the Union Sudanese earlier in the day.'[387] The inference of all press reports is that the decision was taken during the day,[388] so Chart 172 for the Mali Republic is set for 12.00 noon on 22 September 1960, in the capital, Bamako.

MALTA

Malta received independence from Great Britain at 00.00 hrs on 21 September 1964, in the capital, Valletta.[389] Chart 173 is set for this data.

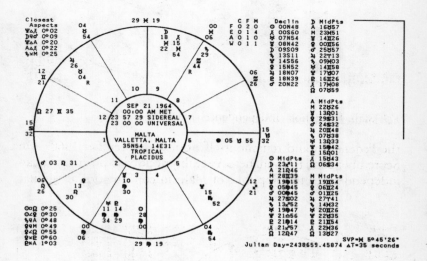

173: Malta, Independence, 1964

MAURETANIA

The independence of Mauretania from France was proclaimed at 00.00 hrs on 28 November 1960 in the capital, Nouakchott.[390] Chart 174 is set for this data.

MAURITIUS

The former British possession of Mauritius received its independence at 00.00 hrs on 12 March 1968, in the capital, Port Louis.[391] Chart 175 is set for this data.

MEXICO

Prior to the Spanish conquest in the sixteenth century the area now

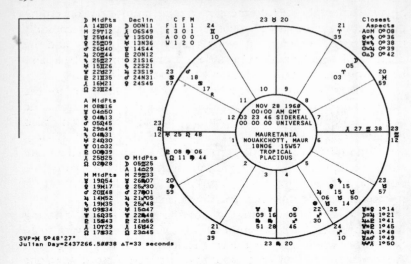

174: Mauretania, Independence, 1960

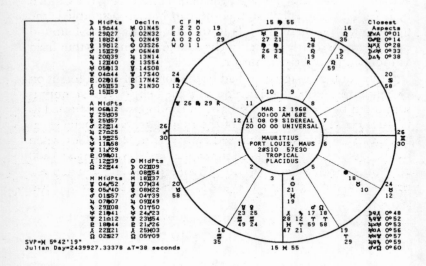

175: Mauritius, Independence, 1968

covered by Mexico was dominated by the Aztec Empire. The Aztec
Emperor Montezuma swore fealty to the King of Spain, Holy Roman
Emperor Charles V, in 1519, in the belief that the coming of the

Spaniards brought the fulfilment of an ancient prophecy concerning the arrival of a white saviour from the east. Charles was thus technically the last Aztec Emperor. Following a revolt by the Aztecs, and the death of Montezuma, the Empire was formally annexed by Spain, becoming the Captain Generalcy of New Spain in 1522.

The main horoscope for modern Mexico should be set for the country's independence, an event traditionally timed from the beginning of the revolt against Spain. Following the conquest of Spain by France, and the declaration of Napoleon's brother, Joseph, as King, on 6 June 1807, Spanish authority throughout the colonial empire entered a rapid decline. The revolt in Mexico finally broke into the open on the night of 15–16 September 1810. However, there is uncertainty concerning the time for this event.

It seems that the revolt broke out prematurely. Originally having been scheduled for 8 December 1810 it was moved forward to 16 September when three of the ringleaders, Aldama, Hidalgo and Allende, realized they were about to be arrested. According to one source, Aldama arrived at Hidalgo's house at 2.00 a.m., finding Allende already there. The three then decided to proclaim the revolt, at mass that morning. Hidalgo, the parish priest, rang the Church bells earlier than usual, and as the parishioners assembled, the uprising was proclaimed.[392] This would suggest a time of around dawn, perhaps shortly before.[393] The date 16 September is thus fixed as Independence Day in Mexico.

Other sources disagree: 'It had been shortly before midnight on 15 September 1810' that Hidalgo rang the bell.[394] This account is supported by the Mexican Embassy in London, who confirmed to Charles Harvey that the time of the ringing is traditionally set at 11.00 p.m.[395] This time is marked every year in Mexico City when the bell, which was brought to the capital in 1896, is rung at 11.00 p.m. on 15 September.[396] Chart 176 for Mexican Independence is therefore set for 11.00 p.m. LMT on 15 September 1810, in the town of Dolores Hidalgo.

A second horoscope for independence could be set for the Plan de Iguala on 24 February 1821, the date given in many reference books as that for independence.[397] The Plan de Iguala was a joint proclamation of independence made by the rebel leader Guerrero and the Spanish commander, Iturbide. Over the following weeks the Plan received support from all rebel and conservative groups, and led to the rapid end of the revolt that had began on 15–16 September 1810.[398] The true end to the war came in September 1821 when Iturbide made his triumphal entry into Mexico City, providing

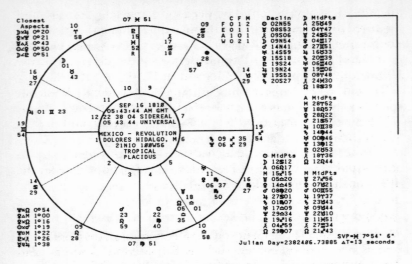

176: Mexico, Revolution, 1810

a third astrologically significant moment.

Various horoscopes are also set for the current 'revolutionary' constitution which dates from the revolutions and civil war of 1910

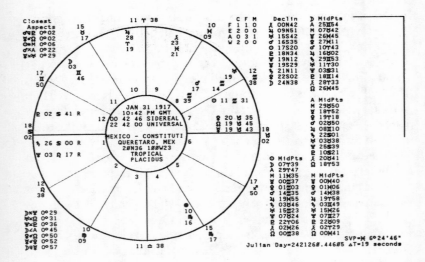

177: Mexico, Constitution, 1917

to 1920. This constitution guaranteed the democratic franchise and restricted the power of the Church, and is the equivalent of the liberal constitutions elsewhere for which horoscopes are cast (see for example Denmark). The constitution was signed by the delegates to the Constitutional Assembly in Queretaro at 11.00 a.m. on 31 January 1917, and signed by First Chief Carranza (subsequently President Carranza) in a public ceremony at 4.00 p.m. that afternoon.[399] Chart 177 for modern Mexico is therefore set for this time and date in Queretaro.

The horoscope for independence should take precedence, but as this event has no undisputed recorded time, the horoscope for the 1917 constitution has added importance.

MONACO

Monaco is a small principality on the Mediterranean coast of France, and is one of those states, such as San Marino, Andorra, and Liechtenstein whose origins in feudal Europe are difficult to trace. In 1191 it was separated from Provence,[400] and since 1297 has been ruled by independent princes,[401] even though these have accepted the military protection of other European powers for most of the state's history. In 1524 it became a Spanish protectorate at the Treaty of Burgos.

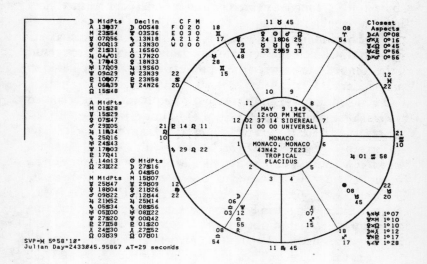

178: Monaco, Rainier III, 1949

After the French revolution military control reverted to France, and in 1814 the state became a protectorate of the Kingdom of Sardinia. In 1918 a *de facto* French protectorate was confirmed.[402] In view of the uncertainty concerning the state's creation, the horoscope should be set for the reign of the current prince. The present ruler, Prince Rainier III succeeded to the throne on 9 May 1949,[403] and was crowned on 11 April 1950.[404] Chart 178 is set for the succession on 9 May 1949, for the town of Monaco-Ville, and, in the absence of accurate information, for 12.00 noon.

As a protectorate, Monaco falls into a category of state that is in general not included in this book, protectorates normally being regarded as colonial possessions. However, in practice the state is regarded internationally as sovereign and independent.

Astrologically significant moments in recent history could include the introduction of universal franchise on 7 May 1910 or the promulgation of the constitution on 5 January 1911.[405]

MONGOLIA

The Mongol Empire was founded in the early years of the thirteenth century by Genghis Khan, the ruler whose armies marched as far west as Poland. At their greatest extent the Mongol dominions extended from Poland to Indonesia, and from Persia to Korea. However, from the installation of the Mongol Manchu dynasty in China in 1636 Mongolia was recognized as under Chinese suzerainty (Inner Mongolia is still a part of China).

By the beginning of the twentieth century Japan and Russia were threatening Chinese power in Mongolia, and it was as a direct result of the competition between these powers that the state achieved its independence.

On 28 February 1919 a provisional government was proclaimed by a Pan Mongolian Congress held at Chita under Japanese auspices. The resulting state was to extend over the whole of Mongolia as far as Tibet. Following the Russian declaration of July 1919 that Mongolia was a free state, the Chinese cancelled Mongolian autonomy on 22 November, but never managed to reassert their control. In February 1921 there was a pro-Soviet coup and on 1 March 1921 the first congress of the Mongolian Peoples' (i.e. Communist) Party, meeting in Kyakhta, decided to liberate the country.[406] On 3 March 1921 this congress issued a declaration of independence,[407] and this date is taken as that for Chart 179 for Mongolia. The chart is set for 12.00 noon LMT, in the absence of accurate information, for Kyakhta, on 3 March 1921.

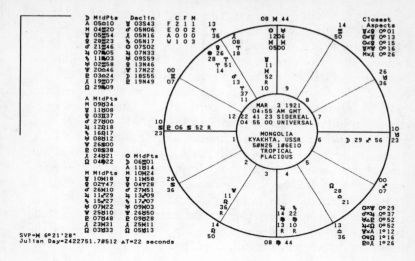

179: Mongolia, Independence, 1921

Subsequent dates in the same year are all cited by reference books as foundation dates. On 17 March a pro-Soviet government was established at Kyakhta,[408] on 6 July[409] or 8 July[410] a Peoples' Revolutionary Government was constituted, and on 5 November 1921 the Russian–Mongolian treaty effectively abrogated Chinese sovereignty, which had hitherto been implicity accepted.[411]

MONTENEGRO
The Balkan state of Montenegro traditionally claimed its independence dated from the Battle of Kossovo in 1389, when it won its independence from Serbia.[412] However, it subsequently came under the domination of the Turkish Empire, which only recognized its independence in 1799.[413] However, complete international independence was not recognized until the Treaty of Berlin, signed at 2.30 p.m. LMT on 13 July 1878 in Berlin.[414] Chart 180 for Montenegro is set for the equivalent time (2.52 p.m. LMT) on 13 July 1878 and for the capital, Ketinje.

In November 1918 Montenegro surrendered its independence by joining the new state of Yugoslavia (see Chart 309).

MOROCCO
Prior to the Roman conquest in 40 BC much of modern Morocco constituted the Kingdom of Mauretania, not to be confused with

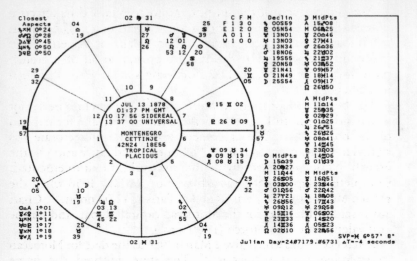

180: Montenegro, Independence, 1878

the modern state of that name (Chart 174). Roman authority collapsed in the early fifth century, to be replaced by the dominion of the Islamic Empire in the eighth century.

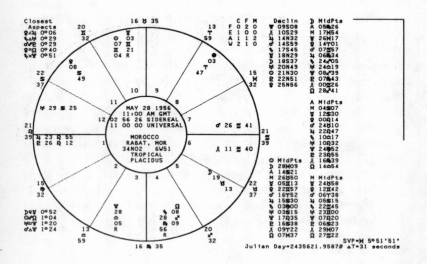

181: Morocco, Independence, 1956

As a remote part of the Empire, Morocco retained its effective independence, though sometimes formed part of a larger state in combination with Arab dominions in Spain or Algeria. This independence was retained until the proclamation of a French protectorate on 30 March 1912, following several years of French interference.[415]

The horoscope for modern Morocco should therefore be set for independence from France, which coincided with the formal end of the protectorate. The agreement ending the protectorate was signed in Paris on 2 March 1956,[416] but required ratification by the French National Assembly before it could be implemented. Complete independence was achieved on 28 May 1956 when the French Moroccan treaty was signed in Paris at 12.00 noon.[417] Chart 181 is set for this date, for the Moroccan capital, Rabat, and for the equivalent time in Morocco (11.00 a.m.).

Reference books which give 2 March 1956 as the date for Moroccan independence are erroneous.[418] The state adopted the name Kingdom of Morocco on 11 August 1957, having been formerly known as the Sherifian Empire.[419]

MOZAMBIQUE

The former Portuguese colony of Mozambique was given its

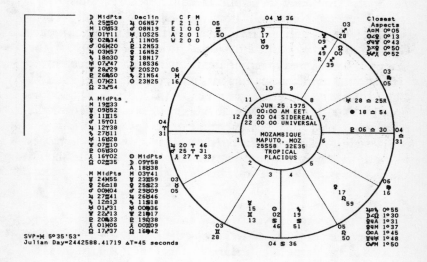

182: Mozambique, Independence, 1975

independence at 00.00 hrs on 25 June 1975.[420] Chart 182 is set for this time and date, and for the capital, Maputo.

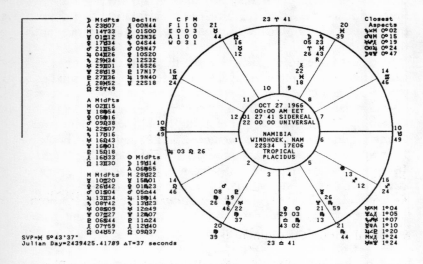

183: Namibia, Termination of Mandate, 1966

NAMIBIA

The South African state of Namibia is administered by South Africa under a mandate (originally from the League of Nations), which is no longer recognized internationally. The mandate over the former German colony was granted to South Africa on 7 May 1919.[421] The United Nations voted to terminate the mandate on 27 September 1966 and the termination came into effect on 27 October 1966.[422] Chart 183 is set for this date, for the capital Windhoek, and for the time of 00.00 hrs, which would be consistent with that for the termination of mandates in other territories.

The state is still under South African occupation, but horoscopes for both the beginning and termination of the mandate should indicate its astrological destiny.

NATAL

The area now covered by Natal was colonized by Boer settlers following the annexation of the Cape Colony by the British from the Dutch in 1806. An attempt to have the settlement incorporated into the British Empire on 27 August 1824 was not recognized by the British Government, and the area was renamed Durban.[423] In 1838 the Boers

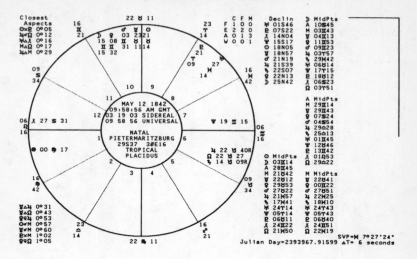

184: Natal, Formal Constitution, 1842

set up the Republic of Natal, or Natalia,[424] with its capital at Pietermaritzburg. In the face of a mounting British threat, the Republic
appears to have formally constituted itself on 12 May 1842,[425] and
Chart 184 is set for this date, for the capital, Pietermaritzburg, and,
in the absence of accurate information, for 12.00 noon.

The state was made a British colony on 8 August 1843, and is now
part of the Republic of South Africa.[426]

NAURU
Nauru is a Pacific island, and is the smallest sovereign state in the
world, having an area of 8.2 square miles. It became a sovereign
independent republic at 00.00 hrs on 31 January 1968.[428] Chart 185
is set for this time and date, and for the longitude of the island.

NEPAL
Nepal is an ancient kingdom, and no historical 'foundation' has been
established, although there are local traditions. The current horoscope
should be that for the coronation of the present king, especially as
this is always elected astrologically: 'King Birendra Bir Bikram Shah
Deva of Nepal was crowned in Katmandu on 24 February. Although
he had succeeded his father on 31 January 1972, the coronation had
been postponed until a date and time (8.37 a.m.) which the court
astrologers regarded as suitably auspicious.'[429] Chart 186 is set for

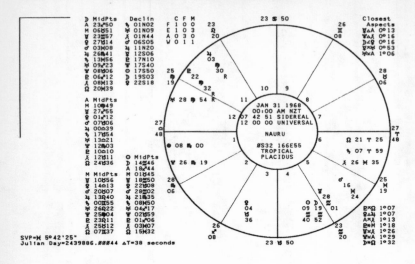

185: Nauru, Independence, 1968

the time and date of the coronation, in the capital, Katmandu. It
must be remembered that the reasoning of the Nepalese astrologers
would be substantially different to that of astrologers in the West.

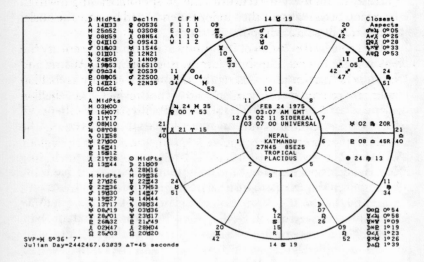

186: Nepal, King Birendra, 1975

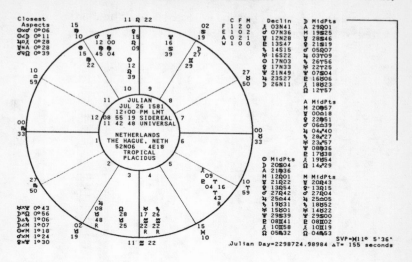

187: Netherlands, Independence, 1581

NETHERLANDS

The modern state of the Netherlands occupies only a part of the area once known as the Netherlands and which included modern Belgium and Luxemburg. During the late feudal age in the fourteenth and fifteenth centuries the prosperous trading towns in the region began to assert their independence, and became the nuclei for a series of small autonomous states.

After rule by the Dukes of Burgundy in the fifteenth century the region passed to the Hapsburg family, rulers of Spain, Austria and the Holy Roman Empire. During the seventeenth century a rebellion broke out, centred on the northern part of the province. The rebellion began in 1568, and in 1576, under the Pacification of Ghent, all the provinces united to drive out the Spanish.[430] However, the southern provinces were reconquered, leaving the north to fight alone for independence. On 2 February 1579 these provinces (including Holland) formed themselves into the Union of Utrecht. On 26 July 1581 the states of the Union of Utrecht signed their declaration of independence at the Hague, under the name of the United Provinces.[431] Chart 187 is set for this date and place, and, in the absence of accurate information, for 12.00 noon LMT.

The state has been through several subsequent political forms, including the Batavian Republic organized under French auspices in the 1790s, and the Kingdom of the Netherlands of 1814 to 1830 that included Belgium, but the horoscope given here is that for the formal foundation of the modern Netherlands.

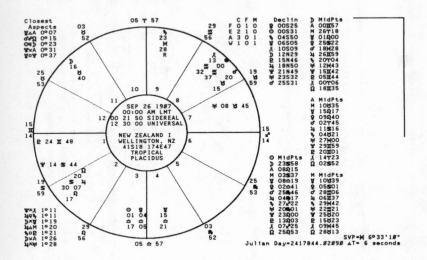

188: New Zealand, Dominion, 1907

NEW ZEALAND

New Zealand's existence as an independent nation dates from the granting of Dominion status within the British Empire at 00.00 hrs on 26 September 1907. Newspaper reports at the time recorded the celebrations that were held, and the toasting of 'The New Dominion', 'just after midnight'.[432] A case can be made for other important charts in the history of New Zealand's constitutional development, both before and after the granting of Dominion status,[433] and the horoscope in *Mundane Astrology* is cast for the public proclamation at 11.00 a.m. on 26 September 1907, in the capital, Wellington.[434]

It should be noted that, although effectively independent in all respects, the country still has constitutional links with the UK.

Chart 188 for New Zealand is set for 00.00 hrs on 26 September 1907 in the capital, Wellington.

NICARAGUA

Independence came to Nicaragua as part of the series of declarations of independence that swept through the cities and provinces of Spanish Central America in 1821. Independence was proclaimed in the city of Leon on 11 October 1821,[435] and Chart 189 for Nicaragua

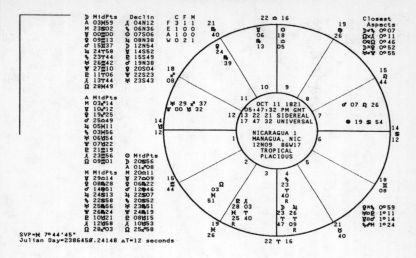

189: Nicaragua, Independence, 1821

is set for this date and place, and, in the absence of accurate
information, for 12.00 noon LMT. This declaration was partly one
of independence from Spain, but also from Guatemala; Nicaragua
had been administered by the Spanish Captain Generalcy of
Guatemala, and so had been technically covered by that country's
declaration of independence on 15 September 1821 (see Chart 113).
As a result of this confusion, and related disputes, the declaration
of 11 October was not accepted across Nicaragua. The more radical
population of the city of Granada supported union with Guatemala,
and in reaction to this the more conservative leaders in Leon proposed
union with Mexico. On 5 January 1822 Guatemala itself joined
Mexico,[436] following which Nicaragua and the other Central
American states were occupied by Mexican troops. On 1 July 1823
Nicaragua won independence from Mexico as part of the United
Provinces of Central America,[437] together with El Salvador,
Guatemala, Honduras and Costa Rica.

This state spent most of its existence moving towards its eventual
disintegration, and Nicaragua finally seceded on 30 April 1839,[438]
although it seems that a previous secession may have taken place
in 1833 or earlier.[439] It would be reasonable to regard this date as
the basis for a second national chart.

Nicaraguan independence may be continuously recorded from
this date, even though the state took part in at least one subsequent

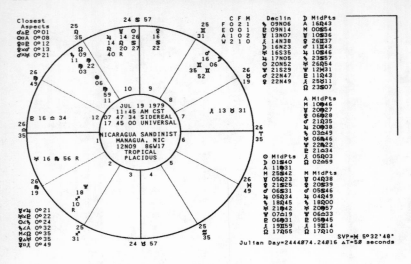

190: Nicaragua, Sandinista Regime, 1979

Central American union. This was the union promulgated between Honduras, Nicaragua and El Salvador on 9 January 1851, and which was ruled by a National Constitutional Congress at Tegucigalpa from 10 October 1852. This state dissolved in 1863 when war broke out between Honduras and Nicaragua.[440]

The present Sandinista regime in Nicaragua took power on 19 July 1979. The USA had attempted to organize a smooth constitutional transition from the previous regime of President Somoza, now represented by President Urcuyo, but Urcuyo refused. The relevant horoscope is therefore for the complete victory of the Sandinista guerrilla army.

The Somoza era came to an end at 5.10 a.m. on 17 July 1979 when the President boarded a plane for exile in Florida,[441] and later in the day the USA told the Sandinista Government-in-Exile that it recognized it as the new Government of Nicaragua.[442] On 18 July the Sandinistas set up a provisional government, which had been named on 15 July,[443] in the city of Leon[444] and President Urcuyo fled to Guatemala.[445] At dawn on 19 July church bells in Managua, the capital, rang to welcome the Sandinista army,[446] and by 11.45 a.m. the citadel of the old regime, the bunker of President Somoza, was in Sandinista hands.[447] The Sandinista Government arrived in Managua that afternoon, but it is 11.45 a.m. that is the key time, and Chart 190 for the Sandinista regime is cast for this time, on 19 July 1979 in Managua. [448]

The civil war which brought the Sandinistas to power had been triggered by the murder by a Government 'death squad' of a liberal newspaper proprietor, Joacquin Chamorro, on 10 January 1978. [449]

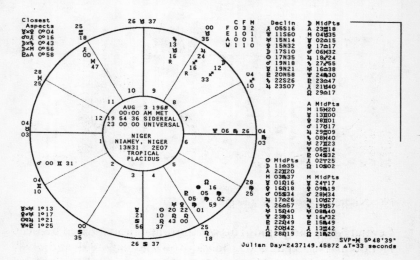

191: Niger, Independence, 1960

NIGER

The former French colony of Niger was granted independence at 00.00 hrs on 3 August 1960 in the capital Niamey. [450] Chart 191 is set for this data.

NIGERIA

The former British colony of Nigeria (Chart 192) was granted its independence at 00.00 hrs on 1 October 1960, in the capital, Lagos. [451] Like the other British possessions which received independence, Nigeria had previously been granted a measure of internal self-rule, in 1954, and at the time of independence retained certain constitutional links with the UK, by retaining the Queen as Head of State. It subsequently became a Republic.

NORWAY

The unification of Norway was begun by Harold I, who reigned from 872 to 930, [452] and the country soon became a regional power, being strong enough to mount an invasion of England in 1066.

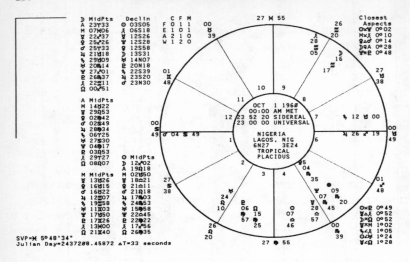

192: Nigeria, Independence, 1960

In 1387 the royal house of Norway was united with those of Sweden and Denmark in a union which, after the subsequent departure of Sweden, was known as the Kingdom of Denmark and Norway.[453]

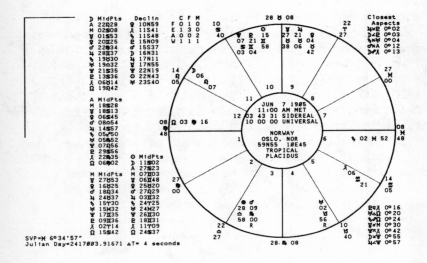

193: Norway, Independence, 1905

Gradually Denmark, which was the more prosperous country, came to dominate its northern neighbour. In 1814 the country was occupied by Sweden, remaining a Swedish possession until 1905.[454]

The horoscope for modern Norway is that for the secession of the country from Sweden on 7 June 1905. This event took place at a session of the Storthing (parliament) in Oslo. The Storthing met at 10.00 a.m. in closed session to consider the motion to secede and at 10.30 a.m. the public were admitted. The Prime Minister then read a short statement announcing the resignation of the Government, followed by the reading of the declaration of the dissolution of the union with Sweden.[455] The horoscope for Norwegian independence (Chart 193) is therefore set for an estimated time of 11.00 a.m, based on this account, for 7 June 1905 in Oslo. This estimated time is supported independently by Norwegian astrologer Andrew Bevan.[456]

Although full legal independence did not come into force until the declaration had been ratified in a plebiscite on 13 August 1905, and a treaty with Sweden signed on 26 October 1905,[457] full *de facto* independence was attained on the morning of 7 June.

OMAN
Oman is a Sultanate occupying the south of the Arabian peninsula.

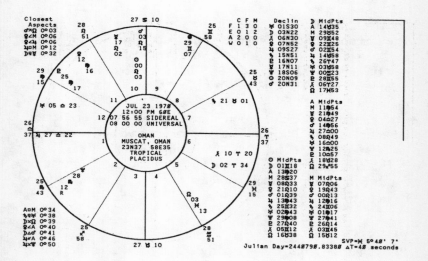

194: Oman, Coup d'État, 1970

Since the nineteenth century it has had close treaty relations with Great Britain, although it is not normally regarded as having been part of the British Empire. Reference books which list independence for Oman from Britain on 23 July 1970 are wrong. In fact this was the date of the coup which should be taken as the basis for the horoscope of modern Oman.

Until 1970 the country had been ruled by the elderly Said bin Taimur, who had resisted all modern influences and had retained all the medieval characteristics of the country, including slavery. The coup of 23 July was led by Qaboos bin Said, the Sultan's son, with the support of the British, who wished the country to modernize.

The old Sultan was arrested on 23 July 1970, and although he was not officially deposed until 26 July,[458] it was from this date that Qaboos exercised effective power, and therefore this date that should be taken as the beginning of his rule.[459]

Chart 194 is set for 23 July 1970, for the capital Muscat, and, in the absence of accurate information, for 12.00 noon. However, as is customary with *coups d'état*, it is likely that the more accurate time was close to dawn. It is important to note that, as Qaboos is an astrologer,[460] the time for the coup could have been astrologically elected, and that if it had been carried out in the early hours of the morning there would have been a close applying trine of the Sun and the Moon.

ORANGE FREE STATE

The area north of the Orange River in South Africa was settled by the Boers in 1836. The British Government proclaimed its authority over the area on 3 February 1848,[461] but was effectively unable to enforce its rule. The Orange Free State formally declared itself independent on 23 February 1854[462] and Chart 197 is set for this date, for the capital, Bloemfontein, and, in the absence of accurate information, for 12.00 noon. The state was annexed by Great Britain on 24 May[463] or 28 May[464] 1900 following the Boer War.

This chart, together with those for Natal and the Transvaal, or South African Republic, is of interest for the continuing strife in modern South Africa.

PAKISTAN

Pakistan is the centre of some of the oldest political civilization in the world. The cities of Monhenjo-Daro had proper planned streets, and plumbing and drainage systems in 2,000 BC. However, Pakistan

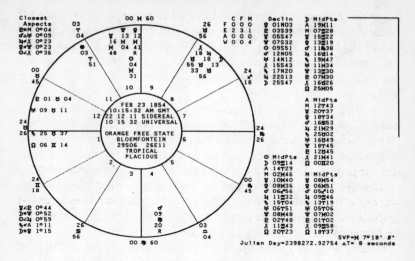

195: Orange Free State, Independence, 1854

never existed as a political unity until independence from the British in 1947. Chart 196 is cast for independence at 00.00 hrs on 15 August 1947 in the capital, Karachi.[465]

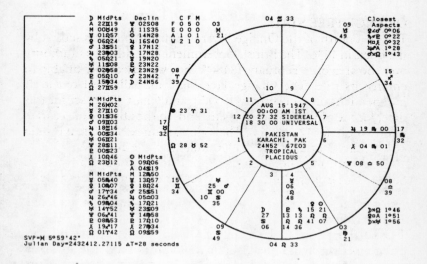

196: Pakistan, Independence, 1947

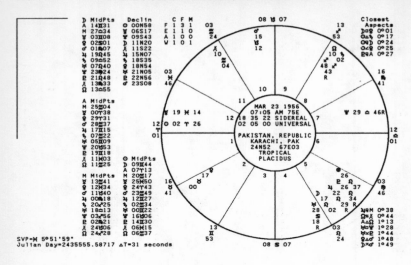

197: Pakistan, Republic, 1956

The horoscope for the proclamation of the Republic of Pakistan may also be considered significant. The Republic was 'created' in a thirty-minute ceremony on the morning of 23 March 1956 in Karachi.[466] The celebrations began with a thirty-one gun salute at 7.00 a.m. and the proclamation was read at 7.05 a.m.[467] Chart 197 is set for 7.05 a.m. on 23 March 1956 in Karachi.

In view of the frequent use made of astrologers by Pakistani politicians, it is likely that this time was elected astrologically.

PALESTINE

The British Mandate in Palestine expired at 00.00 hrs on 15 May 1948,[468] and Chart 198 is set for this date and time for Jerusalem. However, the state of Palestine never came into existence. The Jewish territories had declared their independence as the state of Israel six hours previously (see Chart 135), and the remaining Arab portions were annexed by Jordan. This chart should, however, be used to indicate the aspirations of the Palestinian people for national self-determination.

Other horoscopes which may be used include those for the assigning of the mandate to Britain on 25 April 1920, the approval of this by the League of Nations on 24 July 1922,[469] or the coming into force of the mandate on 29 September 1923.[470] The latter date

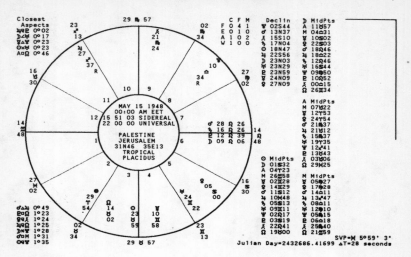

198: Palestine, Termination of Mandate, 1948

is especially recommended; a time of 00.00 hrs should be used, as this would be consistent with the coming into force of mandate powers in other territories, and the chart should be set for Jerusalem.

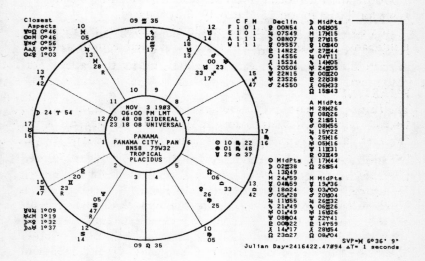

199: Panama, Independence, 1903

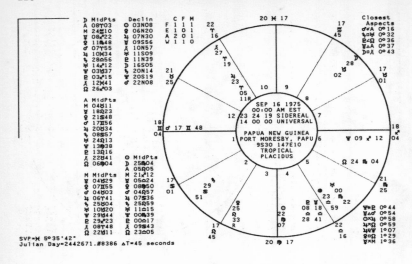

200: Papua New Guinea, Independence, 1975

PANAMA

Panama was ruled by Colombia until 1903. Chart 199 is set for the moment of independence at 6.00 p.m. on 3 November 1903, in the capital, Panama City.[471]

PAPUA NEW GUINEA

Papua New Guinea was administered by Australia until 1975. The state received its independence at 00.00 hrs on 16 September 1975.[472] Chart 200 is set for this date and time, and for the capital, Port Moresby.

PARAGUAY

Paraguay was first organized politically by the Jesuit mission state which controlled the area from 1607 to 1767, in which year the Spanish took control. The independence movement was encouraged here, as in the other Spanish colonial possessions, by the French conquest of Spain. Various dates are given for the Paraguayan declaration of independence from Spain, including 14 August 1811,[473] and 12 October 1811.[474] However effective independence seems to have been gained in a bloodless coup on the night of 14–15 May 1811 when a group of creole military leaders took power from the last Spanish governor.[475]

Chart 201 is set for 12.00 hrs noon on 14 May 1811 in the capital,

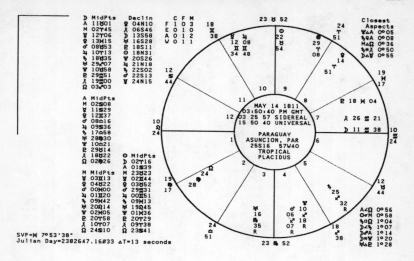

201: Paraguay, Independence 1811

Asuncion, on the grounds that revolutionary events on the previous day could also provide the basis for a national horoscope. The situation remains unclear.

A subsequent declaration of independence was made from Buenos Aires (i.e. Argentina), which claimed authority in the region, in 1813.[476]

PERU

Political organization in Peru extends earlier than recorded history. Prior to the Spanish conquest of 1531–1533, the area was the centre of the Inca Empire. The presence of earlier remains, including the famous giant sculptures on the plain of Nazca are evidence of ancient civilizations of great sophistication.

The last Inca emperor, Atahualpa, was seized by the Spanish on 16 November 1532 and executed in July 1533. From then until 1548 the Spanish conquistadores were virtually independent, although Inca resistance continued until 1572.[477]

Following the French conquest of Spain in 1807, local governments were created throughout the Spanish empire, to rule in the name of Ferdinand VII, the deposed king in 1809–1810.[478] In Peru, as elsewhere, the effect was to encourage an independence movement. Peru (which then included Bolivia) was officially proclaimed independent by José de San Martin at a meeting of the Cabildo (town

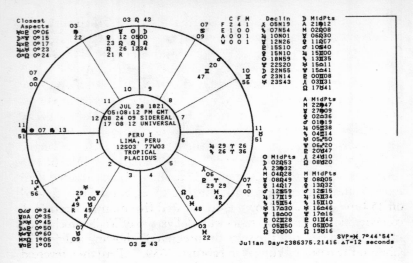

202: Peru, Proclamation, 1821

council) of Lima on 28 July 1821.[479] Chart 202 for the independence of Peru is set for this date and place, and, in the absence of accurate information, for 12.00 noon.

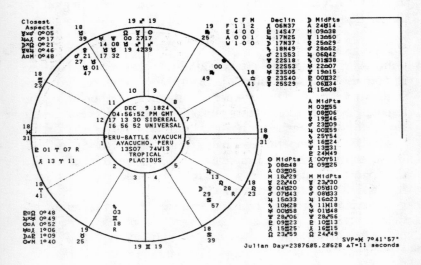

203: Peru, Battle of Ayacucho, 1824

The Spanish viceroy had fled, and San Martin assumed authority as Protector, but the war of independence continued until 1824. Complete independence was gained with the Battle of Ayacucho on 9 December 1824 at which the Venezuelan general Antonio José de Sureré destroyed a Spanish army, delivering 'a death blow to the Spanish Empire in South America'.[480] The battle began at 9.00 a.m. and ended 'in about an hour's time'.[481] The conclusion of the battle is taken as the moment of complete independence in Peru, and Chart 203 is a solar chart set for 12.00 noon on 9 December 1824, Ayacucho.

Bolivia separated from Peru in 1825 (see Chart 27), but the two countries were united again from 1835 to 1839. Bolivia invaded Peru in 1835, and divided the country into two states, South Peru, created on 15 June 1835, and North Peru, created five months later.[482] A confederation of these two states with Bolivia was officially proclaimed in October 1836, but the state disintegrated following a defeat by Chile at the battle of Yungay in February 1839.[483] Peru then reverted to being a single state and independence was finally recognized by Spain in 1869.

PHILIPPINES

Europe became aware of the Philippines on 15 March 1521, when the Spanish seafarer Magellan landed there. A Spanish–Portuguese treaty in 1529 acknowledged the islands as part of the Portuguese

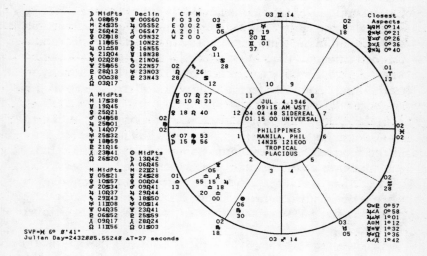

204: Philippines, Independence, 1946

Empire, although they were claimed and conquered by the Spanish after 1583. A war of independence began in 1896, and on 12 June 1898 the nationalist leader Aguinaldo proclaimed independence. [484] However, the USA had secret intentions to annex the islands, and they became an American possession by the Treaty of Paris, signed in Paris at 8.45 p.m. LMT on 10 December 1898. [485]

Independence was granted by the USA on 4 July 1946. The critical moment was the lowering of the American flag at 9.15 a.m. and the hoisting of the Philippines flag. [486] In many of the British possessions it was customary to have a daytime flag-changing ceremony while *de jure* independence had been gained at 00.00 hrs, but in this case it appears that the change of flags marked the actual moment of independence. [487]

Chart 204 for the Philippines is set for 9.15 a.m. on 4 July 1946, in the capital, Manila.

The *New York Times* carried a report that the flag-changing ceremony took place at 10.00 a.m., but the reason for the difference between this and the above time is not clear. [488] The principle has been followed here that a report of the National Historical Institute should be taken as more accurate than a foreign press report.

POLAND

The legendary foundation of Poland is dated to the year 550 (or 555 or 644), when the mythical Lech (or Lechus or Leschus) came from Croatia and settled in what is now the town of Gniezno. [489] The historical origins lie in the unification of six tribes under the leadership of the Polani in the tenth century. The first historical ruler (under German suzerainty) was Mieszko (c. 960–992), and the first king was Boleslav I, who was crowned in 1025. [490] The difficulty of establishing a horoscope for this early period was reported by Polish astrologer Rafal Prinke. [491]

In the early Middle Ages Poland was a major power in Eastern and Central Europe, and after the union with Lithuania (effective in the fourteenth century, formal on 1 July 1569), the country extended over a vast area from the Baltic to the Black Sea. [492]

Poland lost its independence at the end of the eighteenth century when it was divided between Russia, Prussia and Austria in three partitions dated 5 August 1772, 23 January 1793 and 24 October 1795. [493]

A Polish state was recreated by the Treaties of Tilsit between France, Russia and Prussia on 7–9 July 1807. This state, the Grand Duchy of Warsaw, was to consist of the portions of Poland occupied by Prussia in the partitions of 1772 and 1795, and was to be ruled by the Kings of Saxony.[494] By the Treaty of Schonbrunn on 14 October 1809, the Austrian portions of Poland were added to the Grand Duchy.[495]

In 1815 part of the Grand Duchy was returned to Prussia, but the bulk was reconstituted as a new Kingdom of Poland, with the Czar of Russia as hereditary monarch and, on paper at least, complete internal self-government. However, the new state was effectively an extension of the Russian Empire.[496]

In 1830 a revolution broke out and independence was proclaimed, together with union with Lithuania, which was also controlled by Russia. The independent regime was crushed, and what little remained of Polish independence was taken away.[497]

The horoscope for modern Poland should be calculated for the revival of the independent state during the First World War. The situation from 1914 to 1920 was chaotic, with German occupation being followed by civil war and war with Russia, but two dates stand out.

The first chart for Polish independence (Chart 205) is set for 5 November 1916. This was the date of the 'Two Emperors' Declaration (between the Emperors of Germany and Austria), which proclaimed an independent state of Poland, and set up a puppet government, but did not define a territory or constitution.[498] Chart 207 is set for Warsaw on 5 November 1916 and, in the absence of accurate information, for 12.00 noon.

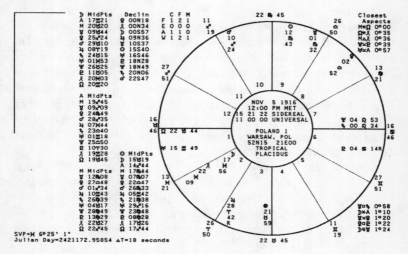

205: Poland, Proclamation, 1916

A serious objection may be made to this chart on grounds of historical invalidity, for the state created by this decree was a German puppet with no real independence. However, this was a significant date which was the beginning of the process leading to independence, and this chart is no more invalid than those for the proclamation of Irish independence in 1916 (Chart 80) or for the declaration of independence in Vietnam while under Japanese occupation (Chart 288). Genuine institutions of government were created which survived into the post-war state.

In March 1917 the Russian Revolution broke out and the Czar was overthrown. On 21 March the Petrograd Soviet of Workers' and Peasants' Deputies, which did not control the Government but which could exert considerable influence, declared Poland independent. [499] On 30 March 1917 the Russian Government issued a proclamation of intent concerning Polish independence, promising to grant this once the country had been liberated from the Germans. [500] The temporary Council of State in Warsaw, representing the Poles, regarded this Russian declaration as a recognition of the state created on 5 November 1916. [501] The anti-German Polish nationalists refused to recognize this state, however, [502] and in the country itself the nationalist leaders were gradually imprisoned. From 15 October 1917 the country was administered by a regency council on behalf of the Germans until the collapse of the Germans in November 1918. On 1 November Poland declared war on the Ukraine, evidence of its existence as a state, and on 3 November a republic was proclaimed at Warsaw. [503] This in itself was not a declaration of independence, but an overthrow of the monarchy proposed on 5 November 1916 but never established. True independence came on 11 November 1918 when Germany accepted its defeat in the war, and Polish troops under the command of General Pilsudski took control of Warsaw. [504] This date represents the full attainment of *de facto* independence in addition to the *de jure* independence granted in 1916, and Chart 206 is set for 11 November in Warsaw, and, in the absence of accurate information, for 12.00 noon.

However, this time may well have some historical validity, for it was at 11.00 a.m. GMT, that the German armies in the west (i.e. France and Belgium) surrendered. [504a] It might be imagined then that until midday the German Army in Warsaw regarded itself as in occupation of the country, but that after then the Polish Army was regarded as the controlling force.

It should be emphasized that there was a legal continuity between the independent state established on 11 November 1918 and the

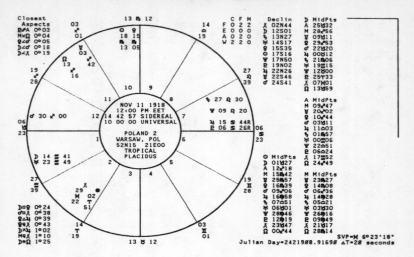

206: Poland, Independence, 1918

nominally independent state legally founded on 5 November 1916, as the German-appointed Regency Council conferred legal power on Pilsudski when it resigned and appointed him Chief of State on 14 November 1918.[505]

The horoscope given for Poland by Charles Carter appears to be based on Pilsudski's appointment as Chief of State, although no reference is given.[506] An astrological study of Poland based on this horoscope is given by Michael Baigent in *Mundane Astrology*.[507]

Poland was again partitioned by Germany and the Soviet Union in 1939, the German Invasion beginning at 4.17 a.m. on 1 September in Danzig.[508] The Polish Government surrendered at 7.30 a.m. on 28 September 1939,[509] and from then until 1944 was to be under first joint German–Soviet and then sole German control. The situation was similar to that in 1916–1918, with factions of Polish nationalists based in east and west. As in 1918 the faction based in the east was to be dominant, and the current Communist regime dates from the entry of Soviet troops into the country.

Polish astrologer Rafal Prinke dates the Polish Peoples' Republic from the announcement on the radio of the manifesto of the Polish National Liberation Committee at 10.45 a.m. on 22 July 1944 in Chelm, (51.08N, 1.34E), the first Polish town to be liberated by Soviet armies.[510]

On 21 April 1945 a provisional government was set up in Lublin

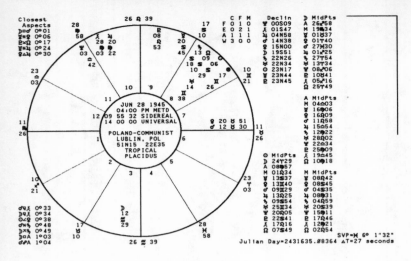

207: Poland, Communist, 1945

under Soviet auspices,[511] and this date could reasonably be taken as the foundation of the Communist regime. However, the British and French supported a rival government-in-exile in London, which had been created on 30 September 1939.[512]

This rivalry was resolved when a joint government of national unity was set up in Lublin on 28 June 1945,[513] and Chart 207 is set for this date and place. The chart is set for 4.00 p.m., the time at which the names of the members of the government were submitted to President Bierut.[514] This horoscope therefore represents the end process of the creation of an internationally recognized post-war regime, and, even though the Government contained non-Communist members, Soviet military occupation ensured that by 1948 the Communists were in absolute control.

PORTUGAL

The origins of Portugal lie in the reconquest of Spain from the Moors by Ferdinand the Great of Leon and Castile (the nucleus of modern Spain) after 1055. The territory, at first consisting of only the northern fraction of the modern country, was organized as a county with Coimbra as the capital. The date for the formal creation of the county of Portugal by Ferdinand should be taken as the foundation date for the state. Several other dates, however, are of sufficient importance

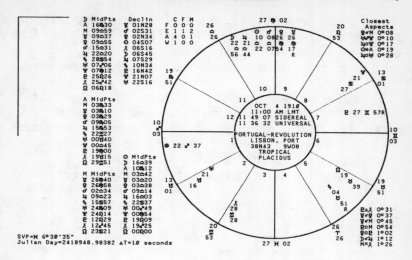

208: Portugal, Revolution, 1910

to merit consideration as the bases for national horoscopes; in 1128 Count Alfonso Henriques asserted his independence from Leon and Castile, and in 1143 he was proclaimed king, Portugal being

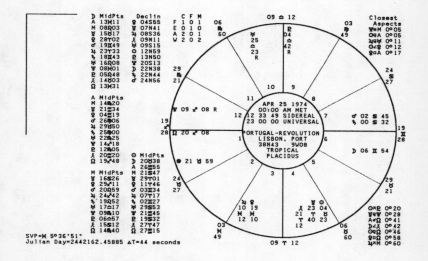

209: Portugal, Revolution, 1974

henceforth an independent kingdom.[515] With the exception of a period of Spanish rule (1580 to 1640) and a brief period of French occupation in 1808 the country has been independent from then until the present day, and has maintained its current borders since 1270.

The horoscope for the modern Portuguese Republic dates from 4 October 1910. Chart 208 is set for the beginning of the insurrection, 11.00 a.m. in Lisbon, when rebellious warships began to bombard the palace of King Manuel II.[516] An additional chart could be set for the proclamation of the Republic on 5 October 1910.[517]

The current democratic regime in Portugal dates from the military coup on 25 April 1974.[519] At 10.45 a.m. GMT the rebel broadcast announced that they controlled most of the country, and the coup had immediate success.[520] Chart 211 is set for Lisbon on 25 April 1974 and, in the absence of accurate information, for 00.00 hrs.

Additional research is necessary into both the question of the foundation of Portugal and the two revolutionary horoscopes presented here.

QATAR

The state of Qatar in the Persian Gulf was bound by treaty relations to Great Britain until September 1971. Even though the relations were so close that in other countries it would have been considered

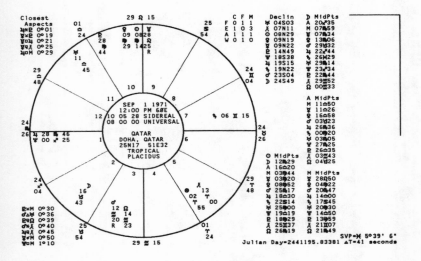

210: Qatar, Independence, 1971

to be a part of the British Empire (as for example Kuwait), like Oman it was not considered a part of the British Empire. Nevertheless, the severance of treaty relations between Qatar and Great Britain on 1 September 1971 was recorded both in the press at the time, and in subsequent reference books, as a declaration of independence.[521]

The event was regarded as of such insignificance at the time that not one major English language newspaper carried a report, except for the *New York Times*, which reported the event seven days later.[522]

There are not even any references in British Parliamentary papers.

The only hint of a time for the event is provided by a Kuwait radio broadcast of 7.00 p.m. GMT on 1 September to the effect that 'Qatar tonight proclaimed its independence and decided to end all agreements with Britain — this was announced in a Qatar radio broadcast. Thus Qatar becomes a fully independent and sovereign state.'[523]

Chart 210 is set for 1 September 1971, for the capital, Doha and, in the absence of accurate information, for 12.00 noon.

ROMAN EMPIRE

The Roman Empire was probably the single most significant political state ever to exist in Europe. For five hundred years it dominated large areas of Europe, North Africa and the Middle East. Its successor state, the Byzantine (or Eastern Roman Empire) continued in the east until 1453, its last remnants, the Despotate of Morea being conquered by the Turks on 29 May 1460 and the Empire of Trebizond disappearing in August 1461.[600] In Europe, the Holy Roman Empire, which had originally claimed a continuity from the Western Roman Empire, was only snuffed out in 1806. The legacy of Rome is felt today through the spread of the 'Romance' languages from France to Spain, Italy and Romania, through the legacy of the Roman legal system and through the domination of the Church of Rome in Christianity.

By 264 BC Rome controlled most of the Italian peninsula, and by 100 BC was the dominant power in the Mediterranean. The return to a monarchical form of government (Rome had been ruled by kings until shortly before 500 BC) became irresistible in the first century BC, but such was the hatred of the word king, that no one leader could afford to use it; Julius Caesar was assassinated because it was feared that he wished to be proclaimed king. Instead there was a gradual gathering of the various offices of the Republic in the hands of two or three men. This process reached a peak in 27 BC, the year historically recognized as the foundation of the Roman Empire. On

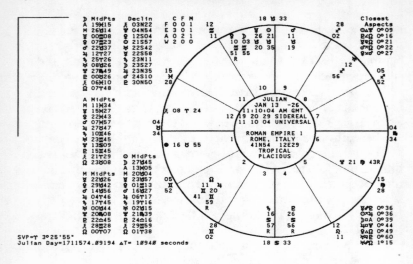

211: Roman Empire (1) 27 BC

13 January 27 BC, Octavian, great nephew and adopted son of Julius Casear, renounced all his republican powers and military commands and returned these to the Senate and people. The outcry was such that Octavian knew the people would grant him absolute power, and by their reaction to his gesture, they had done this. Later in the day Octavian was officially given control of the provinces of Spain, Gaul and Syria, a step which, as he had destroyed Mark Anthony, his last rival in 31 BC, confirmed his position as the most powerful man in the Roman world. He was also in effective control of Egypt, and was virtual Commander-in-Chief of the Roman Army. This day has therefore been called 'the birthday of the new order'.[601] Chart 211 for the Roman Empire is therefore set for 13 January 27 BC,* for Rome, and in the absence of accurate information, for 12.00 noon LMT. (Even though this date is given in old style, there is no need for adjustment to the Gregorian calendar as the Julian calendar reform had taken place only nineteen years earlier.)

At the time there was no recognition that this date marked the foundation of the Empire, as Octavian's *de jure* and *de facto* powers were no greater than those held by a number of previous leaders that century. He himself held power until 17 BC only by virtue of

---

* With regard to Charts 211 and 212, note that, according to Astro Computing Services, – 26 is equivalent to 27 BC.

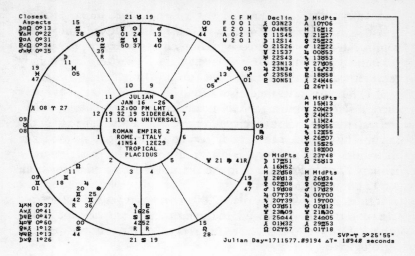

212: Roman Empire (2) 27 BC

his annual tenure of the consulship and *de facto* military command, and the process of creating the role of Emperor did not culminate until 2 BC, when he was given the title of 'Father of His Country'. [602]

However, if there is another date that could stand out as marking the beginning of the Empire, then it is 16 January 27 BC, when Octavian was given the titles that were later to become synonymous with that of Emperor. [603] These titles were Princeps, a traditional republican honour meaning 'first citizen', Imperator, a republican title first used in 43 BC and which was intended to show Octavian's unlimited power in the Greek provinces where he had military command, and Augustus. Augustus has been translated as 'reverend', signifying a person or force bringing prosperity to the state and derived from the root *augere* — to increase. [604] It is also said to be derived from the root *auctoritas*, a word suggesting the absolute power of Imperator, [605] but, through its religious connotations implying moral authority. [606] However, a third possibility is especially interesting; it is said that Octavian chose the name himself because of its derivation from augury, the art of divining the future through examining entrails. [607] Augustus was a shrewd manipulator of popular belief, having published his horoscope [608] and issued coins bearing his Moon sign, Capricorn. [609]

He was quite aware therefore that he was not only implying supreme religious authority for himself as Augustus, but supreme divinatory authority. An Augur was one who looked into the future, and in Rome, where the Augurs were highly respected and influential, commanded the present. Octavian himself was therefore proclaiming himself Lord of Time, not an unlikely claim for a man who regularly represented himself as either the Sun or Jupiter.

If 13 January confirmed Octavian in his *de facto* control of Rome then 16 January must rank as equivalent to a coronation which, through the power of such magical titles as Augustus, helped to secure not only his personal rule but a dynasty and Empire that was to change the world. Chart 212 for the Roman Empire is therefore set for 16 January 27 BC in Rome and, in the absence of accurate information, for 12.00 noon LMT.

It must be a possibility that 12.00 noon was regarded at the time as a propitious moment. When the Emperor Nero was proclaimed on 13 October 54 BC the time of 12.00 noon was elected astrologically. [610]

It would be interesting to compare these charts with those for the Holy Roman Empire, Italy and Rome (Charts 121, 136–8 and 316).

ROMANIA

The modern state of Romania approximates to the ancient Roman province of Dacia, and the name Romania is derived from the former Roman rulership. After the disintegration of the Roman Empire the

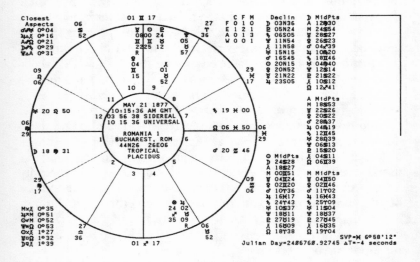

213: Romania, Independence, 1877

region was not politically organized again until the early medieval period, but lost its independence to Hungary in the late fourteenth century. Part of the country was conquered by the Ottoman Turks in the fifteenth century, and it was from the Turkish regions that the state of Romania was created in the nineteenth century. The state came into being as a fusion of the autonomous principalities of Wallachia and Moldavia sometime between 1858[611] and 5 February 1862.[612] In view of the fact that this event saw the creation of a completely new state it could be the basis of a national horoscope, even though it was still a part of the Turkish Empire. However, Chart 213 for Romania is set for the proclamation of independence on 21 May 1877.[613] The chart is set for the capital, Bucharest and, in the absence of accurate information, for 12.00 noon LMT.

Chart 214 is an alternative set for the international recognition of Romanian independence by the great powers (including Turkey) at the signing of the Treaty of Berlin, 2.30 p.m. LMT on 13 July 1878 in Berlin.[614] Chart 214 is cast for the equivalent time in the capital Bucharest — 3.22 p.m. LMT.

The Communist regime was established in Romania during the Soviet occupation after the Second World War. A Communist-dominated government was sworn in on 2 March 1945, but it was not until 30 December 1947 that the king abdicated and 13 April 1948 that a Soviet constitution was adopted.[615]

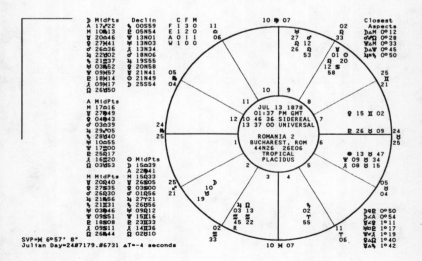

214: Romania, Recognition, 1878

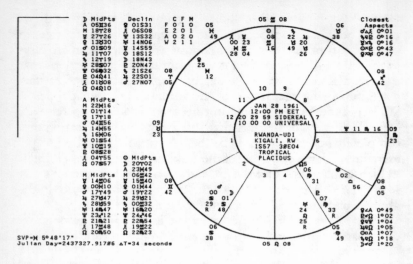

215: Rwanda, UDI, 1961

RWANDA

Rwanda became a part of the German colony of East Africa at the end of the nineteenth century and was transferred to Belgian

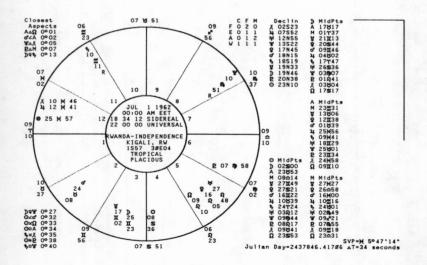

216: Rwanda, Independence, 1962

administration under a League of Nations mandate after the First
World War.

Chart 215 for Rwanda is set for the beginning of the meeting at
which a unilateral declaration of independence was issued on 28
January 1961.[616] One report recorded that the proclamation of
independence took place in the afternoon,[617] although the more
accurate account is that the beginning of a huge public rally at 12.00
noon marked the effective proclamation, and the rest of the afternoon
and evening was spent creating the machinery of government and
the constitution.[618] Chart 215 is cast for 12.00 noon on 28 January
and for the capital, Kigali.

This proclamation failed to receive international recognition, and
full legal independence was granted at 00.00 hrs on 1 July 1962.[619]
Chart 216 is set for this date and time, and for the capital, Rwanda.

The problem of the distinction between charts for revolutionary
moments and full legal independence occurs in many countries. In
some, such as the USA and Eire, the revolutionary moment is accepted
as the basis of the major national horoscope, in others full legal
independence is taken as the true time.

SAHRAWI ARAB DEMOCRATIC REPUBLIC

The Sahrawi Arab Democratic Republic (Chart 217) was proclaimed

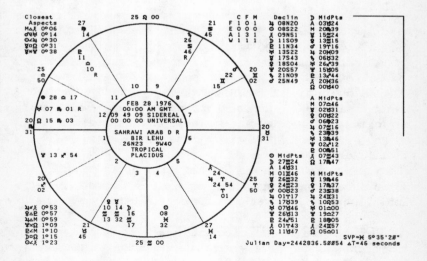

217: Sahrawi Arab Democratic Republic, Proclamation, 1976

in the former colony of the Spanish Sahara at 00.00 hrs on 28 February 1976 near the Bir Lehu oasis in the Western Sahara by the nationalist leader Mohammed Ould Siou.[620] The Spanish withdrew on 26 February and the local desire for independence was thwarted by an immediate Moroccan invasion. Although recognized by several other Arab countries, including Algeria, the Republic has never exerted independent control over the state, and its forces are currently engaged in a guerrilla war against occupying Moroccan troops.

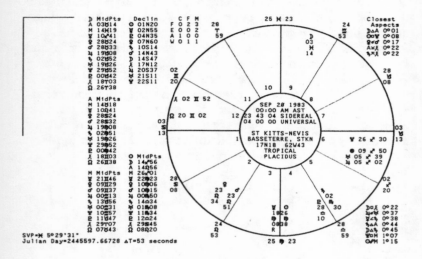

218: St Kitts-Nevis, Independence, 1983

ST KITTS-NEVIS

The Caribbean state of St Kitts-Nevis was given independence by Great Britain at 00.00 hrs on 20 September 1983.[621] Chart 218 is set for this time and date and for the capital, Basseterre.

ST LUCIA

The Caribbean island state of St Lucia was given independence by Great Britain at 00.00 hrs on 22 February 1979.[622] Chart 219 is set for this time and date, and for the capital, Castries.

ST VINCENT AND THE GRENADINES

The Caribbean state of St Vincent and the Grenadines was given independence at 00.00 hrs on 27 October 1979.[623] Chart 220 is set for this time and date and for Kingstown, the capital.

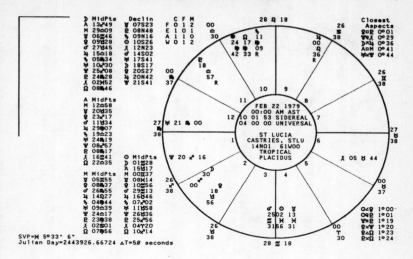

219: St Lucia, Independence, 1979

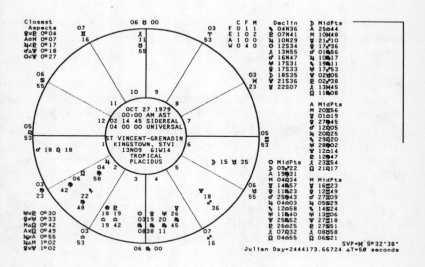

220: St Vincent and the Grenadines, Independence, 1979

SAO-TOMÉ-PRINCIPÉ

The former Portuguese colony of Sao-Tomé-Principé was given independence on the morning of 12 July 1975.[624] The crucial moment

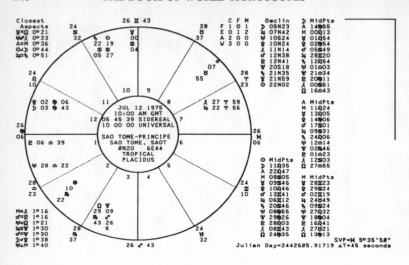

221: Sao-Tomé-Principé, Independence, 1975

seems to have been the flag-changing ceremony at 10.00 a.m. which was the signal for a day of celebrations.[625] Chart 221 is set for this time and date, and for the capital, Sao Tomé.

SAUDI ARABIA

The formation of Saudi Arabia began in 1902, but was not complete until the former rival kingdoms of Hijaz and Nejd lost their separate identity in the Kingdom of Saudi Arabia in 1932.

The kingdom of Nejd, which was the driving force behind the formation of Saudi Arabia was founded in about 1735 in the interior of the Arabian peninsula by the Wahabis, a puritanical Muslim sect, but apart from a brief campaign of conquest in the 1800s, the kingdom did not enter modern history until it captured the city of Riyadh from the Turks in 1902. This event is generally considered to represent the foundation of modern Saudi Arabia.[626]

However, the state in its modern form did not come into being until the conquest of the rival kingdom of Hijaz in the 1920s. Hijaz extended most of the way along the Red Sea coast of the Arabian peninsula and was ruled, under Turkish suzerainty, by the Hashemite family, who were responsible for the control of the Muslim holy places in Mecca and Medina. On 5 June[627] or 7 June[628] 1916, Sherif Hussein of the Hijaz proclaimed himself king of the independent state of

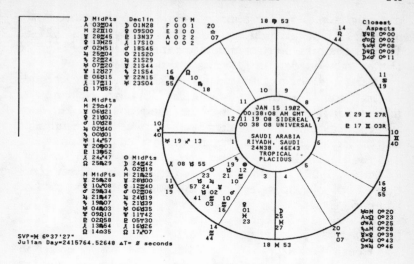

222: Saudi Arabia, Capture of Riyadh, 1902

the Hijaz, and on 29 October 1916[629] adopted the much more ambitious title of King of the Arabs. Hussein hoped that, after the First World War was over, he would be recognized as the ruler of a vast kingdom extending over the entire Arabian peninsula in addition to modern Israel, Jordan, Syria, Lebanon, Kuwait and Iraq. This ambition set him on a collision course with Ibn Saud, Sultan of Nejd, who had similar aspirations. Immediately following the defeat of the Turks in 1918, Ibn Saud began a programme of conquest, annexing the smaller Arabian kings of Asir in 1920, Hail in 1921 and Jauf in 1922. In 1924 he attacked Hijaz and on 8 January 1926 was proclaimed King of Hijaz and Sultan of Nejd,[630] a date which marks a significant step towards the foundation of the modern state. In February 1927 the titles were harmonized so that Ibn Saud became 'King of the Hijaz and Nejd' and in September 1932 the united kingdom was named Saudi Arabia. Major references give either 22 September[631] or 23 September[632] for this event, although the National Day has been fixed for 21 September to harmonize with the Autumn Equinox.[633]

According to this account alone there are three dates for which a horoscope for modern Saudi Arabia may be set: the capture of Riyadh by the Sultanate of Nejd, the proclamation of Ibn Saud as King of Hijaz, and the formal proclamation of Saudi Arabia on the symbolically potent date of 21 September 1932. There may be other dates such as those for the foundation of the ruling Wahabi dynasty in *c*.1735 or the actual military conquest of Hijaz by Nejd in 1924–6. The charts for the proclamation of the independence of Hijaz or of the Arab Kingdom in 1916 might also be relevant.

After consideration of the evidence, the chart given here for Saudi Arabia (Chart 222) is that for the capture of Riyadh by Nejd in 1902, the event quoted widely as that for the foundation of the kingdom and 'the beginning of the modern Saudi Empire'.[634] Ibn Saud crept into the fort at night and the next morning killed the governor and took the city. The horoscope given here is set for 3.45 a.m. LMT on, 15 January 1902. This time is derived from research by Michael Baigent but solar charts set for either 00.00 hrs. at dawn would be appropriate.

SENEGAL

The French West African colony of Senegal was first colonized in the sixteenth century when the fort of St Louis was set up, and was briefly part of the British Empire in the mid eighteenth century. On 4 April 1959 the state, which had become autonomous on 4 April 1959,[635] was combined with Mali, former French Sudan, to form an autonomous federation within the French Union.[636] This federation was given independence at 00.00 hrs on 20 June 1960.[637] However the federation did not survive and on 20 August 1960

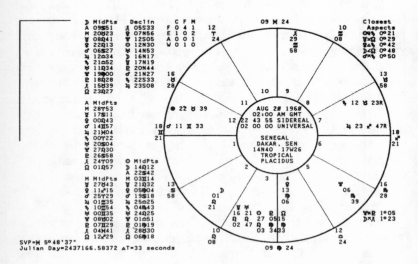

223: Senegal, Independence, 1960

Senegal seceded. The Senegalese cabinet met at 1.00 a.m. on 20 August and took the decision to secede, and by 8.00 a.m. Senegalese troops were in control of the capital, Dakar.[638] The critical time, however, occurred at 2.00 a.m. when the Senegalese Legislative Assembly met and unanimously approved the law proclaiming the independence of the country and its secession from the Mali Federation.[639] Although the report implies that the law might not have been passed until shortly after 2.00 a.m., the horoscope for modern Senegal (Chart 223) is set for this time, on 20 August 1960 and for the capital, Dakar.

SERBIA

The Serbs were Slavs who settled in the Balkans by about 650, when the area was still part of the Byzantine or Eastern Roman Empire. The first attempt to unify the various clans was made by Chaslav, who died in 960. The first king, Mikhail, was crowned in 1077, but it was only after the death of Eastern Roman Emperor Manuel I Comnenus in 1180 that King Stephen Nemanya I was able to assert the country's independence.[640] By the fourteenth century Serbia was the centre of a substantial Balkan empire, but in 1459 was conquered by the Ottoman Turks.[641]

The horoscope for modern Serbia is set for the date of independence from Turkey. A measure of self-government was given

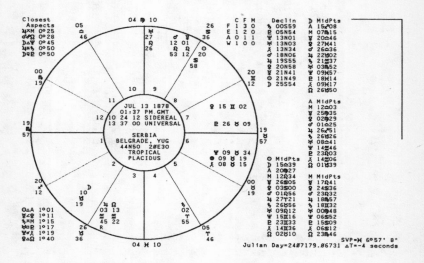

224: Serbia, Independence, 1878

in 1817 and autonomy was guaranteed by the Treaty of Adrianople on 14 September 1829. [642] Full independence was recognized by the Treaty of Berlin, signed at 2.30 p.m. LMT on 13 July 1878 in Berlin. [643] The horoscope given here for Serbia (Chart 224) is set for this date but for the equivalent time (2.58 p.m. LMT) in the capital, Belgrade.

In November 1918 Serbia became a state in the federation of Yugoslavia, along with Montenegro and the former Austrian possessions in Croatia and Bosnia. However, the state itself coalesced around Serbia, whose capital and royal family became those of the new country. Hence it is possible to see Serbia's foundation as the origin of modern Yugoslavia, and in view of the difficulties involved in establishing a horoscope for that country, the chart for Serbia might be used instead. A comparison is found in the use of the 1902 horoscope for the capture of Riyadh by the Sultanate of Nejd as a map for the state of Saudi Arabia, which did not really come into being until union with Hijaz in 1926.

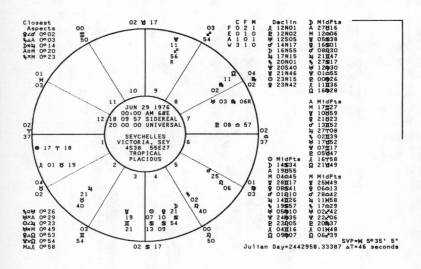

225: Seychelles, Independence, 1976

SEYCHELLES

The Seychelles, a state consisting of a group of islands in the Indian Ocean, was granted independence by Great Britain at 00.00 hrs on 29 June 1976. [644] The horoscope given here (Chart 225) is set for this time and date and for the capital, Victoria.

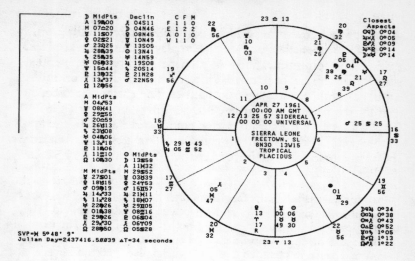

226: Sierra Leone, Independence, 1961

SIERRA LEONE

The former British West African colony of Sierra Leone was granted independence at 00.00 hrs on 27 April 1961.[645] The horoscope given here (Chart 226) is set for this time and date, for the capital, Freetown.

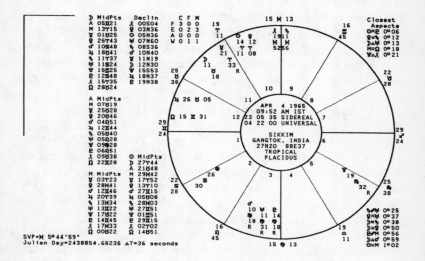

227: Sikkim, Coronation, 1965

SIKKIM

Although self-governing, Sikkim is a protectorate of India, which is therefore responsible for the tiny Himalayan state's foreign affairs, defence and communications. As such it is not a fully independent state. However, it is of particular interest in view of the continuing influential role of astrologers in politics. The current horoscope is that for the coronation of the Chogyal (king) on 4 April 1965.[646] Every moment in the coronation ceremony was elected by the royal astrologers.[647] At 9.22 a.m. the ceremonial procession started from the palace on its route to the royal chapel[648] and at exactly 9.52 a.m. the King was crowned.[649]

> At the royal chapel, in the first floor prayer hall, the Chogyal was robed in brilliant scarlet brocades and his Queen in scarlet and gold. They mounted their thrones, the King's being a foot higher. Then lamas sounded long copper horns, clashed cymbals, and chanted as a fur-rimmed crown was handed to the King who placed it on his head . . . lamas and monks presented the King with the royal insignia of thunderbolt boots, symbolising stability and power, and a thousand-spoked gold wheel, signifying royalty.[650]

The horoscope given here (Chart 227) is set for the astrologically elected moment of 9.52 a.m. on 4 April 1965, in the capital, Gangtok.

SINGAPORE

Singapore was founded by the British adventurer Sir Stamford Raffles in 1819,[651] and a horoscope for this moment could be used as the chart for the modern state. This would be convenient as there are at least three modern times for independence, all of which are given here. Singapore became a self-governing state on 3 June 1959, although still a part of the British Empire.

Independence originally came to Singapore by default due to the delay in the creation of the Federation of Malaysia (Chart 169). Malaysia was scheduled to come into existence at 00.00 hrs on 31 August 1963, and Singapore was due to be transferred from British to Malaysian sovereignty at that moment.[652] As the formation of Malaysia was postponed until 00.00 hrs on 16 September 1963,[653] Singapore became independent at 00.00 hrs on 31 August and enjoyed sixteen days as an independent state.[654] Chart 228 is set for this data. The flamboyant Prime Minister, Lee Kwan Yew, proclaimed independence later in the day,[655] apparently in the evening,[656] and this powerful symbolic moment could also be worthy of astrological investigation.

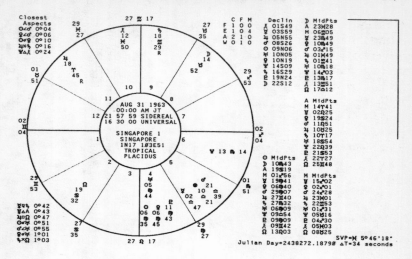

228: Singapore, Independence, 1963

Considerable confusion surrounds the timing of Singapore's secession from Malaysia on 9 August 1965, partly because both prime ministers, Tungku Abdul Rahman of Malaysia and Lee Kwan Yew of Singapore, seem to have played loose with constitutional proprieties, presenting the secession to the Malaysian parliament as a *fait accompli*.

Western reports that the independence of Singapore took place at 00.01 hrs [657] were inaccurate, as there was no legal or public transfer of power at this time. There may have been a *de facto* transfer of a sort as the secession agreement instructed all Malaysian officials in Singapore to transfer their allegiance to the Singapore Government as from 9 August, suggesting *de facto* independence from 00.00 hrs. The *Government Gazette* printed on the 9th referred only to the independence from that day, giving no hint of a time.

In Kualur Lumpur, the Malaysian capital, MPs were informed of the secession at between 9.30 and 9.40 a.m., and five minutes after the later time the independence bill was ready (i.e. 9.45 a.m.). However, Lee Kwan Yew had decided to make a flamboyant gesture, as in 1963, and with or without Malaysian approval, had decided to proclaim independence at 10.00 a.m.:

Just before 10.00 a.m. copies of the [secession] agreement were released, but reporters were barred from getting near telephones until 10.00 a.m.,

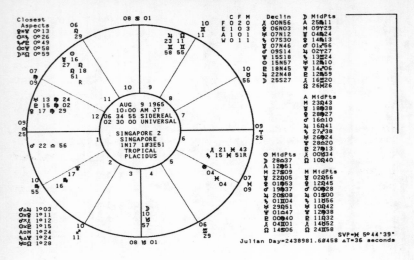

229: Singapore, Independence (1), 1965

the hour of independence . . . sharp on the hour. Radio Singapore went on the air to announce the separation . . . in a number of places it was greeted with a thunderous explosion of firecrackers.[658]

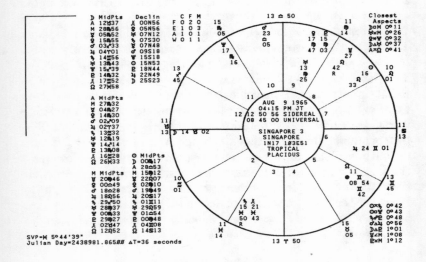

230: Singapore, Independence (2), 1965

The Singapore National Library confirmed that Lee Kwan Yew proclaimed Singapore independent on the steps of City Hall at 10.00 a.m.[659]

Clearly 10.00 a.m. saw a *de facto* proclamation of independence and Chart 229 is set for this time on 9 August 1963 in Singapore.

However, full legal independence could not come until the Malaysian parliament had approved the secession bill. The Prime Minister, Tungku Abdul Rahman, opened parliamentary proceedings in Kualur Lumpur at about 10.00 a.m., and an analysis of the subsequent debates and proceedings shows that they were concluded between 4.00 p.m. and 4.30 p.m., most likely between 4.15 and 4.20 p.m.:[660] 'Simultaneously with the passing of the Bill by both Houses of Parliament, Singapore became independent.'[661]

Supporting evidence of this time is provided by the broadcast of Lee's press conference at 10.00 a.m. on the television at 4.30 p.m., suggesting that this had been delayed until full *de jure* independence had been granted.

Chart 230 is therefore set for 4.15 p.m. on 9 August 1965, in Singapore.

A similar disparity between charts for *de facto* and *de jure* independence occurs in other countries, particularly Israel and the South Yemen.

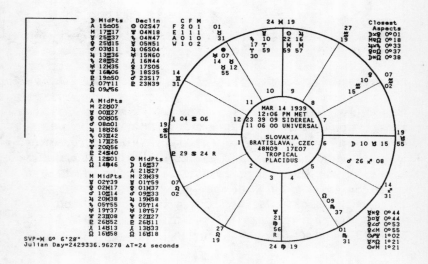

231: Slovakia, Independence, 1939

SLOVAKIA

On 14 March 1939 Czechoslovakia disintegrated into the German protectorate of Bohemia-Moravia and the independent states of Carpatho-Ukraine (Chart 43) and Slovakia. The Slovak Government proclaimed the independence of Slovakia at 12.06 p.m. on 14 March, under severe intimidation from the Germans. [662] On 16 March the country became a German protectorate and was occupied by German troops. The horoscope given here (Chart 231) is set for 12.06 p.m. on 14 March 1939, in the capital, Bratislava. See also the horoscopes for Czechoslovakia and Carpatho-Ukraine.

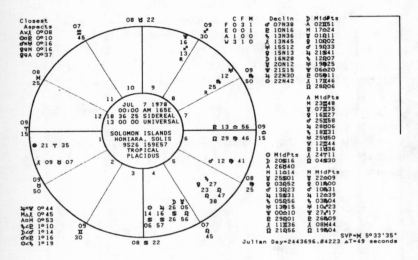

232: Solomon Islands, Independence, 1978

SOLOMON ISLANDS

The Solomon Islands received independence from Great Britain and Australia on 7 July 1978. [663] A time of 00.00 hrs would be consistent with that for the granting of independence to all other former British possessions since 1945 with the exception of Burma (where the time was elected astrologically), and the apparently exceptional cases of the protectorates of the Maldives, Qatar, Kuwait and Bahrain. The horoscope given here (Chart 232) is therefore set for 00.00 hrs on 7 July 1978 and for the capital, Honiara.

SOMALIA

Somalia originally consisted solely of the former colony of British

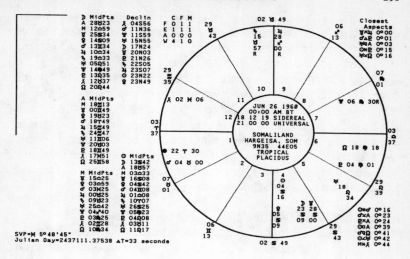

233: Somalia, Independence of Somaliland, 1960

Somaliland, and was given independence under the name of
Somaliland at 00.00 hrs on 26 June 1960.[664] Chart 233 for Somalia
is set for this time and date, and for the capital, Hargeisa.

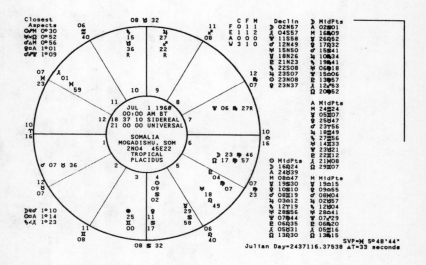

234: Somalia, Independence and Union, 1960

Somalia itself was created at 00.00 hrs on 1 July 1960 when Italian Somaliland simultaneously gained independence from Italian trusteeship and united with Somaliland.[665] Chart 234 is set for this time and date, and for the new capital, Mogadishu.

The question of which chart is more valid is very difficult in this case. The state definitely owes its origins to the independence of Somaliland on 26 June, but the creation of Somalia, combined with the move of capital, on 1 July, was reported in the press at the time as at least as major a development as were the events of 26 June. In each case the events were greeted with massive local celebrations. The question of which, if either chart, has the greater validity on historical grounds must remain open.

SOUTH AFRICAN REPUBLIC (TRANSVAAL)

The South African Republic, more commonly known as the Transvaal, is not to be confused with the modern South African Republic, even though the former was one of the Boer states which eventually united to form the latter.

The area north of the Vaal River in Southern Africa was settled by Boers in the Great Trek of 1835–7, and the Republic seems to have been founded in 1848.[666] A suitable horoscope could be set for the recognition of the independence of the Transvaal by the British on 17 January 1852, a crucial date in the emergence of the republic

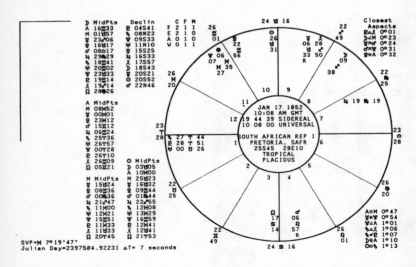

235: South African Republic (Transvaal), Recognition, 1852

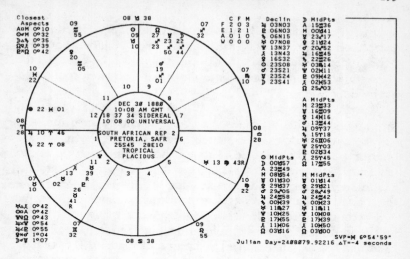

236: South African Republic, Independence, 1880

towards formal organization.[667] The first horoscope given here (Chart 235) is set for this date, and is in the absence of accurate information, for 12.00 noon and for the symbolically important location of the subsequent capital, Pretoria. Pretoria itself was not founded until 1855.

This whole episode is surrounded with confusion and uncertainty, and the Republic does not seem to have been formally organized until 16 December 1856.[668] The state was not recognized by all the Boer groups and Zoutpansberg, Lydenburg and Utrecht continued to function as independent republics. The name South African Republic seems to have been adopted at this time.

Independence was lost on 12 April 1877[669] when the Republic was annexed by Great Britain.

In 1880 the Boers rebelled against British rule, proclaiming their independence on 30 December 1880.[670] Chart 236 is set for this date, for the capital, Pretoria, and, in the absence of accurate information, for 12.00 noon. The new state united with the New Republic (founded in 1884 at Vryheid) in 1888, but was invaded by the British in 1900 and annexed for a second time.

In 1910 independence was restored as part of the Union of South Africa. The significance of the horoscopes of the early Boer Republics lies in a long-term study of the fortunes of the Afrikaaners in modern South Africa.

SOUTH AFRICA

South Africa came into being as the Union of South Africa, an independent state consisting of various British possessions in Southern Africa together with the former Boer republics of the Orange Free State and the South African Republic, which had been conquered in the Boer War of 1899–1902.

Chart 237 is cast for the 31 May 1910, for the capital, Pretoria and for 12.00 noon when 'the Governor General and his first ministers will take the oath and generally assume office with solemn ceremonial'. [671] It must be considered that, as the creation of the new state was a result of legislation passed in the British Parliament, a legal beginning could be fixed for 00.00 hrs. However, the ceremonial proclamation was clearly the most important moment.

A second horoscope in use for South Africa is customarily cast for the formation of the Republic and separation from the British Commonwealth (Chart 238). This event took place on 31 May 1961 at 00.00 hrs. [672] Unlike the creation of the state in 1910, the ceremonial began at 00.00 hrs with the ringing of church bells across the country, although, as reported at the time the whole affair was something of a non-event. However, in that the break with the Commonwealth marked South Africa's refusal to remove apartheid or compromise with the rest of the world, this does represent a highly significant moment.

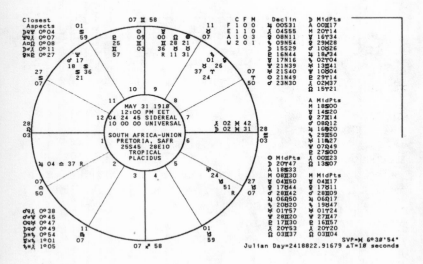

237: South Africa, Union, Independence, 1910

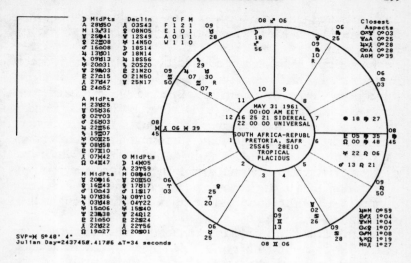

238: South Africa, Republic, 1961

It has been reported that the Republic was proclaimed in
Parliament at 10.14 a.m. on the morning of 31 May, although no
documentary source has been quoted for this event.[673]

In 1984 a new constitution was introduced including separate
parliamentary chambers for 'Asians' and 'Coloureds' though not
for 'Blacks', and under the control of an executive, rather than
ceremonial, president. The critical moment occurred at 10.49 a.m.
when the new President, P. W. Botha, concluded his oath of office
with the words 'so help me God'.[674] At this moment the constitution
was fully implemented.

SPAIN

It is theoretically possible to trace modern Spain back to the Kingdom
of the Visigoths, the first people to unite the Iberian peninsula as
an independent self-governing unit. The Visigoths began the
conquest of Spain from the Vandals in 415 and in 419 the kingdom
was established by Wallia, although the area was technically still under
Roman suzerainty.[675] In 711 a mixed force of Arabs and Berbers
invaded the country, and the Visigothic Kingdom was reduced by
718 to the small northern kingdom of the Asturias.[676] It was from
here that the Christian reconquest of Spain was launched, although
as more land was retaken from the Arabs the result was the creation
of rival kingdoms and counties. However, eventually, all these separate

states coalesced until only two were left — Castile and Portugal. A third state, Aragon, had emerged from the former French possessions in the north.

The creation of Spain was effected by the marriage of Prince Ferdinand of Aragon to Princess Isabella of Castile, and the subsequent succession of each to their respective thrones. The effective union took place on the day that Juan II of Aragon died on 19 January 1479,[677] and the horoscope given here (Chart 239) is set for that date, and, in the absence of accurate information, for 12.00 noon LMT. The chart is set for Madrid, the capital of Castile, which was to become the capital of the united state. The two kingdoms remained constitutionally separate for some time, legal union being effected during the sixteenth century, and the capital being finally established at Madrid in 1560.[678]

A chart for modern Spain is often set for the inauguration of King Juan Carlos on 22 November 1975,[679] a moment which marked not only the restoration of the monarchy, but of parliamentary democracy following the Franco dictatorship. The critical moment seems to have occurred at 12.45 p.m. when the king took the oath of allegiance in Parliament,[680] although other unconfirmed sources quote 12.53 p.m. Coronation was abandoned by Spanish kings in the Middle Ages, although Juan Carlos' inauguration was followed by a Cathedral service on 27 November.[681]

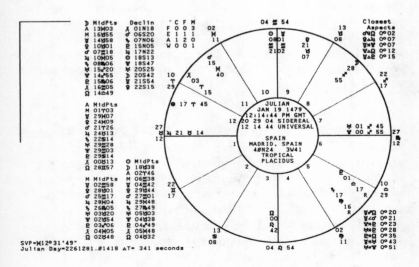

239: Spain, Dynastic Union of Aragon and Castile, 1479

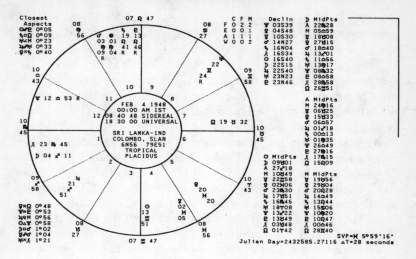

240: Sri Lanka, Independence, 1948

SRI LANKA

The horoscope for modern Sri Lanka is set for the independence of
the state from Great Britain at 00.00 hrs on 4 February 1948, when

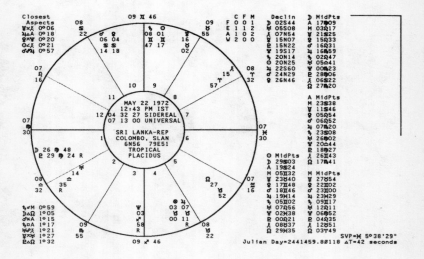

241: Sri Lanka, Republic, 1972

the Ceylon Independence Act came into force.[682] The horoscope given here (Chart 240) is set for this time and date, and for Colombo, the capital.

The ceremonial moment took place when Sir Henry Moore, the Governor of Ceylon, was sworn in as Governor-General of the new state between 7.30 and 7.40 a.m., an event marked by the ringing of church and temple bells and 'public rejoicing'.[683] This moment is worthy of astrological consideration.

Although technically known as the Dominion of Lanka the state was commonly known as Ceylon until the proclamation of the Republic of Sri Lanka on 22 May 1972. The proclamation took place in Colombo at 12.43 p.m., a time elected by the Government's astrologers. 'The day chosen for the birth of the Republic was the most auspicious day of the year and so were all the times fixed for the crucial moments in the drama.'[684]

Presumably this chart is that still used by Sri Lankan politicians (although in its eastern form) and therefore deserves consideration alongside the independence horoscope. Chart 241 is set for this time, date and place.

SUDAN
From 1899 the Sudan was technically ruled jointly by Egypt and Great

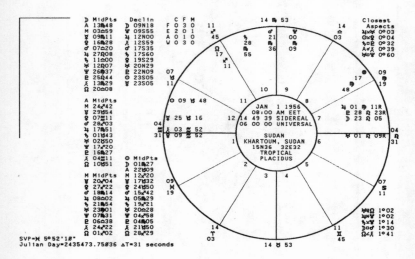

242: Sudan, Independence, 1956

Britain which, as Egypt was for the entire duration under *de jure* or *de facto* British control, meant that Sudan was a part of the British Empire. A proclamation of independence appears to have been made by the prime minister, Ismail El Azhari, on 19 December 1955,[685] although full effective and legal independence was not granted until 1 January 1956. Contempoary reports agreed that the proclamation of independence was during the day,[686] either during the flag-changing ceremony,[687] or, more importantly, during a parliamentary sitting.[688] Reports differed as to whether the parliamentary sitting recognized[689] or declared independence.[690] This is a crucial distinction as, if the sitting recognized independence this would imply it had taken place at an earlier time, perhaps 00.00 hrs. It is clear that Great Britain and Egypt had earlier declared that their joint rule had ended, but that the solemn ceremony in the parliamentary chamber was of sufficient symbolic importance to be taken as the basis of a national horoscope whatever the precise constitutional position. The horoscope given here (Chart 242) is therefore set for 1 January, the capital, Khartoum, and for 8.00 a.m., the time of the solemn recognition of independence by the Sudanese Parliament and Government.[691]

SURINAM

Surinam, the former colony of Dutch Guiana, received its

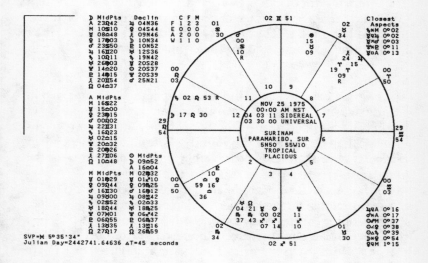

243: Surinam, Independence, 1975

independence at 00.00 hrs on 25 November 1975.[692] The horoscope given here is set for this time and date, and for the capital, Paramaribo.

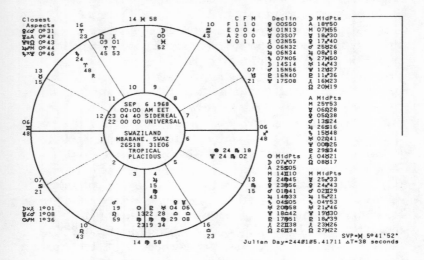

244: Swaziland, Independence, 1968

SWAZILAND

The Southern African state of Swaziland received independence from Great Britain when the protectorate was terminated at 00.00 hrs on 6 September 1968.[693] The horoscope given here (Chart 244) is set for this time and date, and for the capital, Mbabane.

SWEDEN

The origins of Sweden lie in the Svear kingdom which emerged in Scandinavia in the eighth century. The union of the kingdoms of Gothia and Svealand at the beginning of the ninth century seems to mark the beginning of the country's continuous independent existence.[694] It is currently not possible to cast a horoscope for the foundation of Sweden as its origins are so obscure.

The horoscope for modern Sweden should be set for the creation of the liberal parliamentary constitution between 1864 and 1866. Revision of the constitution (the previous constitution of 1809 had confirmed the absolute monarchy), began on 8 December 1864, and the new constitution seems to have come into effect in January 1866.[695] However, the key event occurred on 9 December 1865 when the nobility voted away its privileges. This seems to have been an

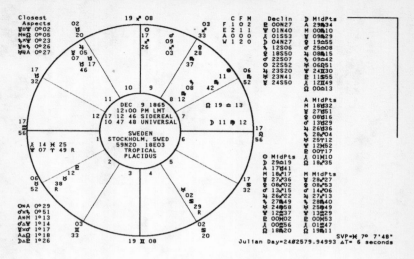

245: Sweden, Constitution, 1865

exciting event, with the hall being surrounded by eager crowds. Once
the nobility had voted away their privileges the clergy followed suit,
and the nobles' vote therefore guaranteed the introduction of the
constitution. [696] The horoscope given here (Chart 245) is calculated
for 9 December 1865, for the capital, Stockholm and, in the absence
of accuration information, for 12.00 noon LMT.

The horoscope for the legal introduction of the constitution in
January 1866 should have equal validity.

The introduction of the parliamentary regime was the catalyst for
a major transformation in Swedish society which then moved from
being a feudal to an industrialized nation. [697]

SWITZERLAND
Switzerland came into being as a result of the gradual rejection of
Hapsburg authority and of the Holy Roman Empire by a group of
towns in the Alps in the thirteenth and fourteenth centuries. While
there is no difficulty in ascertaining precise dates, some historical
investigation is required to determine which are the more important.

The move towards independence began on 26 May 1231 when
the people of Uri obtained from King Henry VII of Germany, the
son of the Holy Roman Emperor Frederick II a charter by which the
canton gained 'Imperial immediacy'. The effect of this was to remove
the town of Uri from the control of its feudal overlords, the Hapsburgs,

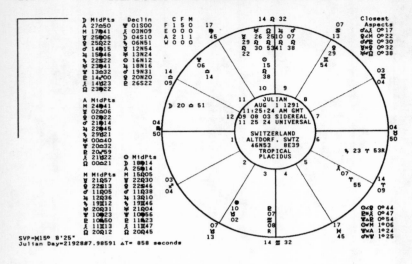

246: Switzerland, Everlasting League, 1291

and place it under the immediate authority of the Emperor. This was an important step towards *de facto* independence which was taken by a great many German towns. However, only in Switzerland did this move result ultimately in *de jure* independence and the charter 'must be considered as the origin of the Confederation [of Switzerland]. The whole structure of our freedom is founded upon it.'[698]

However, the formal beginning of the Swiss Confederation itself is dated from the foundation of the 'Everlasting League' of Schwyz, Uri and Nidwelden. This took place on 1 August 1291 (old style) although it is thought that a secret pact between the three states may have been sworn on an earlier date.[699] The horoscope given here (Chart 246) is therefore set for 1 August 1291 (old style) and, in the absence of accurate information, for 12.00 noon LMT and for Altdorf, the main town of Uri.

The subsequent dates worthy of consideration occurred between 1313 and 1318 and in 1499. On 9 December 1315 (old style) the Pact of Brunnen reaffirmed the pact of 1291 with one additional clause forbidding the making of separate alliances and thus deliberately limiting the cantons' sovereignty. It is said that this marked 'the true foundation of the Confederation',[700] but historically this is far less significant than the original treaty.

Three further dates should be mentioned.

On 19 March 1316 (old style) Emperor Louis IV proclaimed that the Hapsburg Dukes of Austria had forfeited all rights in the three cantons, confirming Imperial Immediacy.[701] This, however, merely repeated the charter of 1231.

On 19 July 1318 (old style) the Hapsburgs signed an armistice which constituted *de facto* recognition of the independence, within the Holy Roman Empire, of the three cantons of the Everlasting League.[702]

On 22 September 1499 (old style) the Peace of Basle was signed recognizing the complete *de jure* independence of the Swiss Confederation from the Holy Roman Empire.[703]

All these dates are worthy of astrological investigation while lacking the historical importance of 1 August 1291.

SYRIA

Although a centre of the earliest recorded civilization, the area covered by modern Syria has been dominated by powerful neighbours from ancient times until the twentieth century. In four thousand years it has formed part of the Babylonian, Assyrian, Egyptian, Persian, Macedonian, Roman, Arabian, Turkish and French Empires.

Following the defeat of Turkey in the First World War, a Syrian State was proclaimed in Damascus by the Emir Feisal, son of the King of the Hijaz[704] However, the region was occupied by the British

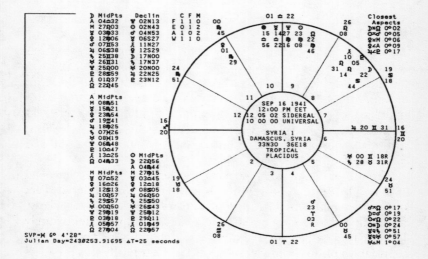

247: Syria, *De Jure* Independence, 1941

and true independence was never gained. On 2 July 1919 and 8 March 1920 requests were made for independence and on 11 March 1920 Feisal was proclaimed King of Syria. However, on 25 April 1920 the mandate over Syria was assigned to France (and confirmed by the League of Nations on 24 July 1922), the French occupied Damascus, Feisal fled[705] and was later appointed King of Iraq by the British.

These two dates represent failed attempts to gain independence and yet are worthy of astrological investigation.

Throughout the 1930s the French offered various degrees of self-government to the Syrians including spurious independence[706] yet always intervened to assert their authority if any local politicians actually started to act independently. It was only the pressure of war that prompted a declaration of independence by France in order to gain Arab support. On 16 September 1941 the Free French leader in Syria, General Georges Catroux, proclaimed Syrian independence in Damascus. The proclamation took place during the day,[707] was in accordance with the French-Syrian Treaty of 9 September 1936[708] and represented complete *de jure* independence.

Chart 247 is set for 16 September 1941 in Damascus and, in the absence of accurate information, for 12.00 noon.

However, the French continued to exercise all the mandate powers, depriving the Syrian government of any real authority. Under British and American pressure the French finally agreed on 27 December

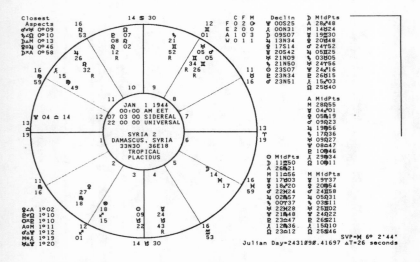

248: Syria, *De Facto* Independence, 1944

1944 to transfer all the mandate powers to the Syrian Government on 1 January 1944,[709] and Chart 248 is set for this date, for the capital, Damascus and, in the absence of accurate information, for 00.00 hrs. An actual time of 00.00 hrs would be consistent with the time for the transfer of mandate powers in other states.

The final evacuation of British and French troops from Syria on 17 April 1946 has been reported in reference works as the date marking final *de facto* independence,[710] but contemporary reports made no such connection.[711]

The problem of which if either chart given here is the more important, can only be solved by detailed investigation.

From 1 February 1958 until 28–29 September 1961 Syria was part of the United Arab Republic in federation with Egypt (see Chart 269).

The current regime in Syria, controlled by the Baath (i.e. radical and nationalist) party has achieved a certain degree of notoriety in the West. The regime was brought to power in a coup led by the current leader, President Assad, at dawn on 13 November 1970.[712] I have found that a chart cast for dawn (approximately 6.00 a.m.) is effective for modern Syria, and may be used instead of, or in addition to, the two independence horoscopes.

TANZANIA

Tanzania is a union of the states of Tanganyika and Zanzibar formed

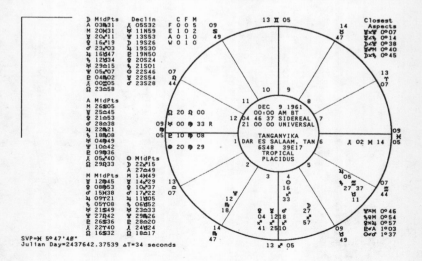

249: Tanzania; Independence of Tanganyika, 1961

in 1964, and the charts for each of these states, as well as for their union, must be considered.

Following the German defeat in the First World War the colony of German East Africa became the British territory of Tanganyika. As Tanganyika the state was given independence at 00.00 hrs on 9 December 1961,[717] Chart 249 is set for this time and date and for the capital, Dar es Salaam.

Zanzibar was until 1856 controlled by the Sultanate of Muscat (now part of Oman), in which year it became independent under Seyyid Majid, a son of the Sultan of Muscat. At that time it controlled a considerable portion of the East African coast, but its power declined and the state became a British protectorate in 1890.[718] Independence was gained from Great Britain at 00.00 hrs on 10 December 1963 when the protectorate was terminated.[719] Chart 250 is set for this time and date, and for the capital, Zanzibar town.

Following a revolution in Zanzibar which overthrew the Sultan, the two countries decided to unite. This union was accomplished during the day of 27 April 1964 when President Nyerere of Tanganyika and President Karume of Zanzibar formally exchanged the instruments of ratification in the Parliament building in Dar es Salaam, an event which was broadcast live.[720] The two presidents were scheduled to exchange the instruments of ratification (the Treaty of Union having been signed on 23 April[721]) at 11.30 a.m., and Chart

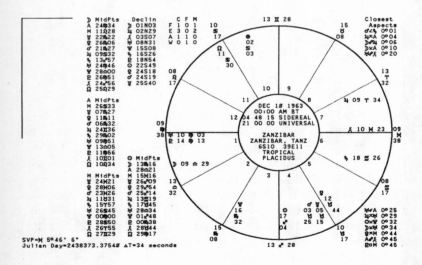

250: Tanzania; Independence of Zanzibar, 1963

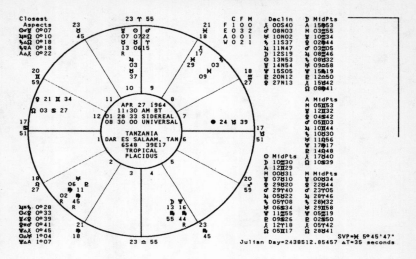

251: Tanzania; Union of Tanganyika and Zanzibar, 1964

251 is set for this time on 27 April 1964 in the capital, Dar es Salaam.

The original name of the state was the United Republic of Tanganyika and Zanzibar, the name being changed to the United Republic of Zanzibar on 30 October 1964. [722]

The obvious question that arises in this case is which horoscope has priority in the modern state. Even though the union chart is important, considerable weight must be attached to the chart of the independence of Tanganyika as the dominant partner in the union.

TEXAS

Spanish exploration of Texas began in 1536, and the region was subsequently incorporated into the Spanish Empire. It gained independence from Spain as part of Mexico (see Chart 176), but American colonization beginning in 1821 led to the rebellion of 1836. The Republic of Texas was proclaimed independent on 2 March 1836 [713] in the town of Washington, and the horoscope given here (Chart 252) is set for this date and place and, in the absence of accurate information, for 12.00 noon LMT. Independence was finally established by the Battle of San Jacinto on 21 April 1836, [714] and the anniversary of this battle was the date chosen to open a Texas Commission in London in 1986. [715]

After nine years of independence the state was annexed by the USA on 19 February 1846, [716] but it would be reasonable to use the

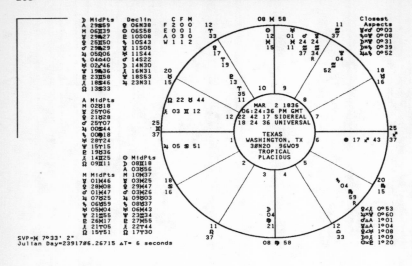

252: Texas, Independence, 1836

independence horoscope as that for the existence of Texas as a state of the USA.

THAILAND

The kingdom of Siam can be traced back to the Middle Ages, although it is not possible to establish a foundation date for the country. In modern Thailand the crucial date is regarded as the foundation of the Chakri Dynasty by Rama I in 1782 and the removal of the capital to Bangkok in the same year.[723] The transfer of the capital was almost certainly undertaken on astrological advice as the same year witnessed the astrologically motivated transfer of the Burmese capital from Ava to Amarapoura.[724] The bicentenary of Bangkok's foundation was celebrated on 6 April 1982,[725] and although the festivities as a whole lasted from 4 to 21 April, the horoscope given here (Chart 253) is set for 6 April 1782. Although it is presumed that the time for the foundation of Bangkok was astrologically elected and that the horoscope must be in circulation in modern Thailand it has not been possible to locate this. The chart is therefore set for 12.00 noon LMT and should be speculatively regarded as a horoscope for the foundation of modern Thailand. In view of the uncertainty surrounding the original event, it should however, be treated with caution.

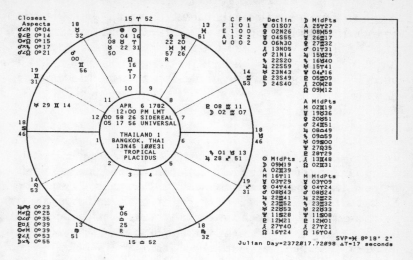

253: Thailand, Foundation of Bangkok, 1982

A second horoscope for modern Thailand is set for the revolution of 24 June 1932 which overthrew the benevolent despotism established in 1860 and initiated the present constitutional system.

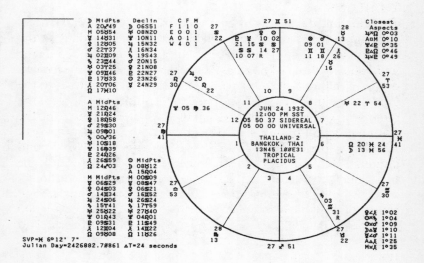

254: Thailand, Constitution, 1932

A military coup took place in the early morning of 24 June and later on the same day the King accepted the principle of constitutional rule. [726] Although confirmation of this acceptance seems to have been issued by the King on 26 June, and the constitution was not signed until 10 December, 24 June would appear to be the key date historically. Chart 255 is set for this date, for the capital Bangkok, and, in the absence of accurate information, for 12.00 noon.

TIMOR

The Democratic Republic of East Timor is a former Portuguese colony in the East Indies now occupied by Indonesia. The first move towards independence from Portugal occurred on 11 August 1975 when the Democratic Union of Timor staged a coup and demanded independence. [727] Independence was proclaimed illegally on 28 November 1975, the President was inaugurated on 29 November and the Government was sworn in on 1 December. [728] The horoscope given here (Chart 255) is set for 28 November, for the capital, Dili, and, in the absence of accurate information, for 12.00 noon.

The country enjoyed only ten days of independent existence. At dawn on 7 December 1975 Indonesian troops invaded and on 17 December a provisional government was formed to promote full integration with Indonesia. Timorese forces are still conducting a guerrilla war against the Indonesian Army.

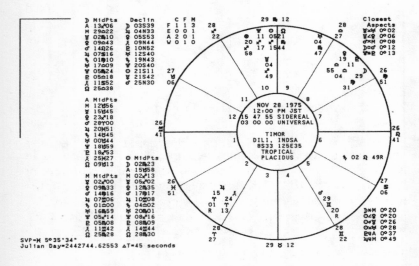

255: Timor, UDI, 1975

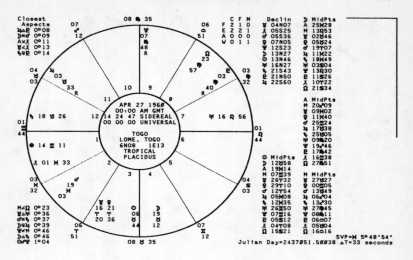

256: Togo, Independence, 1960

TOGO

Togoland became a German colony in 1884. Following the German
defeat in the First World War the country was divided between British
and French mandates. The British section subsequently gained
independence as part of Ghana and the French section was granted
independence as the state of Togo at 00.00 hrs on 27 April 1960.[729]
The horoscope given here (Chart 256) is set for this time and for
the capital, Lomé.

TONGA

The British-ruled island protectorate of Tonga was given independence on 4 June 1970.[730] Contemporary reports indicate that
important ceremonies took place during the day[731] but that they
began during the night,[732] suggesting a time of 00.00 hrs. This would
be consistent with the normal time for the coming into force or
termination of a legal agreement between two countries, unless
specifically stated otherwise. The horoscope given here (Chart 257)
is set for 00.00 hrs on 4 June 1970, and for the capital, Nuku'alofa.

TRANSCAUCASIAN FEDERATIVE REPUBLIC

The Transcaucasian Federative Republic proclaimed independence
from Russia, by which it had been ruled since the early nineteenth

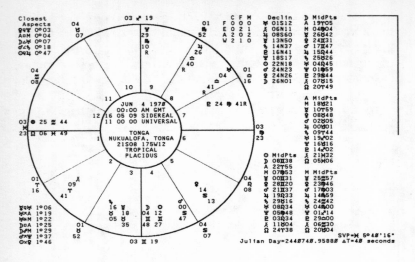

257: Tonga, Independence, 1970

century, on 22 April 1918.[734] The country enjoyed only five weeks
of independent existence before disintegrating into its constituent
states — Georgia, Azerbaijan and Armenia. The horoscope given
here (Chart 258) is set for 22 April 1918 and, in the absence of accurate

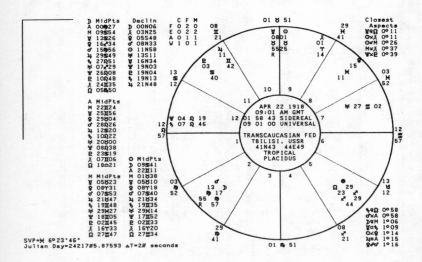

258: Transcaucasian Federative Republic, Independence, 1918

information, for 12.00 noon LMT. The chart is also set for Tbilisi, the capital of Georgia, although it could be reasonably set for the capitals of the other two federated states.

The country was reconstituted on 12 March 1922 as the Communist Transcaucasian Soviet Socialist Republic[735] and agreed to join the USSR on 30 December 1922.

The importance of such charts for current Soviet states lies in the possibility of any substantial revival of nationalist sentiment.

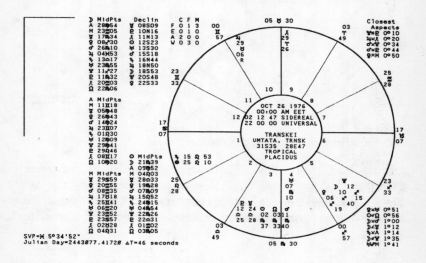

259: Transkei, Independence, 1976

TRANSKEI

The Southern African state of Transkei was created under South Africa's apartheid policy as a 'homeland' for the Xhosa tribe. The state is under the effective control of South Africa, which is itself the only country to recognize its 'independence'. The Transkei received its *de jure* independence at 00.00 hrs on 26 October 1976 in the capital, Umtata.[736] The horoscope given here is cast for this data.

TRINIDAD AND TOBAGO

The Caribbean state of Trinidad and Tobago received its independence from Great Britain at 00.00 hrs on 31 August 1962.[737] The horoscope given here (Chart 260) is set for this time and date, and for the capital, Port-of-Spain.

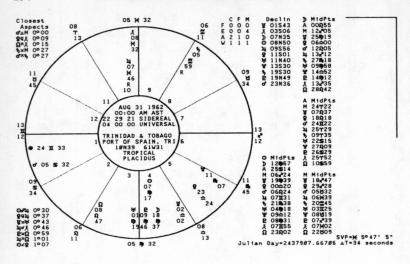

260: Trinidad and Tobago, Independence, 1962

TUNISIA

The area covered by modern Tunisia was colonized by the Phoenicians prior to 500 BC, and subsequently developed its independence as

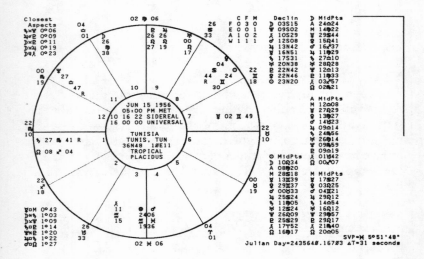

261: Tunisia, Independence, 1956

the centre of the Carthaginian Empire. The region was ruled by Rome from 146 BC to AD 429, when it became the centre of the Vandal Kingdom. In 533 it was reconquered by the Eastern Roman Empire, under whose control it remained until being invaded by the Arabs in 670. The country frequently possessed a large measure of autonomy or independence until conquered by the Turks in the sixteenth century. However, Turkish authority was often weak, and the country slowly reasserted its autonomy. It became a French protectorate in 1881 even though nominally subject to Turkey until 1883, and the modern horoscope for Tunisia should be set for independence from France.

An accord between Tunisia and France agreeing on independence was signed in Paris on 20 March 1956, and this event was widely reported as representing a grant of full independence.[738] However, full independence was not achieved until the signing of the final independence agreement on 15 June 1956.[739] The signing of the agreement, at which moment full independence came into force, took place in Tunis at 5.00 p.m.,[740] and the horoscope given here (Chart 261) is set for this time and place on 15 June 1956.

TURKEY

The Turkish Ottoman Empire was founded by Osman, a Turkish

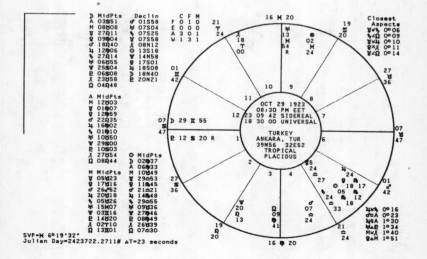

262: Turkey, Republic, 1923

chief who lived from *c.* 1290 to 1326 and founded a principality called Osmanli or Ottoman, in Asia Minor. A programme of conquest followed which resulted in the destruction of the Eastern Roman (Byzantine) Empire and the creation of a realm extending from Algeria to the Persian Gulf and from South Arabia to Central Europe. From the sixteenth century Turkish power declined, reaching its nadir in 1918, after defeat by the Allies in the First World War. A revolutionary movement developed which by 1923 resulted in the creation of a republic, and it is for this that the horoscope for modern Turkey should be set.

As early as April 1920 a revolutionary government in Ankara was disregarding the Sultan, but it was not until 29 October 1923 that the republic was formally created.[741] The proclamation of the republic took place in the National Assembly in Ankara at exactly 8.30 p.m.[742]

Although the proclamation was greeted after midnight by a salute of 101 guns, the time of the proclamation was the crucial moment marking the functional and legal beginning of the republic. Although Kemal Attaturk, the revolutionary leader, was elected President of the Republic by the National Assembly on 9 August 1923 this had been recognized as premature, and he was formally re-elected at 8.45 p.m., fifteen minutes after the proclamation of the republic.[743]

TUVALU

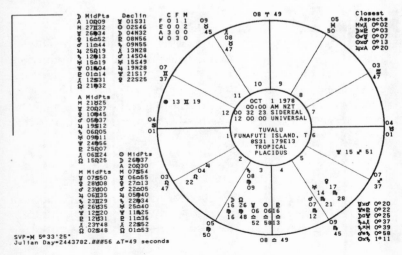

263: Tuvalu, Independence, 1978

The British-ruled Ellice islands in the Pacific Ocean were given independence as the state of Tuvalu at 00.00 hrs on 1 October 1978.[744] The horoscope given here (Chart 263) is set for this time and date and for the capital, Funafuti. After Nauru, Tuvalu is the smallest independent state in the world.

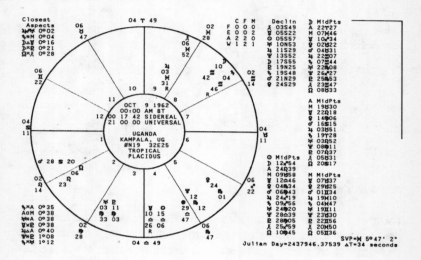

264: Uganda, Independence, 1962

UGANDA

A British protectorate over Uganda was proclaimed in the *London Gazette* on 19 June 1894,[745] although at that time only the kingdom of Buganda was included (see Chart 32). The protectorate was subsequently expanded to include all the territory in the modern state. Uganda became independent from Great Britain at 00.00 hrs on 9 October 1962,[746] and the horoscope given here (Chart 264) is set for this data and for the capital, Kampala.

UKRAINE

Since the Middle Ages the Ukraine has been ruled by Poland, Lithuania, Russia and Turkey, and has enjoyed only three years of nominally independent statehood. A nationalist movement developed following the Russian Revolution of spring 1917, but progress towards complete independence was gradual and owed as much to the disintegration of Russian authority as to positive moves by the Ukrainians.[747] Effective independence was gained while the

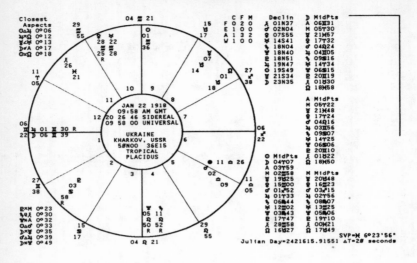

265: Ukraine, Independence, 1918

country still formally considered itself a part of Russia, and the confused circumstances of the times have led to considerable uncertainty in reference books concerning the date of Ukrainian independence.[748]

Independence was finally declared by the Rada (Parliament) on 22 January 1918[749] and the horoscope given here (Chart 265) is set for this date, for the capital, Kharkov and, in the absence of accurate information for 12.00 noon.

For most of its existence the state was swept by civil war between nationalists, bolsheviks and anti-Communist 'white' Russians, and was for eleven months occupied by Germany. Unity and peace were restored by the complete Bolshevik victory on 28 August 1921, but on 30 December 1922 the state surrendered its independence by agreeing to join the USSR.

The Ukraine still has its own flag and seat in the United Nations, and Ukrainian nationalism is an ever-present threat to the Soviet regime.

UNION OF SOVIET SOCIALIST REPUBLICS

The origin of the modern Union of Soviet Socialist Republics, or Soviet Union, may be traced back to the Scandinavian settlement of Russia in the ninth century, simultaneous with the Danish conquests of England, Normandy, Sicily and southern Italy, and the great Viking voyages to North America. The first Russian princes traced their lineage to Rurik, a Scandinavian prince who ruled at Novgorod in the 860s, but it was not until the reign of Ivan III that the different principalities based on cities such as Kiev, Novgorod and Moscow, were united under one ruler. Some accounts put the origins of modern Russia either at the *de facto* assertion of Muscovy's (i.e. the principality of Moscow's) independence from the Mongol Khanate of the Golden Horde in 1452, or Ivan's *de jure* achievement of independence from the Mongols in 1480.[917] Elsewhere the critical date is put at 2 July 1452 when the Mongols failed to sack Moscow, after which its independence was assured.[918] Whatever the date, it is generally agreed that Ivan III, who succeeded in 1462, was the first national ruler of Russia.

The dynasty founded by Rurik died out with Theodore II in 1605, following which the Romanoff Dynasty took power with the election of Michael Romanoff as Czar on 21 February 1613 O/S.[919]

The Russian revolution erupted during February 1917, and although great attention has been paid to the Communist revolution of November, the overthrow of the Czar in February is significant. The wave of strikes which brought the Government down became unstoppable by 22–23 February O/S, and the Czar was deposed only five days later. At exactly 00.00 hrs on 28 February O/S the Executive

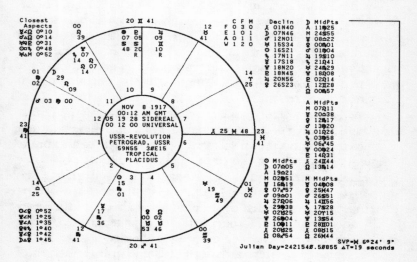

266: USSR, Revolution, 1917

Committee of the State Duma (Parliament) was fully organized and assumed executive authority, after which the abdication of the Czar was a mere formality. [920]

A great many horoscopes have been produced for the Communist revolution, most of which are speculative, or based on embarrassing misreadings of historical accounts. Apart from the chart given here only one, that researched by Michael Baigent, has proper historical credentials. [921]

The horoscope given here is set for the moment that Bolshevik Red Guards under the control of Lenin and Trotsky arrested the Provisional Government, from which time the capital, Petrograd (modern Leningrad) was under Communist control. This time was drawn to my attention by Astrological Association council member Emily Fawcus, who, on a trip around the Winter Palace in Leningrad, was shown the clock in the room in which the Provisional Government had been arrested. The clock had stopped at 2.12.10 a.m., and this, the guide announced, was the time of the revolution. Confirmation of this time was found in Trotsky's *History of the Russian Revolution*, in which the Red Army commander recorded that the Provisional Government had been arrested at 2.10 a.m. [922] The date was 26 October 1917 (8 November 1917), and Chart 266 is set for this date, for 2.12 a.m., and for Petrograd. There is no doubt that this is the principal horoscope for the modern Soviet Union.

The horoscope given in *Mundane Astrology* is set for 2.30 a.m. on 9 November, the time when, according to Michael Baigent, the Bolshevik Kamenev read out the Decree of Constitution of Power establishing a government with Lenin as President of the Council. [923] This moment was significant, and represents a legitimization of the previous night's coup, but on the previous day the new government had already been recognized by army commanders at the front, and had issued decrees. Lenin himself regarded the seizure of the Winter Palace and the arrest of the provisional government as the key time. [924]

Following the Bolshevik seizure of power the Russian Empire disintegrated into about fifteen independent states of which only two, Finland and Poland, survive today. This disintegration was supported by some members of the new government, but as Stalin's power grew, he engineered the reconquest of almost all the newly independent countries. Historically this represented the re-creation of the Russian Empire, and this much was understood by Lenin, who in 1922 equated the formation of the USSR with the revival of Czarism. [925]

On the same day that Lenin published this observation, 30

December 1922, the governments of Russia, Byelorussia, the Ukraine and Transcaucasia formed themselves 'by anticipation, the first congress of Soviets of the USSR'.[926] This date is regarded as the marking the foundation of the USSR, and various horoscopes have been cast for the meeting. However, none gives a source, and the chart given here (Chart 267) is set for 12.00 noon in Moscow. In view of the fact that each of the participating states had been reconquered by Russia and was now under the total control of Moscow, it is appropriate that this be regarded as the chart for the USSR, but the Union itself did not come into force until later.

Legally all that happened on 30 December was a decision to begin the process of unification. The Constitution of the USSR was approved on 6 July 1923 and came into force immediately.[927] This date, then, marked the legal birth of the USSR. The full constitutional process

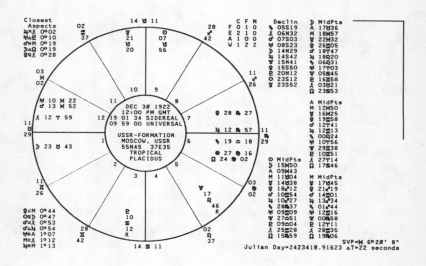

267: USSR, Formation, 1922

was not completed until 31 January 1924, when the Second All Union Congress of Soviets ratified the constitution.[928] This date is clearly of technical importance, although in view of the circumstances it is of no political significance whatsoever.

Historically, there is also no doubt that the horoscope for the revolution in 1917 has far greater significance than that for the formation of the USSR, whichever date is taken for this event.

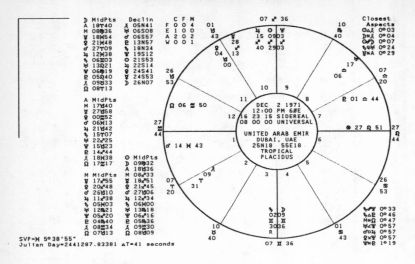

268: United Arab Emirates, Federation, 1971

UNITED ARAB EMIRATES

The United Arab Emirates is a federation on the Persian Gulf consisting of the states of Abu Dhabi, Dubai, Sharja, Ajman, Fujaira and Umm al Quaiwain. Each of these emirates had been subject to treaty obligations to Great Britain which were cancelled by an agreement signed on 1 December 1971, following which they all then enjoyed a few hours of sovereign independence. [750]

On 2 December the rulers of the six newly independent states met to sign an agreement creating the federation, which then came into force. [751] The proclamation of the United Arab Emirates was made at 12.00 noon, [752] and the horoscope given here (Chart 268) is set for this time on 2 December 1971, and for the capital, Dubai.

UNITED ARAB REPUBLIC

The United Arab Republic was a union of Egypt with Syria which came into being on 1 February 1958. [753] The agreement between the two countries was signed in Cairo at 2.53 p.m. GMT and the new state was proclaimed at 3.12 p.m. GMT in Cairo in a live broadcast by President Nasser. [754] The horoscope given here (Chart 269) is set for this data — Cairo was to be the capital.

The formation of the state was subsequently confirmed by a plebiscite, the announcement of the results of which at 9.00 a.m. GMT on 22 February was followed at 9.45 a.m. GMT by a further

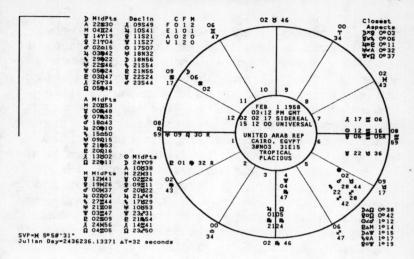

269: United Arab Republic, Proclamation, 1958

broadcast by Nasser.[755] However, as the state had started to function on 1 February, this date should be taken as the true foundation.

The state effectively came to an end when Syria broke away on 29 September 1961.[756] Egypt continued to call itself the United Arab Republic for some years, but on plans to form a new Arab federation, the Federation of Arab Republics, changed its name to the Egyptian Arab Republic.

Although the name 'United Arab Republic' was retained in popular use, on 8 March 1958 the state federated with the North Yemen under the name 'United Arab States'. The federation agreement was signed on 8 March and it seems to have become effective immediately.[1041] Technically only the foreign policies of the UAR and North Yemen were co-ordinated, but in fact Egyptian army officers held considerable influence inside the Yemen. The UAS was dissolved on 26 December 1961. A press report of the 26th reported that President Nasser of Egypt 'tonight' dissolved the federation.[1042]

UNITED KINGDOM
The formation of the United Kingdom of Great Britain and Northern Ireland was the result of a process lasting over a thousand years by which England, Wales, Scotland and Ireland gradually merged into one state (from which the greater part of Ireland has subsequently seceded).

The origins of the British royal dynasty lie in the Scottish kingdom of Dalriada, founded by Fergus MacErc, a Christian Irish chieftain who left Dalriada in the north of Antrim for Argyll in about the year 503 (the Scottish kingdom is generally named after the place of origin of its founder). During the reign of Kenneth I MacAlpin, between 839 and 860, the Scottish kingdom was united with the Pictish kingdom and began to occupy the area approximating to modern Scotland. In 1603 the Scottish royal family, the Stuarts, took control of the English throne, and the modern dynasty may therefore be traced directly back to Fergus MacErc. Horoscopes for the foundation of the kingdom of Dalriada and its union with the Pictish kingdom in the ninth century (if they could be researched), are more than merely maps for Scotland and they should be regarded as horoscopes for the British royal family and for Great Britain.

History, however, is written by the conquerors, and even though a Scottish monarch sat on the throne of England, English economic and military power overwhelmed that of Scotland.

The search for the horoscope of the UK therefore begins with the ancient history of England.

The earliest horoscope that has been produced for England is that for the first invasion of Julius Caesar in 55 BC, and even though both this and the subsequent invasion of 54 BC were unsuccessful, this date is of deep symbolic significance in English history, marking a moment when England became drawn deeply into the orbit of the Roman world.[904] Another interesting horoscope has been cast for the Libran Ingress of AD 410, the closest cardinal solar ingress to the celebrated letter in which the Roman Emperor Honorius advised the British 'civitates' to look after their own defence.[905] This letter represents a recognition of British independence by Rome, and the corresponding horoscope can be read as a map for modern Britain.

In the centuries following the Roman departure, England and Wales disintegrated politically into up to twenty independent kingdoms and principalities, while there were four principal kingdoms in Scotland. However, a tradition of unity seems to have persisted. The evidence suggests that during the fifth century a series of prominent generals exerted control over England, and perhaps Wales, and three names have come down to us — Vortigern, Aurelius Ambrosianus and Arthur. The concept of a unity extending over England itself survived the Anglo-Saxon invasions and from the fifth century the role of Bretwalda was acknowledged. The Bretwalda was an over-king whose suzerainty, however loose, was acknowledged by the other Anglo-Saxon kings. The first king who was listed as a

Bretwalda in the Anglo-Saxon Chronicle was Aelle, King of Sussex from *c.* 477 to 491, and the first who seems to have exerted a real political authority was Aethelbert, King of Kent from *c.* 560 to 616. The final Bretwalda was Egbert, King of Wessex from 812 to 839, under whom dominance irrevocably passed to this kingdom.[906]

However, the complete conquest by Wessex of the whole of England was not complete for another one and a half centuries. After Egbert's death the kingdom's power declined as most of England was overrun by the Danes.

The Danes reached the peak of their power in 878 when they conquered most of Wessex, but under Alfred the Great the fight back began. Alfred's son, Edward the Elder, who reigned from 901 to 924, conquered the midlands (Mercia) and his son Athelstan, king from 924 to 940, conquered the north (Northumbria). Athelstan enlarged the conception of monarchy within Britain, was the first English king to be depicted on coins wearing a crown, and it is from his reign that the unified kingdom of England dates.

However, astrologers habitually cast the horoscope for the unification of England for the coronation of Edgar, who reigned from 959 to 975. The justification of this chart is entirely spurious. It is said that Edgar was the first king to be crowned King of the English. In fact this title had originated with Egbert and was a consistent part of the royal title since the succession of Alfred in 871. Athelstan,

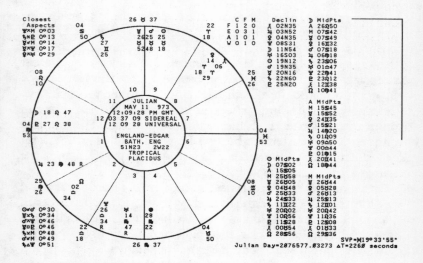

270: United Kingdom; England, Coronation of Edgar, 973

during whose reign England was politically united, was styled 'King of the English and Emperor of Britain'. At least one of Edgar's predecessors, Edwy, had this title conferred in a coronation.

Edgar's erroneous reputation amongst astrologers is probably due to a celebrated public relations event which took place in the year of his coronation, 973. Edgar took a trip to Chester where six or eight of his vassal kings are said to have rowed him down the River Dee in an act of ceremonial and symbolic homage. This event, which some historians suspect may have been invented by subsequent chroniclers, is said by astrologers to mark a symbolically critical point in the unification of England, yet Edgar's predecessor Edwy, had already at his coronation received the homage of kings from Wales, Northumbria and Scotland.

There would therefore seem to be few historical grounds for considering the chart for the coronation of Edgar as a national horoscope, and serious reason to abandon it altogether. However, the horoscope is of interest and is given here (Chart 270).

The chart is set for Whit Sunday (11 May O/S) 973 in Bath, and in the absence of accurate information, for 12.00 noon LMT.[907]

If a historically accurate chart is to be cast for the unification of Anglo-Saxon England, then it should be set either for the coronation of Athelstan or his conquest of Northumbria.

The Norman Conquest

Far more reliable historically than the Edgar chart is the horoscope for the coronation of William the Conqueror as King of England on Christmas Day (25 December O/S) 1066 in Westminster Abbey.[908] Although the cultural and social changes with which the conquest is associated were already well established in 1066, this year marked a major turning point in English history. The country turned away irrevocably from its former close association with the Scandinavian countries and looked to France and Rome instead. The Norman conquest is regarded as the birth of England, and Chart 271 is set for William's coronation. In the absence of accurate information the chart is set for 12.00 noon LMT.

An alternative chart has been set for the Battle of Hastings at which the Norman army routed the English opposition. The battle began at about 9.00 a.m. LMT on 14 October 1066 and concluded when 'as dusk fell Harold [the king] died fighting'.[909] 'The fighting ended in the half light, when a body of Englishmen rallied for a final stand . . . in the darkness William returned to the main battleground knowing that his victory was complete.'[910] The horoscope for the

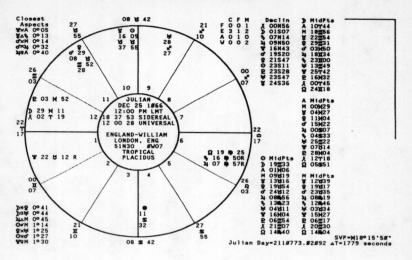

271: United Kingdom, Coronation of William, 1066

conclusion of the battle has been put forward as that for the *de facto* beginning of Norman rule, but even though the popular imagination agrees in dating this from the victory at Hastings and the death of Harold, astrologers in general prefer the coronation map.

The Glorious Revolution

The substance of Britain's modern constitutional system consisting of a parliamentary democracy with limited monarchy dates from the Glorious Revolution of 1689. It is surprising that no astrologer in the past has ever bothered to research this chart in view of the event's significance in British history.

It was in Whitehall on 13 February 1689 that William III and Mary II swore to accept the Declaration of Right, the foundation of the modern constitution, and were immediately afterwards proclaimed King and Queen. Contemporary accounts record that the King, Queen and various other dignitaries arrived at Whitehall at 'about Ten in the Morning' [911] and suggest that the proclamation took place shortly after. The horoscope given here (Chart 272) is therefore given for this data.

Great Britain — The Union with Scotland

The thrones of England and Scotland were combined by the Stuart Dynasty on 24 March 1603 when James VI of Scotland became James

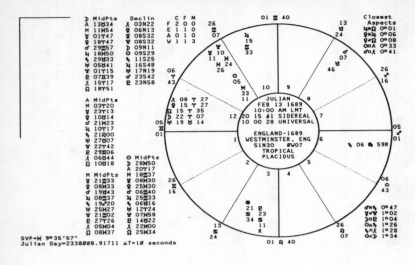

272: United Kingdom, Glorious Revolution, 1689

I of England, but the two countries remained independent and under the reign of Charles I actually went to war against each other. The legal union of the two countries took place under the Act of Union

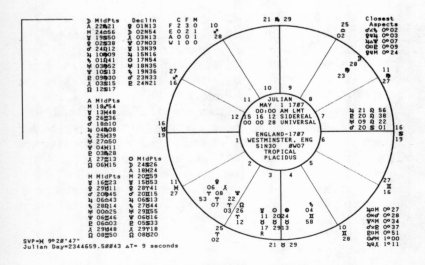

273: United Kingdom; Union of England with Scotland, 1707

which created the kingdom of Great Britain on 1 May 1707.[912] In accordance with general principles, the Act came into effect at 00.00 hrs LMT and the horoscope given here (Chart 273) is set for this time on 1 May 1707, for Westminster. The first move towards unified constitutional government occurred at '10.00 p.m.' (i.e. ten hours after midnight) on 10 May when the first Privy Council of Great Britain was sworn in.[913]

The 1707 horoscope is regarded as, in principle, a major national horoscope, but in practice tends to be ignored in favour of those for the coronations of Edgar or William or the 1801 union with Ireland.

The United Kingdom — The Union with Ireland

The conquest of Ireland by England began with expeditions by the Norman barons in the twelfth century, and Henry II, who reigned from 1154 to 1189 was the first king to be recognized as Overlord of Ireland. However, complete conquest did not become necessary until Ireland, as a Catholic country, came to be seen as a strategic threat, and began seriously under Queen Elizabeth I. This process culminated in the Act of Union which came into effect on 1 January 1801.[914] The Act had received the royal assent on 2 July 1800, and, in accordance with general principles, came into effect at 00.00 hrs

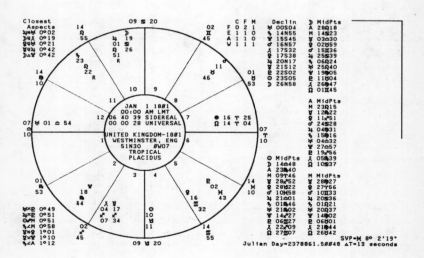

274: United Kingdom; Union of Great Britain and Ireland, 1801

LMT. The horoscope given here (Chart 274) is set for 00.00 hrs LMT on 1 January and for Westminster.

I have found that this horoscope is the most useful for the United Kingdom, being that date on which the modern name of the state came into effect, although the chart for the coronation of William I is also very powerful. Beginners are recommended to use the 1801 horoscope.

An additional horoscope, which refers specifically to the fortunes of the royal family, may be set for the proclamation of George III as the first king of the United Kingdom of Great Britain and Ireland in London at 3.15 p.m. on 1 January.[915]

The United Kingdom — Separation of Southern Ireland

In 1922 the greater part of Ireland became independent and the UK was renamed the United Kingdom of Great Britain and Northern Ireland. It has been argued that the horoscope for this moment should supersede that for the union of 1801, and former Astrological Association Vice-President James Russell investigated this possibility. Russell showed that when the Irish Free State was formed on 6 December 1922 (see Chart 81), Northern Ireland, which since 22 June 1921 had had its own parliament, was obliged to vote formally on whether it wished to join the Free State or remain within the United Kingdom. Russell estimated that this vote took place at shortly

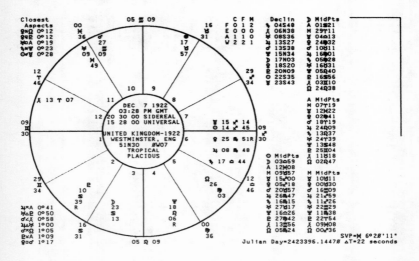

275: United Kingdom, Reorganization, 1922

before 3.30 p.m. on 7 December 1922.[916] The horoscope given here (Chart 275) is set for 3.28 p.m. and is cast for Westminster, although some astrologers prefer to use angles set for Belfast. I have not found this horoscope to be useful in work on the United Kingdom and suggest that its validity may be particular to Northern Ireland.

As the vote in the Northern Irish Parliament merely confirmed a state of affairs which had been in force since the legal creation of the Free State on 6 December, the horoscope for this moment might be worth studying in relation to the United Kingdom. The question remains open.

The Union of England and Wales

Although astrologers have studied the maps for the constitutional unions of England with Scotland and Ireland, the union with Wales has been ignored. The English conquest of Wales commenced shortly after the Norman conquest of England, and English military control was assured after the wars of Edward III. It was not until 1536 that the Act of Union between England and Wales was passed, and the horoscope for this moment, although not presented here, should take its place among the national charts for the United Kingdom.

UNITED NATIONS ORGANIZATION

If there has ever been a moment for which a genuine world horoscope

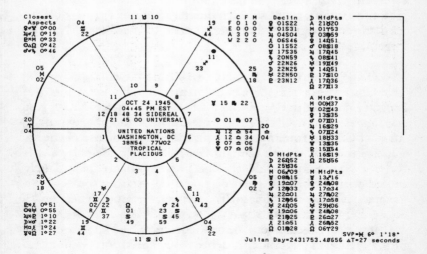

276: United Nations Organization, Legal Foundation, 1945

may be set, then it must be for the creation of the United Nations Organization.

The United Nations came into existence as a result of the conferences held between the Soviet Union, the USA and Great Britain in the closing stages of the Second World War. Initial discussions held at Dumbarton Oaks in 1944–5 resulted in proposals being made public in a document under the heading 'Plan for the Final Defeat of Germany' and issued simultaneously in Washington, Moscow and London at 9.30 p.m. BST on 12 February 1945.[890]

The United Nations Charter itself was signed by fifty participating nations at the conclusion of the San Francisco Conference on 26 June 1945.[891] The signing ceremony began at 6.00 a.m. and was 'not expected to be complete until mid-afternoon'.[892] Following this, each country had to ratify the treaty separately, and the organization was scheduled to come into force when a majority of states had done this.

Shortly after 3.00 p.m. on 24 October 1945 the requisite number of states ratified the treaty when the USSR, Byelorussia and the Ukraine deposited their ratification documents in the US State Department in Washington.[893] At 4.45 p.m. the United Nations came into existence when the US Secretary of State signed a protocol of deposit of ratification,[894] and the horoscope given here (Chart 276) is set for this data.

I am grateful to Ron Howland for pointing out that, as the signing ceremony on 26 June 1945 lasted for most of the day, horoscopes set for the various times at which different nations signed could be used to indicate those nations' attitudes to the United Nations Organization.

UNITED PROVINCES OF CENTRAL AMERICA

The United Provinces of Central America, also known as the Federation of Central America,[760] was the most successful, largest and longest-lived of all the many experiments at union between the states of Central America. The state was formed by five of the six states of the old Spanish Captain Generalcy of Guatemala, which had enjoyed brief independence in 1821, and had then either willingly united with Mexico, or been occupied by Mexican forces. Only Chiapas, which had originally declared independence on 3 September 1821, and which had voluntarily joined Mexico in October of that year, declined to join the new federation.[761] The states which proclaimed their joint independence were El Salvador, Guatemala, Nicaragua, Honduras and Costa Rica. Independence was proclaimed on 1 July 1823[762] and the horoscope given here (Chart 277) is set for this date. In the absence of accurate information the chart is set for 12.00 noon LMT and for Guatemala City, the old capital of the region under Spanish rule. A chart set for the capital of each of the federated states could be used to indicate the circumstances of each

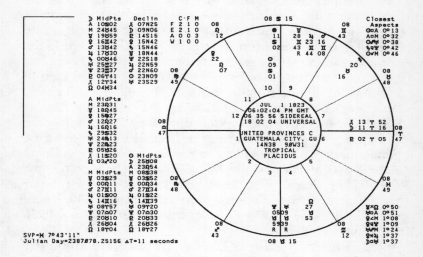

277: United Provinces of Central America, Federation, 1823

state within the federation even though the differences would be slight.

The federation was recognized by Mexico on 20 August 1823[763] and ratified by its constituent states on 1 October 1823.[764]

The federation disintegrated between 1830 and 1840, but the horoscope could be used as the starting point for an analysis of subsequent Central American unions.

Like the United States of America, the United Provinces of Central America appears to have been founded by Freemasons, the seals of each state containing a number of typical masonic occult symbols.

UNITED STATES
Although there is ample documentary evidence pointing to an approximate time of day for the signing of the American Declaration of Independence (the event normally taken as that signifying the 'birth' of the USA), a small industry has developed among astrologers seeking to make a reputation by producing speculative charts, or rectifying existing ones. Once produced, speculative charts may

acquire a spurious historical background, based on rumour, while subsequent rectifications make use of the well-known principle that, if enough factors are used, any horoscope can be used to prove any hypothesis.

For example, one speculative map is set for 2.17 a.m. on 4 July 1776.[929] This ludicrous fiction is contradicted by the journals of congress of the time, which indicate quite clearly the approximate times that sessions ended in the evening and commenced in the morning, and that all delegates were sound asleep at 2.17 a.m. This fact is conveniently ignored and the chart has been the basis of numerous rectifications to, for example. 2.13.32 a.m.,[930] 2.14.15 a.m.[931] or 2.52.10 a.m.[931a] or 3.01.57 a.m.[931b]

Such activities bring astrology into disrepute and are the modern equivalent of the arguments among medieval theologians about the number of angels that could sit on the head of a pin.

Methods of rectification may be occult, as with B. Serrotti's time of 4.30 p.m., based on a dream and 'confirmed' by a horary question,[932] or utterly pointless as with the chart set for 4.49.49 p.m. rectified from 4.50 p.m.[934] Other charts are rectified for 4.46.30 p.m.[938] or 4.47.09 p.m.[939]

Some charts, such as that for 2.20 p.m. are based on documentary accounts which unfortunately conflict with the main body of evidence.[935]

In recent years the most reputable published research into the problem of the date and time of the independence of the USA has been undertaken by Julian Armistead[936] and Michael Baigent,[937] and the following is based substantially on their work.

2 July — The Vote for Independence

The birthday of the USA is celebrated on 4 July, but in fact the crucial vote for independence was taken on 2 July 1776, and constitutional historians such as Carl Becker and Hugh Brogan never tire of pointing this out.[940]

Contemporary press reports were in no doubt that this was so. A report of the 3 July stated that: 'Yesterday the Continental Congress declared the United Colonies are free and independent states.'[941] The declaration in question was entirely unambiguous and read: 'That these United Colonies are, and of right ought to be, Free and Independent States.'[942]

Even the participants in the drama regarded this vote as the vital event in both political and symbolic terms, and in a letter on 3 July 1776 John Adams stated as much to his wife. Adams was the seconder of the motion declaring independence and was from 1797 to 1801 the second President of the USA. In his letter he wrote that:

> Yesterday [i.e. 2 July] the greatest Question was decided, which ever was debated in America. . . . A resolution was passed without one dissenting Colony 'that these united Colonies are . . . free and independent States'.[943]

In what seems to be a second letter Adams continues:

> The Second Day of July 1776, will be the most memorable Epoch in the History of America. I am apt to believe that it will be celebrated by Succeeding Generations as the great anniversary Festival.[944]

The first horoscope given here (Chart 278) is set for Philadelphia on 2 July 1776, but the question of time must be considered separately.

Armistead has attempted to establish the time of the vote by following clues concerning the late arrival at the Congress of Caesar Rodney, a delegate from Delaware. Apparently the independence vote was delayed in order to allow a number of states to change their intentions from opposition to support. As part of this process Rodney was summoned in order to switch the balance in the Delaware

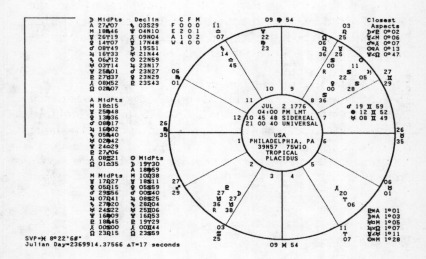

278: United States, Declaration of Independence (1), 2 July 1776, 4.00 p.m.

delegation to support for independence, and there are various accounts of Rodney's arrival in Philadelphia. Armistead quotes two accounts, one stating that Rodney reached Philadelphia 'probably late in the afternoon'[945] and the other that he entered Congress at '4.00 p.m.'[946] Unfortunately neither time is given with any documentary. It is certain that Rodney arrived 'just as the delegates reassembled after lunch',[947] and this could quite conceivably have been around 4.00 p.m.

Bearing this uncertainty in mind, Chart 278 is set for 4.00 p.m. LMT on 2 July 1776 in Philadelphia in keeping with the general principle of this book that horoscopes based on non-astrological sources provide a far superior basis of analysis than those based on spurious pseudo-objective rectifications.

It is recommended that if this time is felt to have insufficient support a solar chart be set for 12.00 noon LMT (Chart 279). It must be remembered that both these times are speculative.

4 July — The Signing of the Declaration
In spite of Adams' expectations, 2 July was forgotten and the signing of the Declaration of Independence on 4 July is remembered as the birthday of the USA, perhaps because the Declaration's lofty tones caught the popular imagination.

So what was the Declaration of Independence? Adams explained

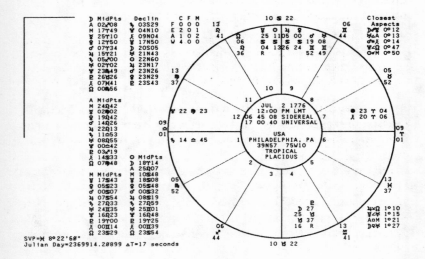

279: United States, Declaration of Independence (2), 2 July 1776, 12.00 p.m.

its purpose vividly in a letter to his wife on 3 July: 'You will see in a few days a Declaration setting forth the Causes which have impelled Us to this mighty Revolution, and the Reasons which will justify it in the sight of God and Man.'[948]

It must be borne in mind that in an age when monarchy was still believed to be the natural and even divinely ordained form of government, a step which to us today seems natural required justification, especially 'in the sight of God'. The Declaration was therefore designed partly to elicit popular support and partly to salve the consciences of the signaturees. 'The primary purpose of the Declaration was not to declare independence, but to proclaim to the World the reasons for declaring independence. It was intended as a formal justification of an act already accomplished.'[949] It has also been called nothing more than 'a public relations document'.[950]

In setting the US horoscope for 4 July rather than the 2nd the astrologer is using a popularly regarded symbolic date rather than a strictly historical date, and to do so is quite legitimate astrological practice, given that the symbolic date also includes an event of great historical significance. The Declaration of Independence is, after all, a profound expression of the American myth, or the American dream as it is commonly known.

The bulk of the documentary evidence points to a time for the signing of the Declaration late in the day. The classic account is that given by Thomas Jefferson, one of the signaturees and from 1801 to 1809 the third US President. Jefferson wrote that:

> The debates having taken up the greater part of the 2nd, 3rd and 4th days of July, were on the evening of the last, closed; the Declaration was reported by the committee, agreed to by the House and signed by every member present except Mr Dickinson.[951]

Another signaturee, Elbridge Gerry, wrote on 5 July, that the Declaration was agreed 'after a day's debate',[952] and historical opinion is in overwhelming agreement that Congress assented in the evening.[953]

Indications of a specific timing are hard to come by. Manley Palmer Hall, writing in 1941, claimed that the writings of Jefferson, Adams and Hancock, another of the signaturees, all agreed on supporting a time of 'late in the day', which he placed between 4.30 and 6.00 p.m. Hall also claimed that the Philadelphia Historical Association stated that the Declaration was signed at approximately 5.00 p.m. or slightly later, but as he gives no source this information has not been checked.[954]

However, Hall's suggestion of 5.00 p.m. finds interesting support
in the fact that the anniversary celebrations on 4 July 1778 began
at 5.00 p.m., and in other years seem to have begun at a similar time,
which the historian Channing (who believed the Declaration was
signed later), regarded as 'early'.[955]

Such evidence leads towards acceptance of the first published chart
for the USA, the so-called 'Sibly chart' with Sagittarius rising. This
horoscope was originally published in 1787, only eleven years after
the signing of the Declaration, five years after the end of the War
of Independence, and two years before George Washington was
inaugurated as the first President of the USA. It was therefore
calculated while the events of 1776 were very much a part of
contemporary politics. Ebenezer Sibly, the astrologer who calculated
the horoscope, was a Freemason and in the 1780s was a member of
Lodges first in Portsmouth and then in Bristol, two cities with intimate
trading connections with the USA. (The first consulate in Britain
was opened in Bristol.) On this basis Michael Baigent has presented
a persuasive case that Sibly was excellently placed to receive an account
of the time the Declaration was signed from those Freemasons in
the USA, including Washington, Franklin and Hancock, who were
responsible for the creation of the new state.[956]

Sibly's horoscope was cast for the stated time of 10.10 p.m. London
time, which corresponds to 5.10 p.m. in Philadelphia[957] but

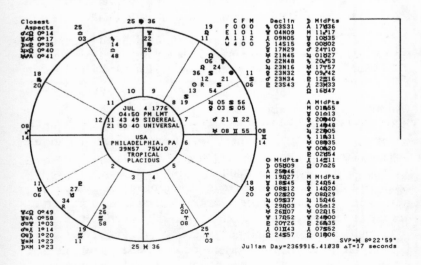

280: United States, Declaration of Independence (3), 4 July 1776, 4.50 p.m.

unfortunately he made several errors in his calculation. The angles
and house cusps appear to be calculated for 9.50 p.m. GMT, but
the Sun, Moon and planets are cast for about 4.50 p.m., which
corresponds to 11.50 a.m. in Philadelphia. It seems that Sibly made
a mistake by setting his chart for twenty minutes earlier than the
stated time, and then reversed the correct procedure, calculating the
house cusps for Greenwich Mean Time and the Planets for Local Mean
Time, instead of vice versa. [958]

The result of this confusion is that there are two rival 'Sibly' charts
in circulation, one set for 4.50 p.m. LMT and the other for 5.10 p.m.
LMT, both for 4 July 1776 in Philadelphia. Both charts are given
here — Chart 280 is set for 4.50 p.m. and Chart 281 is cast for 5.10 p.m.

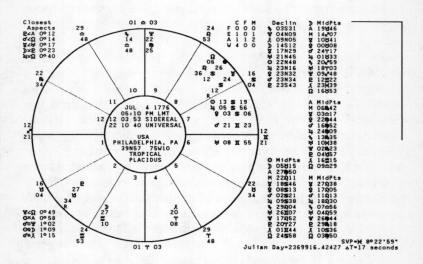

281: United States, Declaration of Independence (4), 4 July 1776, 5.10 p.m.

However, to take the chart for 4.50 p.m. is to become embroiled
in Sibly's series of errors of calculation, and it is recommended that
the 5.10 p.m. chart be taken as the 'genuine' Sibly horoscope. It is
also recommended that, in view of its historical pedigree and in the
light of current evidence, this chart be taken as the best of all
possibilities for the national horoscope of the USA. The short answer
to astrologers who parade their own rectifications with such
intolerance is to ask why theirs is the correct version, and all other
rectified and speculative charts are wrong.

Evidence for a Morning Chart

British researcher Ron Howland has recently uncovered evidence which undermines Jefferson's account of the signing of the Declaration of Independence in the late afternoon, and which points to a time in the morning [1019] Howland's evidence centres on a letter written on 4 July by four members of the Committee of Congress, including Benjamin Franklin. In this letter the four men wrote that:

> The Congress this morning directed us to confer with the Committee of Safety and Inspection, and the Field Officers now in town, about the proper mode of collecting the militia of this province, in order to form a flying camp, to cover Pennsylvania and New Jersey, from the Attacks of the Enemy, who have landed on Statten-Island, and will probably direct their march this way, if they should imagine an attempt on New-York too hazardous. [1020]

The significance of this letter lies in the report that the direction was issued by Congress 'this morning'. Turning to the *Journals* of the Continental Congress, printed from the original manuscript minutes of the Congressional debates, it is clear that on 4 July Congress assembled at 9.00 a.m. and that the debate over the Declaration of Independence was the second item on the agenda following a minor item concerning an application for flints for the troops at New York and a direction to the militia of Maryland and Delaware. [1021] The direction mentioned in the above letter was issued under the fourth item dealt with in the *Journals*, and if, as stated, it was issued 'this morning', this is convincing evidence that the debate on the Declaration itself took place during the morning. Indeed, the conclusion of the editors of 'Letters of Delegates to Congress' at the Library of Congress in Washington was that this evidence 'forced us to call into question Jefferson's version of these events'. [1022]

Indirect support for this account is found in an obvious inaccuracy in Jefferson's account of the signing. Jefferson wrote that 'the Declaration was reported by the committee, agreed to by the House and signed by every member present except Mr Dickinson'. [951] In fact this is incorrect. The Declaration was initially 'authenticated' only by John Hancock, the President of Congress, and Charles Thompson, the Secretary. Some of the members reported as having signed the Declaration on 4 July were not even present in Congress on that day. The printed version of the Declaration inserted in the published version of the *Journals of Congress* containing all the names of the signaturees is an insertion copied from the final signed form of the Declaration, but which is not contained in the original manuscript Journals of Congress.

In view of the fact that Jefferson's account appears to conflict with sound documentary evidence, and can be discredited by a vital internal inconsistency, Paul Smith, the Director of the Manuscripts Division at the Library of Congress is convinced that the Declaration was passed in the morning of 4 July. In a letter to Ron Howland, Smith wrote that

> This statement, that Congress 'this morning' directed the committee . . . provides the best evidence available for determining the approximate time at which the Declaration was adopted, a question that has long puzzled scholars and remained unanswered until the significance of this letter was discovered. . . . And since examination of all available evidence provides no reason to doubt that the committee had indeed been appointed 'this morning', and considerable time undoubtedly elapsed between the adoption of the declaration and the appointment of the committee, one is forced to the conclusion that the vote on the declaration was probably taken somewhere before 11.00 a.m. [1023]

This evidence deserves closer scrutiny from other contemporary sources, but itself highlights certain important points about the entire confusing sequence of events.

Firstly, the above account reports the passing of the Declaration by a vote in Congress, not its signature, even though the two events are often confused. Nowhere in the original *Journals of Congress* for 4 July is there any reference to any signing of the Declaration of Independence by the delegates other than its authentication by Hancock and Thompson.

The original makes no reference to any signing, only that 'The Declaration being again read was agreed to as follows', following which a printed copy of the Declaration has been inserted at a later date. [1024] The reproduction of a printed copy of the final signed version with all the delegates' signatures in the published version of the *Journals* is a misleading addition. The statement that 'The foregoing declaration was, by order of Congress, engrossed, and signed by the following members' [1025] is an equally misleading addition to the original record. Clearly the importance of the Declaration as a public relations exercise was put above the keeping of a chronologically accurate record of events.

Quite simply, the evidence of a morning vote on the Declaration makes no pretence at a morning signing of the Declaration. The recollections of Thomas Jefferson that the Declaration was signed by the delegates 'on the evening' of 4 July may be correct even if his report that it was agreed at the same time is not (although printed copies of the Declaration were not available for signature until the next day).

In support of Jefferson's account, however, Elbridge Gerry's letter should be quoted in full:

> A determined resolution of the Delegates from some of the Colonies to push the question of Independency has had a most happy effect, and after a day's debate, all the Colonies, except New York, whose Delegates are not empowered to give either an affirmative or negative voice, united in a declaration long sought for, solicited, and necessary — the Declaration of Independency.[1026]

Such persuasive evidence must take us back to a further consideration of the manuscript Journals and their significance. These manuscripts are not a verbatim account of events and debates in Congress, but solely a record of decisions taken. They are produced neatly and without corrections which indicates that they were written up by Thompson after the event from notes taken at the time. In this case it is not necessary to assume that Thompson's account accurately reflects the order in which decisions were taken on the day, and hence the Journals do not present absolute evidence that the agreement on the Declaration took place in the morning. In other words, the evidence that the Declaration was passed in the morning is circumstantial, and based on the letter containing the words 'this morning', and on the order in which decisions are recorded in the Journals. There is no direct evidence that the Declaration was passed in the morning, whereas there are two eyewitness accounts, those of Jefferson and Gerry, of an agreement in the late afternoon or early evening.

However, there is a third possibility which might explain the discrepancy between the *Journals of Congress* and the two eyewitness accounts. Jefferson records that 'the Declaration was reported by the committee, agreed to by the house'.[951] The *Journals of Congress* themselves report that a committee of the whole congress was constituted to examine the Declaration and this then reported back 'some time later'. To follow this account we may deduce that a committee of Congress was appointed to examine the Declaration early in the morning, and that while this was under way, the other business of Congress was dealt with, including the direction referred to in the letter as having been made 'this morning'. During the afternoon the committee then reported back to Congress, a final debate was held, and agreement reached. This final agreement was then recorded in the *Journals* under the same item of business under which the committee was set up in the morning.

The relevant committee was 'a Committee of the whole', which suggests that all the delegates were involved. Yet the fact that the *Journals* and Jefferson both make it clear that the committee reported back to the House is evidence that this was not so, and that the third scenario presented above is the most plausible.

The Committee that drafted the Declaration consisted of Franklin, Jefferson and Adams together with Robert Livingstone and Roger Sherman.[1027]

Evidence for an Early Afternoon Chart
Herbert S. Allen, in his biography of John Hancock, *Patriot in Purple* states that

> At last, about two o' clock in the afternoon of the 4th, the great white paper was reported out of committee to the House with a recommendation for approval, and was immediately ratified. Hancock and his secretary, Thompson, were then ordered to authenticate it with their signatures in the customary manner of handling all Congressional measures.[1028]

This account has been used as the basis of a horoscope set for 2.20 p.m.[1029] However, Allen's assumption that the Declaration was reported to the House at 'about two o' clock' appears to be his own deduction on the basis of Hancock's account, rather than the result of a time specified in any primary source. This account may be used as supporting evidence for the Sibly chart, and contradicts the evidence presented above for a morning time.

A second secondary account reports that 'The Declaration had been signed about two o'clock in the afternoon'[1030] although no supporting evidence is quoted.

Additional Charts for the USA
In view of the confusion surrounding the Declaration of Independence it is worth considering other significant moments in the creation of the USA. It should be pointed out that the creation of the state was a process lasting fifteen years and that the Declaration itself was not a declaration of independence of the United States of America. In fact each state became a sovereign independent state

which then joined in a political and military alliance with its twelve fellow rebel colonies. The first priority was the defeat of the British, the second was the formation of the federation of the USA.

There are various horoscopes in circulation for European settlement in North America, and each state also has a foundation date for its foundation as a colony, but all these await further study. The following dates are restricted to those for events between 1775 and 1789.

The American Revolution
The revolution is traditionally timed from the Battle of Lexington which began early in the morning on 19 April 1775. A contemporary report gives the following account: 'At 4.30 a.m. Eight Hundred British troops arrived within 1¼ miles of the meeting house in Lexington. The local American militia was summoned numbering about between 50 and 70 men. The British troops marched to within twelve or thirteen rods of the militia and battle commenced.[1031] It is fair to assume that the fighting, and hence the War of Independence, commenced at around 5.00 a.m.

The Mecklenburg Declaration of Independence
According to secondary accounts, the county of Mecklenburg, based on the city of Charlotte in North Carolina, declared independence from Great Britain on 20 May 1775.[1032] An account written in 1946 gave a time of 2.00 a.m. for this event.[1033]

The First Continental Congress
The first Congress, consisting of delegates from all the rebel colonies, met on 5 September 1774. This body was the ancestor of later federal government. A time of 10.00 a.m. has been given by astrological sources, but not independently confirmed by me.[1034]

Proclamation of Independence
Independence was proclaimed when the Declaration of Independence was read out in State House Square in Philadelphia at noon[959] on 8 July 1776.[960]

De Facto Independence
De facto independence was achieved by the military defeat of the British on 17 October 1781. A time of 10.00 a.m. LMT is given by astrological sources but has not been independently confirmed by me.[1035] Military peace was settled by the Yorktown treaty signed between British General Cornwallis and George Washington on 19

October 1781. A time of 11.00 a.m. is given in astrological sources, but has not been independently confirmed by me.[1036]

Confederation

The first attempt at co-operative government between the States was embodied on the Articles of Confederation, drawn up on 1 March 1781 in Philadelphia. A time of 12.00 noon has been given by an astrological source,[1036a] but not confirmed by me in historical sources. The Confederation was a failure and was replaced in 1787 by the Federation. An attempt to return to Confederation resulted in the Civil War.

De Jure *Independence*

Full legal independence was attained by the preliminary Treaty of Paris of 30 November 1782, which became complete on 3 September 1783.[961] A time of 10.00 a.m. is given for the latter event in astrological sources but has not been independently confirmed by me.[1037]

The Federal Government

The constitution of the United States became effective on 17 September 1787 when it was signed by the 55 delegates to the Federation Convention at 4.00 p.m. in Philadelphia.[1037a] The whole process became complete with the swearing in of the first President, George Washington on 30 April 1789 in New York.[1038] Washington arrived at Federal Hall at 12.30 p.m., went straight inside, was introduced to Congress and took the oath.[1039] If this chronology is correct, the swearing in would have taken place by 12.45 p.m., perhaps by 12.40 p.m. This moment represents the final act in the creation of the United States of America out of the thirteen rebellious English colonies.

URUGUAY

The situation surrounding the independence of Uruguay is even more complicated than that for the independence of some of the other Latin American states, as local nationalist aspirations were opposed by rival claims from neighbouring states as well as by Spain, the colonial power.

The country had been part of the Spanish Empire, but had always been claimed by Portugal so when in 1811–1814 the Spanish were driven out by Uruguayan revolutionaries this was done with the aid of troops from the former Portuguese colony of Buenos Aires (i.e. Brazil). Uruguay was then federated with Brazil, but after a renewed

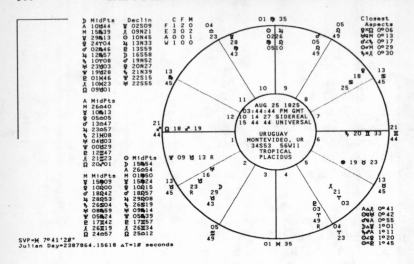

282: Uruguay, Declaration of Independence, 1825

revolution was put down by Brazilian troops the country was formally annexed by its larger neighbour.[757]

Nationalist resentment continued and a declaration of independence was issued on 25 August 1825.[758] The horoscope given here (Chart 282) is set for this date, for the capital, Montevideo and, in the absence of accurate information, for 12.00 noon LMT.

However, the country was not free until after a revolutionary war in which it was supported by Argentina. The country's independence and sovereignty was formally recognized by a treaty between Argentina and Brazil on 27 August 1828,[759] and this date could also be reasonably taken as the basis for an additional national chart.

VANUATU
The Pacific island state of Vanuatu was given independence by Great Britain at 00.00 hrs on 30 July 1980.[765] The horoscope given here is set for this time and date, and for the capital, Port Vila.

THE VATICAN CITY
The Papal State of the Middle Ages was a gradual creation, resulting from the battle waged by the bishops of Rome against their rivals, especially in the east, and the slow accumulation of massive wealth by the Roman Church. It would be quite possible to establish a horoscope for the medieval Roman Church, although there could

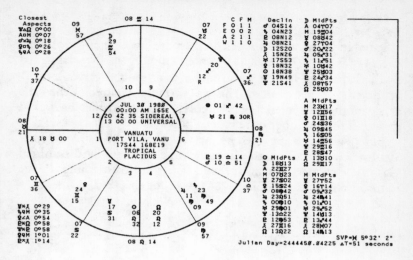

283: Vanuatu, Independence, 1980

be as many as half a dozen major alternatives and the appropriate research is still to be done. The Papal State was occupied by Italy (see Charts 136 and 137) on 20 September 1870 and the Popes lost

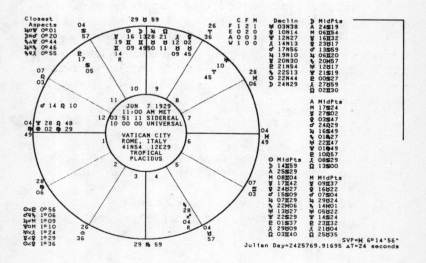

284: Vatican City State, Independence, 1929

their political independence when Rome was formally annexed to Italy on 2 October.[766]

Papal independence was restored by the creation of the Vatican City State in 1929. The Lateran Treaty establishing the state was signed by the Papal and Italian governments at or soon after noon on 11 February 1929 in Rome.[767] This was wrongly reported at the time as the moment of Papal independence,[768] an error which has found its way into a number of reference books.[769]

Independence was gained by the Vatican at 11.00 a.m. on 7 June 1929 when Mussolini, the Italian Prime Minister, and Cardinal Gasparri exchanged the instruments of ratification in Rome.[770] The horoscope given here (Chart 284) is set for this data.

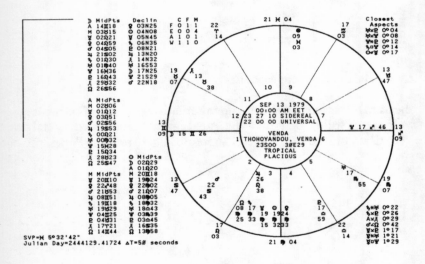

285: Venda, Independence, 1979

VENDA

The southern African state of Venda is one of the so-called African 'homelands', given *de jure* independence by South Africa but in fact under total South African control. Venda was given its 'independence' by South African at 00.00 hrs on 13 September 1979.[771] The horoscope given here (Chart 285) is set for this time and date, and for the capital, Thohoyandou.

VENEZUELA

The independence movement began in Venezuela, as in the other

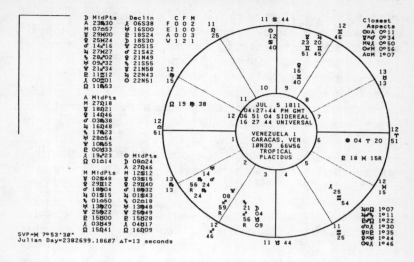

286: Venezuela, Proclamation of Independence, 1811

Spanish American colonies, following the conquest of Spain by the
French under Napoleon. A local revolution took place in 1810, and
although Spanish sovereignty was still recognized[771] this event is in

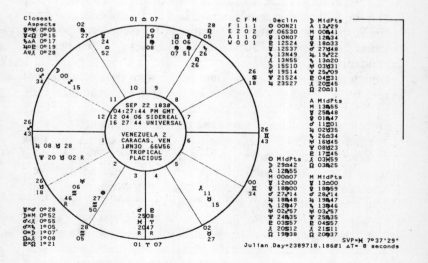

287: Venezuela, Proclamation of Independence, 1830

some references erroneously recorded as a proclamation of independence. [772] True independence was proclaimed on 5 July 1811 in Caracas, and Chart 286 is set for this time. In the absence of accurate information, the time is set for 12.00 noon LMT.

A revolutionary war followed in which the Spanish were partially successful in re-conquering the country, and on 17 December 1819 the revolutionaries themselves united Venezuela with New Granada (i.e. modern Colombia) and Quito (modern Ecuador) to form the Republic of Great Colombia (see Chart 53).

The Venezuelan portion of this new state became effectively independent from Spain at the Battle of Carnabobo on 24 June 1821, immediately after which the capital, Caracas, was returned from Spanish to Venezuelan hands. [773]

The country eventually regained independence when it separated from Great Colombia in April 1830, [774] according to some references on 27 April, [775] the separation becoming final on 22 September 1830. [776] The second horoscope given here, Chart 287, is set for this date in the capital, Caracas and, in the absence of accurate information, for 12.00 noon LMT.

The situation regarding Venezuelan independence is uncertain and requires further research.

VIETNAM

At the beginning of the nineteenth century most of what became French Indo-China (modern Vietnam, Laos and Cambodia) was ruled by the Emperor of Annam, himself under Chinese suzerainty (which explains the modern Chinese resentment at Vietnamese independence).

French expansion in Indo-China began with the occupation of Saigon in 1858 and was complete by the Treaty of Hue on 6 June 1884. [777]

French power collapsed when the region was occupied by Japan in the Second World War, and the Vietnamese themselves took advantage of the Japanese defeat in 1945 to proclaim their independence. In the north of Vietnam the nationalists were dominated by the Communists, led by Ho Chi-Minh, who led the revolution of 8 August 1945 [778] and proclaimed independence on 2 September 1945 in Hanoi. [779] The country was occupied by Chinese, Japanese, British and French troops and the Hanoi Government never exercised complete control, but this proclamation should nevertheless be seen as the foundation of modern Vietnam; the regime founded in Hanoi eventually went on to complete control of North Vietnam

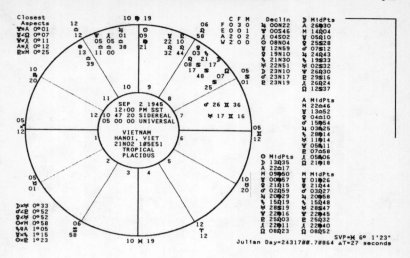

288: Vietnam, Proclamation of Independence, 1945

in 1954 and of the entire country in 1975. The first horoscope given here, Chart 288 is therefore set for 2 September 1945, for Hanoi and, in the absence of accurate information, for 12.00 noon.

However, the French resolved to reconquer Vietnam, which they did in two ways, military and political. The military effort was launched at 10.00 a.m. on 23 November 1946 when French troops invaded the Chinese quarter in Haiphong, the event marking the beginning of the Vietnam War.[780] On the political front the French made Vietnam a Free State within the French Union on 6 March 1946, created the Autonomous Republic of Cochin-China (approximating to South Vietnam) on 1 June 1946, and then reunited the two halves in a state supposedly 'independent' within the French Union on 8 March 1949.[781] As a measure of the ineffectiveness of these steps, Vietnam was again made an 'independent' state within the French Union on 28 April 1954. However, on 6 May 1954 the French suffered a massive military defeat at Dien Bien-Phu, after which the Communist north of the country became effectively independent.

The result of this defeat was the creation of the two separate states of the Democratic Republic of (North) Vietnam and the pro-French state of (South) Vietnam. These two states were effectively created by the Geneva Accord signed at 3.45 a.m. in Geneva on 21 July 1954.[782] Chart 289 for North Vietnam is given for this time (i.e. 2.45

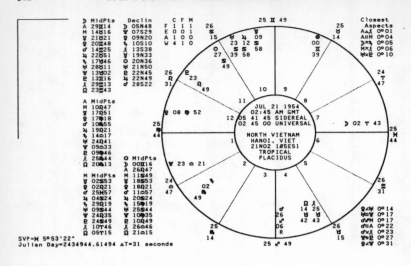

289: Vietnam, North, Geneva Accord, 1954

a.m. GMT) and date and for the capital, Hanoi. Chart 290 for South Vietnam is given for the same time and date, but for the capital, Saigon.

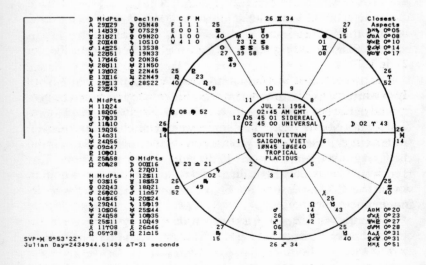

290: Vietnam, South, Geneva Accord, 1954

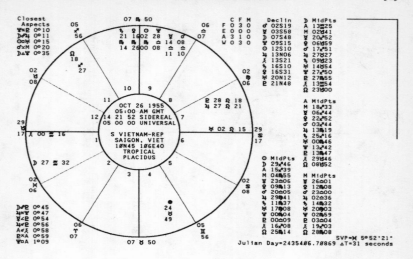

291: Vietnam, South Republic, 1955

However, in spite of the Geneva Accord the French hoped to retain control of South Vietnam by maintaining Bao Dai, the Emperor of Annam, in power as their puppet.

South Vietnam did not achieve true independence from the French until the overthrow of Bao Dai and the subsequent proclamation of the Republic of Vietnam at 5.00 a.m. GMT on 26 October 1955 in Saigon.[783] In studying the history of South Vietnam this chart (Chart 291) should be given at least as much significance as that for 21 July 1954.

The two halves of Vietnam were effectively reunited on 30 April 1975 when the Communist forces of North Vietnam occupied Saigon, capital of the South. The Vietnam War came to an end at 2.28 a.m. GMT when South Vietnamese forces were ordered to surrender,[784] and the liberation of South Vietnam was proclaimed by Hanoi radio as having taken place both at 11.30 a.m.[785] and 12.00 noon.[786]

It would be reasonable to set a chart for the reunited Vietnam for either of these latter times, but in view of the contradictory statements, the horoscope given here is that for the formal reunification of the country on 2 July 1976. Reunification was proclaimed on Hanoi Radio at 8.30 a.m. and the Socialist Republic of Vietnam was born.[787]

Strictly speaking the horoscope given here (Chart 292) is not a foundation chart in the sense that the September 1945 chart marks

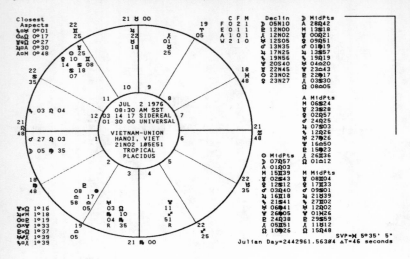

292: Vietnam, Reunification, 1976

the beginning of the country's drive for independence, but unlike the earlier chart, it is set for an exact time, and therefore may be used with greater confidence.

The three horoscopes for North and South Vietnam are of historical interest but should not be used by themselves to plot current developments in Vietnam.

WESTERN SAMOA
The Pacific island state of Western Samoa received its independence from New Zealand at 00.00 hrs on 1 January 1962.[788] The horoscope given here is set for this time and date, and for the capital, Apia.

YEMEN — NORTH
Political organization in the Yemen dates back to ancient history, but the modern state was only defined territorially after the First World War when the country asserted its boundaries and independence in order to resist the encroachment of the Kingdom of Nejd (see Saudi Arabia). The horoscope for the Yemeni Arab Republic (North Yemen) is set for the revolution of 1962. Until 26 December 1962 the country had been in a federation with the United Arab Republic (see Chart 269), during which time a strong left-wing group had built up in the armed forces. Following the death of the King on 19 September 1962 pro-Egyptian officers staged a coup and

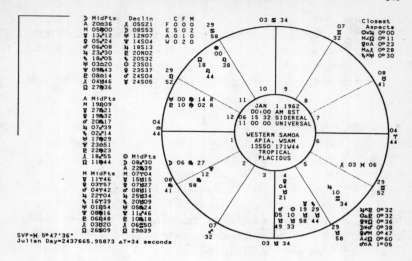

293: Western Samoa, Independence, 1962

on 27 September overthrew the monarchy.[789] Although the republic
was not proclaimed until 31 October,[790] the new regime was firmly
established from 27 September, which is the date taken for the

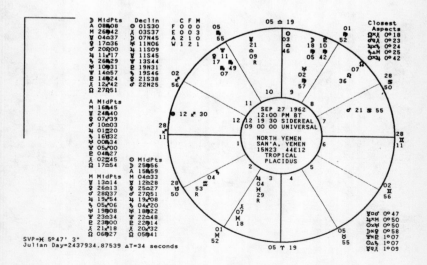

294: Yemen, North, Republic, 1962

horoscope given here (Chart 294). The chart is set for the capital, San'a and, in the absence of accurate information, for 12.00 noon. However, further research might indicate a time closer to dawn as the coup seems to have proceeded without difficulty.

The new regime fought a civil war with pro-Royalist forces until 1967.

YEMEN — SOUTH

The Democratic Republic of (South) Yemen formerly consisted of the British colony of Aden and a group of British protectorates along the south Arabian coast. The state was given independence on 30 April 1967 but the situation was similar to that in Israel, in which *de facto* independence preceded *de jure* independence by a few hours. In each case the time of full legal independence was observed by a British warship offshore after all British troops had been evacuated.

The first horoscope given here (Chart 295), is set for the final evacuation of British troops at 3.00 p.m. on 29 November 1967, the moment considered by *The Times* leader column as that for the end of British rule. The horoscope is set for the capital, Aden. The new President proclaimed independence during the day, but the time for this is not known. [792]

The second horoscope given (Chart 296) is that for full legal independence at 00.00 hrs on 30 September, which was observed

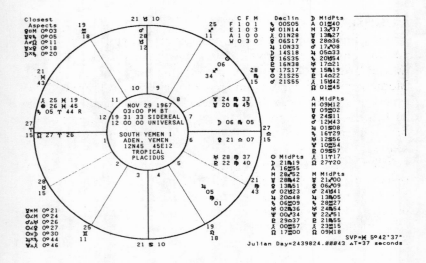

295: Yemen, South, *De Facto* Independence, 1967

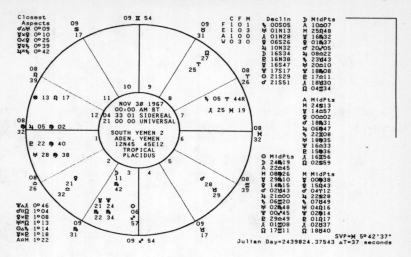

296: Yemen, South, *De Jure* Independence, 1967

by the lowering of the Union Jack, on the aircraft-carrier *Albion*, lying offshore at Aden.[793] The name of the warship adds a symbolic touch, for this moment represented the independence of Britain's last sizeable overseas possession in either Africa or Asia and the end of the country's last major colonial war.

YUGOSLAVIA

The circumstances surrounding the creation of Yugoslavia are highly complicated; the state was formed during the final week of the First World War, partly from the pre-existing states of Serbia and Montenegro, and partly from areas of the Austrian Empire. Press reports at the time focused on the war in France and ignored sideshows such as revolutions in the Balkans, and subsequent reference books have not attempted to unravel the complex and often contradictory sequence of events.

The first proclamation of independence appears to have taken place at the Congress of Oppressed Nationalities held in Rome from 8 to 10 April 1918,[794] although this was probably more a declaration of intent than a serious proclamation. Croatia, which was to be a constituent part of the new state, was proclaimed independent from Austria by the Southern Slav Council at Agram (Zagreb) on 15 October 1918, taking advantage of the apparent Austrian desire to give autonomy to the national regions, although the Austrian Army

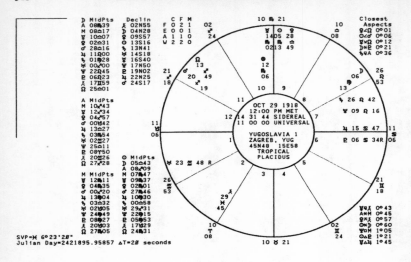

297: Yugoslavia, Proclamation, October 1918

would still have been in control.[795]

On 19 October the National Council at Zagreb proclaimed itself the authoritative body for the Yugoslavs, declaring its intention to

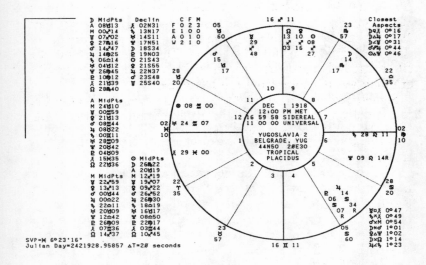

298: Yugoslavia, Proclamation, December 1918

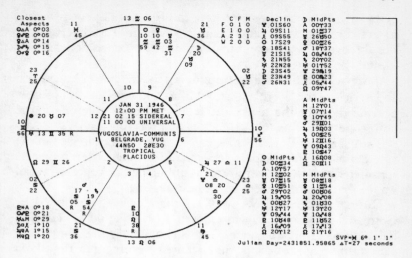

299: Yugoslavia, Communist, 1946

form a union[796] and on 29 October this Yugoslav National Council, which was operating as the *de facto* government of Croatia, proclaimed the existence and independence of Yugoslavia.[797] This was clearly a critical date for, even though the state technically consisted only of Croatia, and perhaps Bosnia, it was recognized on 30 October by the USA.[798] The first horoscope given here (Chart 297) is given for 29 October 1918 in Zagreb and, in the absence of accurate information, for 12.00 noon. This chart represents the effective foundation of modern Yugoslavia, even though the process of union was not complete until December.

Sometime between 29 and 31 October the Kingdom of Greater Serbia was proclaimed at Sarajevo in Bosnia, bringing that state, formerly an Austrian protectorate, into Yugoslavia.[799] On 7 November, another crucial date, the Yugoslav National Conference at Geneva decided on the union of Croatia and Slovenia with Serbia and Montenegro[800] and on 24 November another proclamation appears to have taken place at Zagreb, this time of the United Kingdom of the Serbs, Croats and Slovenes.[801] On 26 November Montenegro (see Chart 180) deposed its king, who opposed union, and voted to join the new state.[802]

The final piece was placed in the jigsaw on 1 December 1918 when the Kingdom which had been proclaimed on 24 November was proclaimed by Alexander Karadjordjevic, the son of King Peter of

Serbia.[803] The state thus became a full functioning entity within its present boundaries, and Chart 298 is set for this date, and, in the absence of accurate information, for 12.00 noon and the new capital, Belgrade.

In view of the uncertainty surrounding the creation of Yugoslavia, and in view of the fact that the capital city and royal family of Serbia became those of the new state, it might be possible to use the horoscope for Serbia (Chart 224) as that for Yugoslavia.

The chart for 1 December is clearly important, but in view of the fact that it is set for the proclamation of the kingdom, it might be considered to have less validity for a current view of Yugoslavia than would that for the present republican regime.

During the Second World War, Yugoslavia was occupied by Germany, and Croatia again enjoyed a brief period of technical independence, though under a German puppet regime. The present Communist regime became the effective government in Yugoslavia following the occupation of Belgrade by Soviet and Yugoslav forces on 20 May 1944.

The Federal Peoples' Republic was proclaimed on 29 November 1945.[804] However, further research may be needed to clarify the situation as the constitution did not come into force until accepted by the Constituent Assembly on the night of 31 January–1 February 1946,[805] the date which was regarded by contemporary press reports as well as some references as that for the foundation of the republic. Chart 298 for Communist Yugoslavia is therefore set for 31 January 1945 in Belgrade and, in the absence of accurate information, for 12.00 noon.

ZAÏRE

Zaïre, formerly the Congo, had a period of *de jure* independence during the nineteenth century as the Congo Free State, with King Leopold of Belgium as Head of State. This state was formally annexed by Belgium following an international scandal provoked by the brutality of the King's regime.

The Belgian colony of the Congo became independent as the Republic of the Congo at 00.00 hrs on 1 July 1960.[806] The horoscope given here is set for this time and date and for the capital Kinshasa.

During the day of 30 June King Baudouin ceremonially handed over power to the new state with the signing and transfer of documents and a speech to Parliament which was broadcast live.[807] As a result most references list 30 June as the date of the country's independence.[808]

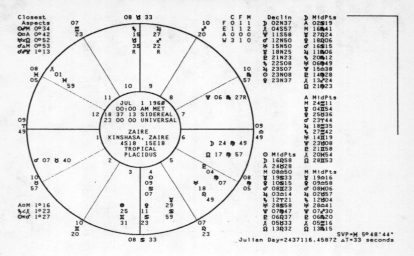

300: Zaïre, Independence, 1960

Two provinces of the new state subsequently seceded. Katanga proclaimed its independence, apparently on the night of 11–12 July 1960,[809] and Kasai also proclaimed its independence in July.[810] Neither state was independent for long, and Katanga, the major rebel, agreed to end its secession on 15 February 1962.[811]

The Congo changed its name to Zaïre in the 1970s.

ZAMBIA

Zambia was formerly the British colony of Northern Rhodesia. This state owes its origins to the charter granted to the British South Africa Company on 29 October 1889 to explore and exploit a vast area of Africa. The area now covered by Zambia was formally constituted as Northern Rhodesia on 17 August 1911 under the administration of the British South Africa Company.[812] There is a good case for experimenting with the horoscopes of countries such as this which were entirely colonial creations, and this is a good example.

The state eventually passed under direct British rule, and was granted independence at 00.00 hrs on 24 October 1964.[813] The horoscope given here (Chart 301) is set for this time and date and for Lusaka, the capital.

ZIMBABWE

The sophistication of political organization in Zimbabwe in medieval

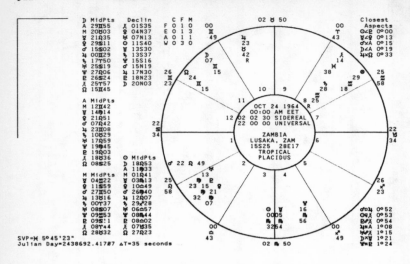

301: Zambia, Independence, 1964

times is attested to by the great ruins which have been variously dated
from the tenth to fifteenth centuries. At one time Europeans thought
that these were too sophisticated for Africans to have built, and their

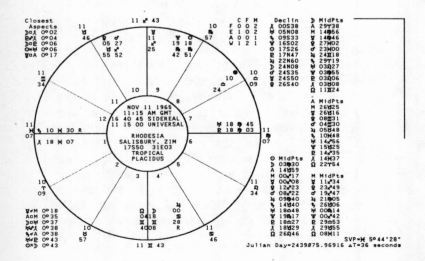

302: Zimbabwe; Rhodesian UDI, 1965

origins were ascribed to Sabaeans from the Yemen or Dravidians from India. Current scholarship, however, assumes that the ruins were indeed constructed by the local Africans.[524]

The British colony of Southern Rhodesia, upon which modern Zimbabwe is based, owes its origins to a charter granted by the British Government to the British South Africa Company (headed by Cecil Rhodes) on 29 October 1889 to settle and exploit the region.[525] The town of Salisbury, now the capital, Harare, was founded by Rhodes on 12 September 1890.[526] The name Rhodesia was introduced on 3 May 1895,[527] and on 1 September 1923 the country became a crown colony, under the administration of the British Government.[528] On 23 October 1953 Southern Rhodesia became a part of the Federation of Rhodesia and Nyasaland, together with Northern Rhodesia (now Zambia) and Nyasaland (now Malawi), with a measure of self-government.[529] It was the British intention to give all three colonies independence as part of this federation, but the opposition of the white supremacists in Southern Rhodesia to this plan, and subsequent British manoeuvres, resulted in the illegal declaration of independence in 1964.

The Federation was dissolved on 1 January 1964,[593] presumably at 00.00 hrs, and after months of crisis the white supremacist government in Southern Rhodesia proclaimed independence on 11 November 1964. Chart 302 for Rhodesia is set for the capital, Salisbury, and the beginning of the live radio broadcast of the proclamation of independence at 11.15 a.m. GMT.[594] The proclamation covered one quarto-size page of type.

The British government declared the proclamation illegal, officially deposed the government and imposed economic sanctions, and from 1967 a guerrilla war was mounted against the regime by African nationalists. The illegal government proclaimed the state a Republic (until then the Queen had been recognized as Head of State) in March 1970. Some references give 1 March as the foundation of the Republic,[595] although contemporary reports suggest that the orders to create the republic were signed on the 1st and that it came into effect sometime between then and 2 March, perhaps at 00.00 hrs on 2 March.[596]

By 1979, under pressure from the nationalist guerrillas, the Government attempted to reach a compromise with African aspirations by creating the state of Zimbabwe-Rhodesia, in which Africans would participate in a government which would still be white-controlled. The state was created in a series of constitutional and political events, from the swearing in of a new house of assembly

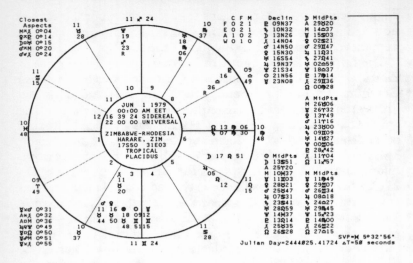

303: Zimbabwe–Rhodesia, Legal Foundation, 1979

on 8 May 1979 to the moment on 1 June when Bishop Muzorewa, the African Prime Minister broadcast to the nation and 'the state of Zimbabwe-Rhodesia finally became effective'.[597] The legal moment

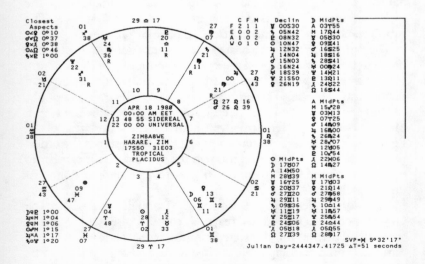

304: Zimbabwe, Independence, 1980

of the beginning of the new state was at 00.00 hrs on 1 June 1979,[598] and Chart 303 is set for this time and for the capital, Salisbury.

However, the new state failed to gain acceptance from the majority of Africans or recognition from Great Britain, and the civil war continued. Within less than a year, in 1980, the country had ended its rebellion and agreed to return to British control, being by then the last British colony in Africa. Under British supervision an agreement was negotiated between the former white government and the African nationalists, the result being the creation of the new state of Zimbabwe. Zimbabwe received its independence from Britain at 00.00 hrs on 18 April 1980,[599] and Chart 304 is set for this time and date, and for the new capital, Harare (formerly Salisbury).

APPENDIX 1
INAUGURATION HOROSCOPES

Inauguration horoscopes are set for the moment that a new government or head of state takes office, and in many cases should be used together with national horoscopes set for more obvious moments such as proclamations of independence. In fact these horoscopes are often so important that they serve as national horoscopes, the chart of the coronation of William the Conqueror as King of England being a prime example.

However, the question of locating the moment of inauguration is complicated and demands a familiarity with the political history of the country under consideration.[814] There are, for example, in any political system, various arms of the government, any of which may increase or decrease in importance. So, the horoscope for the coronation of William the Conqueror in 1066 is still considered to be a national chart for Great Britain, but that for the coronation of Elizabeth II in 1953 is regarded as peripheral. In some instances the introduction of a new constitution may have profound significance yet in others is of no consequence whatsoever. In many cases the critical event surrounds a change in the head of the executive government, yet in these cases there may be doubt as to the moment at which power changes hands. The illegal methods of the military coup as well as constitutional modes of election or selection each contain several key moments. For example, election is followed by subsequent inauguration. In the latter case different countries make their own arrangements; in the UK a Member of Parliament holds power from the moment the election results are declared, but the leader of the winning party must wait for an interview with the Monarch before becoming Prime Minister, while in the USA both congressmen and President must wait for a formal public inauguration. Even in *coups d'état*, rebel leaders may either proclaim themselves heads of state or attempt to legitimize their rule through some subsequent ceremony.

The situation is therefore complex, yet satisfactory solutions may be reached through study of the political circumstances of each significant event with regard to the *de facto*, *de jure* and symbolic consequences.

That this has not so far been the practice is a poor tribute to the standards expected by astrologers of their own work. So long as some astrological societies and schools, as well as individuals, continue to promote low standards in their work, mundane astrology does not deserve the respect of the world at large.

The secular origins of kingship are inseparable from the sacred, and in Greece, Asia Minor, Babylonia and Syria the institution in the first and second millennia BC, seems to have involved a number of rituals based on the religious observation of the seasons.[815] The vital role of astrologers in the politics of Mesopotamia after 2000 BC has also been well-documented,[816] although the first coronation horoscope known to modern historians was cast for Antiochus I, apparently for 6 or 7 July 62 BC.[817] Antiochus was the ruler of the small state of Commagene in eastern Asia Minor, and the horoscope was carved in a massive relief 7,000 feet above sea level on the Nimrud Dagh, high in the Taurus Mountains, presumably to show to the world that his rule was ordained by heaven.

However, the political use of astrology was frequently a matter of great secrecy, for horoscopes could be used equally to predict the deaths of rulers and plot their overthrow. This could be one reason why, although a great many Roman Emperors used astrology, only one, Nero, is said to have had the time of his proclamation (midday, 13 October 54 BC) elected astrologically.[818]

Throughout the medieval era the use of astrology to elect times for coronations was probably far less frequent than astrologers would like to think. For example, the use of a noon solar chart for the coronation of William the Conqueror is often justified by the claim that medieval kings were often crowned at noon for symbolic astrological reasons. Yet a study of the circumstances of the successions of English kings shows that the prime consideration was to secure coronation as quickly as possible in order to pre-empt potential rivals. Sacred support was sought from the bishops and archbishops, not from the position of the Sun.[903]

Charlemagne himself, the greatest model for medieval monarchy was crowned Emperor at morning mass (see Chart 121 for the Holy Roman Empire).

A notable example of the astrological election of a coronation is found in the service performed for Queen Elizabeth I by John Dee. [819] That Dee elected the time for the coronation is well attested, and the incident is discussed in the many biographies of this great scholar. [820] However, there is no horoscope in any of the publicly available Dee papers and it is likely that the astrologer's advice was regarded as so secret that it is still languishing in some royal archive.

This book is primarily a study of national horoscopes, although some twenty of the charts in the main collection are inauguration charts, set for the swearing in of governments (e.g. the second Australian chart, democratic Greece, Nazi Germany) the succession of monarchs (e.g. Monaco, Spain), their proclamation (Egypt, Iraq) or coronation (Bhutan, Sikkim, Nepal, England, the German Empire). Others are set for *coups d'état* (e.g. Afghanistan, Iraq, Syria, the Russian Revolution). There is also a sense in which every national chart involves an inauguration of some kind, for proclamations of independence themselves involve formal alterations in the nature of the government.

The horoscopes presented here represent a sample of those inauguration charts which are not included as national maps yet are nevertheless vital for an astrological view of politics in the closing decades of the twentieth century.

RONALD REAGAN

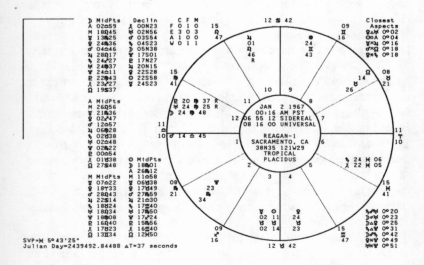

305: Reagan, Inauguration, California, 1967

Ronald Reagan's career in US politics may be said to have begun formally with his inauguration as Governor of California in Sacramento at 00.16 hrs on 2 January 1967. This chart (Chart 305) is especially worthy of study in view of the possibility that it was astrologically elected. Most gubernatorial inaugurations take place during the day at public ceremonies for obvious public relations reasons, and the time chosen by Reagan was noted as strange by all the major US papers. The time was regarded as 'unusual',[821] 'without precedent in the history of California'[822] and 'without parallel'.[823] Reagan's presumed interest in astrology was the reason given for the midnight inauguration.

> Originally associates of Governor Brown (the outgoing Democratic governor) had attributed the selection of the past midnight hour to a Reagan belief in astrology, but this was hotly denied by the new Governor's aides. They declared this was to be no 'star-gazing' administration.[824]

The horoscope given here (Chart 305) is set for this 00.16 hrs on 2 January 1967 in Sacramento.

Reagan's presidential career began at 11.57 a.m. on 20 January 1981, when he was inaugurated in Washington,[825] and Chart 306 is given for this data. This horoscope should be that for the Reagan

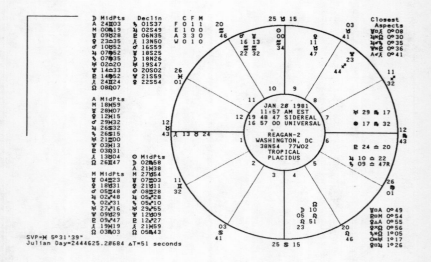

306: Reagan, Inauguration, Washington, 1981

Presidency, with all its internal and international repercussions, yet it is a point of debate as to whether this, or that for the inauguration of his second term, at noon on 20 January 1985 in Washington, [826] should be taken to judge the second half of his eight-year term of office.

The institution of the Presidency itself is covered by the horoscope for the inauguration of the first President, George Washington, at shortly after 12.30 p.m. on 30 April 1789 in New York. [827]

Such horoscopes are obviously essential when the President's birth data is uncertain. There are for example, up to thirty horoscopes in circulation for Ronald Reagan. [828]

MIKHAIL GORBACHEV

Mikhail Gorbachev's rule in the Soviet Union is timed from his appointment as General Secretary of the Soviet Communist Party. This event took place between 6.00 p.m. and 7.00 p.m. on 11 March 1985, [829] and the horoscope given here (Chart 307) is set for 6.00 p.m. (which the evidence suggests is the most likely time). This horoscope is of great significance for developments in the Soviet Union during the last part of the twentieth century, and attempts at rectification will be contrary to the principles of this book.

Gorbachev was born on 2 March 1931 in Stavropol.

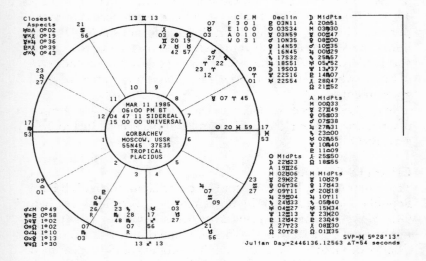

307: Gorbachev, Appointment, 1985

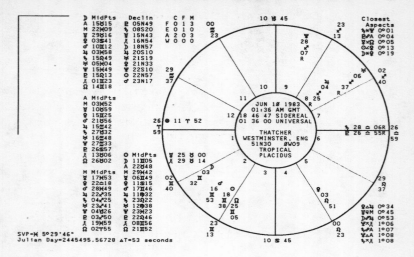

308: Thatcher, Re-election, 1983

MARGARET THATCHER

Significant moments during a politician's career may be indicative of national trends. The horoscope given here (Chart 308) is that for the moment at which the Conservative Party achieved a majority of seats in the House of Commons at 1.36 a.m. GMT on 10 June 1983.[830] Although Thatcher has stood and been elected in many previous elections, and had been Prime Minister since 1979, the horoscope for this moment contains clear signatures of the beliefs and behaviour of 'Thatcherism' relevant both to her second term of office (which her re-election made certain) and to her previous government.

In the 1987 general election, the Conservative Party became assured of a majority in the House of Commons at between 2.30 and 2.33 a.m. BST.[830a]

CHARLES DE GAULLE

The contemporary horoscope for France is that for the French Fifth Republic, founded at 00.00 hrs on 5 October 1958 in Paris (see Chart 98). However, this legal moment lacks symbolic power and represented but a stage in the consolidation of the personal rule of Charles de Gaulle. Two additional horoscopes could be examined for any astrological analysis of the Fifth Republic: those for de Gaulle's election as Prime Minister and his appointment as President.

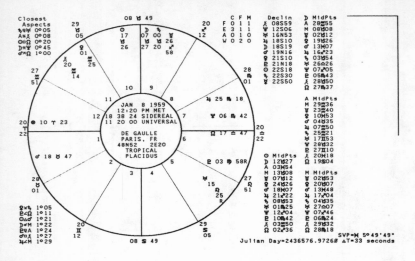

309: De Gaulle, Inauguration, 1959

De Gaulle's rule began when he was elected Prime Minister of the Fourth Republic in Paris between 7.35 p.m. and 7.45 p.m. on 1 June 1958.[831] This time represents the beginning of the Gaullist era in France, and could reasonably be taken as a 'seed-moment' for the Fifth Republic.

De Gaulle's inauguration as President followed his creation of the Fifth Republic, and as the new constitution allowed for an executive President, marked the full operational beginning of the new regime.[832] The horoscope for this moment is certainly indicative of De Gaulle's rule as President, and could reasonably be used as an additional chart for the Fifth Republic. Chart 309 is set for the time De Gaulle was inaugurated, 12.20 p.m. on 8 January 1959 in Paris.[833]

APPENDIX 2
POLITICAL PARTIES

The nature and activities of the major political parties in a state, especially the ruling party, are of obvious consequence for the condition of any country at a particular time. There has in the past been little effort amongst astrologers to research or use such charts, and the horoscopes presented here represent the summary of such work as has been directed towards the question of the major British political parties.

THE CONSERVATIVE PARTY

The modern British Conservative Party traces its origins to those royal supporters in the sixteenth-century House of Commons who backed the monarch against the demands of various interest groups for more power. The birth of the party has been traced to 1558, the year of Queen Elizabeth I's accession to the throne, following which support for, or opposition to, monarchical authority in Parliament became a major national issue. Throughout the seventeenth and eighteenth centuries there was always a King's or Queen's party in the House of Commons, although during the eighteenth century the leader of this group tended to accumulate power at the expense of the monarch.

However, there were no formal party groupings, and factions were grouped around particular leaders. In the last half of the eighteenth century the name 'Tory' entered common usage as a term of abuse meaning Irish bandit, but eventually the party took the name over as its own. Thus at the end of the century a 'Tory' party was based around the leadership of William Pitt.

This party disintegrated in April 1830, following which the process began by which the modern Conservative Party was created. A critical stage in this process occurred on 18 December 1834 when the new leader, Sir Robert Peel, issued the 'Tamworth Manifesto', a political

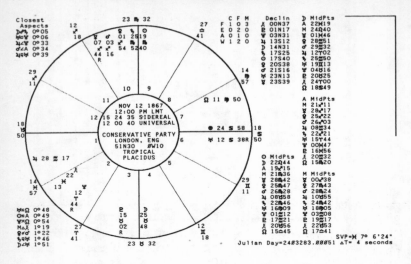

310: Conservative Party, 1867

address which was published and became the first policy document to be issued in such a form.[835] While undoubtedly a significant moment in British politics, this event does not represent a nativity for the party.

A further crucial event occurred in January–February 1846 when the party split and a new grouping coalesced around Benjamin Disraeli, who is today regarded as the father of the modern party. Unfortunately it has not been possible to establish the date for a meeting in February at which the new group met, and which could reasonably be regarded as the birth date for the modern party.[836]

The chart given here is set for the date for a major reorganization of the party under Disraeli's control. On 12 November 1867 a meeting of delegates of local Conservative and Constitutional Associations took place in Freemason's Hall in London at which the name National Union of Conservative and Constitutional Associations was adopted.[837] However, this meeting represented more than just a change of name, for the events brought into being the modern mass party, a response to the recent extension of the franchise in the second Reform Act.

This chart was used by Charles Carter, who considered that it was not a nativity for the party.[838] It remains, however, the closest to a nativity that we have at present, and should be used as such.

Unfortunately it has been reported to the author that the minutes of the 1867 meeting do not indicate the times at which votes were taken, although this has not been verified,[839] and contemporary reports do not give times for the meeting. The chart here (Chart 310) is therefore set for 12.00 noon on 12 November 1867 in London.

However, Charles Carter based his chart on a time for the opening of the meeting of 10.00 a.m., and it would be appropriate to experiment by resetting the horoscope for this time.

LABOUR PARTY

The modern Labour Party does not seem to have had a single clear foundation, but is the result of two decades of experimentation and organizational upheaval in socialist organizations at the turn of the century. The date classically given for the formation of the party is 27 February 1900, when the two main existing socialist parties, the Social Democratic Federation and the Independent Labour Party, together with the Trades Union Congress and other socialist groups, such as the Fabians, formed the Labour Representation Committee. This was not a political party as such, but a committee designed to pool the resources of the participating groups and secure the election of Labour MPs. At the 1900 general election the LRC put up fifteen candidates and only two were elected. In any case the Social Democratic Federation soon withdrew its support, 95 per cent of the trade unions failed to affiliate and some groups were openly

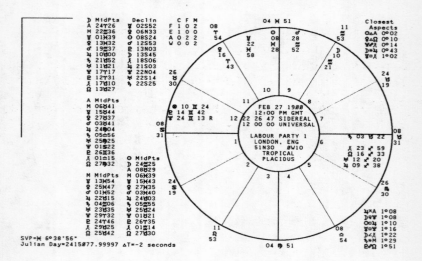

311: Labour Party; Labour Representation Committee, 1900

hostile.[841] Historically there may be some doubt as to whether this date truly represents the foundation of the Labour Party, yet it is undoubtedly a major step towards the creation of the modern party. The first horoscope given here (Chart 311) is set for London on 27 February 1900 and, in the absence of accurate information, for 12.00 noon.

The final critical date in the party's foundation occurred on the afternoon of 12 February 1906 when the twenty-nine MPs elected under the wing of the Labour Representation Committee formed their own organization, electing a chairman (Keir Hardy), other officers and whips.[842] This move established the independence of Labour MPs from the Liberals to whom they had previously been affiliated, and was regarded as the core of 'the new Labour Party'.[843]

At the time there was considerable uncertainty concerning the status of the new group. It was confused with the Independent Labour party,[844] and at the subsequent Labour Representation Committee Conference, Keir Hardy referred to the twenty-nine MPs as a 'Liberal-Labour' group, allied with, but separate from, the Liberal Party. It is clear that at the time the events of 12 February were not seen as marking the foundation of a party, but with hindsight they may be seen as the culmination of a long process during which the Labour Party gradually came into being. From this date the Labour Party in Parliament acted as a totally independent group.

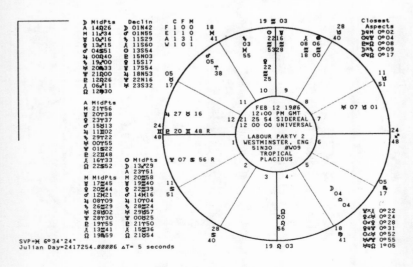

312: Labour Party; Parliamentary Labour Party, 1906

The second horoscope given here (Chart 312) is set for 12 February 1906, for Westminster and, in the absence of accurate information, for 12.00 noon.

Further evidence that 1906 rather than 1900 was seen as the date of formation of the Labour Party, is provided by Alan Leo's claim that he forecast from the Capricorn Ingress of 1905 the formation of a new working-class party in the House of Commons, a prediction he saw fulfilled in the January 1906 General Election.[845]

Although there is doubt as to which date, if any, may be taken as that for the foundation of the Labour Party, the 1906 chart is clearly that for the foundation of the Parliamentary Labour Party.

LIBERAL PARTY

The Liberal Party traces its origins to the opponents of the Monarch and royal power in the sixteenth-century House of Commons. Known as the Whigs through the eighteenth century, the party, like the Tories, existed only as a succession of groupings around particular leaders. By the mid nineteenth century the name Liberal had been adopted as opposed to that of Whig, and, like the Conservatives, the Liberals were prompted into creating a party organization by the Reform Bill of August 1867. This extended the franchise and made it necessary for the parties to canvass and organize locally and nationally in order to win votes.

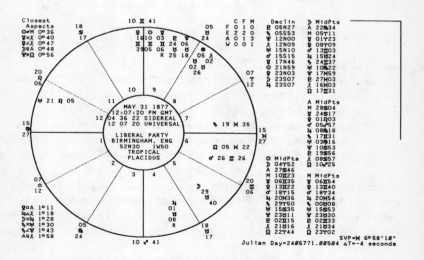

313: Liberal Party, 1877

The chart given here (Chart 313) is cast for 31 May 1877, the day when the National Liberal Federation was formed.[846] This is not a nativity for the party, but it is a significant moment in the creation of the modern party, and may therefore serve as a nativity. The horoscope is set for 31 May 1877, for Birmingham and, in the absence of accurate information, for 12.00 noon.

A horoscope has been used set for 6.00 p.m., a time without published supporting evidence, but which may have some validity.

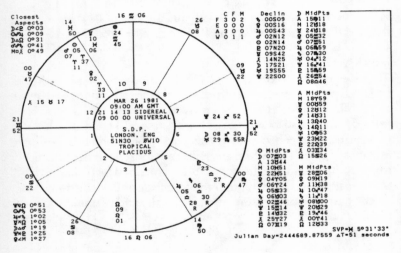

314: Social Democratic Party, 1981

SOCIAL DEMOCRATIC PARTY

The Social Democratic Party, a breakaway from the Labour Party, was officially launched at 9.00 a.m. on 26 March 1981 in London.[847] The horoscope given here (Chart 314) is set for this data.

The first step towards the formation of the party took place on 25 January 1981 when four dissident Labour Party members, Roy Jenkins, David Owen, William Rodgers and Shirley Williams issued the 'Limehouse Declaration' setting out their principles. On 26 January the four dissidents formed the Council for Social Democracy and on 2 March twelve Labour MPs and nine Peers constituted the Parliamentary Committee of the Council for Social Democracy. The creation of the SDP on 26 March was the culmination of these moves.

LIBERAL–SOCIAL DEMOCRATIC PARTY ALLIANCE

The electoral alliance between the Liberals and the Social Democrats

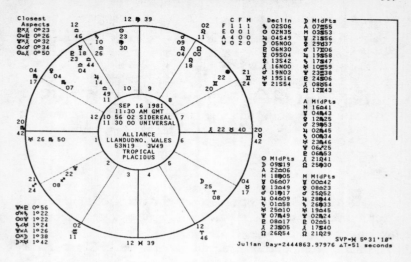

315: Liberal–SDP Alliance, 1981

came into being after a vote in favour at the Liberal Party Conference at Llandudno at 12.30 p.m. on 16 September 1981.[848] Although not strictly speaking a political party, the Alliance parties co-ordinated their policies and national activities as far as is possible, and between 1981 and 1987 were widely perceived to operate as a single party.

The horoscope given here (Chart 315) is set for the data given above.

THE SOCIAL AND LIBERAL DEMOCRATIC PARTY

Following a process initiated in June 1987, the Liberal Party and the SDP merged to form the Social and Liberal Democratic Party (SLDP). The party was formally launched at a press conference in Westminster on 3 March 1988 and came into legal and constitutional existence at 00.00 hrs on 7 March 1988 (see the *Guardian*, 4 March 1988, p. 1). A group in the SDP led by Dr David Owen refused to acknowledge the merger and maintained an independent existence, claiming descent from the SDP founded in 1981.

APPENDIX 3
THE HOROSCOPES OF TOWNS AND CITIES

The search for the horoscopes of towns and cities has long been an accepted part of astrological practice, but there exists no reputable modern collection of such charts.

A thorough introduction to the subject was given by Charles Harvey in *Mundane Astrology*,[849] which remains the best guide to the available literature.

An essential collection of data for English towns and cities is Harold Wigglesworth's *The Astrology of Towns and Cities*, published by the Astrological Association.

The two examples given here — for Rome and London — are given as indications of the current muddled state of the art.

ROME
Rome is the most important city in Western civilization, and the fact that much of the world adheres to the Roman Catholic Church and that so many countries base their legal systems on Roman Law is testimony to the legacy of the Roman Empire. In Asia Minor the last vestiges of the Empire did not disappear until 1462, and in Europe the title Roman Emperor was not dropped until 1806. Until the fifteenth century, Latin, the Roman language, was the international tongue of European scholarship, and until the 1970s a qualification in this language was required for admission to certain British universities.

It is not difficult to make out a case that the horoscope for the founding of Rome could be interpreted as the key to European civilization. Yet how is it possible to arrive at a nativity for this city?

The current traditional rulership of Rome is Leo, an obvious choice for the Imperial City (although not perhaps so relevant to the 'Eternal City'). This rulership was in use at least as far back as the Renaissance,[850] and is repeated by modern authors.[851]

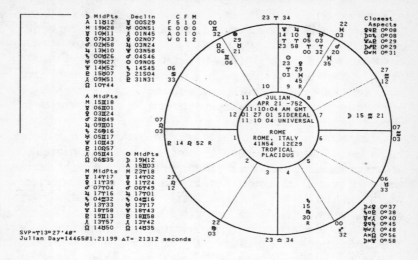

316: Rome, Foundation, 753 BC

However, the Romans had their own ideas. In cases when the date of foundation was uncertain (such as in that of Rome), Ptolemy, writing in the early second century, advised that the Midheaven of the king or other ruler be used as a sensitive degree, especially that of the ruler who was responsible for the foundation. However, it was preferable to cast a horoscope, in which case the Sun, Moon and angles (especially the Ascendant) would be the most significant points.[852]

Ptolemy was probably aware that in the first century BC about two hundred years earlier, an astrologer named Lucius Tarrutius had cast a horoscope for Rome based on the traditional date of foundation 21 April, apparently in 772-771 BC.[853] This incident is quoted in most popular histories of astrology, although the details vary from book to book.[854] The casting of the horoscope clearly had an impact at the time, for Tarrutius' claim that Rome's Moon was in Libra finds an echo in Manilius' belief, about fifty years later, that both Rome and Italy were ruled by this sign.[855] Tarrutius placed the Sun in Taurus, the Moon in Libra, Jupiter in Pisces and the remaining four planets in Scorpio, a physical impossibility. Clearly the Romans had a very different understanding of the role of the signs of the zodiac and felt no need to place their city under imperialistic Leo. One modern author calculated the horoscope for 753 BC, the traditional date of Rome's foundation and felt it necessary to move the Sun from Taurus to Aries in order to find a date in April when the Moon was in Libra.[856]

The horoscope given here for Rome (Chart 316) is set for 21 April (the date given by Tarrutius), for 753 BC, the traditional year of the city's foundation, and in the Gregorian calendar.[857] The chart was calculated by Astro-Computing Services in the tropical zodiac, but might be reset using a vernal point of 8° Aries, which seems to have been assumed by the Romans of the time.[858]

The question of the foundation of the city of Rome is therefore virtually impossible to settle, even using classical sources.

Yet clues might still be found in later horoscopes, such as those for the foundation of the Roman Empire or the Holy Roman Empire, or for the Vatican City State. An interesting extension of the study is allowed by an examination of the horoscopes for Constantinople, which replaced Rome as the capital of the Empire, and which was officially known as 'New Rome which is Constantinople'.[859]

A traditional date is given by astrologers for the laying of the city's foundation stone on the basis of astrological election of 26 November AD 326 'at the hour of the Crab'.[860] This account is the basis of the belief in both Renaissance and modern texts that the city is ruled by Cancer.[861] Although the foundations of the city were laid in 326,[862] the city was inaugurated in a great ceremony on 11 May 330, a date which is considered to represent the birth of the Eastern Roman, or Byzantine, Empire.[863] The horoscope for 11 May could be considered a supplementary chart for the city.

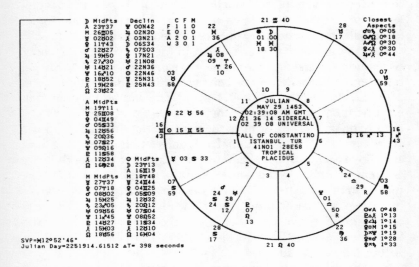

317: Fall of Constantinople, 1453

Other horoscopes for the city circulated during the Renaissance. One chart is taken from a chart collection published in 1558 and which purports to be set for 7.34 a.m. on 2 May AD 638, a date with no conceivable historical importance.[864]

However, there is ample historical data that could allow at least an analysis of the sensitive degrees of the chart for Constantinople, or Istanbul as it is now known. Such degrees would be those that seem to be especially prominent during critical periods of the city's history, using the inauguration date (11 May AD 330) as a basis.

After the foundation, the major event in the city's existence was its capture by the Turks in 1543, a date which marks a watershed in European history. The horoscope for this event (Chart 317) is therefore worthy of study as more than just a map for the city of Constantinople. The Turkish assault on the city began at 1.30 a.m. on Tuesday 29 May 1453, and at 'sunrise' or 'daybreak' the Turks broke through the city walls, capturing the city immediately after.[865]

The city subsequently became the capital of the Turkish Ottoman Empire, and the horoscope for its capture could therefore be seen as a chart for that Empire, and therefore deserves comparison with the horoscope for Turkey given above (Chart 262) which is cast for the end of that Empire.

LONDON

The astrological character of London is derived from tradition, 'empirical' astrological research and horoscopes based on actual events.

The city is traditionally ruled by Gemini, and some astrologers have been so precise as to specify the eighteenth degree (i.e. 17°) or 17° 54′ of that sign.[866] The origin of this rulership may lie in a simple association of the sign of the twins with the giants Gog and Magog who were reputedly involved in the city's history.

Working within that tradition, and a traditional foundation of the city with the Sun at 25° Gemini,[867] astrologers as early as the seventeenth century attempted an empirical analysis of London's sensitive degrees by analysing past traumas, mainly fires, in its past. One such astrologer, Frances Bernard, physician to James II concluded that London's sensitive degrees were 14° Gemini, 25° Gemini, 8° Aquarius and 14° Aquarius.[868]

Subsequent research concluded that London's Midheaven was 9° Gemini and its Ascendant 14° Virgo,[869] and that the ninth and fourteenth degrees of all the mutable signs are significant.[870]

An additional approach followed by modern astrologers is that

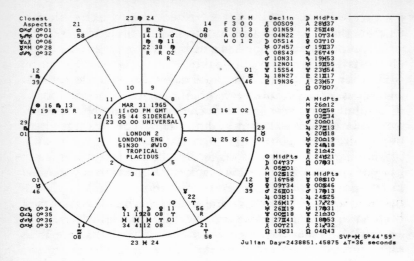

318: London, Greater London Council, 1965

of assigning Midheaven degrees on the basis of degrees of Latitude under which system London may have a Midheaven of anywhere between 9° Pisces and 5° Gemini,[871] although variations on such

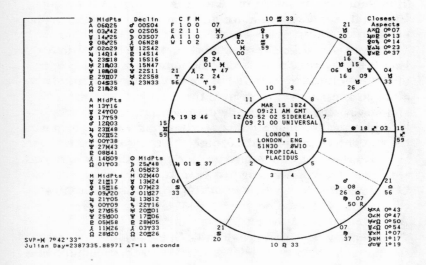

319: London, London Bridge, 1824

practices can produce still wider differences. One of the most logical systems was that of Sepharial who equated 0° Latitude with 0° Aries, 1° West with 1° Aries and so on. Under this system London has a Midheaven of 29° 55′ Pisces, and on this basis it is possible to create a house grid for the city: when 29° 55′ Pisces is on the Midheaven at London 26° 33′ Cancer is rising, the second cusp (Placidus) is 12° Leo and so on. The result is a horoscope through which planets may be transited, conjunctions with angles being of critical importance.

Horoscopes for London should be set for major stages in the city's political organization. Until 1986 the working horoscope was that for the Greater London Council, which came into existence at 00.00 hrs on 1 April 1965 (Chart 318). [872] Although this council has now been abolished and London now has no single administration, as a significant moment in the recent history of the city it could be expected to have continued relevance.

The second horoscope given here (Chart 319) is that given in Alfred Pearce's *Textbook of Astrology*. Pearce set his chart for the beginning of the building of London Bridge in 1824, but considered that the map was relevant to the city as a whole.

THE TRADITIONAL RULERSHIPS OF TOWNS AND CITIES

The following list of astrological rulerships of towns and cities is taken principally from William Lilly's *Christian Astrology* published in 1647, and *Mundane Astrology*, Raphael's work published in the nineteenth century, with additions from H. S. Green's *Mundane Astrology* and Charles Carter's *Introduction to Political Astrology*.

Green wrote that 'most of the rulerships of towns . . . given in this list may be taken as correct, for they have been carefully observed and fully corroborated by experience' (p.76).

In fact, the lists seem to be reproduced by successive authors with little thought, proving little more than the proposition that, with the appropriate perspective, any sign will seem correct.

Carter, who was always more cautious, regarded the accepted attributions as tentative in the extreme, and they are reproduced here — not that they might be blindly copied, but as a reference list for the questioning astrologer.

When considering astrological rulerships of towns and cities, it is advisable to refer back to first principles, as Carter suggests. These are, after all, the principles from which medieval astrologers worked. For example, Carter concludes that the administrative areas of towns are ruled by Capricorn (hence this sign's rulership of Westminster and Whitehall) and that Luton, where hats are made, is ruled by Aries. The assumption here is that the astrological rulership of a place changes with its evolving human use, although some would argue that the human use follows the astrological character.

These rulerships should be compared to those in the table of midheaven degrees.

Alexandria	♓	Cadiz	♋
Algiers	♋	Caesarea	♈
Amsterdam	♋	Capua	♈
Ancona	♈	Cardiff	♓
Antwerp	♎	Cesena	♓
(Raphael gives 21°)		Charleston	♎
Arles	♎	Cheltenham	♍
Ashton-under-Lyme	♑	Chicago	♌
Augusta	♈	(Raphael gives the	
Avignon	♐	1st decanate)	
Baltimore	♏	Christchurch	♓
Bamberg	♓	Cincinnati	♏
Basle	♍	Cleves	♑
Bath	♌	Cologne	♐
Bergama	♈	Compostella	♓
Berne	♋	Constantinople (Istanbul)	♋
Birmingham	♈	Cordoba	♓
Blackburn	♈	Corinth	♍
Blackpool	♌	Cowes	♓
Bombay	♌	Cracow	♈
Bononia	♑	Cremona	♌
Boston	♍	Cullen	♐
Bournemouth	♓	Damascus	♌
Bradford	♐	Delhi	♑
Brandenburg	♑	Deptford	♋
Bremen	♒	Dover	♏
Brighton	♒	Dublin	♑
Brindisi	♍	Eastbourne	♑
Bristol	♌	East Grinstead	♏
Bruges	♓	Farnham	♓
Brunswick	♈	Ferrara	♈
Brussels	♑	Florence	♈
Budapest	♐	Frankfurt	♎
Bury	♍	Freiburg	♎

City	Sign	City	Sign
Gaeta	♎	Metz	♓
Genoa	♋	Mexico City	♑
Ghent	♑	Milan	♋
Glossop	♏	Milwaukee	♏
Grimsby	♓	(Raphael gives 7°)	
Halifax	♏	Montserrat	♒
Hamborough	♒	Moscow	♒
Hamburg	♒	Nantes	♉
Hastings	♉	Naples	♈
Heidelberg	♍	Narbonne	♐
Hull	♏	Newcastle	♏
Ingolstadt	♒, ♄	New Orleans	♏
Jerusalem	♍	New York	♋
Keighly	♑	Neuremburg	☽, ♓
King's Lynn	♓	Nottingham, according	
Lancaster	♓	to Raphael	♐
Leeds	♎	according to Carter	♎
Leicester	♈	Novgorod	♉
Leipzig	♉	Oldham	♈
Leningrad	♒	Oxford	♑
Lintz	♌	Padua	♈
Lisbon	♎	Palermo (Panormus)	♉
Liverpool	♏	Paris	☿, ♍
London	♓	(Raphael gives 29°)	
(Raphael gives 17°54′)		Parma	♉
Los Angeles, according to		Philadelphia	♌
Raphael	♍	Pisa	♒
according to Carter	♌	Placenza	♎
Louvaine	♓	Plymouth	♓
Lubeck	♋	Port Said	♑
Lucerne	♉	Portsmouth	♌
Lyons	♍	Prague	♌
Magdeburg	♋	Preston	♓
Maidstone	♍	Ratisbon	♓
Manchester	♋	Ravenna	♄, ♌
Mantua	♉	Reading	♍
Marseilles	♈	Regensburg	♓
Mecklin	♑	Rheims	♓
Melbourne	♓	Rhodes	♉
(Raphael gives 10°29′)		Rochdale	♋
Messina, according to Lilly	♎	Rome	♌
according to Raphael 18°	♏	Rottenburg	♐

St Andrews	♋	Toledo	♐
St Johns, Newfoundland	♏	Tortona	♑
(Raphael gives 2°)		Toulouse	♍
St Louis	♑	Trent	♒
Salisbury, according to		Tunis	♋
Raphael	♒	Turin	♀
according to Green	♑	Urbino	♏
San Francisco	♓	Utrecht	♈
Saragossa	♈	Valencia	♏
Seville	♓	Venice	♋
Southport	♓	Verona	♈
Speyer (Spires)	♎	Versailles	♓
Stargard	♐	Washington D.C.	♏
Stockholm, according to		Wednesbury	♓
Raphael	♋	West Bromwich	♐
according to Carter	♒	Westminster	♑
Stockport	♏	Wittenberg	♋
Strasbourg	♍	Whitehall	♑
Stuttgart	♐	Wolverhampton	♓
Syracuse	♌	Worms	♓
Taranto	♐	Worthing	♏
Taunton	♌	(Raphael gives 7°)	
Tiverton	♓	York	♋
Todmorden	♍		

COMPARATIVE TABLE OF MIDHEAVEN DEGREES FOR MAJOR CITIES

This table, originally compiled by Charles Harvey in *Mundane Astrology*, shows the midheaven degrees for various major cities based on systems of correspondences between degrees of celestial longitude and terrestrial longitude (i.e. the zodiac). Andersen's correlations are based on his own systems of earth zodiacs rather than correlations between longitude and the zodiac. (The rationale behind each of these systems is given in detail in *Mundane Astrology* by Baigent, Campion and Harvey.)

In general only planetary transits over midheaven degrees have been used to demonstrate the validity of these schemes, although interesting results can be obtained by casting a full horoscope based on the latitude of any particular place, and using the midheaven degree as the basis for the other houses. For example, Sepharial's midheaven degree for London of 29° 55′ Pisces correlates with an ascendant (for 51° 31′ north) of 26° Cancer; a second cusp (placidus)

	Sepharial Geodetic	Hamburg School	Johndro (1930)	Andersen Earth	Andersen Sun	Ritter	Wise	Hitschler	Ronald Davison	David Williams	Henri de Boullainviller
Madrid	26PI19	25PI58	29AR27	21AR19	25CP00	8GE41	11AR19	29AR34	3AR41	10AR09	1CN19
London	29PI55	29PI54	1TA12	24AR55	9PI00	5GE07	14AR55	26AR07	0AR05	13AR45	27GE45
Paris	2AR20	2AR32	3TA45	27AR20	4AQ00	2GE40	17AR20	23AR33	27PI40	16AR10	25GE18
Berlin	13AR23	14AR30	15TA02	8TA23	10-14VI*	21TA37	28AR23	12AR30	16PI37	27AR13	14GE15
Cape Town	18AR30	19AR54	20TA17	13TA30	10SG00	16TA30	3TA30	—	11PI00	2TA20	9GE08
Warsaw	21AR00	22AR40	22TA41	16TA00	12VI00	14TA00	6TA00	—	9PI00	5TA00	6GE38
Cairo	1TA17	3TA28	2GE30	26TA17	00SC00	3TA43	16TA17	24PI36	28AQ43	15TA07	26TA21
Jerusalem	5TA13	7TA34	6GE15	00GE13	22LI00	29AR47	20TA13	20PI40	24AQ47	19TA03	22TA25
Moscow	7TA38	9TA52	8GE29	2GE38	23LE00	27AR22	22TA38	18PI15	22AQ22	21TA28	20TA00
Tehran	21TA29	23TA29	21GE21	16GE29	27VI00	13AR31	6GE29	4PI24	8AQ31	5GE19	6TA09
Delhi	17GE13	18GE03	15CN06	12CN13	12VI00	27AQ47	2CN13	18CP40	12CP47	1CN03	20PI25
Peking	26CN25	24CN10	23LE19	21LE25	7LE00	8AQ35	11LE25	29SG28	3SG35	10LE15	1PI13
Tokyo	19LE48	16LE55	17VI56	14VI48	23CN30	15CP12	4VI48	6SG05	10SC12	3VI38	7AQ50
Canberra	26LE51	26LE29	28VI08	21VI51	***	7CP09	11VI51	28SC02	3SC09	10VI41	29CP47
San Fransisco	27SC52	00SG05	27SG02	22SG52	6TA00	7LI08	12SG52	28LE01	2LE08	11SG42	29LI46
Washington	13CP00	12CP06	9AQ43	8AQ00	8AR30	22LE00	28CP00	12CN53	17II00	27CP00	14VI38
New York	16CP10	14CP57	12AQ41	11AQ10	10AR00*	18LE50	1AQ10	9CN43	13II50	0AQ00	11VI28
Buenos Aires	1AQ32	29CP32	28AQ39	26AQ32	***	3LE28	16AQ32	24GE21	28TA28	15AQ22	26LE06

* It is difficult to give precise values for areas close to the pole of zodiac.
** Estimated value from map.
*** Not available.

of 12° Leo and so on. The planets may then be plotted by transit through the entire system of houses.

APPENDIX 4.
ECONOMIC ORGANIZATIONS

An attempt to produce a thorough collection of horoscopes for companies and businesses was made by Carol S. Mull in *Standard and Poor's Five Hundred*, published in 1984 by the American Federation of Astrologers. Louise McWhirter's *Astrology and Stock Forecasting* and Hans Gerhard Lenz's *The Stock Market, the Dollar and Interest Rate Developments 1985 to 1990* also contain valuable data although the latter is especially lacking in failing to provide adequate sources for horoscopes apparently based on recorded times.

There is still no comprehensive and reliable collection of horoscopes for economic institutions, banks, stock exchanges companies and trade unions, and this appendix includes only four of the major horoscopes of economic relevance in the contemporary world.

THE NEW YORK STOCK EXCHANGE
The New York Stock Exchange is arguably the most important of the three exchanges (the others being London and Tokyo) which dominate the markets of the world. Although stock trading is known to have taken place on Wall Street before May 1792, this month is taken as that of the formal foundation of the Exchange. On 17 May 1792 a group of traders concluded the so-called Buttonwood Agreement when they met under an old buttonwood tree on Wall Street and decided to regulate and co-ordinate their activities. [873] The horoscope given here (Chart 320) is set for this time and date and, in the absence of accurate information, for 12.00 noon LMT.

THE EUROPEAN ECONOMIC COMMUNITY
The European Economic Community (Common Market) is the largest and richest trading bloc in the history of the world, and current intentions are that it should slowly mature into a political federation.

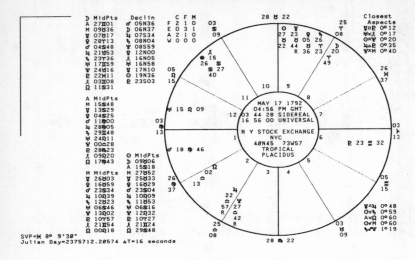

320: New York Stock Exchange, 1792

It already ranks as a confederation in which each member has surrendered its sovereignty over certain important aspects of policy. The prototype for the EEC was the European Coal and Steel

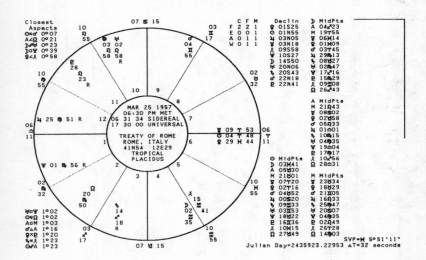

321: EEC; Treaty of Rome, 1957

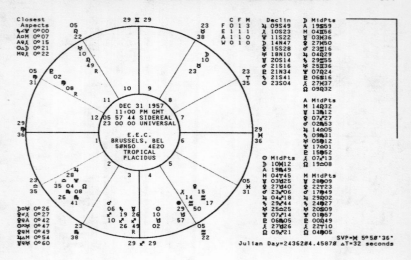

322: EEC; Legal Foundation, 1958

Community which was created on 1 July 1952 and which was the result of a series of initiatives involving political and economic co-operation between the states of Western Europe.

The EEC itself came into being as a result of the Treaty of Rome, which was signed at 6.30 p.m. on 25 March 1957 in Rome.[874] This horoscope has been used as a chart for the EEC itself, and is given here (Chart 321).

The EEC came into existence at 00.00 hrs on 1 January 1958[875] and Chart 322 is set for this data, and for the administrative capital, Brussels. This horoscope, rather than that for the Treaty of Rome, should be seen as that for the organization.

The horoscope for the Treaty of Rome will be important for indicating the implementation of its provisions by the EEC, and hence should indicate many of the crises to which this organization has been prone.

OPEC

OPEC, the Organization of Petroleum Exporting Countries, came into being as a result of the Baghdad Conference on 14 September 1960. According to research by Michael Baigent using *The BBC Summary of World Broadcast*, the decision to form OPEC was taken at the final session of the Conference, which began at 11.00 a.m. Following the decision, the acting Iraqi Oil Minister made a speech

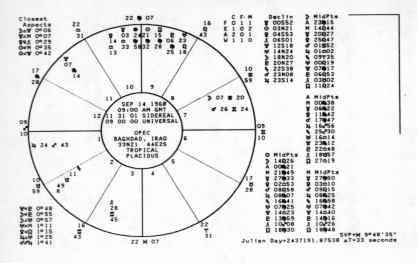

323: OPEC, 1960

and the resolution was signed.[1040] Michael Baigent deduced that the likely time of signature was therefore 12.00 noon, and the horoscope given here (Chart 323), is set for 12.00 noon on 14 September 1960 in Baghdad. Apart from this decision, there was no ceremonial or legal inception for the organization, which gradually assumed its full form as a result of subsequent conferences between the oil-producing states.

APPENDIX 5.
MILITARY ORGANIZATIONS

NORTH ATLANTIC TREATY ORGANIZATION

The North Atlantic Treaty Organization (NATO) came into being as the result of a treaty signed on 4 April 1949. The horoscope for this date is highly descriptive and is sometimes used as that for the creation of NATO itself, which it is definitely not. The treaty was signed in Washington at around 5.00 p.m., although a literal reading of press reports suggests a time of 4.52 p.m. for the completion of the signing ceremony.[878]

The organization came into being at 11.42 a.m. on 24 August 1949 when, following the ratification of the treaty by France (the final country to do so), President Truman signed the document

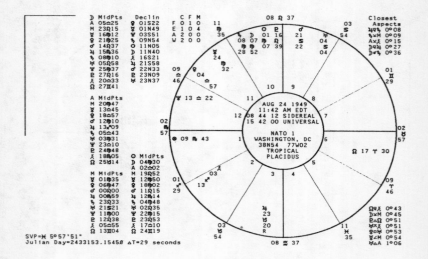

bringing the treaty into force.[879] The horoscope given here (Chart 320) is set for this time and date in Washington the location of Truman's signing.

THE US DEFENCE DEPARTMENT

The United States Defence Department was created by the National Security Act, signed by President Truman on 26 July 1947. Contemporary press reports suggested that the President signed the Act a few minutes before his plane took off from Washington at 12.30 p.m.,[880] and the horoscope given is set for this time (Chart 325). Research by Ron Howland, using Truman's appointments book for 26 July shows that this source records that the Act was signed at 12.15 p.m.[1043]

The Act was designed to create the apparatus 'to protect the internal security of the USA', and 'to take operations by land, sea and air' to guarantee this. Ron Howland has shown how, although the Defence Department itself came into being immediately the Act was signed, various other institutions set up under the terms of the Act such as the National Security Council, the Air Force and the Central Intelligence Agency came into being at subsequent times.

The Central Intelligence Agency came into being on 26 September 1947 when the first director, Ray Kline, was appointed sometime between 10.00 a.m. and 10.15 a.m.[1044] Howland estimates the time as between 10.05 a.m. and 10.10 a.m.

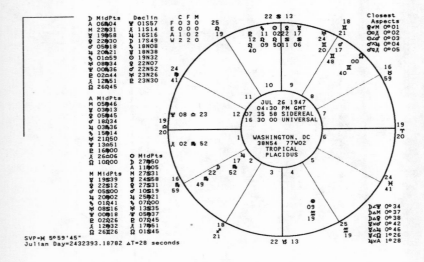

325: US Defence Department (including CIA), 1947

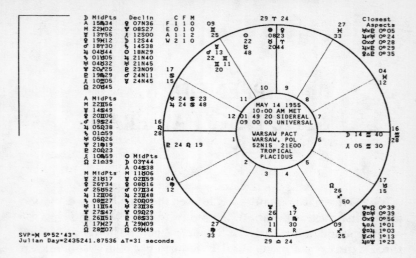

326: Warsaw Pact, 1955

WARSAW PACT

The Warsaw Pact, the Soviet Union's response to NATO, is dated from the signature of the treaty of Warsaw on 14 May 1955. According to research by Michael Baigent the Soviet Union and its allies — Poland, Czechoslovakia, Romania, Hungary and Bulgaria — held a conference in Warsaw to discuss the pact beginning at 10.00 a.m. on 10 May, and the signing took place at 10.00 a.m. on 14 May.[881] The horoscope given here (Chart 326) is set for this time and date and for Warsaw.

APPENDIX 6.
THE NUCLEAR ERA

It is a cliché that the world was forever changed by the explosion of the first nuclear bomb to be used in war in 1945, and that the current period of history is the 'Nuclear Era'. The horoscopes given here are three of the most critical in the history of man's use of nuclear energy, although there are many more moments of powerful significance. These may be easily researched for there are ample records in this field. [994]

Data for the scientific discoveries that made nuclear power possible has been collected by Nick Kollerstrom and will hopefully be published.

THE FIRST CONTROLLED NUCLEAR REACTION

The first controlled nuclear reaction took place at 3.25 p.m. on 2 December 1942 in Chicago. [995] The reaction ceased at 3.53 p.m., at which moment the scientists, led by Enrico Fermi, judged, that the reaction was in danger of becoming out of control.

A dispute has arisen concerning the time standard in use in Chicago on this date. The horoscope given here is calculated in Central War Time, equivalent to Central Standard Time, the normal standard time, minus one hour. This is in accordance with the practice of this book which is to use information supplied by Astro Computing Services and the *American Atlas*. Previous charts for the same moment have been set for Central Standard Time on the authority of Doris Chase Doane's *Time Changes in the USA*, giving 25° Taurus Ascendant for the beginning of the reaction, and Uranus conjunct the Ascendant for the close.

THE FIRST ATOMIC EXPLOSION

The first atom bomb was exploded at 12.29.21 p.m. GMT on 16

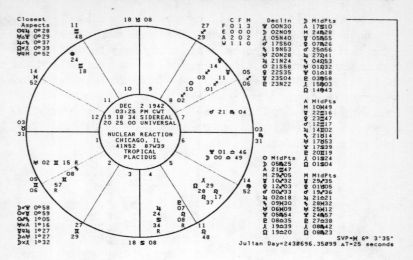

327: Controlled Nuclear Reaction, 1942

July 1945 at Alamogordo in New Mexico,[996] and Chart 328 is set for this time. In the past, confusion has surrounded the exact time for this event due to uncertainty over time zone differences, although

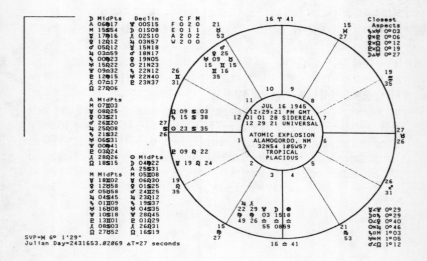

328: First Atom Bomb, 1945

recently Michael Harding has brought a true account to light.[997] Originally the time recorded was that used by the scientists recording the explosion in Los Alamos, who were using the same time as that of the research laboratory in Berkeley (GMT minus 8 hrs) rather than that of New Mexico (GMT minus 7 hrs). The result of this confusion was that an additional hour was added to the time at which it was thought the explosion took place. The true time came to light as a result of the record of seismic tremors made by the California Institute of Technology.

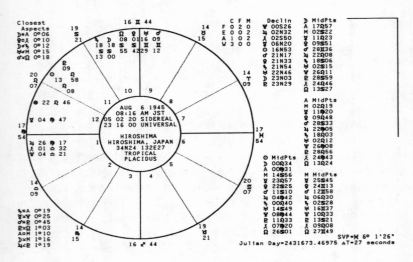

329: Hiroshima Atom Bomb, 1945

THE HIROSHIMA ATOM BOMB
The age of nuclear war was opened with the dropping of the first atom bomb to be used in war on Hiroshima in Japan at 8.16 a.m. on 6 August 1945.[998] The horoscope given here (Chart 329) is set for this moment. The second atom bomb was dropped on Nagasaki at 11.02 a.m. on 9 August 1945.[999]

APPENDIX 7.
THE ERA OF MANNED FLIGHT AND SPACE TRAVEL

The invention of mechanical means for human beings to fly has revolutionized life on Earth and has shown the way forward to space travel and even life on other planets. To the author's knowledge there has been no fully comprehensive astrological study of the history of manned flight. This is a pity, for the research involved is free of the source problems that afflict the quest for national charts. The records are available, and in most cases the data is quite unambiguous for all major flights have taken place at well-documented times.

A true history should start with the history of the hot-air balloon. The first balloon ascent in modern times was undertaken by the Montgolfier brothers on 21 November 1783 at Paris, and the habit caught on quickly. The first balloon flight in England took place at 4.00 a.m. on 2 October 1784 in Oxford. [1000]

However, no real advance was made until the invention of the aeroplane and powered flight.

THE FIRST POWERED FLIGHT
The first manned powered flight took place when the Wright brothers' plane, the Kitty Hawk, lifted off at 10.35 a.m. on 17 December 1903 at Kill Devil Hills in North Carolina. The horoscope given here (Chart 330) is for this data. A discussion of this chart is included in *Mundane Astrology*. [1001]

Flight technology improved rapidly, and it was just over seven years later, at 10.00 a.m. on 1 January 1911, that the first commercial scheduled flight took off from St Petersburg, Florida. [1002]

SPUTNIK — THE BEGINNING OF THE SPACE ERA
The Sputnik, the first artificial Earth satellite was launched by the Soviet Union on 4 October 1957, inaugurating the era of space

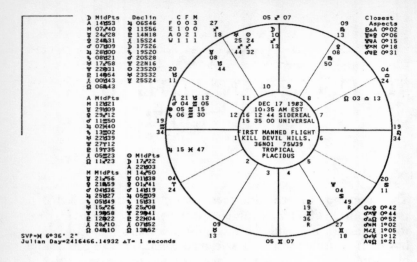

330: First Manned Powered Flight, 1903

exploration and travel. Although the Soviet scientists did not accounce
either the launch site or time, their United States counterparts
calculated the time to be 9.00 p.m. GMT and the site as a point

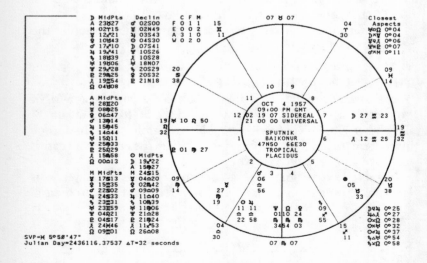

331: First Artificial Space Satellite (Sputnik), 1957

north of the Caspian Sea.[1003] The horoscope given here (Chart 331) is set for this data and for the assumed location of the Baikonur Cosmodrome in Kazakhstan. The Soviet Government announced the launch of the Sputnik via TASS, the official Soviet news agency at 00.00 hrs (presumably Moscow time) on 5 October. This horoscope (Chart 331) is the inceptional map for all space travel.

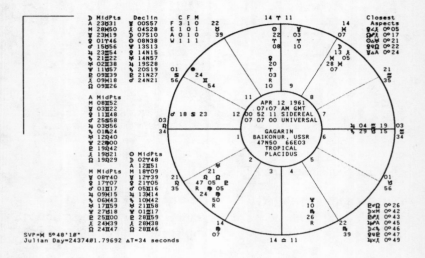

332: First Manned Space Flight, 1961

THE FIRST MANNED SPACE FLIGHT
The first manned space flight, carrying cosmonaut Yuri Gagarin on one orbit around the Earth, was launched at 09.07 a.m. Moscow time on 12 April 1961 from the Baikonur Cosmodrome in Kazakhstan.[1004] The horoscope for this moment (Chart 332) is that for all manned space flight, and in particular for the Soviet manned space programme.

THE FIRST US MANNED SPACE FLIGHT
The first US manned space flight was launched at 9.24 a.m. on 5 May 1961 from Cape Canaveral in Florida (Chart 333). The flight carried Alan Shepard vertically into space and back down to Earth without going into orbit, and lasted 15 minutes and 22 seconds.[1005] This horoscope is relevant to the US manned space programme, although I believe that the chart for the first Soviet manned space flight may take precedence.

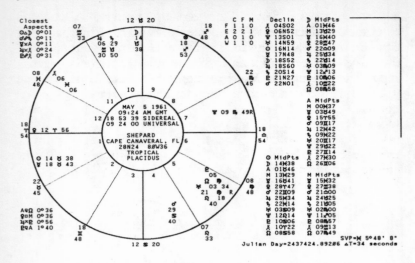

333: First US Manned Space Flight, 1961

THE MOON LANDING

The culmination of the space programme so far was the manned landing on the Moon in 1969. A complete account of all the stages

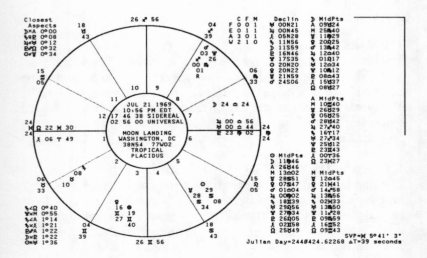

334: First Manned Moon Landing, 1969

involved in the flight together with times, is given in *Keesing's Contemporary Archives*. The spaceship, Apollo 11, was launched at 9.32 a.m. EDT on 16 July 1969, [1006] and Neil Armstrong stepped onto the Moon at 10.56 p.m. EDT (3.56 p.m. BST) on 21 July 1969. [1007] The horoscope given here (Chart 334) is set for this time. It was hoped to calculate a lunacentric horoscope for this moment, but this proved not to be possible for this book, so the chart is cast for Washington. Obviously there is no adequate location on the Earth for which to cast this chart, although a chart set for Washington should indicate the future of the United States in interplanetary travel, and as the enterprise was American, have greater relevance than horoscopes set for other locations.

APPENDIX 8.
EARTH ZODIACS

The first known attempt to ascribe zodiacal rulerships to nations (see Figure 3) is found in the *Astronomica* by the Roman astrologer Marcus Manilius, written at around the beginning of the Christian era.[970] Manilius was in no doubt as to the total unity of the cosmos connecting the nations of the earth and the signs of the zodiac in one grand system:

> Thus is the world for ever distributed among the twelve signs, and from the signs themselves must the laws prevailing among them be applied to the areas they govern; for these areas maintain between themselves the same relationships as exist between the signs; and just as the signs unite with each other or clash in enmity, now confronting one another across the sky and now linked in triangular federation, or as some other principle directs them to their various feelings, even so is land joined with land, city with city, and shores are at war with shores, realms with realms. So must every man shun or seek a place to live in, so hope for loyalty or be forewarned of peril, according to the character which has come down to earth from high heaven.[971]

The second, and more enduring set of correlations between nations and signs (see Figure 4) was drawn up by Claudius Ptolemy in the first to second centuries AD, and published in his astrological text, the *Tetrabiblos*.[972] Ptolemy divided the world into four quarters, each ruled by one triplicity, and subdivided into smaller regions ruled by one of the twelve signs. In the middle of the known world was an area of overlapping influences in which each of the signs ruled an additional territory. The four major quarters were also ruled by the planetary rulers of the respective triplicity, while each region was also the dominion of the planetary ruler of its respective sign.

The Muslim astrologers of the ninth to twelfth centuries preserved a model based on that of Ptolemy, but had little knowledge of, or

Figure 3: Astrological Rulerships According to Manilius *c.* AD 0.

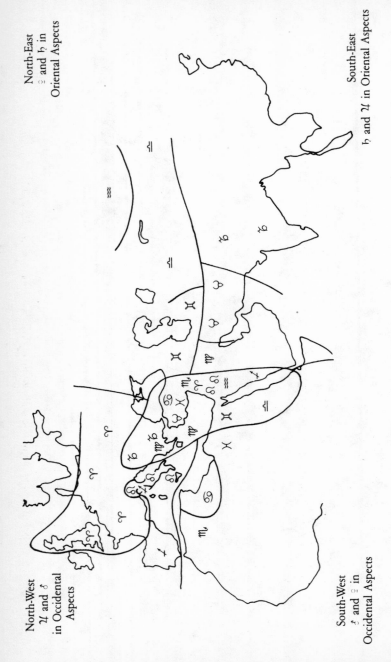

Figure 4: Astrological Rulerships According to Ptolemy *c.* AD 120.

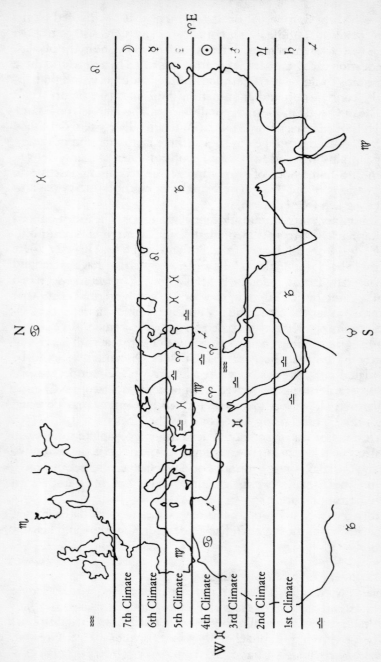

Figure 5: Astrological Rulerships, Climates and Points of the Compass According to Al Biruni, 1029

concern with, Europe. Al Biruni, writing in 1029, divided North Africa and the Middle East among the twelve signs and combined these with a system of seven climates, each ruled by one of the planets. In addition each point of the compass was ruled by a sign, and these rulerships could be used both for finding lost objects and perhaps in the construction and alignment of buildings (see Figure 5).[973]

The medieval Europeans naturally focused their models on Europe and borrowed heavily from Ptolemy. William Lilly's system published in 1647 contains strange omissions (there is no mention of India), but contains many additions for European states probably derived from the horoscopes of contemporary or recent monarchs and coronations. Some changes were made; for example Turkey was now ruled by Leo (see Figure 6).[974]

Subsequent lists contain additional variations. The lists produced by Raphael,[975] Green,[976] Sepharial[977] and, somewhat disdainfully, by Carter[978] are all derived from Ptolemy and Lilly. However, there seems to be no rationale for Lilly and Carter's claim that Switzerland was ruled by Taurus, or for the belief of Green, Raphael and Sepharial that it came under Virgo, in view of Ptolemy's original claim that it came under the Fire triplicity and most likely under Aries.

Sometimes rulerships are based on name association. For example Raphael clearly links the American state of Virginia with Virgo and Carter argues that the Australian state of Queensland should be associated with Leo even though he reluctantly places it under Scorpio.

Other rulerships are derived from national horoscopes: Cheiro's belief that all of North America is ruled by Gemini may be taken from the Gemini rising horoscope for the USA.[979]

One major list of zodiacal rulerships is a complete innovation bearing no relationship to any previous work. This is the list drawn up by Alice Bailey using intuitive or clairvoyant faculties, but which, unlike much of her work, appears to have had little impact on astrological practice.[980]

For a review of other approaches to this question see Charles Harvey, 'The Search for the Earth Zodiac' in Baigent, Campion and Harvey, *Mundane Astrology*.

Additional Zodiacal Rulerships

Since Lilly's day further rulerships have been added which in some cases extend the correlations of Ptolemy and Lilly, and in others contradict them. The following list is derived from the additional rulerships given by Raphael in *Mundane Astrology*, H. S. Green in *Mundane Astrology*, Charles Carter in *An Introduction to Political*

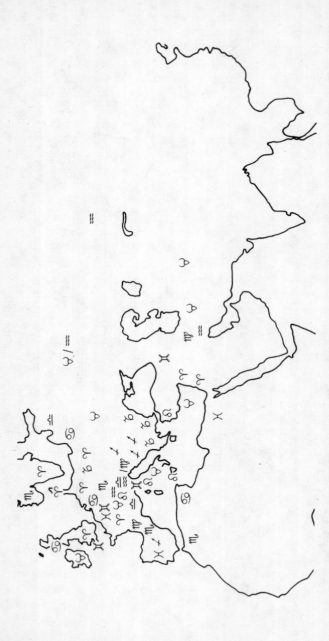

Figure 6: Astrological Rulerships According to William Lilly, 1647. Lilly appears to have retained the same major rulerships as Ptolemy but given sub-rulerships to various feudal principalities. For reasons of space not all the variations are given here. Lilly included one new rulership, the West Indies, which he placed under Capricorn.

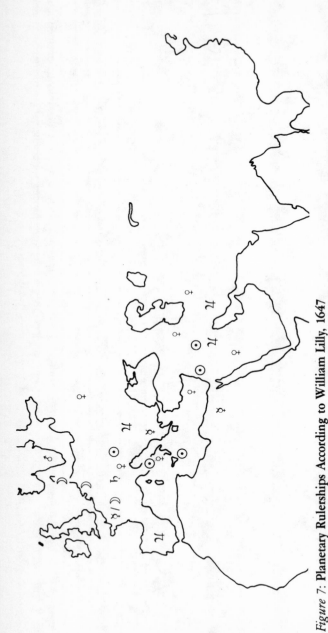

Figure 7: **Planetary Rulerships According to William Lilly, 1647**
In some cases Lilly's planetary rulers correspond to the traditional zodiacal rulers. For example Jupiter and Sagittarius both rule Spain, the Sun and Leo both rule Italy, the Moon and Cancer both rule Holland, and Venus and Taurus both rule Poland. In other cases there is disagreement between zodiacal and planetary rulers. For example, Mercury and Pisces both rule Egypt. Lilly also referred to the system of climates found in Al Biruni. However, he gave astrological rulerships to only two climates: Jupiter to the second and Venus (instead of Mercury) to the sixth.

Astrology and Sepharial in *The World Horoscope.*

In some cases these lists contradict each other. In most there are internal contradictions due to repetition of the differences between Ptolemy and Lilly, or to the fact that political boundaries have moved.

Some of the rulerships appear to be based on assessment of national characteristics while others are derived from independence or other significant political dates.

This list is reproduced purely as a reference for those interested in this field, and it is not recommended that any of the attributions be used in preference to national horoscopes.

Afghanistan	♑	Georgia	♀
Africa	♋	Germany, according to	
Africa, North East Coast	♓	Sepharial	♏
Africa, North and West	♋	according to Carter	♋
Alaska	♍	Iceland	♏
Arabia	♌	Indo China	♎
Argentina, according to		Indonesia	♈
Raphael and Green	♎	Iraq	♌
according to Sepharial	♀	(according to Raphael,	
who places Patagonia		'Chaldea to Bassorah')	
under	♍	Iran	♑
Armenia	♓	(according to Green,	
Asia Minor	♀	area around Circon and	
Australia	♐	Maracan)	
Bolivia	♍	Japan,	
Burma	♎	according to Raphael	♈
Canada	♍	according to Carter	♎/♌
Caucasus	♀	Jordan	♏
China, according to		Judea (i.e. Palestine)	♏
Raphael	♎	Jutland	♏
according to Carter	♋	Korea	♌
Commonwealth of Nations	♈	Kurdistan	♍
Cuba	♌	Lithuania	♑
England, West of,	♓	Madagascar	♐
England, North East	♏	Mauritius	♋
England, Yorkshire	♐	Mexico, according to	
Ethiopia (Abyssinia)	♒	Raphael and Green	♑
European Economic		according to Sepharial	♀
Community	♌	New Zealand	♓
Finland	♏	Norway	♏
France	♌	Nubia	♓

Orkney Islands	♑	Raphael	♒
Panama Canal Zone	♌	Carter mentions	
Paraguay	♋	traditional rulership by	♉
Peru	♎	Switzerland	♍
Provence, France,	♐	Syria	♏
Prussia	♒	Tibet	♎
Queensland, Australia	♏	Transvaal	♏
Romania, according to		Turkey	♍
Sepharial	♐	UAR	♎
according to Carter	♌	USA	♊
north only according		Vietnam	♍
to Raphael	♌	Wales	♊
Sahara Desert	♓	West Indies	♍
Sardinia	♊	Zaïre (Congo)	♊
Silesia	♍	Zambia	
South Africa	♋	(Northern Rhodesia)	♏
Sudan	♊	Zimbabwe	
Sweden, according to		(Southern Rhodesia)	♏

APPENDIX 9.
WORLD HOROSCOPES

The quest for the world horoscope can be traced back at least 1,600 years. Although astrological theories of world history were first written down by Plato in the fourth century BC, Plato himself was building on the work of earlier Greek philosophers such as Empedocles and Pythagoras, and operating within a cosmological framework that seems to have been established in Sumer and Akkad prior to 2,000 BC.

It is important to distinguish two types of world horoscope — those cast for the creation of the world itself, and those cast for the beginning of major epochs in history. It is also necessary to remember that some charts are cast on the basis of astronomical and historical research, while others are purely symbolic.

Plato, whose views were extremely influential, believed that every 36,000 years the seven wandering stars (the Sun, the Moon, Mercury, Venus, Mars, Jupiter and Saturn), formed a mean conjunction at the same position as their creation. At this point the world was destroyed in a major cataclysm which became the birth moment for a fresh 36,000 year period.[882] In the original Babylonian tradition the multiple conjunctions occurred alternately at 0° Cancer (bringing fire) and 0° Capricorn (bringing flood),[883] but in later Arab and European astrology the conjunction was fixed at 0° Aries.

THE HERMETIC BIRTHDAY OF THE UNIVERSE
The Roman astrologer Julius Firmicus Maternus, writing in the fourth century AD some 800 years after Plato, described a birth chart for the universe in which all the planets were in their dignities, Mercury, Venus, Mars, Jupiter and Saturn being in their diurnal dignities (Chart 335). He did not consider this to be a literal chart for the creation for, following in the Platonic tradition, he believed that the

335: The Hermetic Birthday of the Universe (*The Mathesis*, Book III, Chapter 1)

universe was eternal and that its existence was punctuated by great cataclysms.

Firmicus relates that he copied the chart from a book called the *Myriogenesis* by the Alexandrian hermetic writer Aesculapius, but said the doctrine owed as much to the other semi-mythical hermetic teachers, Petosiris, Nechepso and Hanubius. The purpose of the chart was purely symbolic — to show all the planets in their most perfect positions as an inspirational model for the perfect human life.

According to Firmicus 'The divine wise men of old invented this birthchart of the universe so that it would be an example for astrologers to follow in the charts of men.'[884]

JOHN GADBURY'S WORLD NATIVITY

In his *Collection of Nativities*, published in London in 1662, John Gadbury included a discussion of the various dates chosen by

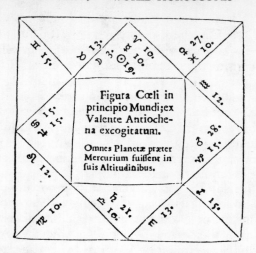

336: John Gadbury's World Nativity (*Collectio Genitarum*, p. 1)
Above: The horoscope as it appears in the original text.
Below: In the modern style.

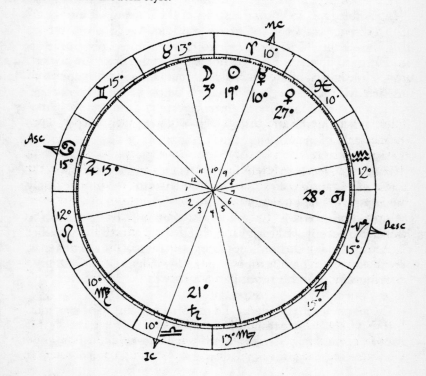

astrologers for the beginning of the world. [885] He reported opinions
to the effect that the world was created with the Sun at 4° Aries,
19° Aries, 0° Leo or 0° Libra. However, Gadbury follows closely upon
Firmicus by denying the possibility of a horoscope based on an exact
moment for the creation.

Unlike Firmicus, Gadbury believed in the creation of the world
by God, but did not believe that this occurred at a particular moment
in the year, but rather that all seasons were created simultaneously.
This is an interesting argument which could lead to the conclusion
that all times were created simultaneously, and that past, present
and future exist contemporaneously.

Gadbury therefore chose a symbolic horoscope for his world nativity
(Chart 336), following Firmicus in placing the Ascendant at 15°
Cancer, but instead of locating the planets in their diurnal dignities
he placed them in their exaltation degrees, all that is except Mercury.
Clearly, Gadbury was imitating Firmicus by erecting a horoscope
of symbolic power which was intended as a model of perfection, so
why was Mercury not placed in its exaltation?

The astrologer himself gives us the answer when he denies that
it is possible truly to know the secret of the universe: if even Jesus
Christ did not know the end of the world how could any man have
this knowledge? 'The gods', he wrote, 'our minds do muddle up
in clouds.' [886] To cast the perfect horoscope would therefore be both
impossible and by inference, blasphemous, and Gadbury therefore
inserted a deliberate flaw into the chart: Mercury, ruler of knowledge,
wisdom and Reason, is in the 'intemperate and violent' [887] sign of
Aries, indicating the arrogance which makes men wish to penetrate
the mysteries of the universe, and is itself weakened by being under
the Sun's Beams. [888]

The astrologer cleverly tells his readers that the erection of a world
horoscope is a futile exercise, and uses the chart to demonstrate firmly
the arguments he puts more mildly in his text.

In its fundamentals, Gadbury's horoscope was copied from the
World Horoscope of Rossigliano, itself a reproduction of earlier
Sassanian and Indian horoscopes for the great man or the first man
(see below — 'The Creation of Man' — Chart 341) Gadbury's
contribution lay in his moving of Mercury to the Midheaven, and
his curious but subtle interpretation.

The argument that Gadbury did not place Mercury in its exaltation
degree because it is astronomically impossible for it to be in this
place while the Sun is in its exaltation, is not relevant as the horoscope
is based on symbolism, not astronomy.

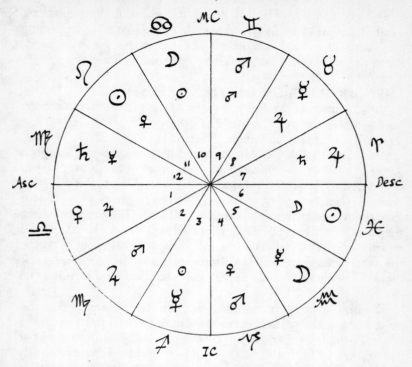

337: Sepharial's World Horoscope for AD 2000. Planets to the outside of the circle are the main house rulers, those on the inside are the secondary rulers.

SEPHARIAL'S WORLD HOROSCOPE

A modern attempt to create a world horoscope by Sepharial was based, like those of Firmicus and Gadbury, on symbolism rather than a fixed point of the creation. Sepharial focused his work on cycles of time based on the number 36 (in accordance with Babylonian and Platonic tradition) through which the planets and signs move in reverse or direct order.[889] Each thirty-six-year period is ruled by a single horoscope with each year having its own sub-horoscope. The charts are arranged so that each house contains two planets, a major ruler and a minor ruler, and the interpretation is then carried out in accordance with the basic principles of astrology, the sign and house positions of the planets, and the signs on the angles, being the critical factors.

The horoscope given here (Chart 337) is the sub-horoscope for the year 2000, the symbolic beginning of the twenty-first century.

The horoscope may be adapted to individual nations by taking the traditional national ruling sign as the rising sign at the beginning of a thirty-six-year sub-period. For example in the case of England, the rising sign would be Aries, the Ptolemaic ruler.

THE WORLD HOROSCOPE OF ALLAEUS

In a 1932 edition of the *British Journal of Astrology*, Vivian Robson outlined the theory of a world horoscope he attributed to the seventeenth-century astrologer Allaeus.[981]

According to Robson, Allaeus based his horoscope on an epoch dated to 3960 BC, assuming that at that time the Sun was at exactly 0° Gemini at the vernal equinox (presumably Allaeus was using the sidereal zodiac, revealing a rare early interest in precession). Allaeus fixed the Ascendant at the 'last degree' of Taurus. Three of the planets, the Sun, Mercury and Mars were located at 0° Aries, the traditional location of all the planets at the junction of a world age. However, the other planets were all in different signs — the Moon was at 0° Libra, Venus at 0° Taurus, Saturn at 0° Aquarius and Jupiter at 0° Pisces.

The horoscope was not static, but could be progressed. Robson believed that the planets themselves were to be kept in the same places (although other astrologers might consider using transits or progressions), but that the Ascendant progressed backwards through the zodiac at a rate of 1° in twelve years.

Apparently Allaeus dated his second epoch to the traditional beginning of the Christian era in 0 AD. He claimed that the planets occupied exactly the same degrees as at the first epoch (Robson does not reveal whether they had moved in the intervening period) while the Ascendant was at 0° Gemini, also exactly conjunct its position in 3960 BC.

However, this position is inconsistent with the earlier statement that the Ascendant progresses through the zodiac at the rate of 1° in twelve years. At this rate the true position would have been 0° Cancer in 0 AD and the accompanying horoscope (Chart 338) is set for this degree, and with equal houses. Robson does not state whether Allaeus had a preferred system, and if so, whether to adjust the Midheaven and intermediate cusps for varying altitudes, but this issue is raised by Allaeus's use of aspects to planets from the progressed house cusps. It is clear that every 330 years the progressed cusps will aspect all the planets, bringing critical historical points. Since 0 AD such points have occurred in the years 330, 660, 990, 1320, 1650 and 1980. The progressed Ascendant for 1988 is 14° 20' Capricorn,

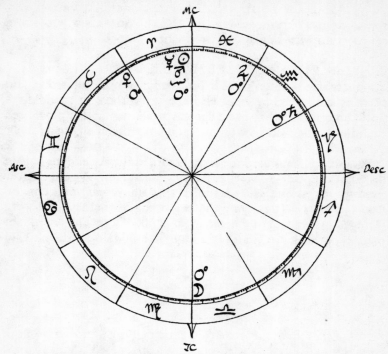

338: The World Horoscope for AD 0 According to Allaeus and Vivian Robson. The Ascendant for 1988 is 14° 20′ Capricorn.

approximately midway between two such critical points.

Each country also has its own horoscope derived from the world horoscope. National horoscopes are worked out in the following way. Assuming that the equator is equivalent to a celestial longitude of 12° Cancer, each two degrees of north latitude are then equivalent to a deviation of 1° of celestial longitude. The latitude of the capital city then provides the national Ascendant, and when the World Ascendant progresses over this same degree, the national horoscope is activated. From that date the national Ascendant then progresses backwards at a rate of 1° every six years.

According to Robson, Spain's national horoscope was activated in the year 742 and England's in 801, but this is inconsistent with the rules given. For example, England's capital, London, occupies a latitude of 51° 31′ North, giving a deviation from the Equator of 25° 45′ of celestial longitude and a national Ascendant of 7° 45′ Leo (or if northerly latitudes move backwards through the zodiac, of 16° 15′ Gemini). Yet in AD 801, the world Ascendant was, according to Robson's account, at 23° 15′ Aries, nowhere near a conjunction with England's Ascendant.

E. H. BAILEY'S UNIVERSAL HOROSCOPE

Two years after Robson's article on Allaeus's world horoscope, and perhaps influenced by it, E. H. Bailey published his model for a world horoscope, which like Allaeus's, was dynamic, but progressed according to the precession of the equinoxes rather than to a symbolic measure.[982]

Whereas Allaeus used the vernal point as the Ascendant only in his original Epoch of 2960 BC, Bailey's Ascendant was permanently fixed to precession. Bailey assumed that the vernal point entered Pisces in AD 321 (signifying the beginning of the Age of Pisces), giving an Ascendant in the same year of 30° Pisces. The Ascendant then progresses backwards through the zodiac at the rate of

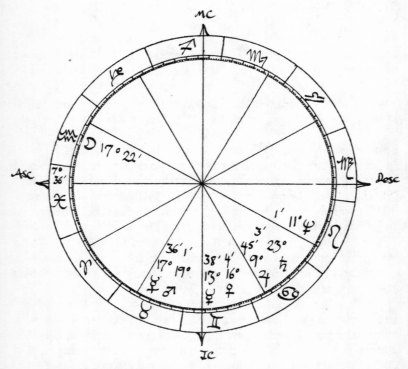

339: E. H. Bailey's Universal Horoscope for 1934.

precession, about one degree every seventy-two years. The planets themselves progress according to the positions of their respective ascending (i.e. north) nodes.

The accompanying horoscope (Chart 339) is Bailey's universal horoscope for 1934. The Ascendant is due to enter Aquarius in the year 2481, the year in which Bailey believed that the Age of Aquarius would begin.

It will be noticed that the horoscope does not include the Sun and Pluto. The Sun, by definition does not have any nodes, and cannot be included, although since the Ascendant is fixed by the vernal point, the Sun's sidereal location at the vernal equinox, the Ascendant itself is a solar point.

The reason for Pluto's non-inclusion is more mundane. The planet had only been discovered four years previously, and was clearly not in general use.

THE BIBLICAL CREATION OF THE WORLD

When in 1662 John Gadbury published his gentle rebuke of those who dared to calculate the horoscope of the world, he was probably aware of the work of James Ussher, Bishop of Armagh and Primate of Ireland. In 1658 Ussher had published his *The Annals of the World*, in which he had worked out an exact chronology for every event in the bible. Ussher worked out that the creation began at the beginning of the night preceding 23 October 4004 BC,[895] that is, 6.00 p.m. on 22 October.[896] Chart 340 is set for this date,* for 6.00 p.m. LMT, and, in the absence of any specification by Ussher, for Jerusalem, the symbolic and spiritual centre of the Christian world. Ussher's chronology was widely accepted by the Anglican Church, and a chart set for 6.00 p.m. LMT for London (or perhaps for Canterbury), the focus of the Church of England, might also be of interest.

Like Gadbury, Ussher was well aware of the classical astrological interest in the horoscope of the world, and quoted the work of Firmicus Maternus.[985]

The fact that the Ascendant and Midheaven in this horoscope occupy 28° Pisces and 29° Sagittarius respectively, in this computer-calculated version, suggests that Ussher's intention was that the Ascendant should be 0° Aries and the Midheaven 0° Capricorn. This would accord with the astrological tradition of world horoscopes.

* Note that, according to Astro Computing Services, −4003 is equivalent to 4004 BC.

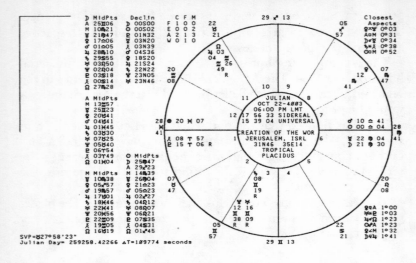

340: The Biblical Creation of the World, 4004 BC

THE CREATION OF MAN

The earliest example of a horoscope for the ideal man predates Firmicus's horoscope for the ideal world by over a hundred years and is dated to AD 269/70 in India. The Indian horoscope of the ideal great man (Mahapurusa) placed all the planets in their exaltations, with the possible exception of Mercury. The Indian practice was taken over by the Sassanians, rulers of Persia, who used this horoscope as that of Gayomart, the first man, whose birth was taken to coincide with the beginning of all planetary motion.[986] The Sassanians used the Greek exaltation degrees, which differ from the Indian, and it is in this form that the horoscope found its way into a work by an early sixteenth-century astrologer, Tiberio Rossigliano Sisto of Calabria. Rossigliano presented the horoscope as that of the world, although it is included here (Chart 344) as an early view of the archetypal horoscope of man.

It was not until the seventeenth century that a supposedly objective attempt was made to work out the exact minute of man's creation by God. In 1642 Dr John Lightfoot, a biblical scholar, published *A Few and New Observations upon the Booke of Genesis* in which he wrote that 'Man [was] created by the Trinity about the third hour of the day, or nine of the clocke in the morning.'[987] It is likely that Lightfoot was familiar with Ussher's work (see above — 'The Biblical Creation'),[988] or that both men were familiar with common sources.

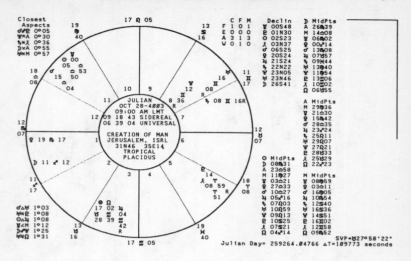

341: The Biblical Creation of Man, 4004 BC

The Book of Genesis claims that man was created on the sixth day, which in Ussher's chronology corresponds to Friday, 28 October 4004 BC in the Julian calendar. By reconciling the two chronologies it is found that man was created at 9.00 a.m. on 28 October 4004 BC, and Chart 341 is set for this data.* Probably Lightfoot envisaged the creation taking place in the Garden of Eden, but in the absence of precise geographical co-ordinates for this fabled land, the chart is set for LMT in Jerusalem, the symbolic focus of Christianity. However, a horoscope set for England might be more evocative of Lightfoot's intentions.

RENAISSANCE WORLD HOROSCOPES
World horoscopes were published during the Renaissance, often purporting to be based on earlier traditions, and maintaining the critical importance of the cardinal degrees. For example, Tiberio Rossigliano in the 1510s published a horoscope for the world according to 'the Jews and Chaldeans' (Chart 342) and another (Chart 343) according to 'the Arabs and Egyptians'.[993] Mercury was omitted from the original of Chart 343.

---

* Note that, according to Astro Computing Services, −4003 is equivalent to 4004 BC.

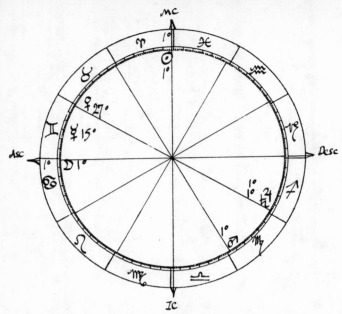

342: World Horoscope 'According to the Jews and Chaldeans'.

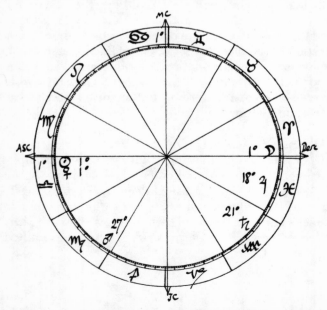

343: World Horoscopes 'According to the Arabs and Egyptians'.

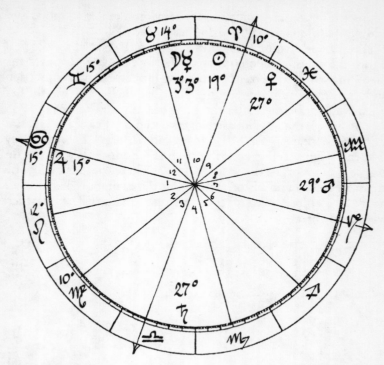

344: Sassanian Horoscope for the First Man. Saturn is shown at 27° Libra, whereas its exaltation degree is 21° Libra. This may be a transcription error. Similarly with Mars. A touch of astronomical accuracy is added by removing Mercury from its exaltation degree, which places it an impossible distance from the Sun. However, its conjunction with the Moon is clearly of symbolic importance (the birth of Reason?).

THE HOROSCOPE OF MAN

Parallel with the tradition of world horoscopes existed a practice of casting horoscopes for man. The Indians used a horoscope for the 'Great Man', taken up later by the Sassanians, rulers of Persia, in a form which clearly provided a model, if an indirect one, for Gadbury's world horoscope. Chart 344 is the Sassanian horoscope for the First Man.[993]

WORLD EPOCHS — THE ERA OF NABONASSAR

The great Muslim astrologers of the ninth to twelfth centuries, such as Al Biruni, Abu Mashar and Masha'Allah, devoted much of their time to working out a comprehensive theory of astrological history, taking earlier sources from Greece, Babylon, Persia and India, and adding additional detail and sophistication.

History was divided into epochs, each with its own astrological signification, usually demonstrated through the horoscopes of the preceding vernal equinox, the preceding Jupiter–Saturn conjunction and the vernal equinox preceding that. One such epoch was the Era of Nabonassar, named after the King of Babylon from 747 to 735 BC. Although the Muslim astrologers dated the Era of Nabonassar from 26 February 746 BC,[989] Cyril Fagan has argued convincingly that the origins of this epoch were closely bound up with certain astrological events in the year 786 BC.[990] There could therefore be an astronomical and historical basis for the exaltation degrees and hence for all those charts for the ideal man or the ideal world which have used these.

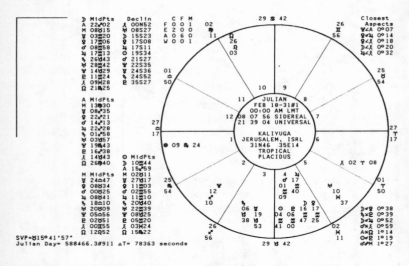

345: The Biblical Flood; the Commencement of the Kali Yuga

WORLD EPOCHS — THE GREAT FLOOD

The epoch of which the Era of Nabonassar formed a sub-division was believed by the Muslims, Al Biruni, Abu Ma'shar and Masha'Allah, to have commenced with the great world deluge known in the Bible as the Flood of Noah and preserved in Mesopotamian tradition in the Epic of Gilgamesh. It was thought that the rains which brought the flood commenced exactly at dawn on Friday, 18 February 3101 BC. It was agreed, however, that the epoch that commenced with the flood began at exactly midnight (00.00 hrs) on 18 February and the chart given here (Chart 345) is set for this data.[991]

Added significance was given to this event by the adaptation of traditions from other cultures. From the Greeks was taken the concept of the Platonic Great Year which began with a conjunction of all the planets at their creation points, and it was assumed that at 00.00 hrs on 18 February all the planets were in a mean conjunction at 0° Aries. From Persian and Indian tradition was taken the concept of the Kaliyuga, a length of time the Muslims determined as 360,000 years (although the Indians reckon it as 432,000 years). The horoscope given here is therefore a chart for the biblical Flood, the current Great Year and the Current Kaliyuga synthesized into one by the Muslims. It is important to remember that this chart has been recalculated with the original data and it is not as the Muslims would have seen it. Although the Muslim horoscopes for some other epochs, especially for the birth of Christ, passed into European use, medieval astrologers do not seem to have expressed much interest in this chart. In 1658 Bishop Ussher calculated that the rains of the deluge began on Sunday, 7 December 2348 BC in the Julian calendar.[992]

The concept of the Kaliyuga was revived by Madame Blavatsky, the founder of Theosophy. Blavatsky propounded the view that the age was about to come to an end and that the world was approaching the New Age. This belief was translated into the conviction that the Age of Aquarius was approaching (see below).

THE CHRISTIAN ERA — HOROSCOPES FOR CHRIST

Now when Jesus was born in Bethlehem of Judea in the days of Herod the King, behold, wise men from the East came to Jerusalem, saying, 'Where is he who has been born king of the Jews? For we have seen his star in the East, and have come to worship him.'

Matthew 2: 1–3

Jesus said to them, 'Why do you discuss the fact that you have no bread? Do you not understand? Are your hearts hardened? Having eyes do you not see, and having ears do you not hear? And do you not remember? When I broke the five loaves for the five thousand, and how many baskets full of broken pieces did you take up?' They said to him, 'Twelve'. 'And the seven for the four thousand, how many baskets full of broken pieces did you take up?' And they said to him, 'Seven'. And he said to them, 'Do you still not understand?'

Mark 8: 17–21

The Muslim astrologers accepted the birth of Christ as the beginning of a major epoch of world history, and set out to explain and analyse this astrologically. Masha'Allah is one whose work has survived.

There is no record of Masha'Allah calculating the nativity of Christ, perhaps because the relevant work has been lost or destroyed, perhaps because he considered it blasphemous to do so, or perhaps because he focused on astronomical events rather than events on earth as the basis for horoscopes. Masha'Allah calculated the horoscopes for the vernal equinox preceding the Jupiter–Saturn conjunction in Sagittarius of 45 BC, indicating the Christ, the vernal equinox preceding the Jupiter–Saturn conjunction in Leo of 25 BC, indicating

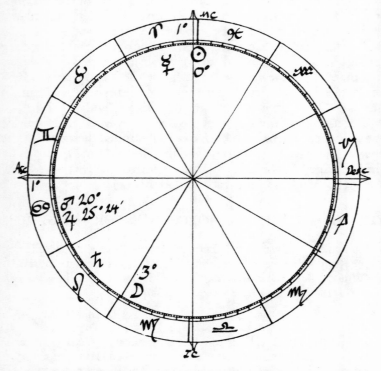

346: The Horoscope Indicating the Nativity of Christ[1008] According to Masha'Allah (the horoscope for the vernal equinox prior to the Jupiter–Saturn conjunction of 25 BC). Venus was not included on the original, and Mercury and Saturn were not given exact degrees. When the positions were recalculated by Kennedy and Pingree it was found that the Moon was at 2° Virgo, Mercury at 26° Aquarius, Venus at 21° Aries, the Sun at 21° Pisces, Mars at 3° Cancer, Jupiter at 21° Cancer and Saturn at 29° Cancer.

the nativity of Christ, and the vernal equinox for 12 BC, the supposed year of Christ's birth.[1008]

The horoscope given here (Chart 346) is that for the vernal equinox preceding the Jupiter–Saturn conjunction in Leo, and is notable for its connections to the series of world horoscopes and Alan Leo's horoscope indicating the world teacher (see 'The Age of Aquarius'). Like so many of the world horoscopes, this chart has 1° Cancer rising, picking up the point at which ancient Babylonian tradition held that a cataclysm would occur by fire. The main indications of the prophet are found in the location of the Sun on the Midheaven in a fiery trine to Saturn and to be in a fiery trine with Jupiter once it makes its conjunction with Saturn. There was also an Islamic tradition that prophets were born with the Sun conjunct the Ascendant at 0° Cancer.

In the previous horoscope for the vernal equinox prior to the Jupiter–Saturn conjunction in Sagittarius the indications of the arrival of a prophet had been stronger. The Sun, Mercury and the Ascendant

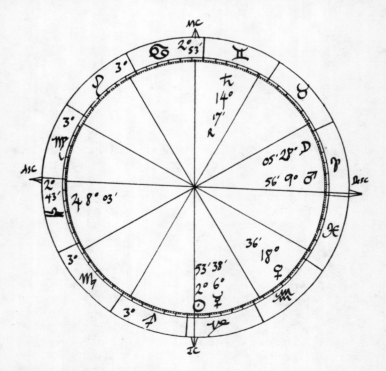

347: Cardan's Horoscope for Christ

in Aries had been in a trine to Saturn in Sagittarius in the ninth
house, ruler of religion (even though according to strict rules the
birth of a prophet was indicated by a conjunction in the tenth house).

A brief study of the later European desire to cast the nativity of
Christ is contained in J. D. North's *Horoscopes and History*,[1009]
focusing on the connections between these charts and those for the
series of world nativities. Through these charts runs a strong tendency
to retain the early degrees of the cardinal signs on the angles, although
some astrologers did make a break with this practice. Chart 347,
erected by Cardan, an astrologer active in the late fifteenth and early
sixteenth centuries, proved to be quite influential in this respect.
The most popular chart amongst English astrologers was that
supposedly cast by Dr John Butler, chaplain to James, Duke of
Ormonde and published in 1671,[1010] reproduced here as Chart 348.
On closer inspection it is clear that contrary to the impression he
managed to convey to English astrologers, all Butler had done was
to rectify Cardan's birth time for Christ.

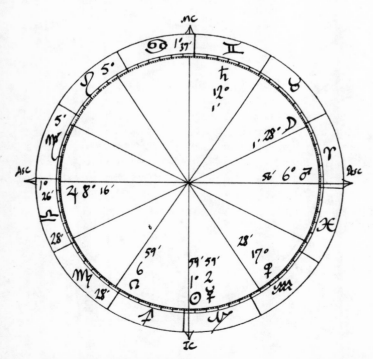

348: John Butler's Horoscope for Christ

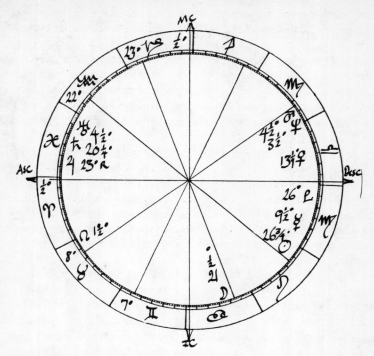

349: John Addey's Horoscope for Christ

The most recent horoscope produced for Christ was that calculated by the late John Addey and reproduced in his *Selected Writings*.[1011] Addey recalculated the horoscope using astronomical data and assuming that the famous 'Star of Bethlehem' was the Jupiter–Saturn conjunction in Pisces of 7 BC, an interesting throwback to the concerns of Masha'Allah and the Muslims. Addey also retained the symbolically significant early degrees of the cardinal signs on the angles.

THE AGE OF AQUARIUS
The belief in the coming of the Age of Aquarius is a relatively recent one, extending back no further than the late nineteenth century, but derived from a far more ancient millennarian tradition in which great epochs in history were marked out by astrological phenomena.

Prior to the seventeenth century a belief in the great precessional ages was contrary to the fundamentals of astrology which argued that the fixed stars were immovable and immutable (even though

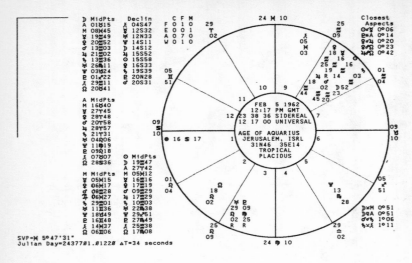

350: Age of Aquarius (1), Jeanne Dixon's Chart for the Anti-Christ

the theory of precession was understood from the works of Hipparchus and Ptolemy). If they precessed this would undermine the belief system of the time, and so it was only with the revival of astrology

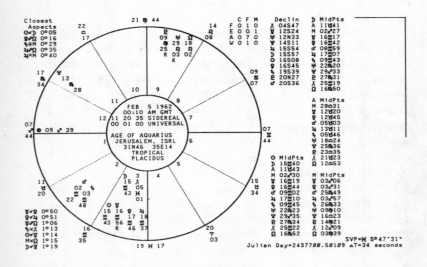

351: Age of Aquarius (2), New Moon 5 February 1962

that the theory of the great ages of Pisces, Aquarius and so on, was developed.

In spite of the fact that I have in my possession some seventy dates for the beginning of the Age of Aquarius over a period of 1,500 years, it has only been possible to locate a few feasible horoscopes for the beginning of the Age.

Before proceeding it is best to call to mind Charles Carter's opinion that 'It is probable that there is no branch of Astrology upon which more nonsense has been poured forth than the doctrine of the precession of the equinoxes.'[897]

THE WORK OF ELBERT BENJAMIN
One horoscope for the Age of Aquarius is that taken from the work of Elbert Benjamin (C. C. Zain) who, on the basis that there are 1881 pyramid inches in the base of the Great Pyramid, concluded that the Aquarian Age began at the Sun's entry into tropical Aquarius at 3.48.24 p.m. LMT on 19 January 1881 in Washington.[898] John Addey experimented with this data, recasting it for various capital cities in Europe and in a letter to Charles Harvey described the results as 'pretty staggering'.[899]

1962 — CHRIST OR ANTI-CHRIST?
In the 1890s the French hoaxer Gabriel Jogand created the myth of an anti-Christ to be born in 1962 as a deliberate fraud to upset superstitious Catholics, but Jogand's trick has found a curious echo in recent times.[900]

On 5 February 1962 noted American clairvoyant Jeanne Dixon had a vision that somewhere in the Middle East a baby was born who would become a world teacher, but who would lead humanity away from Christianity — he would be the anti-Christ. Dixon glanced at her clock at 7.17 a.m. and assumed that the child had been born shortly after 7.00 a.m.[901] At the time Dixon was in Washington, so her vision occurred at 12.17 p.m. GMT and the horoscope given here, Chart 350, is set for this time on 5 February 1962, and for Jerusalem, the symbolic centre of Christianity.

It was later commentators who assumed that the birth of Dixon's baby symbolized the beginning of the Age of Aquarius, and transformed the anti-Christ into the World Teacher,[902] perhaps equivalent to the Maitreya of Theosophical and related groups. Dixon's time therefore becomes the basis of a horoscope for the Age of Aquarius.

It just so happens that at 00.10 hrs GMT on 5 February 1962 there was a solar eclipse at 15° Aquarius, at which time every one of the traditional seven planets was in this sign (Chart 351). According to all the tenets of astrology this event should mark a major turning point in history, and is a far more logical time to take for the beginning of the Age of Aquarius (if such a thing exists) than any of the times supposedly based on precession. In India 5 February was greeted with panic by those who believed the eclipse heralded some great cataclysm. It did not, but in retrospect it is not difficult to relate this horoscope to some of the major changes in the world during the late decades of the twentieth century.[902a]

ALAN LEO AND THE WORLD TEACHER

When Jogand perpetrated his anti-Christ hoax in the 1890s the members of the Theosophical Society, founded in 1875, were looking forward to the coming of the new World Teacher, known variously as the Christ or the Lord Maitreya.

Alan Leo was a devoted Theosophist, and during a visit to the Theosophical headquarters at Adyar in India in 1911, participated in the founding of an organization known as the Order of the Rising Sun, a name later to be changed to the more familiar Order of the Star in the East. The organization, founded on 11 January 1911, was headed by Krishnamurti, then believed to be the vehicle of the Lord Maitreya, bearing the same relationship to him as John the Baptist to Jesus Christ.

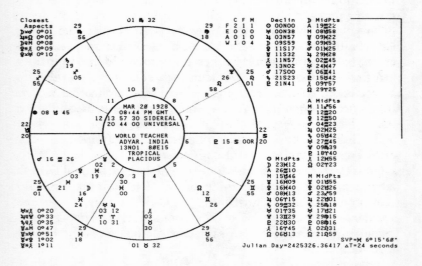

352: Age of Aquarius (3), Alan Leo's chart for the World Teacher

On his return to England Leo reported the founding of the Order in his journal, *Modern Astrology*, and speculated that the Aries Ingress of 21 March 1928 would bring either the World Teacher himself, or at least a further stage in the religious preparations for his coming. Leo was impressed by the grand trine (albeit loose) between the Sun, Jupiter, Saturn, Uranus and Neptune, and by the fact that Saturn was in Sagittarius, the ninth (i.e. religious) sign.[983] Similar configurations were noted by Masha'Allah in his horoscopes concerning Christ (see above).

Leo himself did not mention the Age of Aquarius, but his wife Bessie did. In 1925 she wrote that the anticipated appearance of the Christ/Lord Maitreya/World Teacher in 1928 would herald the beginning of the Age of Aquarius.[984]

The accompanying horoscope (Chart 353) is set for the solar ingress into Aries of 1928, and for the symbolically important location of Adyar, the Theosophical headquarters in India. Leo himself had referred to the ingress of 21 March 1928 even though the GMT date was 20 March. This could be either because he expected the ingress to be on the 21st, this being the usual date, and did not check, or because he had also cast a horoscope for Adyar, the ingress occurring there on the 21st.

THE START OF THE AGE OF AQUARIUS

By definition the 'Age of Aquarius' begins when the First Point of Aries in the tropical zodiac precesses either into the equal thirty degree division of the sidereal sign of Aquarius or into the unequal sidereal constellation of Aquarius. The moment this occurs will depend on exactly where the boundary of this sign or constellation is fixed. Opinion varies considerably from school to school and astrologer to astrologer, as witnessed by the wide variations in Ayanamshas (the difference between 0° Aries in the tropical and sidereal zodiacs) in use in India and elsewhere.

The following list is an update of that originally given in *Mundane Astrology*,[1012] and is a compilation of the various dates for the beginning of the Age of Aquarius either given or implied by astrologers. When the date is not taken from a stated text but is calculated on the basis of the author's Ayanamsha or other information, this may mean that the date given may be slightly different to that intended by the author. This is due to the differing rates of precession employed by different authors. The rate of precession assumed in such cases is 50.25″ per annum. The true rate of precession is $50.2564 + 0.0222T$ arc seconds per annum where

T is the time in Julian Centuries from 1900.[1045]

Some of the following dates are not based on astronomical measurement but on a symbolic reading of world history.

1762   Cheiro, *Book of World Predictions*, p. 170.

1789   Mme Blavatsky, the founder of Theosophy, cited in an editorial in *AQ*, Vol. 9, no. 2, p. 52, June 1935.

1811   (January) Quoted in *Prediction Annual*, 1983, p. 85.

1844   David Williams in *The Aquarian Age, AJ*, Vol. XX, no. 1, 1977/78.

1881   Sepharial, quoted in David Williams, op. cit.; Elbert Benjamin (C. C. Zain — see accompanying text, Chart 332; W. P. Swaison in *The Occult Review* (February 1925), quoted in Julius Bennet, *The Riddle of the Aquarian Age*, p. 20, published by the London Astrological Research Society, 1926.

1900   Gerald Massey in *The Hebrew and Other Creations* quoted by H. S. Green in *Modern Astrology*, April 1912; Magazine of the American Rosae Crucis, cited by correspondent in *BJA*, September 1916, Vol. IX, no. 12.

1904   Alistair Crowley, in *The Book of the Law*, p. 12. Crowley was not referring directly to the Age of Aquarius but to his own version of the New Age, a New Aeon of 2,000 years ruled by the Egyptian solar deity, Horus. *The Book of the Law* was dedicated between noon and 1.00 p.m. in Cairo on 8–10 April 1904 (p. 5). Interestingly, L. Ron Hubbard, the founder of Scientology, who was drawn into Crowley's circle in 1945, was interested in establishing this New Aeon (see John Symonds, *The Great Beast*, pp. 446, 451). Scientology may therefore be seen as one attempt to promote the New Age, even though most 'New Agers' may not like the implications of this.

1905   Gerald Massey, assuming a starting date for the Age of Pisces in 255 BC and a rate of precession of 30° in 2,160 years, cited by Dane Rudhyar in *Astrological Timing: The Transition to the New Age*, San Francisco, NY and London 1969. Rudhyar himself used this rate of precession (see p. 115).

1911   (28 December) Jean Overton Fuller in *AQ*, Vol. 56, no. 4, p. 140. This was the date when Lord Maitreya first spoke through Krishnamurti, regarded by Jean Overton Fuller as 'the day the dawn of the Age of Aquarius began'. This moment could be used as the basis for an additional horoscope for the New Age. See also 1928, below.

1927   Elizabeth Aldrich in *MA*, Vol. 37, no. 2, p. 53, 1926. Aldrich was citing the ingress of Uranus into Aquarius in 1927, and the horoscope for this moment could be an additional horoscope for the New Age. However, in 1927 Uranus entered Aries, having been in Aquarius between 1912 and 1920. It is possible Aldrich had her dates muddled up, or that she meant Aries rather than Aquarius, perhaps from the symbolism of the new ruler of Aquarius entering the first sign of the zodiac.

1928   (vernal equinox) Alan and Bessie Leo. See accompanying text, Chart 352.

1930s   Alice Bailey, *The Externalisation of the Hierarchy*, pp. 3, 4, 567.

1962   (5 February) John Sturgess, *The Piscean Age and the Aquarian Age*, p. 1. See accompanying text, Charts 350 and 351. See also John Sedgwick, *Harmonics of History* (New York, 1985).

1969   (10.56 p.m. EDT, 16 July) Alan Oken. This was the moment when Neil Armstrong became the first man to step on the Moon (see Appendix 7). Oken does not regard this as the literal beginning of the Age of Aquarius, but as the critical symbolic moment during the cuspal period between the Ages of Pisces and Aquarius (lecture given at Astrological Lodge of London, 23 March 1987).

1975   Quoted in A. Woldben, *After Nostradamus*, p. 24.

1977   (19 July) Angela Borodzicz, cited in *AQ*, Vol. 56, no. 4, p. 140.

1980   (approx.) Rabbi Joel Dobin in *The Astrological Secrets of the Hebrew Sages* (1983), p. 65.

1980-81 W. Baron, *AQ*, Winter 1983.

1982   Charles Berlitz in *Doomsday 1999 AD*, p. 39 (London, 1981). Berlitz associated this date with the dire predictions given in Gribbin and Plageman, *The Jupiter Effect*.

1983   (approx.) Nefert (pseudonym), *MA*, Vol. 23 (Vol. 9 new series), no. 10, p. 439, October 1912.

1997   C. G. Jung, *The Sign of the Fishes*, in Collected Works, Vol.
-2200   9, Part 2; *Aion*, Chapter 6, p. 92. As Hand points out (see 2813, below), Nostradamus was part of the inspiration for Jung's thinking.

1998   (January) Pamela M. Strauss, 'House Movement to Allow for the Precession of the Equinoxes', *CAO Times*, 1984, Vol. 6, no. 1, p. 37.

2000   Quoted in A. Woldben, op. cit., p. 24; Alfred Jeremias, *Handbuch der Altorientalischen Geisteskultur*, 2nd edn., (Berlin and Leipzig, 1929), pp. 240–2, assuming that the Age of Gemini began in 6200 BC, the Age of Taurus in 4400 BC, the Age of Aries in 2200 BC, and the Age of Pisces in 100 BC, A. E. Thierens, *Astrology in Mesopotamian Culture* (Leiden, Brill, 1935), p. 15; Trygne Kougshady in *MA*, Vol. 33, no. 8, p. 254, August 1932, assuming the Age of Pisces began in AD 498 and a rate of precession of 54″ per annum. Margarate Hone, *The Modern Textbook of Astrology*, p. 279 gives 'about AD 2000' as a symbolic date. P. V. Neugebauer in *Astronomische Chronologie*, Vol. I, p. 27.

2010   Peter Lemesurier, *The Gospel of the Stars* (Compton Press, Tisbury, 1977), p. 48, citing the French Institut Geographique.

2012   Jose Arguelles, *The Mayan Factor*, pp. 145, 175. Arguelles relates his own system of cycles to precession without explicitly mentioning the Age of Aquarius. Arguelles' work was the inspiration for the 'Harmonic Convergence' of 16-17 August 1987 (recalculated by the Mayan calendar as occurring in 1988).

2023   A. Woldben, op. cit., p. 24.

2035   Thierens, cited by Dane Rudhyar, op. cit., assuming the Age of Pisces began in 125 BC.

2059   Dane Rudhyar in *The Lunation Cycle*, p. 149.

2070   Kugler, *In Bannkreis Babels* (Munster, 1910), p. 149, assuming the Age of Gemini began in 6534 BC the Age of Taurus in 4383 BC and the Age of Aries in 2252 BC.

2130   Quoted in A. Woldben, op. cit., p. 24.

2156   Cited in *Prediction Annual*, 1983, p. 85.

2159   (August) Robert de Luce, *Constellational Astrology According to the Hindu System*.

2160   Charles Carter, *Introduction to Political Astrology*, p. 76; Vera Reid, *Towards Aquarius*, p. 8; Paul Councel, *Your Stars of Destiny*, quoted by David Williams, op. cit.

2260   Gavin Arthur, quoted in James Webb, *The Occult Establishment* (1981), p. 454.

2299   *Waite's Compendium of Natal Astrology* cited in Bennet, op. cit.

2320   Zip Dobyns, *The Zodiac as a Key to History*, p. 24.

2321   *Waite's Compendium of Natal Astrology*, cited in Bennet, op. cit.

2325   (approx.) W. Hamaker in *The Theosophist*, cited by Bennet, op. cit.

2360   Rupert Gleadow, *Your Character in the Zodiac* (London, 1968), p. 137.

2369   Cyril Fagan, *Zodiacs Old and New*, p. 29.

2370   Gleadow, op. cit., p. 137.

2375-6 Powell and Treadgold, *The Sidereal Zodiac*; Cyril Fagan in *AFA Bulletin*, March 1950, quoted in David Williams, op. cit. Powell in *AJ* March–April 1987, p. 92.

2395   Graha Lghav, quoted in S. Rajagopola Iyer, *Directions in New Age Astrology*, p. 332. The author's calculations suggest June.

late 24th century   Peter Nockolds on the basis of Robert Hand's work (see below).

2432   Based on Lahiri's Ephemeris Ayanamsha, quoted in Iyer, op. cit., p. 332. The author's calculations suggest October.

2441   Based on Chitra Ayanamsha and L. Narain Roa Ayanamsha, quoted in Iyer, op. cit., p. 332. The author's calculations suggest April for the former Ayanamsha and December for the latter.

2449   Sepharial, *Why the War Will End in 1917*. Sepharial actually refers to the coming of the 'blessed Millennium', rather than to the Age of Aquarius, although the latter is the subject of concern.

2480   Calculated by Peter Nockolds on the basis of the star calendar zodiac used by followers of Rudolf Steiner. See *AQ*, Vol. 6.

2481   vernal equinox: Sepharial, *The World Horoscope*, p. 59, assuming the Age of Pisces started in AD 321; E. H. Bailey, according to report of lecture given by him in *BJA*, August 1939, p. 200, and article in *BJA*, Vol. 27, no. 5, p. 88. See also E. H. Bailey, 'The Universal Horoscope' in *BJA*, Vol. 27 no. 6, p. 107, March 1934, in which he also assumes the Age of Pisces commenced in AD 321.

2500   David Davidson, cited by David Williams, op. cit.

2521   Quoted by B. V. Raman, *A Manual of Hindu Astrology*, p. 51.

2455   Based on Madras Ephemeris Ayanamsha, quoted in Iyer, op. cit. The author's calculations suggest February.

2554   Quoted in B. V. Raman, op. cit., p. 51.

2557   ibid., p. 51. Walter Koch regarded this as the earliest possible starting date, *In Search*, Vol. II, no. 2, Spring 1959, pp. 80–81.

2568   'According to the Rosicrucians', quoted by Bennet, op. cit., p. 22.

2594   (approx.) N. Chidambaram Iyer in *Brihat Samhita*, based on an Ayanamsha of 19° 26' 7" in 1910, quoted by Alan Leo in *MA*, April 1912.

2600   Calculated by Peter Nockolds on the basis of the International Astronomical Union's definition of the constellations in 1928, placing Aldaberan at 15° Taurus and adapting this to an equal sign Sidereal Zodiac. Letter to author.

2622   Sepharial in *MA*, Vol. 11, no. 1, p. 31, January 1902.

2640   From *Astrology for All*, cited by Bennet, op. cit.

2647   Sepharial, *Manual of Astrology* (London, 1967), p. 178, assuming the Age of Pisces started in AD 498, also quoted by H. S. Green in *MA*, April 1912, p. 139.

2656   Gavin Arthur, based on Max Heindel, assuming the Age of Pisces began in AD 496; see also Rudhyar, *Astrological Timing*.

2658   Max Heindel, *Simplified Scientific Astrology*, pp. 134–5; B. V. Raman, op. cit., p. 51.

2685   E. H. Bailey, *BJA*, Vol. XII, no. 3, December 1918.

2700   H. S. Green, speculating in *MA*, April 1912, on the basis of the theosophical theory of history.

2708   *MA*, Vol. 44, no. 5, p. 198, September–October 1933.

2715   Bennet, op. cit., p. 23, quoting unknown source.

2730   Walter Koch, quoting Burgess, *In Search*, Vol. II, no. 2, Spring 1959, p. 80.

2740   Margaret Hone, *The Modern Textbook of Astrology*, p. 279, 'by astronomical computation' (see 2000).

2753   (approx.) G. E. Sutcliffe, *The Hindu Zodiac*, based on Ayanamsha of 18° 9′ 13″ in 1900, quoted by Alan Leo in *MA*, April 1912.

2813   Robert Hand, *Essays on Astrology* (Para Research, 1982), Chapter 13, 'The Age and Constellation of Pisces'. This date, like Jung's (see 1997, above), is based on the precession of the Vernal Point through the actual irregular morphomaton constellation of Pisces, and not the regular 30° sidereal sign. It makes the Aries Point's contact with the westernmost marking star of the constellation, Beta Pisces, 'the Mouth of the Western Fish'.

3000+   Rupert Gleadow, *Origins of the Zodiac*, p. 171, based on figures given in Fagan, op. cit., p. 21, on the basis of Langdon's writing.

3278   This was the last possible date mentioned by Alan Leo in *MA*, March 1910, on the basis of a review of various Ayanamshas between 19° and 27° in 1910.

3550   Ernest Tied, in *MA*, Vol. 23 (Vol. 9 new series), no. 8, p. 356, August 1912. On p. 349 the Era of Nabonassar is cited as the beginning of the Age of Aries (see Appendix 9, 'World Epochs — The Era of Nabonassar', above).

THE DISCOVERY OF THE NEW PLANETS

It is accepted by most astrologers that the times of discovery of the new planets are significant. It has not been possible to include the horoscopes in this volume, but the data is given below.

Discovery of Uranus

According to Herschel's own account, he discovered Uranus at 'between ten and eleven in the evening' on Tuesday, 13 March 1781, in Bath. [1013]

Discovery of Neptune

Neptune was first sighted by Galle in the 'evening' of 23 September 1846 in Berlin. [1014] According to Nick Kollerstrom, who has researched the discovery for his 'Project Eureka', the actual date was 24 September and the time was 00.14 hrs LMT in Berlin. The existence of Neptune was first recorded by Galileo, who observed the planet at 3.00 a.m. LMT on 28 December 1612 in Florence, but mistakenly thought that the new body was a moon of Jupiter. [1015]

Discovery of Pluto

Pluto was first observed by Clyde Tombaugh at 4.00 p.m. on 18 February 1930 at the Lowell Observatory, Flagstaff, Arizona. [1016] The events leading up to the naming of Pluto were described by Patrick Moore in an article in *Sky and Telescope*, November 1984. The name was first mooted a few minutes after 8.00 a.m. on 14 March 1930 and formally accepted on 1 May. The 14 March horoscope shows Pluto exactly on the IC. [1017]

Discovery of Chiron

Chiron was first observed by Charles Kowal at about 10.00 a.m. PST on 1 November 1977 at Pasadena, California. [1018]

APPENDIX 10
INDEXES OF PLANETARY, ASCENDANT AND MIDHEAVEN DEGREES

There are a number of minor typographical errors and abbreviations in the following indexes, most of which are obvious, such as IND for Independence and REP for Republic. *Philippines, Guinea-Bissau, Burkina-Faso* and *Colombia* have all been spelt incorrectly, and for degree positions for charts for ENGLAND, see under horoscopes for the *United Kingdom* in the main text.

Please note that *Germany–East, Biblical Flood* and *Age of Aquarius 3* data has had to be omitted from these indexes due to their late insertion into the main text. Please refer to the individual charts for this information.

Positions given in the indexes for *Chiron* differ very slightly to those in the charts. This is due to the regular updating by Astro Computing Services of their data, and as a consequence the indexes show the most accurate information available.

PLANET-BY-PLANET INDEX

SUN ☉

0 ♈ 31	GUATEMALA - 3
2 ♈ 26	PAKISTAN, REPUBLIC
4 ♈ 28	GREECE REVOLUTION
4 ♈ 48	TREATY OF ROME
4 ♈ 56	BANGLADESH 1
5 ♈ 37	S.D.P.
11 ♈ 01	LONDON 2
11 ♈ 06	IRAN - ISLAMIC REP
14 ♈ 11	SIKKIM
15 ♈ 23	CHILE 2
15 ♈ 36	FAR EAST REPUBLIC
16 ♈ 31	THAILAND 1
22 ♈ 08	GAGARIN
22 ♈ 28	U.S. CIVIL WAR
23 ♈ 02	ROME
26 ♈ 35	BANGLADESH 2
27 ♈ 01	GUATEMALA - 2
27 ♈ 21	KAMPUCHEA, COMM
27 ♈ 35	EIRE 3
28 ♈ 02	ZIMBABWE
1 ♉ 25	TRANSCAUCASIAN FED
3 ♉ 59	EIRE 1
4 ♉ 23	PORTUGAL-REVOLUTION
6 ♉ 30	SIERRA LEONE
6 ♉ 44	TOGO
7 ♉ 06	TANZANIA
8 ♉ 12	JAPAN - SOVEREIGNTY
9 ♉ 54	NICARAGUA 2
14 ♉ 11	GERMANY WEST SOVEREIGN
14 ♉ 38	SHEPARD
18 ♉ 29	MONACO
20 ♉ 29	ENGLAND-1707
21 ♉ 14	NATAL
22 ♉ 23	ECUADOR 2
22 ♉ 48	WARSAW PACT
22 ♉ 54	PARAGUAY
23 ♉ 40	ISRAEL
23 ♉ 59	PALESTINE
25 ♉ 18	ENGLAND-EDGAR
27 ♉ 22	N Y STOCK EXCHANGE
28 ♉ 45	CUBA - INDEPENDENCE 2
0 ♊ 25	ROMANIA 1
1 ♊ 17	SRI LANKA-REP
1 ♊ 27	GERMANY WEST PROCLAM
3 ♊ 35	JORDAN
3 ♊ 42	ARGENTINA - REVOLUTION
4 ♊ 18	GEORGIA
4 ♊ 18	ARMENIA
4 ♊ 27	GUYANA
6 ♊ 12	AZERBAIJAN
7 ♊ 04	MOROCCO
7 ♊ 59	BIAFRA
9 ♊ 03	SOUTH AFRICA-UNION
9 ♊ 13	SOUTH AFRICA-REPUBLIC
9 ♊ 51	ZIMBABWE-RHODESIA
10 ♊ 05	LIBERAL PARTY
11 ♊ 14	BHUTAN
12 ♊ 27	TONGA
14 ♊ 36	DENMARK
15 ♊ 55	FALL OF CONSTANTINOPLE
15 ♊ 58	NORWAY
16 ♊ 09	VATICAN CITY
18 ♊ 38	THATCHER
19 ♊ 09	ITALY - REPUBLIC
22 ♊ 43	KHALISTAN
24 ♊ 30	TUNISIA
25 ♊ 29	FRANCE-VICHY REPUBLIC
26 ♊ 13	ICELAND
27 ♊ 24	EGYPT - REPUBLIC
27 ♊ 50	KUWAIT
28 ♊ 40	MALI - FEDERATION
2 ♋ 27	THAILAND 2
2 ♋ 46	MOZAMBIQUE
4 ♋ 16	MADAGASCAR
4 ♋ 16	SOMALILAND
5 ♋ 07	DJIBOUTI
6 ♋ 29	POLAND-COMMUNIST
7 ♋ 13	SEYCHELLES
8 ♋ 36	BURUNDI
8 ♋ 36	RWANDA-INDEPENDENCE
9 ♋ 01	UNITED PROVINCES C A
9 ♋ 02	SOMALIA
9 ♋ 07	ZAIRE
9 ♋ 20	CANADA
10 ♋ 05	ITALY - KINGDOM 2
10 ♋ 18	VIETNAM-UNION
10 ♋ 59	ALGERIA
11 ♋ 13	USA 2
11 ♋ 22	USA 1
11 ♋ 40	VENEZUELA 1
12 ♋ 40	PHILLIPINES
12 ♋ 56	CAPE VERDE ISLANDS
13 ♋ 19	USA 3
13 ♋ 19	USA 4
13 ♋ 41	COMOROS 1
13 ♋ 52	MALAWI
14 ♋ 06	SOLOMON ISLANDS
17 ♋ 14	ARGENTINA - INDEPENDENCE
17 ♋ 46	BAHAMAS
18 ♋ 36	KIRIBATI
19 ♋ 27	SAO TOME-PRINCIPE
20 ♋ 58	BULGARIA - AUTONOMY
20 ♋ 58	SERBIA
20 ♋ 58	ROMANIA 2
21 ♋ 08	MONTENEGRO
21 ♋ 35	IRAQ - REPUBLIC
23 ♋ 35	ATOMIC EXPLOSION
24 ♋ 06	AFGHANISTAN
26 ♋ 27	NICARAGUA SANDINISTA
27 ♋ 49	SOUTH VIETNAM
27 ♋ 49	LAOS 2
27 ♋ 49	NORTH VIETNAM
28 ♋ 38	KAMPUCHEA - INDEP
29 ♋ 08	MOON LANDING
0 ♌ 03	OMAN
0 ♌ 49	GREECE DEMOCRACY
2 ♌ 47	LIECHTENSTEIN
2 ♌ 50	CIA
3 ♌ 04	LIBERIA
5 ♌ 12	MALDIVES
6 ♌ 32	PERU 1
8 ♌ 42	VANUATU
8 ♌ 49	BENIN
10 ♌ 37	BYELO RUSSIA
12 ♌ 34	NIGER
12 ♌ 39	BURKINO-FASSO
13 ♌ 08	NETHERLANDS
13 ♌ 16	HIROSHIMA
13 ♌ 49	JAMAICA
14 ♌ 29	BOLIVIA
15 ♌ 58	IVORY COAST
16 ♌ 18	SWITZERLAND
16 ♌ 33	SINGAPORE 2
18 ♌ 17	SINGAPORE 3
20 ♌ 12	CHAD
20 ♌ 58	CENTRAL AFRICAN REPUBLIC
21 ♌ 07	BAHRAIN
21 ♌ 07	HYDERABAD
21 ♌ 07	PAKISTAN
22 ♌ 00	INDIA - INDEPENDENCE
23 ♌ 02	CONGO
24 ♌ 02	KOREA - SOUTH
27 ♌ 03	CYPRUS
29 ♌ 26	GABON
1 ♍ 07	SENEGAL
6 ♍ 35	IRAQ - KINGDOM
7 ♍ 01	NATO 1
7 ♍ 17	URUGUAY
7 ♍ 25	SINGAPORE 1
	MALAYA
	TRINIDAD & TOBAGO
	COSTA RICA 2

MOON ☽

Deg	Sign	Min	Name
28	♈	34	ALBANIA-PEOPLES REPUBLIC
1	♉	43	MEXICO - REVOLUTION
2	♉	21	LAOS 1
2	♉	31	FRANCE - NAPOLEON
3	♉	27	GHANA
5	♉	15	NAT KHOREZEM SOVIET REP
5	♉	31	CENTRAL AFRICAN REPUBLIC
5	♉	43	INDIA - REPUBLIC
10	♉	06	BOLIVIA
10	♉	23	E.E.C.
11	♉	18	SIKKIM
11	♉	19	GUINEA
11	♉	20	BELGIUM
12	♉	26	AUSTRALIA 1
13	♉	00	MALI - FEDERATION
15	♉	12	GUATEMALA - 1
15	♉	36	U.S. CIVIL WAR
16	♉	40	NEW ZEALAND 1
17	♉	23	ICELAND
18	♉	14	CHILE 1
19	♉	02	CHINA - NATIONALIST
19	♉	12	TOGO
20	♉	05	AUSTRALIA 2
21	♉	54	CHINA - REPUBLIC
23	♉	43	USSR-FORMATION
24	♉	04	MALAWI
25	♉	23	ITALY - KINGDOM 1
25	♉	47	CONSERVATIVE PARTY
26	♉	56	LATVIA
27	♉	02	LESOTHO
27	♉	18	CAPE VERDE ISLANDS
29	♉	41	USSR-REPUBLIC
0	♊	16	CONGO
1	♊	13	ESTONIA
3	♊	20	BAHRAIN
3	♊	32	THATCHER
3	♊	46	MEXICO - CONSTITUTION
3	♊	54	LIBYA, COUP
4	♊	48	TONGA
6	♊	11	ZIMBABWE
6	♊	26	GUATEMALA - 3
6	♊	39	UKRAINE
6	♊	46	IRAN - ISLAMIC REP
6	♊	52	NICARAGUA SANDINISTA
6	♊	54	PORTUGAL-REVOLUTION
7	♊	09	BRAZIL
7	♊	15	ZAMBIA
7	♊	41	COMOROS 1
9	♊	36	UNITED ARAB EMIR
11	♊	48	CYPRUS
13	♊	49	VATICAN CITY
15	♊	14	NATAL
15	♊	26	VENDA
15	♊	33	BULGARIA - COMMUNIST
17	♊	57	IRAQ - REPUBLIC
18	♊	08	RHODESIA
19	♊	45	GUATEMALA - 2
21	♊	51	GREECE INDEPENDENCE
22	♊	37	UNITED NATIONS
22	♊	48	BUGANDA
23	♊	16	GUINEA - BUISSAU
24	♊	13	GABON
25	♊	21	EQUATORIAL GUINEA
25	♊	23	RWANDA-INDEPENDENCE
25	♊	23	BURUNDI
27	♊	28	NETHERLANDS
27	♊	44	JAPAN - MEIJI CONST
28	♊	27	FRANCE-FIFTH REPUBLIC
28	♊	41	JAPAN - SOVEREIGNTY
29	♊	55	TURKEY
1	♋	48	RWANDA-UDI
1	♋	55	MALDIVES
2	♋	19	BARBADOS
3	♋	41	BELIZE
6	♋	02	UNITED ARAB REP
6	♋	29	CANADA
7	♋	20	OPEC
10	♋	42	EIRE 2
12	♋	05	KAMPUCHEA, COMM
17	♋	48	VIETNAM
18	♋	00	HIROSHIMA
19	♋	26	UNITED KINGDOM-1801
21	♋	54	SEYCHELLES
22	♋	44	SYRIA 1
22	♋	45	LIECHTENSTEIN
23	♋	09	SOMALILAND
23	♋	09	MADAGASCAR
23	♋	13	UNITED KINGDOM-1922
23	♋	47	ETHIOPIA
25	♋	53	ALBANIA - INDEPENDENCE
26	♋	26	SOLOMON ISLANDS
27	♋	06	INDIA - INDEPENDENCE
27	♋	06	PAKISTAN
27	♋	06	HYDERABAD
27	♋	44	ALGERIA
27	♋	47	FAR EAST REPUBLIC
29	♋	57	PERU-BATTLE AYACUCHO
0	♌	24	NICARAGUA 2
0	♌	33	PERU 1
1	♌	21	SENEGAL
4	♌	21	ISRAEL
5	♌	23	REAGAN-2
6	♌	07	NORWAY
7	♌	07	EL SALVADOR
7	♌	26	NEPAL
9	♌	06	PALESTINE
12	♌	59	MAURITIUS
17	♌	02	PAKISTAN, REPUBLIC
17	♌	30	SURINAM
17	♌	51	ZIMBABWE-RHODESIA
18	♌	22	GUYANA
18	♌	44	ENGLAND-EDGAR
20	♌	42	GRENADA
23	♌	05	SUDAN
24	♌	03	CZECHOSLOVAKIA 2
26	♌	38	MALAYSIA
29	♌	09	USSR-REVOLUTION
3	♍	43	SAO TOME-PRINCIPE
4	♍	21	TEXAS
4	♍	25	HAITI
4	♍	35	VIETNAM-UNION
5	♍	48	KUWAIT
6	♍	13	YUGOSLAVIA 1
7	♍	52	NATO 1
8	♍	54	CHINA - COMMUNIST 1
11	♍	12	SWEDEN
11	♍	59	FINLAND
15	♍	56	PHILLIPINES
16	♍	14	CZECHOSLOVAKIA-COMMUNIST
16	♍	16	TUVALU
17	♍	57	TRANSCAUCASIAN FED
18	♍	05	NORTH YEMEN
18	♍	31	ROMANIA 1
18	♍	37	TRINIDAD & TOBAGO
19	♍	59	CREATION OF THE WORLD
21	♍	26	SIERRA LEONE
21	♍	43	EGYPT - REPUBLIC
23	♍	46	SOMALIA
24	♍	48	REAGAN-1
24	♍	49	ZAIRE
26	♍	01	GAMBIA
26	♍	38	TUNISIA
26	♍	48	SRI LANKA-REP
26	♍	50	LONDON 1
28	♍	23	ENGLAND-1707
29	♍	31	TIMOR
29	♍	56	COSTA RICA 2
0	♎	49	NUCLEAR REACTION
4	♎	04	LABOUR PARTY 2
4	♎	32	GREECE DEMOCRACY
6	♎	03	MONACO
8	♎	13	BOPHUTHATSWANA
8	♎	29	CUBA - COMMUNIST
9	♎	29	ZANZIBAR
14	♎	23	EGYPT - INDEPENDENCE
15	♎	08	ATOMIC EXPLOSION
16	♎	08	JAMAICA
17	♎	56	BURMA
18	♎	05	MALI - REPUBLIC
20	♎	07	EGYPT - KINGDOM
20	♎	50	SWITZERLAND
22	♎	56	PORTUGAL-REVOLUTION
23	♎	16	ESPIRITU SANTO
24	♎	24	MOON LANDING
27	♎	57	GERMANY WEST SOVEREIGN
29	♎	04	LIBYA - INDEP
3	♏	26	KENYA
4	♏	26	ITALY - REPUBLIC
5	♏	33	DJIBOUTI
6	♏	05	SOUTH YEMEN 1
6	♏	27	WESTERN SAMOA
8	♏	51	BHUTAN
9	♏	58	CUBA - INDEPENDENCE 2
11	♏	42	SOUTH YEMEN 2
12	♏	52	LITHUANIA
13	♏	00	CUBA - INDEPENDENCE 1
13	♏	17	ECUADOR 1
13	♏	55	TANZANIA
14	♏	12	BENIN
14	♏	17	YUGOSLAVIA 2
15	♏	01	FRANCE-VICHY REPUBLIC
15	♏	16	ICELAND
18	♏	26	MALAYA
19	♏	40	BAHAMAS
22	♏	34	COSTA RICA 1
22	♏	49	CIA
23	♏	48	GORBACHEV
0	♐	15	VENEZUELA 2
1	♐	12	IRAQ - INDEPENCENCE
4	♐	06	FRANCE-1st REPUBLIC 1
4	♐	11	SRI LANKA-IND
6	♐	26	FRANCE-FOURTH REPUBLIC
8	♐	26	BANGLADESH 3
8	♐	30	S.D.P.
9	♐	24	GEORGIA
9	♐	24	ARMENIA
9	♐	36	DENMARK
9	♐	38	CREATION OF MAN
9	♐	50	SOUTH AFRICAN REP 1
10	♐	13	BRUNEI
10	♐	14	FIRST MANNED FLIGHT
10	♐	34	DOMINICA
10	♐	40	TRANSKEI
10	♐	53	HATAY
12	♐	33	NIGER
15	♐	29	CONFEDERATE STATES AMER
17	♐	35	GREECE REVOLUTION
18	♐	56	SOUTH AFRICA-REPUBLIC
22	♐	22	KHALISTAN
22	♐	44	SOUTH AFRICAN REP 2
23	♐	37	COMOROS 2
24	♐	06	GERMANY - EMPIRE
25	♐	41	ANTIGUA-BARBUDA
27	♐	57	TANGANYIKA
28	♐	54	SPAIN
29	♐	56	MONGOLIA
0	♑	00	ST LUCIA
0	♑	53	COLUMBIA
1	♑	06	KOREA - SOUTH
1	♑	32	EIRE 3
4	♑	08	VENEZUELA 1
4	♑	35	ARAB FEDERATION
5	♑	02	AZERBAIJAN
7	♑	27	DE GAULLE
8	♑	29	FRANCE-THIRD REPUBLIC
8	♑	57	ITALY - KINGDOM 2
9	♑	42	CARPATHO-UKRAINE
10	♑	15	SLOVAKIA

10 ♑ 19	SERBIA
10 ♑ 19	ROMANIA 2
10 ♑ 19	MONTENEGRO
10 ♑ 19	BULGARIA - AUTONOMY
10 ♑ 20	KOREA - NORTH
10 ♑ 34	BANGLADESH 2
10 ♑ 57	SINGAPORE 2
12 ♑ 50	BURKINO-FASSO
13 ♑ 11	BOKHARA NAT'L SOVIET REP
13 ♑ 56	ORANGE FREE STATE
14 ♑ 02	SINGAPORE 3
14 ♑ 17	LIBERIA
14 ♑ 38	SHEPARD
14 ♑ 52	SINGAPORE 1
15 ♑ 19	DANZIG
15 ♑ 35	ST VINCENT-GRENADINES
16 ♑ 43	QATAR
17 ♑ 09	MOZAMBIQUE
17 ♑ 17	FEDERATION OF ARAB REPUB
19 ♑ 00	GERMANY - WEIMAR
19 ♑ 13	ARGENTINA - INDEPENDENCE
19 ♑ 13	MOROCCO
20 ♑ 09	YUGOSLAVIA-COMMUNIST
24 ♑ 36	LUXEMBOURG
25 ♑ 15	USA 2
25 ♑ 39	KAMPUCHEA - REP
27 ♑ 38	USA 1
28 ♑ 02	PAPUA NEW GUINEA
28 ♑ 11	ECUADOR 2
28 ♑ 25	EIRE 1
29 ♑ 40	LIBERAL PARTY
29 ♑ 43	URUGUAY
1 ♒ 28	CHINA - COMMUNIST 2
2 ♒ 07	THAILAND 1
2 ♒ 35	TREATY OF ROME
2 ♒ 41	FIJI
3 ♒ 45	ROMAN EMPIRE 1
7 ♒ 33	HONDURAS
8 ♒ 33	AUSTRIA
8 ♒ 41	AFGHANISTAN
9 ♒ 39	CAMEROON
9 ♒ 59	BULGARIA - INDEPENDENCE
10 ♒ 21	LABOUR PARTY 1
10 ♒ 42	UGANDA
11 ♒ 11	FRANCE-1st REPUBLIC 2

11 ♒ 38	PARAGUAY
11 ♒ 49	KIRIBATI
12 ♒ 29	POLAND-COMMUNIST
12 ♒ 55	IVORY COAST
14 ♒ 40	WARSAW PACT
14 ♒ 41	POLAND 2
15 ♒ 02	ROME
15 ♒ 37	AGE OF AQUARIUS-2
16 ♒ 17	NIGERIA
16 ♒ 17	SAHRAWI ARAB D R
19 ♒ 52	NAURU
22 ♒ 06	ANGOLA
23 ♒ 20	AGE OF AQUARIUS-1
25 ♒ 11	BYELO RUSSIA
26 ♒ 45	BIAFRA
26 ♒ 58	USA 3
27 ♒ 10	USA 4
27 ♒ 23	SPUTNIK
27 ♒ 32	S VIETNAM-REP
28 ♒ 42	DOMINICAN REPUBLIC
29 ♒ 54	VANUATU
0 ♓ 30	FALL OF CONSTANTINOPLE
0 ♓ 52	SWAZILAND
2 ♓ 31	CISKEI
2 ♓ 31	SOUTH AFRICA-UNION
3 ♓ 14	ST KITTS-NEVIS
4 ♓ 00	ARGENTINA - REVOLUTION
10 ♓ 54	ROMAN EMPIRE 2
11 ♓ 40	LEBANON I
12 ♓ 59	HUNGARY
13 ♓ 28	GAGARIN
13 ♓ 56	THAILAND 2
14 ♓ 17	LEBANON 2
14 ♓ 17	SYRIA 2
17 ♓ 56	POLAND 1
18 ♓ 22	MALTA
19 ♓ 02	JORDAN
19 ♓ 22	HOLY ROMAN EMPIRE
21 ♓ 03	CYPRUS - TURKISH
25 ♓ 27	SAUDI ARABIA
26 ♓ 59	BANGLADESH 1
27 ♓ 27	CZECHOSLOVAKIA 3
28 ♓ 12	LONDON 2
29 ♓ 08	ENGLAND-WILLIAM

MERCURY ☿

3 ♈ 10	GAGARIN
4 ♈ 48	ZIMBABWE
4 ♈ 57R	GREECE REVOLUTION
5 ♈ 00	ROME
7 ♈ 45	GORBACHEV
9 ♈ 53	TREATY OF ROME
10 ♈ 55	CARPATHO-UKRAINE
10 ♈ 59	SLOVAKIA
12 ♈ 13	JAPAN - SOVEREIGNTY
15 ♈ 25	GUATEMALA - 3
16 ♈ 20	TOGO
17 ♈ 49	CHILE 2
21 ♈ 33R	SIKKIM
22 ♈ 06	BANGLADESH 1
22 ♈ 56R	LONDON 2
23 ♈ 07	PORTUGAL-REVOLUTION
26 ♈ 22	KAMPUCHEA, COMM
0 ♉ 49	SIERRA LEONE
1 ♉ 06R	BANGLADESH 2
2 ♉ 50	EIRE 3
7 ♉ 13R	TANZANIA
8 ♉ 55R	TRANSCAUCASIAN FED
9 ♉ 24	GEORGIA
9 ♉ 24	ARMENIA
11 ♉ 11R	GUATEMALA - 2
11 ♉ 17R	ENGLAND-1707
11 ♉ 36	AZERBAIJAN
14 ♉ 49	EIRE 1
16 ♉ 02	SRI LANKA-REP
18 ♉ 35	TONGA
18 ♉ 43	SHEPARD
23 ♉ 11	NATAL
23 ♉ 44R	N Y STOCK EXCHANGE
25 ♉ 00	THATCHER
26 ♉ 15	JORDAN
26 ♉ 51	ENGLAND-EDGAR
27 ♉ 38	NORWAY
27 ♉ 55	GERMANY WEST SOVEREIGN
28 ♉ 58	NICARAGUA 2
0 ♊ 36R	SOUTH AFRICA-UNION
2 ♊ 49	TUNISIA
2 ♊ 04	GUYANA
3 ♊ 06R	LIBERAL PARTY
3 ♊ 21R	MOROCCO
8 ♊ 22R	ROMANIA 1
9 ♊ 48	MONACO
10 ♊ 22	ISRAEL
10 ♊ 31	ICELAND
10 ♊ 58	PALESTINE
11 ♊ 24R	KHALISTAN
12 ♊ 15	ZIMBABWE-RHODESIA
12 ♊ 34	PARAGUAY
12 ♊ 55	ECUADOR 2
13 ♊ 11	WARSAW PACT
15 ♊ 13	MOZAMBIQUE
17 ♊ 02	BURUNDI
17 ♊ 02	RWANDA-INDEPENDENCE
17 ♊ 13	GERMANY WEST PROCLAM

19 ♊ 14R	VATICAN CITY
19 ♊ 21	SEYCHELLES
19 ♊ 28	ALGERIA
19 ♊ 40	CUBA - INDEPENDENCE 2
21 ♊ 35	CAPE VERDE ISLANDS
22 ♊ 23	COMOROS 1
23 ♊ 51	VENEZUELA 1
25 ♊ 08	VIETNAM-UNION
26 ♊ 36	ARGENTINA - REVOLUTION
27 ♊ 17	BIAFRA
28 ♊ 43R	UNITED PROVINCES C A
29 ♊ 28	ITALY - KINGDOM 2
0 ♋ 04	SAO TOME-PRINCIPE
1 ♋ 11	ITALY - REPUBLIC
1 ♋ 15	DJIBOUTI
2 ♋ 26	SOUTH AFRICA-REPUBLIC
5 ♋ 33	FALL OF CONSTANTINOPLE
4 ♋ 36	BHUTAN
6 ♋ 33R	ARGENTINA - INDEPENDENCE
8 ♋ 11	DENMARK
9 ♋ 40R	KUWAIT
9 ♋ 58	LAOS 2
9 ♋ 58	NORTH VIETNAM
9 ♋ 58	SOUTH VIETNAM
10 ♋ 18	KAMPUCHEA - INDEP
10 ♋ 52	GREECE DEMOCRACY
13 ♋ 07	THAILAND 2
17 ♋ 06	CIA
17 ♋ 31	VANUATU
19 ♋ 13	FRANCE-VICHY REPUBLIC
20 ♋ 45	POLAND-COMMUNIST
20 ♋ 52	BENIN
20 ♋ 58	EGYPT - REPUBLIC
21 ♋ 56	NIGER
23 ♋ 28	BURKINO-FASSO
23 ♋ 33	MALI - FEDERATION
23 ♋ 53	MALAWI
24 ♋ 12R	USA 4
24 ♋ 12R	USA 3
25 ♋ 00R	USA 1
25 ♋ 04R	USA 2
25 ♋ 23	IVORY COAST
28 ♋ 00	MADAGASCAR
28 ♋ 00	SOMALILAND
28 ♋ 34	MOON LANDING
29 ♋ 42R	AFGHANISTAN
29 ♋ 58	SOMALIA
29 ♋ 59	ZAIRE
0 ♌ 18	CHAD
0 ♌ 40R	BYELO RUSSIA
1 ♌ 12	MONTENEGRO
1 ♌ 12	SERBIA
1 ♌ 12	ROMANIA 2
1 ♌ 12	BULGARIA - AUTONOMY
2 ♌ 53R	BAHAMAS
3 ♌ 18	CENTRAL AFRICAN REPUBLIC
4 ♌ 58	CANADA
5 ♌ 56	SOLOMON ISLANDS

6 ♌ 36	CONGO
6 ♌ 48	PAKISTAN
6 ♌ 48	INDIA - INDEPENDENCE
6 ♌ 48	HYDERABAD
7 ♌ 27	PHILLIPINES
8 ♌ 16	CYPRUS
10 ♌ 08	GABON
12 ♌ 26R	PERU I
12 ♌ 50	KIRIBATI
14 ♌ 20R	NICARAGUA SANDINISTA
14 ♌ 47	IRAQ - REPUBLIC
16 ♌ 02	SENEGAL
17 ♌ 02	OMAN
19 ♌ 24	ATOMIC EXPLOSION
21 ♌ 20	JAMAICA
21 ♌ 57R	LIBERIA
22 ♌ 32	VIETNAM
25 ♌ 38	KOREA - SOUTH
27 ♌ 42R	SINGAPORE 3
27 ♌ 51R	SINGAPORE 2
28 ♌ 19	MALDIVES
28 ♌ 24R	FEDERATION OF ARAB REPUB
28 ♌ 25R	QATAR
29 ♌ 06	IRAQ - KINGDOM
29 ♌ 22	SWITZERLAND
29 ♌ 25	LIECHTENSTEIN
0 ♍ 04	NETHERLANDS
0 ♍ 42R	HATAY
4 ♍ 47	HIROSHIMA
5 ♍ 09	COSTA RICA 2
7 ♍ 33	BOLIVIA
10 ♍ 26R	BAHRAIN
10 ♍ 30	MALTA
10 ♍ 52	LUXEMBOURG
11 ♍ 51R	BULGARIA - COMMUNIST
18 ♍ 08R	ST KITTS-NEVIS
18 ♍ 55	FRANCE-1st REPUBLIC 2
19 ♍ 15	VENDA
20 ♍ 43R	FRANCE-1st REPUBLIC 1
21 ♍ 54	CREATION OF THE WORLD
23 ♍ 48	BRAZIL
23 ♍ 53	GUATEMALA - 1
24 ♍ 32	NATO 1
24 ♍ 42R	MALAYA
26 ♍ 17R	PORTUGAL-REVOLUTION
27 ♍ 19	SPUTNIK
28 ♍ 43	URUGUAY
0 ♎ 43	CREATION OF MAN
1 ♎ 06R	MALAYSIA
2 ♎ 02	TRINIDAD & TOBAGO
2 ♎ 05	KAMPUCHEA - REP
2 ♎ 47	SINGAPORE 1
2 ♎ 56	FIJI
3 ♎ 33	OPEC
3 ♎ 48	GUINEA
4 ♎ 32	EL SALVADOR
5 ♎ 53	GUINEA - BUISSAU
6 ♎ 08	SWAZILAND
6 ♎ 52	TUVALU
7 ♎ 29	LIBYA, COUP
8 ♎ 25	FRANCE-THIRD REPUBLIC
9 ♎ 20	ETHIOPIA
10 ♎ 26R	UGANDA
10 ♎ 46	FRANCE-FIFTH REPUBLIC
12 ♎ 23	KOREA - NORTH
13 ♎ 19R	CHINA - COMMUNIST 2
13 ♎ 51	IRAQ - INDEPENDENCE
14 ♎ 11	S VIETNAM-REP
14 ♎ 22	SYRIA 1
15 ♎ 21	NEW ZEALAND I
16 ♎ 34	MALI - REPUBLIC
18 ♎ 01	MEXICO - REVOLUTION
18 ♎ 41	PAPUA NEW GUINEA
18 ♎ 44	ALLIANCE
19 ♎ 07R	CHINA - COMMUNIST 1
20 ♎ 14	ANTIGUA-BARBUDA
20 ♎ 53	BOTSWANA
21 ♎ 09R	NORTH YEMEN
22 ♎ 01	ECUADOR 1
22 ♎ 23	NAT KHOREZEM SOVIET REP
24 ♎ 13	BELIZE
24 ♎ 27	TURKEY
24 ♎ 28	TRANSKEI
24 ♎ 52	VENEZUELA 2
26 ♎ 08R	EQUATORIAL GUINEA
26 ♎ 18	CZECHOSLOVAKIA 1
27 ♎ 01	LESOTHO
27 ♎ 13	HONDURAS
27 ♎ 15R	BELGIUM
28 ♎ 57	NIGERIA
29 ♎ 37	PANAMA
1 ♏ 32	POLAND 1
5 ♏ 54	ZAMBIA
6 ♏ 13	NICARAGUA 1
7 ♏ 10	BULGARIA - INDEPENDENCE
7 ♏ 23	ANGOLA
12 ♏ 28	CZECHOSLOVAKIA 2
14 ♏ 02	YUGOSLAVIA 1
15 ♏ 27	UNITED NATIONS
16 ♏ 28	MAURETANIA
17 ♏ 36	USSR-REVOLUTION
18 ♏ 05	BARBADOS
19 ♏ 49	LEBANON I
20 ♏ 45	DOMINICAN REPUBLIC
20 ♏ 49	SOUTH YEMEN 1
21 ♏ 22	SOUTH YEMEN 2
23 ♏ 11	LAOS I
24 ♏ 44R	DANZIG
26 ♏ 45	ST VINCENT-GRENADINES
26 ♏ 59	NAMIBIA
27 ♏ 16	FRANCE-FOURTH REPUBLIC
27 ♏ 16	COSTA RICA 1
28 ♏ 21	FRANCE - NAPOLEON
29 ♏ 47	DOMINICA
0 ♐ 07	SURINAM
0 ♐ 48	GERMANY - WEIMAR
1 ♐ 25	CYPRUS - TURKISH
3 ♐ 01	AUSTRIA
3 ♐ 42	POLAND 2
4 ♐ 49	TIMOR
6 ♐ 41	HUNGARY
7 ♐ 44R	CONSERVATIVE PARTY
7 ♐ 57	CISKEI
8 ♐ 08	CZECHOSLOVAKIA 3
11 ♐ 01	NUCLEAR REACTION
11 ♐ 25	RHODESIA
12 ♐ 25	TANGANYIKA
13 ♐ 45	EIRE 2
13 ♐ 47	LATVIA
14 ♐ 37	HOLY ROMAN EMPIRE
15 ♐ 14	UNITED KINGDOM-1922
15 ♐ 34R	BANGLADESH 3
16 ♐ 59R	LIBYA - INDEP
17 ♐ 34	UNITED KINGDOM-1801
18 ♐ 02	CUBA - COMMUNIST
19 ♐ 12	ESTONIA
23 ♐ 50	SOUTH AFRICAN REP 2
24 ♐ 37	ALBANIA - INDEPENDENCE
24 ♐ 54	CAMEROON
25 ♐ 28R	CHINA - REPUBLIC
26 ♐ 23	CHINA - NATIONALIST
26 ♐ 49R	E.E.C.
26 ♐ 58	DE GAULLE
27 ♐ 03	AUSTRALIA 1
27 ♐ 42	PERU-BATTLE AYACUCHO
27 ♐ 52	AUSTRALIA 2
28 ♐ 13	UNITED ARAB EMIR
29 ♐ 48	YUGOSLAVIA 2
29 ♐ 52	ICELAND
1 ♑ 03	FINLAND
2 ♑ 02	REAGAN-1
2 ♑ 40	ALBANIA-PEOPLES REPUBLIC
4 ♑ 38	BOPHUTHATSWANA
5 ♑ 15	ZANZIBAR
6 ♑ 30	BUGANDA
6 ♑ 33R	SOUTH AFRICAN REP 1
7 ♑ 00	COLUMBIA
7 ♑ 14	UKRAINE
7 ♑ 42	CUBA - INDEPENDENCE 1
7 ♑ 46	SWEDEN
8 ♑ 00	KENYA
8 ♑ 01	LITHUANIA
8 ♑ 35R	BRUNEI
8 ♑ 44	FIRST MANNED FLIGHT
12 ♑ 39	BURMA
16 ♑ 37	ENGLAND-WILLIAM
18 ♑ 11	HAITI
18 ♑ 41R	INDIA - REPUBLIC
19 ♑ 43	MEXICO - CONSTITUTION
19 ♑ 58	WESTERN SAMOA
20 ♑ 07	ESPIRITU SANTO
21 ♑ 20	USSR-FORMATION
22 ♑ 36	UNITED ARAB REP
23 ♑ 47	INDONESIA
24 ♑ 43R	LEBANON 2
24 ♑ 43R	SYRIA 2
25 ♑ 16	SUDAN
26 ♑ 19	ROMAN EMPIRE 1
26 ♑ 34	COMOROS 2
27 ♑ 00R	GERMANY - EMPIRE
27 ♑ 36	CHILE 1
1 ♒ 02	SPAIN
1 ♒ 48	ROMAN EMPIRE 2
2 ♒ 02	SAUDI ARABIA
3 ♒ 31	YUGOSLAVIA-COMMUNIST
5 ♒ 46	GERMANY - THIRD REICH
6 ♒ 03	IRAN - KHOMEINI
10 ♒ 33	NEPAL
11 ♒ 53	ARAB FEDERATION
13 ♒ 32	REAGAN-2
14 ♒ 32	SAHRAWI ARAB D R
16 ♒ 19R	AGE OF AQUARIUS-1
16 ♒ 28	LABOUR PARTY 2
16 ♒ 37	USSR-REPUBLIC
16 ♒ 56R	AGE OF AQUARIUS-2
19 ♒ 11	CONFEDERATE STATES AMER
23 ♒ 04	RWANDA-UDI
23 ♒ 49	MAURITIUS
24 ♒ 13	GAMBIA
24 ♒ 34R	TEXAS
24 ♒ 49R	CZECHOSLOVAKIA-COMMUNIST
26 ♒ 10	EGYPT - INDEPENDENCE
26 ♒ 35	EGYPT - KINGDOM
28 ♒ 01	NAURU
29 ♒ 07R	GREECE INDEPENCENCE
0 ♓ 38R	JAPAN - MEIJI CONST
2 ♓ 00	LONDON 1
2 ♓ 05	SRI LANKA-IND
2 ♓ 35	GHANA
5 ♓ 56	GRENADA
10 ♓ 06	S.D.P.
10 ♓ 42R	BOKHARA NAT'L SOVIET REP
11 ♓ 26	ENGLAND-1689
11 ♓ 52R	MONGOLIA
13 ♓ 31	ST LUCIA
16 ♓ 48	ORANGE FREE STATE
19 ♓ 14	PAKISTAN, REPUBLIC
20 ♓ 26	THAILAND 1
22 ♓ 58	LABOUR PARTY 1
24 ♓ 42R	ITALY - KINGDOM 1
24 ♓ 56	U.S. CIVIL WAR
27 ♓ 16R	IRAN - ISLAMIC REP
27 ♓ 51	FAR EAST REPUBLIC

VENUS ♀

Position	Name	Position	Name
17 ♏ 07	NORTH YEMEN	21 ♑ 07	SPAIN
17 ♏ 28	TUVALU	21 ♑ 15	GERMANY - THIRD REICH
17 ♏ 39	HUNGARY	21 ♑ 33	BANGLADESH 3
17 ♏ 55R	DOMINICA	22 ♑ 00	CONFEDERATE STATES AMER
18 ♏ 12	TURKEY	22 ♑ 51	ESTONIA
18 ♏ 20	LIBYA - INDEP	23 ♑ 36	CUBA - COMMUNIST
18 ♏ 54	CZECHOSLOVAKIA 3	24 ♑ 23	REAGAN-1
19 ♏ 09	CREATION OF MAN	24 ♑ 38	DOMINICAN REPUBLIC
19 ♏ 17	CHINA - COMMUNIST 2	26 ♑ 22	CISKEI
19 ♏ 18	EQUATORIAL GUINEA	26 ♑ 35R	GRENADA
19 ♏ 38	ST VINCENT-GRENADINES	29 ♑ 26	HAITI
22 ♏ 45	KAMPUCHEA - REP	29 ♑ 50	CHINA - NATIONALIST
22 ♏ 57	FIJI	29 ♑ 52	ENGLAND-WILLIAM
23 ♏ 28	ESPIRITU SANTO	0 ♒ 51	FINLAND
23 ♏ 54	LATVIA	0 ♒ 01R	ARAB FEDERATION
24 ♏ 01	UGANDA	1 ♒ 25	DE GAULLE
24 ♏ 03	SPUTNIK	3 ♒ 37	LITHUANIA
24 ♏ 39	NICARAGUA 1	6 ♒ 05R	UNITED ARAB REP
25 ♏ 47	CHINA - REPUBLIC	7 ♒ 50	GERMANY - EMPIRE
25 ♏ 51R	UNITED KINGDOM-1922	9 ♒ 39R	ROMAN EMPIRE 2
26 ♏ 11R	EIRE 2	9 ♒ 52	SUDAN
27 ♏ 18	SYRIA 2	10 ♒ 11	CARPATHO-UKRAINE
27 ♏ 18	LEBANON 2	10 ♒ 13	SAHRAWI ARAB D R
28 ♏ 19	CAMEROON	10 ♒ 15	SLOVAKIA
28 ♏ 27	USSR-FORMATION	10 ♒ 42	YUGOSLAVIA-COMMUNIST
28 ♏ 37	SWEDEN	10 ♒ 52R	ROMAN EMPIRE 1
28 ♏ 38	COMOROS 2	12 ♒ 31	BURMA
29 ♏ 30	BRUNEI	13 ♒ 54R	INDIA - REPUBLIC
1 ♐ 52	HOLY ROMAN EMPIRE	15 ♒ 01	INDONESIA
1 ♐ 54	CONSERVATIVE PARTY	15 ♒ 17	E.E.C.
2 ♐ 19	BOPHUTHATSWANA	15 ♒ 51	GAMBIA
2 ♐ 30	FRANCE-FOURTH REPUBLIC	16 ♒ 28	CHILE 1
4 ♐ 32R	CUBA - INDEPENDENCE 1	16 ♒ 32	UNITED KINGDOM-1801
4 ♐ 41	TANGANYIKA	17 ♒ 46	AGE OF AQUARIUS-2
6 ♐ 19	TRANSKEI	18 ♒ 05	AGE OF AQUARIUS-1
10 ♐ 14	AUSTRALIA 1	19 ♒ 59	LONDON 1
10 ♐ 16	YUGOSLAVIA 2	20 ♒ 05	SOUTH AFRICAN REP 2
10 ♐ 22	ICELAND	22 ♒ 25	LABOUR PARTY 2
10 ♐ 54	AUSTRALIA 2	22 ♒ 56	SOUTH AFRICAN REP 1
12 ♐ 43	BARBADOS	24 ♒ 14	USSR-REPUBLIC
13 ♐ 48	COSTA RICA 1	24 ♒ 37	BUGANDA
14 ♐ 03	NUCLEAR REACTION	25 ♒ 24	MAURITIUS
25 ♐ 26	ANTIGUA-BARBUDA	26 ♒ 02	BANGLADESH 1
25 ♐ 27	IRAN - KHOMEINI	28 ♒ 25R	UKRAINE
27 ♐ 11	DANZIG	1 ♓ 23	SAUDI ARABIA
0 ♑ 53	USSR-REVOLUTION	3 ♓ 56	IRAN - ISLAMIC REP
4 ♑ 00	UNITED ARAB EMIR	5 ♓ 10	GHANA
4 ♑ 21	WESTERN SAMOA	12 ♓ 02	ITALY - KINGDOM 1
4 ♑ 36	NAURU	12 ♓ 41R	ORANGE FREE STATE
5 ♑ 55	RHODESIA	15 ♓ 11	TRANSCAUCASIAN FED
11 ♑ 47	REAGAN-2	19 ♓ 10	PORTUGAL-REVOLUTION
11 ♑ 57	COLUMBIA	19 ♓ 11	GREECE REVOLUTION
12 ♑ 28	ALBANIA - INDEPENDENCE	20 ♓ 20	SRI LANKA-IND
12 ♑ 44	ZANZIBAR	22 ♓ 18	BANGLADESH 2
15 ♑ 13	KENYA	22 ♓ 22	GREECE INDEPENCENCE
15 ♑ 14	MAURETANIA	22 ♓ 57R	THAILAND 1
15 ♑ 34	ALBANIA-PEOPLES REPUBLIC	24 ♓ 40	NICARAGUA 2
18 ♑ 56	ST LUCIA	25 ♓ 12	RWANDA-UDI
20 ♑ 35	MEXICO - CONSTITUTION	29 ♓ 44	TREATY OF ROME
20 ♑ 55	LEBANON I	29 ♓ 45R	ROME
21 ♑ 01	PERU-BATTLE AYACUCHO		

MARS ♂

Position	Name	Position	Name
5 ♈ 38	LABOUR PARTY 2	25 ♉ 48	ENGLAND-EDGAR
7 ♈ 11	S.D.P.	25 ♉ 55	ALGERIA
12 ♈ 13	BAHAMAS	28 ♉ 02	GUYANA
12 ♈ 42	LEBANON I	29 ♉ 11	BENIN
13 ♈ 37	MONGOLIA	0 ♊ 31	NIGER
13 ♈ 40	DENMARK	0 ♊ 56	THAILAND 1
14 ♈ 27	BOKHARA NAT'L SOVIET REP	1 ♊ 18	THAILAND 2
16 ♈ 10	AFGHANISTAN	1 ♊ 52	BURKINO-FASSO
17 ♈ 59	MAURITIUS	1 ♊ 54	GUINEA
20 ♈ 49	EIRE 3	2 ♊ 19	FRANCE-FIFTH REPUBLIC
21 ♈ 11	CONFEDERATE STATES AMER	3 ♊ 10	IVORY COAST
22 ♈ 15	TANZANIA	3 ♊ 31	NATAL
23 ♈ 03R	SYRIA 1	4 ♊ 56	TREATY OF ROME
24 ♈ 51	LIBERIA	5 ♊ 26R	SYRIA 2
25 ♈ 22	IRAQ - REPUBLIC	5 ♊ 26R	LEBANON 2
25 ♈ 31	MOZAMBIQUE	5 ♊ 45	CHAD
25 ♈ 59	NICARAGUA 2	6 ♊ 02	U.S. CIVIL WAR
27 ♈ 23	GORBACHEV	7 ♊ 10	CENTRAL AFRICAN REPUBLIC
29 ♈ 43	MALI - FEDERATION	8 ♊ 19	CONGO
3 ♉ 08	CAPE VERDE ISLANDS	8 ♊ 56	CYPRUS
3 ♉ 42	COMOROS 1	9 ♊ 12	HIROSHIMA
4 ♉ 00	SOMALILAND	9 ♊ 24	ARGENTINA - REVOLUTION
4 ♉ 00	MADAGASCAR	9 ♊ 35	GABON
6 ♉ 59	MONACO	10 ♊ 53	KIRIBATI
7 ♉ 36	SOMALIA	11 ♊ 33	SENEGAL
7 ♉ 40	ZAIRE	13 ♊ 00	MALAWI
7 ♉ 55	SAO TOME-PRINCIPE	13 ♊ 13	CHILE 1
11 ♉ 44	ZIMBABWE-RHODESIA	16 ♊ 08	UNITED PROVINCES C A
11 ♉ 46	UNITED KINGDOM-1801	16 ♊ 26	GERMANY WEST SOVEREIGN
12 ♉ 30	POLAND-COMMUNIST	16 ♊ 35	NICARAGUA SANDINISTA
15 ♉ 15	DJIBOUTI	16 ♊ 53	THATCHER
16 ♉ 54	GERMANY WEST PROCLAM	17 ♊ 32R	COMOROS 2
17 ♉ 12	CUBA - INDEPENDENCE 2	17 ♊ 48	CIA
17 ♉ 37	CUBA - COMMUNIST	17 ♊ 48	PAPUA NEW GUINEA
18 ♉ 27	ITALY - KINGDOM 1	18 ♊ 49R	ESPIRITU SANTO
18 ♉ 47	DE GAULLE	19 ♊ 18	JAMAICA
19 ♉ 11	GRENADA	19 ♊ 52	USA 2
22 ♉ 32	GHANA	19 ♊ 57	USA 1
24 ♉ 08	BURUNDI	20 ♊ 47	PERU I
24 ♉ 08	RWANDA-INDEPENDENCE	21 ♊ 22	USA 3
24 ♉ 21	CHINA - REPUBLIC	21 ♊ 23	USA 4
25 ♉ 15	ATOMIC EXPLOSION	22 ♊ 15	SAHRAWI ARAB D R

Pos	Sign	Deg	Name
22	♊	20	WARSAW PACT
26	♊	24	OPEC
26	♊	36	VIETNAM
29	♊	20R	TIMOR
0	♋	10R	SURINAM
0	♋	29R	RWANDA-UDI
0	♋	35	PAKISTAN
0	♋	35	INDIA - INDEPENDENCE
0	♋	35	HYDERABAD
0	♋	41	MALI - REPUBLIC
0	♋	47	TONGA
2	♋	31R	ANGOLA
2	♋	45	PORTUGAL-REVOLUTION
3	♋	13	EGYPT - REPUBLIC
4	♋	49	NIGERIA
5	♋	13	CHILE 2
5	♋	32	TRINIDAD & TOBAGO
6	♋	14	SRI LANKA-REP
8	♋	21R	BUGANDA
17	♋	05R	YUGOSLAVIA-COMMUNIST
18	♋	17R	MAURETANIA
18	♋	21	SOUTH AFRICA-UNION
18	♋	23	GAGARIN
19	♋	25	FRANCE-VICHY REPUBLIC
20	♋	01	ENGLAND-1707
21	♋	22	NATO 1
21	♋	55	NORTH YEMEN
22	♋	18	GUATEMALA - 1
22	♋	43	VENDA
23	♋	36	BOLIVIA
23	♋	59	UNITED NATIONS
24	♋	18R	ALBANIA-PEOPLES REPUBLIC
24	♋	24	FALL OF CONSTANTINOPLE
24	♋	25	SIERRA LEONE
25	♋	48	BHUTAN
25	♋	54	EL SALVADOR
27	♋	24	FRANCE-THIRD REPUBLIC
28	♋	20	UGANDA
29	♋	40	SHEPARD
2	♌	16	LIECHTENSTEIN
3	♌	15	OMAN
3	♌	31	MALTA
5	♌	03R	COLUMBIA
5	♌	49	URUGUAY
6	♌	57R	SOUTH AFRICAN REP 1
7	♌	26	NICARAGUA 1
7	♌	38	SWITZERLAND
7	♌	47	IRAQ - INDEPENDENCE
8	♌	40R	CUBA - INDEPENDENCE 1
8	♌	42	CHINA - COMMUNIST 1
9	♌	04	ALLIANCE
11	♌	15	BOPHUTHATSWANA
12	♌	02	BELIZE
12	♌	38	IRAQ - KINGDOM
12	♌	53	MONTENEGRO
12	♌	53	BULGARIA - AUTONOMY
12	♌	53	SERBIA
12	♌	53	ROMANIA 2
13	♌	21	SOUTH AFRICA-REPUBLIC
14	♌	10	VATICAN CITY
14	♌	48	CHINA - COMMUNIST 2
15	♌	13	ICELAND
15	♌	50	JORDAN
16	♌	00	COSTA RICA 1
16	♌	14	EIRE 1
16	♌	56	ARGENTINA - INDEPENDENCE
18	♌	18	ST VINCENT-GRENADINES
19	♌	59	SWAZILAND
22	♌	10	BOTSWANA
22	♌	49	ZAMBIA
23	♌	51	ST KITTS-NEVIS
23	♌	59	MEXICO - REVOLUTION
24	♌	23	KUWAIT
24	♌	35	ITALY - REPUBLIC
24	♌	37	LESOTHO
24	♌	53R	CZECHOSLOVAKIA-COMMUNIST
25	♌	06	SEYCHELLES
25	♌	08	HONDURAS
26	♌	14	HATAY
26	♌	39	ZIMBABWE
27	♌	03	VIETNAM-UNION
27	♌	49	GREECE DEMOCRACY
28	♌	18	ISRAEL
28	♌	26	PALESTINE
1	♍	38	DOMINICAN REPUBLIC
3	♍	00	USSR-REVOLUTION
3	♍	09R	SRI LANKA-IND
5	♍	27	CANADA
6	♍	17	CHINA - NATIONALIST
6	♍	24	ANTIGUA-BARBUDA
7	♍	28	BURMA
7	♍	53	PHILLIPINES
8	♍	26	NAMIBIA
9	♍	20R	ORANGE FREE STATE
10	♍	18R	SIKKIM
11	♍	02R	LONDON 2
11	♍	09R	GUATEMALA - 2
11	♍	35	AUSTRALIA 1
11	♍	40	AUSTRALIA 2
12	♍	41	SOLOMON ISLANDS
12	♍	45	NETHERLANDS
12	♍	55	EQUATORIAL GUINEA
13	♍	22	ESTONIA
13	♍	55R	TRANSCAUCASIAN FED
14	♍	16	MALAYA
17	♍	04	FINLAND
18	♍	46	N Y STOCK EXCHANGE
18	♍	55	GEORGIA
18	♍	55	ARMENIA
19	♍	16	LITHUANIA
19	♍	32	AZERBAIJAN
19	♍	35R	GERMANY - THIRD REICH
22	♍	43	COSTA RICA 2
22	♍	44	KAMPUCHEA - REP
23	♍	03	FIJI
23	♍	53	LAOS I
24	♍	06	CISKEI
25	♍	27R	GAMBIA
26	♍	54	BULGARIA - INDEPENDENCE
27	♍	55	BARBADOS
28	♍	08	CYPRUS - TURKISH
28	♍	12	GUINEA - BUISSAU
29	♍	40	ETHIOPIA
0	♎	28	INDONESIA
2	♎	09	UKRAINE
5	♎	34	GERMANY - EMPIRE
6	♎	56	SPUTNIK
7	♎	14	ITALY - KINGDOM 2
7	♎	22	BULGARIA - COMMUNIST
7	♎	24	TURKEY
8	♎	07	PORTUGAL-REVOLUTION
8	♎	07R	LONDON 1
8	♎	10	S VIETNAM-REP
9	♎	23	INDIA - REPUBLIC
10	♎	36	CREATION OF THE WORLD
10	♎	51	VANUATU
14	♎	44	MALDIVES
14	♎	45	REAGAN-1
15	♎	00	CREATION OF MAN
15	♎	04	BIAFRA
16	♎	26	LIBYA - INDEP
17	♎	29	KOREA - SOUTH
18	♎	57	LUXEMBOURG
20	♎	12	HOLY ROMAN EMPIRE
21	♎	39	SINGAPORE 1
22	♎	56	SINGAPORE 2
23	♎	05	SINGAPORE 3
24	♎	29	BRUNEI
29	♎	39	FRANCE - NAPOLEON
2	♏	12	MALAYSIA
3	♏	41	BRAZIL
5	♏	40	KOREA - NORTH
7	♏	12	TUVALU
9	♏	00R	NORWAY
9	♏	58	BYELO RUSSIA
11	♏	32R	JAPAN - SOVEREIGNTY
11	♏	40	TRANSKEI
11	♏	45	ECUADOR 1
11	♏	57R	KHALISTAN
21	♏	04	NUCLEAR REACTION
21	♏	36	SUDAN
23	♏	00	FRANCE-FOURTH REPUBLIC
24	♏	24	VENEZUELA 1
25	♏	47	FRANCE-1st REPUBLIC 1
28	♏	40	ALBANIA - INDEPENDENCE
29	♏	05	FRANCE-1st REPUBLIC 2
0	♐	48	DOMINICA
3	♐	00	MOON LANDING
3	♐	16	CONSERVATIVE PARTY
6	♐	07R	PARAGUAY
6	♐	10	E.E.C.
9	♐	03	SWEDEN
10	♐	24	POLAND 1
11	♐	27	EGYPT - INDEPENDENCE
11	♐	37	EGYPT - KINGDOM
12	♐	15	CZECHOSLOVAKIA 1
15	♐	08	GREECE INDEPENCENCE
17	♐	02	NAT KHOREZEM SOVIET REP
18	♐	10	TANGANYIKA
19	♐	01	SOUTH AFRICAN REP 2
19	♐	31	LIBYA, COUP
19	♐	48	FAR EAST REPUBLIC
20	♐	17	CAMEROON
26	♐	19	YUGOSLAVIA 1
26	♐	00R	KAMPUCHEA - INDEP
26	♐	06R	SOUTH VIETNAM
26	♐	06R	LAOS 2
26	♐	06R	NORTH VIETNAM
26	♐	06	CARPATHO-UKRAINE
26	♐	08	SLOVAKIA
27	♐	52	RHODESIA
28	♐	24	UNITED ARAB REP
28	♐	31	GERMANY - WEIMAR
29	♐	39	AUSTRIA
0	♑	00	POLAND 2
0	♑	33	PANAMA
1	♑	32	HUNGARY
2	♑	17	CZECHOSLOVAKIA 3
3	♑	25	ZANZIBAR
3	♑	33	HAITI
4	♑	56	KENYA
5	♑	18	LATVIA
5	♑	49	WESTERN SAMOA
7	♑	28	ARAB FEDERATION
7	♑	46	ENGLAND-1689
8	♑	18	BANGLADESH 1
11	♑	18	ROMAN EMPIRE 1
13	♑	40	ROMAN EMPIRE 2
15	♑	12	PAKISTAN, REPUBLIC
15	♑	17	YUGOSLAVIA 2
15	♑	21	ICELAND
20	♑	15	NEW ZEALAND I
20	♑	44	DANZIG
21	♑	01	BANGLADESH 2
24	♑	40	NEPAL
27	♑	47	PERU-BATTLE AYACUCHO
27	♑	55	GUATEMALA - 3
28	♑	12	SOUTH YEMEN 1
28	♑	29	SOUTH YEMEN 2
2	♒	22	AGE OF AQUARIUS-2
2	♒	45	AGE OF AQUARIUS-1
4	♒	05	FIRST MANNED FLIGHT
8	♒	28	ENGLAND-WILLIAM
9	♒	01	IRAN - KHOMEINI
10	♒	16	SAUDI ARABIA
12	♒	20R	FEDERATION OF ARAB REPUB
12	♒	20R	QATAR

15	≈	55R	BAHRAIN
16	≈	22	REAGAN-2
17	≈	39	MEXICO - CONSTITUTION
20	≈	42	ECUADOR 2
20	≈	46	ROMANIA 1
24	≈	37	TEXAS
25	≈	31	ST LUCIA
26	≈	26	LIBERAL PARTY
26	≈	27	EIRE 2
26	≈	41	MOROCCO
27	≈	09	UNITED KINGDOM-1922
28	≈	52	LABOUR PARTY 1
4	♓	43	KAMPUCHEA, COMM
6	♓	36	TUNISIA

8	♓	58	USSR-REPUBLIC
13	♓	52	USSR-FORMATION
14	♓	43	UNITED ARAB EMIR
15	♓	40	SPAIN
16	♓	24	NAURU
18	♓	25	GREECE REVOLUTION
19	♓	03	TOGO
20	♓	34	ROME
22	♓	29R	BELGIUM
23	♓	27	BANGLADESH 3
25	♓	14	JAPAN - MEIJI CONST
25	♓	20R	VENEZUELA 2
25	♓	37	IRAN - ISLAMIC REP

JUPITER ♃

5	♈	12	LIBYA - INDEP
5	♈	52	GREECE REVOLUTION
7	♈	16	KAMPUCHEA, COMM
9	♈	10	FALL OF CONSTANTINOPLE
9	♈	34	ZANZIBAR
9	♈	37	KENYA
10	♈	46	SOUTH AFRICAN REP 2
10	♈	58	ROME
15	♈	01R	TIMOR
15	♈	09R	SURINAM
15	♈	13	ESPIRITU SANTO
15	♈	29	COMOROS 2
16	♈	13R	ANGOLA
17	♈	01	EIRE 1
17	♈	19R	MALAYSIA
18	♈	45R	SINGAPORE 1
20	♈	37R	DOMINICAN REPUBLIC
20	♈	46	MOZAMBIQUE
22	♈	10	CAPE VERDE ISLANDS
22	♈	16	COMOROS 1
22	♈	56	SAO TOME-PRINCIPE
23	♈	05R	PAPUA NEW GUINEA
24	♈	00R	COSTA RICA 1
24	♈	01	SAHRAWI ARAB D R
26	♈	09R	NICARAGUA 1
27	♈	19	MEXICO - CONSTITUTION
28	♈	33R	EL SALVADOR
28	♈	42R	POLAND 1
29	♈	06R	GUATEMALA - 1
29	♈	26	PERU I
29	♈	56	JAPAN - SOVEREIGNTY
2	♉	38	USSR-REPUBLIC
3	♉	37	TANZANIA
6	♉	45	FRANCE-VICHY REPUBLIC
14	♉	13	ARGENTINA - REVOLUTION
18	♉	32	GAMBIA
18	♉	53	MALAWI
21	♉	06	NORWAY
21	♉	14	SPAIN
21	♉	40	SEYCHELLES
22	♉	18	VIETNAM-UNION
23	♉	42R	ZAMBIA
25	♉	26	LONDON 2
26	♉	04R	MALTA
26	♉	05	SIKKIM
27	♉	16	LABOUR PARTY 2
28	♉	50	VATICAN CITY
29	♉	06R	TRANSKEI
1	♊	23	MEXICO - REVOLUTION
1	♊	30R	UKRAINE
4	♊	48R	LITHUANIA
5	♊	28R	FINLAND
6	♊	03	BRAZIL
6	♊	33R	ESTONIA
8	♊	48	PARAGUAY
9	♊	10R	USSR-REVOLUTION
9	♊	24	EGYPT - REPUBLIC
10	♊	22	GUATEMALA - 3
11	♊	42	TRANSCAUCASIAN FED
17	♊	16R	GERMANY - EMPIRE
18	♊	02R	LEBANON 1
18	♊	50	DJIBOUTI
19	♊	05	GEORGIA
19	♊	05	ARMENIA
19	♊	32	AZERBAIJAN
20	♊	31	SYRIA 1
20	♊	42R	ROMAN EMPIRE 2
20	♊	45	VENEZUELA 1
20	♊	59R	ROMAN EMPIRE 1
21	♊	20	MALDIVES
23	♊	44	UNITED PROVINCES C A
23	♊	55	FRANCE-THIRD REPUBLIC
23	♊	58	SINGAPORE 2
24	♊	01	SINGAPORE 3
26	♊	23R	LAOS 1
0	♋	28R	RHODESIA
0	♋	35R	FRANCE - NAPOLEON
1	♋	37	LONDON 1
1	♋	19R	BOPHUTHATSWANA
4	♋	09	GUYANA
5	♋	26	USA 2
5	♋	28	USA 1
5	♋	51	TEXAS
5	♋	56	USA 3
5	♋	56	USA 4
6	♋	45	LIBERIA
8	♋	47	ITALY - KINGDOM 2
12	♋	58	SOUTH VIETNAM
12	♋	58	LAOS 2

12	♋	58	NORTH VIETNAM
13	♋	10	KAMPUCHEA - INDEP
14	♋	33R	ICELAND
14	♋	34R	YUGOSLAVIA 2
15	♋	24	CZECHOSLOVAKIA 1
15	♋	28R	LATVIA
15	♋	38R	CZECHOSLOVAKIA 3
15	♋	40R	HUNGARY
15	♋	44R	POLAND 2
15	♋	44R	AUSTRIA
15	♋	46	CZECHOSLOVAKIA 2
15	♋	46R	GERMANY - WEIMAR
15	♋	47	YUGOSLAVIA 1
16	♋	57	SOLOMON ISLANDS
23	♋	30	GERMANY WEST SOVEREIGN
24	♋	34R	NUCLEAR REACTION
24	♋	48	WARSAW PACT
29	♋	04	IRAN - ISLAMIC REP
0	♌	36R	BOTSWANA
0	♌	36R	ST LUCIA
0	♌	55	LESOTHO
1	♌	07	BIAFRA
1	♌	46R	REAGAN-1
1	♌	51R	UNITED KINGDOM-1801
3	♌	02R	IRAN - KHOMEINI
3	♌	26	NAMIBIA
4	♌	21R	BARBADOS
4	♌	22	TUVALU
5	♌	12	ZIMBABWE-RHODESIA
7	♌	17	NEW ZEALAND I
8	♌	14	DOMINICA
9	♌	54	COSTA RICA 2
10	♌	41	SWITZERLAND
12	♌	56	KIRIBATI
13	♌	28R	PERU-BATTLE AYACUCHO
14	♌	40	NICARAGUA SANDINISTA
17	♌	00R	U.S. CIVIL WAR
17	♌	12	DENMARK
18	♌	08R	ITALY - KINGDOM 1
20	♌	22	THAILAND 2
21	♌	56	ENGLAND-1707
22	♌	02	BOLIVIA
22	♌	29R	PAKISTAN, REPUBLIC
22	♌	51R	CONFEDERATE STATES AMER
22	♌	53	ICELAND
23	♌	55	MOROCCO
24	♌	24	BYELO RUSSIA
26	♌	10	URUGUAY
26	♌	19	TUNISIA
26	♌	32R	LEBANON 2
26	♌	32R	SYRIA 2
26	♌	38	VENDA
27	♌	21	S VIETNAM-REP
28	♌	19R	MAURITIUS
0	♍	21R	ZIMBABWE
1	♍	11R	SUDAN
3	♍	30R	NAURU
4	♍	41	BULGARIA - INDEPENDENCE
4	♍	58	ST VINCENT-GRENADINES
5	♍	01	SOUTH YEMEN 1
5	♍	02	SOUTH YEMEN 2
7	♍	14	NAT KHOREZEM SOVIET REP
7	♍	57R	ENGLAND-WILLIAM
8	♍	51R	NICARAGUA 2
9	♍	42	BULGARIA - COMMUNIST
11	♍	09	VANUATU
11	♍	28	IRAQ - INDEPENCENCE
14	♍	05R	BOKHARA NAT'L SOVIET REP
14	♍	13R	MONGOLIA
15	♍	17	DANZIG
15	♍	43	SWAZILAND
20	♍	22	POLAND-COMMUNIST
20	♍	24R	GERMANY - THIRD REICH
22	♍	47	IRAQ - KINGDOM
22	♍	49	ATOMIC EXPLOSION
23	♍	30	EQUATORIAL GUINEA
23	♍	48R	ENGLAND-EDGAR
26	♍	51R	TREATY OF ROME
26	♍	17	HIROSHIMA
28	♍	23R	GHANA
0	♎	56	MOON LANDING
1	♎	38	VIETNAM
4	♎	31	MALAYA
4	♎	37R	SOUTH AFRICA-UNION
5	♎	28R	S.D.P.
6	♎	25	HONDURAS
8	♎	37	LIBYA, COUP
10	♎	22	REAGAN-2
11	♎	58	SPUTNIK

12 ♎ 08R	GUATEMALA - 2	
12 ♎ 54	UNITED NATIONS	
13 ♎ 48R	FAR EAST REPUBLIC	
14 ♎ 49	ALLIANCE	
15 ♎ 49	BELIZE	
16 ♎ 29R	EGYPT - KINGDOM	
16 ♎ 32R	EGYPT - INDEPENDENCE	
17 ♎ 29R	ITALY - REPUBLIC	
18 ♎ 00	PHILLIPINES	
18 ♎ 04R	JORDAN	
21 ♎ 44	PORTUGAL-REVOLUTION	
22 ♎ 40	IRAQ - REPUBLIC	
22 ♎ 57R	N Y STOCK EXCHANGE	
24 ♎ 38	ANTIGUA-BARBUDA	
25 ♎ 54	ALBANIA-PEOPLES REPUBLIC	
26 ♎ 40R	TONGA	
27 ♎ 11	YUGOSLAVIA-COMMUNIST	
27 ♎ 22	OMAN	
28 ♎ 35	E.E.C.	
0 ♏ 28	ARGENTINA - INDEPENDENCE	
1 ♏ 19	CISKEI	
1 ♏ 21	UNITED ARAB REP	
1 ♏ 40	ARAB FEDERATION	
2 ♏ 10	HAITI	
2 ♏ 32	CUBA - INDEPENDENCE 1	
2 ♏ 47	FRANCE-1st REPUBLIC 1	
3 ♏ 45	FRANCE-1st REPUBLIC 2	
4 ♏ 36	GUINEA	
5 ♏ 25	FRANCE-FIFTH REPUBLIC	
6 ♏ 56	FRANCE-FOURTH REPUBLIC	
8 ♏ 37	EIRE 2	
8 ♏ 48	UNITED KINGDOM-1922	
9 ♏ 42	KAMPUCHEA - REP	
9 ♏ 49	FIJI	
12 ♏ 57	USSR-FORMATION	
17 ♏ 52	CIA	
19 ♏ 00	INDIA - INDEPENDENCE	
19 ♏ 00	HYDERABAD	
19 ♏ 00	PAKISTAN	
19 ♏ 19	SOUTH AFRICAN REP 1	
24 ♏ 12	CUBA - COMMUNIST	
24 ♏ 17	TURKEY	
25 ♏ 18	DE GAULLE	
27 ♏ 14	BAHRAIN	
28 ♏ 46	QATAR	
28 ♏ 46	FEDERATION OF ARAB REPUB	
4 ♐ 25R	THATCHER	
4 ♐ 34	ST KITTS-NEVIS	
4 ♐ 02	CHINA - REPUBLIC	
5 ♐ 31R	BANGLADESH 2	
6 ♐ 27R	BANGLADESH 1	
9 ♐ 38	LABOUR PARTY 1	
13 ♐ 33	CHINA - NATIONALIST	
15 ♐ 25	CYPRUS - TURKISH	
15 ♐ 40	UNITED ARAB EMIR	
15 ♐ 46	BURMA	
18 ♐ 44	CAMEROON	
18 ♐ 52	BANGLADESH 3	
19 ♐ 06R	KOREA - SOUTH	
20 ♐ 13	KOREA - NORTH	
21 ♐ 51	SRI LANKA-IND	
21 ♐ 57	ALBANIA - INDEPENDENCE	
23 ♐ 47R	SENEGAL	
23 ♐ 48R	GABON	
23 ♐ 49R	CYPRUS	
23 ♐ 50R	CONGO	
23 ♐ 52R	CENTRAL AFRICAN REPUBLIC	
23 ♐ 55R	CHAD	
24 ♐ 04R	IVORY COAST	
24 ♐ 09R	BURKINO-FASSO	
24 ♐ 16R	NIGER	
24 ♐ 23R	BENIN	
24 ♐ 43	OPEC	
25 ♐ 18	CZECHOSLOVAKIA-COMMUNIST	
25 ♐ 25	MALI - REPUBLIC	
25 ♐ 50	BRUNEI	
25 ♐ 52	AUSTRALIA 1	
25 ♐ 59	AUSTRALIA 2	
26 ♐ 19	NIGERIA	
27 ♐ 22R	ZAIRE	
27 ♐ 22R	SOMALIA	
27 ♐ 37R	PALESTINE	
27 ♐ 39R	ISRAEL	
28 ♐ 00R	MADAGASCAR	
28 ♐ 00R	SOMALILAND	
28 ♐ 45R	MALI - FEDERATION	
28 ♐ 51	THAILAND 1	
0 ♑ 57	JAPAN - MEIJI CONST	
1 ♑ 08R	LIBERAL PARTY	
2 ♑ 09R	ROMANIA 1	
3 ♑ 33R	TOGO	
4 ♑ 52	CHILE 1	
5 ♑ 17	SWEDEN	
6 ♑ 25	MAURETANIA	
6 ♑ 51	GREECE INDEPENCENCE	
7 ♑ 11R	SRI LANKA-REP	
8 ♑ 28	VENEZUELA 2	
8 ♑ 48R	NETHERLANDS	
9 ♑ 21	BELGIUM	
10 ♑ 04R	KHALISTAN	
12 ♑ 01	CHILE 2	
13 ♑ 57	BUGANDA	
17 ♑ 40R	ECUADOR 2	
18 ♑ 33	ORANGE FREE STATE	
20 ♑ 26	RWANDA-UDI	
22 ♑ 21	CHINA - COMMUNIST 1	
22 ♑ 35	CHINA - COMMUNIST 2	
22 ♑ 40R	NATAL	
23 ♑ 20R	NATO 1	
24 ♑ 41	SAUDI ARABIA	
0 ♒ 32	EIRE 3	
1 ♒ 58	MONACO	
2 ♒ 10R	GERMANY WEST PROCLAM	
3 ♒ 45R	BULGARIA - AUTONOMY	
3 ♒ 45R	MONTENEGRO	
3 ♒ 45R	SERBIA	
3 ♒ 45R	ROMANIA 2	
4 ♒ 19	GAGARIN	
5 ♒ 29	INDONESIA	
5 ♒ 29R	CREATION OF MAN	
5 ♒ 37R	CREATION OF THE WORLD	
5 ♒ 37	TANGANYIKA	
5 ♒ 52	SIERRA LEONE	
6 ♒ 13R	KUWAIT	
6 ♒ 30	SHEPARD	
7 ♒ 07R	SOUTH AFRICA-REPUBLIC	
7 ♒ 09	GORBACHEV	
8 ♒ 57R	AFGHANISTAN	
9 ♒ 43R	BAHAMAS	
10 ♒ 34	WESTERN SAMOA	
12 ♒ 22	INDIA - REPUBLIC	
15 ♒ 24	COLUMBIA	
15 ♒ 33	ENGLAND-1689	
16 ♒ 50	CUBA - INDEPENDENCE 2	
18 ♒ 37	AGE OF AQUARIUS-2	
18 ♒ 44	AGE OF AQUARIUS-1	
23 ♒ 01	GRENADA	
25 ♒ 45R	HATAY	
28 ♒ 17	CONSERVATIVE PARTY	
0 ♓ 23R	LIECHTENSTEIN	
0 ♓ 44R	LUXEMBOURG	
3 ♓ 31R	UGANDA	
4 ♓ 29R	NORTH YEMEN	
7 ♓ 30R	CANADA	
7 ♓ 46R	TRINIDAD & TOBAGO	
9 ♓ 31	HOLY ROMAN EMPIRE	
10 ♓ 12	PORTUGAL-REVOLUTION	
10 ♓ 48R	JAMAICA	
12 ♓ 02R	ETHIOPIA	
12 ♓ 20R	GUINEA - BUISSAU	
12 ♓ 41	RWANDA-INDEPENDENCE	
12 ♓ 41R	BURUNDI	
13 ♓ 28R	ALGERIA	
13 ♓ 28R	PANAMA	
14 ♓ 52R	ECUADOR 1	
14 ♓ 47	FIRST MANNED FLIGHT	
15 ♓ 54	BHUTAN	
16 ♓ 57	CARPATHO-UKRAINE	
16 ♓ 57	SLOVAKIA	
17 ♓ 26R	GREECE DEMOCRACY	
24 ♓ 35	NEPAL	

SATURN ♄

2 ♈ 55	BULGARIA - AUTONOMY	
2 ♈ 55	MONTENEGRO	
2 ♈ 55	ROMANIA 2	
2 ♈ 55	SERBIA	
5 ♈ 44R	SOUTH YEMEN 2	
5 ♈ 44R	SOUTH YEMEN 1	
6 ♈ 20R	BULGARIA - INDEPENDENCE	
6 ♈ 23	DENMARK	
7 ♈ 59	NAURU	
9 ♈ 38R	ECUADOR 1	
9 ♈ 56	BIAFRA	
12 ♈ 21	MAURITIUS	
14 ♈ 58	GREECE REVOLUTION	
17 ♈ 09R	HATAY	
17 ♈ 30	CARPATHO-UKRAINE	
17 ♈ 30	SLOVAKIA	
18 ♈ 02	LIECHTENSTEIN	
20 ♈ 17R	DOMINICAN REPUBLIC	
22 ♈ 08	SOUTH AFRICAN REP 2	
22 ♈ 19R	EQUATORIAL GUINEA	
22 ♈ 24R	COSTA RICA 1	
23 ♈ 40R	NICARAGUA 1	
23 ♈ 53R	SWITZERLAND	
24 ♈ 48R	SWAZILAND	
25 ♈ 09R	EL SALVADOR	
25 ♈ 31R	GUATEMALA - 1	
26 ♈ 23	N Y STOCK EXCHANGE	
26 ♈ 36	PERU 1	
27 ♈ 44	SOUTH AFRICAN REP 1	
0 ♉ 37R	FRANCE-1st REPUBLIC 2	
0 ♉ 55R	FRANCE-1st REPUBLIC 1	
1 ♉ 37	SOUTH AFRICA-UNION	
4 ♉ 51R	PORTUGAL-REVOLUTION	
8 ♉ 10	MOON LANDING	
8 ♉ 48R	LIBYA, COUP	
9 ♉ 56R	BRAZIL	
10 ♉ 43	FRANCE-VICHY REPUBLIC	
13 ♉ 30R	CHINA - REPUBLIC	
16 ♉ 05	TONGA	
19 ♉ 36	BANGLADESH 1	
19 ♉ 46	LONDON 1	
20 ♉ 16	UNITED PROVINCES C A	
21 ♉ 01	OMAN	
21 ♉ 34R	FIJI	

21 ♉ 36R	KAMPUCHEA - REP
22 ♉ 06	BANGLADESH 2
24 ♉ 22R	LEBANON 1
25 ♉ 37	ORANGE FREE STATE
28 ♉ 31R	SYRIA 1
0 ♊ 11R	ALBANIA - INDEPENDENCE
1 ♊ 25R	BANGLADESH 3
2 ♊ 30R	UNITED ARAB EMIR
3 ♊ 18R	PERU-BATTLE AYACUCHO
4 ♊ 58	ENGLAND-1707
5 ♊ 24	BAHRAIN
6 ♊ 15	QATAR
6 ♊ 15	FEDERATION OF ARAB REPUB
7 ♊ 47	SRI LANKA-REP
8 ♊ 57R	NUCLEAR REACTION
9 ♊ 03R	CREATION OF MAN
9 ♊ 06R	CREATION OF THE WORLD
19 ♊ 01	BOLIVIA
20 ♊ 33	URUGUAY
21 ♊ 52R	LEBANON 2
21 ♊ 52R	SYRIA 2
27 ♊ 18	BAHAMAS
27 ♊ 25	ENGLAND-EDGAR
28 ♊ 07	AFGHANISTAN
28 ♊ 11R	GRENADA
29 ♊ 39	ICELAND
0 ♋ 32	PORTUGAL-REVOLUTION
4 ♋ 42	BHUTAN
9 ♋ 05	BULGARIA - COMMUNIST
11 ♋ 16	EIRE 1
11 ♋ 22	GREECE DEMOCRACY
12 ♋ 15R	NEPAL
13 ♋ 02	KAMPUCHEA, COMM
13 ♋ 18	POLAND-COMMUNIST
15 ♋ 38	GUINEA - BUISSAU
16 ♋ 34	ROMAN EMPIRE 2
16 ♋ 42R	ETHIOPIA
16 ♋ 46	ROMAN EMPIRE 1
16 ♋ 57R	HIROSHIMA
18 ♋ 13	MOZAMBIQUE
19 ♋ 51	YUGOSLAVIA-COMMUNIST
19 ♋ 54R	CAPE VERDE ISLANDS
21 ♋ 12	VIETNAM
21 ♋ 17	COMOROS 1
21 ♋ 18	ALBANIA-PEOPLES REPUBLIC
21 ♋ 30R	JORDAN
21 ♋ 36	SAO TOME-PRINCIPE
22 ♋ 05	ITALY - REPUBLIC
23 ♋ 21	USSR-REPUBLIC
24 ♋ 16R	UNITED NATIONS
24 ♋ 45	MEXICO - CONSTITUTION
26 ♋ 00R	SAHRAWI ARAB D R
26 ♋ 12	PHILLIPINES
26 ♋ 46R	PAPUA NEW GUINEA
29 ♋ 51	POLAND 1
0 ♌ 34	COMOROS 2
1 ♌ 06R	ESPIRITU SANTO
2 ♌ 40	SEYCHELLES
2 ♌ 49R	TIMOR
2 ♌ 53R	SURINAM
2 ♌ 58	ANGOLA
3 ♌ 04	VIETNAM-UNION
7 ♌ 46	TRANSCAUCASIAN FED
8 ♌ 22	FRANCE-FOURTH REPUBLIC
9 ♌ 30	GEORGIA
9 ♌ 32	ARMENIA
9 ♌ 40	AZERBAIJAN
10 ♌ 09	FRANCE - NAPOLEON
11 ♌ 52R	CIA
12 ♌ 04	UKRAINE
13 ♌ 36	ECUADOR 2
13 ♌ 36	PAKISTAN
14 ♌ 14	HYDERABAD
14 ♌ 20R	INDIA - INDEPENDENCE
14 ♌ 27R	USSR-REVOLUTION
14 ♌ 32R	LITHUANIA
14 ♌ 38	FINLAND
14 ♌ 46R	ESTONIA
15 ♌ 53	DJIBOUTI
16 ♌ 25	GREECE INDEPENCENCE
16 ♌ 26	TRANSKEI
16 ♌ 27R	ISRAEL
17 ♌ 57R	PALESTINE
19 ♌ 41R	JAPAN - MEIJI CONST
21 ♌ 50R	CZECHOSLOVAKIA-COMMUNIST
22 ♌ 18R	SRI LANKA-IND
23 ♌ 22R	BURMA
25 ♌ 37	CHINA - NATIONALIST
25 ♌ 50	UNITED KINGDOM-1801
26 ♌ 26	KOREA - SOUTH
26 ♌ 38	CZECHOSLOVAKIA 1
26 ♌ 42	VENEZUELA 2
27 ♌ 24	CZECHOSLOVAKIA 2
27 ♌ 29	YUGOSLAVIA 1
27 ♌ 30	GERMANY - WEIMAR
27 ♌ 36	AUSTRIA
27 ♌ 39	POLAND 2
27 ♌ 43	HUNGARY
27 ♌ 47	CZECHOSLOVAKIA 3
27 ♌ 49	BELGIUM
28 ♌ 11	SOLOMON ISLANDS
28 ♌ 11	LATVIA
29 ♌ 09	YUGOSLAVIA 2
29 ♌ 22	ICELAND
29 ♌ 28R	KOREA - NORTH
29 ♌ 43	MONACO
0 ♍ 31	EIRE 3
3 ♍ 05R	GERMANY WEST PROCLAM
4 ♍ 34R	BOPHUTHATSWANA
0 ♍ 31	HOLY ROMAN EMPIRE
3 ♍ 05R	U.S. CIVIL WAR
4 ♍ 34R	ITALY - KINGDOM 1
7 ♍ 30	ZIMBABWE-RHODESIA
7 ♍ 41R	CONFEDERATE STATES AMER
8 ♍ 09	TUVALU
8 ♍ 18R	IRAN - ISLAMIC REP
8 ♍ 28	NATO 1
10 ♍ 15	KIRIBATI
10 ♍ 27	BYELO RUSSIA
11 ♍ 03	NICARAGUA SANDINISTA
11 ♍ 09R	ST LUCIA
11 ♍ 36	DOMINICA
11 ♍ 55	CHINA - COMMUNIST 1
12 ♍ 40R	IRAN - KHOMEINI
13 ♍ 08	CHINA - COMMUNIST 2
16 ♍ 50R	ENGLAND-WILLIAM
17 ♍ 16R	SPAIN
17 ♍ 33	VENDA
17 ♍ 47	NAT KHOREZEM SOVIET REP
18 ♍ 47R	INDIA - REPUBLIC
19 ♍ 26	INDONESIA
21 ♍ 11R	ZIMBABWE
22 ♍ 05R	BOKHARA NAT'L SOVIET REP
22 ♍ 10R	MONGOLIA
22 ♍ 38	DANZIG
22 ♍ 48	ST VINCENT-GRENADINES
23 ♍ 49	VANUATU
24 ♍ 25	IRAQ - KINGDOM
3 ♎ 22R	FAR EAST REPUBLIC
3 ♎ 27	HAITI
5 ♎ 03R	EGYPT - KINGDOM
5 ♎ 05R	EGYPT - INDEPENDENCE
6 ♎ 30R	S.D.P.
6 ♎ 39R	JAPAN - SOVEREIGNTY
9 ♎ 47R	REAGAN-2
10 ♎ 26	ALLIANCE
11 ♎ 01	BELIZE
14 ♎ 05	LIBYA - INDEP
14 ♎ 45	USA 2
14 ♎ 45	USA 1
14 ♎ 48	USA 3
14 ♎ 48	USA 4
15 ♎ 58	ANTIGUA-BARBUDA
17 ♎ 39	EIRE 2
17 ♎ 44	UNITED KINGDOM-1922
19 ♎ 18	USSR-FORMATION
19 ♎ 25	CISKEI
20 ♎ 34R	EGYPT - REPUBLIC
24 ♎ 29R	FALL OF CONSTANTINOPLE
24 ♎ 33	TURKEY
28 ♎ 06R	THATCHER
0 ♏ 01	LAOS 1
2 ♏ 30	ST KITTS-NEVIS
2 ♏ 49	SOUTH VIETNAM
2 ♏ 49	LAOS 2
2 ♏ 50	NORTH VIETNAM
2 ♏ 50	KAMPUCHEA - INDEP
4 ♏ 59R	TEXAS
6 ♏ 59R	ENGLAND-1689
8 ♏ 12	SWEDEN
8 ♏ 02	CYPRUS - TURKISH
10 ♏ 24R	KHALISTAN
13 ♏ 55	BRUNEI
15 ♏ 30R	ROME
17 ♏ 30R	WARSAW PACT
17 ♏ 46R	CANADA
18 ♏ 10R	GERMANY WEST SOVEREIGN
19 ♏ 20	LUXEMBOURG
21 ♏ 14	S VIETNAM-REP
26 ♏ 52	CONSERVATIVE PARTY
26 ♏ 43R	NICARAGUA 2
27 ♏ 41R	TUNISIA
28 ♏ 05	HONDURAS
28 ♏ 07R	GORBACHEV
28 ♏ 55	SUDAN
28 ♏ 56R	MOROCCO
2 ♐ 43R	PAKISTAN, REPUBLIC
7 ♐ 58	MALAYA
9 ♐ 35	MEXICO - REVOLUTION
9 ♐ 41R	GUATEMALA - 2
9 ♐ 55	SPUTNIK
12 ♐ 39R	ARGENTINA - REVOLUTION
14 ♐ 02	GHANA
14 ♐ 18R	TREATY OF ROME
15 ♐ 14	CUBA - INDEPENDENCE 1
19 ♐ 26	E.E.C.
20 ♐ 14	GUINEA
20 ♐ 22R	IRAQ - REPUBLIC
20 ♐ 29	FRANCE-FIFTH REPUBLIC
21 ♐ 56R	VENEZUELA 1
21 ♐ 59	FRANCE-THIRD REPUBLIC
22 ♐ 42	UNITED ARAB REP
23 ♐ 45	ARAB FEDERATION
25 ♐ 32R	PARAGUAY
28 ♐ 04R	VATICAN CITY
29 ♐ 37	CUBA - COMMUNIST
0 ♑ 20	DE GAULLE
1 ♑ 13	THAILAND 1
3 ♑ 22	LABOUR PARTY 1
4 ♑ 01	GERMANY - EMPIRE
6 ♑ 19R	ITALY - KINGDOM 2
7 ♑ 39	AUSTRALIA 1
7 ♑ 43	AUSTRALIA 2
9 ♑ 27	CAMEROON
11 ♑ 49R	OPEC
11 ♑ 51	MALI - REPUBLIC
12 ♑ 00	NIGERIA
12 ♑ 23R	SENEGAL
12 ♑ 32R	GABON
12 ♑ 34R	CYPRUS
12 ♑ 37R	CONGO
12 ♑ 37R	CENTRAL AFRICAN REPUBLIC
12 ♑ 49R	CHAD
13 ♑ 02R	IVORY COAST
13 ♑ 09R	BURKINO-FASSO

13	♑	16R	NIGER	17	♒	29R	MALAYSIA
13	♑	24R	BENIN	18	♒	26	ZANZIBAR
14	♑	09R	NATAL	18	♒	29R	SINGAPORE 1
15	♑	35R	ZAIRE	18	♒	35	KENYA
15	♑	36R	SOMALIA	23	♒	04R	ARGENTINA - INDEPENDENCE
15	♑	50	MAURETANIA	26	♒	22R	NETHERLANDS
15	♑	57R	MADAGASCAR	28	♒	25R	ZAMBIA
15	♑	57R	SOMALILAND	29	♒	44R	MALTA
16	♑	22R	MALI - FEDERATION	2	♓	52	NORWAY
18	♑	26	TOGO	3	♓	09	TANZANIA
19	♑	21	SAUDI ARABIA	3	♓	55	LABOUR PARTY 2
19	♑	31	BUGANDA	4	♓	41R	MALAWI
22	♑	49	RWANDA-UDI	6	♓	34	GAMBIA
27	♑	11	TANGANYIKA	6	♓	35	GUATEMALA - 3
27	♑	41R	CUBA - INDEPENDENCE 2	6	♓	45	CHILE 1
28	♑	07	IRAQ - INDEPENCENCE	10	♓	30R	RHODESIA
28	♑	36R	KUWAIT	11	♓	34	LONDON 2
29	♑	15	GAGARIN	11	♓	56	SIKKIM
29	♑	30R	SOUTH AFRICA-REPUBLIC	12	♓	05R	LIBERIA
29	♑	43	SIERRA LEONE	12	♓	57	CHILE 2
29	♑	44	WESTERN SAMOA	15	♓	50R	SINGAPORE 3
29	♑	50	SHEPARD	15	♓	51R	SINGAPORE 2
3	♒	17	PANAMA	16	♓	35R	MALDIVES
3	♒	31R	THAILAND 2	19	♓	00	ROMANIA 1
3	♒	52	AGE OF AQUARIUS-2	19	♓	35	LIBERAL PARTY
3	♒	52	AGE OF AQUARIUS-1	22	♓	55	BARBADOS
4	♒	46R	UGANDA	23	♓	01R	COSTA RICA 2
4	♒	53R	NORTH YEMEN	23	♓	28R	NEW ZEALAND I
5	♒	59R	TRINIDAD & TOBAGO	23	♓	43R	NAMIBIA
6	♒	30	FIRST MANNED FLIGHT	24	♓	06	REAGAN-1
7	♒	37	GERMANY - THIRD REICH	24	♓	19	COLUMBIA
7	♒	40R	JAMAICA	25	♓	11R	LESOTHO
10	♒	02R	ALGERIA	25	♓	29R	BOTSWANA
10	♒	11R	RWANDA-INDEPENDENCE	27	♓	57	GUYANA
10	♒	11R	BURUNDI				

URANUS ⛢

3	♈	32	ROME	12	♋	12	LUXEMBOURG
10	♈	45	VATICAN CITY	12	♋	24R	LIBYA - INDEP
13	♈	24	GUATEMALA - 3	12	♋	38R	CONSERVATIVE PARTY
18	♈	14R	LIBERIA	17	♋	26	EGYPT - REPUBLIC
19	♈	56	GERMANY - THIRD REICH	23	♋	05	LAOS I
21	♈	48R	COSTA RICA 2	23	♋	39	NORTH VIETNAM
21	♈	50R	IRAQ - INDEPENCENCE	23	♋	39	SOUTH VIETNAM
22	♈	54	THAILAND 2	23	♋	39	LAOS 2
25	♈	02	DENMARK	23	♋	42	KAMPUCHEA - INDEP
0	♉	26	SOUTH AFRICAN REP 1	24	♋	06	GERMANY WEST SOVEREIGN
9	♉	11	ORANGE FREE STATE	24	♋	23	WARSAW PACT
14	♉	55	CARPATHO-UKRAINE	24	♋	24R	GERMANY - EMPIRE
14	♉	55	SLOVAKIA	25	♋	09	FRANCE-THIRD REPUBLIC
17	♉	29	LIECHTENSTEIN	25	♋	48	ITALY - KINGDOM 2
19	♉	47R	HATAY	28	♋	12	FALL OF CONSTANTINOPLE
19	♉	14	ENGLAND-1689	28	♋	18R	PAKISTAN, REPUBLIC
23	♉	57	FRANCE-VICHY REPUBLIC	29	♋	25	MOROCCO
28	♉	07R	LEBANON I	0	♌	17	TUNISIA
0	♊	18R	SYRIA 1	1	♌	09R	SUDAN
2	♊	15R	NUCLEAR REACTION	2	♌	15	S VIETNAM-REP
5	♊	34R	LEBANON 2	2	♌	58R	TREATY OF ROME
5	♊	34R	SYRIA 2	3	♌	24R	GHANA
8	♊	02R	CONFEDERATE STATES AMER	8	♌	58R	ARAB FEDERATION
8	♊	24	ITALY - KINGDOM 1	9	♌	09	MALAYA
8	♊	49	USA 2	9	♌	22	ENGLAND-1707
8	♊	49	USA 1	9	♌	30R	UNITED ARAB REP
8	♊	55	USA 3	10	♌	39	IRAQ - REPUBLIC
8	♊	55	USA 4	10	♌	49R	E.E.C.
9	♊	21	U.S. CIVIL WAR	10	♌	50	SPUTNIK
9	♊	59	ICELAND	15	♌	09	N Y STOCK EXCHANGE
13	♊	06	BULGARIA - COMMUNIST	15	♌	10	GUINEA
13	♊	35R	YUGOSLAVIA-COMMUNIST	15	♌	20	FRANCE-FIFTH REPUBLIC
14	♊	05R	ALBANIA-PEOPLES REPUBLIC	15	♌	25R	DE GAULLE
14	♊	38	POLAND-COMMUNIST	15	♌	38R	CUBA - COMMUNIST
15	♊	35	ATOMIC EXPLOSION	16	♌	56	TOGO
16	♊	06R	CREATION OF MAN	18	♌	18	MALI - FEDERATION
16	♊	07R	CREATION OF THE WORLD	18	♌	34	SOMALILAND
16	♊	29	HIROSHIMA	18	♌	34	MADAGASCAR
16	♊	42	JORDAN	18	♌	49	SOMALIA
17	♊	02R	UNITED NATIONS	18	♌	49	ZAIRE
17	♊	16	VIETNAM	20	♌	32R	CAMEROON
17	♊	40	ITALY - REPUBLIC	20	♌	35	BENIN
17	♊	01	PHILLIPINES	20	♌	43	NIGER
21	♊	25R	FRANCE-FOURTH REPUBLIC	20	♌	50	ROMANIA 1
22	♊	07R	CZECHOSLOVAKIA-COMMUNIST	20	♌	58	BURKINO-FASSO
22	♊	24R	SRI LANKA-IND	20	♌	58	IVORY COAST
23	♊	23R	BURMA	21	♌	05	LIBERAL PARTY
23	♊	49R	CHINA - NATIONALIST	21	♌	12	CHAD
24	♊	20	CIA	21	♌	20	CENTRAL AFRICAN REPUBLIC
24	♊	21	ISRAEL	21	♌	27	CONGO
24	♊	22	PALESTINE	21	♌	31	CYPRUS
25	♊	10	INDIA - INDEPENDENCE	21	♌	35	GABON
25	♊	10	PAKISTAN	21	♌	39R	SIERRA LEONE
25	♊	10	HYDERABAD	21	♌	40	SHEPARD
27	♊	20	EIRE 3	21	♌	46	FRANCE-1st REPUBLIC 1
28	♊	15	MONACO	21	♌	47	SENEGAL
28	♊	47	GERMANY WEST PROCLAM	21	♌	47R	GAGARIN
29	♊	14	THAILAND 1	22	♌	00	FRANCE-1st REPUBLIC 2
29	♊	26	KOREA - SOUTH	22	♌	00	SOUTH AFRICA-REPUBLIC
0	♋	19	KOREA - NORTH	22	♌	46	KUWAIT
1	♋	42R	INDIA - REPUBLIC	23	♌	18	OPEC
2	♋	29R	SWEDEN	23	♌	44	MALI - REPUBLIC
2	♋	53R	INDONESIA	24	♌	10	NIGERIA
4	♋	04	NATO I	24	♌	25R	RWANDA-UDI
4	♋	50	CHINA - COMMUNIST 1	25	♌	48	MAURETANIA
4	♋	58	CHINA - COMMUNIST 2	26	♌	30	SWITZERLAND
8	♋	38	CANADA	27	♌	26	BULGARIA - AUTONOMY
10	♋	39	JAPAN - SOVEREIGNTY				

Deg	Sign	Min	Name
27	♌	26	SERBIA
27	♌	26	ROMANIA 2
27	♌	26	MONTENEGRO
27	♌	48	BURUNDI
27	♌	48	RWANDA-INDEPENDENCE
27	♌	55	ALGERIA
29	♌	02R	AGE OF AQUARIUS-1
29	♌	03R	AGE OF AQUARIUS-2
29	♌	46	JAMAICA
0	♍	14R	WESTERN SAMOA
0	♍	33R	TANGANYIKA
1	♍	19	TRINIDAD & TOBAGO
2	♍	57	NORTH YEMEN
3	♍	33	UGANDA
5	♍	44	SINGAPORE 1
6	♍	02R	TANZANIA
6	♍	43	MALAYSIA
7	♍	08	MALAWI
10	♍	03	ZANZIBAR
10	♍	04	KENYA
11	♍	31R	SIKKIM
11	♍	34	MALTA
11	♍	38R	LONDON 2
12	♍	38	MALDIVES
13	♍	23	ZAMBIA
13	♍	23R	GAMBIA
13	♍	24	SINGAPORE 2
13	♍	25	SINGAPORE 3
13	♍	43R	SOUTH AFRICAN REP 2
15	♍	29	GUYANA
18	♍	45	RHODESIA
20	♍	17	BIAFRA
21	♍	04	BOTSWANA
21	♍	18	LESOTHO
22	♍	37	NAMIBIA
24	♍	00	BARBADOS
24	♍	25R	REAGAN-1
25	♍	56	FRANCE - NAPOLEON
27	♍	26R	MAURITIUS
28	♍	34	SWAZILAND
28	♍	37	SOUTH YEMEN 1
28	♍	38	SOUTH YEMEN 2
28	♍	54R	NAURU
0	♎	44	MOON LANDING
0	♎	51	EQUATORIAL GUINEA
1	♎	54	UNITED KINGDOM-1801
2	♎	53	LIBYA, COUP
4	♎	41R	TONGA
5	♎	23	OMAN
9	♎	35	KAMPUCHEA - REP
9	♎	37	FIJI
10	♎	50	BAHRAIN
10	♎	53R	BANGLADESH 2
11	♎	45	QATAR
11	♎	45	FEDERATION OF ARAB REPUB
11	♎	49R	BANGLADESH 1
14	♎	35R	SRI LANKA-REP
16	♎	02	HAITI
17	♎	06	UNITED ARAB EMIR
17	♎	40	BANGLADESH 3
19	♎	01	BAHAMAS
19	♎	07	AFGHANISTAN
21	♎	52R	JAPAN - MEIJI CONST
23	♎	52	GREECE DEMOCRACY
24	♎	02R	BHUTAN
25	♎	23R	PORTUGAL-REVOLUTION
25	♎	39	GUINEA - BUISSAU
25	♎	46	ETHIOPIA
26	♎	31	HOLY ROMAN EMPIRE
27	♎	46R	GRENADA
28	♎	21R	COMOROS 1
28	♎	22R	CAPE VERDE ISLANDS
28	♎	22	SAO TOME-PRINCIPE
28	♎	25R	MOZAMBIQUE
0	♏	22	PAPUA NEW GUINEA
0	♏	35R	KAMPUCHEA, COMM
2	♏	20R	NEPAL
3	♏	04R	VIETNAM-UNION
3	♏	06R	SEYCHELLES
3	♏	46	ANGOLA
4	♏	37	SURINAM
4	♏	47	TIMOR
6	♏	12	ESPIRITU SANTO
6	♏	22	COMOROS 2
6	♏	01R	SAHRAWI ARAB D R
7	♏	10	TRANSKEI
7	♏	51R	DJIBOUTI
11	♏	22R	ARGENTINA - REVOLUTION
11	♏	37	MEXICO - REVOLUTION
12	♏	25R	SOLOMON ISLANDS
14	♏	00	BOPHUTHATSWANA
14	♏	21	TUVALU
14	♏	47R	ENGLAND-EDGAR
14	♏	56R	VENEZUELA 1
16	♏	20	DOMINICA
16	♏	35R	PARAGUAY
16	♏	56R	NICARAGUA SANDINISTA
17	♏	01R	KIRIBATI
17	♏	55	VENDA
18	♏	06R	ZIMBABWE-RHODESIA
20	♏	11	ST VINCENT-GRENADINES
20	♏	27R	IRAN - ISLAMIC REP
20	♏	45	IRAN - KHOMEINI
21	♏	00	ST LUCIA
21	♏	30R	VANUATU
24	♏	36R	ZIMBABWE
26	♏	50	ALLIANCE
27	♏	01	BELIZE
29	♏	04	ANTIGUA-BARBUDA
29	♏	17	REAGAN-2
29	♏	55R	S.D.P.
1	♐	04	CISKEI
4	♐	45	SPAIN
4	♐	43	CUBA - INDEPENDENCE 1
5	♐	39	ST KITTS-NEVIS
6	♐	37R	THATCHER
7	♐	54R	ARGENTINA - INDEPENDENCE
8	♐	20	CYPRUS - TURKISH
11	♐	05R	KHALISTAN
11	♐	07	BRUNEI
12	♐	20	LABOUR PARTY 1
12	♐	56	ROMAN EMPIRE 1
13	♐	05	ROMAN EMPIRE 2
14	♐	17	AUSTRALIA 1
14	♐	19	AUSTRALIA 2
17	♐	56	GORBACHEV
19	♐	13	SAUDI ARABIA
19	♐	27	CHILE 1
20	♐	07R	CHILE 2
20	♐	09R	CUBA - INDEPENDENCE 2
23	♐	17	PANAMA
24	♐	43	COLUMBIA
25	♐	24	ECUADOR 1
25	♐	44	FIRST MANNED FLIGHT
28	♐	27	ENGLAND-WILLIAM
29	♐	10	GUATEMALA - 1
29	♐	13	EL SALVADOR
29	♐	37	NICARAGUA-1
29	♐	49R	PERU 1
0	♑	09	COSTA RICA 1
1	♑	52	DOMINICAN REPUBLIC
2	♑	56R	NORWAY
3	♑	03	GREECE REVOLUTION
3	♑	24R	BRAZIL
7	♑	01	LABOUR PARTY 2
8	♑	45	NEW ZEALAND 1
9	♑	39R	UNITED PROVINCES C A
13	♑	00	BULGARIA - INDEPENDENCE
14	♑	17	PERU-BATTLE AYACUCHO
15	♑	16	LONDON 1
16	♑	23R	URUGUAY
16	♑	57R	BOLIVIA
21	♑	16	PORTUGAL-REVOLUTION
24	♑	51R	SOUTH AFRICA-UNION
28	♑	16	CHINA - REPUBLIC
0	♒	33	ALBANIA - INDEPENDENCE
6	♒	36R	BELGIUM
6	♒	46R	VENEZUELA 2
6	♒	52	GREECE INDEPENCENCE
10	♒	28	ECUADOR 2
15	♒	49	POLAND 1
17	♒	22R	NETHERLANDS
19	♒	14	MEXICO - CONSTITUTION
19	♒	20	EIRE 1
19	♒	49	USSR-REVOLUTION
20	♒	09	ESTONIA
20	♒	32	FINLAND
20	♒	47	LITHUANIA
22	♒	28	UKRAINE
23	♒	48R	YUGOSLAVIA 1
23	♒	48	GERMANY - WEIMAR
23	♒	48R	CZECHOSLOVAKIA 2
23	♒	49	AUSTRIA
23	♒	49	POLAND 2
23	♒	50	HUNGARY
23	♒	50	CZECHOSLOVAKIA 3
23	♒	53	LATVIA
23	♒	54R	CZECHOSLOVAKIA 1
24	♒	07	YUGOSLAVIA 2
24	♒	07	ICELAND
27	♒	02	TRANSCAUCASIAN FED
27	♒	42	ARMENIA
27	♒	42	GEORGIA
27	♒	42	AZERBAIJAN
1	♓	11	TEXAS
1	♓	45	DANZIG
2	♓	26R	NAT KHOREZEM SOVIET REP
4	♓	41R	BYELO RUSSIA
6	♓	00	MONGOLIA
6	♓	04	BOKHARA NAT'L SOVIET REP
8	♓	00R	IRAQ - KINGDOM
8	♓	45R	HONDURAS
9	♓	48	EIRE 2
9	♓	49	UNITED KINGDOM-1922
10	♓	22	USSR-FORMATION
10	♓	23	EGYPT - INDEPENDENCE
10	♓	25	EGYPT - KINGDOM
11	♓	34	NICARAGUA 2
11	♓	35	FAR EAST REPUBLIC
13	♓	54R	TURKEY
14	♓	49	GUATEMALA - 2
27	♓	14	NATAL

NEPTUNE ♆

Deg	Sign	Min	Name
7	♈	49R	SWEDEN
12	♈	44R	CONSERVATIVE PARTY
14	♈	23	ROME
14	♈	24R	LUXEMBOURG

15	♈	00	CANADA
19	♈	07	GERMANY - EMPIRE
21	♈	24R	FRANCE-THIRD REPUBLIC
22	♈	03	ENGLAND-1787
23	♈	54	ITALY - KINGDOM 2
5	♉	57	ROMANIA 1
6	♉	18	LIBERAL PARTY
9	♉	34	BULGARIA - AUTONOMY
9	♉	34	MONTENEGRO
9	♉	34	ROMANIA 2
9	♉	34	SERBIA
11	♉	39R	SOUTH AFRICAN REP 2
22	♉	12R	ENGLAND-WILLIAM
29	♉	31	JAPAN - MEIJI CONST
10	♊	22R	CREATION OF MAN
10	♊	25R	CREATION OF THE WORLD
23	♊	30R	CUBA - INDEPENDENCE 1
24	♊	13R	LABOUR PARTY 1
27	♊	31R	AUSTRALIA 2
27	♊	32R	AUSTRALIA 1
29	♊	27R	SAUDI ARABIA
29	♊	58	CUBA - INDEPENDENCE 2
4	♋	49R	FIRST MANNED FLIGHT
5	♋	47R	PANAMA
7	♋	03	NORWAY
7	♋	56R	LABOUR PARTY 2
14	♋	44	NEW ZEALAND I
16	♋	39	NETHERLANDS
17	♋	03	BULGARIA - INDEPENDENCE
17	♋	36	SOUTH AFRICA-UNION
21	♋	27	PORTUGAL-REVOLUTION
22	♋	46R	CHINA - REPUBLIC
25	♋	47R	ALBANIA - INDEPENDENCE
29	♋	55	EIRE 1
2	♌	36R	USSR-REPUBLIC
3	♌	17R	MEXICO - CONSTITUTION
4	♌	19	TRANSCAUCASIAN FED
4	♌	45	GEORGIA
4	♌	45	ARMENIA
4	♌	48	AZERBAIJAN
4	♌	53	POLAND 1
5	♌	50R	UKRAINE
6	♌	50R	LITHUANIA
6	♌	55R	FINLAND
7	♌	01	ESTONIA
7	♌	07	USSR-REVOLUTION
9	♌	09	CZECHOSLOVAKIA 1
9	♌	14R	ICELAND
9	♌	14R	YUGOSLAVIA 2
9	♌	16	CZECHOSLOVAKIA 2
9	♌	16	YUGOSLAVIA 1
9	♌	19R	LATVIA
9	♌	20R	GERMANY - WEIMAR
9	♌	20R	CZECHOSLOVAKIA 3
9	♌	20	AUSTRIA
9	♌	20	HUNGARY
9	♌	20	POLAND 2
11	♌	10	BYELO RUSSIA
11	♌	34R	BOKHARA NAT'L SOVIET REP
11	♌	36R	MONGOLIA
13	♌	09	NAT KHOREZEM SOVIET REP
13	♌	16R	FAR EAST REPUBLIC
13	♌	36R	EGYPT - KINGDOM
13	♌	36R	EGYPT - INDEPENDENCE
13	♌	46	DANZIG
14	♌	06	IRAQ - KINGDOM
17	♌	46R	USSR-FORMATION
18	♌	06R	UNITED KINGDOM-1922
18	♌	07R	EIRE 2
20	♌	13	TURKEY
28	♌	48	VATICAN CITY
5	♍	36	THAILAND 2
8	♍	55	IRAQ - INDEPENCENCE
9	♍	33R	GERMANY - THIRD REICH
19	♍	12	LIECHTENSTEIN
20	♍	25	HATAY
21	♍	41R	ROMAN EMPIRE 2
21	♍	43R	ROMAN EMPIRE 1
21	♍	56R	SLOVAKIA
21	♍	56R	CARPATHO-UKRAINE
22	♍	23	USA 2
22	♍	23	USA 1
22	♍	25	USA 3
22	♍	25	USA 4
22	♍	46	FRANCE-VICHY REPUBLIC
27	♍	16	SYRIA 1
29	♍	31	LEBANON I
1	♎	28	ICELAND
1	♎	46	NUCLEAR REACTION
1	♎	50R	FALL OF CONSTANTINOPLE
3	♎	20	BULGARIA - COMMUNIST
3	♎	42	POLAND-COMMUNIST
3	♎	55	ATOMIC EXPLOSION
4	♎	14	SYRIA 2
4	♎	14	LEBANON 2
4	♎	21	HIROSHIMA
5	♎	11	VIETNAM
5	♎	51R	ITALY - REPUBLIC
5	♎	55	PHILLIPINES
5	♎	59R	JORDAN
6	♎	14	SWITZERLAND
6	♎	25R	THAILAND 1
7	♎	05	UNITED NATIONS
8	♎	23	CIA
8	♎	30R	YUGOSLAVIA-COMMUNIST
8	♎	37R	ALBANIA-PEOPLES REPUBLIC
8	♎	50	PAKISTAN
8	♎	50	INDIA - INDEPENDENCE
8	♎	50	HYDERABAD
9	♎	18	FRANCE-FOURTH REPUBLIC
10	♎	31	HOLY ROMAN EMPIRE
10	♎	34R	PALESTINE
10	♎	35R	ISRAEL
10	♎	59	KOREA - SOUTH
11	♎	52	KOREA - NORTH
12	♎	32R	CZECHOSLOVAKIA-COMMUNIST
12	♎	40R	GERMANY WEST PROCLAM
12	♎	52	CHINA - NATIONALIST
12	♎	53R	SRI LANKA-IND
12	♎	55R	MONACO
12	♎	57	BURMA
13	♎	22	NATO 1
13	♎	26R	EIRE 3
14	♎	16	CHINA - COMMUNIST 1
14	♎	38	CHINA - COMMUNIST 2
17	♎	13	INDONESIA
17	♎	20R	INDIA - REPUBLIC
19	♎	51R	JAPAN - SOVEREIGNTY
21	♎	10R	EGYPT - REPUBLIC
21	♎	27	LIBYA - INDEP
23	♎	21	SOUTH VIETNAM
23	♎	21	LAOS 2
23	♎	21	NORTH VIETNAM
23	♎	22	KAMPUCHEA - INDEP
23	♎	51	LAOS 1
26	♎	11R	WARSAW PACT
26	♎	24R	GERMANY WEST SOVEREIGN
26	♎	34R	ENGLAND-EDGAR
27	♎	42R	N Y STOCK EXCHANGE
27	♎	47R	TUNISIA
28	♎	05R	MOROCCO
28	♎	0B	S VIETNAM-REP
28	♎	28	FRANCE-1st REPUBLIC 1
28	♎	38	FRANCE-1st REPUBLIC 2
29	♎	46R	PAKISTAN, REPUBLIC
0	♏	09	SUDAN
0	♏	28	MALAYA
1	♏	34	SPUTNIK
1	♏	56R	TREATY OF ROME
2	♏	00R	IRAQ - REPUBLIC
2	♏	20R	GHANA
3	♏	31	GUINEA
3	♏	39	FRANCE-FIFTH REPUBLIC
4	♏	26	E.E.C.
4	♏	45R	ARAB FEDERATION
4	♏	47	UNITED ARAB REP
6	♏	25	BENIN
6	♏	26	NIGER
6	♏	27R	ZAIRE
6	♏	27R	SOMALIA
6	♏	28	BURKINO-FASSO
6	♏	28	IVORY COAST
6	♏	30R	MADAGASCAR
6	♏	30R	SOMALILAND
6	♏	31	CHAD
6	♏	33	CENTRAL AFRICAN REPUBLIC
6	♏	34	CONGO
6	♏	34R	MALI - FEDERATION
6	♏	35	CYPRUS
6	♏	35	CUBA - COMMUNIST
6	♏	36	GABON
6	♏	39	SENEGAL
6	♏	42	DE GAULLE
7	♏	14	OPEC
7	♏	28	MALI - REPUBLIC
7	♏	45	NIGERIA
7	♏	48R	TOGO
8	♏	41	CAMEROON
8	♏	48R	KUWAIT
9	♏	10R	SOUTH AFRICA-REPUBLIC
9	♏	49R	SHEPARD
9	♏	51	MAURETANIA
10	♏	03R	SIERRA LEONE
10	♏	26R	GAGARIN
10	♏	46	JAMAICA
10	♏	49	ALGERIA
10	♏	49R	BUGANDA
10	♏	51R	RWANDA-INDEPENDENCE
10	♏	51R	BURUNDI
11	♏	07	TRINIDAD & TOBAGO
11	♏	16	RWANDA-UDI
11	♏	49	NORTH YEMEN
12	♏	12	UGANDA
12	♏	47	TANGANYIKA
12	♏	58	WESTERN SAMOA
13	♏	14	SINGAPORE 1
13	♏	28	AGE OF AQUARIUS-2
13	♏	28	AGE OF AQUARIUS-1
13	♏	35	MALAYSIA
14	♏	56	FRANCE - NAPOLEON
15	♏	11R	MALAWI
15	♏	52	MALTA
16	♏	32	ZANZIBAR
16	♏	36	KENYA
16	♏	44R	TANZANIA
16	♏	56	ZAMBIA
17	♏	14R	MALDIVES
17	♏	16	SINGAPORE 2
17	♏	16	SINGAPORE 3
18	♏	44	UNITED KINGDOM-1801
19	♏	32R	SIKKIM
19	♏	35R	LONDON 2
19	♏	42	RHODESIA
20	♏	00	GAMBIA
20	♏	19	BOTSWANA
20	♏	26R	GUYANA
21	♏	26	LESOTHO
21	♏	13	NAMIBIA
22	♏	25	BARBADOS
22	♏	34R	BIAFRA
23	♏	34	REAGAN-1
24	♏	02	SWAZILAND
24	♏	33	SOUTH YEMEN 1
24	♏	34	SOUTH YEMEN 2
24	♏	56	EQUATORIAL GUINEA
25	♏	06	HAITI
26	♏	01R	MOON LANDING
26	♏	0B	LIBYA, COUP

26 ♏ 19	NAURU	20 ♐ 02R	ARGENTINA - INDEPENDENCE
26 ♏ 29R	MAURITIUS	20 ♐ 12R	VANUATU
28 ♏ 12R	OMAN	20 ♐ 16	ST LUCIA
29 ♏ 03	KAMPUCHEA - REP	20 ♐ 29R	IRAN - ISLAMIC REP
29 ♏ 04	FIJI	22 ♐ 08	ALLIANCE
29 ♏ 10R	TONGA	22 ♐ 11	BELIZE
0 ♐ 18	BAHRAIN	22 ♐ 31R	ZIMBABWE
0 ♐ 25	QATAR	22 ♐ 59	ANTIGUA-BARBUDA
0 ♐ 25	FEDERATION OF ARAB REPUB	23 ♐ 44	REAGAN-2
0 ♐ 55	SPAIN	24 ♐ 06	CISKEI
2 ♐ 36R	BANGLADESH 2	24 ♐ 52	S.D.P.
2 ♐ 58R	BANGLADESH 1	25 ♐ 57	CHILE 1
3 ♐ 03	UNITED ARAB EMIR	26 ♐ 29R	CHILE 2
3 ♐ 34	BANGLADESH 3	26 ♐ 30	ST KITTS-NEVIS
3 ♐ 58R	SRI LANKA-REP	27 ♐ 39	CYPRUS - TURKISH
4 ♐ 55R	AFGHANISTAN	28 ♐ 07R	THATCHER
5 ♐ 01R	BAHAMAS	28 ♐ 16	COLUMBIA
6 ♐ 29	MEXICO - REVOLUTION	28 ♐ 21	ECUADOR 1
6 ♐ 59	GUINEA - BUISSAU	29 ♐ 20	BRUNEI
7 ♐ 00	ETHIOPIA	0 ♑ 15R	KHALISTAN
7 ♐ 01R	GREECE DEMOCRACY	0 ♑ 18	GUATEMALA - 1
7 ♐ 47R	ARGENTINA - REVOLUTION	0 ♑ 19	EL SALVADOR
8 ♐ 10R	BHUTAN	0 ♑ 32	NICARAGUA 1
8 ♐ 59R	VENEZUELA 1	0 ♑ 49R	PERU 1
9 ♐ 08R	PORTUGAL-REVOLUTION	0 ♑ 51	COSTA RICA 1
9 ♐ 12	PAPUA NEW GUINEA	1 ♑ 55	DOMINICAN REPUBLIC
9 ♐ 19	GRENADA	2 ♑ 30R	BRAZIL
9 ♐ 26R	SAO TOME-PRINCIPE	3 ♑ 02	GREECE REVOLUTION
9 ♐ 33R	COMOROS 1	3 ♑ 27	GORBACHEV
9 ♐ 34R	CAPE VERDE ISLANDS	5 ♑ 59R	UNITED PROVINCES C A
9 ♐ 49R	MOZAMBIQUE	8 ♑ 32	PERU-BATTLE AYACUCHO
10 ♐ 18R	PARAGUAY	9 ♑ 13R	URUGUAY
10 ♐ 39	ANGOLA	9 ♑ 26	LONDON 1
11 ♐ 10	SURINAM	9 ♑ 33R	BOLIVIA
11 ♐ 17	TIMOR	20 ♑ 01	BELGIUM
11 ♐ 29R	KAMPUCHEA, COMM	20 ♑ 02R	VENEZUELA 2
11 ♐ 42	NEPAL	21 ♑ 09	GREECE INDEPENCENCE
11 ♐ 51R	VIETNAM-UNION	22 ♑ 42R	ECUADOR 2
11 ♐ 56R	SEYCHELLES	4 ♒ 52	TEXAS
12 ♐ 15	TRANSKEI	7 ♒ 39	HONDURAS
12 ♐ 21	ESPIRITU SANTO	10 ♒ 22	NICARAGUA 2
12 ♐ 30	COMOROS 2	12 ♒ 25	GUATEMALA - 2
13 ♐ 54	SAHRAWI ARAB D R	19 ♒ 15	NATAL
14 ♐ 13R	DJIBOUTI	29 ♒ 02	GUATEMALA - 3
15 ♐ 47	BOPHUTHATSWANA	29 ♒ 41R	LIBERIA
15 ♐ 51	TUVALU	1 ♓ 01R	COSTA RICA 2
16 ♐ 13R	SOLOMON ISLANDS	4 ♓ 50	DENMARK
16 ♐ 42	DOMINICA	7 ♓ 27	SOUTH AFRICAN REP 1
17 ♐ 46	VENDA	10 ♓ 24	ENGLAND-1689
18 ♐ 10R	NICARAGUA SANDINISTA	13 ♓ 04	ORANGE FREE STATE
18 ♐ 20R	KIRIBATI	27 ♓ 33	CONFEDERATE STATES AMER
18 ♐ 36	ST VINCENT-GRENADINES	28 ♓ 58	ITALY - KINGDOM 1
19 ♐ 23R	ZIMBABWE-RHODESIA	29 ♓ 57	U.S. CIVIL WAR
19 ♐ 49	IRAN - KHOMEINI		

PLUTO ♇

0 ♈ 14R	BRAZIL	20 ♊ 23R	PANAMA
1 ♈ 07R	PERU-BATTLE AYACUCHO	20 ♊ 48R	LABOUR PARTY 2
1 ♈ 24	LONDON 1	21 ♊ 04	NORWAY
2 ♈ 05	UNITED PROVINCES C A	24 ♊ 48	NEW ZEALAND 1
3 ♈ 49R	URUGUAY	25 ♊ 50R	BULGARIA - INDEPENDENCE
4 ♈ 05R	BOLIVIA	25 ♊ 57	SOUTH AFRICA-UNION
4 ♈ 43R	NETHERLANDS	27 ♊ 45R	CHINA - REPUBLIC
6 ♈ 53	GREECE INDEPENCENCE	27 ♊ 57R	PORTUGAL-REVOLUTION
8 ♈ 33R	BELGIUM	29 ♊ 29R	ALBANIA - INDEPENDENCE
8 ♈ 47R	VENEZUELA 2	1 ♋ 32	EIRE 1
9 ♈ 03	ECUADOR 2	2 ♋ 23R	USSR-REPUBLIC
13 ♈ 35	TEXAS	2 ♋ 41R	MEXICO - CONSTITUTION
16 ♈ 36R	HONDURAS	3 ♋ 40	TRANSCAUCASIAN FED
16 ♈ 56	NICARAGUA 2	3 ♋ 58R	UKRAINE
17 ♈ 38	GUATEMALA - 2	4 ♋ 14R	POLAND 1
21 ♈ 09	NATAL	4 ♋ 16	GEORGIA
24 ♈ 50	GUATEMALA - 3	4 ♋ 16	ARMENIA
26 ♈ 56	LIBERIA	4 ♋ 19	AZERBAIJAN
27 ♈ 44R	COSTA RICA 2	4 ♋ 48R	LITHUANIA
28 ♈ 24	DENMARK	4 ♋ 53R	FINLAND
28 ♈ 51	SOUTH AFRICAN REP 1	5 ♋ 02R	ESTONIA
1 ♉ 04	ORANGE FREE STATE	5 ♋ 20R	USSR-REVOLUTION
7 ♉ 34	CONFEDERATE STATES AMER	6 ♋ 07R	ICELAND
8 ♉ 03	ITALY - KINGDOM 1	6 ♋ 07R	YUGOSLAVIA 2
8 ♉ 35	U.S. CIVIL WAR	6 ♋ 20R	LATVIA
12 ♉ 38R	SWEDEN	6 ♋ 23R	CZECHOSLOVAKIA 3
15 ♉ 02R	CONSERVATIVE PARTY	6 ♋ 24R	HUNGARY
15 ♉ 46	CANADA	6 ♋ 26R	POLAND 2
16 ♉ 00R	LUXEMBOURG	6 ♋ 26R	AUSTRIA
17 ♉ 00R	GERMANY - EMPIRE	6 ♋ 27R	GERMANY - WEIMAR
18 ♉ 53R	FRANCE-THIRD REPUBLIC	6 ♋ 34R	YUGOSLAVIA 1
19 ♉ 29	ITALY - KINGDOM 2	6 ♋ 34R	CZECHOSLOVAKIA 2
24 ♉ 12	ROMANIA 1	6 ♋ 38R	CZECHOSLOVAKIA 1
24 ♉ 25	LIBERAL PARTY	6 ♋ 51R	BOKHARA NAT'L SOVIET REP
26 ♉ 09	BULGARIA - AUTONOMY	6 ♋ 52R	MONGOLIA
26 ♉ 09	MONTENEGRO	7 ♋ 57R	EGYPT - KINGDOM
26 ♉ 09	ROMANIA 2	7 ♋ 57R	EGYPT - INDEPENDENCE
26 ♉ 09	SERBIA	7 ♋ 59	FAR EAST REPUBLIC
26 ♉ 41R	SOUTH AFRICAN REP 2	8 ♋ 04	BYELO RUSSIA
2 ♊ 14R	CREATION OF MAN	8 ♋ 40R	DANZIG
2 ♊ 18R	CREATION OF THE WORLD	8 ♋ 54	NAT KHOREZEM SOVIET REP
4 ♊ 00R	JAPAN - MEIJI CONST	9 ♋ 37	IRAQ - KINGDOM
14 ♊ 38R	CUBA - INDEPENDENCE 1	10 ♋ 12R	USSR-FORMATION
14 ♊ 42	LABOUR PARTY 1	10 ♋ 39R	UNITED KINGDOM-1922
16 ♊ 16R	AUSTRALIA 2	10 ♋ 40R	EIRE 2
16 ♊ 16R	AUSTRALIA 1	12 ♋ 20R	TURKEY
17 ♊ 03R	SAUDI ARABIA	17 ♋ 05	VATICAN CITY
17 ♊ 42	CUBA - INDEPENDENCE 2	21 ♋ 10	THAILAND 2
19 ♊ 36R	FIRST MANNED FLIGHT	21 ♋ 58R	GERMANY - THIRD REICH

17 ♓ 00	ARGENTINA - REVOLUTION
18 ♓ 04	PARAGUAY
18 ♓ 15R	VENEZUELA 1
24 ♓ 02	CHILE 1
24 ♓ 08R	ARGENTINA - INDEPENDENCE
25 ♓ 20	CHILE 2
25 ♓ 31	COLUMBIA
27 ♓ 18R	ECUADOR 1

27 ♓ 47R	DOMINICAN REPUBLIC
28 ♓ 09R	COSTA RICA 1
28 ♓ 23	GREECE REVOLUTION
28 ♓ 25R	NICARAGUA 1
28 ♓ 49R	EL SALVADOR
28 ♓ 56R	GUATEMALA - 1
29 ♓ 43R	PERU I

CHIRON ⚷

0 ♈ 17R	EQUATORIAL GUINEA
0 ♈ 17R	DOMINICAN REPUBLIC
0 ♈ 22R	CZECHOSLOVAKIA 1
0 ♈ 50	GREECE REVOLUTION
1 ♈ 08R	COSTA RICA 1
1 ♈ 25	TRANSCAUCASIAN FED
1 ♈ 47R	NICARAGUA 1
1 ♈ 54R	SWAZILAND
2 ♈ 42R	EL SALVADOR
2 ♈ 55	GEORGIA
2 ♈ 55	ARMENIA
2 ♈ 59R	GUATEMALA - 1
2 ♈ 59	AZERBAIJAN
3 ♈ 06	GERMANY - EMPIRE
4 ♈ 39R	PERU I
5 ♈ 41R	LIBYA, COUP
5 ♈ 50R	FRANCE-THIRD REPUBLIC
5 ♈ 36R	DANZIG
6 ♈ 49R	MOON LANDING
7 ♈ 12R	BRAZIL
7 ♈ 45R	FIJI
7 ♈ 46R	KAMPUCHEA - REP
8 ♈ 26R	NAT KHOREZEM SOVIET REP
8 ♈ 27	MONGOLIA
8 ♈ 30	BOKHARA NAT'L SOVIET REP
9 ♈ 22R	BANGLADESH 3
9 ♈ 24	ROMAN EMPIRE 1
9 ♈ 25	ROMAN EMPIRE 2
9 ♈ 30	BANGLADESH 1
9 ♈ 32R	UNITED ARAB EMIR
9 ♈ 42	TONGA
9 ♈ 47	ROME
10 ♈ 20R	OMAN
10 ♈ 30R	BYELO RUSSIA
10 ♈ 39R	SWITZERLAND
10 ♈ 42	LONDON 1
10 ♈ 46	ITALY - KINGDOM 2
10 ♈ 47	BANGLADESH 2
11 ♈ 27R	PERU-BATTLE AYACUCHO
12 ♈ 02R	CREATION OF MAN
12 ♈ 06	HOLY ROMAN EMPIRE
12 ♈ 08R	CREATION OF THE WORLD
12 ♈ 10	UNITED PROVINCES C A
12 ♈ 14	SPAIN
12 ♈ 23	EGYPT - INDEPENDENCE
12 ♈ 24	EGYPT - KINGDOM
13 ♈ 01R	FEDERATION OF ARAB REPUB
13 ♈ 01R	QATAR
13 ♈ 08	USSR-FORMATION
13 ♈ 16R	UNITED KINGDOM-1922
13 ♈ 17R	EIRE 2
13 ♈ 32R	BAHRAIN
13 ♈ 35R	IRAQ - KINGDOM
13 ♈ 39	FALL OF CONSTANTINOPLE
13 ♈ 40	FAR EAST REPUBLIC
15 ♈ 57	SRI LANKA-REP
15 ♈ 58R	NETHERLANDS
16 ♈ 16	ENGLAND-1689
16 ♈ 54	ENGLAND-WILLIAM
16 ♈ 54	ENGLAND-EDGAR
17 ♈ 09	GRENADA
17 ♈ 13	USA 2
17 ♈ 13	USA 1
17 ♈ 15	USA 3
17 ♈ 15	USA 4
17 ♈ 51	ENGLAND-1707
18 ♈ 09R	TURKEY
19 ♈ 18R	URUGUAY
19 ♈ 42R	BOLIVIA
20 ♈ 49	BAHAMAS
20 ♈ 53	AFGHANISTAN
21 ♈ 12	PORTUGAL-REVOLUTION
21 ♈ 16	NEPAL
23 ♈ 11	BHUTAN
23 ♈ 36R	COMOROS 2
23 ♈ 37R	ESPIRITU SANTO
23 ♈ 38R	ETHIOPIA
23 ♈ 43R	GUINEA - BUISSAU
24 ♈ 10	KAMPUCHEA, COMM
24 ♈ 13R	TIMOR
24 ♈ 19R	SURINAM
24 ♈ 30	GREECE DEMOCRACY
24 ♈ 52R	ANGOLA
24 ♈ 55	SAHRAWI ARAB D R
27 ♈ 19R	PAPUA NEW GUINEA
27 ♈ 33	MOZAMBIQUE
27 ♈ 51	CAPE VERDE ISLANDS
27 ♈ 52	COMOROS 1
27 ♈ 59	SAO TOME-PRINCIPE
29 ♈ 26R	TRANSKEI
1 ♉ 15	GREECE INDEPENCENCE
1 ♉ 19	SEYCHELLES
1 ♉ 25	VIETNAM-UNION
1 ♉ 32	ROMANIA 1
1 ♉ 43R	BOPHUTHATSWANA
2 ♉ 05	LIBERAL PARTY
4 ♉ 57	DJIBOUTI
5 ♉ 11	IRAN - KHOMEINI
5 ♉ 44	ST LUCIA
5 ♉ 52	THAILAND 1
6 ♉ 36	ECUADOR 2
7 ♉ 15R	DOMINICA
7 ♉ 35	IRAN - ISLAMIC REP
7 ♉ 57	SERBIA
7 ♉ 57	MONTENEGRO
7 ♉ 57	BULGARIA - AUTONOMY
7 ♉ 57	ROMANIA 2
8 ♉ 47R	TUVALU
9 ♉ 00R	BELGIUM
9 ♉ 07	SOLOMON ISLANDS
9 ♉ 28R	VENEZUELA 2
11 ♉ 20	ZIMBABWE-RHODESIA
11 ♉ 55R	ST VINCENT-GRENADINES
12 ♉ 15	VATICAN CITY
12 ♉ 33	ZIMBABWE
12 ♉ 47R	SOUTH AFRICAN REP 2
13 ♉ 15	KIRIBATI
13 ♉ 24R	REAGAN-2
13 ♉ 31	NICARAGUA SANDINISTA
13 ♉ 38R	VENDA
15 ♉ 17	S.D.P.
18 ♉ 00	VANUATU
19 ♉ 19R	CISKEI
20 ♉ 58R	ANTIGUA-BARBUDA
22 ♉ 34R	BELIZE
22 ♉ 40R	ALLIANCE
23 ♉ 40R	GERMANY - THIRD REICH
26 ♉ 22	THAILAND 2
28 ♉ 19R	IRAQ - INDEPENCENCE
28 ♉ 28R	BRUNEI
29 ♉ 14	THATCHER
0 ♊ 47R	CYPRUS - TURKISH
1 ♊ 14	TEXAS
2 ♊ 52R	ST KITTS-NEVIS
3 ♊ 47	GORBACHEV
4 ♊ 33	KHALISTAN
17 ♊ 19	NICARAGUA 2
23 ♊ 51	GUATEMALA - 2
27 ♊ 46R	HONDURAS
4 ♋ 13	CARPATHO-UKRAINE
4 ♋ 13	SLOVAKIA
5 ♋ 39	LIECHTENSTEIN
6 ♋ 32R	JAPAN - MEIJI CONST
8 ♋ 34	HATAY
9 ♋ 29	N Y STOCK EXCHANGE
19 ♋ 36	FRANCE-VICHY REPUBLIC
21 ♋ 52	FRANCE-1st REPUBLIC 1
22 ♋ 09	FRANCE-1st REPUBLIC 2
24 ♋ 23	NATAL
10 ♌ 39	SYRIA 1
14 ♌ 44	LEBANON I
29 ♌ 28	NUCLEAR REACTION
11 ♍ 05	ICELAND
16 ♍ 02R	SYRIA 2
16 ♍ 02R	LEBANON 2
20 ♍ 55	BULGARIA - COMMUNIST
28 ♍ 16	POLAND-COMMUNIST
29 ♍ 38	ATOMIC EXPLOSION
1 ♎ 44	HIROSHIMA
5 ♎ 12	VIETNAM
12 ♎ 46	UNITED NATIONS
15 ♎ 09R	ITALY - REPUBLIC
15 ♎ 11	LIBERIA
15 ♎ 28R	JORDAN
22 ♎ 33	PHILLIPINES
17 ♎ 52R	GUATEMALA - 3
20 ♎ 59	ALBANIA-PEOPLES REPUBLIC
21 ♎ 33	YUGOSLAVIA-COMMUNIST
28 ♎ 18	FRANCE-FOURTH REPUBLIC
3 ♏ 04	CIA
4 ♏ 08	COSTA RICA 2
4 ♏ 13	HYDERABAD
4 ♏ 13	PAKISTAN
4 ♏ 13	INDIA - INDEPENDENCE
6 ♏ 56	FRANCE - NAPOLEON
18 ♏ 20R	DENMARK
19 ♏ 15	KOREA - SOUTH
20 ♏ 14	CHINA - NATIONALIST
21 ♏ 07	KOREA - NORTH
21 ♏ 22	BURMA
21 ♏ 36R	PALESTINE
21 ♏ 38R	ISRAEL
23 ♏ 56	SRI LANKA-IND
24 ♏ 48	CZECHOSLOVAKIA-COMMUNIST
26 ♏ 57	UNITED KINGDOM-1801
3 ♐ 10	NATO 1
4 ♐ 50	CHINA - COMMUNIST 1
5 ♐ 38	CHINA - COMMUNIST 2
6 ♐ 18	CUBA - INDEPENDENCE 1
6 ♐ 30R	GERMANY WEST PROCLAM

NORTH NODE ☊

Deg	Sign	Min	Name
11	♊	18	ROMAN EMPIRE 2
11	♊	41	ROMAN EMPIRE 1
11	♊	54	SINGAPORE 3
11	♊	55	SINGAPORE 2
12	♊	08	FRANCE-FOURTH REPUBLIC
12	♊	45	MALDIVES
15	♊	12	ARGENTINA - INDEPENDENCE
15	♊	31	SIKKIM
15	♊	53	BRUNEI
16	♊	02	LONDON 2
16	♊	11	CYPRUS - TURKISH
20	♊	02	ST KITTS-NEVIS
20	♊	19	GAMBIA
20	♊	37	PHILLIPINES
20	♊	48	ITALY - REPUBLIC
20	♊	54	JORDAN
24	♊	15	ZAMBIA
25	♊	05	THATCHER
27	♊	35	MALTA
29	♊	26	YUGOSLAVIA-COMMUNIST
29	♊	27	BULGARIA - INDEPENDENCE
29	♊	48	ALBANIA-PEOPLES REPUBLIC
0	♋	51	ITALY - KINGDOM 2
1	♋	49	UNITED NATIONS
2	♋	03	MALAWI
3	♋	27	TANZANIA
7	♋	25	VIETNAM
8	♋	55	HIROSHIMA
9	♋	03	ATOMIC EXPLOSION
9	♋	10	POLAND-COMMUNIST
9	♋	58	GERMANY - EMPIRE
11	♋	24	KENYA
11	♋	30	ZANZIBAR
17	♋	14	SOUTH AFRICAN REP 1
17	♋	56	FRANCE-THIRD REPUBLIC
18	♋	35	MALAYSIA
19	♋	32	SINGAPORE 1
20	♋	30	NEW ZEALAND 1
20	♋	57	JAPAN - MEIJI CONST
23	♋	12	CISKEI
25	♋	31	ANTIGUA-BARBUDA
26	♋	28	BULGARIA - COMMUNIST
28	♋	02	ICELAND
0	♌	00	BELIZE
0	♌	18	ALLIANCE
0	♌	42	SPAIN
4	♌	23	UGANDA
6	♌	36	USA 1
6	♌	36	USA 2
6	♌	36	USA 3
6	♌	36	USA 4
7	♌	02	SYRIA 2
7	♌	02	LEBANON 2
7	♌	36	NORTH YEMEN
8	♌	47	TRINIDAD & TOBAGO
8	♌	55	JAMAICA
9	♌	01	S.D.P.
9	♌	03	ALGERIA
9	♌	10	RWANDA-INDEPENDENCE
9	♌	10	BURUNDI
10	♌	51	REAGAN-2
18	♌	02	AGE OF AQUARIUS-1
18	♌	02	AGE OF AQUARIUS-2
18	♌	44	WESTERN SAMOA
20	♌	00	TANGANYIKA
20	♌	12	VANUATU
20	♌	56	LABOUR PARTY 2
25	♌	53	SWITZERLAND
27	♌	16	ZIMBABWE
28	♌	37	NUCLEAR REACTION
29	♌	00	KUWAIT
0	♍	48	SOUTH AFRICA-REPUBLIC
3	♍	16	NORWAY
3	♍	18	SHEPARD
4	♍	26	SIERRA LEONE
5	♍	24	GAGARIN
6	♍	31	RWANDA-UDI
6	♍	42	ST VINCENT-GRENADINES
6	♍	52	DENMARK
8	♍	00	BUGANDA
8	♍	25	VENDA
9	♍	22	NICARAGUA SANDINISTA
9	♍	33	KIRIBATI
9	♍	41	TURKEY
9	♍	59	BELGIUM
10	♍	07	VENEZUELA 2
11	♍	44	MAURETANIA
11	♍	50	CONSERVATIVE PARTY
13	♍	06	ZIMBABWE-RHODESIA
14	♍	18	LUXEMBOURG
15	♍	25	NIGERIA
15	♍	28	OPEC
15	♍	31	MALI - REPUBLIC
15	♍	33	SENEGAL
15	♍	42	GABON
15	♍	43	CHAD
15	♍	45	CYPRUS
15	♍	45	IVORY COAST
15	♍	46	CENTRAL AFRICAN REPUBLIC
15	♍	46	CONGO
15	♍	53	BURKINO-FASSO
16	♍	02	NIGER
16	♍	06	BENIN
16	♍	41	CANADA
16	♍	48	ECUADOR 2
17	♍	15	IRAN - ISLAMIC REP
17	♍	33	ST LUCIA
17	♍	57	SOMALIA
17	♍	57	ZAIRE
17	♍	58	IRAN - KHOMEINI
18	♍	18	MADAGASCAR
18	♍	18	SOMALILAND
19	♍	25	ENGLAND-WILLIAM
19	♍	28	MALI - FEDERATION
19	♍	38	VENEZUELA 1
19	♍	45	LEBANON 1
19	♍	55	GREECE INDEPENCENCE
21	♍	31	COSTA RICA 2
22	♍	46	SYRIA 1
23	♍	57	TOGO
24	♍	02	USSR-FORMATION
24	♍	18	FRANCE-1st REPUBLIC 1
24	♍	19	FRANCE-1st REPUBLIC 2
24	♍	28	PARAGUAY
25	♍	53	DOMINICA
26	♍	03	UNITED KINGDOM-1922
26	♍	13	EIRE 2
26	♍	48	TUVALU
28	♍	02	CAMEROON
29	♍	46	SOLOMON ISLANDS
2	♎	13	N Y STOCK EXCHANGE
2	♎	34	ENGLAND-EDGAR
3	♎	13	FIRST MANNED FLIGHT
5	♎	35	MEXICO - REVOLUTION
6	♎	33	PANAMA
8	♎	44	FAR EAST REPUBLIC
8	♎	45	EGYPT - INDEPENDENCE
8	♎	45	EGYPT - KINGDOM
12	♎	27	LIBERIA
13	♎	21	BOPHUTHATSWANA
13	♎	31	ARGENTINA - REVOLUTION
17	♎	47	DE GAULLE
17	♎	47	FRANCE-VICHY REPUBLIC
18	♎	19	CUBA - COMMUNIST
18	♎	54	GUATEMALA - 3
19	♎	00	IRAQ - KINGDOM
19	♎	13	SWEDEN
21	♎	24	DJIBOUTI
22	♎	16	GUINEA
24	♎	20	FRANCE-FIFTH REPUBLIC
27	♎	37	IRAQ - REPUBLIC
28	♎	17	BOKHARA NAT'L SOVIET REP
28	♎	21	MONGOLIA
3	♏	33	TRANSKEI
4	♏	11	ARAB FEDERATION
4	♏	20	CUBA - INDEPENDENCE 2
5	♏	24	UNITED ARAB REP
6	♏	25	DANZIG
6	♏	42	NAT KHOREZEM SOVIET REP
8	♏	41	E.E.C.
9	♏	37	SLOVAKIA
9	♏	38	CARPATHO-UKRAINE
10	♏	18	SAUDI ARABIA
10	♏	35	VIETNAM-UNION
10	♏	54	SPUTNIK
11	♏	02	SEYCHELLES
11	♏	09	BYELO RUSSIA
12	♏	54	MALAYA
15	♏	03	SAHRAWI ARAB D R
20	♏	45	HATAY
20	♏	50	TREATY OF ROME
20	♏	55	COMOROS 2
20	♏	59	ESPIRITU SANTO
21	♏	43	SURINAM
21	♏	44	TIMOR
21	♏	48	ANGOLA
21	♏	48	GHANA
24	♏	04	PAPUA NEW GUINEA
24	♏	28	LIECHTENSTEIN
29	♏	43	SAO TOME-PRINCIPE
0	♐	15	COMOROS 1
0	♐	15	CAPE VERDE ISLANDS
0	♐	39	MOZAMBIQUE
1	♐	18	AUSTRALIA 1
1	♐	19	AUSTRALIA 2
1	♐	20	KAMPUCHEA, COMM
5	♐	47	NEPAL
8	♐	04	TUNISIA
8	♐	09	MOROCCO
10	♐	48	PAKISTAN, REPUBLIC
13	♐	03	ICELAND
13	♐	03	YUGOSLAVIA 2
13	♐	03	LATVIA
13	♐	12	CZECHOSLOVAKIA 3
13	♐	14	GERMANY - WEIMAR
13	♐	14	HUNGARY
13	♐	16	AUSTRIA
13	♐	16	POLAND 2
13	♐	49	YUGOSLAVIA 1
13	♐	53	CZECHOSLOVAKIA 2
14	♐	14	CZECHOSLOVAKIA 1
14	♐	31	ETHIOPIA
14	♐	36	GUINEA - BUISSAU
16	♐	13	FALL OF CONSTANTINOPLE
16	♐	33	LABOUR PARTY 1
17	♐	11	SUDAN
18	♐	19	URUGUAY
18	♐	27	S VIETNAM-REP
18	♐	35	GREECE DEMOCRACY
19	♐	25	BOLIVIA
19	♐	25	BHUTAN
20	♐	08	PORTUGAL-REVOLUTION
22	♐	13	ARMENIA
22	♐	13	GEORGIA
22	♐	13	AZERBAIJAN
23	♐	44	TRANSCAUCASIAN FED
26	♐	50	WARSAW PACT
27	♐	06	GERMANY WEST SOVEREIGN
27	♐	23	SOUTH AFRICAN REP 2
27	♐	27	GRENADA
0	♑	19	PERU-BATTLE AYACUCHO
1	♑	18	UKRAINE
1	♑	34	LITHUANIA
1	♑	37	ESTONIA
1	♑	40	FINLAND
2	♑	46	USSR-REVOLUTION

5 ♑ 19	HOLY ROMAN EMPIRE	14 ♒ 23 QATAR
7 ♑ 39	BAHAMAS	14 ♒ 23 FEDERATION OF ARAB REPUB
7 ♑ 40	AFGHANISTAN	14 ♒ 27 HAITI
8 ♑ 43	CUBA - INDEPENDENCE 1	14 ♒ 32 BAHRAIN
14 ♑ 41	KAMPUCHEA - INDEP	15 ♒ 48 BRAZIL
14 ♑ 2	LAOS 2	21 ♒ 07 BANGLADESH 2
14 ♑ 42	NORTH VIETNAM	22 ♒ 59 BANGLADESH 1
14 ♑ 42	SOUTH VIETNAM	27 ♒ 40 JAPAN - SOVEREIGNTY
16 ♑ 06	LONDON 1	28 ♒ 48 DOMINICAN REPUBLIC
17 ♑ 24	U.S. CIVIL WAR	1 ♓ 57 KAMPUCHEA - REP
18 ♑ 34	USSR-REPUBLIC	1 ♓ 57 FIJI
19 ♑ 45	MEXICO - CONSTITUTION	2 ♓ 35 COSTA RICA 1
20 ♑ 06	ITALY - KINGDOM 1	2 ♓ 43 LIBYA - INDEP
22 ♑ 27	NATAL	3 ♓ 13 OMAN
22 ♑ 41	CONFEDERATE STATES AMER	3 ♓ 51 NICARAGUA 1
22 ♑ 44	POLAND 1	4 ♓ 33 GUATEMALA - 1
27 ♑ 52	SRI LANKA-REP	4 ♓ 33 EL SALVADOR
27 ♑ 53	UNITED PROVINCES C A	4 ♓ 48 PERU I
28 ♑ 25	NETHERLANDS	5 ♓ 22 LIBERAL PARTY 1
28 ♑ 34	LAOS I	6 ♓ 49 TONGA
2 ♒ 39	CREATION OF MAN	6 ♓ 50 ROMANIA 1
3 ♒ 27	CREATION OF THE WORLD	8 ♓ 01 GERMANY - THIRD REICH
3 ♒ 28	EIRE 1	13 ♓ 29 GREECE REVOLUTION
3 ♒ 51	EGYPT - REPUBLIC	16 ♓ 56 IRAQ - INDEPENCENCE
5 ♒ 56	BANGLADESH 3	20 ♓ 24 THAILAND 2
6 ♒ 50	UNITED ARAB EMIR	21 ♓ 10 LIBYA, COUP
13 ♒ 22	SERBIA	22 ♓ 30 MOON LANDING
13 ♒ 22	BULGARIA - AUTONOMY	22 ♓ 47 ECUADOR I
13 ♒ 22	MONTENEGRO	24 ♓ 31 GUATEMALA - 2
13 ♒ 22	ROMANIA 2	

ASCENDANT A

0 ♈ 48	BAHAMAS	11 ♊ 49 INDONESIA
2 ♈ 37	SEYCHELLES	13 ♊ 09 VENDA
3 ♈ 37	DJIBOUTI	13 ♊ 12 TRINIDAD & TOBAGO
3 ♈ 37	SOMALILAND	15 ♊ 14 NEW ZEALAND I
4 ♈ 31	MOZAMBIQUE	15 ♊ 40 MALAYSIA
4 ♈ 11	INDIA - REPUBLIC	15 ♊ 59 LONDON 1
6 ♈ 11	MADAGASCAR	16 ♊ 01 CYPRUS
6 ♈ 44	ESPIRITU SANTO	16 ♊ 43 FALL OF CONSTANTINOPLE
7 ♈ 26	COMOROS 2	18 ♊ 04 PAPUA NEW GUINEA
8 ♈ 20	BURUNDI	18 ♊ 21 SENEGAL
8 ♈ 28	SOUTH AFRICAN REP 2	19 ♊ 54 MEXICO - REVOLUTION
9 ♈ 10	RWANDA-INDEPENDENCE	21 ♊ 41 BANGLADESH 3
9 ♈ 15	SOLOMON ISLANDS	21 ♊ 52 S.D.P.
9 ♈ 49	ZAIRE	23 ♊ 17 BOTSWANA
10 ♈ 16	SOMALIA	24 ♊ 48 LABOUR PARTY 2
12 ♈ 01	PAKISTAN, REPUBLIC	25 ♊ 37 TEXAS
13 ♈ 01	HAITI	25 ♊ 53 LESOTHO
13 ♈ 05	KIRIBATI	29 ♊ 09 EIRE 2
13 ♈ 31	BUGANDA	29 ♊ 24 SIKKIM
14 ♈ 04	CHINA - REPUBLIC	0 ♋ 49 NIGERIA
16 ♈ 22	BIAFRA	2 ♋ 38 BOKHARA NAT'L SOVIET REP
18 ♈ 18	MALAWI	3 ♋ 13 ST KITTS-NEVIS
18 ♈ 54	SHEPARD	4 ♋ 01 TUVALU
20 ♈ 04	UNITED NATIONS	5 ♋ 11 UGANDA
20 ♈ 22	DE GAULLE	4 ♋ 22 CZECHOSLOVAKIA-COMMUNIST
21 ♈ 40	NEPAL	4 ♋ 41 GUATEMALA - 3
22 ♈ 07	AUSTRALIA 2	4 ♋ 52 HATAY
22 ♈ 17	ENGLAND-WILLIAM	7 ♋ 22 FIJI
23 ♈ 28	SOUTH AFRICAN REP 1	8 ♋ 47 TURKEY
26 ♈ 59	THATCHER	8 ♋ 31 LABOUR PARTY 1
27 ♈ 15	SOUTH YEMEN 1	8 ♋ 48 BELIZE
29 ♈ 19	EGYPT - REPUBLIC	9 ♋ 10 AGE OF AQUARIUS-1
0 ♉ 39	BENIN	10 ♋ 23 MONGOLIA
3 ♉ 31	NUCLEAR REACTION	10 ♋ 49 NAMIBIA
4 ♉ 03	NIGER	11 ♋ 39 CARPATHO-UKRAINE
4 ♉ 34	ROMAN EMPIRE 1	12 ♋ 59 BANGLADESH 1
8 ♉ 21	VANUATU	13 ♋ 09 GREECE DEMOCRACY
8 ♉ 46	AFGHANISTAN	13 ♋ 25 GUINEA
9 ♉ 08	ROMAN EMPIRE 2	15 ♋ 32 MALTA
9 ♉ 23	RWANDA-UDI	15 ♋ 32 TRANSKEI
11 ♉ 29	USSR-FORMATION	17 ♋ 51 TANZANIA
11 ♉ 32	ALBANIA-PEOPLES REPUBLIC	18 ♋ 02 MEXICO - CONSTITUTION
12 ♉ 43	REAGAN-2	18 ♋ 46 THAILAND 1
13 ♉ 42	CHILE 1	19 ♋ 23 GREECE REVOLUTION
13 ♉ 32	IVORY COAST	19 ♋ 40 IRAQ - REPUBLIC
15 ♉ 52	CUBA - INDEPENDENCE 1	19 ♋ 55 SLOVAKIA
16 ♉ 24	KAMPUCHEA, COMM	22 ♋ 34 ZAMBIA
17 ♉ 16	PANAMA	24 ♋ 38 IRAQ - INDEPENCENCE
17 ♉ 32	PAKISTAN	24 ♋ 50 FRANCE-FIFTH REPUBLIC
18 ♉ 24	BURKINO-FASSO	25 ♋ 32 CHILE 2
20 ♉ 57	JAMAICA	27 ♋ 26 ATOMIC EXPLOSION
22 ♉ 03	GERMANY - EMPIRE	28 ♋ 38 GUATEMALA - 2
22 ♉ 19	GABON	1 ♌ 57 BANGLADESH 2
24 ♉ 26	ORANGE FREE STATE	3 ♌ 34 GAGARIN
24 ♉ 32	CONGO	5 ♌ 16 ST VINCENT-GRENADINES
26 ♉ 06	CHAD	5 ♌ 16 NATAL
26 ♉ 56	HYDERABAD	6 ♌ 49 FAR EAST REPUBLIC
27 ♉ 07	GERMANY - THIRD REICH	7 ♌ 03 ROME
27 ♉ 12	SPAIN	8 ♌ 03 KAMPUCHEA - INDEP
28 ♉ 47	CENTRAL AFRICAN REPUBLIC	8 ♌ 55 UNITED ARAB REP
0 ♊ 35	CONFEDERATE STATES AMER	9 ♌ 35 BHUTAN
0 ♊ 53	INDIA - INDEPENDENCE	9 ♌ 45 NICARAGUA 2
1 ♊ 07	MALAYA	10 ♌ 24 PARAGUAY
2 ♊ 04	SINGAPORE 1	11 ♌ 30 FRANCE-FOURTH REPUBLIC
2 ♊ 16	GREECE INDEPENCENCE	11 ♌ 30 ANTIGUA-BARBUDA
5 ♊ 01	ENGLAND-1689	12 ♌ 31 ANGOLA
6 ♊ 22	UKRAINE	12 ♌ 57 TRANSCAUCASIAN FED
6 ♊ 48	SWAZILAND	12 ♌ 58 DOMINICA
8 ♊ 27	EGYPT - KINGDOM	16 ♌ 20 WARSAW PACT
8 ♊ 20	UNITED KINGDOM-1922	17 ♌ 57 IRAN - ISLAMIC REP
9 ♊ 31	GUINEA - BUISSAU	18 ♌ 06 LIBYA, COUP
9 ♊ 47	JAPAN - MEIJI CONST	18 ♌ 27 ECUADOR 2
10 ♊ 56	YUGOSLAVIA-COMMUNIST	19 ♌ 31 ARGENTINA - REVOLUTION

19 ♌ 32	SPUTNIK	23 ♏ 12	BULGARIA - AUTONOMY
20 ♌ 25	EIRE 1	24 ♏ 20	BOLIVIA
20 ♌ 46	GERMANY WEST SOVEREIGN	24 ♏ 25	ROMANIA 2
21 ♌ 10	MONACO	24 ♏ 25	QATAR
21 ♌ 39	MOROCCO	25 ♏ 21	BULGARIA - COMMUNIST
21 ♌ 48	VIETNAM-UNION	26 ♏ 05	LUXEMBOURG
23 ♌ 12	MAURETANIA	26 ♏ 35	USA 1
23 ♌ 13	LAOS 1	27 ♏ 18	KOREA - NORTH
28 ♌ 03	SOUTH AFRICA-UNION	27 ♏ 38	ST LUCIA
29 ♌ 54	SURINAM	29 ♏ 01	LONDON 2
0 ♍ 17	CUBA - INDEPENDENCE 2	3 ♐ 54	BAHRAIN
0 ♍ 30	CISKEI	3 ♐ 58	ITALY - KINGDOM 1
1 ♍ 12	AUSTRIA	5 ♐ 06	EIRE 3
2 ♍ 02	PHILLIPINES	5 ♐ 12	VIETNAM
3 ♍ 13	N Y STOCK EXCHANGE	6 ♐ 55	COSTA RICA 2
4 ♍ 32	BOPHUTHATSWANA	7 ♐ 44	AGE OF AQUARIUS-2
4 ♍ 49	VATICAN CITY	8 ♐ 14	USA 3
4 ♍ 53	ENGLAND-EDGAR	8 ♐ 24	CHINA - COMMUNIST 1
4 ♍ 54	IRAQ - KINGDOM	9 ♐ 10	OPEC
6 ♍ 29	ROMANIA 1	10 ♐ 03	PORTUGAL-REVOLUTION
7 ♍ 30	SRI LANKA-REP	10 ♐ 40	SAUDI ARABIA
8 ♍ 32	SOUTH YEMEN 2	10 ♐ 40	BURMA
8 ♍ 37	ARMENIA	12 ♐ 21	USA 4
8 ♍ 48	NORWAY	12 ♐ 26	GHANA
8 ♍ 59	GEORGIA	13 ♐ 36	BELGIUM
9 ♍ 05	TANGANYIKA	16 ♐ 20	SYRIA 1
9 ♍ 17	BARBADOS	16 ♐ 33	HOLY ROMAN EMPIRE
9 ♍ 38	ZANZIBAR	16 ♐ 34	CHINA - COMMUNIST 2
9 ♍ 57	KENYA	17 ♐ 15	BULGARIA - INDEPENDENCE
10 ♍ 12	AZERBAIJAN	17 ♐ 56	NAT KHOREZEM SOVIET REP
11 ♍ 27	JORDAN	18 ♐ 52	MALI - REPUBLIC
12 ♍ 19	ALGERIA	18 ♐ 58	GUATEMALA - 1
15 ♍ 27	LIBERAL PARTY	19 ♐ 58	PORTUGAL-REVOLUTION
17 ♍ 05	LIBYA - INDEP	20 ♐ 20	EGYPT - INDEPENDENCE
17 ♍ 53	GORBACHEV	21 ♐ 44	URUGUAY
17 ♍ 54	HIROSHIMA	22 ♐ 19	KHALISTAN
19 ♍ 11	DENMARK	23 ♐ 48	CYPRUS - TURKISH
22 ♍ 32	LAOS 2	24 ♐ 43	EL SALVADOR
22 ♍ 52	FRANCE - NAPOLEON	25 ♐ 26	CZECHOSLOVAKIA 1
23 ♍ 41	USSR-REVOLUTION	26 ♐ 43	MAURITIUS
25 ♍ 44	NORTH VIETNAM	26 ♐ 43	VENEZUELA 2
26 ♍ 06	SAO TOME-PRINCIPE	27 ♐ 44	FRANCE-VICHY REPUBLIC
26 ♍ 14	SOUTH VIETNAM	28 ♐ 11	NORTH YEMEN
27 ♍ 41	THAILAND 2	29 ♐ 16	ICELAND
29 ♍ 36	E.E.C.	0 ♑ 32	JAPAN - SOVEREIGNTY
0 ♎ 05	KUWAIT	3 ♑ 56	CZECHOSLOVAKIA 2
2 ♎ 13	ICELAND	4 ♑ 57	GERMANY WEST PROCLAM
3 ♎ 29	CHINA - NATIONALIST	5 ♑ 20	DANZIG
4 ♎ 39	BRUNEI	6 ♑ 23	POLAND 2
4 ♎ 44	WESTERN SAMOA	11 ♑ 06	YUGOSLAVIA 1
6 ♎ 11	TREATY OF ROME	11 ♑ 13	SINGAPORE 3
6 ♎ 30	CAMEROON	11 ♑ 41	GERMANY - WEIMAR
7 ♎ 01	CANADA	12 ♑ 13	EQUATORIAL GUINEA
7 ♎ 10	UNITED KINGDOM-1801	13 ♑ 41	FRANCE-THIRD REPUBLIC
7 ♎ 23	AUSTRALIA 1	14 ♑ 12	NICARAGUA 1
8 ♎ 47	UNITED PROVINCES C A	16 ♑ 19	ENGLAND-1707
9 ♎ 01	USA 2	16 ♑ 33	SIERRA LEONE
9 ♎ 25	SINGAPORE 2	16 ♑ 38	LATVIA
11 ♎ 10	REAGAN-1	16 ♑ 46	POLAND 1
12 ♎ 36	LEBANON 2	18 ♑ 46	ECUADOR 1
12 ♎ 51	VENEZUELA 1	18 ♑ 50	CONSERVATIVE PARTY
13 ♎ 19	SYRIA 2	22 ♑ 05	CZECHOSLOVAKIA 3
13 ♎ 46	ITALY - KINGDOM 2	23 ♑ 14	ESTONIA
14 ♎ 18	COMOROS 1	25 ♑ 33	FRANCE-1st REPUBLIC 1
17 ♎ 13	CUBA - COMMUNIST	27 ♑ 08	HONDURAS
18 ♎ 54	CAPE VERDE ISLANDS	29 ♑ 17	S VIETNAM-REP
19 ♎ 20	CIA	29 ♑ 52	COSTA RICA 1
20 ♎ 45	LIECHTENSTEIN	0 ♒ 03	HUNGARY
23 ♎ 02	ISRAEL	1 ♒ 38	ZIMBABWE
24 ♎ 02	ARGENTINA - INDEPENDENCE	1 ♒ 44	TOGO
25 ♎ 14	BYELO RUSSIA	4 ♒ 31	SUDAN
26 ♎ 35	NICARAGUA SANDINISTA	5 ♒ 39	FINLAND
26 ♎ 37	OMAN	14 ♒ 48	PALESTINE
27 ♎ 48	NAURU	17 ♒ 56	SWEDEN
0 ♏ 33	NETHERLANDS	19 ♒ 34	FIRST MANNED FLIGHT
1 ♏ 46	KAMPUCHEA - REP	22 ♒ 13	ALBANIA - INDEPENDENCE
2 ♏ 57	MATO 1	26 ♒ 41	TIMOR
3 ♏ 33	MALDIVES	27 ♒ 29	BRAZIL
4 ♏ 24	LIBERIA	27 ♒ 41	GUYANA
4 ♏ 50	SWITZERLAND	27 ♒ 44	UNITED ARAB EMIR
6 ♏ 50	FRANCE-1st REPUBLIC 2	0 ♓ 44	LEBANON 1
6 ♏ 51	KOREA - SOUTH	2 ♓ 10	YUGOSLAVIA 2
9 ♏ 53	GAMBIA	3 ♓ 23	TONGA
10 ♏ 45	SRI LANKA-IND	5 ♓ 07	DOMINICAN REPUBLIC
11 ♏ 26	POLAND-COMMUNIST	5 ♓ 31	LITHUANIA
11 ♏ 28	USSR-REPUBLIC	6 ♓ 35	MALI - FEDERATION
11 ♏ 51	PERU 1	8 ♓ 45	SOUTH AFRICA-REPUBLIC
12 ♏ 07	CREATION OF MAN	10 ♓ 48	ZIMBABWE-RHODESIA
14 ♏ 05	GRENADA	11 ♓ 07	RHODESIA
14 ♏ 26	ETHIOPIA	18 ♓ 21	ARAB FEDERATION
17 ♏ 24	ITALY - REPUBLIC	18 ♓ 31	PERU-BATTLE AYACUCHO
18 ♏ 14	FEDERATION OF ARAB REPUB	21 ♓ 44	IRAN - KHOMEINI
18 ♏ 57	MONTENEGRO	24 ♓ 24	MOON LANDING
19 ♏ 57	SERBIA	24 ♓ 43	COLUMBIA
20 ♏ 31	SAHRAWI ARAB D R	27 ♓ 06	U.S. CIVIL WAR
20 ♏ 42	ALLIANCE	28 ♓ 41	CREATION OF THE WORLD
22 ♏ 10	TUNISIA		

MIDHEAVEN M

0 ♈ 30	FRANCE-FIFTH REPUBLIC	5 ♈ 57	NEW ZEALAND I
2 ♈ 00	BELIZE	6 ♈ 23	IRAQ - REPUBLIC
2 ♈ 47	GREECE REVOLUTION	8 ♈ 49	TUVALU
3 ♈ 46	BANGLADESH 1	10 ♈ 30	LESOTHO
4 ♈ 30	BOTSWANA	11 ♈ 28	GUINEA
4 ♈ 49	UGANDA	11 ♈ 38	MEXICO - CONSTITUTION

2 ♑ 46	DJIBOUTI	
2 ♑ 49	SOMALILAND	
3 ♑ 06	INDIA - REPUBLIC	
4 ♑ 36	MOZAMBIQUE	
5 ♑ 59	MADAGASCAR	
6 ♑ 20	ESPIRITU SANTO	
6 ♑ 50	COMOROS 2	
7 ♑ 13	BURUNDI	
7 ♑ 51	RWANDA-INDEPENDENCE	
8 ♑ 07	PAKISTAN, REPUBLIC	
8 ♑ 22	SOLOMON ISLANDS	
8 ♑ 32	SOMALIA	
8 ♑ 33	ZAIRE	
8 ♑ 38	SOUTH AFRICAN REP 2	
8 ♑ 41	CHINA - REPUBLIC	
8 ♑ 42	ENGLAND-WILLIAM	
8 ♑ 49	DE GAULLE	
9 ♑ 19	HAITI	
10 ♑ 45	THATCHER	
10 ♑ 57	KIRIBATI	
11 ♑ 10	UNITED NATIONS	
11 ♑ 25	BUGANDA	
12 ♑ 20	SHEPARD	
13 ♑ 13	BIAFRA	
14 ♑ 11	USSR-FORMATION	
14 ♑ 19	NEPAL	
17 ♑ 27	MALAWI	
18 ♑ 08	NUCLEAR REACTION	
18 ♑ 33	ROMAN EMPIRE 1	
19 ♑ 05	EGYPT - REPUBLIC	
21 ♑ 10	SOUTH YEMEN 1	
21 ♑ 19	ROMAN EMPIRE 2	
23 ♑ 20	ALBANIA-PEOPLES REPUBLIC	
24 ♑ 16	SOUTH AFRICAN REP 1	
24 ♑ 17	AFGHANISTAN	
24 ♑ 23	AUSTRALIA 2	
25 ♑ 13	BENIN	
25 ♑ 15	REAGAN-2	
25 ♑ 20	GERMANY - THIRD REICH	
25 ♑ 29	GERMANY - EMPIRE	
26 ♑ 37	NIGER	
1 ♒ 40	ENGLAND-1689	
3 ♒ 46	CUBA - INDEPENDENCE 1	
4 ♒ 21	UKRAINE	
4 ♒ 33	PAKISTAN	
4 ♒ 54	SPAIN	
5 ♒ 08	RWANDA-UDI	
5 ♒ 09	UNITED KINGDOM-1922	
7 ♒ 59	KAMPUCHEA, COMM	
8 ♒ 14	VANUATU	
9 ♒ 03	IVORY COAST	

9 ♒ 35	BURKINO-FASSO	
9 ♒ 35	PANAMA	
10 ♒ 01	JAMAICA	
10 ♒ 33	LONDON 1	
10 ♒ 38	GREECE INDEPENCENCE	
12 ♒ 24	CONFEDERATE STATES AMER	
13 ♒ 06	YUGOSLAVIA-COMMUNIST	
14 ♒ 35	INDIA - INDEPENDENCE	
15 ♒ 52	HYDERABAD	
16 ♒ 06	S.D.P.	
17 ♒ 01	CHAD	
17 ♒ 20	GABON	
18 ♒ 55	JAPAN - MEIJI CONST	
19 ♒ 03	LABOUR PARTY 2	
19 ♒ 42	CHILE 1	
21 ♒ 00	EGYPT - KINGDOM	
21 ♒ 03	EIRE 2	
21 ♒ 16	CONGO	
21 ♒ 40	FALL OF CONSTANTINOPLE	
22 ♒ 37	CENTRAL AFRICAN REPUBLIC	
25 ♒ 24	CYPRUS	
25 ♒ 32	MALAYA	
27 ♒ 17	SINGAPORE 1	
0 ♓ 57	GUINEA - BUISSAU	
1 ♓ 00	ORANGE FREE STATE	
1 ♓ 39	CZECHOSLOVAKIA-COMMUNIST	
4 ♓ 51	LABOUR PARTY 1	
5 ♓ 32	TRINIDAD & TOBAGO	
7 ♓ 51	MEXICO - REVOLUTION	
8 ♓ 28	BANGLADESH 3	
8 ♓ 44	MONGOLIA	
8 ♓ 58	TEXAS	
9 ♓ 24	SENEGAL	
9 ♓ 58	BOKHARA NAT'L SOVIET REP	
11 ♓ 23	INDONESIA	
11 ♓ 42	MALAYSIA	
13 ♓ 08	CARPATHO-UKRAINE	
14 ♓ 58	SWAZILAND	
15 ♓ 13	SIKKIM	
15 ♓ 26	HATAY	
16 ♓ 20	TURKEY	
20 ♓ 17	PAPUA NEW GUINEA	
21 ♓ 04	VENDA	
24 ♓ 10	AGE OF AQUARIUS-1	
24 ♓ 19	SLOVAKIA	
24 ♓ 42	GREECE DEMOCRACY	
25 ♓ 23	ST KITTS-NEVIS	
27 ♓ 55	NIGERIA	
28 ♓ 30	GUATEMALA - 3	
29 ♓ 19	MALTA	

INTEGRATED PLANETARY INDEX

11 ♈ 38	M	MEXICO - CONSTITUTION
11 ♈ 52	●	THATCHER
12 ♈ 01	A	PAKISTAN, REPUBLIC
12 ♈ 02R	⚷	CREATION OF MAN
12 ♈ 04	●	FRANCE-FIPTH REPUBLIC
12 ♈ 06	⚷	HOLY ROMAN EMPIRE
12 ♈ 08	♀	SIKKIM
12 ♈ 08R	⚷	CREATION OF THE WORLD
12 ♈ 10	⚷	UNITED PROVINCES C A
12 ♈ 13	☿	JAPAN - SOVEREIGNTY
12 ♈ 13	♂	BAHAMAS
12 ♈ 14	⚷	SPAIN
12 ♈ 21	♄	MAURITIUS
12 ♈ 23	⚷	EGYPT - INDEPENDENCE
12 ♈ 24	⚷	EGYPT - KINGDOM
12 ♈ 38	●	ITALY - KINGDOM 2
12 ♈ 42	♂	LEBANON I
12 ♈ 44R	♆	CONSERVATIVE PARTY
12 ♈ 47	M	IRAQ - INDEPENCENCE
12 ♈ 48	☊	INDONESIA
12 ♈ 51	☊	NICARAGUA 2
12 ♈ 56	♀	SHEPARD
13 ♈ 00	♀	GERMANY WEST SOVEREIGN
13 ♈ 01R	⚷	FEDERATION OF ARAB REPU
13 ♈ 01	A	HAITI
13 ♈ 01R	⚷	QATAR
13 ♈ 05	A	KIRIBATI
13 ♈ 08	⚷	USSR-FORMATION
13 ♈ 16R	⚷	UNITED KINGDOM-1922
13 ♈ 17R	♀	SIERRA LEONE
13 ♈ 17R	⚷	EIRE 2
13 ♈ 24	♅	GUATEMALA - 3
13 ♈ 31	A	BUGANDA
13 ♈ 32R	⚷	BAHRAIN
13 ♈ 35R	⚷	IRAQ - KINGDOM
13 ♈ 35	♇	TEXAS
13 ♈ 37	♂	MONGOLIA
13 ♈ 39	⚷	FALL OF CONSTANTINOPLE
13 ♈ 40	♂	DENMARK
13 ♈ 40	⚷	FAR EAST REPUBLIC
14 ♈ 04	A	CHINA - REPUBLIC
14 ♈ 04	☊	UNITED KINGDOM-18Ø1
14 ♈ 11	M	GAGARIN
14 ♈ 11	☉	SIKKIM
14 ♈ 15	♀	CUBA - INDEPENDENCE 2
14 ♈ 18	♀	ENGLAND-EDGAR
14 ♈ 19	●	BELIZE
14 ♈ 23	♆	ROME
14 ♈ 24R	♆	LUXEMBOURG
14 ♈ 27	♂	BOKHARA NAT'L SOVIET RE
14 ♈ 47	♀	U.S. CIVIL WAR
14 ♈ 51	♀	PARAGUAY
14 ♈ 51	M	FAR EAST REPUBLIC
14 ♈ 58	♄	GREECE REVOLUTION
14 ♈ 58	☽	KAMPUCHEA - INDEP
15 ♈ 00	♆	CANADA
15 ♈ 01R	♃	TIMOR
15 ♈ 09R	♃	SURINAM
15 ♈ 13	♃	ESPIRITU SANTO
15 ♈ 23	☉	CHILE 2
15 ♈ 25	☿	GUATEMALA - 3
15 ♈ 27	♀	ENGLAND-1689
15 ♈ 28	●	BULGARIA - INDEPENDENCE
15 ♈ 29	♃	COMOROS 2
15 ♈ 35	☊	ENGLAND-1689
15 ♈ 36	☉	FAR EAST REPUBLIC
15 ♈ 50	●	LIBERIA
15 ♈ 52	M	THAILAND 1
15 ♈ 55	●	BANGLADESH 2
15 ♈ 57	⚷	SRI LANKA-REP
15 ♈ 58R	⚷	NETHERLANDS
16 ♈ 10	♂	AFGHANISTAN
16 ♈ 13R	♃	ANGOLA
16 ♈ 15	♀	CZECHOSLOVAKIA-COMMUNIS
16 ♈ 16	⚷	ENGLAND-1689
16 ♈ 17	☊	THAILAND 1
16 ♈ 20	☿	TOGO
16 ♈ 22	A	BIAFRA
16 ♈ 25	●	UNITED KINGDOM-18Ø1
16 ♈ 31	☉	THAILAND 1
16 ♈ 36R	♇	HONDURAS
16 ♈ 41	M	ATOMIC EXPLOSION
16 ♈ 43	♀	LABOUR PARTY 1
16 ♈ 43	☊	CHINA - COMMUNIST 2
16 ♈ 43	☊	CHINA - COMMUNIST 1
16 ♈ 47	☽	CHILE 2
16 ♈ 54	⚷	ENGLAND-WILLIAM
16 ♈ 54	⚷	ENGLAND-EDGAR
16 ♈ 56	♇	NICARAGUA 2
17 ♈ 01	♃	EIRE 1
17 ♈ 09	⚷	GRENADA
17 ♈ 09R	♄	HATAY
17 ♈ 13	⚷	USA 2
17 ♈ 13	⚷	USA 1
17 ♈ 15	⚷	USA 3
17 ♈ 15	⚷	USA 4
17 ♈ 18	●	SEYCHELLES
17 ♈ 19R	♃	MALAYSIA
17 ♈ 19	♀	TEXAS
17 ♈ 28	M	FIJI
17 ♈ 30	♄	CARPATHO-UKRAINE
17 ♈ 30	♄	SLOVAKIA
17 ♈ 30	☊	NATO 1
17 ♈ 38	♇	GUATEMALA - 2
17 ♈ 38	☽	GERMANY - THIRD REICH
17 ♈ 45	●	SPAIN
17 ♈ 49	☿	CHILE 2
17 ♈ 51	⚷	ENGLAND-17Ø7
17 ♈ 59	♂	MAURITIUS
18 ♈ 02	♄	LIECHTENSTEIN
18 ♈ 09	●	GERMANY - EMPIRE
18 ♈ 09R	⚷	TURKEY
18 ♈ 14R	♅	LIBERIA
18 ♈ 18	A	MALAWI
18 ♈ 45R	♃	SINGAPORE 1
18 ♈ 54	A	SHEPARD
18 ♈ 58	☊	MAURITIUS
19 ♈ 04	☽	IRAQ - KINGDOM
19 ♈ 07	♆	GERMANY - EMPIRE
19 ♈ 18R	⚷	URUGUAY
19 ♈ 42R	⚷	BOLIVIA
19 ♈ 56	♅	GERMANY - THIRD REICH
20 ♈ 03R	♀	GAGARIN
20 ♈ 04	A	UNITED NATIONS
20 ♈ 14	●	U.S. CIVIL WAR
20 ♈ 17R	♄	DOMINICAN REPUBLIC
20 ♈ 22	A	DE GAULLE
20 ♈ 37R	♃	DOMINICAN REPUBLIC
20 ♈ 46	♃	MOZAMBIQUE
20 ♈ 49	♂	EIRE 3
20 ♈ 49	☽	N Y STOCK EXCHANGE
20 ♈ 49	⚷	BAHAMAS
20 ♈ 53	⚷	AFGHANISTAN
21 ♈ 09	♇	NATAL
21 ♈ 11	♂	CONFEDERATE STATES AMER
21 ♈ 12	♀	GEORGIA
21 ♈ 12	♀	ARMENIA
21 ♈ 12	⚷	PORTUGAL-REVOLUTION
21 ♈ 16	⚷	NEPAL
21 ♈ 23	♀	CHILE 2
21 ♈ 24R	♆	FRANCE-THIRD REPUBLIC
21 ♈ 25	☊	NAURU
21 ♈ 33R	☿	SIKKIM
21 ♈ 35	●	SOLOMON ISLANDS
21 ♈ 36	♀	TOGO
21 ♈ 40	A	NEPAL
21 ♈ 48R	♅	COSTA RICA 2
21 ♈ 50R	♅	IRAQ - INDEPENCENCE
22 ♈ 03	♆	ENGLAND-17Ø7
22 ♈ 06	☿	BANGLADESH 1
22 ♈ 07	☽	ENGLAND-1689
22 ♈ 07	A	AUSTRALIA 2
22 ♈ 08	☉	GAGARIN
22 ♈ 08	♄	SOUTH AFRICAN REP 2
22 ♈ 10	♃	CAPE VERDE ISLANDS
22 ♈ 12	♀	GORBACHEV
22 ♈ 15	♂	TANZANIA
22 ♈ 16	♃	COMOROS 1
22 ♈ 17	A	ENGLAND-WILLIAM
22 ♈ 19R	♄	EQUATORIAL GUINEA
22 ♈ 24R	♄	COSTA RICA 1
22 ♈ 28	☉	U.S. CIVIL WAR
22 ♈ 30	●	SOMALILAND
22 ♈ 31	●	CYPRUS - TURKISH
22 ♈ 52	♀	JAPAN - SOVEREIGNTY
22 ♈ 54	♅	THAILAND 2
22 ♈ 56R	☿	LONDON 2
22 ♈ 56	♃	SAO TOME-PRINCIPE
23 ♈ 02	☉	ROME
23 ♈ 03R	♂	SYRIA 1
23 ♈ 04	●	USA 2
23 ♈ 05R	♃	PAPUA NEW GUINEA
23 ♈ 11	⚷	BHUTAN
23 ♈ 22	♀	GUATEMALA - 3
23 ♈ 25	♀	AZERBAIJAN
23 ♈ 28	A	SOUTH AFRICAN REP 1
23 ♈ 31	●	PAKISTAN
23 ♈ 34	M	ROME
23 ♈ 35	♀	GUYANA
23 ♈ 36R	⚷	COMOROS 2
23 ♈ 37R	⚷	ESPIRITU SANTO
23 ♈ 38R	⚷	ETHIOPIA
23 ♈ 40	☿	PORTUGAL-REVOLUTION
23 ♈ 40R	♄	NICARAGUA 1
23 ♈ 41	M	NAMIBIA
23 ♈ 43R	⚷	GUINEA - BUISSAU
23 ♈ 44	♀	WARSAW PACT
23 ♈ 47	☽	NICARAGUA 1
23 ♈ 53R	♄	SWITZERLAND
23 ♈ 54	♆	ITALY - KINGDOM 2
23 ♈ 55	M	TANZANIA
24 ♈ 00R	♃	COSTA RICA 1
24 ♈ 01	♃	SAHRAWI ARAB D R
24 ♈ 10	⚷	KAMPUCHEA, COMM
24 ♈ 13R	⚷	TIMOR
24 ♈ 15	●	ECUADOR 2
24 ♈ 19R	⚷	SURINAM
24 ♈ 23	●	KAMPUCHEA - INDEP
24 ♈ 30	⚷	GREECE DEMOCRACY
24 ♈ 33	●	IRAQ - KINGDOM
24 ♈ 48R	♄	SWAZILAND
24 ♈ 50	♇	GUATEMALA - 3
24 ♈ 51	♂	LIBERIA
24 ♈ 51	M	FRANCE-FOURTH REPUBLIC
24 ♈ 52R	⚷	ANGOLA
24 ♈ 54	☽	PANAMA
24 ♈ 55	⚷	SAHRAWI ARAB D R
25 ♈ 02	♅	DENMARK
25 ♈ 03	●	MADAGASCAR
25 ♈ 08	☽	ALLIANCE
25 ♈ 09R	♄	EL SALVADOR
25 ♈ 14	☊	GERMANY WEST PROCLAM
25 ♈ 20	♀	SOUTH AFRICA-REPUBLIC
25 ♈ 22	♂	IRAQ - REPUBLIC
25 ♈ 31R	♄	GUATEMALA - 1
25 ♈ 31	♂	MOZAMBIQUE
25 ♈ 33	☊	MONACO
25 ♈ 39	☊	EIRE 3
25 ♈ 58	●	ARGENTINA - INDEPENDENC
25 ♈ 59	♂	NICARAGUA 2
26 ♈ 09R	♃	NICARAGUA 1
26 ♈ 12	☊	ENGLAND-17Ø7
26 ♈ 22	☿	KAMPUCHEA, COMM
26 ♈ 23	♄	N Y STOCK EXCHANGE
26 ♈ 24	♀	SOUTH AFRICA-UNION
26 ♈ 35	☉	BANGLADESH 2

26 ♈ 36	PERU 1
26 ♈ 51	MONGOLIA
26 ♈ 56	LIBERIA
26 ♈ 59	THATCHER
27 ♈ 01	GUATEMALA - 2
27 ♈ 05	BANGLADESH 2
27 ♈ 08	GUATEMALA - 2
27 ♈ 15	SOUTH YEMEN 1
27 ♈ 19R	PAPUA NEW GUINEA
27 ♈ 21	KAMPUCHEA, COMM
27 ♈ 23	GORBACHEV
27 ♈ 25	SOUTH YEMEN 2
27 ♈ 26	SOUTH YEMEN 1
27 ♈ 33	MOZAMBIQUE
27 ♈ 35	EIRE 3
27 ♈ 43	BOKHARA NAT'L SOVIET RE
27 ♈ 44R	COSTA RICA 2
27 ♈ 44	SOUTH AFRICAN REP 1
27 ♈ 51	CAPE VERDE ISLANDS
27 ♈ 51	EIRE 3
27 ♈ 52	COMOROS 1
27 ♈ 59	SAO TOME-PRINCIPE
28 ♈ 02	ZIMBABWE
28 ♈ 11	CHINA - REPUBLIC
28 ♈ 14	MONGOLIA
28 ♈ 19	MEXICO - CONSTITUTION
28 ♈ 24	DENMARK
28 ♈ 25	CARPATHO-UKRAINE
28 ♈ 33R	EL SALVADOR
28 ♈ 34	ALBANIA-PEOPLES REPUBLI
28 ♈ 42R	POLAND - 1
28 ♈ 51	SOUTH AFRICAN REP 1
29 ♈ 06R	GUATEMALA - 1
29 ♈ 08	PARAGUAY
29 ♈ 19	EGYPT - REPUBLIC
29 ♈ 24	WARSAW PACT
29 ♈ 25	FAR EAST REPUBLIC
29 ♈ 26	PERU 1
29 ♈ 26R	TRANSKEI
29 ♈ 43	MALI - FEDERATION
29 ♈ 54	PALESTINE
29 ♈ 56	JAPAN - SOVEREIGNTY
0 ♉ 26	SOUTH AFRICAN REP 1
0 ♉ 37R	FRANCE-1st REPUBLIC 2
0 ♉ 39	BENIN
0 ♉ 49	SIERRA LEONE
0 ♉ 55R	FRANCE-1st REPUBLIC 1
1 ♉ 04	ORANGE FREE STATE
1 ♉ 06R	BANGLADESH 2
1 ♉ 15	GREECE INDEPENCENCE
1 ♉ 19	SEYCHELLES
1 ♉ 25	VIETNAM-UNION
1 ♉ 25	TRANSCAUCASIAN FED
1 ♉ 32	ROMANIA 1
1 ♉ 37	SOUTH AFRICA-UNION
1 ♉ 43	MEXICO - REVOLUTION
1 ♉ 43R	BOPHUTHATSWANA
1 ♉ 48	HONDURAS
1 ♉ 51	TRANSCAUCASIAN FED
2 ♉ 05	LIBERAL PARTY
2 ♉ 08	BHUTAN
2 ♉ 21	LAOS 1
2 ♉ 27	BOKHARA NAT'L SOVIET RE
2 ♉ 31	FRANCE - NAPOLEON
2 ♉ 38	USSR-REPUBLIC
2 ♉ 45	VATICAN CITY
2 ♉ 46	UNITED ARAB REP
2 ♉ 50	EIRE 3
2 ♉ 50	ZAMBIA
2 ♉ 56	HYDERABAD
3 ♉ 08	CAPE VERDE ISLANDS
3 ♉ 27	GHANA
3 ♉ 31	NUCLEAR REACTION
3 ♉ 37	TANZANIA
3 ♉ 42	COMOROS 1
3 ♉ 59	EIRE 1
4 ♉ 00	SOMALILAND
4 ♉ 00	MADAGASCAR
4 ♉ 03	NIGER
4 ♉ 22	THAILAND 1
4 ♉ 23	PORTUGAL-REVOLUTION
4 ♉ 28	EIRE 1
4 ♉ 34	ROMAN EMPIRE 1
4 ♉ 39	BHUTAN
4 ♉ 42	NORWAY
4 ♉ 51R	PORTUGAL-REVOLUTION
4 ♉ 57	DJIBOUTI
5 ♉ 02	LIBERAL PARTY
5 ♉ 11	IRAN - KHOMEINI
5 ♉ 15	NAT KHOREZEM SOVIET REP
5 ♉ 30	TRANSKEI
5 ♉ 31	CENTRAL AFRICAN REPUBLI
5 ♉ 36	N Y STOCK EXCHANGE
5 ♉ 43	INDIA - REPUBLIC
5 ♉ 44	ST LUCIA
5 ♉ 52	THAILAND 1
5 ♉ 57	ROMANIA 1
6 ♉ 00	ST VINCENT-GRENADINES
6 ♉ 09	KOREA - NORTH
6 ♉ 18	LIBERAL PARTY
6 ♉ 29	BIAFRA
6 ♉ 30	SIERRA LEONE
6 ♉ 44	ECUADOR 2
6 ♉ 44	TOGO
6 ♉ 45	FRANCE-VICHY REPUBLIC
6 ♉ 48	FRANCE - NAPOLEON
6 ♉ 53	INDIA - INDEPENDENCE
6 ♉ 58	GERMANY WEST SOVEREIGN
7 ♉ 06	MONACO
7 ♉ 06	TANZANIA
7 ♉ 12	SPUTNIK
7 ♉ 12	SLOVAKIA
7 ♉ 13R	TANZANIA
7 ♉ 15R	DOMINICA
7 ♉ 34	CONFEDERATE STATES AMER
7 ♉ 35	IRAN - ISLAMIC REP
7 ♉ 36	SOMALIA
7 ♉ 40	ZAIRE
7 ♉ 55	SAO TOME-PRINCIPE
7 ♉ 57	BULGARIA - AUTONOMY
7 ♉ 57	MONTENEGRO
7 ♉ 57	ROMANIA 2
7 ♉ 57	SERBIA
8 ♉ 03	ITALY - KINGDOM 1
8 ♉ 10	MOON LANDING
8 ♉ 12	JAPAN - SOVEREIGNTY
8 ♉ 20	WARSAW PACT
8 ♉ 21	VANUATU
8 ♉ 30	KOREA - SOUTH
8 ♉ 35	U.S. CIVIL WAR
8 ♉ 46	AFGHANISTAN
8 ♉ 47R	TUVALU
8 ♉ 48R	LIBYA,-COUP
8 ♉ 49	CHILE 2
8 ♉ 55R	TRANSCAUCASIAN FED
9 ♉ 00	KAMPUCHEA - INDEP
9 ♉ 00R	BELGIUM
9 ♉ 07	SOLOMON ISLANDS
9 ♉ 08	ROMAN EMPIRE 2
9 ♉ 11	ORANGE FREE STATE
9 ♉ 19	MONTENEGRO
9 ♉ 23	RWANDA-UDI
9 ♉ 24	GEORGIA
9 ♉ 24	ARMENIA
9 ♉ 28R	VENEZUELA 2
9 ♉ 34	BULGARIA - AUTONOMY
9 ♉ 34	MONTENEGRO
9 ♉ 34	SERBIA
9 ♉ 34	ROMANIA 2
9 ♉ 54	NICARAGUA 2
9 ♉ 56R	BRAZIL
10 ♉ 06	BOLIVIA
10 ♉ 18	FRANCE-THIRD REPUBLIC
10 ♉ 23	E.E.C.
10 ♉ 33	IRAN - ISLAMIC REP
10 ♉ 39	NICARAGUA 2
10 ♉ 43	FRANCE-VICHY REPUBLIC
10 ♉ 56	ANTIGUA-BARBUDA
11 ♉ 11R	GUATEMALA - 2
11 ♉ 17R	ENGLAND-1707
11 ♉ 18	SIKKIM
11 ♉ 19	GUINEA
11 ♉ 20	ZIMBABWE-RHODESIA
11 ♉ 20	BELGIUM
11 ♉ 29	USSR-FORMATION
11 ♉ 32	ALBANIA-PEOPLES REPUBLI
11 ♉ 34	LIBYA, COUP
11 ♉ 35	BYELO RUSSIA
11 ♉ 36	GUYANA
11 ♉ 36	AZERBAIJAN
11 ♉ 39R	SOUTH AFRICAN REP 2
11 ♉ 44	ZIMBABWE-RHODESIA
11 ♉ 45	EGYPT - REPUBLIC
11 ♉ 45	MONACO
11 ♉ 46	UNITED KINGDOM-1801
11 ♉ 55R	ST VINCENT-GRENADINES
12 ♉ 08	KUWAIT
12 ♉ 15	VATICAN CITY
12 ♉ 18	CHILE 1
12 ♉ 26	AUSTRALIA 1
12 ♉ 30	POLAND-COMMUNIST
12 ♉ 33	ZIMBABWE
12 ♉ 34	BULGARIA - AUTONOMY
12 ♉ 38R	SWEDEN
12 ♉ 43	LIBYA, COUP
12 ♉ 43	REAGAN-2
12 ♉ 47R	SOUTH AFRICAN REP 2
13 ♉ 00	MALI - FEDERATION
13 ♉ 07	DOMINICA
13 ♉ 15	KIRIBATI
13 ♉ 24R	REAGAN-2
13 ♉ 30R	CHINA - REPUBLIC
13 ♉ 31	NICARAGUA SANDINISTA
13 ♉ 38R	VENDA
13 ♉ 41	DENMARK
13 ♉ 42	CHILE 1
13 ♉ 47	ROMANIA 2
14 ♉ 02	PALESTINE
14 ♉ 02	ISRAEL
14 ♉ 11	GERMANY WEST SOVEREIGN
14 ♉ 13	ARGENTINA - REVOLUTION
14 ♉ 26	REAGAN-1
14 ♉ 38	SHEPARD
14 ♉ 49	EIRE 1
14 ♉ 51	EIRE 1
14 ♉ 55	CARPATHO-UKRAINE
14 ♉ 55	SLOVAKIA
15 ♉ 09	CONSERVATIVE PARTY
15 ♉ 09	SURINAM
15 ♉ 12	GUATEMALA - 1
15 ♉ 15	DJIBOUTI
15 ♉ 17	S.D.P.
15 ♉ 32	IVORY COAST
15 ♉ 36	U.S. CIVIL WAR
15 ♉ 46	CANADA
15 ♉ 56	CUBA - INDEPENDENCE 1
15 ♉ 56	CHILE 2
16 ♉ 00R	LUXEMBOURG
16 ♉ 02	SRI LANKA-REP
16 ♉ 05	TONGA
16 ♉ 07	BARBADOS
16 ♉ 12	NAMIBIA
16 ♉ 24	KAMPUCHEA, COMM
16 ♉ 33	LESOTHO
16 ♉ 35	MOROCCO

16 ♉ 40	☽	NEW ZEALAND I
16 ♉ 41	☊	BOTSWANA
16 ♉ 42	●	IRAN - KHOMEINI
16 ♉ 46	●	ROMAN EMPIRE 1
16 ♉ 47	●	GRENADA
16 ♉ 47	☊	CZECHOSLOVAKIA-COMMUNIS
16 ♉ 50	♀	ZIMBABWE-RHODESIA
16 ♉ 54	♂	GERMANY WEST PROCLAM
17 ♉ 00R	♇	GERMANY - EMPIRE
17 ♉ 00	♀	PAKISTAN, REPUBLIC
17 ♉ 12	♂	CUBA - INDEPENDENCE 2
17 ♉ 16	●	FRANCE-VICHY REPUBLIC
17 ♉ 16	A	PANAMA
17 ♉ 23	☽	ICELAND
17 ♉ 29	♅	LIECHTENSTEIN
17 ♉ 32	A	PAKISTAN
17 ♉ 37	♂	CUBA - COMMUNIST
17 ♉ 47R	♅	HATAY
18 ♉ 00	⚷	VANUATU
18 ♉ 10	●	MAURITIUS
18 ♉ 14	☽	CHILE 1
18 ♉ 24	A	BURKINO-FASSO
18 ♉ 27	♂	ITALY - KINGDOM 1
18 ♉ 29	⊙	MONACO
18 ♉ 32	♃	GAMBIA
18 ♉ 35	☿	TONGA
18 ♉ 43	☿	SHEPARD
18 ♉ 47	♂	DE GAULLE
18 ♉ 48	●	ZIMBABWE-RHODESIA
18 ♉ 53	♃	MALAWI
18 ♉ 53R	♇	FRANCE-THIRD REPUBLIC
19 ♉ 02	☽	CHINA - NATIONALIST
19 ♉ 11	♂	GRENADA
19 ♉ 12	☽	TOGO
19 ♉ 14	♅	ENGLAND-1689
19 ♉ 19R	⚷	CISKEI
19 ♉ 23	●	URUGUAY
19 ♉ 29	♇	ITALY - KINGDOM 2
19 ♉ 32	☊	SRI LANKA-IND
19 ♉ 36	♄	BANGLADESH 1
19 ♉ 39	☊	PORTUGAL-REVOLUTION
19 ♉ 46	♄	LONDON 1
19 ♉ 49	●	ARGENTINA - REVOLUTION
19 ♉ 49	♀	DJIBOUTI
19 ♉ 57	☊	GORBACHEV
20 ♉ 05	☽	AUSTRALIA 2
20 ♉ 07	●	YUGOSLAVIA-COMMUNIST
20 ♉ 09	M	ANGOLA
20 ♉ 12	●	MALAYSIA
20 ♉ 16	♄	UNITED PROVINCES C A
20 ♉ 29	⊙	ENGLAND-17Ø7
20 ♉ 42	●	GORBACHEV
20 ♉ 51	♀	POLAND-COMMUNIST
20 ♉ 57	A	JAMAICA
20 ♉ 58R	⚷	ANTIGUA-BARBUDA
21 ♉ 00	M	VIETNAM-UNION
21 ♉ 01	♄	OMAN
21 ♉ 06	♃	NORWAY
21 ♉ 11	☊	VATICAN CITY
21 ♉ 14	⊙	NATAL
21 ♉ 14	♃	SPAIN
21 ♉ 31	●	SOUTH AFRICA-UNION
21 ♉ 34R	♄	FIJI
21 ♉ 36R	♄	KAMPUCHEA - REP
21 ♉ 40	♃	SEYCHELLES
21 ♉ 54	☽	CHINA - REPUBLIC
21 ♉ 59	●	POLAND 1
22 ♉ 03	A	GERMANY - EMPIRE
22 ♉ 06	♄	BANGLADESH 2
22 ♉ 11	M	NATAL
22 ♉ 12R	♆	ENGLAND-WILLIAM
22 ♉ 12	☊	BURMA
22 ♉ 18	♃	VIETNAM-UNION
22 ♉ 19	A	GABON
22 ♉ 23	⊙	ECUADOR 2
22 ♉ 32	♂	GHANA
22 ♉ 34R	⚷	BELIZE
22 ♉ 39	●	SENEGAL
22 ♉ 40R	⚷	ALLIANCE
22 ♉ 44	☊	TEXAS
22 ♉ 46	●	HUNGARY
22 ♉ 48	⊙	WARSAW PACT
22 ♉ 53	☊	CHINA - NATIONALIST
22 ♉ 54	⊙	PARAGUAY
22 ♉ 56	♀	FALL OF CONSTANTINOPLE
23 ♉ 01	M	AUSTRIA
23 ♉ 11	☿	NATAL
23 ♉ 20	M	MAURETANIA
23 ♉ 21	M	ECUADOR 2
23 ♉ 23	M	LAOS I
23 ♉ 40	⊙	ISRAEL
23 ♉ 40R	⚷	GERMANY - THIRD REICH
23 ♉ 42R	♃	ZAMBIA
23 ♉ 43	☽	USSR-FORMATION
23 ♉ 44R	☿	N Y STOCK EXCHANGE
23 ♉ 52	M	PARAGUAY
23 ♉ 57	♅	FRANCE-VICHY REPUBLIC
23 ♉ 59	⊙	PALESTINE
24 ♉ 04	☽	MALAWI
24 ♉ 08	♂	RWANDA-INDEPENDENCE
24 ♉ 08	♂	BURUNDI
24 ♉ 12	♇	ROMANIA 1
24 ♉ 13	●	ENGLAND-17Ø7
24 ♉ 21	♂	CHINA - REPUBLIC
24 ♉ 22R	♄	LEBANON I
24 ♉ 23	♀	MONACO
24 ♉ 25	♇	LIBERAL PARTY
24 ♉ 26	A	ORANGE FREE STATE
24 ♉ 32	A	CONGO
24 ♉ 35	●	DOMINICAN REPUBLIC
24 ♉ 49	●	S VIETNAM-REP
25 ♉ 00	☿	THATCHER
25 ♉ 15	♂	ATOMIC EXPLOSION

25 ♉ 18	☊	GUYANA
25 ♉ 18	⊙	ENGLAND-EDGAR
25 ♉ 23	☽	ITALY - KINGDOM 1
25 ♉ 26	♃	LONDON 2
25 ♉ 37	♄	ORANGE FREE STATE
25 ♉ 42	♀	GUATEMALA - 2
25 ♉ 47	☽	CONSERVATIVE PARTY
25 ♉ 48	♂	ENGLAND-EDGAR
25 ♉ 55	♂	ALGERIA
26 ♉ 04R	♃	MALTA
26 ♉ 05	♃	SIKKIM
26 ♉ 06	A	CHAD
26 ♉ 09	♇	MONTENEGRO
26 ♉ 09	♇	SERBIA
26 ♉ 09	♇	BULGARIA - AUTONOMY
26 ♉ 09	♇	ROMANIA 2
26 ♉ 15	☿	JORDAN
26 ♉ 22	⚷	THAILAND 2
26 ♉ 37	M	ENGLAND-EDGAR
26 ♉ 41R	♇	SOUTH AFRICAN REP 2
26 ♉ 51	☿	ENGLAND-EDGAR
26 ♉ 56	A	HYDERABAD
26 ♉ 56	☽	LATVIA
27 ♉ 02	☽	LESOTHO
27 ♉ 07	A	GERMANY - THIRD REICH
27 ♉ 12	A	SPAIN
27 ♉ 16	♃	LABOUR PARTY 2
27 ♉ 18	☽	CAPE VERDE ISLANDS
27 ♉ 22	⊙	N Y STOCK EXCHANGE
27 ♉ 27	●	LAOS 2
27 ♉ 38	☿	NORWAY
27 ♉ 55	☿	GERMANY WEST SOVEREIGN
28 ♉ 02	♂	GUYANA
28 ♉ 07R	♅	LEBANON I
28 ♉ 08	M	NORWAY
28 ♉ 11	☊	SOUTH AFRICA-UNION
28 ♉ 16	●	CZECHOSLOVAKIA 3
28 ♉ 19R	⚷	IRAQ - INDEPENCENCE
28 ♉ 22	M	N Y STOCK EXCHANGE
28 ♉ 28R	⚷	BRUNEI
28 ♉ 31R	♄	SYRIA 1
28 ♉ 45	⊙	CUBA - INDEPENDENCE 2
28 ♉ 47	A	CENTRAL AFRICAN REPUBLI
28 ♉ 50	♃	VATICAN CITY
28 ♉ 52	☊	PAKISTAN
28 ♉ 52	☊	INDIA - INDEPENDENCE
28 ♉ 52	☊	HYDERABAD
28 ♉ 58	☿	NICARAGUA 2
29 ♉ 03	●	ROME
29 ♉ 06R	♃	TRANSKEI
29 ♉ 11	♂	BENIN
29 ♉ 14	⚷	THATCHER
29 ♉ 31	♆	JAPAN - MEIJI CONST
29 ♉ 38	M	CUBA - INDEPENDENCE 2
29 ♉ 41	☽	USSR-REPUBLIC
29 ♉ 59	M	VATICAN CITY
0 ♊ 11R	♄	ALBANIA - INDEPENDENCE
0 ♊ 16	☽	CONGO
0 ♊ 18R	♅	SYRIA 1
0 ♊ 25	⊙	ROMANIA 1
0 ♊ 31	♂	NIGER
0 ♊ 35	A	CONFEDERATE STATES AMER
0 ♊ 36R	☿	SOUTH AFRICA-UNION
0 ♊ 39	●	NORTH VIETNAM
0 ♊ 40	☊	CIA
0 ♊ 47R	⚷	CYPRUS - TURKISH
0 ♊ 53	A	INDIA - INDEPENDENCE
0 ♊ 56	♂	THAILAND 1
1 ♊ 07	A	MALAYA
1 ♊ 08	●	SOUTH VIETNAM
1 ♊ 13	☽	ESTONIA
1 ♊ 14	⚷	TEXAS
1 ♊ 17	M	ROMANIA 1
1 ♊ 17	⊙	SRI LANKA-REP
1 ♊ 18	♂	THAILAND 2
1 ♊ 23	♃	MEXICO - REVOLUTION
1 ♊ 25R	♄	BANGLADESH 3
1 ♊ 27	⊙	GERMANY WEST PROCLAM
1 ♊ 29	●	SIERRA LEONE
1 ♊ 30R	♃	UKRAINE
1 ♊ 52	♂	BURKINO-FASSO
1 ♊ 54	♂	GUINEA
2 ♊ 04	A	SINGAPORE 1
2 ♊ 14R	♇	CREATION OF MAN
2 ♊ 15R	♅	NUCLEAR REACTION
2 ♊ 16	A	GREECE INDEPENCENCE
2 ♊ 18R	♇	CREATION OF THE WORLD
2 ♊ 19	♂	FRANCE-FIFTH REPUBLIC
2 ♊ 22	M	IRAQ - KINGDOM
2 ♊ 30R	♄	UNITED ARAB EMIR
2 ♊ 49	☿	TUNISIA
2 ♊ 51	M	SURINAM
2 ♊ 52R	⚷	ST KITTS-NEVIS
3 ♊ 04	☿	GUYANA
3 ♊ 06R	☿	LIBERAL PARTY
3 ♊ 10	♂	IVORY COAST
3 ♊ 14	M	PHILLIPINES
3 ♊ 18R	♄	PERU-BATTLE AYACUCHO
3 ♊ 20	☽	BAHRAIN
3 ♊ 21R	☿	MOROCCO
3 ♊ 31	♂	NATAL
3 ♊ 32	☽	THATCHER
3 ♊ 35	⊙	JORDAN
3 ♊ 42	⊙	ARGENTINA - REVOLUTION
3 ♊ 46	☽	MEXICO - CONSTITUTION
3 ♊ 47	⚷	GORBACHEV
3 ♊ 54	☽	LIBYA, COUP
4 ♊ 00R	♇	JAPAN - MEIJI CONST
4 ♊ 15	♀	ROMANIA 1
4 ♊ 18	⊙	GEORGIA
4 ♊ 18	⊙	ARMENIA
4 ♊ 27	⊙	GUYANA
4 ♊ 33	M	ARGENTINA - REVOLUTION

20 ♊ 48	☊	ITALY - REPUBLIC
20 ♊ 48R	♇	LABOUR PARTY 2
20 ♊ 54	☊	JORDAN
20 ♊ 59R	♀	MALAWI
20 ♊ 59R	♃	ROMAN EMPIRE 1
21 ♊ 00	M	FRANCE - NAPOLEON
21 ♊ 04	♇	NORWAY
21 ♊ 20	♃	MALDIVES
21 ♊ 22	♂	USA 3
21 ♊ 23	♂	USA 4
21 ♊ 25R	♅	FRANCE-FOURTH REPUBLIC
21 ♊ 34	♀	TANZANIA
21 ♊ 35	☿	CAPE VERDE ISLANDS
21 ♊ 41	A	BANGLADESH 3
21 ♊ 51	☽	GREECE INDEPENCENCE
21 ♊ 52	A	S.D.P.
21 ♊ 52R	♄	SYRIA 2
21 ♊ 52R	♄	LEBANON 2
21 ♊ 57	●	KHALISTAN
22 ♊ 05	♀	KHALISTAN
22 ♊ 05	♀	ARGENTINA - REVOLUTION
22 ♊ 07R	♅	CZECHOSLOVAKIA-COMMUNIS
22 ♊ 15	♂	SAHRAWI ARAB D R
22 ♊ 20	●	ALLIANCE
22 ♊ 20	♂	WARSAW PACT
22 ♊ 23	☿	COMOROS 1
22 ♊ 24R	♅	SRI LANKA-IND
22 ♊ 37	☽	UNITED NATIONS
22 ♊ 43	☉	KHALISTAN
22 ♊ 48	☽	BUGANDA
22 ♊ 50	M	LAOS 2
23 ♊ 16	☽	GUINEA - BUISSAU
23 ♊ 17	A	BOTSWANA
23 ♊ 23R	♅	BURMA
23 ♊ 30R	♆	CUBA - INDEPENDENCE 1
23 ♊ 36	♀	ICELAND
23 ♊ 44	♃	UNITED PROVINCES C A
23 ♊ 49R	♅	CHINA - NATIONALIST
23 ♊ 51	☿	VENEZUELA 1
23 ♊ 51	⚷	GUATEMALA - 2
23 ♊ 55	♃	FRANCE-THIRD REPUBLIC
23 ♊ 58	♃	SINGAPORE 2
24 ♊ 01	♃	SINGAPORE 3
24 ♊ 13	☽	GABON
24 ♊ 13R	♆	LABOUR PARTY 1
24 ♊ 15	♀	VANUATU
24 ♊ 15	☊	ZAMBIA
24 ♊ 20	♅	CIA
24 ♊ 21	♅	ISRAEL
24 ♊ 22	♅	PALESTINE
24 ♊ 30	☉	TUNISIA
24 ♊ 33	●	TRINIDAD & TOBAGO
24 ♊ 43	●	REAGAN-1
24 ♊ 48	A	LABOUR PARTY 2
24 ♊ 48	♇	NEW ZEALAND I
24 ♊ 54	●	GAGARIN
25 ♊ 00	●	SOMALIA
25 ♊ 05	☊	THATCHER
25 ♊ 08	☿	VIETNAM-UNION
25 ♊ 10	♅	HYDERABAD
25 ♊ 10	♅	PAKISTAN
25 ♊ 10	♅	INDIA - INDEPENDENCE
25 ♊ 21	☽	EQUATORIAL GUINEA
25 ♊ 23	☽	BURUNDI
25 ♊ 23	☽	RWANDA-INDEPENDENCE
25 ♊ 26	●	ROMAN EMPIRE 2
25 ♊ 29	☉	FRANCE-VICHY REPUBLIC
25 ♊ 31	●	ZAIRE
25 ♊ 37	A	TEXAS
25 ♊ 49	M	NORTH VIETNAM
25 ♊ 50R	♇	BULGARIA - INDEPENDENCE
25 ♊ 53	A	LESOTHO
25 ♊ 57	♇	SOUTH AFRICA-UNION
26 ♊ 13	☉	ICELAND
26 ♊ 23R	♃	LAOS I
26 ♊ 24	♂	OPEC
26 ♊ 34	M	SOUTH VIETNAM
26 ♊ 36	♂	VIETNAM
26 ♊ 36	☿	ARGENTINA - REVOLUTION
26 ♊ 43	M	SAO TOME-PRINCIPE
26 ♊ 54	●	JORDAN
27 ♊ 17	☿	BIAFRA
27 ♊ 18	♄	BAHAMAS
27 ♊ 20	♅	EIRE 3
27 ♊ 24	☉	EGYPT - REPUBLIC
27 ♊ 25	♄	ENGLAND-EDGAR
27 ♊ 28	☽	NETHERLANDS
27 ♊ 31R	♆	AUSTRALIA 2
27 ♊ 32R	♆	AUSTRALIA 1
27 ♊ 35	☊	MALTA
27 ♊ 44	☽	JAPAN - MEIJI CONST
27 ♊ 45R	♇	CHINA - REPUBLIC
27 ♊ 46R	⚷	HONDURAS
27 ♊ 50	⚷	KUWAIT
27 ♊ 51	M	THAILAND 2
27 ♊ 55	♀	MALI - FEDERATION
27 ♊ 57R	♇	PORTUGAL-REVOLUTION
28 ♊ 07	♄	AFGHANISTAN
28 ♊ 11R	♄	GRENADA
28 ♊ 15	♅	MONACO
28 ♊ 24	♀	BOLIVIA
28 ♊ 27	☽	FRANCE-FIFTH REPUBLIC
28 ♊ 40	☉	MALI - FEDERATION
28 ♊ 41	☽	JAPAN - SOVEREIGNTY
28 ♊ 43R	☿	UNITED PROVINCES C A
28 ♊ 57	♅	GERMANY WEST PROCLAM
29 ♊ 04	●	BOPHUTHATSWANA
29 ♊ 07	●	OMAN
29 ♊ 09	A	EIRE 2
29 ♊ 14	♅	THAILAND 1
29 ♊ 20R	♂	TIMOR
29 ♊ 24	A	SIKKIM
29 ♊ 26	☊	YUGOSLAVIA-COMMUNIST
29 ♊ 26	♅	KOREA - SOUTH
29 ♊ 27R	♆	SAUDI ARABIA
29 ♊ 27	☊	BULGARIA - INDEPENDENCE
29 ♊ 28	☿	ITALY - KINGDOM 2
29 ♊ 29	M	E.E.C.
29 ♊ 29R	♇	ALBANIA - INDEPENDENCE
29 ♊ 39	♄	ICELAND
29 ♊ 48	☊	ALBANIA-PEOPLES REPUBLI
29 ♊ 54	♀	SWITZERLAND
29 ♊ 55	☽	TURKEY
29 ♊ 58	♆	CUBA - INDEPENDENCE 2
0 ♋ 04	☿	SAO TOME-PRINCIPE
0 ♋ 05	M	KUWAIT
0 ♋ 10R	♂	SURINAM
0 ♋ 19	♅	KOREA - NORTH
0 ♋ 24	♀	USA 2
0 ♋ 28R	♃	RHODESIA
0 ♋ 29R	♂	RWANDA-UDI
0 ♋ 32	♄	PORTUGAL-REVOLUTION
0 ♋ 35	♂	HYDERABAD
0 ♋ 35	♂	INDIA - INDEPENDENCE
0 ♋ 35	♂	PAKISTAN
0 ♋ 35R	♃	FRANCE - NAPOLEON
0 ♋ 36	♀	USA 1
0 ♋ 41	♂	MALI - REPUBLIC
0 ♋ 47	♂	TONGA
0 ♋ 49	A	NIGERIA
0 ♋ 51	☊	ITALY - KINGDOM 2
1 ♋ 11	☿	ITALY - REPUBLIC
1 ♋ 15	☿	DJIBOUTI
1 ♋ 32	♀	JORDAN
1 ♋ 32	♇	EIRE 1
1 ♋ 37	♃	LONDON 1
1 ♋ 42	♀	HIROSHIMA
1 ♋ 42R	♅	INDIA - REPUBLIC
1 ♋ 48	☽	RWANDA-UDI
1 ♋ 49	☊	UNITED NATIONS
1 ♋ 55	☽	MALDIVES
2 ♋ 03	☊	MALAWI
2 ♋ 03	●	ZANZIBAR
2 ♋ 19	☽	BARBADOS
2 ♋ 23R	♇	USSR-REPUBLIC
2 ♋ 26	☿	SOUTH AFRICA-REPUBLIC
2 ♋ 27	☉	THAILAND 2
2 ♋ 28	A	BOKHARA NAT'L SOVIET RE
2 ♋ 29R	♅	SWEDEN
2 ♋ 31R	♂	ANGOLA
2 ♋ 41R	♇	MEXICO - CONSTITUTION
2 ♋ 45	♂	PORTUGAL-REVOLUTION
2 ♋ 46	☉	MOZAMBIQUE
2 ♋ 53R	♅	INDONESIA
3 ♋ 05	♀	USA 3
3 ♋ 06	♀	USA 4
3 ♋ 13	♂	EGYPT - REPUBLIC
3 ♋ 13	A	ST KITTS-NEVIS
3 ♋ 19R	♃	BOPHUTHATSWANA
3 ♋ 27	☊	TANZANIA
3 ♋ 29	♀	GREECE DEMOCRACY
3 ♋ 31	M	CHINA - NATIONALIST
3 ♋ 32	M	ICELAND
3 ♋ 33	☿	FALL OF CONSTANTINOPLE
3 ♋ 34	M	WESTERN SAMOA
3 ♋ 40	♇	TRANSCAUCASIAN FED
3 ♋ 41	☽	BELIZE
3 ♋ 58R	♇	UKRAINE
4 ♋ 01	A	TUVALU
4 ♋ 04	♅	NATO 1
4 ♋ 04	M	BRUNEI
4 ♋ 08	M	AUSTRALIA 1
4 ♋ 09	♃	GUYANA
4 ♋ 11	A	UGANDA
4 ♋ 13	⚷	CARPATHO-UKRAINE
4 ♋ 13	⚷	SLOVAKIA
4 ♋ 14R	♇	POLAND 1
4 ♋ 16	☉	SOMALILAND
4 ♋ 16	☉	MADAGASCAR
4 ♋ 16	♇	GEORGIA
4 ♋ 16	♇	ARMENIA
4 ♋ 18	♀	SRI LANKA-REP
4 ♋ 19	♇	AZERBAIJAN
4 ♋ 22	A	CZECHOSLOVAKIA-COMMUNIS
4 ♋ 36	☿	BHUTAN
4 ♋ 41	A	GUATEMALA - 3
4 ♋ 42	♄	BHUTAN
4 ♋ 44R	♀	TUNISIA
4 ♋ 48R	♇	LITHUANIA
4 ♋ 48	♀	ISRAEL
4 ♋ 49R	♆	FIRST MANNED FLIGHT
4 ♋ 49	♂	NIGERIA
4 ♋ 50	♅	CHINA - COMMUNIST 1
4 ♋ 52	●	INDIA - REPUBLIC
4 ♋ 52	A	HATAY
4 ♋ 53R	♇	FINLAND
4 ♋ 58	♅	CHINA - COMMUNIST 2
5 ♋ 00	♀	PALESTINE
5 ♋ 01	●	BANGLADESH 1
5 ♋ 02R	♇	ESTONIA
5 ♋ 07	☉	DJIBOUTI
5 ♋ 09	♀	MADAGASCAR
5 ♋ 09	♀	SOMALILAND
5 ♋ 13	♂	CHILE 2
5 ♋ 20R	♇	USSR-REVOLUTION
5 ♋ 26	♃	USA 2
5 ♋ 28	♃	USA 1
5 ♋ 32	♂	TRINIDAD & TOBAGO
5 ♋ 38	M	CAMEROON
5 ♋ 39	⚷	LIECHTENSTEIN
5 ♋ 47R	♆	PANAMA
5 ♋ 51	♃	TEXAS
5 ♋ 56	♃	USA 3
5 ♋ 56	♃	USA 4
6 ♋ 02	☽	UNITED ARAB REP
6 ♋ 07R	♇	ICELAND

6 S 07R			YUGOSLAVIA 2
6 S 14			SRI LANKA-REP
6 S 16			KIRIBATI
6 S 20R			LATVIA
6 S 23R			CZECHOSLOVAKIA 3
6 S 24R			HUNGARY
6 S 26			POLAND 2
6 S 26R			AUSTRIA
6 S 27R			GERMANY - WEIMAR
6 S 29			CANADA
6 S 29			POLAND-COMMUNIST
6 S 32R			JAPAN - MEIJI CONST
6 S 33R			ARGENTINA - INDEPENDENC
6 S 34R			YUGOSLAVIA 1
6 S 34R			CZECHOSLOVAKIA 2
6 S 38R			CZECHOSLOVAKIA 1
6 S 45			LIBERIA
6 S 51R			BOKHARA NAT'L SOVIET RE
6 S 52R			MONGOLIA
7 S 03			NORWAY
7 S 13			SEYCHELLES
7 S 15			TREATY OF ROME
7 S 20			OPEC
7 S 22			FIJI
7 S 25			VIETNAM
7 S 47			TURKEY
7 S 48			USSR-REVOLUTION
7 S 56R			LABOUR PARTY 2
7 S 57R			EGYPT - KINGDOM
7 S 57R			EGYPT - INDEPENDENCE
7 S 59			FAR EAST REPUBLIC
8 S 00			KOREA - SOUTH
8 S 01			SINGAPORE 2
8 S 04			BYELO RUSSIA
8 S 11			DENMARK
8 S 15			UNITED PROVINCES C A
8 S 21R			BUGANDA
8 S 31			LABOUR PARTY 1
8 S 31			CANADA
8 S 34			HATAY
8 S 36			BURUNDI
8 S 36			RWANDA-INDEPENDENCE
8 S 38			CANADA
8 S 40R			DANZIG
8 S 47			ITALY - KINGDOM 2
8 S 48			BELIZE
8 S 49			MOROCCO
8 S 54			NAT KHOREZEM SOVIET REP
8 S 55			HIROSHIMA
9 S 01			UNITED PROVINCES C A
9 S 02			SOMALIA
9 S 03			ATOMIC EXPLOSION
9 S 05			BULGARIA - COMMUNIST
9 S 07			ZAIRE
9 S 10			POLAND-COMMUNIST
9 S 10			AGE OF AQUARIUS-1
9 S 20			CANADA
9 S 20			UNITED KINGDOM-1801
9 S 29			N Y STOCK EXCHANGE
9 S 37			IRAQ - KINGDOM
9 S 40R			KUWAIT
9 S 58			LAOS 2
9 S 58			SOUTH VIETNAM
9 S 58			NORTH VIETNAM
9 S 58			GERMANY - EMPIRE
10 S 05			ITALY - KINGDOM 2
10 S 09			SEYCHELLES
10 S 12R			USSR-FORMATION
10 S 14R			THAILAND 2
10 S 18			VIETNAM-UNION
10 S 18			KAMPUCHEA - INDEP
10 S 22			USA 2
10 S 23			MONGOLIA
10 S 39			JAPAN - SOVEREIGNTY
10 S 39R			UNITED KINGDOM-1922
10 S 40R			EIRE 2
10 S 42			EIRE 2
10 S 44R			FRANCE-VICHY REPUBLIC
10 S 49			NAMIBIA
10 S 52			GREECE DEMOCRACY
10 S 59			ALGERIA
11 S 02			COMOROS 1
11 S 02			UNITED PROVINCES C A
11 S 06			ARGENTINA - INDEPENDENC
11 S 08			EGYPT - INDEPENDENCE
11 S 13			USA 2
11 S 16			EIRE 1
11 S 17			SOMALIA
11 S 22			GREECE DEMOCRACY
11 S 22			USA 1
11 S 23			ZAIRE
11 S 24			KENYA
11 S 30			PHILLIPINES
11 S 30			ENGLAND-WILLIAM
11 S 39			ZANZIBAR
11 S 39			CARPATHO-UKRAINE
11 S 44			VENEZUELA 1
12 S 05			KAMPUCHEA, COMM
12 S 12			LUXEMBOURG
12 S 15R			NEPAL
12 S 20R			TURKEY
12 S 24R			LIBYA - INDEP
12 S 38R			CONSERVATIVE PARTY
12 S 40			VENEZUELA 1
12 S 42			REAGAN-1
12 S 56			CAPE VERDE ISLANDS
12 S 58			LAOS 2
12 S 58			NORTH VIETNAM
12 S 58			SOUTH VIETNAM
12 S 59			BANGLADESH 1
13 S 02			KAMPUCHEA, COMM
13 S 09			GREECE DEMOCRACY
13 S 10			KAMPUCHEA - INDEP
13 S 18			POLAND-COMMUNIST
13 S 19			USA 3
13 S 19			GUINEA
13 S 25			GUINEA
13 S 41			COMOROS 1
13 S 46			LEBANON 2
13 S 52			MALAWI
14 S 06			SOLOMON ISLANDS
14 S 07			VIETNAM-UNION
14 S 11			BELGIUM
14 S 13			TONGA
14 S 30			SYRIA 2
14 S 33R			ICELAND
14 S 34R			YUGOSLAVIA 2
14 S 36			CUBA - COMMUNIST
14 S 44			NEW ZEALAND I.
14 S 53			LIBYA - INDEP
15 S 07			THAILAND 2
15 S 24			CZECHOSLOVAKIA 1
15 S 28R			LATVIA
15 S 32			MALTA
15 S 38			ATOMIC EXPLOSION
15 S 38R			CZECHOSLOVAKIA 3
15 S 40R			HUNGARY
15 S 44R			POLAND 2
15 S 44R			AUSTRIA
15 S 46			CZECHOSLOVAKIA 2
15 S 46R			GERMANY - WEIMAR
15 S 47			YUGOSLAVIA 1
16 S 07			ARGENTINA - INDEPENDENC
16 S 12			ITALY - KINGDOM 2
16 S 17			AGE OF AQUARIUS-1
16 S 20			NAT KHOREZEM SOVIET REP
16 S 22			NICARAGUA SANDINISTA
16 S 34			GUINEA - BUISSAU
16 S 39			NETHERLANDS
16 S 42R			ROMAN EMPIRE 2
16 S 46			ETHIOPIA
16 S 57			SOLOMON ISLANDS
16 S 57R			ROMAN EMPIRE 1
17 S 03			BULGARIA - INDEPENDENCE
17 S 05			VATICAN CITY
17 S 05R			YUGOSLAVIA-COMMUNIST
17 S 06			CIA
17 S 07			TRANSKEI
17 S 14			ARGENTINA - INDEPENDENC
17 S 14			SOUTH AFRICAN REP 1
17 S 19			CUBA - COMMUNIST
17 S 26			EGYPT - REPUBLIC
17 S 31			VANUATU
17 S 36			SOUTH AFRICA-UNION
17 S 46			BAHAMAS
17 S 48			VIETNAM
17 S 51			TANZANIA
17 S 56			CAPE VERDE ISLANDS
17 S 56			FRANCE-THIRD REPUBLIC
18 S 00			HIROSHIMA
18 S 02			MEXICO - CONSTITUTION
18 S 13			HIROSHIMA
18 S 17R			MAURETANIA
18 S 17			LATVIA
18 S 21			SOUTH AFRICA-UNION
18 S 23			GAGARIN
18 S 25			URUGUAY
18 S 35			MALAYSIA
18 S 36			KIRIBATI
18 S 46			THAILAND 1
18 S 50			ESTONIA
19 S 13			FRANCE-VICHY REPUBLIC
19 S 23			GREECE REVOLUTION
19 S 25			FRANCE-VICHY REPUBLIC
19 S 26			UNITED KINGDOM-1801
19 S 27			SAO TOME-PRINCIPE
19 S 32			SINGAPORE 1
19 S 36			FRANCE-VICHY REPUBLIC
19 S 40			IRAQ - REPUBLIC
19 S 47			IRAQ - KINGDOM
19 S 51			MOZAMBIQUE
19 S 54			NICARAGUA 1
19 S 54R			YUGOSLAVIA-COMMUNIST
19 S 55			SLOVAKIA
20 S 01			ENGLAND-1707
20 S 30			NEW ZEALAND I
20 S 45			POLAND-COMMUNIST
20 S 52			BENIN
20 S 57			JAPAN - MEIJI CONST
20 S 58			EGYPT - REPUBLIC
20 S 58			SERBIA
20 S 58			MONTENEGRO
20 S 58			ROMANIA 2
21 S 02			BULGARIA - AUTONOMY
21 S 02			ITALY - REPUBLIC
21 S 08			IRAQ - REPUBLIC
21 S 10			THAILAND 2
21 S 12			CAPE VERDE ISLANDS
21 S 17			VIETNAM
21 S 18			COMOROS 1
21 S 22			NATO 1
21 S 27			PORTUGAL-REVOLUTION
21 S 30R			ALBANIA-PEOPLES REPUBLI
21 S 34			ENGLAND-1689
21 S 36			JORDAN
21 S 52			FRANCE-1st REPUBLIC 1
21 S 54			USA 3
21 S 54			SEYCHELLES
21 S 55			NORTH YEMEN
21 S 56			NIGER
21 S 57			BIAFRA
21 S 58R			GERMANY - THIRD REICH
22 S 05			SAO TOME-PRINCIPE
22 S 09			FRANCE-1st REPUBLIC 2
22 S 11			CIA
22 S 13			CIA

22 ♋ 18	♂	GUATEMALA - 1
22 ♋ 34	A	ZAMBIA
22 ♋ 43	♂	VENDA
22 ♋ 44	☽	SYRIA 1
22 ♋ 45	☽	LIECHTENSTEIN
22 ♋ 46R	♆	CHINA - REPUBLIC
23 ♋ 05	♅	LAOS I
23 ♋ 09	☽	MADAGASCAR
23 ♋ 09	☽	SOMALILAND
23 ♋ 11R	♇	ENGLAND-1689
23 ♋ 12	☊	CISKEI
23 ♋ 13	☽	UNITED KINGDOM-1922
23 ♋ 21	♄	ITALY - REPUBLIC
23 ♋ 22	♇	IRAQ - INDEPENCENCE
23 ♋ 28	☿	BURKINO-FASSO
23 ♋ 30	♃	GERMANY WEST SOVEREIGN
23 ♋ 33	☿	MALI - FEDERATION
23 ♋ 35	☉	ATOMIC EXPLOSION
23 ♋ 36	♂	BOLIVIA
23 ♋ 37	●	EGYPT - REPUBLIC
23 ♋ 39	♅	SOUTH VIETNAM
23 ♋ 39	♅	NORTH VIETNAM
23 ♋ 39	♅	LAOS 2
23 ♋ 42	♅	KAMPUCHEA - INDEP
23 ♋ 50	●	JAMAICA
23 ♋ 50	M	NAURU
23 ♋ 53	☿	MALAWI
23 ♋ 59	♂	UNITED NATIONS
24 ♋ 06	☉	AFGHANISTAN
24 ♋ 06	♅	GERMANY WEST SOVEREIGN
24 ♋ 12R	☿	USA 4
24 ♋ 12R	☿	USA 3
24 ♋ 16R	♄	USSR-REPUBLIC
24 ♋ 17	●	KENYA
24 ♋ 18R	♂	ALBANIA-PEOPLES REPUBLI
24 ♋ 23	⚷	NATAL
24 ♋ 23	♅	WARSAW PACT
24 ♋ 24	♂	FALL OF CONSTANTINOPLE
24 ♋ 24R	♅	GERMANY - EMPIRE
24 ♋ 34R	♃	NUCLEAR REACTION
24 ♋ 38	A	IRAQ - INDEPENCENCE
24 ♋ 45	♄	UNITED NATIONS
24 ♋ 48	♃	WARSAW PACT
24 ♋ 50	A	FRANCE-FIFTH REPUBLIC
24 ♋ 57	M	NICARAGUA SANDINISTA
24 ♋ 58	●	CONSERVATIVE PARTY
25 ♋ 00R	☿	USA 1
25 ♋ 02	M	ISRAEL
25 ♋ 04R	☿	USA 2
25 ♋ 09	♅	FRANCE-THIRD REPUBLIC
25 ♋ 23	☿	IVORY COAST
25 ♋ 25	♂	SIERRA LEONE
25 ♋ 31	☊	ANTIGUA-BARBUDA
25 ♋ 47R	♆	ALBANIA - INDEPENDENCE
25 ♋ 47	☽	ETHIOPIA
25 ♋ 48	♅	ITALY - KINGDOM 2
25 ♋ 48	♂	BHUTAN
25 ♋ 53	☽	ALBANIA - INDEPENDENCE
25 ♋ 54	♂	EL SALVADOR
26 ♋ 00R	♄	MEXICO - CONSTITUTION
26 ♋ 00	M	LIECHTENSTEIN
26 ♋ 12	♄	PHILLIPINES
26 ♋ 12	●	USA 4
26 ♋ 26	☽	SOLOMON ISLANDS
26 ♋ 27	☉	NICARAGUA SANDINISTA
26 ♋ 28	☊	BULGARIA - COMMUNIST
26 ♋ 30	●	SIKKIM
26 ♋ 40	●	N Y STOCK EXCHANGE
26 ♋ 46R	♄	SAHRAWI ARAB D R
26 ♋ 52R	♇	ROMAN EMPIRE 2
26 ♋ 53	A	CHILE 2
26 ♋ 56R	♇	ROMAN EMPIRE 1
27 ♋ 06	☽	HYDERABAD
27 ♋ 06	☽	PAKISTAN
27 ♋ 06	☽	INDIA - INDEPENDENCE
27 ♋ 10	M	OMAN
27 ♋ 24	♂	FRANCE-THIRD REPUBLIC
27 ♋ 26	A	ATOMIC EXPLOSION
27 ♋ 44	☽	ALGERIA
27 ♋ 47	☽	FAR EAST REPUBLIC
27 ♋ 49	☉	LAOS 2
27 ♋ 49	☉	NORTH VIETNAM
27 ♋ 49	☉	SOUTH VIETNAM
28 ♋ 00	☿	MADAGASCAR
28 ♋ 00	☿	SOMALILAND
28 ♋ 02	☊	ICELAND
28 ♋ 12	♅	FALL OF CONSTANTINOPLE
28 ♋ 17	●	CHILE 2
28 ♋ 18R	♅	PAKISTAN, REPUBLIC
28 ♋ 20	♂	UGANDA
28 ♋ 34	☿	MOON LANDING
28 ♋ 38	☉	KAMPUCHEA - INDEP
28 ♋ 38	A	GUATEMALA - 2
29 ♋ 04	♃	IRAN - ISLAMIC REP
29 ♋ 08	☉	MOON LANDING
29 ♋ 24R	♇	SLOVAKIA
29 ♋ 24R	♇	CARPATHO-UKRAINE
29 ♋ 25	♅	MOROCCO
29 ♋ 40	♂	SHEPARD
29 ♋ 42R	☿	AFGHANISTAN
29 ♋ 46	♇	LIECHTENSTEIN
29 ♋ 51	♄	PAPUA NEW GUINEA
29 ♋ 55	♆	EIRE 1
29 ♋ 56	M	KAMPUCHEA - REP
29 ♋ 57	☽	PERU-BATTLE AYACUCHO
29 ♋ 58	☿	SOMALIA
29 ♋ 59	☿	ZAIRE
0 ♌ 00	☊	BELIZE
0 ♌ 03	☉	OMAN
0 ♌ 05	M	MALDIVES
0 ♌ 17	♅	TUNISIA
0 ♌ 18	☊	ALLIANCE
0 ♌ 18	☿	CHAD

0 ♌ 21	♃	BOTSWANA
0 ♌ 24	☽	NICARAGUA 2
0 ♌ 33	☽	PERU I
0 ♌ 34	♄	POLAND 1
0 ♌ 36R	♃	ST LUCIA
0 ♌ 38	●	WESTERN SAMOA
0 ♌ 40R	☿	BYELO RUSSIA
0 ♌ 42	☊	SPAIN
0 ♌ 45	♇	HATAY
0 ♌ 49	☉	GREECE DEMOCRACY
0 ♌ 55	♃	LESOTHO
1 ♌ 06R	♄	COMOROS 2
1 ♌ 07	♃	BIAFRA
1 ♌ 08	●	KAMPUCHEA, COMM
1 ♌ 09R	♅	SUDAN
1 ♌ 12	☿	SERBIA
1 ♌ 12	☿	ROMANIA 2
1 ♌ 12	☿	BULGARIA - AUTONOMY
1 ♌ 12	☿	MONTENEGRO
1 ♌ 21	☽	SENEGAL
1 ♌ 21	M	LIBERIA
1 ♌ 25R	♄	ESPIRITU SANTO
1 ♌ 27	♇	FRANCE-VICHY REPUBLIC
1 ♌ 46R	♃	REAGAN-1
1 ♌ 51R	♃	UNITED KINGDOM-18Ø1
1 ♌ 57	A	BANGLADESH 2
2 ♌ 15	♅	S VIETNAM-REP
2 ♌ 16	♂	LIECHTENSTEIN
2 ♌ 36R	♆	USSR-REPUBLIC
2 ♌ 40	♄	SEYCHELLES
2 ♌ 43	●	BAHAMAS
2 ♌ 47	☉	LIECHTENSTEIN
2 ♌ 49R	♄	TIMOR
2 ♌ 50	☉	CIA
2 ♌ 51	☉	LIBERIA
2 ♌ 53R	♄	SURINAM
2 ♌ 53R	☿	BAHAMAS
2 ♌ 58	♄	ANGOLA
2 ♌ 58R	♅	TREATY OF ROME
3 ♌ 02R	♃	IRAN - KHOMEINI
3 ♌ 04	♄	VIETNAM-UNION
3 ♌ 04	☉	MALDIVES
3 ♌ 08	♀	VIETNAM
3 ♌ 15	♂	OMAN
3 ♌ 17R	♆	MEXICO - CONSTITUTION
3 ♌ 18	☿	CENTRAL AFRICAN REPUBLI
3 ♌ 24R	♅	GHANA
3 ♌ 26	♃	NAMIBIA
3 ♌ 31	♂	MALTA
3 ♌ 34	A	GAGARIN
3 ♌ 36	♀	KOREA - NORTH
3 ♌ 37	●	GERMANY - THIRD REICH
3 ♌ 43	M	PERU I
3 ♌ 51	♀	THATCHER
3 ♌ 58	●	TREATY OF ROME
4 ♌ 02	●	DJIBOUTI
4 ♌ 19	♆	TRANSCAUCASIAN FED
4 ♌ 21	☽	ISRAEL
4 ♌ 21R	♃	BARBADOS
4 ♌ 22	♃	TUVALU
4 ♌ 41	M	BYELO RUSSIA
4 ♌ 45	♆	GEORGIA
4 ♌ 45	♆	ARMENIA
4 ♌ 48	♆	AZERBAIJAN
4 ♌ 53	♆	POLAND 1
4 ♌ 58	☿	CANADA
5 ♌ 03R	♂	COLUMBIA
5 ♌ 12	♃	ZIMBABWE-RHODESIA
5 ♌ 12	☉	PERU I
5 ♌ 14	♇	SYRIA 1
5 ♌ 23	☽	REAGAN-2
5 ♌ 42R	♇	LEBANON I
5 ♌ 49	♂	URUGUAY
5 ♌ 50R	♆	UKRAINE
5 ♌ 53	A	ST VINCENT-GRENADINES
5 ♌ 56	☿	SOLOMON ISLANDS
5 ♌ 56	♀	LIBYA, COUP
6 ♌ 07	☽	NORWAY
6 ♌ 09	●	BENIN
6 ♌ 16	A	NATAL
6 ♌ 23	☊	UGANDA
6 ♌ 32	☉	VANUATU
6 ♌ 36	☊	USA 1
6 ♌ 36	☊	USA 2
6 ♌ 36	☿	CONGO
6 ♌ 36	☊	USA 3
6 ♌ 36	☊	USA 4
6 ♌ 48	☿	PAKISTAN
6 ♌ 48	☿	HYDERABAD
6 ♌ 48	☿	INDIA - INDEPENDENCE
6 ♌ 49	A	FAR EAST REPUBLIC
6 ♌ 50R	♆	LITHUANIA
6 ♌ 55R	♆	FINLAND
6 ♌ 57R	♂	SOUTH AFRICAN REP 1
7 ♌ 01R	♆	ESTONIA
7 ♌ 02	☊	SYRIA 2
7 ♌ 02	☊	LEBANON ∠
7 ♌ 03	A	ROME
7 ♌ 07	♆	USSR-REVOLUTION
7 ♌ 07	☽	EL SALVADOR
7 ♌ 08R	♇	NUCLEAR REACTION
7 ♌ 09	♇	ICELAND
7 ♌ 13	♇	FALL OF CONSTANTINOPLE
7 ♌ 17	♃	NEW ZEALAND I
7 ♌ 26	☽	NEPAL
7 ♌ 26	♂	NICARAGUA 1
7 ♌ 27	☿	PHILLIPINES
7 ♌ 36	☊	NORTH YEMEN
7 ♌ 38	♂	SWITZERLAND
7 ♌ 46	♄	TRANSCAUCASIAN FED
7 ♌ 47	M	SRI LANKA-IND
7 ♌ 47	♂	IRAQ - INDEPENCENCE
8 ♌ 03	A	KAMPUCHEA - INDEP

8 ♌ 12R	SYRIA 2
8 ♌ 12R	LEBANON 2
8 ♌ 14	DOMINICA
8 ♌ 16	CYPRUS
8 ♌ 22	FRANCE-FOURTH REPUBLIC
8 ♌ 29	CHILE 1
8 ♌ 37	NATO 1
8 ♌ 40	GAMBIA
8 ♌ 40R	CUBA - INDEPENDENCE 1
8 ♌ 42	BENIN
8 ♌ 42	CHINA - COMMUNIST 1
8 ♌ 47	TRINIDAD & TOBAGO
8 ♌ 49	BYELO RUSSIA
8 ♌ 53	POLAND-COMMUNIST
8 ♌ 55	JAMAICA
8 ♌ 58R	ARAB FEDERATION
8 ♌ 59	UNITED ARAB REP
9 ♌ 01	S.D.P.
9 ♌ 02	EIRE 3
9 ♌ 03	ALGERIA
9 ♌ 04	ALLIANCE
9 ♌ 06	PALESTINE
9 ♌ 09	MALAYA
9 ♌ 09	CZECHOSLOVAKIA 1
9 ♌ 10	BURUNDI
9 ♌ 10	RWANDA-INDEPENDENCE
9 ♌ 14R	ICELAND
9 ♌ 14R	YUGOSLAVIA 2
9 ♌ 16	CZECHOSLOVAKIA 2
9 ♌ 16	YUGOSLAVIA 1
9 ♌ 19R	LATVIA
9 ♌ 20	GERMANY - WEIMAR
9 ♌ 20R	CZECHOSLOVAKIA 3
9 ♌ 20	AUSTRIA
9 ♌ 20R	HUNGARY
9 ♌ 20	POLAND 2
9 ♌ 22	ENGLAND-1787
9 ♌ 22	ATOMIC EXPLOSION
9 ♌ 26	BULGARIA - COMMUNIST
9 ♌ 30	GEORGIA
9 ♌ 30	ARMENIA
9 ♌ 30R	UNITED ARAB REP
9 ♌ 35	BHUTAN
9 ♌ 40	AZERBAIJAN
9 ♌ 41	JORDAN
9 ♌ 45	NICARAGUA 2
9 ♌ 54	COSTA RICA 2
9 ♌ 58	ITALY - REPUBLIC
9 ♌ 58	HIROSHIMA
10 ♌ 08	GABON
10 ♌ 09	FRANCE - NAPOLEON
10 ♌ 24	PARAGUAY
10 ♌ 31	PHILLIPINES
10 ♌ 37	NIGER
10 ♌ 38R	YUGOSLAVIA-COMMUNIST
10 ♌ 39	IRAQ - REPUBLIC
10 ♌ 39	SYRIA 1
10 ♌ 41	SWITZERLAND
10 ♌ 44	VIETNAM
10 ♌ 49R	E.E.C.
10 ♌ 50	SPUTNIK
10 ♌ 51	REAGAN-♌
11 ♌ 05R	ALBANIA-PEOPLES REPUBLI
11 ♌ 09	CIA
11 ♌ 10	BYELO RUSSIA
11 ♌ 15	BOPHUTHATSWANA
11 ♌ 22	NETHERLANDS
11 ♌ 30	FRANCE-FOURTH REPUBLIC
11 ♌ 33	ANTIGUA-BARBUDA
11 ♌ 34R	BOKHARA NAT'L SOVIET RE
11 ♌ 36R	MONGOLIA
11 ♌ 39	GUATEMALA - 1
11 ♌ 43	UNITED NATIONS
11 ♌ 52R	UKRAINE
11 ♌ 55	BAHAMAS
12 ♌ 02	BELIZE
12 ♌ 04	ECUADOR 2
12 ♌ 09	ETHIOPIA
12 ♌ 21	BOLIVIA
12 ♌ 26R	PERU I
12 ♌ 31	ANGOLA
12 ♌ 32	MALAYA
12 ♌ 34	BURKINO-FASSO
12 ♌ 38	IRAQ - KINGDOM
12 ♌ 39	ISRAEL
12 ♌ 39	PALESTINE
12 ♌ 39	NETHERLANDS
12 ♌ 40	CIA
12 ♌ 41	GRENADA
12 ♌ 50	KIRIBATI
12 ♌ 53	ROMANIA 2
12 ♌ 53	SERBIA
12 ♌ 53	MONTENEGRO
12 ♌ 53	BULGARIA - AUTONOMY
12 ♌ 56	KIRIBATI
12 ♌ 57	TRANSCAUCASIAN FED
12 ♌ 58	KOREA - SOUTH
12 ♌ 58	DOMINICA
12 ♌ 59	MAURITIUS
13 ♌ 08	HIROSHIMA
13 ♌ 09	NAT KHOREZEM SOVIET REP
13 ♌ 14	HYDERABAD
13 ♌ 14	PAKISTAN
13 ♌ 14	INDIA - INDEPENDENCE
13 ♌ 16	JAMAICA
13 ♌ 16R	FAR EAST REPUBLIC
13 ♌ 16R	CZECHOSLOVAKIA-COMMUNIS
13 ♌ 17	SOUTH YEMEN 2
13 ♌ 18	FRANCE-FOURTH REPUBLIC
13 ♌ 21	SOUTH AFRICA-REPUBLIC
13 ♌ 28R	PERU-BATTLE AYACUCHO
13 ♌ 30	MALTA
13 ♌ 36	HYDERABAD
13 ♌ 36	INDIA - INDEPENDENCE
13 ♌ 36	PAKISTAN
13 ♌ 36R	EGYPT - KINGDOM
13 ♌ 36R	EGYPT - INDEPENDENCE
13 ♌ 46	DANZIG
13 ♌ 46R	SRI LANKA-IND
13 ♌ 49	BOLIVIA
14 ♌ 06	IRAQ - KINGDOM
14 ♌ 10	VATICAN CITY
14 ♌ 10R	EIRE 3
14 ♌ 11	MONACO
14 ♌ 18	USSR-REVOLUTION
14 ♌ 18	GERMANY WEST PROCLAM
14 ♌ 20R	LITHUANIA
14 ♌ 20R	NICARAGUA SANDINISTA
14 ♌ 27R	FINLAND
14 ♌ 27R	BURMA
14 ♌ 29	IVORY COAST
14 ♌ 32	SWITZERLAND
14 ♌ 32R	ESTONIA
14 ♌ 38	DJIBOUTI
14 ♌ 38R	CHINA - NATIONALIST
14 ♌ 40	NICARAGUA SANDINISTA
14 ♌ 44	LEBANON I
14 ♌ 46R	GREECE INDEPENCENCE
14 ♌ 47	IRAQ - REPUBLIC
14 ♌ 48	CHINA - COMMUNIST 2
14 ♌ 48	KOREA - SOUTH
14 ♌ 52R	ROME
15 ♌ 09	NETHERLANDS
15 ♌ 09	N Y STOCK EXCHANGE
15 ♌ 10	GUINEA
15 ♌ 13	ICELAND
15 ♌ 20	FRANCE-FIFTH REPUBLIC
15 ♌ 25R	DE GAULLE
15 ♌ 36	KOREA - NORTH
15 ♌ 38R	CUBA - COMMUNIST
15 ♌ 38	SWITZERLAND
15 ♌ 41	INDIA - INDEPENDENCE
15 ♌ 41	PAKISTAN
15 ♌ 41	HYDERABAD
15 ♌ 50	JORDAN
15 ♌ 53	TRANSKEI
16 ♌ 00	COSTA RICA 1
16 ♌ 02	SENEGAL
16 ♌ 05	RWANDA-INDEPENDENCE
16 ♌ 05	BURUNDI
16 ♌ 14	EIRE 1
16 ♌ 18	SINGAPORE 2
16 ♌ 25	ISRAEL
16 ♌ 26	PALESTINE
16 ♌ 27R	JAPAN - MEIJI CONST
16 ♌ 28	WARSAW PACT
16 ♌ 33	SINGAPORE 3
16 ♌ 39	NATO 1
16 ♌ 43	BYELO RUSSIA
16 ♌ 56	ARGENTINA - INDEPENDENC
16 ♌ 56	TOGO
17 ♌ 00R	U.S. CIVIL WAR
17 ♌ 02	PAKISTAN, REPUBLIC
17 ♌ 02	OMAN
17 ♌ 05	CREATION OF MAN
17 ♌ 12	DENMARK
17 ♌ 16R	INDIA - REPUBLIC
17 ♌ 17	IRAN - ISLAMIC REP
17 ♌ 18	BAHRAIN
17 ♌ 25	CHINA - COMMUNIST 1
17 ♌ 30	SURINAM
17 ♌ 38	CHINA - COMMUNIST 2
17 ♌ 46R	USSR-FORMATION
17 ♌ 51	ZIMBABWE-RHODESIA
17 ♌ 53R	INDONESIA
17 ♌ 57R	CZECHOSLOVAKIA-COMMUNIS
17 ♌ 59	MOZAMBIQUE
17 ♌ 59	FRANCE-THIRD REPUBLIC
18 ♌ 00	BRAZIL
18 ♌ 02	AGE OF AQUARIUS-1
18 ♌ 02	AGE OF AQUARIUS-2
18 ♌ 06	LIBYA, COUP
18 ♌ 06R	UNITED KINGDOM-1922
18 ♌ 07R	EIRE 2
18 ♌ 08R	ITALY - KINGDOM 1
18 ♌ 17	CHAD
18 ♌ 18	MALI - FEDERATION
18 ♌ 18	ST VINCENT-GRENADINES
18 ♌ 22	GUYANA
18 ♌ 24	FRANCE-1st REPUBLIC 2
18 ♌ 27	ECUADOR 2
18 ♌ 34	SOMALILAND
18 ♌ 34	MADAGASCAR
18 ♌ 40	PHILLIPINES
18 ♌ 44	ENGLAND-EDGAR
18 ♌ 44	WESTERN SAMOA
18 ♌ 49	SOMALIA
18 ♌ 49	ZAIRE
18 ♌ 58	ALGERIA
19 ♌ 24	JAPAN - SOVEREIGNTY
19 ♌ 28	ATOMIC EXPLOSION
19 ♌ 28	ALBANIA-PEOPLES REPUBLI
19 ♌ 31	ARGENTINA - REVOLUTION
19 ♌ 32	SPUTNIK
19 ♌ 32	BENIN
19 ♌ 48	SRI LANKA-IND
19 ♌ 59	AFGHANISTAN
19 ♌ 59	SWAZILAND
20 ♌ 00	TANGANYIKA
20 ♌ 12	CENTRAL AFRICAN REPUBLI
20 ♌ 12	VANUATU
20 ♌ 13	TURKEY
20 ♌ 22	THAILAND 2
20 ♌ 25	EIRE 1
20 ♌ 32R	CAMEROON
20 ♌ 35	BENIN

20 ♌ 38	♇	ENGLAND-17Ø7
20 ♌ 38	●	BOLIVIA
20 ♌ 42	☽	GRENADA
20 ♌ 43	♅	NIGER
20 ♌ 46	A	GERMANY WEST SOVEREIGN
20 ♌ 50	♅	ROMANIA 1
20 ♌ 50	♅	BURKINO-FASSO
20 ♌ 56	☊	LABOUR PARTY 2
20 ♌ 58	♅	IVORY COAST
20 ♌ 58	☉	BAHRAIN
21 ♌ 05	♅	LIBERAL PARTY
21 ♌ 07	☉	INDIA - INDEPENDENCE
21 ♌ 07	☉	PAKISTAN
21 ♌ 07	☉	HYDERABAD
21 ♌ 10	A	MONACO
21 ♌ 12	♅	CHAD
21 ♌ 18	♇	EGYPT - REPUBLIC
21 ♌ 20	♅	CENTRAL AFRICAN REPUBLI
21 ♌ 20R	♇	LIBYA - INDEP
21 ♌ 20	☿	JAMAICA
21 ♌ 27	♅	CONGO
21 ♌ 31	♅	CYPRUS
21 ♌ 35	♅	GABON
21 ♌ 39	A	MOROCCO
21 ♌ 39R	♅	SIERRA LEONE
21 ♌ 40	♅	SHEPARD
21 ♌ 46	♅	FRANCE-1st REPUBLIC 1
21 ♌ 47	♅	SENEGAL
21 ♌ 47R	♅	GAGARIN
21 ♌ 48	A	VIETNAM-UNION
21 ♌ 50R	♄	BURMA
21 ♌ 56	♃	ENGLAND-17Ø7
21 ♌ 57R	☿	LIBERIA
22 ♌ 00	♀	NIGER
22 ♌ 00	♅	FRANCE-1st REPUBLIC 2
22 ♌ 02	♃	BOLIVIA
22 ♌ 06	♅	SOUTH AFRICA-REPUBLIC
22 ♌ 07	☉	CONGO
22 ♌ 07	♀	UNITED PROVINCES C A
22 ♌ 10	♂	BOTSWANA
22 ♌ 11	☉	KOREA - SOUTH
22 ♌ 18R	♄	CHINA - NATIONALIST
22 ♌ 29R	♃	PAKISTAN, REPUBLIC
22 ♌ 32	☿	VIETNAM
22 ♌ 46	●	HIROSHIMA
22 ♌ 46	♅	KUWAIT
22 ♌ 49	♂	ZAMBIA
22 ♌ 51R	♃	CONFEDERATE STATES AMER
22 ♌ 53	♃	ICELAND
23 ♌ 02	☉	CYPRUS
23 ♌ 05	☽	SUDAN
23 ♌ 12	A	MAURETANIA
23 ♌ 13	A	LAOS I
23 ♌ 18	♅	OPEC
23 ♌ 21	♀	PERU I
23 ♌ 22R	♄	UNITED KINGDOM-18Ø1
23 ♌ 23	●	ICELAND
23 ♌ 34	♀	ST KITTS-NEVIS
23 ♌ 38	♀	SOLOMON ISLANDS
23 ♌ 44	♅	MALI - REPUBLIC
23 ♌ 48	M	FEDERATION OF ARAB REPU
23 ♌ 49	♇	LAOS 2
23 ♌ 49	♇	SOUTH VIETNAM
23 ♌ 49	♇	NORTH VIETNAM
23 ♌ 50	♇	KAMPUCHEA - INDEP
23 ♌ 51	♂	ST KITTS-NEVIS
23 ♌ 55	♃	MOROCCO
23 ♌ 59	♂	MEXICO - REVOLUTION
24 ♌ 02	☉	GABON
24 ♌ 03	☽	CZECHOSLOVAKIA 2
24 ♌ 10	♅	NIGERIA
24 ♌ 18R	♇	GERMANY WEST SOVEREIGN
24 ♌ 19	♇	WARSAW PACT
24 ♌ 19	●	BULGARIA - COMMUNIST
24 ♌ 23	♂	KUWAIT
24 ♌ 24	♃	BYELO RUSSIA
24 ♌ 25R	♅	RWANDA-UDI
24 ♌ 31	♀	BURKINO-FASSO
24 ♌ 35	♂	ITALY - REPUBLIC
24 ♌ 37	♂	LESOTHO
24 ♌ 43	♇	LAOS I
24 ♌ 52	♀	ITALY - KINGDOM 2
24 ♌ 53R	♂	CZECHOSLOVAKIA-COMMUNIS
25 ♌ 00	M	SAHRAWI ARAB D R
25 ♌ 06	♂	SEYCHELLES
25 ♌ 08	♂	HONDURAS
25 ♌ 10	●	TRANSKEI
25 ♌ 24R	♅	BUGANDA
25 ♌ 33R	♀	PAPUA NEW GUINEA
25 ♌ 37	♄	KOREA - SOUTH
25 ♌ 38	☿	KOREA - SOUTH
25 ♌ 48	♅	MAURETANIA
25 ♌ 50	♄	CZECHOSLOVAKIA 1
25 ♌ 53	☊	SWITZERLAND
26 ♌ 10	♃	URUGUAY
26 ♌ 12	♇	MOROCCO
26 ♌ 14	♂	HATAY
26 ♌ 15	♀	IRAQ - INDEPENCENCE
26 ♌ 19	♃	TUNISIA
26 ♌ 26	♄	VENEZUELA 2
26 ♌ 27	♇	TUNISIA
26 ♌ 30	♅	SWITZERLAND
26 ♌ 32R	♃	SYRIA 2
26 ♌ 32R	♃	LEBANON 2
26 ♌ 34R	♇	PAKISTAN, REPUBLIC
26 ♌ 35	●	CHINA - REPUBLIC
26 ♌ 37	●	PAKISTAN, REPUBLIC
26 ♌ 38	♄	CZECHOSLOVAKIA 2
26 ♌ 38	♃	VENDA
26 ♌ 38	☽	MALAYSIA
26 ♌ 39	♂	ZIMBABWE
26 ♌ 39	M	POLAND-COMMUNIST
26 ♌ 42	♄	YUGOSLAVIA 1

26 ♌ 53	♀	BULGARIA - INDEPENDENCE
26 ♌ 59	♀	IVORY COAST
27 ♌ 03	♂	VIETNAM-UNION
27 ♌ 03	☉	SENEGAL
27 ♌ 03	♀	CAPE VERDE ISLANDS
27 ♌ 16	☊	ZIMBABWE
27 ♌ 21	♃	S VIETNAM-REP
27 ♌ 24	♄	GERMANY - WEIMAR
27 ♌ 26	♅	ROMANIA 2
27 ♌ 26	♅	BULGARIA - AUTONOMY
27 ♌ 26	♅	SERBIA
27 ♌ 26	♅	MONTENEGRO
27 ♌ 29	♄	AUSTRIA
27 ♌ 30	♄	POLAND 2
27 ♌ 36	♄	HUNGARY
27 ♌ 38	♇	ENGLAND-EDGAR
27 ♌ 39	♄	CZECHOSLOVAKIA 3
27 ♌ 40	♀	COMOROS 1
27 ♌ 42R	☿	SINGAPORE 3
27 ♌ 43	♄	BELGIUM
27 ♌ 47	♄	SOLOMON ISLANDS
27 ♌ 48	♅	BURUNDI
27 ♌ 48	♅	RWANDA-INDEPENDENCE
27 ♌ 49	♂	GREECE DEMOCRACY
27 ♌ 49	♄	LATVIA
27 ♌ 51	●	UNITED ARAB EMIR
27 ♌ 51R	☿	SINGAPORE 2
27 ♌ 55	♅	ALGERIA
28 ♌ 03	A	SOUTH AFRICA-UNION
28 ♌ 11	♄	YUGOSLAVIA 2
28 ♌ 11	♄	ICELAND
28 ♌ 18	♇	S VIETNAM-REP
28 ♌ 18	♂	ISRAEL
28 ♌ 18	M	ST LUCIA
28 ♌ 19	☿	MALDIVES
28 ♌ 19R	♃	MAURITIUS
28 ♌ 23R	♇	SUDAN
28 ♌ 23R	♇	TREATY OF ROME
28 ♌ 24R	☿	FEDERATION OF ARAB REPU
28 ♌ 25R	☿	QATAR
28 ♌ 26	♂	PALESTINE
28 ♌ 37	☊	NUCLEAR REACTION
28 ♌ 44	M	ITALY - REPUBLIC
28 ♌ 48	♆	VATICAN CITY
28 ♌ 49R	♇	GHANA
29 ♌ 00	☊	KUWAIT
29 ♌ 02R	♅	AGE OF AQUARIUS-1
29 ♌ 03R	♅	AGE OF AQUARIUS-2
29 ♌ 06	☿	IRAQ - KINGDOM
29 ♌ 09	☽	USSR-REVOLUTION
29 ♌ 09	♄	KOREA - NORTH
29 ♌ 15	M	QATAR
29 ♌ 22	☿	SWITZERLAND
29 ♌ 22	♄	MONACO
29 ♌ 25	☿	LIECHTENSTEIN
29 ♌ 26	☉	IRAQ - KINGDOM
29 ♌ 28	⚷	NUCLEAR REACTION
29 ♌ 28R	♄	EIRE 3
29 ♌ 43	♄	GERMANY WEST PROCLAM
29 ♌ 46	♅	JAMAICA
29 ♌ 54	A	SURINAM
0 ♍ 02	♀	ECUADOR 1
0 ♍ 04	☿	NETHERLANDS
0 ♍ 14R	♅	WESTERN SAMOA
0 ♍ 17	A	CUBA - INDEPENDENCE 2
0 ♍ 17	●	NATAL
0 ♍ 21R	♃	ZIMBABWE
0 ♍ 23	♇	MALAYA
0 ♍ 30	A	CISKEI
0 ♍ 31	♄	BOPHUTHATSWANA
0 ♍ 33R	♅	TANGANYIKA
0 ♍ 42	♇	IRAQ - REPUBLIC
0 ♍ 42R	☿	HATAY
0 ♍ 48	☊	SOUTH AFRICA-REPUBLIC
0 ♍ 49	♀	MALDIVES
0 ♍ 51R	♄	HOLY ROMAN EMPIRE
1 ♍ 04	●	SRI LANKA-IND
1 ♍ 07	☉	NATO 1
1 ♍ 11R	♃	SUDAN
1 ♍ 12	A	AUSTRIA
1 ♍ 14R	♇	ARAB FEDERATION
1 ♍ 19	♅	TRINIDAD & TOBAGO
1 ♍ 27	♇	SPUTNIK
1 ♍ 32R	♇	UNITED ARAB REP
1 ♍ 35	M	URUGUAY
1 ♍ 38	♂	DOMINICAN REPUBLIC
1 ♍ 51	♀	CHAD
1 ♍ 56	♀	GUINEA - BUISSAU
2 ♍ 02	A	PHILLIPINES
2 ♍ 05	☉	URUGUAY
2 ♍ 06	♀	SAO TOME-PRINCIPE
2 ♍ 06	M	TUNISIA
2 ♍ 08R	♇	E.E.C.
2 ♍ 10	●	AUSTRALIA 2
2 ♍ 29	●	VATICAN CITY
2 ♍ 31	M	MONTENEGRO
2 ♍ 57	♅	NORTH YEMEN
3 ♍ 00	♂	USSR-REVOLUTION
3 ♍ 05R	♄	U.S. CIVIL WAR
3 ♍ 09R	♂	SRI LANKA-IND
3 ♍ 11	♇	GUINEA
3 ♍ 13	A	N Y STOCK EXCHANGE
3 ♍ 16	☊	NORWAY
3 ♍ 17	●	CAPE VERDE ISLANDS
3 ♍ 17	♇	FRANCE-FIFTH REPUBLIC
3 ♍ 18	☊	SHEPARD
3 ♍ 30R	♃	NAURU
3 ♍ 33	♅	UGANDA
3 ♍ 40R	♇	TOGO
3 ♍ 43	☽	SAO TOME-PRINCIPE
3 ♍ 54	♇	MALI - FEDERATION
3 ♍ 58R	♇	DE GAULLE
4 ♍ 01	♇	MADAGASCAR

15 ♍ 45	☊	IVORY COAST
15 ♍ 46	☊	CENTRAL AFRICAN REPUBLI
15 ♍ 46	☊	CONGO
15 ♍ 48R	♇	GUYANA
15 ♍ 53	☊	BURKINO-FASSO
15 ♍ 55	M	MAURITIUS
15 ♍ 56	☽	PHILLIPINES
16 ♍ 02	☊	NIGER
16 ♍ 02R	⚷	SYRIA 2
16 ♍ 02R	⚷	LEBANON 2
16 ♍ 06	☊	BENIN
16 ♍ 10	●	BURMA
16 ♍ 14	☽	CZECHOSLOVAKIA-COMMUNIS
16 ♍ 16	●	BAHRAIN
16 ♍ 16	☽	TUVALU
16 ♍ 18	☉	LUXEMBOURG
16 ♍ 35	☉	BULGARIA - COMMUNIST
16 ♍ 41	☊	CANADA
16 ♍ 48	☊	ECUADOR 2
16 ♍ 50R	♄	ENGLAND-WILLIAM
16 ♍ 52	●	GREECE' DEMOCRACY
16 ♍ 55	☉	GUINEA - BUISSAU
17 ♍ 00	M	LUXEMBOURG
17 ♍ 04	♂	FINLAND
17 ♍ 05	A	LIBYA - INDEP
17 ♍ 15	☊	IRAN - ISLAMIC REP
17 ♍ 16R	♄	SPAIN
17 ♍ 29	♀	SINGAPORE 2
17 ♍ 33	♄	VENDA
17 ♍ 33	☊	ST LUCIA
17 ♍ 47	♄	NAT KHOREZEM SOVIET REP
17 ♍ 47	♀	SINGAPORE 3
17 ♍ 48	●	SUDAN
17 ♍ 53	A	GORBACHEV
17 ♍ 54	A	HIROSHIMA
17 ♍ 57	☽	TRANSCAUCASIAN FED
17 ♍ 57	☊	SOMALIA
17 ♍ 57	☊	ZAIRE
17 ♍ 58	☊	IRAN - KHOMEINI
17 ♍ 58	♇	BIAFRA
18 ♍ 03	♇	RHODESIA
18 ♍ 04	♀	COSTA RICA 2
18 ♍ 05	☽	NORTH YEMEN
18 ♍ 08R	☿	ST KITTS-NEVIS
18 ♍ 18	☊	MADAGASCAR
18 ♍ 18	☊	SOMALILAND
18 ♍ 24	●	EQUATORIAL GUINEA
18 ♍ 27	●	SOUTH AFRICA-REPUBLIC
18 ♍ 31	♀	LIBERIA
18 ♍ 31	☽	ROMANIA 1
18 ♍ 37	☽	TRINIDAD & TOBAGO
18 ♍ 45	♅	RHODESIA
18 ♍ 46	♂	N Y STOCK EXCHANGE
18 ♍ 47R	♄	INDIA - REPUBLIC
18 ♍ 53	M	SAUDI ARABIA
18 ♍ 55	♇	BOTSWANA
18 ♍ 55	♂	GEORGIA
18 ♍ 55	♂	ARMENIA
18 ♍ 55	☿	FRANCE-1st REPUBLIC 2
19 ♍ 03	♇	LESOTHO
19 ♍ 08	☉	ETHIOPIA
19 ♍ 11	A	DENMARK
19 ♍ 12	♆	LIECHTENSTEIN
19 ♍ 15	☉	KOREA - NORTH
19 ♍ 15	☿	VENDA
19 ♍ 16	♂	LITHUANIA
19 ♍ 17	M	AGE OF AQUARIUS-2
19 ♍ 25	☊	ENGLAND-WILLIAM
19 ♍ 26	♄	INDONESIA
19 ♍ 28	♄	MALI - FEDERATION
19 ♍ 32	♂	AZERBAIJAN
19 ♍ 32	☉	VENDA
19 ♍ 35R	♂	GERMANY - THIRD REICH
19 ♍ 38	☊	VENEZUELA 1
19 ♍ 45	☊	LEBANON I
19 ♍ 46	♇	NAMIBIA
19 ♍ 55	☊	GREECE INDEPENCENCE
19 ♍ 59	☽	CREATION OF THE WORLD
20 ♍ 17	♅	BIAFRA
20 ♍ 22	♃	POLAND-COMMUNIST
20 ♍ 25	♆	HATAY
20 ♍ 29	●	TANGANYIKA
20 ♍ 30	♇	BARBADOS
20 ♍ 37R	♇	REAGAN-1
20 ♍ 43R	☿	FRANCE-1st REPUBLIC 1
20 ♍ 59	⚷	BULGARIA - COMMUNIST
21 ♍ 04	♅	BOTSWANA
21 ♍ 05	●	ETHIOPIA
21 ♍ 07	♀	ZAMBIA
21 ♍ 11R	♄	ZIMBABWE
21 ♍ 18	♅	LESOTHO
21 ♍ 22	●	GUATEMALA - 2
21 ♍ 26	☽	SIERRA LEONE
21 ♍ 27	♀	BELGIUM
21 ♍ 31	☊	COSTA RICA 2
21 ♍ 32	☉	OPEC
21 ♍ 33R	♇	MAURITIUS
21 ♍ 41R	♆	ROMAN EMPIRE 2
21 ♍ 43	☽	EGYPT - REPUBLIC
21 ♍ 43R	♆	ROMAN EMPIRE 1
21 ♍ 54	☿	CREATION OF THE WORLD
21 ♍ 56R	♆	SLOVAKIA
21 ♍ 56R	♆	CARPATHO-UKRAINE
22 ♍ 05R	♄	BOKHARA NAT'L SOVIET RE
22 ♍ 06	☉	MALAYSIA
22 ♍ 07	☉	PAPUA NEW GUINEA
22 ♍ 07	M	OPEC
22 ♍ 10R	♄	MONGOLIA
22 ♍ 19	♇	SWAZILAND
22 ♍ 23	♆	USA 2
22 ♍ 23	♆	USA 1
22 ♍ 24R	♃	GERMANY - THIRD REICH
22 ♍ 25	♆	USA 3
22 ♍ 25	♆	USA 4
22 ♍ 31	☉	GUATEMALA - 1
22 ♍ 32R	♇	NAURU
22 ♍ 32	A	LAOS 2
22 ♍ 37	♅	NAMIBIA
22 ♍ 38	♄	DANZIG
22 ♍ 40	♇	SOUTH YEMEN 1
22 ♍ 40	☉	MEXICO - REVOLUTION
22 ♍ 40	♇	SOUTH YEMEN 2
22 ♍ 43	♂	COSTA RICA 2
22 ♍ 44	♂	KAMPUCHEA - REP
22 ♍ 45	M	MALI - REPUBLIC
22 ♍ 46	☊	SYRIA 1
22 ♍ 46	♆	FRANCE-VICHY REPUBLIC
22 ♍ 47	♃	IRAQ - KINGDOM
22 ♍ 48	♄	ST VINCENT-GRENADINES
22 ♍ 49	♃	ATOMIC EXPLOSION
22 ♍ 52	A	FRANCE - NAPOLEON
23 ♍ 02	♇	MOON LANDING
23 ♍ 03	♂	FIJI
23 ♍ 08	☉	SYRIA 1
23 ♍ 24	M	LONDON 2
23 ♍ 30	☉	ALLIANCE
23 ♍ 30	♃	EQUATORIAL GUINEA
23 ♍ 38	♇	EQUATORIAL GUINEA
23 ♍ 41	A	USSR-REVOLUTION
23 ♍ 46	☽	SOMALIA
23 ♍ 48R	♃	ENGLAND-EDGAR
23 ♍ 48	☿	BRAZIL
23 ♍ 49	♄	VANUATU
23 ♍ 52	M	GUATEMALA - 1
23 ♍ 53	☿	GUATEMALA - 1
23 ♍ 53	♂	LAOS I
23 ♍ 57	☊	TOGO
24 ♍ 00	♅	BARBADOS
24 ♍ 02	☊	USSR-FORMATION
24 ♍ 02	M	ITALY - KINGDOM 1
24 ♍ 06	♂	CISKEI
24 ♍ 13	●	NEPAL
24 ♍ 18	☊	FRANCE-1st REPUBLIC 1
24 ♍ 19	☊	FRANCE-1st REPUBLIC 2
24 ♍ 23	♇	LIBYA, COUP
24 ♍ 25	♄	IRAQ - KINGDOM
24 ♍ 25R	♅	REAGAN-1
24 ♍ 28	☊	PARAGUAY
24 ♍ 32	☿	NATO 1
24 ♍ 33	♀	VENDA
24 ♍ 41R	♇	TONGA
24 ♍ 42R	☿	MALAYA
24 ♍ 42	●	ST LUCIA
24 ♍ 48	☽	REAGAN-1
24 ♍ 49	☽	ZAIRE
24 ♍ 58	●	OPEC
25 ♍ 17	♇	OMAN
25 ♍ 27R	♂	GAMBIA
25 ♍ 36	M	USA 3
25 ♍ 44	A	NORTH VIETNAM
25 ♍ 46	M	CHINA - COMMUNIST 1
25 ♍ 51R	♃	TREATY OF ROME
25 ♍ 53	☊	DOMINICA
25 ♍ 56	♅	FRANCE - NAPOLEON
25 ♍ 58	♀	BOTSWANA
26 ♍ 01	☽	GAMBIA
26 ♍ 03	☊	UNITED KINGDOM-1922
26 ♍ 06	A	SAO TOME-PRINCIPE
26 ♍ 13	☊	EIRE 2
26 ♍ 14	A	SOUTH VIETNAM
26 ♍ 17	♃	HIROSHIMA
26 ♍ 17R	☿	PORTUGAL-REVOLUTION
26 ♍ 25	♀	PANAMA
26 ♍ 35	●	BUGANDA
26 ♍ 37	♀	MALAYSIA
26 ♍ 38	☉	ST KITTS-NEVIS
26 ♍ 38	☽	TUNISIA
26 ♍ 41	♀	GUINEA
26 ♍ 48	☊	TUVALU
26 ♍ 48	☽	SRI LANKA-REP
26 ♍ 50	☽	LONDON 1
26 ♍ 54	♂	BULGARIA - INDEPENDENCE
26 ♍ 54	♀	PORTUGAL-REVOLUTION
27 ♍ 02	M	PORTUGAL-REVOLUTION
27 ♍ 16	♀	JAMAICA
27 ♍ 16	♆	SYRIA 1
27 ♍ 16	●	USSR-FORMATION
27 ♍ 19	☿	SPUTNIK
27 ♍ 26R	♅	MAURITIUS
27 ♍ 38R	♇	BANGLADESH 2
27 ♍ 41	A	THAILAND 2
27 ♍ 50	☉	CHINA - COMMUNIST 1
27 ♍ 54	♇	KAMPUCHEA - REP
27 ♍ 55	♂	BARBADOS
27 ♍ 55	♇	FIJI
28 ♍ OC	☉	MALTA
28 ♍ 02	☊	CAMEROON
28 ♍ 08	♇	BAHRAIN
28 ♍ 08	♂	CYPRUS - TURKISH
28 ♍ 10	☉	BELIZE
28 ♍ 11R	♇	BANGLADESH 1
28 ♍ 12	♂	GUINEA - BUISSAU
28 ♍ 16	⚷	POLAND-COMMUNIST
28 ♍ 23	☽	ENGLAND-1707
28 ♍ 23R	♃	GHANA
28 ♍ 23	☉	EL SALVADOR
28 ♍ 34	♅	SWAZILAND
28 ♍ 35	●	ANTIGUA-BARBUDA
28 ♍ 37	♅	SOUTH YEMEN 1
28 ♍ 38	♅	SOUTH YEMEN 2
28 ♍ 43	☿	URUGUAY
28 ♍ 44	♇	QATAR
28 ♍ 44	♇	FEDERATION OF ARAB REPU
28 ♍ 54R	♅	NAURU
29 ♍ 05	●	ALGERIA
29 ♍ 08	☉	VENEZUELA 2

29 ♍ 17	☉	FRANCE-1st REPUBLIC 1
29 ♍ 24R	♇	SRI LANKA-REP
29 ♍ 28	☉	MALI - REPUBLIC
29 ♍ 31	♆	LEBANON I
29 ♍ 31	☽	TIMOR
29 ♍ 36	A	E.E.C.
29 ♍ 38	⚷	ATOMIC EXPLOSION
29 ♍ 40	♂	ETHIOPIA
29 ♍ 46	☊	SOLOMON ISLANDS
29 ♍ 56	☽	COSTA RICA 2
29 ♍ 58	☉	CREATION OF THE WORLD
0 ♎ 05	A	KUWAIT
0 ♎ 18	M	EL SALVADOR
0 ♎ 28	♂	INDONESIA
0 ♎ 43	☿	CREATION OF MAN
0 ♎ 44	♅	MOON LANDING
0 ♎ 49	☽	NUCLEAR REACTION
0 ♎ 51	♅	EQUATORIAL GUINEA
0 ♎ 56	♃	MOON LANDING
0 ♎ 57	♀	LESOTHO
1 ♎ 03	M	USA 4
1 ♎ 06R	☿	MALAYSIA
1 ♎ 07	M	VENEZUELA 2
1 ♎ 17	☉	NEW ZEALAND I
1 ♎ 17R	♇	SPAIN
1 ♎ 22	M	SYRIA 1
1 ♎ 25	♀	ANGOLA
1 ♎ 28	♆	ICELAND
1 ♎ 34	♀	FRANCE-FIFTH REPUBLIC
1 ♎ 38	♃	VIETNAM
1 ♎ 44	♇	UNITED ARAB EMIR
1 ♎ 44	⚷	HIROSHIMA
1 ♎ 46	♆	NUCLEAR REACTION
1 ♎ 50R	♆	FALL OF CONSTANTINOPLE
1 ♎ 53	♇	BAHAMAS
1 ♎ 54	♅	UNITED KINGDOM-18Ø1
1 ♎ 57	♇	BANGLADESH 3
2 ♎ 00	♇	AFGHANISTAN
2 ♎ 02	☿	TRINIDAD & TOBAGO
2 ♎ 05	☿	KAMPUCHEA - REP
2 ♎ 09	♂	UKRAINE
2 ♎ 13	A	ICELAND
2 ♎ 13	☊	N Y STOCK EXCHANGE
2 ♎ 25	⊕	MALDIVES
2 ♎ 34	☊	ENGLAND-EDGAR
2 ♎ 47	☿	SINGAPORE 1
2 ♎ 52	♀	POLAND 1
2 ♎ 53	♅	LIBYA, COUP
2 ♎ 56	⊕	RWANDA-UDI
2 ♎ 56	☿	FIJI
3 ♎ 13	☊	FIRST MANNED FLIGHT
3 ♎ 20	♆	BULGARIA - COMMUNIST
3 ♎ 22R	♄	FAR EAST REPUBLIC
3 ♎ 27	♄	HAITI
3 ♎ 29	A	CHINA - NATIONALIST
3 ♎ 33	☿	OPEC
3 ♎ 42	♆	POLAND-COMMUNIST
3 ♎ 46	☉	NORTH YEMEN
3 ♎ 48	☿	GUINEA
3 ♎ 55	♆	ATOMIC EXPLOSION
3 ♎ 55	☉	FRANCE-1st REPUBLIC 2
4 ♎ 04	☽	LABOUR PARTY 2
4 ♎ 05	♀	NEW ZEALAND I
4 ♎ 06	M	EGYPT - INDEPENDENCE
4 ♎ 06R	♇	BHUTAN
4 ♎ 10	⊕	CANADA
4 ♎ 14	♆	LEBANON 2
4 ♎ 14	♆	SYRIA 2
4 ♎ 21	♆	HIROSHIMA
4 ♎ 29	♀	SWAZILAND
4 ♎ 29	♇	GREECE DEMOCRACY
4 ♎ 31	♃	MALAYA
4 ♎ 32	☽	GREECE DEMOCRACY
4 ♎ 32	☿	EL SALVADOR
4 ♎ 37R	♃	SOUTH AFRICA-UNION
4 ♎ 39	A	BRUNEI
4 ♎ 41R	♅	TONGA
4 ♎ 42R	♇	PORTUGAL-REVOLUTION
4 ♎ 44	A	WESTERN SAMOA
4 ♎ 53	M	EIRE 3
4 ♎ 57	♀	NATO 1
5 ♎ 03R	♄	EGYPT - KINGDOM
5 ♎ 05R	♄	EGYPT - INDEPENDENCE
5 ♎ 06	♀	LAOS I
5 ♎ 11	♆	VIETNAM
5 ♎ 12	⚷	VIETNAM
5 ♎ 19	M	NORTH YEMEN
5 ♎ 23	♅	OMAN
5 ♎ 28R	♃	S.D.P.
5 ♎ 34	♂	GERMANY - EMPIRE
5 ♎ 35	☊	MEXICO - REVOLUTION
5 ♎ 43	☉	CREATION OF MAN
5 ♎ 51R	♆	ITALY - REPUBLIC
5 ♎ 53	☿	GUINEA - BUISSAU
5 ♎ 55	♆	PHILLIPINES
5 ♎ 56	♇	GUINEA - BUISSAU
5 ♎ 59R	♆	JORDAN
6 ♎ 01	♇	ETHIOPIA
6 ♎ 03	☽	MONACO
6 ♎ 08	☿	SWAZILAND
6 ♎ 08	♀	CYPRUS - TURKISH
6 ♎ 11	A	TREATY OF ROME
6 ♎ 14	♆	SWITZERLAND
6 ♎ 18	☉	BOTSWANA
6 ♎ 25R	♆	THAILAND 1
6 ♎ 25	♃	HONDURAS
6 ♎ 30	A	CAMEROON
6 ♎ 30	♇	MOZAMBIQUE
6 ♎ 30R	♄	S.D.P.
6 ♎ 31	M	CHINA - COMMUNIST 2
6 ♎ 33	☊	PANAMA
6 ♎ 34	♇	CAPE VERDE ISLANDS
6 ♎ 35	♇	COMOROS 1
6 ♎ 35R	♇	GRENADA
6 ♎ 39	♇	SAO TOME-PRINCIPE
6 ♎ 49	♀	BULGARIA - COMMUNIST
6 ♎ 51	☉	NAT KHOREZEM SOVIET REP
6 ♎ 52	☿	TUVALU
6 ♎ 56	♂	SPUTNIK
6 ♎ 58	⊕	HATAY
6 ♎ 58	☉	TUVALU
7 ♎ 01	A	CANADA
7 ♎ 05	♆	UNITED NATIONS
7 ♎ 06	♀	UNITED NATIONS
7 ♎ 10	A	UNITED KINGDOM-18Ø1
7 ♎ 14	♂	ITALY - KINGDOM 2
7 ♎ 21	☉	GUINEA
7 ♎ 22R	♇	KAMPUCHEA, COMM
7 ♎ 22	♂	BULGARIA - COMMUNIST
7 ♎ 23	A	AUSTRALIA 1
7 ♎ 24	♂	TURKEY
7 ♎ 29	☿	LIBYA, COUP
7 ♎ 39	☉	CHINA - COMMUNIST 2
7 ♎ 39	M	KHALISTAN
7 ♎ 46	☉	NIGERIA
8 ♎ 07	♂	PORTUGAL-REVOLUTION
8 ♎ 07R	♂	LONDON 1
8 ♎ 10	♂	S VIETNAM-REP
8 ♎ 13	☽	BOPHUTHATSWANA
8 ♎ 21	M	HOLY ROMAN EMPIRE
8 ♎ 23	♆	CIA
8 ♎ 25	☿	FRANCE-THIRD REPUBLIC
8 ♎ 28	♇	PAPUA NEW GUINEA
8 ♎ 29	☽	CUBA - COMMUNIST
8 ♎ 30R	♆	YUGOSLAVIA-COMMUNIST
8 ♎ 37R	♆	ALBANIA-PEOPLES REPUBLI
8 ♎ 37	♃	LIBYA, COUP
8 ♎ 44	☊	FAR EAST REPUBLIC
8 ♎ 45	☊	EGYPT - INDEPENDENCE
8 ♎ 45R	♇	NEPAL
8 ♎ 45	☊	EGYPT - KINGDOM
8 ♎ 47	A	UNITED PROVINCES C A
8 ♎ 50	♆	PAKISTAN
8 ♎ 50	♆	INDIA - INDEPENDENCE
8 ♎ 50	♆	HYDERABAD
8 ♎ 57	♇	SEYCHELLES
8 ♎ 58	♇	VIETNAM-UNION
9 ♎ 01	A	USA 2
9 ♎ 12	M	PORTUGAL-REVOLUTION
9 ♎ 18	♆	FRANCE-FOURTH REPUBLIC
9 ♎ 20	☿	ETHIOPIA
9 ♎ 23	♂	INDIA - REPUBLIC
9 ♎ 25	A	SINGAPORE 2
9 ♎ 29	☽	ZANZIBAR
9 ♎ 32	M	NAT KHOREZEM SOVIET REP
9 ♎ 35	♅	KAMPUCHEA - REP
9 ♎ 37	♅	FIJI
9 ♎ 39R	♄	JAPAN - SOVEREIGNTY
9 ♎ 47R	♄	REAGAN-2
9 ♎ 57	⊕	GREECE INDEPENCENCE
10 ♎ 09	M	BULGARIA - INDEPENDENCE
10 ♎ 14	☉	LESOTHO
10 ♎ 21	⊕	SINGAPORE 1
10 ♎ 22	♃	REAGAN-2
10 ♎ 22	☉	PORTUGAL-REVOLUTION
10 ♎ 24	⊕	RHODESIA
10 ♎ 26R	☿	UGANDA
10 ♎ 26	☉	IRAQ - INDEPENCENCE
10 ♎ 26	♄	ALLIANCE
10 ♎ 31	♆	HOLY ROMAN EMPIRE
10 ♎ 34	♇	ANGOLA
10 ♎ 34R	♆	PALESTINE
10 ♎ 35R	♆	ISRAEL
10 ♎ 36	♂	CREATION OF THE WORLD
10 ♎ 43	⊕	LIECHTENSTEIN
10 ♎ 44	☉	BELGIUM
10 ♎ 46	☿	FRANCE-FIFTH REPUBLIC
10 ♎ 50	♅	BAHRAIN
10 ♎ 51	♂	VANUATU
10 ♎ 53R	♅	BANGLADESH 2
10 ♎ 59	♆	KOREA - SOUTH
10 ♎ 59	♇	SURINAM
11 ♎ 01	♄	BELIZE
11 ♎ 04	♇	TIMOR
11 ♎ 10	A	REAGAN-1
11 ♎ 10R	♇	SAHRAWI ARAB D R
11 ♎ 12	☉	FRANCE-FIFTH REPUBLIC
11 ♎ 22	☉	SPUTNIK
11 ♎ 24	♇	DJIBOUTI
11 ♎ 26	⊕	UKRAINE
11 ♎ 37	♇	ESPIRITU SANTO
11 ♎ 39	♇	COMOROS 2
11 ♎ 45	♅	QATAR
11 ♎ 45	♅	FEDERATION OF ARAB REPU
11 ♎ 45	♀	FRANCE-1st REPUBLIC 1
11 ♎ 45	☉	BULGARIA - INDEPENDENCE
11 ♎ 49R	♅	BANGLADESH 1
11 ♎ 52	♆	KOREA - NORTH
11 ♎ 52	M	CYPRUS - TURKISH
11 ♎ 58	♃	SPUTNIK
12 ♎ 08R	♃	GUATEMALA - 2
12 ♎ 15	⊕	ALBANIA - INDEPENDENCE
12 ♎ 23	☿	KOREA - NORTH
12 ♎ 25	♇	TRANSKEI
12 ♎ 27	☊	LIBERIA
12 ♎ 32R	♆	CZECHOSLOVAKIA-COMMUNIS
12 ♎ 36	A	LEBANON 2
12 ♎ 40R	♆	GERMANY WEST PROCLAM
12 ♎ 44	♀	MALAYA
12 ♎ 46	⚷	UNITED NATIONS
12 ♎ 51	A	VENEZUELA 1
12 ♎ 52	♆	CHINA - NATIONALIST
12 ♎ 53R	♆	SRI LANKA-IND
12 ♎ 54	♃	UNITED NATIONS
12 ♎ 55R	♆	MONACO
12 ♎ 57	⊕	IRAN - ISLAMIC REP

12 ♎ 57	♆	BURMA
13 ♎ 19R	☿	CHINA - COMMUNIST 2
13 ♎ 19	A	SYRIA 2
13 ♎ 21	☊	BOPHUTHATSWANA
13 ♎ 22	♆	NATO 1
13 ♎ 26R	♆	EIRE 3
13 ♎ 31	☊	ARGENTINA - REVOLUTION
13 ♎ 39	●	VIETNAM
13 ♎ 45	M	BELGIUM
13 ♎ 46	A	ITALY - KINGDOM 2
13 ♎ 48R	♃	FAR EAST REPUBLIC
13 ♎ 50	M	SINGAPORE 3
13 ♎ 51	☿	IRAQ - INDEPENCENCE
13 ♎ 56	♇	SOLOMON ISLANDS
14 ♎ 05	♄	LIBYA - INDEP
14 ♎ 11	☿	S VIETNAM-REP
14 ♎ 13	♀	OPEC
14 ♎ 16	♆	CHINA - COMMUNIST 1
14 ♎ 18	A	COMOROS 1
14 ♎ 22	☿	SYRIA 1
14 ♎ 23	☽	EGYPT - INDEPENDENCE
14 ♎ 35R	♅	SRI LANKA-REP
14 ♎ 38	♆	CHINA - COMMUNIST 2
14 ♎ 44	♂	MALDIVES
14 ♎ 45	♂	REAGAN-1
14 ♎ 45	♄	USA 2
14 ♎ 45	♄	USA 1
14 ♎ 48	♄	USA 3
14 ♎ 48	♄	USA 4
14 ♎ 49	♃	ALLIANCE
14 ♎ 54	●	JAPAN - MEIJI CONST
15 ♎ 00	♂	CREATION OF MAN
15 ♎ 02	♀	CZECHOSLOVAKIA 1
15 ♎ 04	♂	BIAFRA
15 ♎ 06	☉	UGANDA
15 ♎ 08	☽	ATOMIC EXPLOSION
15 ♎ 09R	⚷	ITALY - REPUBLIC
15 ♎ 11	⚷	LIBERIA
15 ♎ 17	☉	KAMPUCHEA - REP
15 ♎ 21	☿	NEW ZEALAND I
15 ♎ 28R	⚷	JORDAN
15 ♎ 33	⚷	PHILLIPINES
15 ♎ 47	☉	FIJI
15 ♎ 49	♃	BELIZE
15 ♎ 56	●	SYRIA 1
15 ♎ 58	♄	ANTIGUA-BARBUDA
16 ♎ 02	♅	HAITI
16 ♎ 08	♇	BOPHUTHATSWANA
16 ♎ 08	M	EQUATORIAL GUINEA
16 ♎ 08	☽	JAMAICA
16 ♎ 13	♇	TUVALU
16 ♎ 17	♀	FRANCE - NAPOLEON
16 ♎ 19	☉	ECUADOR 1
16 ♎ 26	♂	LIBYA - INDEP
16 ♎ 29	♇	KIRIBATI
16 ♎ 29R	♃	EGYPT - KINGDOM
16 ♎ 32R	♃	EGYPT - INDEPENDENCE
16 ♎ 34	☿	MALI - REPUBLIC
16 ♎ 34	♇	NICARAGUA SANDINISTA
16 ♎ 36	♀	SURINAM
16 ♎ 36R	♇	ZIMBABWE-RHODESIA
17 ♎ 05	●	VIETNAM-UNION
17 ♎ 06	♅	UNITED ARAB EMIR
17 ♎ 13	A	CUBA - COMMUNIST
17 ♎ 13	♆	INDONESIA
17 ♎ 20R	♆	INDIA - REPUBLIC
17 ♎ 29R	♃	ITALY - REPUBLIC
17 ♎ 29	♂	KOREA - SOUTH
17 ♎ 31	♇	DOMINICA
17 ♎ 38	♀	FRANCE-1st REPUBLIC 2
17 ♎ 39	♄	EIRE 2
17 ♎ 40	♅	BANGLADESH 3
17 ♎ 44	♄	UNITED KINGDOM-1922
17 ♎ 47	☊	DE GAULLE
17 ♎ 47	☊	FRANCE-VICHY REPUBLIC
17 ♎ 52R	⚷	GUATEMALA - 3
17 ♎ 56	☽	BURMA
17 ♎ 59	♇	VENDA
18 ♎ 00	♃	PHILLIPINES
18 ♎ 01	☿	MEXICO - REVOLUTION
18 ♎ 02R	♇	IRAN - ISLAMIC REP
18 ♎ 04R	♃	JORDAN
18 ♎ 05	☉	NICARAGUA 1
18 ♎ 05	☽	MALI - REPUBLIC
18 ♎ 19	☊	CUBA - COMMUNIST
18 ♎ 19	●	ST VINCENT-GRENADINES
18 ♎ 41	●	BURKINO-FASSO
18 ♎ 41	☿	PAPUA NEW GUINEA
18 ♎ 44	☿	ALLIANCE
18 ♎ 54	☊	GUATEMALA - 3
18 ♎ 54	●	MOZAMBIQUE
18 ♎ 54	A	CAPE VERDE ISLANDS
18 ♎ 57	♂	LUXEMBOURG
18 ♎ 57R	♇	ST LUCIA
18 ♎ 59	●	ATOMIC EXPLOSION
19 ♎ 00	☊	IRAQ - KINGDOM
19 ♎ 01	♅	BAHAMAS
19 ♎ 07	♅	AFGHANISTAN
19 ♎ 07R	☿	CHINA - COMMUNIST 1
19 ♎ 11	☉	EQUATORIAL GUINEA
19 ♎ 12R	♇	IRAN - KHOMEINI
19 ♎ 13	☊	SWEDEN
19 ♎ 14	♇	VANUATU
19 ♎ 18	♄	USSR-FORMATION
19 ♎ 20	A	CIA
19 ♎ 25	♄	CISKEI
19 ♎ 42	♇	ST VINCENT-GRENADINES
19 ♎ 51R	♆	JAPAN - SOVEREIGNTY
19 ♎ 52	♀	HONDURAS
19 ♎ 53	M	ECUADOR 1
19 ♎ 55	♀	TIMOR
20 ♎ 07	☽	EGYPT - KINGDOM
20 ♎ 11R	♇	ZIMBABWE
20 ♎ 12	♂	HOLY ROMAN EMPIRE
20 ♎ 14	☿	ANTIGUA-BARBUDA
20 ♎ 16	M	JAPAN - SOVEREIGNTY
20 ♎ 34R	♄	EGYPT - REPUBLIC
20 ♎ 45	A	LIECHTENSTEIN
20 ♎ 50	☽	SWITZERLAND
20 ♎ 53	☿	BOTSWANA
20 ♎ 59	⚷	ALBANIA-PEOPLES REPUBLI
21 ♎ 07	♀	SOUTH YEMEN 1
21 ♎ 09R	☿	NORTH YEMEN
21 ♎ 10R	♆	EGYPT - REPUBLIC
21 ♎ 24	☊	DJIBOUTI
21 ♎ 27	♆	LIBYA - INDEP
21 ♎ 32	♀	SOUTH YEMEN 2
21 ♎ 33	⚷	YUGOSLAVIA-COMMUNIST
21 ♎ 39	♂	SINGAPORE 1
21 ♎ 44	♃	PORTUGAL-REVOLUTION
21 ♎ 52R	♅	JAPAN - MEIJI CONST
22 ♎ 01	☿	ECUADOR 1
22 ♎ 16	☊	GUINEA
22 ♎ 16	M	NICARAGUA 1
22 ♎ 20	☊	FRANCE-FIFTH REPUBLIC
22 ♎ 23	☿	NAT KHOREZEM SOVIET REP
22 ♎ 40	♃	IRAQ - REPUBLIC
22 ♎ 56	♂	SINGAPORE 2
22 ♎ 56	☽	PORTUGAL-REVOLUTION
22 ♎ 57R	♃	N Y STOCK EXCHANGE
23 ♎ 02	A	ISRAEL
23 ♎ 04	♇	ALLIANCE
23 ♎ 05	♂	SINGAPORE 3
23 ♎ 13	M	SIERRA LEONE
23 ♎ 14	♇	BELIZE
23 ♎ 14	♀	GUATEMALA - 1
23 ♎ 16	☽	ESPIRITU SANTO
23 ♎ 21	♆	NORTH VIETNAM
23 ♎ 21	♆	SOUTH VIETNAM
23 ♎ 21	♆	LAOS 2
23 ♎ 22	♆	KAMPUCHEĂ - INDEP
23 ♎ 24	♀	TRINIDAD & TOBAGO
23 ♎ 27R	♇	S.D.P.
23 ♎ 46	●	CZECHOSLOVAKIA 2
23 ♎ 50	♆	LAOS I
23 ♎ 52	♅	GREECE DEMOCRACY
23 ♎ 59	●	PAPUA NEW GUINEA
24 ♎ 02	A	ARGENTINA - INDEPENDENC
24 ♎ 02R	♅	BHUTAN
24 ♎ 12	♀	MALI - REPUBLIC
24 ♎ 13	☿	BELIZE
24 ♎ 16	☉	CZECHOSLOVAKIA 1
24 ♎ 17	●	FIJI
24 ♎ 20	♇	REAGAN-2
24 ♎ 24	☽	MOON LANDING
24 ♎ 27	☿	TURKEY
24 ♎ 28	☿	TRANSKEI
24 ♎ 29R	♄	FALL OF CONSTANTINOPLE
24 ♎ 29	♂	BRUNEI
24 ♎ 33	♄	TURKEY
24 ♎ 38	♃	ANTIGUA-BARBUDA
24 ♎ 49	♀	HATAY
24 ♎ 51	♇	ANTIGUA-BARBUDA
24 ♎ 52	☿	VENEZUELA 2
25 ♎ 14	A	BYELO RUSSIA
25 ♎ 23R	♅	PORTUGAL-REVOLUTION
25 ♎ 39	♅	GUINEA - BUISSAU
25 ♎ 46	♅	ETHIOPIA
25 ♎ 54	♃	ALBANIA-PEOPLES REPUBLI
26 ♎ 01	♇	CISKEI
26 ♎ 08R	☿	EQUATORIAL GUINEA
26 ♎ 11R	♆	WARSAW PACT
26 ♎ 18	☿	CZECHOSLOVAKIA 1
26 ♎ 24R	♆	GERMANY WEST SOVEREIGN
26 ♎ 31	♅	HOLY ROMAN EMPIRE
26 ♎ 34R	♆	ENGLAND-EDGAR
26 ♎ 35	A	NICARAGUA SANDINISTA
26 ♎ 37	A	OMAN
26 ♎ 40R	♃	TONGA
26 ♎ 55R	♇	THATCHER
27 ♎ 01	☿	LESOTHO
27 ♎ 11	♃	YUGOSLAVIA-COMMUNIST
27 ♎ 13	☿	HONDURAS
27 ♎ 15R	☿	BELGIUM
27 ♎ 22	♃	OMAN
27 ♎ 34	♀	CZECHOSLOVAKIA 2
27 ♎ 37	☊	IRAQ - REPUBLIC
27 ♎ 42R	♆	N Y STOCK EXCHANGE
27 ♎ 46R	♅	GRENADA
27 ♎ 47R	♆	TUNISIA
27 ♎ 48	A	NAURU
27 ♎ 57	☽	GERMANY WEST SOVEREIGN
28 ♎ 05R	♆	MOROCCO
28 ♎ 06R	♄	THATCHER
28 ♎ 08	M	CZECHOSLOVAKIA 1
28 ♎ 08	♆	S VIETNAM-REP
28 ♎ 10	♇	ST KITTS-NEVIS
28 ♎ 17	●	SAHRAWI ARAB D R
28 ♎ 17	☊	BOKHARA NAT'L SOVIET RE
28 ♎ 18	⚷	FRANCE-FOURTH REPUBLIC
28 ♎ 21	☊	MONGOLIA
28 ♎ 21R	♅	COMOROS 1
28 ♎ 22R	♅	CAPE VERDE ISLANDS
28 ♎ 22	♅	SAO TOME-PRINCIPE
28 ♎ 25R	♅	MOZAMBIQUE
28 ♎ 28	♆	FRANCE-1st REPUBLIC 1
28 ♎ 35	♃	E.E.C.
28 ♎ 38	♆	FRANCE-1st REPUBLIC 2
28 ♎ 49	♀	YUGOSLAVIA 1
28 ♎ 57	☿	NIGERIA
28 ♎ 58	●	NORWAY
29 ♎ 04	☉	LAOS I
29 ♎ 04	☽	LIBYA - INDEP
29 ♎ 17	M	ZIMBABWE
29 ♎ 19	M	FRANCE-VICHY REPUBLIC
29 ♎ 30R	♇	KHALISTAN

29 ≏ 37	☿	PANAMA
29 ≏ 39	♂	FRANCE - NAPOLEON
29 ≏ 43	♀	NAMIBIA
29 ≏ 46R	♆	PAKISTAN, REPUBLIC
29 ≏ 47	●	UGANDA
0 ♏ 01	♄	LAOS I
0 ♏ 09	♆	SUDAN
0 ♏ 15	●	NICARAGUA 2
0 ♏ 22	♇	CYPRUS - TURKISH
0 ♏ 22	♅	PAPUA NEW GUINEA
0 ♏ 28	♃	ARGENTINA - INDEPENDENC
0 ♏ 28	♆	MALAYA
0 ♏ 31	♀	EL SALVADOR
0 ♏ 31	☉	ZAMBIA
0 ♏ 33	A	NETHERLANDS
0 ♏ 35R	♅	KAMPUCHEA, COMM
0 ♏ 38	♀	NAT KHOREZEM SOVIET REP
0 ♏ 49	●	PERU-BATTLE AYACUCHO
1 ♏ 07	☉	UNITED NATIONS
1 ♏ 19	♃	CISKEI
1 ♏ 21	♃	UNITED ARAB REP
1 ♏ 29	♀	SYRIA 1
1 ♏ 32	☿	POLAND 1
1 ♏ 34	♆	SPUTNIK
1 ♏ 40	♃	ARAB FEDERATION
1 ♏ 46	A	KAMPUCHEA - REP
1 ♏ 47	♇	BRUNEI
1 ♏ 48	●	PANAMA
1 ♏ 56R	♆	TREATY OF ROME
2 ♏ 00	☉	S VIETNAM-REP
2 ♏ 00R	♆	IRAQ - REPUBLIC
2 ♏ 10	♃	HAITI
2 ♏ 12	♂	MALAYSIA
2 ♏ 20R	♅	NEPAL
2 ♏ 20R	♆	GHANA
2 ♏ 30	♄	ST KITTS-NEVIS
2 ♏ 32	♃	CUBA - INDEPENDENCE 1
2 ♏ 37	☉	TRANSKEI
2 ♏ 47	♃	FRANCE-1st REPUBLIC 1
2 ♏ 49	♄	NORTH VIETNAM
2 ♏ 49	♄	LAOS 2
2 ♏ 49	♄	SOUTH VIETNAM
2 ♏ 50	♄	KAMPUCHEA - INDEP
2 ♏ 54	☉	HONDURAS
2 ♏ 57	A	NATO 1
3 ♏ 02	☉	NAMIBIA
3 ♏ 04R	♅	VIETNAM-UNION
3 ♏ 04	⚷	CIA
3 ♏ 06R	♅	SEYCHELLES
3 ♏ 08	☉	ST VINCENT-GRENADINES
3 ♏ 26	☽	KENYA
3 ♏ 26	●	EL SALVADOR
3 ♏ 31	♆	GUINEA
3 ♏ 33	☊	TRANSKEI
3 ♏ 33	A	MALDIVES
3 ♏ 39	♆	FRANCE-FIFTH REPUBLIC
3 ♏ 41	♂	BRAZIL
3 ♏ 45	♃	FRANCE-1st REPUBLIC 2
3 ♏ 46	♅	ANGOLA
3 ♏ 54	●	FINLAND
3 ♏ 56	☉	FRANCE-FOURTH REPUBLIC
4 ♏ 00	☉	COSTA RICA 1
4 ♏ 07	♀	ALLIANCE
4 ♏ 08	⚷	COSTA RICA 2
4 ♏ 11	☊	ARAB FEDERATION
4 ♏ 13	⚷	INDIA - INDEPENDENCE
4 ♏ 13	⚷	HYDERABAD
4 ♏ 13	⚷	PAKISTAN
4 ♏ 13	☉	CZECHOSLOVAKIA 2
4 ♏ 20	☊	CUBA - INDEPENDENCE 2
4 ♏ 24	A	LIBERIA
4 ♏ 26R	♇	GORBACHEV
4 ♏ 26	♆	E.E.C.
4 ♏ 26	☽	ITALY - REPUBLIC
4 ♏ 35	♀	NIGERIA
4 ♏ 36	♃	GUINEA
4 ♏ 37	♅	SURINAM
4 ♏ 45R	♆	ARAB FEDERATION
4 ♏ 47	♆	UNITED ARAB REP
4 ♏ 47	♅	TIMOR
4 ♏ 50	A	SWITZERLAND
4 ♏ 59R	♄	TEXAS
5 ♏ 13	☉	YUGOSLAVIA 1
5 ♏ 18	☉	TURKEY
5 ♏ 24	☊	UNITED ARAB REP
5 ♏ 25	♃	FRANCE-FIFTH REPUBLIC
5 ♏ 33	☽	DJIBOUTI
5 ♏ 40	♂	KOREA - NORTH
5 ♏ 54	☿	ZAMBIA
6 ♏ 05	☽	SOUTH YEMEN 1
6 ♏ 12	♅	ESPIRITU SANTO
6 ♏ 13	☿	NICARAGUA 1
6 ♏ 18	●	KIRIBATI
6 ♏ 22	♅	COMOROS 2
6 ♏ 25	♆	BENIN
6 ♏ 25	☊	DANZIG
6 ♏ 26	♆	NIGER
6 ♏ 27R	♆	ZAIRE
6 ♏ 27R	♆	SOMALIA
6 ♏ 27	☽	WESTERN SAMOA
6 ♏ 27	♆	BURKINO-FASSO
6 ♏ 28	♆	IVORY COAST
6 ♏ 30R	♆	SOMALILAND
6 ♏ 30R	♆	MADAGASCAR
6 ♏ 30	●	PHILLIPINES
6 ♏ 31	♆	CHAD
6 ♏ 33	♆	CENTRAL AFRICAN REPUBLI
6 ♏ 34	♆	CONGO
6 ♏ 34R	♆	MALI - FEDERATION
6 ♏ 35	♆	CYPRUS
6 ♏ 35	♆	CUBA - COMMUNIST
6 ♏ 36	♆	GABON
6 ♏ 37	●	CAMEROON
6 ♏ 39	♆	SENEGAL
6 ♏ 42	♆	DE GAULLE
6 ♏ 42	☊	NAT KHOREZEM SOVIET REP
6 ♏ 50	A	FRANCE-1st REPUBLIC 2
6 ♏ 50	♀	MEXICO - REVOLUTION
6 ♏ 51	A	KOREA - SOUTH
6 ♏ 56	⚷	FRANCE - NAPOLEON
6 ♏ 56	♃	FRANCE-FOURTH REPUBLIC
6 ♏ 59R	♄	ENGLAND-1689
7 ♏ 00	M	HONDURAS
7 ♏ 01R	♅	SAHRAWI ARAB D R
7 ♏ 10	☿	BULGARIA - INDEPENDENCE
7 ♏ 10	♅	TRANSKEI
7 ♏ 12	♂	TUVALU
7 ♏ 13	●	PERU I
7 ♏ 14	♆	OPEC
7 ♏ 23	☿	ANGOLA
7 ♏ 28	♆	MALI - REPUBLIC
7 ♏ 36	♀	CHINA - COMMUNIST 1
7 ♏ 45	♆	NIGERIA
7 ♏ 47	M	CZECHOSLOVAKIA 2
7 ♏ 48R	♆	TOGO
7 ♏ 50	M	S VIETNAM-REP
7 ♏ 51R	♅	DJIBOUTI
8 ♏ 00	●	NAURU
8 ♏ 07	M	COSTA RICA 1
8 ♏ 12	♄	SWEDEN
8 ♏ 35	M	TOGO
8 ♏ 37	♃	EIRE 2
8 ♏ 39	☉	ANTIGUA-BARBUDA
8 ♏ 41	☊	E.E.C.
8 ♏ 41	♆	CAMEROON
8 ♏ 48R	♆	KUWAIT
8 ♏ 48	♃	UNITED KINGDOM-1922
8 ♏ 50	♀	FIRST MANNED FLIGHT
8 ♏ 51	☽	BHUTAN
8 ♏ 54	●	GERMANY WEST PROCLAM
9 ♏ 00R	♂	NORWAY
9 ♏ 02	♄	CYPRUS - TURKISH
9 ♏ 10R	♆	SOUTH AFRICA-REPUBLIC
9 ♏ 20	●	NIGERIA
9 ♏ 37	☊	SLOVAKIA
9 ♏ 38	☊	CARPATHO-UKRAINE
9 ♏ 40	♀	BELIZE
9 ♏ 41	M	GERMANY WEST PROCLAM
9 ♏ 42	♃	KAMPUCHEA - REP
9 ♏ 43	●	NATO 1
9 ♏ 49	♃	FIJI
9 ♏ 49R	♆	SHEPARD
9 ♏ 51	♆	MAURETANIA
9 ♏ 53	A	GAMBIA
9 ♏ 58	♂	BYELO RUSSIA
9 ♏ 58	☽	CUBA - INDEPENDENCE 2
10 ♏ 03R	♆	SIERRA LEONE
10 ♏ 16	●	MEXICO - CONSTITUTION
10 ♏ 18	☊	SAUDI ARABIA
10 ♏ 21	M	YUGOSLAVIA 1
10 ♏ 22	☉	PANAMA
10 ♏ 22	●	SAO TOME-PRINCIPE
10 ♏ 23	☉	DOMINICA
10 ♏ 24R	♄	KHALISTAN
10 ♏ 26R	♆	GAGARIN
10 ♏ 35	☊	VIETNAM-UNION
10 ♏ 45	A	SRI LANKA-IND
10 ♏ 46	♆	JAMAICA
10 ♏ 49R	♆	ALGERIA
10 ♏ 49	♆	BUGANDA
10 ♏ 51R	♆	RWANDA-INDEPENDENCE
10 ♏ 51R	♆	BURUNDI
10 ♏ 54	☊	SPUTNIK
11 ♏ 02	☊	SEYCHELLES
11 ♏ 07	♆	TRINIDAD & TOBAGO
11 ♏ 09	☊	BYELO RUSSIA
11 ♏ 16	♆	RWANDA-UDI
11 ♏ 22R	♅	ARGENTINA - REVOLUTION
11 ♏ 26	A	POLAND-COMMUNIST
11 ♏ 28	A	USSR-REPUBLIC
11 ♏ 32R	♂	JAPAN - SOVEREIGNTY
11 ♏ 37	♅	MEXICO - REVOLUTION
11 ♏ 40	♂	TRANSKEI
11 ♏ 42	●	SWEDEN
11 ♏ 42	☽	SOUTH YEMEN 2
11 ♏ 45	♂	ECUADOR 1
11 ♏ 49	♆	NORTH YEMEN
11 ♏ 51	A	PERU I
11 ♏ 57R	♂	KHALISTAN
12 ♏ 06	●	YUGOSLAVIA 1
12 ♏ 07	A	CREATION OF MAN
12 ♏ 12	♆	UGANDA
12 ♏ 18	♆	TANGANYIKA
12 ♏ 25R	♅	SOLOMON ISLANDS
12 ♏ 28	☿	CZECHOSLOVAKIA 2
12 ♏ 33	♀	CREATION OF THE WORLD
12 ♏ 37	♀	GERMANY - WEIMAR
12 ♏ 43	☉	POLAND 1
12 ♏ 52	☽	LITHUANIA
12 ♏ 54	☊	MALAYA
12 ♏ 57	♃	USSR-FORMATION
12 ♏ 58	♆	WESTERN SAMOA
13 ♏ 00	☽	CUBA - INDEPENDENCE 1
13 ♏ 12	M	POLAND 2
13 ♏ 14	♆	SINGAPORE 1
13 ♏ 17	☽	ECUADOR 1
13 ♏ 28	♆	AGE OF AQUARIUS-2
13 ♏ 28	♆	AGE OF AQUARIUS-1
13 ♏ 35	♆	MALAYSIA
13 ♏ 55	☽	TANZANIA
13 ♏ 55	♄	BRUNEI
13 ♏ 58	●	IVORY COAST
14 ♏ 00	♅	BOPHUTHATSWANA
14 ♏ 02	☿	YUGOSLAVIA 1
14 ♏ 05	A	GRENADA
14 ♏ 12	☽	BENIN

14 ♏ 17	☽	YUGOSLAVIA 2
14 ♏ 21	♅	TUVALU
14 ♏ 26	A	ETHIOPIA
14 ♏ 30	♀	AUSTRIA
14 ♏ 41	●	ANGOLA
14 ♏ 47R	♅	ENGLAND-EDGAP
14 ♏ 53	M	SUDAN
14 ♏ 56	♆	FRANCE - NAPOLEON
14 ♏ 56R	♅	VENEZUELA 1
15 ♏ 01	☽	FRANCE-VICHY REPUBLIC
15 ♏ 01	☉	USSR-REVOLUTION
15 ♏ 03	☊	SAHRAWI ARAB D R
15 ♏ 05	♀	POLAND 2
15 ♏ 11R	♆	MALAWI
15 ♏ 16	☽	ICELAND
15 ♏ 19	M	DANZIG
15 ♏ 22	☿	UNITED NATIONS
15 ♏ 30R	♄	ROME
15 ♏ 52	♆	MALTA
16 ♏ 02	M	FRANCE-THIRD REPUBLIC
16 ♏ 13	●	LONDON 2
16 ♏ 15	☉	GERMANY - WEIMAR
16 ♏ 20	♅	DOMINICA
16 ♏ 26	♀	S VIETNAM-REP
16 ♏ 28	☿	MAURETANIA
16 ♏ 32	♆	ZANZIBAR
16 ♏ 35R	♅	PARAGUAY
16 ♏ 36	♆	KENYA
16 ♏ 44R	♆	TANZANIA
16 ♏ 56	♆	ZAMBIA
16 ♏ 56R	♅	NICARAGUA SANDINISTA
17 ♏ 01R	♅	KIRIBATI
17 ♏ 07	♀	NORTH YEMEN
17 ♏ 14R	♆	MALDIVES
17 ♏ 16	♆	SINGAPORE 2
17 ♏ 16	♆	SINGAPORE 3
17 ♏ 24	A	ITALY - REPUBLIC
17 ♏ 28	♀	TUVALU
17 ♏ 30R	♄	WARSAW PACT
17 ♏ 32	●	REAGAN-2
17 ♏ 36	☿	USSR-REVOLUTION
17 ♏ 39	♀	HUNGARY
17 ♏ 45	☉	AUSTRIA
17 ♏ 46R	♄	CANADA
17 ♏ 52	♃	CIA
17 ♏ 55	♅	VENDA
17 ♏ 55R	♀	DOMINICA
17 ♏ 56	☉	ANGOLA
18 ♏ 05	☿	BARBADOS
18 ♏ 06R	♅	ZIMBABWE-RHODESIA
18 ♏ 10R	♄	GERMANY WEST SOVEREIGN
18 ♏ 12	♀	TURKEY
18 ♏ 13	☉	POLAND 2
18 ♏ 14	A	FEDERATION OF ARAB REPU
18 ♏ 20	♀	LIBYA - INDEP
18 ♏ 20R	⚷	DENMARK
18 ♏ 26	☽	MALAYA
18 ♏ 38	M	GERMANY - WEIMAR
18 ♏ 44	☉	FRANCE - NAPOLEON
18 ♏ 44	♆	UNITED KINGDOM-18Ø1
18 ♏ 51	☉	RHODESIA
18 ♏ 54	♀	CZECHOSLOVAKIA 3
19 ♏ 00	♃	HYDERABAD
19 ♏ 00	♃	INDIA - INDEPENDENCE
19 ♏ 00	♃	PAKISTAN
19 ♏ 00	●	FAR EAST REPUBLIC
19 ♏ 09	♀	CREATION OF MAN
19 ♏ 15	⚷	KOREA - SOUTH
19 ♏ 17	♀	CHINA - COMMUNIST 2
19 ♏ 18	♀	EQUATORIAL GUINEA
19 ♏ 19	♃	SOUTH AFRICAN REP 1
19 ♏ 20	♄	LUXEMBOURG
19 ♏ 28	●	CHINA - COMMUNIST 1
19 ♏ 32R	♆	SIKKIM
19 ♏ 35R	♆	LONDON 2
19 ♏ 38	♀	ST VINCENT-GRENADINES
19 ♏ 40	☉	CONSERVATIVE PARTY
19 ♏ 40	☽	BAHAMAS
19 ♏ 42	♆	RHODESIA
19 ♏ 49	☿	LEBANON I
19 ♏ 57	A	MONTENEGRO
19 ♏ 57	A	SERBIA
20 ♏ 00	♆	GAMBIA
20 ♏ 04	●	BRAZIL
20 ♏ 11	♅	ST VINCENT-GRENADINES
20 ♏ 14	⚷	CHINA - NATIONALIST
20 ♏ 16	⚷	HUNGARY
20 ♏ 19	♆	BOTSWANA
20 ♏ 26R	♆	GUYANA
20 ♏ 26	♆	LESOTHO
20 ♏ 27R	♅	IRAN - ISLAMIC REP
20 ♏ 31	A	SAHRAWI ARAB D R
20 ♏ 42	A	ALLIANCE
20 ♏ 45	☿	DOMINICAN REPUBLIC
20 ♏ 45	♅	IRAN - KHOMEINI
20 ♏ 45	☊	HATAY
20 ♏ 49	☿	SOUTH YEMEN 1
20 ♏ 50	☊	TREATY OF ROME
20 ♏ 55	☊	COMOROS 2
20 ♏ 59	☊	ESPIRITU SANTO
21 ♏ 00	♅	ST LUCIA
21 ♏ 04	♂	NUCLEAR REACTION
21 ♏ 07	⚷	KOREA - NORTH
21 ♏ 13	♆	NAMIBIA
21 ♏ 14	♄	S VIETNAM-REP
21 ♏ 16	☉	CZECHOSLOVAKIA 3
21 ♏ 21	●	CISKEI
21 ♏ 22	⚷	BURMA
21 ♏ 22	☿	SOUTH YEMEN 2
21 ♏ 29	M	ENGLAND-17Ø7
21 ♏ 30R	♅	VANUATU
21 ♏ 36	♂	SUDAN
21 ♏ 36R	⚷	PALESTINE
21 ♏ 38R	⚷	ISRAEL
21 ♏ 43	☊	SURINAM
21 ♏ 44	☊	TIMOR
21 ♏ 48	☊	ANGOLA
21 ♏ 48	☊	GHANA
22 ♏ 01	●	AUSTRIA
22 ♏ 10	A	TUNISIA
22 ♏ 20	☉	CYPRUS - TURKISH
22 ♏ 29	♆	BARBADOS
22 ♏ 34	☽	COSTA RICA 1
22 ♏ 34R	♆	BIAFRA
22 ♏ 45	M	POLAND 1
22 ♏ 45	☉	DANZIG
22 ♏ 45	♀	KAMPUCHEA - REP
22 ♏ 49	☽	CIA
22 ♏ 57	♀	FIJI
23 ♏ 00	♂	FRANCE-FOURTH REPUBLIC
23 ♏ 11	☿	LAOS I
23 ♏ 12	A	BULGARIA - AUTONOMY
23 ♏ 21	●	AFGHANISTAN
23 ♏ 28	♀	ESPIRITU SANTO
23 ♏ 32	M	CONSERVATIVE PARTY
23 ♏ 34	♆	REAGAN-1
23 ♏ 48	☽	GORBACHEV
23 ♏ 54	♀	LATVIA
23 ♏ 56	⚷	SRI LANKA-IND
24 ♏ 01	♀	UGANDA
24 ♏ 02	♆	SWAZILAND
24 ♏ 03	♀	SPUTNIK
24 ♏ 04	☊	PAPUA NEW GUINEA
24 ♏ 12	♃	CUBA - COMMUNIST
24 ♏ 17	♃	TURKEY
24 ♏ 18	●	SWAZILAND
24 ♏ 20	A	BOLIVIA
24 ♏ 24	♂	VENEZUELA 1
24 ♏ 25	A	ROMANIA 2
24 ♏ 26	A	QATAR
24 ♏ 28	☊	LIECHTENSTEIN
24 ♏ 32	M	CZECHOSLOVAKIA 3
24 ♏ 33	♆	SOUTH YEMEN 1
24 ♏ 34	♆	SOUTH YEMEN 2
24 ♏ 36R	♅	ZIMBABWE
24 ♏ 39	♀	NICARAGUA 1
24 ♏ 44R	☿	DANZIG
24 ♏ 48	⚷	CZECHOSLOVAKIA-COMMUNIS
24 ♏ 56	♆	EQUATORIAL GUINEA
25 ♏ 06	♆	HAITI
25 ♏ 17	☉	LATVIA
25 ♏ 18	♃	DE GAULLE
25 ♏ 21	A	BULGARIA - COMMUNIST
25 ♏ 47	♂	FRANCE-1st REPUBLIC 1
25 ♏ 47	♀	CHINA - REPUBLIC
25 ♏ 51R	♀	UNITED KINGDOM-1922
25 ♏ 52	♄	CONSERVATIVE PARTY
26 ♏ 00	M	FRANCE-1st REPUBLIC 1
26 ♏ 01R	♆	MOON LANDING
26 ♏ 05	A	LUXEMBOURG
26 ♏ 08	♆	LIBYA, COUP
26 ♏ 09	M	BRAZIL
26 ♏ 11R	♀	EIRE 2
26 ♏ 19	♆	NAURU
26 ♏ 29R	♆	MAURITIUS
26 ♏ 35	A	USA 1
26 ♏ 43R	♄	NICARAGUA 2
26 ♏ 45	☿	ST VINCENT-GRENADINES
26 ♏ 50	♅	ALLIANCE
26 ♏ 57	⚷	UNITED KINGDOM-18Ø1
26 ♏ 59	☿	NAMIBIA
27 ♏ 01	♅	BELIZE
27 ♏ 14	♃	BAHRAIN
27 ♏ 15	☿	FRANCE-FOURTH REPUBLIC
27 ♏ 16	☿	COSTA RICA 1
27 ♏ 18	A	KOREA - NORTH
27 ♏ 18	♀	SYRIA 2
27 ♏ 18	♀	LEBANON 2
27 ♏ 38	A	ST LUCIA
27 ♏ 41R	♄	TUNISIA
28 ♏ 05	♄	HONDURAS
28 ♏ 05	M	HUNGARY
28 ♏ 07R	♄	GORBACHEV
28 ♏ 12R	♆	OMAN
28 ♏ 19	●	ENGLAND-EDGAR
28 ♏ 19	♀	CAMEROON
28 ♏ 21	☿	FRANCE - NAPOLEON
28 ♏ 27	♀	USSR-FORMATION
28 ♏ 37	♀	SWEDEN
28 ♏ 38	♀	COMOROS 2
28 ♏ 40	♂	ALBANIA - INDEPENDENCE
28 ♏ 46	♃	QATAR
28 ♏ 46	♃	FEDERATION OF ARAB REPU
28 ♏ 55	♄	SUDAN
28 ♏ 56R	♄	MOROCCO
28 ♏ 59	M	LATVIA
29 ♏ 01	A	LONDON 2
29 ♏ 03	♆	KAMPUCHEA - REP
29 ♏ 04	♆	FIJI
29 ♏ 04	♅	ANTIGUA-BARBUDA
29 ♏ 05	♂	FRANCE-1st REPUBLIC 2
29 ♏ 10R	♆	TONGA
29 ♏ 12	M	TIMOR
29 ♏ 17	♅	REAGAN-2
29 ♏ 30	♀	BRUNEI
29 ♏ 43	☊	SAO TOME-PRINCIPE
29 ♏ 47	☿	DOMINICA
29 ♏ 55R	♅	S.D.P.
29 ♏ 57	M	PALESTINE
0 ♐ 07	☿	SURINAM
0 ♐ 15	☊	COMOROS 1
0 ♐ 15	☊	CAPE VERDE ISLANDS
0 ♐ 15	☽	VENEZUELA 2
0 ♐ 18	♆	BAHRAIN
0 ♐ 25	♆	QATAR
0 ♐ 25	♆	FEDERATION OF ARAB REPU

0 ♐ 39	☊	MOZAMBIQUE
0 ♐ 48	♂	DOMINICA
0 ♐ 48	☿	GERMANY - WEIMAR
0 ♐ 55	♆	SPAIN
1 ♐ 04	♅	CISKEI
1 ♐ 12	☽	IRAQ - INDEPENCENCE
1 ♐ 18	☊	AUSTRALIA 1
1 ♐ 19	☊	AUSTRALIA 2
1 ♐ 20	☊	KAMPUCHEA, COMM
1 ♐ 25	☿	CYPRUS - TURKISH
1 ♐ 42	●	VANUATU
1 ♐ 45	♅	SPAIN
1 ♐ 52	♀	HOLY ROMAN EMPIRE
1 ♐ 54	♀	CONSERVATIVE PARTY
2 ♐ 14	☉	SURINAM
2 ♐ 19	♀	BOPHUTHATSWANA
2 ♐ 30	♀	FRANCE-FOURTH REPUBLIC
2 ♐ 36R	♆	BANGLADESH 2
2 ♐ 43R	♄	PAKISTAN, REPUBLIC
2 ♐ 58R	♆	BANGLADESH 1
3 ♐ 00	♂	MOON LANDING
3 ♐ 01	☿	AUSTRIA
3 ♐ 03	♆	UNITED ARAB EMIR
3 ♐ 16	♂	CONSERVATIVE PARTY
3 ♐ 19	M	TONGA
3 ♐ 22	⚷	NATO 1
3 ♐ 23	M	GUYANA
3 ♐ 34	♆	BANGLADESH 3
3 ♐ 42	☿	POLAND 2
3 ♐ 46	☉	LEBANON I
3 ♐ 54	A	BAHRAIN
3 ♐ 58R	♆	SRI LANKA-REP
3 ♐ 58	A	ITALY - KINGDOM 1
4 ♐ 06	☽	FRANCE-1st REPUBLIC 1
4 ♐ 11	☽	SRI LANKA-IND
4 ♐ 25R	♃	THATCHER
4 ♐ 32R	♀	CUBA - INDEPENDENCE 1
4 ♐ 34	♃	CHINA - REPUBLIC
4 ♐ 41	♀	TANGANYIKA
4 ♐ 41	M	ICELAND
4 ♐ 43	♅	CUBA - INDEPENDENCE 1
4 ♐ 49	☿	TIMOR
4 ♐ 50	⚷	CHINA - COMMUNIST 1
4 ♐ 55R	♆	AFGHANISTAN
5 ♐ 01R	♆	BAHAMAS
5 ♐ 02	♃	ST KITTS-NEVIS
5 ♐ 06	A	EIRE 3
5 ♐ 07	M	FIRST MANNED FLIGHT
5 ♐ 12	A	VIETNAM
5 ♐ 15	☉	TIMOR
5 ♐ 31R	♃	BANGLADESH 2
5 ♐ 38	⚷	CHINA - COMMUNIST 2
5 ♐ 38	☉	ESTONIA
5 ♐ 39	♅	ST KITTS-NEVIS
5 ♐ 46	☉	MAURETANIA
5 ♐ 47	☊	NEPAL
5 ♐ 51	☉	ALBANIA - INDEPENDENCE
6 ♐ 00	●	ICELAND
6 ♐ 07R	♂	PARAGUAY
6 ♐ 10	♂	E.E.C.
6 ♐ 18	⚷	CUBA - INDEPENDENCE 1
6 ♐ 19	♀	TRANSKEI
6 ♐ 27R	♃	BANGLADESH 1
6 ♐ 29	♆	MEXICO - REVOLUTION
6 ♐ 30R	⚷	GERMANY WEST PROCLAM
6 ♐ 34	☉	SOUTH YEMEN 1
6 ♐ 37R	♅	THATCHER
6 ♐ 41	☿	HUNGARY
6 ♐ 55	☽	FRANCE-FOURTH REPUBLIC
6 ♐ 55	A	COSTA RICA 2
6 ♐ 57	☉	SOUTH YEMEN 2
6 ♐ 59	♆	GUINEA - BUISSAU
7 ♐ 00	♆	ETHIOPIA
7 ♐ 01R	♆	GREECE DEMOCRACY
7 ♐ 16	●	HAITI
7 ♐ 26R	⚷	MONACO
7 ♐ 30	☉	BARBADOS
7 ♐ 36	M	UNITED ARAB EMIR
7 ♐ 39	●	AGE OF AQUARIUS-2
7 ♐ 44R	☿	CONSERVATIVE PARTY
7 ♐ 44	A	AGE OF AQUARIUS-2
7 ♐ 47R	♆	ARGENTINA - REVOLUTION
7 ♐ 54R	♅	ARGENTINA - INDEPENDENC
7 ♐ 57	☿	CISKEI
7 ♐ 58	♄	MALAYA
8 ♐ 03	●	KUWAIT
8 ♐ 04	☊	TUNISIA
8 ♐ 06	M	SOUTH AFRICA-REPUBLIC
8 ♐ 08	☿	CZECHOSLOVAKIA 3
8 ♐ 09	☊	MOROCCO
8 ♐ 10R	♆	BHUTAN
8 ♐ 14	A	USA 3
8 ♐ 20	♅	CYPRUS - TURKISH
8 ♐ 24	A	CHINA - COMMUNIST 1
8 ♐ 26	☽	BANGLADESH 3
8 ♐ 27	☉	YUGOSLAVIA 2
8 ♐ 29	M	ESTONIA
8 ♐ 30	☽	S.D.P.
8 ♐ 32	☉	ICELAND
8 ♐ 38R	⚷	EIRE 3
8 ♐ 41	M	ALBANIA - INDEPENDENCE
8 ♐ 59R	♆	VENEZUELA 1
9 ♐ 03	♂	SWEDEN
9 ♐ 08R	♆	PORTUGAL-REVOLUTION
9 ♐ 10	A	OPEC
9 ♐ 12	♆	PAPUA NEW GUINEA
9 ♐ 14	☉	DOMINICAN REPUBLIC
9 ♐ 19	♆	GRENADA
9 ♐ 24	☽	GEORGIA
9 ♐ 24	☽	ARMENIA
9 ♐ 26R	♆	SAO TOME-PRINCIPE
9 ♐ 28	☽	DENMARK
9 ♐ 29	☉	UNITED ARAB EMIR
9 ♐ 33R	♆	COMOROS 1
9 ♐ 34R	♆	CAPE VERDE ISLANDS
9 ♐ 35	♄	MEXICO - REVOLUTION
9 ♐ 36	☽	CREATION OF MAN
9 ♐ 38	☽	SOUTH AFRICAN REP 1
9 ♐ 38	♃	LABOUR PARTY 1
9 ♐ 41R	♄	GUATEMALA - 2
9 ♐ 49R	♆	MOZAMBIQUE
9 ♐ 50	●	ST KITTS-NEVIS
9 ♐ 50	☽	BRUNEI
9 ♐ 55	♄	SPUTNIK
10 ♐ 02	☉	NUCLEAR REACTION
10 ♐ 03	A	PORTUGAL-REVOLUTION
10 ♐ 13	☽	FIRST MANNED FLIGHT
10 ♐ 14	♀	AUSTRALIA 1
10 ♐ 16	♀	YUGOSLAVIA 2
10 ♐ 18R	♆	PARAGUAY
10 ♐ 22	♀	ICELAND
10 ♐ 24	♂	POLAND 1
10 ♐ 34	☽	DOMINICA
10 ♐ 39	♆	ANGOLA
10 ♐ 40	☽	TRANSKEI
10 ♐ 40	A	SAUDI ARABIA
10 ♐ 40	A	BURMA
10 ♐ 48	☊	PAKISTAN, REPUBLIC
10 ♐ 53	☽	HATAY
10 ♐ 54	♀	AUSTRALIA 2
11 ♐ 01	☿	NUCLEAR REACTION
11 ♐ 05R	♅	KHALISTAN
11 ♐ 07	♅	BRUNEI
11 ♐ 10	♆	SURINAM
11 ♐ 17	♆	TIMOR
11 ♐ 24	M	ZIMBABWE-RHODESIA
11 ♐ 25	☿	RHODESIA
11 ♐ 27	♂	EGYPT - INDEPENDENCE
11 ♐ 29R	♆	KAMPUCHEA, COMM
11 ♐ 33	●	UNITED NATIONS
11 ♐ 37	♂	EGYPT - KINGDOM
11 ♐ 40	☉	CISKEI
11 ♐ 42	♆	NEPAL
11 ♐ 43	M	RHODESIA
11 ♐ 44	M	DOMINICAN REPUBLIC
11 ♐ 51R	♆	VIETNAM-UNION
11 ♐ 56R	♆	SEYCHELLES
11 ♐ 57	M	LEBANON I
12 ♐ 13	M	MALI - FEDERATION
12 ♐ 15	♆	TRANSKEI
12 ♐ 15	♂	CZECHOSLOVAKIA 1
12 ♐ 20	♅	LABOUR PARTY 1
12 ♐ 21	A	USA 4
12 ♐ 21	♆	ESPIRITU SANTO
12 ♐ 25	☿	TANGANYIKA
12 ♐ 26	A	GHANA
12 ♐ 30	●	NORTH YEMEN
12 ♐ 30	♆	COMOROS 2
12 ♐ 33	☽	NIGER
12 ♐ 39R	♄	ARGENTINA - REVOLUTION
12 ♐ 43	♀	BARBADOS
12 ♐ 56	♅	ROMAN EMPIRE 1
13 ♐ 03	☊	ICELAND
13 ♐ 03	☊	YUGOSLAVIA 2
13 ♐ 03	☊	LATVIA
13 ♐ 05	♅	ROMAN EMPIRE 2
13 ♐ 12	●	NAMIBIA
13 ♐ 12	☊	CZECHOSLOVAKIA 3
13 ♐ 14	☊	GERMANY - WEIMAR
13 ♐ 14	☊	HUNGARY
13 ♐ 16	☊	AUSTRIA
13 ♐ 16	☊	POLAND 2
13 ♐ 33	♃	CHINA - NATIONALIST
13 ♐ 34	A	BELGIUM
13 ♐ 40	☉	BOPHUTHATSWANA
13 ♐ 45	☉	FINLAND
13 ♐ 45	☿	EIRE 2
13 ♐ 47	☿	LATVIA
13 ♐ 48	♀	COSTA RICA 1
13 ♐ 48	☉	EIRE 2
13 ♐ 49	☊	YUGOSLAVIA 1
13 ♐ 53	☊	CZECHOSLOVAKIA 2
13 ♐ 54	♆	SAHRAWI ARAB D R
14 ♐ 02	♄	GHANA
14 ♐ 03	♀	NUCLEAR REACTION
14 ♐ 13R	♆	DJIBOUTI
14 ♐ 14	☊	CZECHOSLOVAKIA 1
14 ♐ 17	♅	AUSTRALIA 1
14 ♐ 18R	♄	TREATY OF ROME
14 ♐ 19	♅	AUSTRALIA 2
14 ♐ 31	☊	ETHIOPIA
14 ♐ 36	☊	GUINEA - BUISSAU
14 ♐ 37	☿	HOLY ROMAN EMPIRE
14 ♐ 45	☉	UNITED KINGDOM-1922
15 ♐ 08	♂	GREECE INDEPENCENCE
15 ♐ 14	♄	CUBA - INDEPENDENCE 1
15 ♐ 14	☿	UNITED KINGDOM-1922
15 ♐ 23	⚷	INDONESIA
15 ♐ 25	♃	CYPRUS - TURKISH
15 ♐ 29	☽	CONFEDERATE STATES AMER
15 ♐ 34R	☿	BANGLADESH 3
15 ♐ 40	♃	UNITED ARAB EMIR
15 ♐ 46	♃	BURMA
15 ♐ 47	♆	BOPHUTHATSWANA
15 ♐ 49	M	FINLAND
15 ♐ 51	♆	TUVALU
16 ♐ 11	M	YUGOSLAVIA 2
16 ♐ 13	☊	FALL OF CONSTANTINOPLE
16 ♐ 13R	♆	SOLOMON ISLANDS
16 ♐ 20	A	SYRIA 1
16 ♐ 33	☊	LABOUR PARTY 1
16 ♐ 33	☉	TANGANYIKA
16 ♐ 33	A	HOLY ROMAN EMPIRE
16 ♐ 34	A	CHINA - COMMUNIST 2
16 ♐ 42	♆	DOMINICA
16 ♐ 59R	☿	LIBYA - INDEP

17 ♐ 02	♂	NAT KHOREZEM SOVIET REP
17 ♐ 04	☉	ZANZIBAR
17 ♐ 11	☊	SUDAN
17 ♐ 15	A	BULGARIA - INDEPENDENCE
17 ♐ 26	☉	SWEDEN
17 ♐ 32	●	LEBANON 2
17 ♐ 34	☿	UNITED KINGDOM-18Ø1
17 ♐ 35	☽	GREECE REVOLUTION
17 ♐ 39	☉	PERU-BATTLE AYACUCHO
17 ♐ 43	●	TEXAS
17 ♐ 46	♆	VENDA
17 ♐ 56	♅	GORBACHEV
17 ♐ 56	A	NAT KHOREZEM SOVIET REP
18 ♐ 03	●	LONDON 1
18 ♐ 10R	♆	NICARAGUA SANDINISTA
18 ♐ 10	♂	TANGANYIKA
18 ♐ 15	●	SYRIA 2
18 ♐ 19	☊	URUGUAY
18 ♐ 20R	♆	KIRIBATI
18 ♐ 27	☊	S VIETNAM-REP
18 ♐ 33	⚷	INDIA - REPUBLIC
18 ♐ 35	☊	GREECE DEMOCRACY
18 ♐ 36	♆	ST VINCENT-GRENADINES
18 ♐ 44	♃	CAMEROON
18 ♐ 50	☉	LITHUANIA
18 ♐ 52	♃	BANGLADESH 3
18 ♐ 52	A	MALI - REPUBLIC
18 ♐ 52	☉	CUBA - INDEPENDENCE 1
18 ♐ 53	●	SHEPARD
18 ♐ 56	☽	SOUTH AFRICA-REPUBLIC
18 ♐ 58	A	GUATEMALA - 1
19 ♐ 01	♂	SOUTH AFRICAN REP 2
19 ♐ 03	☿	CUBA - COMMUNIST
19 ♐ 06	☉	KENYA
19 ♐ 06R	♃	KOREA - SOUTH
19 ♐ 08	M	SWEDEN
19 ♐ 12	☿	ESTONIA
19 ♐ 13	♅	SAUDI ARABIA
19 ♐ 19	M	PERU-BATTLE AYACUCHO
19 ♐ 23R	♆	ZIMBABWE-RHODESIA
19 ♐ 25	☊	BOLIVIA
19 ♐ 25	☊	BHUTAN
19 ♐ 26	♄	E.E.C.
19 ♐ 27	♅	CHILE 1
19 ♐ 28	A	PORTUGAL-REVOLUTION
19 ♐ 31	♂	LIBYA, COUP
19 ♐ 34	♂	CZECHOSLOVAKIA 2
19 ♐ 48	♂	FAR EAST REPUBLIC
19 ♐ 49	♆	IRAN - KHOMEINI
20 ♐ 02R	♆	ARGENTINA - INDEPENDENC
20 ♐ 07R	♅	CHILE 2
20 ♐ 08	☊	PORTUGAL-REVOLUTION
20 ♐ 09R	♅	CUBA - INDEPENDENCE 2
20 ♐ 12R	♆	VANUATU
20 ♐ 13	♃	KOREA - NORTH
20 ♐ 14	♄	GUINEA
20 ♐ 16	♆	ST LUCIA
20 ♐ 17	♂	CAMEROON
20 ♐ 19	♂	YUGOSLAVIA 1
20 ♐ 20	A	EGYPT - INDEPENDENCE
20 ♐ 22R	♄	IRAQ - REPUBLIC
20 ♐ 29R	♆	IRAN - ISLAMIC REP
20 ♐ 29	♄	FRANCE-FIFTH REPUBLIC
20 ♐ 58	●	TIMOR
21 ♐ 43	M	LITHUANIA
21 ♐ 44	A	URUGUAY
21 ♐ 51	♃	SRI LANKA-IND
21 ♐ 56R	♄	VENEZUELA 1
21 ♐ 57	♃	ALBANIA - INDEPENDENCE
21 ♐ 59	♄	FRANCE-THIRD REPUBLIC
22 ♐ 08	♆	ALLIANCE
22 ♐ 11	♆	BELIZE
22 ♐ 13	☊	GEORGIA
22 ♐ 13	☊	ARMENIA
22 ♐ 13	☊	AZERBAIJAN
22 ♐ 19	A	KHALISTAN
22 ♐ 22	☽	KHALISTAN
22 ♐ 30	●	MAURETANIA
22 ♐ 31R	♆	ZIMBABWE
22 ♐ 37	●	PORTUGAL-REVOLUTION
22 ♐ 42	♄	UNITED ARAB REP
22 ♐ 44	☽	SOUTH AFRICAN REP 2
22 ♐ 48	M	ARAB FEDERATION
22 ♐ 59	♆	ANTIGUA-BARBUDA
23 ♐ 17	♅	PANAMA
23 ♐ 37	☽	COMOROS 2
23 ♐ 44	☊	TRANSCAUCASIAN FED
23 ♐ 44	♆	REAGAN-2
23 ♐ 45	♄	ARAB FEDERATION
23 ♐ 47R	♃	SENEGAL
23 ♐ 48R	♃	GABON
23 ♐ 48	A	CYPRUS - TURKISH
23 ♐ 49R	♃	CYPRUS
23 ♐ 50R	♃	CONGO
23 ♐ 50	☉	BANGLADESH 3
23 ♐ 50	☿	SOUTH AFRICAN REP 2
23 ♐ 52R	♃	CENTRAL AFRICAN REPUBLI
23 ♐ 55R	♃	CHAD
24 ♐ 04R	♃	IVORY COAST
24 ♐ 06	♆	CISKEI
24 ♐ 06	☽	GERMANY - EMPIRE
24 ♐ 09R	♃	BURKINO-FASSO
24 ♐ 16R	♃	NIGER
24 ♐ 23R	♃	BENIN
24 ♐ 32	☉	FIRST MANNED FLIGHT
24 ♐ 35	●	ROMANIA 1
24 ♐ 37	☿	ALBANIA - INDEPENDENCE
24 ♐ 43	A	EL SALVADOR
24 ♐ 43	♅	COLUMBIA
24 ♐ 43	♃	OPEC
24 ♐ 52	♆	S.D.P.
24 ♐ 53	⚷	LABOUR PARTY 1
24 ♐ 54	☿	CAMEROON
24 ♐ 57	☉	COLUMBIA
25 ♐ 12	M	IRAN - KHOMEINI
25 ♐ 18	♃	CZECHOSLOVAKIA-COMMUNIS
25 ♐ 24	♅	ECUADOR 1
25 ♐ 25	♃	MALI - REPUBLIC
25 ♐ 26	♀	ANTIGUA-BARBUDA
25 ♐ 26	A	CZECHOSLOVAKIA 1
25 ♐ 27	♀	IRAN - KHOMEINI
25 ♐ 28R	☿	CHINA - REPUBLIC
25 ♐ 32R	♄	PARAGUAY
25 ♐ 39	●	BOTSWANA
25 ♐ 41	☽	ANTIGUA-BARBUDA
25 ♐ 44	♅	FIRST MANNED FLIGHT
25 ♐ 50	M	COLUMBIA
25 ♐ 50	♃	BRUNEI
25 ♐ 52	♃	AUSTRALIA 1
25 ♐ 57	♆	CHILE 1
25 ♐ 59	♃	AUSTRALIA 2
26 ♐ 00R	♂	KAMPUCHEA - INDEP
26 ♐ 06R	♂	SOUTH VIETNAM
26 ♐ 06R	♂	LAOS 2
26 ♐ 06R	♂	NORTH VIETNAM
26 ♐ 06	♂	CARPATHO-UKRAINE
26 ♐ 08	♂	SLOVAKIA
26 ♐ 19	♃	NIGERIA
26 ♐ 23	☿	CHINA - NATIONALIST
26 ♐ 29R	♆	CHILE 2
26 ♐ 30	A	MAURITIUS
26 ♐ 30	♆	ST KITTS-NEVIS
26 ♐ 31	⚷	SOUTH AFRICAN REP 1
26 ♐ 43	A	VENEZUELA 2
26 ♐ 49R	☿	E.E.C.
26 ♐ 50	☊	WARSAW PACT
26 ♐ 56	M	MOON LANDING
26 ♐ 58	☿	DE GAULLE
27 ♐ 03	☿	AUSTRALIA 1
27 ♐ 06	☊	GERMANY WEST SOVEREIGN
27 ♐ 11	♀	DANZIG
27 ♐ 22R	♃	ZAIRE
27 ♐ 22R	♃	SOMALIA
27 ♐ 23	☊	SOUTH AFRICAN REP 2
27 ♐ 27	☊	GRENADA
27 ♐ 37R	♃	PALESTINE
27 ♐ 39R	♃	ISRAEL
27 ♐ 39	♆	CYPRUS - TURKISH
27 ♐ 42	☿	PERU-BATTLE AYACUCHO
27 ♐ 44	A	FRANCE-VICHY REPUBLIC
27 ♐ 52	♂	RHODESIA
27 ♐ 52	☿	AUSTRALIA 2
27 ♐ 57	☽	TANGANYIKA
28 ♐ 00R	♃	MADAGASCAR
28 ♐ 00R	♃	SOMALILAND
28 ♐ 04R	♄	VATICAN CITY
28 ♐ 07R	♆	THATCHER
28 ♐ 11	A	NORTH YEMEN
28 ♐ 13	☿	UNITED ARAB EMIR
28 ♐ 14	M	U.S. CIVIL WAR
28 ♐ 16	♆	COLUMBIA
28 ♐ 21	♆	ECUADOR 1
28 ♐ 27	♅	ENGLAND-WILLIAM
28 ♐ 28	♂	UNITED ARAB REP
28 ♐ 31	♂	GERMANY - WEIMAR
28 ♐ 45R	♃	MALI - FEDERATION
28 ♐ 51	♃	THAILAND 1
28 ♐ 54	☽	SPAIN
29 ♐ 10	♅	GUATEMALA - 1
29 ♐ 13	M	CREATION OF THE WORLD
29 ♐ 13	♅	EL SALVADOR
29 ♐ 16	A	ICELAND
29 ♐ 20	♆	BRUNEI
29 ♐ 26	●	COSTA RICA 2
29 ♐ 28	⚷	AUSTRALIA 1
29 ♐ 29	●	TRANSCAUCASIAN FED
29 ♐ 31	⚷	AUSTRALIA 2
29 ♐ 37	♅	NICARAGUA 1
29 ♐ 37	♄	CUBA - COMMUNIST
29 ♐ 38	⚷	HAITI
29 ♐ 39	♂	AUSTRIA
29 ♐ 48	☿	YUGOSLAVIA 2
29 ♐ 49R	♅	PERU I
29 ♐ 52	☿	ICELAND
29 ♐ 56	☽	MONGOLIA
0 ♑ 00	♂	POLAND 2
0 ♑ 00	☽	ST LUCIA
0 ♑ 09	♅	COSTA RICA 1
0 ♑ 15R	♆	KHALISTAN
0 ♑ 18	♆	GUATEMALA - 1
0 ♑ 19	☊	PERU-BATTLE AYACUCHO
0 ♑ 19	♆	EL SALVADOR
0 ♑ 20	♄	DE GAULLE
0 ♑ 32	A	JAPAN - SOVEREIGNTY
0 ♑ 32	♆	NICARAGUA 1
0 ♑ 33	M	BAHAMAS
0 ♑ 33	♂	PANAMA
0 ♑ 49R	♆	PERU I
0 ♑ 51	♆	COSTA RICA 1
0 ♑ 53	☽	COLUMBIA
0 ♑ 53	♀	USSR-REVOLUTION
0 ♑ 57	♃	JAPAN - MEIJI CONST
1 ♑ 03	☿	FINLAND
1 ♑ 06	☽	KOREA - SOUTH
1 ♑ 08R	♃	LIBERAL PARTY
1 ♑ 13	♄	THAILAND 1
1 ♑ 16	☉	LIBYA - INDEP
1 ♑ 18	☊	UKRAINE
1 ♑ 32	☽	EIRE 3
1 ♑ 32	♂	HUNGARY
1 ♑ 34	☊	LITHUANIA
1 ♑ 37	☊	ESTONIA
1 ♑ 40	☊	FINLAND
1 ♑ 52	♅	DOMINICAN REPUBLIC
1 ♑ 55	♆	DOMINICAN REPUBLIC
2 ♑ 00	☉	CHINA - NATIONALIST

18 ♉ 08	M	NUCLEAR REACTION
18 ♉ 11	☿	HAITI
18 ♉ 26	♄	TOGO
18 ♉ 33	♃	ORANGE FREE STATE
18 ♉ 33	M	ROMAN EMPIRE 1
18 ♉ 34	☊	USSR-REPUBLIC
18 ♉ 41R	☿	INDIA - REPUBLIC
18 ♉ 49	⚷	PANAMA
18 ♉ 50	A	CONSERVATIVE PARTY
18 ♉ 56	♀	ST LUCIA
19 ♉ 00	☽	GERMANY - WEIMAR
19 ♉ 05	M	EGYPT - REPUBLIC
19 ♉ 10	☽	ARGENTINA - INDEPENDENC
19 ♉ 13	☽	MOROCCO
19 ♉ 21	♄	SAUDI ARABIA
19 ♉ 31	♄	BUGANDA
19 ♉ 32R	⚷	EGYPT - REPUBLIC
19 ♉ 43	☿	MEXICO - CONSTITUTION
19 ♉ 45	☊	MEXICO - CONSTITUTION
19 ♉ 58	☿	WESTERN SAMOA
20 ♉ 01	♆	BELGIUM
20 ♉ 02R	♆	VENEZUELA 2
20 ♉ 06	☊	ITALY - KINGDOM 1
20 ♉ 07	☿	ESPIRITU SANTO
20 ♉ 09	☽	YUGOSLAVIA-COMMUNIST
20 ♉ 15	♂	NEW ZEALAND I
20 ♉ 26	♃	RWANDA-UDI
20 ♉ 35	♀	MEXICO - CONSTITUTION
20 ♉ 38	☉	ALBANIA-PEOPLES REPUBLI
20 ♉ 44	♂	DANZIG
20 ♉ 55	♀	LEBANON I
20 ♉ 56	⊗	MALI - FEDERATION
21 ♉ 01	♂	BANGLADESH 2
21 ♉ 01	♀	PERU-BATTLE AYACUCHO
21 ♉ 07	♀	SPAIN
21 ♉ 09	♆	GREECE INDEPENCENCE
21 ♉ 10	M	SOUTH YEMEN 1
21 ♉ 15	♀	GERMANY - THIRD REICH
21 ♉ 16	♅	PORTUGAL-REVOLUTION
21 ♉ 19	M	ROMAN EMPIRE 2
21 ♉ 20	☿	USSR-FORMATION
21 ♉ 33	♀	BANGLADESH 3
21 ♉ 34	☉	ROMAN EMPIRE 1
21 ♉ 46	⚷	FIRST MANNED FLIGHT
21 ♉ 59	⊗	PORTUGAL-REVOLUTION
22 ♉ 00	♀	CONFEDERATE STATES AMER
22 ♉ 05	A	CZECHOSLOVAKIA 3
22 ♉ 21	♃	CHINA - COMMUNIST 1
22 ♉ 27	☊	NATAL
22 ♉ 35	♃	CHINA - COMMUNIST 2
22 ♉ 36	☿	UNITED ARAB REP
22 ♉ 40R	♃	NATAL
22 ♉ 41	☊	CONFEDERATE STATES AMER
22 ♉ 42R	♆	ECUADOR 2
22 ♉ 44	☊	POLAND 1
22 ♉ 49	♄	RWANDA-UDI
22 ♉ 51	♀	ESTONIA
23 ♉ 14	A	ESTONIA
23 ♉ 20R	♃	NATO 1
23 ♉ 20	M	ALBANIA-PEOPLES REPUBLI
23 ♉ 36	♀	CUBA - COMMUNIST
23 ♉ 47	☿	INDONESIA
23 ♉ 57	☉	SAUDI ARABIA
24 ♉ 16	M	S^UTH AFRICAN REP 1
24 ♉ 17	M	AFGHANISTAN
24 ♉ 23	M	AUSTRALIA 2
24 ♉ 23	♀	REAGAN-1
24 ♉ 36	☉	ROMAN EMPIRE 2
24 ♉ 36	☽	LUXEMBOURG
24 ♉ 38	♀	DOMINICAN REPUBLIC
24 ♉ 39	⊗	TANZANIA
24 ♉ 40	♂	NEPAL
24 ♉ 41	♃	SAUDI ARABIA
24 ♉ 43R	☿	LEBANON 2
24 ♉ 43R	☿	SYRIA 2
24 ♉ 51R	♅	SOUTH AFRICA-UNION
25 ♉ 13	M	BENIN
25 ♉ 15	M	REAGAN-2
25 ♉ 15	☽	USA 2
25 ♉ 16	☿	SUDAN
25 ♉ 20	M	GERMANY - THIRD REICH
25 ♉ 22	⊗	ESPIRITU SANTO
25 ♉ 29	M	GERMANY - EMPIRE
25 ♉ 33	A	FRANCE-1st REPUBLIC 1
25 ♉ 39	☽	KAMPUCHEA - REP
25 ♉ 45R	⚷	KAMPUCHEA - INDEP
25 ♉ 48R	⚷	NORTH VIETNAM
25 ♉ 48R	⚷	SOUTH VIETNAM
25 ♉ 48R	⚷	LAOS 2
26 ♉ 02	⊗	EIRE 2
26 ♉ 19	☿	ROMAN EMPIRE 1
26 ♉ 22	♀	CISKEI
26 ♉ 31	☉	SOUTH AFRICAN REP 1
26 ♉ 34	☿	COMOROS 2
26 ♉ 35R	♀	GRENADA
26 ♉ 37	M	NIGER
27 ♉ 00R	☿	GERMANY - EMPIRE
27 ♉ 08	A	HONDURAS
27 ♉ 11	♄	TANGANYIKA
27 ♉ 34R	♇	USA 4
27 ♉ 34R	♇	USA 3
27 ♉ 36	☿	CHILE 1
27 ♉ 36R	♇	USA 1
27 ♉ 37R	♇	USA 2
27 ♉ 38	☽	USA 1
27 ♉ 41R	♄	CUBA - INDEPENDENCE 2
27 ♉ 47	♂	PERU-BATTLE AYACUCHO
27 ♉ 52	☊	SRI LANKA-REP
27 ♉ 53	☊	UNITED PROVINCES C A
27 ♉ 55	⊗	ARAB FEDERATION
27 ♉ 55	♂	GUATEMALA - 3
28 ♉ 00	☉	GERMANY - EMPIRE
28 ♉ 02	☽	PAPUA NEW GUINEA

28 ♉ 07	♄	IRAQ - INDEPENCENCE
28 ♉ 11	☽	ECUADOR 2
28 ♉ 12	♂	SOUTH YEMEN 1
28 ♉ 16	♅	CHINA - REPUBLIC
28 ♉ 25	☊	NETHERLANDS
28 ♉ 25	☽	EIRE 1
28 ♉ 29	♂	SOUTH YEMEN 2
28 ♉ 34	☊	LAOS I
28 ♉ 36R	♄	KUWAIT
28 ♉ 57	⊗	MEXICO - REVOLUTION
29 ♉ 15	♄	GAGARIN
29 ♉ 17	A	S VIETNAM-REP
29 ♉ 26	♀	HAITI
29 ♉ 30R	♄	SOUTH AFRICA-REPUBLIC
29 ♉ 34	⊗	LITHUANIA
29 ♉ 40	☽	LIBERAL PARTY
29 ♉ 43	☽	URUGUAY
29 ♉ 43	♄	SIERRA LEONE
29 ♉ 44	♄	WESTERN SAMOA
29 ♉ 50	♀	CHINA - NATIONALIST
29 ♉ 50	♄	SHEPARD
29 ♉ 52	♀	ENGLAND-WILLIAM
29 ♉ 52	A	COSTA RICA 1
29 ♉ 57	⊗	E.E.C.
0 ♒ 03	A	HUNGARY
0 ♒ 19	⚷	S VIETNAM-REP
0 ♒ 32	♃	EIRE 3
0 ♒ 33	♅	ALBANIA - INDEPENDENCE
0 ♒ 34	☉	REAGAN-2
0 ♒ 37	⊗	NEW ZEALAND I
0 ♒ 44	⊗	GHANA
0 ♒ 51	♀	FINLAND
1 ♒ 01R	♀	ARAB FEDERATION
1 ♒ 02	☿	SPAIN
1 ♒ 25	♀	DE GAULLE
1 ♒ 28	☽	CHINA - COMMUNIST 2
1 ♒ 36	☉	UKRAINE
1 ♒ 38	A	ZIMBABWE
1 ♒ 40	M	ENGLAND-1689
1 ♒ 44	A	TOGO
1 ♒ 48	☿	ROMAN EMPIRE 2
1 ♒ 58	♃	MONACO
2 ♒ 02	☿	SAUDI ARABIA
2 ♒ 07	☽	THAILAND 1
2 ♒ 10R	♃	GERMANY WEST PROCLAM
2 ♒ 22	♂	AGE OF AQUARIUS-2
2 ♒ 23	⊗	USSR-REPUBLIC
2 ♒ 35	☽	TREATY OF ROME
2 ♒ 39	☊	CREATION OF MAN
2 ♒ 41	☽	FIJI
2 ♒ 45	♂	AGE OF AQUARIUS-1
2 ♒ 58	⊗	ITALY - KINGDOM 1
3 ♒ 17	♄	PANAMA
3 ♒ 27	☊	CREATION OF THE WORLD
3 ♒ 28	☊	EIRE 1
3 ♒ 31R	♄	THAILAND 2
3 ♒ 31	☿	YUGOSLAVIA-COMMUNIST
3 ♒ 45R	♃	ROMANIA 2
3 ♒ 45R	♃	BULGARIA - AUTONOMY
3 ♒ 45R	♃	SERBIA
3 ♒ 45R	♃	MONTENEGRO
3 ♒ 45	☽	ROMAN EMPIRE 1
3 ♒ 46	M	CUBA - INDEPENDENCE 1
3 ♒ 48	♄	AGE OF AQUARIUS-2
3 ♒ 51	☊	EGYPT - REPUBLIC
3 ♒ 52	♄	AGE OF AQUARIUS-1
3 ♒ 55	⚷	SUDAN
4 ♒ 05	♂	FIRST MANNED FLIGHT
4 ♒ 19	♃	GAGARIN
4 ♒ 21	M	UKRAINE
4 ♒ 31	A	SUDAN
4 ♒ 33	M	PAKISTAN
4 ♒ 33	⊗	GERMANY WEST SOVEREIGN
4 ♒ 46R	♄	UGANDA
4 ♒ 52	♆	TEXAS
4 ♒ 53R	♄	NORTH YEMEN
4 ♒ 54	M	SPAIN
5 ♒ 08	M	RWANDA-UDI
5 ♒ 09	M	UNITED KINGDOM-1922
5 ♒ 15	⊗	FIRST MANNED FLIGHT
5 ♒ 29	♃	INDONESIA
5 ♒ 29R	♃	CREATION OF MAN
5 ♒ 33	⚷	GERMANY WEST SOVEREIGN
5 ♒ 34R	⚷	WARSAW PACT
5 ♒ 37	♀	LITHUANIA
5 ♒ 37R	♃	CREATION OF THE WORLD
5 ♒ 37	♃	TANGANYIKA
5 ♒ 39	A	FINLAND
5 ♒ 40	☉	INDIA - REPUBLIC
5 ♒ 46	☿	GERMANY - THIRD REICH
5 ♒ 52	♃	SIERRA LEONE
5 ♒ 56	☊	BANGLADESH 3
5 ♒ 59R	♄	TRINIDAD & TOBAGO
6 ♒ 00	⊗	LABOUR PARTY 2
6 ♒ 05R	♀	UNITED ARAB REP
6 ♒ 06	☿	IRAN - KHOMEINI
6 ♒ 13R	♃	KUWAIT
6 ♒ 29	♇	HOLY ROMAN EMPIRE
6 ♒ 30	♃	SHEPARD
6 ♒ 30	♄	FIRST MANNED FLIGHT
6 ♒ 36R	♅	BELGIUM
6 ♒ 46R	♅	VENEZUELA 2
6 ♒ 50	☊	UNITED ARAB EMIR
6 ♒ 51R	⚷	NORWAY
6 ♒ 52	♅	GREECE INDEPENCENCE
7 ♒ 07R	♃	SOUTH AFRICA-REPUBLIC
7 ♒ 08R	♇	SWITZERLAND
7 ♒ 09	♃	GORBACHEV
7 ♒ 33	☽	HONDURAS
7 ♒ 37	♄	GERMANY - THIRD REICH
7 ♒ 39	♆	HONDURAS
7 ♒ 40R	♄	JAMAICA
7 ♒ 50	♀	GERMANY - EMPIRE

Deg	Min	Name
7 ≋	59	KAMPUCHEA, COMM
8 ≋	00	YUGOSLAVIA 2
8 ≋	11	THAILAND 1
8 ≋	14	VANUATU
8 ≋	16	RWANDA-UDI
8 ≋	21	SPAIN
8 ≋	28	ENGLAND-WILLIAM
8 ≋	33	AUSTRIA
8 ≋	41	AFGHANISTAN
8 ≋	44	LABOUR PARTY 2
8 ≋	57R	AFGHANISTAN
9 ≋	01	IRAN - KHOMEINI
9 ≋	03	IVORY COAST
9 ≋	19	CIA
9 ≋	35	BURKINO-FASSO
9 ≋	35	PANAMA
9 ≋	39R	ROMAN EMPIRE 2
9 ≋	39	CAMEROON
9 ≋	40	NAURU
9 ≋	43R	BAHAMAS
9 ≋	52	SUDAN
9 ≋	59	BULGARIA - INDEPENDENCE
10 ≋	01	JAMAICA
10 ≋	02R	ALGERIA
10 ≋	07	PAKISTAN, REPUBLIC
10 ≋	11R	RWANDA-INDEPENDENCE
10 ≋	11R	BURUNDI
10 ≋	11	CARPATHO-UKRAINE
10 ≋	13	SAHRAVI ARAB D R
10 ≋	15	SLOVAKIA
10 ≋	16	SAUDI ARABIA
10 ≋	20	AUSTRALIA 1
10 ≋	21	LABOUR PARTY 1
10 ≋	22	NICARAGUA 2
10 ≋	28	ECUADOR 2
10 ≋	33	NEPAL
10 ≋	33	LONDON 1
10 ≋	34	WESTERN SAMOA
10 ≋	38	GREECE INDEPENCENCE
10 ≋	42	UGANDA
10 ≋	42	YUGOSLAVIA-COMMUNIST
10 ≋	52R	ROMAN EMPIRE 1
10 ≋	59	YUGOSLAVIA-COMMUNIST
11 ≋	07	GERMANY - THIRD REICH
11 ≋	11	FRANCE-1st REPUBLIC 2
11 ≋	18R	TUNISIA
11 ≋	30	CUBA - INDEPENDENCE 2
11 ≋	31	MEXICO - CONSTITUTION
11 ≋	38	PARAGUAY
11 ≋	43R	MOROCCO
11 ≋	45	IRAN - KHOMEINI
11 ≋	49	KIRIBATI
11 ≋	53	ARAB FEDERATION
12 ≋	08	KAMPUCHEA - REP
12 ≋	10	SAUDI ARABIA
12 ≋	16	UNITED ARAB REP
12 ≋	20R	FEDERATION OF ARAB REPU
12 ≋	20R	QATAR
12 ≋	22	INDIA - REPUBLIC
12 ≋	24	CONFEDERATE STATES AMER
12 ≋	25	GUATEMALA - 2
12 ≋	28R	SPUTNIK
12 ≋	29	POLAND-COMMUNIST
12 ≋	31	BURMA
12 ≋	41	LESOTHO
12 ≋	55	IVORY COAST
13 ≋	06	YUGOSLAVIA-COMMUNIST
13 ≋	22	BULGARIA - AUTONOMY
13 ≋	22	SERBIA
13 ≋	22	ROMANIA 2
13 ≋	22	MONTENEGRO
13 ≋	32	REAGAN-2
13 ≋	40R	MALAYA
13 ≋	51	SRI LANKA-IND
13 ≋	54R	INDIA - REPUBLIC
13 ≋	58R	NEW ZEALAND 1
14 ≋	07	CENTRAL AFRICAN REPUBLI
14 ≋	10	GREECE INDEPENCENCE
14 ≋	11R	MEXICO - REVOLUTION
14 ≋	11	TOGO
14 ≋	23	QATAR
14 ≋	23	FEDERATION OF ARAB REPU
14 ≋	27	HAITI
14 ≋	28	GHANA
14 ≋	32	BAHRAIN
14 ≋	32	SAHRAWI ARAB D R
14 ≋	35	INDIA - INDEPENDENCE
14 ≋	40	WARSAW PACT
14 ≋	41	POLAND 2
14 ≋	43	ECUADOR 1
14 ≋	48	PALESTINE
14 ≋	53	E.E.C.
15 ≋	01	INDONESIA
15 ≋	02	ROME
15 ≋	17	E.E.C.
15 ≋	24	COLUMBIA
15 ≋	33	ENGLAND-1689
15 ≋	37	AGE OF AQUARIUS-2
15 ≋	42	AGE OF AQUARIUS-2
15 ≋	44	TREATY OF ROME
15 ≋	48	BRAZIL
15 ≋	49	POLAND 1
15 ≋	51	GAMBIA
15 ≋	52	HYDERABAD
15 ≋	55R	BAHRAIN
15 ≋	58	CONFEDERATE STATES AMER
16 ≋	06	S.D.P.
16 ≋	14	AGE OF AQUARIUS-1
16 ≋	16	NIGERIA
16 ≋	17	SAHRAWI ARAB D R
16 ≋	19R	AGE OF AQUARIUS-1
16 ≋	22	REAGAN-2
16 ≋	28	LABOUR PARTY 2
16 ≋	28	CHILE 1
16 ≋	32	UNITED KINGDOM-1801
16 ≋	37	USSR-REPUBLIC
16 ≋	50	CUBA - INDEPENDENCE 2
16 ≋	56R	AGE OF AQUARIUS-2
17 ≋	01	CHAD
17 ≋	08	UNITED ARAB REP
17 ≋	20	GABON
17 ≋	22R	NETHERLANDS
17 ≋	23	GUINEA
17 ≋	29R	MALAYSIA
17 ≋	39	MEXICO - CONSTITUTION
17 ≋	46	AGE OF AQUARIUS-2
17 ≋	56	SWEDEN
17 ≋	58R	FRANCE-FIFTH REPUBLIC
18 ≋	00	GRENADA
18 ≋	04R	GUINEA
18 ≋	05	ARAB FEDERATION
18 ≋	25	AGE OF AQUARIUS-1
18 ≋	26	ZANZIBAR
18 ≋	27	COSTA RICA 1
18 ≋	29R	SINGAPORE 1
18 ≋	35	KENYA
18 ≋	37	AGE OF AQUARIUS-2
18 ≋	37R	ARGENTINA - REVOLUTION
18 ≋	44	AGE OF AQUARIUS-1
18 ≋	55	JAPAN - MEIJI CONST
19 ≋	01R	BULGARIA - INDEPENDENCE
19 ≋	03	LABOUR PARTY 2
19 ≋	11	CONFEDERATE STATES AMER
19 ≋	14	MEXICO - CONSTITUTION
19 ≋	15	NATAL
19 ≋	20	EIRE 1
19 ≋	34	FIRST MANNED FLIGHT
19 ≋	42	CHILE 1
19 ≋	49	USSR-REVOLUTION
19 ≋	52	NAURU
19 ≋	53	CUBA - COMMUNIST
19 ≋	59	LONDON 1
20 ≋	05	SOUTH AFRICAN REP 2
20 ≋	06	ANGOLA
20 ≋	09	ESTONIA
20 ≋	16	DE GAULLE
20 ≋	22	FINLAND
20 ≋	30	CHINA - NATIONALIST
20 ≋	32	LITHUANIA
20 ≋	42	ECUADOR 2
20 ≋	46	ROMANIA 1
20 ≋	47	USSR-REPUBLIC
21 ≋	00	EGYPT - KINGDOM
21 ≋	01	JAPAN - SOVEREIGNTY
21 ≋	07	BANGLADESH 2
21 ≋	16	CONGO
21 ≋	32R	FRANCE-1st REPUBLIC 2
21 ≋	37R	FRANCE-1st REPUBLIC 1
21 ≋	40	FALL OF CONSTANTINOPLE
21 ≋	40R	IRAQ - REPUBLIC
22 ≋	13	ALBANIA - INDEPENDENCE
22 ≋	25	LABOUR PARTY 2
22 ≋	28	UKRAINE
22 ≋	37	CENTRAL AFRICAN REPUBLI
22 ≋	37	JAPAN - MEIJI CONST
22 ≋	53	LABOUR PARTY 2
22 ≋	56	SOUTH AFRICAN REP 1
22 ≋	59	BANGLADESH 1
23 ≋	01	GRENADA
23 ≋	04R	ARGENTINA - INDEPENDENC
23 ≋	04R	VENEZUELA 1
23 ≋	20	RWANDA-UDI
23 ≋	20	AGE OF AQUARIUS-1
23 ≋	27	CHILE 1
23 ≋	32	N Y STOCK EXCHANGE
23 ≋	40	PARAGUAY
23 ≋	48R	YUGOSLAVIA 1
23 ≋	48	GERMANY - WEIMAR
23 ≋	48R	CZECHOSLOVAKIA 2
23 ≋	49	AUSTRIA
23 ≋	49	MAURITIUS
23 ≋	49	POLAND 2
23 ≋	50	HUNGARY
23 ≋	50	CZECHOSLOVAKIA 3
23 ≋	53	LATVIA
23 ≋	54R	CZECHOSLOVAKIA 1
24 ≋	07	YUGOSLAVIA 2
24 ≋	07	ICELAND
24 ≋	13	GAMBIA
24 ≋	14	USSR-REPUBLIC
24 ≋	18	NUCLEAR REACTION
24 ≋	24	TUNISIA
24 ≋	27	CAMEROON
24 ≋	34R	TEXAS
24 ≋	37	TEXAS
24 ≋	37	BUGANDA
24 ≋	45	S.D.P.
24 ≋	49R	CZECHOSLOVAKIA-COMMUNIS
25 ≋	01	ARAB FEDERATION
25 ≋	11	BYELO RUSSIA
25 ≋	24	CYPRUS
25 ≋	24	MAURITIUS
25 ≋	31	ST LUCIA
25 ≋	32	MALAYA
25 ≋	39	CONFEDERATE STATES AMER
25 ≋	45R	TONGA
25 ≋	45R	HATAY
26 ≋	02	BANGLADESH 1
26 ≋	10	EGYPT - INDEPENDENCE
26 ≋	22R	NETHERLANDS
26 ≋	26	LIBERAL PARTY
26 ≋	27	EIRE 2
26 ≋	30	LAOS 1
26 ≋	35	EGYPT - KINGDOM
26 ≋	41	MOROCCO

26 ♒ 41	A	TIMOR
26 ♒ 45	☽	BIAFRA
26 ♒ 58	☽	USA 3
27 ♒ 02	♅	TRANSCAÚCASIAN FED
27 ♒ 09	♂	UNITED KINGDOM-1922
27 ♒ 10	☽	USA 4
27 ♒ 17	M	SINGAPORE 1
27 ♒ 23	☽	SPUTNIK
27 ♒ 29	A	BRAZIL
27 ♒ 32	☽	S VIETNAM-REP
27 ♒ 40	☊	JAPAN - SOVEREIGNTY
27 ♒ 40	⚷	MAURETANIA
27 ♒ 41	A	GUYANA
27 ♒ 42	♅	ARMENIA
27 ♒ 42	♅	GEORGIA
27 ♒ 42	♅	AZERBAIJAN
27 ♒ 43	●	HOLY ROMAN EMPIRE
27 ♒ 44	A	UNITED ARAB EMIR
27 ♒ 50	●	VENEZUELA 2
27 ♒ 54	●	DANZIG
28 ♒ 01	☿	NAURU
28 ♒ 07R	⚷	NIGERIA
28 ♒ 17	♃	CONSERVATIVE PARTY
28 ♒ 25R	♄	ZAMBIA
28 ♒ 25R	♀	UKRAINE
28 ♒ 26	⚷	ITALY - KINGDOM 1
28 ♒ 26R	⚷	MALI - REPUBLIC
28 ♒ 30	●	MALAWI
28 ♒ 42	☽	DOMINICAN REPUBLIC
28 ♒ 46R	⚷	OPEC
28 ♒ 47R	⚷	PORTUGAL-REVOLUTION
28 ♒ 48	☊	DOMINICAN REPUBLIC
28 ♒ 52	⚷	BUGANDA
28 ♒ 52	♂	LABOUR PARTY 1
29 ♒ 02	☿	GUATEMALA - 3
29 ♒ 07R	☿	GREECE INDEPENCENCE
29 ♒ 08	⊙	GAMBIA
29 ♒ 18	●	ZAMBIA·
29 ♒ 41R	♆	LIBERIA
29 ♒ 44R	♄	MALTA
29 ♒ 54	☽	VANUATU
29 ♒ 56	⚷	U.S. CIVIL WAR
29 ♒ 59R	⚷	SENEGAL
0 ♓ 09R	⚷	GABON
0 ♓ 12R	⚷	CYPRUS
0 ♓ 15R	⚷	CONGO
0 ♓ 20R	⚷	CENTRAL AFRICAN REPUBLI
0 ♓ 23R	♃	LIECHTENSTEIN
0 ♓ 26R	⚷	CHAD
0 ♓ 29	⚷	RWANDA-UDI
0 ♓ 30	☽	FALL OF CONSTANTINOPLE
0 ♓ 38R	☿	JAPAN - MEIJI CONST
0 ♓ 38R	⚷	IVORY COAST
0 ♓ 43R	⚷	BURKINO-FASSO
0 ♓ 44	A	LEBANON I
0 ♓ 44R	♃	LUXEMBOURG
0 ♓ 49R	⚷	NIGER
0 ♓ 52	☽	SWAZILAND
0 ♓ 54R	⚷	BENIN
0 ♓ 57R	♇	FRANCE - NAPOLEON
0 ♓ 57	M	GUINEA - BUISSAU
1 ♓ 00	M	ORANGE FREE STATE
1 ♓ 01R	♆	COSTA RICA 2
1 ♓ 11	♅	TEXAS
1 ♓ 17	●	FALL OF CONSTANTINOPLE
1 ♓ 23	♀	SAUDI ARABIA
1 ♓ 34	⚷	TOGO
1 ♓ 39	M	CZECHOSLOVAKIA-COMMUNIS
1 ♓ 45	♅	DANZIG
1 ♓ 57	☊	KAMPUCHEA - REP
1 ♓ 57	☊	FIJI
2 ♓ 00	☿	LONDON 1
2 ♓ 01R	⚷	ZAIRE
2 ♓ 01R	⚷	SOMALIA
2 ♓ 05	☿	SRI LANKA-IND
2 ♓ 07R	⚷	MADAGASCAR
2 ♓ 07R	⚷	SOMALILAND
2 ♓ 10	A	YUGOSLAVIA 2
2 ♓ 13R	⚷	MALI - FEDERATION
2 ♓ 16	⚷	TANGANYIKA
2 ♓ 24	●	TURKEY
2 ♓ 26R	♅	NAT KHOREZEM SOVIET REP
2 ♓ 31	☽	CISKEI
2 ♓ 31	☽	SOUTH AFRICA-UNION
2 ♓ 35	☿	GHANA
2 ♓ 35	☊	COSTA RICA 1
2 ♓ 41	●	CONGO
2 ♓ 43	♇	UNITED KINGDOM-18Ø1
2 ♓ 43	☊	LIBYA - INDEP
2 ♓ 52	♄	NORWAY
2 ♓ 56	⊙	ST LUCIA
3 ♓ 01	⚷	SOUTH AFRICA-UNION
3 ♓ 07	⚷	WESTERN SAMOA
3 ♓ 09	♄	TANZANIA
3 ♓ 13	☊	OMAN
3 ♓ 14	☽	ST KITTS-NEVIS
3 ♓ 23	A	TONGA
3 ♓ 31R	♃	UGANDA
3 ♓ 39	⚷	CHINA - REPUBLIC
3 ♓ 51	☊	NICARAGUA 1
3 ♓ 52	♇	ENGLAND-WILLIAM
3 ♓ 55	♄	LABOUR PARTY 2
3 ♓ 56	♀	IRAN - ISLAMIC REP
4 ♓ 00	☽	ARGENTINA - REVOLUTION
4 ♓ 04	●	SINGAPORE 2
4 ♓ 29R	♃	NORTH YEMEN
4 ♓ 31	⊙	ORANGE FREE STATE
4 ♓ 33	☊	GUATEMALA - 1
4 ♓ 33	☊	EL SALVADOR
4 ♓ 41R	♅	BYELO RUSSIA
4 ♓ 41R	♄	MALAWI
4 ♓ 43	♂	KAMPUCHEA, COMM
4 ♓ 48	☊	PERU I
4 ♓ 50	♆	DENMARK
4 ♓ 51	M	LABOUR PARTY 1
4 ♓ 53	⊙	NEPAL
5 ♓ 02	⚷	AGE OF AQUARIUS-2
5 ♓ 04	⚷	AGE OF AQUARIUS-1
5 ♓ 07	A	DOMINICAN REPUBLIC
5 ♓ 09	⚷	GAGARIN
5 ♓ 10	♀	GHANA
5 ♓ 22	☊	LIBERAL PARTY
5 ♓ 31	A	LITHUANIA
5 ♓ 32	M	TRINIDAD & TOBAGO
5 ♓ 33	⊙	ENGLAND-1689
5 ♓ 46	⊙	CZECHOSLOVAKIA-COMMUNIS
5 ♓ 49	⚷	SIERRA LEONE
5 ♓ 56	☿	GRENADA
6 ♓ 00	♅	MONGOLIA
6 ♓ 04	♅	BOKHARA NAT'L SOVIET RE
6 ♓ 07	⚷	SHEPARD
6 ♓ 33	♇	HAITI
6 ♓ 34	♄	GAMBIA
6 ♓ 35	●	SOUTH AFRICAN REP 1
6 ♓ 35	A	MALI - FEDERATION
6 ♓ 35	♄	GUATEMALA - 3
6 ♓ 36	♂	TUNISIA
6 ♓ 39	●	FRANCE - NAPOLEON
6 ♓ 40	⚷	SOUTH AFRICA-REPUBLIC
6 ♓ 41R	⚷	KUWAIT
6 ♓ 45	♄	CHILE 1
6 ♓ 46	⚷	ALBANIA - INDEPENDENCE
6 ♓ 49	☊	TONGA
6 ♓ 50	☊	ROMANIA 1
6 ♓ 53R	⚷	UGANDA
7 ♓ 19R	⚷	NORTH YEMEN
7 ♓ 27	♀	SOUTH AFRICAN REP 1
7 ♓ 30R	♃	CANADA
7 ♓ 46R	♃	TRINIDAD & TOBAGO
7 ♓ 51	M	MEXICO - REVOLUTION
8 ♓ 00R	♅	IRAQ - KINGDOM
8 ♓ 01	☊	GERMANY - THIRD REICH
8 ♓ 28	⊙	LABOUR PARTY 1
8 ♓ 28	M	BANGLADESH 3
8 ♓ 32	⊙	SAHRAWI ARAB D R
8 ♓ 34R	⚷	TRINIDAD & TOBAGO
8 ♓ 44	M	MONGOLIA
8 ♓ 45R	♅	HONDURAS
8 ♓ 45	A	SOUTH AFRICA-REPUBLIC
8 ♓ 46	⊙	USSR-REPUBLIC
8 ♓ 58	M	TEXAS
8 ♓ 58	♂	USSR-REPUBLIC
9 ♓ 03	●	VENDA
9 ♓ 24	M	SENEGAL
9 ♓ 31	♃	HOLY ROMAN FMPIRE
9 ♓ 42R	⚷	JAMAICA
9 ♓ 47	●	ZIMBABWE
9 ♓ 48	♅	EIRE 2
9 ♓ 49	♅	UNITED KINGDOM-1922
9 ♓ 58	M	BOKHARA NAT'L SOVIET RE
10 ♓ 06	☿	S.D.P.
10 ♓ 12	♃	PORTUGAL-REVOLUTION
10 ♓ 22	♅	USSR-FORMATION
10 ♓ 23	♅	EGYPT - INDEPENDENCE
10 ♓ 24	♆	ENGLAND-1689
10 ♓ 25	♅	EGYPT - KINGDOM
10 ♓ 25	⚷	ZANZIBAR
10 ♓ 27	⚷	KENYA
10 ♓ 30R	♄	RHODESIA
10 ♓ 42R	☿	BOKHARA NAT'L SOVIET RE
10 ♓ 44R	⚷	ALGERIA
10 ♓ 47R	⚷	RWANDA-INDEPENDENCE
10 ♓ 47R	⚷	BURUNDI
10 ♓ 48	A	ZIMBABWE-RHODESIA
10 ♓ 48R	♃	JAMAICA
10 ♓ 54	☽	ROMAN EMPIRE 2
11 ♓ 07	A	RHODESIA
11 ♓ 23	M	INDONESIA
11 ♓ 26	☿	ENGLAND-1689
11 ♓ 34	♅	NICARAGUA 2
11 ♓ 34	♄	LONDON 2
11 ♓ 35	♅	FAR EAST REPUBLIC
11 ♓ 40	☽	LEBANON I
11 ♓ 42	M	MALAYSIA
11 ♓ 52R	☿	MONGOLIA
11 ♓ 56	♄	SIKKIM
12 ♓ 02R	♃	ETHIOPIA
12 ♓ 02	♀	ITALY - KINGDOM 1
12 ♓ 05	⊙	MONGOLIA
12 ♓ 05R	♄	LIBERIA
12 ♓ 06R	⚷	MALAYSIA
12 ♓ 15	⊙	TEXAS
12 ♓ 20R	♃	GUINEA - BUISSAU
12 ♓ 41R	♀	ORANGE FREE STATE
12 ♓ 41	♃	BURUNDI
12 ♓ 41	♃	RWANDA-INDEPENDENCE
12 ♓ 41R	♃	ALGERIA
12 ♓ 51R	⚷	SINGAPORE 1
12 ♓ 57	♄	CHILE 2
12 ♓ 59	☽	HUNGARY
13 ♓ 04	♆	ORANGE FREE STATE
13 ♓ 08	M	CARPATHO-UKRAINE
13 ♓ 12	⊙	BOKHARA NAT'L SOVIET RE
13 ♓ 28R	♃	PANAMA
13 ♓ 28	☽	GAGARIN
13 ♓ 29	☊	GREECE REVOLUTION
13 ♓ 31	☿	ST LUCIA
13 ♓ 36	⚷	SWEDEN
13 ♓ 44	●	ARMENIA
13 ♓ 52	♂	USSR-FORMATION
13 ♓ 54R	♅	TURKEY
13 ♓ 56	☽	THAILAND 2
14 ♓ 03	●	DENMARK
14 ♓ 05	●	GEORGIA
14 ♓ 06	●	FRANCE-1st REPUBLIC 2
14 ♓ 17	☽	LEBANON 2

14 ♓ 17	☽	SYRIA 2
14 ♓ 27	●	GERMANY - WEIMAR
14 ♓ 39R	⚷	ZAMBIA
14 ♓ 43	♂	UNITED ARAB EMIR
14 ♓ 49	♅	GUATEMALA - 2
14 ♓ 52R	♃	ECUADOR 1
14 ♓ 58	M	SWAZILAND
15 ♓ 10	☉	GHANA
15 ♓ 11	♀	TRANSCAUCASIAN FED
15 ♓ 13	M	SIKKIM
15 ♓ 25	M	HATAY
15 ♓ 36R	⚷	ARGENTINA - INDEPENDENC
15 ♓ 40	♂	SPAIN
15 ♓ 46	●	KOREA - SOUTH
15 ♓ 47	♃	FIRST MANNED FLIGHT
15 ♓ 50R	♄	SINGAPORE 3
15 ♓ 51R	♄	SINGAPORE 2
15 ♓ 52	●	GUINEA - BUISSAU
15 ♓ 52R	♇	MEXICO - REVOLUTION
15 ♓ 54	♃	BHUTAN
15 ♓ 55R	⚷	MALTA
16 ♓ 20	M	TURKEY
16 ♓ 24	♂	NAURU
16 ♓ 35R	♄	MALDIVES
16 ♓ 48	☿	ORANGE FREE STATE
16 ♓ 56	☊	IRAQ - INDEPENCENCE
16 ♓ 57	♃	CARPATHO-UKRAINE
16 ♓ 57	♃	SLOVAKIA
17 ♓ 00	♇	ARGENTINA - REVOLUTION
17 ♓ 09	⚷	GAMBIA
17 ♓ 26R	♃	GREECE DEMOCRACY
17 ♓ 30	⚷	TANZANIA
17 ♓ 41	⚷	CHILE 1
17 ♓ 56	☽	POLAND 1
18 ♓ 04	♇	PARAGUAY
18 ♓ 08R	⚷	RHODESIA
18 ♓ 15R	♇	VENEZUELA 1
18 ♓ 21	A	ARAB FEDERATION
18 ♓ 22	☽	MALTA
18 ♓ 22	●	KOREA - NORTH
18 ♓ 25	♂	GREECE REVOLUTION
18 ♓ 31	A	PERU-BATTLE AYACUCHO
18 ♓ 43	●	CREATION OF THE WORLD
18 ♓ 43R	⚷	MALAWI
19 ♓ 00	♄	ROMANIA 1
19 ♓ 02	☽	JORDAN
19 ♓ 03	♂	TOGO
19 ♓ 10	♀	PORTUGAL-REVOLUTION
19 ♓ 11	♀	GREECE REVOLUTION
19 ♓ 14	☿	PAKISTAN, REPUBLIC
19 ♓ 22	☽	HOLY ROMAN EMPIRE
19 ♓ 35	♄	LIBERAL PARTY
19 ♓ 42	⚷	LONDON 2
19 ♓ 53	⚷	SIKKIM
20 ♓ 17	M	PAPUA NEW GUINEA
20 ♓ 20	♀	SRI LANKA-IND
20 ♓ 24	☊	THAILAND 2
20 ♓ 26	☿	THAILAND 1
20 ♓ 34	♂	ROME
20 ♓ 52	⚷	CHILE 2
20 ♓ 59	☉	GORBACHEV
21 ♓ 03	☽	CYPRUS - TURKISH
21 ♓ 04	M	VENDA
21 ♓ 10	☊	LIBYA, COUP
21 ♓ 19	☉	MAURITIUS
21 ♓ 28R	⚷	CONSERVATIVE PARTY
21 ♓ 41R	⚷	BARBADOS
21 ♓ 44R	⚷	SINGAPORE 3
21 ♓ 44R	⚷	SINGAPORE 2
21 ♓ 44	A	IRAN - KHOMEINI
22 ♓ 00	●	COMOROS 2
22 ♓ 02	●	SOUTH AFRICAN REP 2
22 ♓ 06	⚷	REAGAN-1
22 ♓ 10R	⚷	MALDIVES
22 ♓ 18	♀	BANGLADESH 2
22 ♓ 18R	⚷	NAMIBIA
22 ♓ 22R	⚷	POLAND 1
22 ♓ 22	♀	GREECE INDEPENCENCE
22 ♓ 29R	♂	BELGIUM
22 ♓ 29	●	GABON
22 ♓ 30	☊	MOON LANDING
22 ♓ 47	☊	ECUADOR 1
22 ♓ 50	⚷	COLUMBIA
22 ♓ 55	♄	BARBADOS
22 ♓ 56	☉	CARPATHO-UKRAINE
22 ♓ 57R	♀	THAILAND 1
22 ♓ 58	☿	LABOUR PARTY 1
22 ♓ 59	☉	SLOVAKIA
23 ♓ 01R	♄	COSTA RICA 2
23 ♓ 11R	⚷	LESOTHO
23 ♓ 21R	⚷	BOTSWANA
23 ♓ 27	♂	BANGLADESH 3
23 ♓ 28R	♄	NEW ZEALAND I
23 ♓ 32	⚷	MEXICO - CONSTITUTION
23 ♓ 34	☉	EGYPT - INDEPENDENCE
23 ♓ 43R	♄	NAMIBIA
23 ♓ 55R	⚷	LUXEMBOURG
23 ♓ 58	☉	EGYPT - KINGDOM
24 ♓ 02	♇	CHILE 1
24 ♓ 06	♄	REAGAN-1
24 ♓ 08R	♇	ARGENTINA - INDEPENDENC
24 ♓ 10	M	AGE OF AQUARIUS-1
24 ♓ 19	M	SLOVAKIA
24 ♓ 19	♄	COLUMBIA
24 ♓ 24	A	MOON LANDING
24 ♓ 31	☊	GUATEMALA - 2
24 ♓ 35	♃	NEPAL
24 ♓ 40	♀	NICARAGUA 2
24 ♓ 42R	☿	ITALY - KINGDOM 1
24 ♓ 42	M	GREECE DEMOCRACY
24 ♓ 43	A	COLUMBIA
24 ♓ 46	⚷	EIRE 1
24 ♓ 47	☉	LONDON 1
24 ♓ 56	☿	U.S. CIVIL WAR
24 ♓ 59	⚷	USSR-REPUBLIC
25 ♓ 07	●	BURUNDI
25 ♓ 11R	♄	LESOTHO
25 ♓ 12	♀	RWANDA-UDI
25 ♓ 14	♂	JAPAN - MEIJI CONST
25 ♓ 20	♇	CHILE 2
25 ♓ 20R	⚷	SOUTH YEMEN 2
25 ♓ 20R	⚷	SOUTH YEMEN 1
25 ♓ 20R	♂	VENEZUELA 2
25 ♓ 23	M	ST KITTS-NEVIS
25 ♓ 27	☽	SAUDI ARABIA
25 ♓ 29R	♄	BOTSWANA
25 ♓ 31	♇	COLUMBIA
25 ♓ 36R	⚷	FINLAND
25 ♓ 37	⚷	LITHUANIA
25 ♓ 37	♂	IRAN - ISLAMIC REP
25 ♓ 39R	⚷	ESTONIA
25 ♓ 44	⚷	GUYANA
25 ♓ 56R	⚷	CANADA
25 ♓ 57	●	RWANDA-INDEPENDENCE
26 ♓ 00R	⚷	USSR-REVOLUTION
26 ♓ 23	☉	ITALY - KINGDOM 1
26 ♓ 32	⚷	UKRAINE
26 ♓ 35	⚷	NAURU
26 ♓ 45	●	SOUTH YEMEN 1
26 ♓ 59	☽	BANGLADESH 1
27 ♓ 06	A	U.S. CIVIL WAR
27 ♓ 14	●	FEDERATION OF ARAB REPU
27 ♓ 14	♅	NATAL
27 ♓ 16R	☿	IRAN - ISLAMIC REP
27 ♓ 18R	♇	ECUADOR 1
27 ♓ 27	☽	CZECHOSLOVAKIA 3
27 ♓ 33	♆	CONFEDERATE STATES AMER
27 ♓ 47R	♇	DOMINICAN REPUBLIC
27 ♓ 51	☿	FAR EAST REPUBLIC
27 ♓ 55	M	NIGERIA
27 ♓ 57	♄	GUYANA
27 ♓ 58R	⚷	ECUADOR 1
28 ♓ 09R	♇	COSTA RICA 1
28 ♓ 12	☽	LONDON 2
28 ♓ 23	♇	GREECE REVOLUTION
28 ♓ 25R	♇	NICARAGUA 1
28 ♓ 30	M	GUATEMALA - 3
28 ♓ 41	A	CREATION OF THE WORLD
28 ♓ 48	⚷	MAURITIUS
28 ♓ 49R	♇	EL SALVADOR
28 ♓ 56R	♇	GUATEMALA - 1
28 ♓ 58	♆	ITALY - KINGDOM 1
29 ♓ 08	☽	ENGLAND-WILLIAM
29 ♓ 11R	⚷	ICELAND
29 ♓ 12R	⚷	YUGOSLAVIA 2
29 ♓ 19	M	MALTA
29 ♓ 20	⚷	BIAFRA
29 ♓ 23R	⚷	LATVIA
29 ♓ 28R	⚷	CZECHOSLOVAKIA 3
29 ♓ 30R	⚷	HUNGARY
29 ♓ 33R	⚷	POLAND 2
29 ♓ 34R	⚷	AUSTRIA
29 ♓ 36R	⚷	GERMANY - WEIMAR
29 ♓ 43R	♇	PERU I
29 ♓ 44	♀	TREATY OF ROME
29 ♓ 45R	♀	ROME
29 ♓ 57R	⚷	YUGOSLAVIA 1
29 ♓ 57	♆	U.S. CIVIL WAR
29 ♓ 59R	⚷	CZECHOSLOVAKIA 2

REFERENCES

Abbreviations:

Newspapers:
DT, *Daily Telegraph*; FT, *Financial Times*; G, *Guardian* and *Manchester Guardian*; IHT, *International Herald Tribune*; NYHT, *New York Herald Tribune*; NYT, *New York Times*; OFNS, *Observer Foreign News Service*; ST, *Sunday Times*; T, *Times*; SWB, *BBC Summary of World Broadcasts*; KCA *Keesing's Contemporary Archives.*

Astrological Journals:
AJ, *Astrological Journal*; AQ, *Astrology Quarterly*; BJA, *British Journal of Astrology*; MA, *Modern Astrology.*

When a horoscope in the text is set for a precise given time, only the source giving that time is cited below. Sources cited following the words 'see also', provide additional information. When a horoscope in the text is not set for a precise given time all the sources used are cited below.

1. T, 19 July 1973, p. 6.
2. T, 18 July 1973, p. 8.
3. SWB, 2nd Series, Pt 3, FE/4349, 18 July 1973.
4. Marmullaku, *Albania and the Albanians*, p. 28; Stavroskendi, *The Albanian National Awakening, 1878–1912.*
5. Marmullaku, op. cit.
6. NYHT, 4 July 1962.
7. *Le Monde*, 4 July 1962; G, 4 July 1962.
8. T, 12 November 1975; KCA.
9. G, 1 November 1981; see also T, 2 November 1981, p. 4, KCA, pp. 31381–2.

10. KCA, p. 16017.

11. *Daily Express*, 15 July 1958.

12. Wright, I. S., and Neckham, L. M., *Historical Dictionary of Argentina*, pp. 538–40; see also Leven, Rivardo, *Ensayo Historico Sabre la Revolucion de Mayo y Mariano Moreno*, 2 vols., Buenos Aires, 1920.

13. Wright and Neckham, op. cit., pp. 202–3; see also Gianello, Leonico, *Historico del Congero de Tucumán*, Academia Nacional de Historia, Buenos Aires, 1966.

14. ISCWA Bulletin No. 4.

15. Letter to the author from Ernesto Cordero.

16. Long, D. M., *A Modern History of Georgia*; Dmtryshyn, Basil, *USSR: A Concise History*.

17. Pipes, Richard, *The Formation of the Soviet Union, Communism and Nationalism, 1917–1923*, p. 298.

18. T, 2 December 1918, p. 7.

19. Langer, *Encyclopaedia of World History*, p. 979.

20. Long, D. M., op. cit.; Langer op. cit., p. 1032.

21. T, 2 January 1901, p. 3.

22. ibid; NYT, 2 January 1901, p. 5.

23. Clark, C. M. H., *A History of Australia*, 2 vols., *Australian Encyclopaedia*.

24. T, 29 October 1946, p. 3.

25. Strong, David F., Austria, *Transition from Empire to Republic*.

26. NYT, 1 November 1918, p. 1.

27. Strong, op. cit., pp. 113–14.

28. ibid., pp. 115–16.

29. McCartney, C. A., *The Hapsburg Empire, 1790–1918*, p. 833.

30. Longville, *Austria*, p. 8.

31. NYT, 1 November 1918, p. 1.

32. Pipes, op. cit., p. 298; Dmytryshyn, op. cit., p. 80; Long, op. cit., p. 207.

33. SWB, 2nd Series, Pt 4, ME/13764/E/1–E/3, 18 August 1971; see also M. H. Abdullah, *The United Arab Emirates, A Modern History*.

34. KCA, p. 25994; NYT, 11 July 1973, p. 2.

35. SWB, 2nd Series, Pt 3 FE/3645/B/13.

36. T, 27 March 1971, p. 1.

37. SWB, 2nd Series, Pt 3 FE/3645/B/17.

38. See for example Dom Moraes, *Mrs Gandhi*, p. 186.

39. SWB, 2nd Series Pt 3 FE/3662/B/4.

40. NYT, 16 December 1971, p. 16.

41. T, 17 December 1971, p. 1.
42. SWB, 2nd Series Pt 3 FE/3868/c/6, 18 December 1971.
43. SWB, 2nd Series Pt 3 FE/3872/c/1, 23 December 1971.
44. T, 30 November 1966, p. 6; KCA, p. 21754.
45. T, 8 October 1830, pp. 2–3.
46. G, 21 November 1981.
47. KCA, p. 17569.
48. KCA, p. 27536.
48a. The Nigerian Mid-Western State proclaimed its independence on 18 August 1967, having set up an internal administration on 15 August. On 20 September the state proclaimed itself the Autonomous Republic of Benin, and on the same day was invaded by Nigerian forces. See KCA, 1967.
49. KCA, p. 25412.
50. KCA, p. 26580.
51. T, 3 June 1974, p. 6.
52. *Whittaker's Almanack* 1986.
53. NYT, 28 May 1967, p. 1.
54. NYT, 31 May 1967, pp. 1, 14; see also T, 31 May 1967, p. 1, KCA, p. 22088, Langer, op. cit., p. 1267.
55. *Whittaker's Almanack* 1925, 1928.
56. Joslin, D. (ed.), *Bolivia: Land, Location and Politics Since 1825*, p. 12.
57. Werlich, David, *Peru: A Short History*, p. 61.
58. ibid., p. 65.
59. Joslin (ed.), op. cit., pp. 12–13.
60. Welich, op. cit., p. 16.
61. ibid., p. 6.
62. ibid., pp. 44–5.
63. DT, 5 December 1977; G, 6 December 1977; see also KCA, p. 28850. NB, T, 6 December 1977, wrongly implies 00.00 hrs on 5 December 1977.
64. T, 30 September 1966.
65. Bombo, Hocha, *Brazilian History*.
66. KCA.
67. KCA, p. 17982.
68. KCA, p. 18396.
69. T, 6 October 1908, p. 5.
70. T, 15 July 1878, p. 8.
71. T, 6 October 1908, p. 5.
72. ibid.
73. Bulgarian Academy of Science (ed.), *Information Bulgaria*, pp. 231–2.

74. NYT, 5 August 1960; *Le Monde*, 5 August 1960.
75. KCA, p. 9035.
76. T, 5 January 1949.
77. NYT, 1 July 1962; *Le Soir*, 1/2 July 1962.
78. Pipes, op. cit., p. 151.
79. NYT, 1 January 1960.
80. NYT, 2 July 1867, p. 1.
81. Official Timetable supplied by Canada House, London.
82. KCA, p. 27260.
83. Shirer, W., *The Rise and Fall of the Third Reich*, pp. 449–50.
84. KCA, p. 17612.
85. Langer, op. cit., p. 1268.
86. KCA, p. 28172.
87. KCA, p. 28811.
88. KCA, p. 17612.
89. Langer, op. cit., p. 840.
90. Bizzaro, Salvatore, *Historical Dictionary of Chile*, p. 195.
91. McAleavy, Henry, *Modern History of China*, p. 182, 279.
92. ibid., Langer, op. cit., p. 916.
93. Sun Yat-sen, *Autobiography*.
94. McAleavy, op. cit.
95. SWB, Summary of New China News Agency broadcast of 9.00 p.m. GMT, 21 September 1949.
96. T, 22 September 1949, p. 4.
97. NYT, 1 October 1949, p. 1.
98. SWB, Summary of New China News Agency broadcast of 1 October 1949.
99. T, 2 October 1949.
100. NYT, 3 October 1949, p. 2.
101. Carter, Charles, *An Introduction to Political Astrology*, p. 65, citing the *Astrological Magazine* (Bangalore), March 1950, p. 213.
102. NYT, 26 December 1947, p. 3.
103. *Rand Daily Mail*, 4 December 1981, FT, 4 December 1981.
104. Langer, op. cit.
105. KCA, p. 27282; NYT, FT, IHT, 7 July 1975.
106. KCA, p. 27561.
107. Official Records of the First Session of the Provisional Congress of the Confederate States of America in *Official Records of the War of the Rebellion*, Series V, US Government Printing Office, 1880–1901; see Long, E. B., *The Civil War Day by Day*.
108. Langer, op. cit.

109. *Sunday Mail Magazine*, 7–13 April 1985, p. 3.
110. KCA, p. 17612.
111. Langer, op. cit., p. 1269.
112. ibid., p. 878.
113. ibid., p. 880.
114. Bancroft, Hubert Bowe, *History of Central America*, Vol. III, p. 49.
115. ibid., pp. 209, 230.
116. NYT, 11 December 1898, p. 1.
117. ibid., p. 4.
118. NYT, 21 May 1902, p. 1.
119. See for example, the *Observer* magazine, 27 January 1983, p. 28.
120. NYT, 4 January 1959, p. 1.
121. T, 16 August 1960, p. 6.
122. SWB, Pt 4, 2nd Series, ME/7492, 16 November 1983.
123. Opocensky, Jan, *The Collapse of the Austro-Hungarian Empire and the Rise of the Czechoslovak State*. p. 42.
124. ibid., pp. 51–2.
125. Masaryk, Thomas, *The Making of a State*, p. 270. According to S. Harrison Thomson in *Czechoslovakia in European History* (London, 1965), p. 324, the Czech National Council in Paris also declared independence on 18 October 1918.
126. Opocensky, op. cit., p. 93.
127. ibid.
128. ibid., p. 102.
129. ibid., p. 117; Thomson, op. cit.
130. Opocensky, op. cit., p. 117.
131. Thomson, op. cit., p. 214.
132. Opocensky, op. cit., p. 214.
133. ibid., p. 64.
134. ibid., p. 214.
135. ibid., p. 215.
136. Thomson, op. cit., pp. 446–7.
137. T, 16 November 1920.
138. Hovde, B. J., *The Scandinavian Countries, 1720–1865*; see also Lauring, Palle, *A History of the Kingdom of Denmark*.
139. T, DT, 27 June 1977.
140. T, 2 November 1978, 4 November 1978; FT, 3 November 1978.
141. Langer, op. cit., p. 861.
142. ibid., pp. 862, 1073.
143. ibid., p. 842.

144. Delpar, Helen (ed.), *Encyclopaedia of Latin America*.

145. ibid; Langer, op. cit., p. 851.

146. Depar, op. cit.

147. Hansard, 28 February 1922, p. 225; see also Correspondence Respecting Affairs in Egypt, 1922, Cmnd 1592 (*Parliamentary Accounts and Papers 1922, Vol. XXIII, 25*); *Egyptian Mail*, 28 February, 1922, p. 1.

148. Hansard, 14 March 1922, col. 2126.

149. *Egyptian Gazette*, 16 March 1922.

150. *Egyptian Mail*, 16 march 1922, p. 1; see also T, 17, 20, 22 March 1922.

151. T, 24 July 1952, p. 6., SWB, Pt IV, no. 280, p. 24, 29 July 1952.

152. SWB, Pt IV, no. 281, 1 August, 1952, p. 44.

153. SWB, Pt IV, no. 373, p. 26, 23 June 1953.

154. NYT, 19 June 1953, p. 1.

155. T, 26 April 1916, p. 6.

156. T, 7 December 1922, p. 12. James Russell in AJ, Vol. 3, June 1961, argued that 00.00 hrs on 6 December 1922 was effectively regarded as the moment of independence, citing *The Times*, 7 December 1922 and the terms of the Irish Treaty of 6 December 1921. However, I remain unconvinced on the basis of my own reading of the account of the signing of the Irish Treaty (see *Irish Times*, 7 December 1921, p. 5) and of accounts of the independence of the Irish Free State given in the *Irish Times*, 6 and 7 December 1922. The latter makes it clear that the state came into existence when the King signed the proclamation bringing the constitution into operation. The Parliament itself assembled in Dublin at 5.05 p.m. on 6 December and the swearing in of members began at 5.15 p.m. (see *Irish Times*, 7 December 1921). It is clear that the Irish Government itself waited until after the King signed the proclamation.

It is worth noting that contemporary press comment made much of the fact that independence in fact was of little consequence, and that the Free State had had home-rule for the previous year. Historical evidence therefore diminishes the importance of the 1922 horoscope, necessarily reinforcing the significance of that for 1916.

156a. Russel, op. cit., reports that the King held a privy council meeting starting at 1.00 p.m. and concluding before 3.00 p.m., at which the proclamation may have been signed.

157. T, 19 April 1949, p. 4.

158. Bancroft, op. cit., p. 48.
159. ibid., p. 168.
160. NYT, 13 October 1968, G, 14 October 1968.
161. NYT, 31 December 1975.
162. Langer, op. cit., p. 971; Dmytryshyn, op. cit., p. 80.
163. Langer, op. cit., p. 971; Pipes, op. cit., p. 298; *Whittaker's Almanack* 1925.
164. Bilmanis, Alfred, *A History of Latvia*, p. 303.
165. Halliday, Fred, and Molyneux, Maxine, *The Ethiopian Revolution*.
166. DT, 27 February 1974; see also NYT, 27 February 1974.
167. T, 13 September 1974; see also FT, 13 September 1974.
168. T, 22 march 1975; IHT, 22, 27 March 1975.
169. T, 13 September 1974.
170. Langer, op. cit., p. 1032.
171. SWB, ME/3778/i, 2 September 1971.
172. ibid.
173. ibid.
174. G, 3 October 1984, p. 8.
175. OFNS, no. 28168, 8 October 1970; T, FT, DT, NYT, *Straits Times*, 10 October 1970; Hindu, 11 October 1970.
176. Bowder, R, Kerensky, A, *The Russian Provisional Government, 1917*, chap. 7:303, p. 341.
177. ibid., chap. 7:305.
178. ibid., chap. 7:311.
179. Wuorinen, John H., *A History of Finland*, p. 215; Carr, E. H., *The Bolshevik Revolution*, Vol. 1, p. 294.
180. Houtin, Albert, *Les Séances des députés du clergé aux États Généraux de 1789*, p. 139. For the early history of France see James, Edward, *The Origins of France, 500–1000* (London, 1982); Latouche, Robert, *Caesar to Charlemagne* (London, 1965).
181. Hibbert, Christopher, *The French Revolution*, p. 59; Leathers, Stanley (ed.), *Cambridge Modern History*, Vol. VIII, p. 155.
182. Journal Officiel de la Convention Nationale: La Convention Nationale, 1792, 21 September 1792. See also Collection Générale Des Loix, Proclamations, Instructions Et Autre Actes Du Pouvoir Executif, p. 556.
183. Overture de la Convention National, pp. 3–4.
184. Leathers (ed.), op. cit., Vol. VIII, p. 261.
185. ibid., p. 686.
186. Langer, op. cit., p. 686.

187. Collier, Richard, *1940, The World in Flames*.

188. Royal Institute for International Affairs Press Library, Chatham House, London.

189. NYT, 2 June 1958.

190. Carter, op. cit., p. 61.

191. *BBC Daily Digest of World Broadcasts*, no. 2642, p. 1A1, 15 October 1946.

192. T, G, NYHT, 6 October 1958.

193. G, T, 7 October 1958. The horoscope for the fixing of the great seal is of prime symbolic significance and has been used as a national chart by French astrologers, According to one such, Alexander Volguine, writing in the *Astrological Journal*, the seal was fixed to the Constitution sometime between 6.20 p.m. and 6.45 p.m. in Paris.

194. G, 8 January 1958.

195. NYT, 2 June 1958.

196. KCA, p. 17612.

197. T, 18 February 1965.

198. Long, D. M., op. cit., p. 207.

199. Langer, op. cit., p. 1032.

200. Tulloch, B. D., *The Life of the Emperor William*, p. 70.

201. T, 20 January 1871, p. 5. NYT, 22 January 1871, p. 1. The fact that the Imperial Constitution had already been adopted may account for the lack of general interest in the coronation in the press.

202. NYT, 22 January 1871, p. 1.

203. NYT, 21 December 1870.

204. Strauss, G. L. M., *Emperor William*, p. 330.

205. Forbes, Archibald, *William of Germany: A Succinct Biography*, p. 297.

206. NYT, 11 November 1918, p. 1.

207. ibid., NYT, 13 November 1918, p. 2.

208. NYT, 11 November 1918, p. 1.

209. Carter, op. cit., p. 61.

210. Strasser, Otto, *Hitler and I*, p. 154.

211. Shirer, op. cit., p. 188.

212. Goering, Herman, *Germany Reborn*, p. 114.

213. Carter, op. cit., p. 61.

214. Fest, Joachim, *Hitler*, pp. 365–6.

215. Shirer, op. cit., p. 226.

216. ibid., p. 1133, 1136.

217. Whiting, Charles, *Finale at Flensburg*; Steinert, Maurice,

Capitulation 1945: The Story of the Donitz Regime; see also Longmate, Norman, *When We Won the War*, giving the date of the arrest as 22 May.

218. NYT, 8 October 1949, p. 122.
219. SWB, Pt III, no. 6, p. 13, 1 June 1949.
220. SWB, Pt III, no. 254, pp. 2–3, 31 March 1954; see also T, 26 March 1954, p. 6.
221. SWB, Pt III, no. 6, p. 40, 1 June 1949.
222. T, 6 May 1955, p. 10.
223. T, 6 March 1957, 7 March 1957.
224. Clogey, Richard, *A Short History of Modern Greece*, p. 53; SWB, Pt. IV, no. 65930, March 1956, p. 3.
225. Clogey, Richard, op. cit., p. 5.
226. Finlay, G., *History of Greece*, Vol 7, p. 53.
227. G, 24 July 1984, p. 17; see also T, 25 July 1974, p. 1.
228. T, 7 February 1974, p. 1.
229. Bancroft, op. cit., p. 33.
230. ibid., pp. 160, 189.
231. ibid., pp. 207–8.
232. DT, NYT, 1 October 1958.
234. NYT, 30 September 1958.
235. DT, 30 September 1958.
236. KCA, p. 16600.
236a. G, T, DT, FT, 27 September 1973; *Le Monde*, 28 September 1973.
236b. SWB, 2nd Series, Pt. 4, ME/4701/B14, 12 September 1974.
236c. *Christian Science Monitor* (London edn), 9 September 1973; G, 9, 10 September 1973.
237. KCA, p. 21428; see also T, 26 May 1966.
238. Perusse, Roland, *Historical Dictionary of Haiti*, p. XII.
239. ibid., p. XIII.
240. ibid.
241. ibid.
242. Langer, op. cit., p. 1090.
243. 'Annales regni Francorum' in Sullivan, Richard E. (ed.), *The Coronation of Charlemagne*.
244. Bancroft, op. cit., p. 164.
245. Opočensky, op. cit., p. 103.
246. Strong, David, op. cit., p. 100. Langer, op. cit., p. 1019, gives 17 October 1918 for the proclamation of the republic, though not independence.
247. NYT, 1 November 1918, p. 1.

248. NYT, 30 October 1918.
249. Sinor, Denis, *A History of Hungary*, p. 282.
250. NYT, 4 November 1918.
251. Strong, op. cit., p. 114.
252. Siner, op. cit., p. 283; Langer, op. cit., p. 1019.
253. See NYT, 1 February 1949.
254. NYT, 14 September 1948, p. 1.
256. Gjersel, Knut, *History of Iceland*, p. 448.
257. NYT, 17 June 1944, p. 3.
258. T, 19 June 1944, p. 3.
259. T, 15 August 1947, p. 4.
260. NYT, 26 January 1950, p. 1.
261. Langer, op. cit., p. 1334.
262. NYT, 5 May 1947, p. 10.
263. NYT, 28 December 1949, p. 1.
264. NYT, 11 August 1954, p. 1.
265. G, 21 August 1985.
266. Langer, op. cit., p. 897.
267. ibid., p. 1097.
268. According to research by Michael Baigent.
269. Langer, op. cit., p. 1099.
270. According to research by Michael Baigent.
271. Langer, op. cit., p. 1099.
272. NYT, 17 January 1977, p. 1.
273. NYT, 12 February 1979, p. 1.
274. NYT, 2 February 1979, p. 1.
275. According to research by Michael Baigent.
276. FT, 2 April 1979. IHT, 2 April 1979, reported that Khomeini's proclamation was read by an announcer.
277. DT, 2 April 1979.
278. NYT, 1 April 1979.
279. FT, IHT, G, NYT, 2 April 1979.
280. T, 24 August 1921, p. 7.
281. T, 5 October 1932, p. 13.
282. *Daily Express*, 15 July 1958; also research by Michael Baigent citing SWB.
283. *Le Monde*, 15 July 1958, gives 'vers sept heures'.
284. *Daily Express*, 15 July 1958.
285. KCA, p. 19323.
286. Bar-Zohar, Michael, *Ben Gurion*, p. 162.
287. ibid., p. 159.
288. ibid., p. 162.

289. ibid., p. 151.

290. ibid., p. 162.

291. ibid.

292. Baigent, Michael; Campion, Nicholas; Harvey, Charles, *Mundane Astrology*, p. 459.

293. ibid., p. 163.

294. ibid.

295. T, 20 September 1870.

296. T, 18 March 1861, p. 9.

297. It was, however, possible that the *Official Gazette* was published in the evening. See the report of 18 March in *The Times*; see T, 3 July 1871, p. 5.

298. Baigent, Campion, Harvey, op. cit., p. 454.

299. NYT, 22 September 1870, p. 1; T, 22 September 1870, p. 3; T, 24 September 1870, p. 5.

300. T, 4 July 1871, p. 12.

301. NYT, 11 June 1946, p. 12; see also p. 1.

302. NYT, 14 June 1946, p. 1, 3; T, 14 June 1946, p. 4.

303. Leathers (ed.), *Cambridge Modern History*, Vol. VIII, p. 797.

304. KCA, p. 17569.

305. NYT, 7 August 1962, p. 14; see also T, 6 August 1962, p. 6, *Sunday Telegraph*, 5 August 1962.

306. Langer, op. cit., p. 150.

307. T, 14 February 1889, p. 5; Storry, Richard, *A History of Modern Japan*, p. 116.

308. Report by Japanese astrologer Toshitaka Hifumi of Yokahama to James Russell, Vice-President of the Astrological Association.

309. NYT, 4 November 1946, p. 1.

310. T, 5 may 1947, p. 4, see also NYT, 3 May 1947, p. 1.

311. *Daily Herald*, 29 April 1952.

312. NYT, 28 April 1952.

313. NYT, 28 April 1952, p. 1, 29 April 1952.

314. NYT, 28 April 1952, p. 1.

315. G, 26 April 1952.

316. Langer, op. cit., p. 1091.

317. *Whittaker's Almanack*, 1944, p. 828, 830.

318. Langer, op. cit., p. 1091.

319. ibid.

320. *Whittaker's Almanack*, 1925.

321. T, 22 March 1946, p. 3, 23 March 1946, p. 4; NYT, 23 March 1946, p. 6; KCA, p. 73839, 13–20 April 1946.

322. T, 23 March 1946, p. 4; NYT, 23 March 1946, p. 6.

323. T, 26 May 1946, p. 3, 27 May 1946, p. 4; NYT, 26 May 1946, p. 1.

324. NYT, 21 July 1954.

325. SWB, 2nd Series, FE/3333/A3/7, 19 March 1970.

326. SWB, 2nd Series, FE/3504/A3/6, 10 October 1970.

327. T, 18 April 1975.

328. T, 12 December 1963.

329. Information supplied to the author by *Guardian* journalist Paul Keel, who was present at the meeting; see also G, 14 June 1984, p. 3.

330. IHT, 13 July 1979.

331. *Statesman's Year Book* 1985.

332. Langer, op. cit.

333. SWB, Pt. III, no. 64. 19 August 1948.

334. NYT, 16 August 1948.

335. G, 20 June 1961; T, 20 June 1961, p. 12.

336. Exchange of Notes regarding Relations between the United Kingdom of Great Britain and Northern Ireland and the State of Kuwait, Kuwait, 19 June 1961, 1960–61, Cmnd 1409, Vol. XXXIV, p. 621.

337. G, 20 June 1961; ST, 25 June 1961.

338. Langer, op. cit., p. 1332.

339. ibid.

340. *Le Monde*, 23 October 1953; see also NYT, T, G, 23 October 1953, *Le Monde*, G, 24 October 1953.

341. NYT, 21 July 1954.

342. KCA, p. 22779.

343. Dmytryshyn, op. cit., p. 80.

344. Langer, op. cit., p. 971; Pipes, op. cit., p. 298.

345. Bilmanis, op. cit., p. 303.

346. ibid., pp. 307–8; *Whittaker's Almanack* 1925; Langer, op. cit., p. 1046.

347. Langer, op. cit., p. 1214.

348. NYT, 27 November 1941, p. 11; T, 27 November 1941, p. 11.

349. NYT, 12 November 1843, p. 1.

350. NYT, 23 November 1943, p. 5.

351. *Statesman's Year Book*, 1957.

352. T, 4 October 1966; KCA, p. 35669; KCA gives 'midnight' on 3 October, meaning 24.00 hrs (see p. 21669).

353. Langer, op. cit., p. 811.

354. ibid., p. 875; see also Dunn and Holsoe, *Historical Dictionary*

of Liberia, p. XIII, NYT, 27 April 1947, p. 51.

355. *Le Monde, Le Stampa*, 25 December 1951; see also NYT, 25 December 1951, p. 1.

356. T, 3 September 1969, p. 1, quoting Middle East News Agency.

357. Le Duc Astraude, *Les Petits Etats D'Europe*.

358. *Whittaker's Almanack*, 1986.

359. Langer, op. cit., p. 340.

360. Bowder, Kerensky, op. cit., chap. 7:372, p. 406.

361. ibid., chap 7:373, p. 406.

362. Pipes, op. cit., p. 298; Langer, op. cit., p. 1031; Dmytryshyn, op. cit., p. 80.

363. *Whittaker's Almanack*, 1925.

364. T, 21 February 1928, p. 15.

365. Langer, op. cit., p. 1214.

366. Steinberg, S. H., *Historical Tables*.

367. Forbes, op. cit., p. 208.

368. Langer, op. cit.

369. KCA, p. 17514, 26 June 1960; *Whittaker's Almanack*, 1986.

370. NYHT, 27 June 1960; T, 27 June 1960.

371. T, 6 July 1964; KCA, p. 20157.

372. T, 31 August 1957, p. 7.

373. Information supplied to K. C. Foong of Malaysia by the National Archive of Kuala Lumpur.

374. Information supplied to author by K. C. Foong of Malaysia.

375. Campion, N., *British Foreign Policy with Particular Reference to the Strategic Importance of Malaysia and Singapore in the Period Immediately Following Independence, 1961–1963*.

376. T, 16 September 1963, p. 8; *Straits Times*, 16 September 1963, p. 1; KCA, p. 19720.

377. *Straits Times*, 16 September 1963, p. 1.

378. Information supplied to author by K. C. Foong of Malaysia.

379. Dawn, 28 July 1965.

380. Agreement between Her Majesty's Government of the United Kingdom of Great Britain and Northern Ireland and the Government of the Maldive Islands (with Exchange of Letters), Colombo, 26 July 1965, 1964–65, Cmnd 2749, Vol. XXXIV, p. 409.

381. DT, 27 July 1965.

383. *The Hindu*, 26 July 1965.

384. T, 27 July 1965, 'the Maldive Islands are to become fully independent'.

385. KCA. p. 17513.

386. KCA, p. 17685.
387. KCA, p. 17687.
388. *Le Monde*, NYHT, T, 23 September 1960; *Le Monde*, NYT, DT, 24 September 1960.
389. T, 22 September 1964, p. 10; see also KCA, p. 20311, which refers to the 'instruments of independence being handed over after the flag was hoisted at midnight' on the previous day, i.e. 24.00 hrs on 20 September 1964.
390. KCA, p. 17799.
391. KCA, p. 22596; see also *Whittaker's Almanack*, 1986.
392. Mayer, Michael C., Sherman, William L., *The Course of Mexican History*, p. 287.
393. Briggs, Donald C., Alisky, Marvin, *Historical Dictionary of Mexico*.
394. Atkin, Ronald, *Revolution: Mexico 1910–1920*, p. 5.
395. Letter from the Librarian of the Mexican Embassy in London to Charles Harvey, 1984 (copy in the possession of the author); see also the account given in Bancroft, *History of Central America*.
396. See Atkin, op. cit., p. 5.
397. Langer, op. cit., p. 843.
398. Mayer, Sherman, op. cit., pp. 295–6.
399. NYT, 1 February 1917, p. 7.
400. Le Duc Astraude, *Le Principauté de Monaco*, p. 4.
401. KCA, p. 9994.
402. Astraude, op. cit., pp. 5–13.
403. KCA, p. 9994.
404. KCA, p. 10676.
405. Astraude, op. cit., p. 9.
406. Carr, op. cit., Vol. 3, pp. 494–6, 507.
407. *Statesman's Year Book*, 1986.
408. Carr, op. cit., p. 507.
409. Langer, op. cit., p. 1106.
410. Carr, op. cit., p. 507.
411. ibid., p. 513.
412. *Whittaker's Almanack* 1913.
413. Langer, op. cit., p. 762.
414. T, 15 July 1878, p. 8.
415. Langer, op. cit., p. 874.
416. G, T, *Scotsman*, NYT, NYHT, 3 March 1956; *Le Monde*, 5 March 1956; T, NYHT, 6 March 1956; NYHT, 9 March 1956.
417. *Le Monde*, 29 May 1956; see also T, *Combat, Christian Science*

Monitor, 29 May 1956, T, 30 May 1956.

418. See for example Langer, op. cit., p. 1288.

419. ibid.

420. KCA, p. 27245.

421. Langer, op. cit., p. 1083.

422. ibid., p. 1277.

423. ibid., p. 885.

424. ibid.

425. Vincent, Benjamin, *Haydn's Book of Dates*, p. 938.

426. ibid.; Langer, op. cit., p. 885.

427. *Whittaker's Almanack* 1925.

428. NYT, 31 January 1968; *Le Monde*, 1 February 1968; see also KCA, p. 22500, T, 1 February 1968, p. 5.

429. KCA, p. 27062.

430. Langer, op. cit., p. 408.

431. Motley, *The Rise of the Dutch Republic*, Vol. 5, p. 225.

432. T, 27 September 1907, p. 7.

433. The author has in his possession several articles by New Zealand astrologer Dennis Frank which it is hoped to make available through the ISCWA *Bulletin of Mundane Astrology*.

434. Baigent, Campion and Harvey, op. cit., p. 461.

435. Bancroft, op. cit., p. 47.

436. Langer, op. cit., p. 843.

437. ibid.

438. Bancroft, op. cit., p. 178; see also Mayer, Harvey, K., *Historical Dictionary of Nicaragua*, p. 295, Longville, op. cit., p. 111, Delpar, op. cit., p. 415.

439. Bancroft, op. cit., p. 168.

440. Bancroft, op. cit., p. 210.

441. DT, 18 July 1979.

442. NYT, 18 July 1979.

443. DT, 16 July 1979.

444. G, 19 July 1979.

445. NYT, 20 July 1979.

446. DT, 20 July 1979.

447. G, 21 July 1979.

448. See summary of press reports in *Bulletin of Mundane Astrology*, no. 7, December 1983, pp. 11–12.

449. G, 20 July 1979.

450. KCA, p. 17569.

451. T, 1 October 1960.

452. Langer, op. cit., p. 219.

453. ibid., p. 336.
454. ibid., p. 747.
455. T, 8 June 1905, p. 5.
456. Bevan Andrew, 'The National Chart of Norway' in *CAO Times*, Vol. 6, no. 1, 1984.
457. Langer, op. cit., p. 749.
458. T, 27 July 1970, 31 July 1970.
459. *Statesman's Year Book*, 1986.
460. G, 26 April 1982, p. 8; G, 3 December 1982, p. 13; Akehurst, John, *We Won a War*.
461. Vincent, op. cit., p. 1010; Langer, op. cit., p. 886.
462. Vincent, op. cit., p. 1010.
463. Langer, op. cit., p. 890.
464. Vincent, op. cit., p. 1010.
465. T, 15 August 1947, p. 4.
466. DT, 24 March 1956; see also NYT, 23 March 1956.
467. Dawn, 25 March 1956.
468. Bar Zohar, op. cit., p. 162.
469. Langer, op. cit., p. 1091.
470. According to research by Michael Baigent.
471. NYT, 4 November 1903, p. 1.
472. T, 16 September 1975, p. 7.
473. Langer, op. cit., p. 840.
474. Steinberg, op. cit.
475. Delpar, op. cit.
476. Langer, op. cit., p. 840.
477. Werlich, op. cit., pp. 39–40.
478. ibid., p. 58.
479. Werlich, op. cit., p. 61; see also Vincent, op. cit., p. 1063; Langer, op. cit., p. 840–1.
480. Werlich, op. cit., p. 65.
481. ibid.
482. ibid., pp. 44–5.
483. ibid., pp. 70–72.
484. Langer, op. cit., p. 937.
485. NYT, 11 December 1898, p. 1.
486. Letter to Philippines astrologer Serafin Lanot from the National Historical Institute, confirmed by local newspaper reports of 5 July 1946.
487. ibid.
488. NYT, 4 July 1946, p. 1.
489. Rafal Prinke, 'Poland', in *CAO Times*, Vol. 5, no. 1, 16 February

1982, p. 16.

490. Langer, op. cit., p. 257.

491. Prinke, op. cit.

492. Langer, op. cit., p. 442.

493. ibid., p. 512.

494. ibid., p. 642.

495. ibid., p. 644.

496. ibid., p. 750.

497. ibid.

498. Browder and Kerensky, op. cit., chap. 7:282–3; Davies, Norman, *God's Playground: A History of Poland*, Vol. 2, p. 384; Langer, op. cit.

499. Davies, op. cit., p. 386.

500. Browder and Kerensky, op. cit., chap. 7:279; Davies, op. cit., p. 386.

501. Browder and Kerensky, op. cit., chap. 7:283.

502. ibid.

503. Langer, op. cit., p. 1037.

504. Davies, op. cit., p. 391.

504a. There is some doubt concerning the time zone in use in Poland on 11 November 1918. Polish astrologer Rafal Prinke in *CAO Times*, vol. 7, no. 1, stated that in November 1918 Poland was using Central European Time (GMT plus 1 hour), in which case the German surrender in the West at 11.00 a.m. GMT would have taken place at 12.00 noon Warsaw time. However, in the *International Atlas*, Thomas Shanks reports that in November 1918 Warsaw was using GMT plus two hours, in which case the time in Warsaw at the surrender of the German armies in the West would have been 1.00 p.m., and 12.00 noon in Warsaw corresponded to 10.00 a.m. GMT. In spite of Rafal Prinke's obvious authority as a Polish astrologer, for the sake of consistency throughout this book, the zone difference used here is that given in the *International Atlas*. The horoscope for 11 November in Warsaw is therefore set for 10.00 a.m. GMT, one hour before the German surrender in the West. The question is in urgent need of further investigation.

505. Davies, op. cit., p. 391.

506. Carter, op. cit., p. 62; see also Prinke, op. cit.

507. Baigent, Campion, Harvey, op. cit., pp. 373–9.

508. Bethell, *The War Hitler Won, September 1939*.

509. Cooper and Lucas, *Hitler's Elite*.

510. Prinke, *CAO Times*, Vol. 5, no. 1, 16 February 1982, p. 18.
511. Langer, op. cit., p. 1219.
512. ibid.
513. Langer, op. cit., p. 1220.
514. SWB, July 1945.
515. Langer, op. cit., p. 253.
516. Livermore, H. V., *A New History of Portugal*, p. 317.
517. Langer, op. cit., p. 699.
518. Livermore, op. cit.
519. See the NYT, DT, T, 26 April 1974.
520. G, 26 April 1974, p. 1.
521. Abdullah, Mohammed Morry, *The United Arab Emirates, A Modern History*, p. 141; NYT, 8 September 1971.
522. NYT, 8 September 1971.
523. SWB, 2nd Series ME/3777/A/9, 3 September 1971.
524. Langer, op. cit., p. 353.
525. ibid., p. 888.
526. ibid.
527. ibid., p. 889.
528. ibid., p. 1084.
529. ibid., p. 1274.
593. ibid.
594. SWB, 2nd Series ME/2010/E/1 CB, 12 November 1965.
595. Langer, op. cit., p. 1275.
596. See SWB, 3 March 1970.
597. KCA, p. 29759.
598. G, 1 June 1985, p. 7; see also G, 2 June 1985, p. 5.
599. T, 18 April 1980; see also T, 19 April 1980.
600. Langer, op. cit., p. 352; Nicol, D. M., *The End of the Byzantine Empire*, p. 89.
601. Boak, Arthur E., Sinnigen, William, *A History of Rome to AD 565*, p. 254; see also Scullard, H. H., *From the Gracchi to Nero*, p. 210.
602. Boak and Sinnigen, op. cit., p. 255; Scullard, op. cit., p. 210.
603. ibid.
604. Boak and Sinnigen, op. cit., p. 255.
605. ibid.
606. Scullard, op. cit., p. 212.
607. *Encyclopaedia Britannica*.
608. Dio Cassius, *History*, Book LVI:25.
609. See Campion, N., *An Introduction to the History of Astrology*.
610. Tacitus, *Annales*, Book XII, chapters LXVIII to LXIX; see

Campion, N., 'Roman Astrology' in *AQ*, Vol. 58, no. 1, Spring 1984.

611. Fullard, Harold, and Treharne, R. F. (ed.), *Muir's Historical Atlas*, p. 33.
612. Langer, op. cit., p. 766.
613. ibid., p. 767.
614. T, 15 July 1878, p. 8.
615. Langer, op. cit., p. 1213.
616. NYT, DT, 30 January 1961.
617. *Le Soir*, 29–30 January 1961.
618. OFNS., no. 16617, 31 January 1961.
619. NYT, 1 July 1962, *Le Soir*, 1–2 July 1962.
620. KCA, p. 27747.
621. G, 20 September 1983.
622. NYT, 22 February 1979; DT, 23 February 1979; FT, 24 February 1979.
623. G, 26 October 1979; NYT, 28 October 1979.
624. *Le Soir*, 16 July 1975.
625. Hsinhua News Agency, 13 July 1975.
626. Langer, op. cit., p. 1094; G, 2 April 1986, p. 17.
627. *Whittaker's Almanack* 1925.
628. Langer, op. cit., p. 965.
629. ibid.
630. ibid., p. 1093; *Statesman's Year Book*, 1984–5.
631. Langer, op. cit., p. 1093.
632. *Statesman's Year Book*, 1984–5.
633. G, 2 April 1986, p. 17.
634. ibid., *Whittaker's Almanack* 1925.
635. KCA, p. 17685.
636. Langer, op. cit., p. 1265.
637. KCA, p. 17513.
638. ibid., p. 17685.
639. ibid.
640. Langer, op. cit., p. 265.
641. ibid.
642. ibid., p. 757.
643. T, 15 July 1878, p. 8.
644. KCA, p. 27852.
645. T, 27 April 1961, p. 14.
646. *Hindu*, 28 March 1965.
647. NYT, 4 April 1965.
648. *Hindu*, 5 April 1965.

649. T, 5 April 1965.

650. ibid.

651. Langer, op. cit., p. 908.

652. See Campion, *British Foreign Policy with Particular Reference to the Strategic Importance of Malaysia and Singapore in the Period Immediately Following Independence, 1961–1963*.

653. T, 16 September 1963, p. 1; *Straits Times*, 16 September 1963, p. 1; KCA, p. 19720.

654. *Straits Times*, 31 August 1963; see also *Sunday Telegraph*, 1 September 1963.

655. T, 2 September 1963; *Sunday Times* (Malaysia), 1 September 1963; *Sunday Telegraph*, 1 September 1963; KCA.

656. *Straits Times*, 31 August 1965.

657. NYT, 10 August 1965.

658. *Straits Times*, 10 August 1963.

659. Letter to the author from K. C. Foong.

660. Campion, N., *Historical and Chronological Analaysis for Malaya, 1957–1963, Malaysia, 1963–1975*, Appendix 1; see also *Straits Times*, 10 August 1963, *Sunday Times* of Singapore, 15 August 1963.

661. *Straits Times*, 10 August 1963.

662. Brissaud, André, *The Nazi Secret Service*; see also Shirer, op. cit., p. 442.

663. KCA, p. 29371; see also T, 7 July 1978, p. 9.

664. T, G, *Daily Express*, 27 June 1960.

665. T, NYT, G, 1 July 1960; see also *Daily Herald*, 29 June 1960.

666. Vincent, op. cit., p. 1381.

667. Langer, op. cit., p. 886.

668. ibid.

669. ibid.

670. ibid.

671. T, 31 May 1910.

672. T, 31 May 1961.

673. Letter from South African astrologer George Taylor to Derek Appleby, see AQ, Spring 1983, Vol. 57, no. 1, p. 37.

674. ibid.; also letter from South African Embassy to the author confirming sequence and significance of events.

675. Langer, op. cit., p. 134.

676. ibid., p. 177–8.

677. Hillgarth, J. N., *The Spanish Kingdoms*, 1250–1576, Vol. 2, p. 361; see also Prescott, W. H., *History of the Reign of Ferdinand and Isabella*.

678. Langer, op. cit., p. 417.
679. See the NYT, 23 November 1975; G, 24 November 1975, p. 1.
680. According to research by Michael Baigent.
681. NYT, 23 November 1975; G, 28 November 1975, p. 3.
682. *Times of Ceylon*, 4 February 1948, p. 1.
683. ibid.
684. SWB, monitoring Colombo Home Service Broadcast in English, 12.45 p.m. GMT, 22 May 1972.
685. NYHT, 2 January 1956.
686. Cairo Radio monitored by SWB, Pt IV, no. 635, p. 41.
687. NYT, G, 2 January 1956.
688. T, NYT, G, 2 January 1956.
689. NYT, T, 2 January 1956.
690. G, 2 January 1956.
691. *La Bourse Egyptienne*, 2 January 1956.
692. FT, 25 November 1975; *Hindu*, 26 November 1975; *Le Monde*, 28 November 1975.
693. T, 6 September 1968; see also T, 7 September 1968.
694. Oakley, Stewart, *The Story of Sweden*; Langer, op. cit., pp. 185–7, 219.
695. Langer, op. cit., p. 747.
696. Oakley, op. cit., p. 538.
697. ibid., p. 204.
698. Martin, W., *A History of Switzerland*, p. 31.
699. ibid., pp. 36–8; *Encyclopaedia Britannica*, Vol. 17, pp. 879–81.
700. Martin, op. cit., p. 43.
701. ibid., p. 44.
702. ibid.
704. Langer, op. cit., p. 1088.
705. ibid., pp. 1088–9.
706. T, 29 September 1941, p. 3.
707. NYT, 17 September 1941, p. 3.
708. Langer, op. cit., p. 1090.
710. See for example *Statesman's Year Book* 1957.
711. See for example NYT, 18 April 1946, p. 4.
712. T, 16 November 1970, p. 8.
713. Newston, Lewis, M., *Texas Yesterday and Today*, p. 142; Bancroft, op. cit., Vol. XVI, *History of North Mexican States and Texas*, Vol. II, 1801–1889, chap. V, p. 211, citing *Texas Law Report 1838*: 6–7, *Nile's Register* lxiii, p. 195; see also Yoakum, H., *History of Texas*.
714. Langer, op. cit., p. 813.

715. ST, 5 January 1986, p. 5.
716. Bancroft, op. cit., Vol. XVI, chapt. XIV, p. 383; Langer, op. cit., p. 814, gives 1 March 1845.
717. T, 9 December 1961, p. 6.
718. *Whittaker's Almanack* 1913.
719. T, 10 December 1963, p. 10; KCA, p. 19778.
720. T, 25 April 1965, p. 7, 28 April 1965, p. 11; *Nationalist*, 28 April 1965.
721. KCA, 1964.
722. ibid.
723. Langer, op. cit., p. 580.
724. Coutald, Caroline, *In Search of Burma*, p. 55.
725. Address given by Dr Sipponondhu Ketudat, Minister of Education, to Diplomatic Missions and International Organizations at Government House, Bangkok, 9 September 1981.
726. T, 25 June 1932, p. 12; NYT, 25 June 1932, p. 1.
727. KCA, p. 27533.
728. ibid., p. 27534–5.
729. NYT, T, 28 April 1960.
730. Exchange of Letters, Termination of United Kingdom Responsibility for the External Relations of Tonga, 19 May 1970, Bs 14/806, 1970–71/Cmnd 4990 viii, 1135.
731. NYT, 5 June 1970.
732. T, 4 June 1970.
734. Pipes, op. cit., p. 298; Langer, op. cit., p. 1031.
735. Pipes, op. cit., p. 299; Langer, op. cit., p. 1032.
736. T, 26 October 1976.
737. T, 31 August 1962, p. 7.
738. *Observer*, NYT, 18 March 1956; NYHT, 19 March 1956; T, NYT, NYHT, FT, 21 March 1956; *Le Monde*, 22 March 1956.
739. NYT, *Scotsman*, 16 June 1956; see also NYHT, G, 31 May 1956.
740. *Le Figaro*, 17 June 1956.
741. *Statesman's Year Book*, 1927; Langer, op. cit., p. 1087.
742. Lewis, Bernard, *The Emergence of Modern Turkey*, London 1961, p. 256.
743. ibid., p. 255–6.
744. G, 28 September 1978; T, IHT, 2 October 1978.
745. *Whittaker's Almanack*, 1913, p. 643; Langer, op. cit., p. 883.
746. T, 9 October 1962.
747. See Browder and Kerensky, op. cit., chap. 7:331, 349, 356,

363; Carr, op. cit., Vol. 1, pp. 298–304; Hrushevsky, Michael, *Ukraine*, pp. 534–9.

748. See for example, *Whittaker's Almanack*, 1925; Langer, op. cit., pp. 971, 1031.

749. Carr, op. cit., p. 304; Pipes, op. cit., p. 298.

750. SWB, 2nd Series, Pt 4, ME/3856/A/5.

751. *Egyptian Gazette*, G, FT, IHT, 3 December 1971.

752. NYT, 3 December 1971.

753. KCA, pp. 16005, 16085.

754. SWB, Pt IV, no. 466, 3 February 1958, p. 1.

755. SWB, Pt IV, no. 484, 24 February 1958.

756. Langer, op. cit., p. 1294.

757. ibid., p. 840.

758. Vincent, op. cit., p. 1460; Steinberg, op. cit., p. 192.

759. Langer, op. cit., p. 849.

760. Delpar, op. cit., p. 415.

761. Bancroft, op. cit., p. 39.

762. Langer, op. cit., p. 843.

763. ibid.

764. Bancroft, op. cit., p. 68.

765. KCA, p. 30641.

766. Langer, op. cit., p. 708.

767. NYT, 12 February 1929, p. 1.

768. ibid.

769. See for example, Langer, op. cit., p. 1002.

770. NYT, 8 June 1929, p. 1.

771. Langer, op. cit., p. 841.

772. Delpar, op. cit., p. 616.

773. Langer, op. cit., p. 842.

774. Delpar, op. cit., p. 147.

775. Steinberg, op. cit.

776. Langer, op. cit., p. 854.

777. ibid., p. 907.

778. KCA, p. 10494.

779. ibid.; Langer, op. cit., p. 1324.

780. Werth, *France, 1940–55*, p. 10.

781. Langer, op. cit., p. 1324.

782. G, 22 July 1954. *Christian Science Monitor*, 21 July 1954 reports 3.30 a.m.; DT, 21 July 1954, reports 2.30 a.m., NYT, 21 July 1954 reports signing ceremony began at 3.42 a.m.; NYHT 21 July 1954 reports signing ceremony completed by 3.50 a.m. The Accords allowed for the temporary division of

Vietnam into northern and southern sectors, to be reunited following free elections. These never took place and the two halves of the country continued as two separate states until reunification in 1975.

783. SWB, Pt. V, no. 505, 1 November 1953, pp. 41–2. The proclamation speech began at 5.00 a.m. GMT.

784. SWB, FE/4893/A3.

785. SWB, FE/4893/A3/1.

786. SWB, FE/4893/A3/6.

787. SWB, 2nd Series, Pt 3, FE/5250, 3 July 1976; see also T, 3 July 1976.

788. G, 1 January 1962; see also KCA, p. 18524.

789. T, 28 September 1962.

790. Langer, op. cit., p. 1307.

791. T, 30 November 1967.

792. ibid.

793. ibid.

794. Langer, op. cit., p. 1021.

795. Strong, op. cit., p. 100. An independent state of Croatia was also created during the Second World War, although it was in effect a German puppet.

796. Langer, op. cit., p. 1021.

797. ibid., p. 973; Singleton, *Twentieth Century Yugoslavia*; McCarney, op. cit., p. 832 reports this date for the independence of Croatia and Slovenia.

798. NYT, 30 October 1918.

799. NYT, 1 November 1918, p. 2, despatch received 31 October 1918.

800. Langer, op. cit., pp. 973–4.

801. ibid.

802. ibid., p. 1021; Singleton, op. cit., p. 66; *Whittaker's Almanack*, 1925 gives 29 November 1918; Langer, op. cit., p. 974, also gives 1 December 1918.

804. Langer, op. cit., p. 1207.

805. NYT, 2 February 1946, p. 4, report of 1 February 1946 quotes 'last night'; Singleton, op. cit., p. 105 gives 31 January 1946; see also Langer, op. cit., p. 1027.

806. KCA, p. 17594.

807. ibid., T, 1 July 1960, p. 12.

808. Langer, op. cit.; *Whittaker's Almanack*.

809. NYT, 12 July 1960, p. 1, quotes Katanga 'declared itself an independent state tonight in a live broadcast'.

810. Langer, op. cit., p. 1270.
811. ibid., p. 1271.
812. ibid., p. 888, 892.
813. T, 24 October 1964.
814. For an outline of this problem see 'The National Horoscope: Mundane Astrology and Political Theory' in Baigent, Campion and Harvey, op. cit., pp. 95–111.
815. See for example, Graves, Robert, *The Greek Myths*, Vol. 2, p. 106.
816. See for example, Lindsay, Jack, *The Origins of Astrology*, chap. 1, 2.
817. ibid., pp. 137–40; Neugebauer, O., Van Hoesen, H. B., *Greek Horoscopes*, pp. 14–16, 161.
818. Tacitus, *Annales*, Bk XII, chap. LXVIII; Campion, N., 'Roman Astrology', in AQ, Vol. 58, no. 1, Spring 1984.
819. See Campion, N., *The Practical Astrologer*, for a summary of the likely reasoning behind this chart, which was discussed at the Astrological Lodge of London history seminar in 1985 by Derek Appleby, Annabella Kitson, Olivia Barclay and Geoffrey Cornelius.
820. See for example, Richard Deacon, *John Dee*, p. 46.
821. *Washington Post*, 3 January 1967, p. 1.
822. *San Francisco Chronicle*, 2 July 1987, p. 1.
823. NYT, 3 January, 1967, p. 24.
824. ibid.
825. Time taken by the author from live transmission.
826. ibid.
827. *Washington Post*, 4 March 1929, quoted *New York Daily Advertiser*, *New York Daily Gazette*, 1 May 1789.
828. For horoscopes with supporting background see Lois Rodden, *The American Book of Charts*, *CAO Times*, Vol. 5, no. 1, p. 21.
829. For reasoning see *Bulletin of Mundane Astrology*, no. 12, p. 9, April 1985, based on sources in Christian Science Monitor, 16–22 March 1985, p. 1, G, 12 March 1984, p. 1; see also Campion, N., *Astrological Chronology for the Soviet Union*.
830. Time taken by the author from live transmission.
830a. ibid.
831. NYT, 2 June 1958; see also Campion, N., *Political, Economic and Social Analysis and Chronology for France: The Fourth Republic, 1946–1958*.
832. DT, 7 January 1959.
833. G, 9 January 1959; see also NYHT, 8 January 1959, *Le Monde*

9 January 1959, suggesting 12.00 noon; see also Campion, N., *Political, Economic and Social Analysis and Chronology for France: The Fifth Republic, 1958–1974.*

834. Fieling, Keith, *History of the Conservative Party.*

835. Cornelius, Geoffrey, 'The Tamworth Manifesto and the Conservative Party', AQ, Vol. 57, no. 5, p. 158, Winter 1983/84.

836. Blake, *The Conservative Party*, p. 60.

837. T, 13 November 1867, p. 5.

838. AQ, Vol. 41, no. 2, p. 35, Summer 1967.

839. Letter to the author from the Bodleian Library, Oxford.

840. AQ, Vol. 41, no. 2, p. 35, Summer 1967.

841. Cole, G. D. H., *British Working Class Politics 1832–1914.*

842. T, 13 February 1906, p. 9.

843. ibid.

844. See the *Times* index for 1906.

845. Leo, Bessie, *Life and Times of Alan Leo*, pp. 110–11.

846. *Birmingham Post*, 1 June 1877.

847. G, 27 March 1981, gives 9.02 a.m.; LBC radio news, 9.00 a.m., 27 March 1981, reported 'a few minutes ago'.

848. Telephone communication to the author from Liberal Party head office. This vote was the second of two. The first was taken at 12.15 p.m.

849. Baigent, Campion, Harvey, op. cit., pp. 291–317.

850. Lilly, William, *Christian Astrology*, p. 96.

851. Carter, op. cit., p. 97; Raphael, *Mundane Astrology*, p. 76; Green, H. S., *Mundane Astrology*, p. 75.

852. Ptolemy, Claudius, *Tetrabiblos*, II:3.

853. Cicero, *De Diviniatione*, II:XLVII; see also Lindsay, op. cit., p. 224.

854. See for example, Hall, Manley Palmer, *The Story of Astrology*, p. 87; McCaffery, Ellen, *Astrology and its Influence in the Western World*, p. 100.

855. Manilius, Marcus, *Astronomica*, 4:774–8.

856. Gleadow, Rupert, *The Origin of the Zodiac*, p. 68.

857. Tarrutius' calculation was probably made soon after the Julian calendar reform, before the anomalies in that system had become apparent. Therefore 21 April Julian in the first century BC corresponds to 21 April Gregorian, and Tarrutius would therefore have believed that the Sun on 21 April in the eighth century BC therefore occupied the same zodiacal longitude as on 21 September in the first century BC.

858. Manilius, op. cit., introduction, pp lxxxii–lxxxiii; Pliny, *De Natura Rerum*, Bk II, XVII:81.

859. Runciman, Steven, *Byzantine Civilisation*, p. 27.

860. Baigent, Campion, Harvey, op. cit., quoting Knappich (the date given on p. 312 is a misprint). See also Pingreee, David, 'The Horoscope of Constantinople' in *Prismata Festchrift*, pp. 305–15.

861. Lilly, op. cit., p. 95; Carter, op. cit., p. 97; Green, op. cit., p. 74; Raphael, op. cit., p. 76.

862. Langer, op. cit., p. 133.

863. Runciman, op. cit., pp. 29–30; see also Langer, op. cit., p. 133; Robinson, Charles Alexander, *Ancient History,* p. 648. N.B. The city was based on the old colony of Byzantium, founded in about the seventh century BC by the Greeks; see Robinson, op. cit., p.148.

864. Prior, Thomas, *Speculum Astrologiae, Universam, Mathematicam, Scientiam etc.*, Vol. 1, p. 813.

865. Runciman, Steven, *The Fall of Constantinople*, p. 138; Nicol, D. M., *The End of the Byzantine Empire*.

866. Lilly's Almanack for 1661 quoted by Alfred Pearce, *The Text Book of Astrology*, p. 272; Leigh, Barry, *Francis Bernard: Astrologer and Physician to James II*, quoting Lilly. Raphael, op. cit., p. 79.

867. Pearce, op. cit., p. 272, quoting Lilly.

868. See Leigh, op. cit.

869. Sepharial, *The Law of Values*.

870. Naylor, John, 'Sensitive Points in Mundane Astrology', in AQ, Vol. 54, no. 1–2, Spring 1980, Summer 1980.

871. Baigent, Campion, Harvey, op. cit., p. 305; see Sepharial, *The Theory of Geodetic Equivalents*.

872. See T, DT, G, 1 April 1965; Wrigglesworth, Harold, *The Astrology of Towns and Cities*.

873. Little, Jeffrey B., and Rhodes, Lucien, *Understanding Wall Street*.

874. Letter from Secretariat Général des Conseils des Communautés Européennes to James Russell, copy in the possession of the author.

875. The event attracted little interest at the time. The *Guardian* carried no mention on either 1 or 2 January 1958. On 1 January 1958, *The Times*, p. 1, carried a report dated 31 December to the effect that the EEC comes into force tomorrow, i.e. 1 January.

877. T, 15 September 1960, p. 11, KCA, p. 17682.

878. NYT, 4 April 1949, p. 1; see also KCA, pp. 9869, 10159, 10192.

879. NYT, 25 August 1949, p. 1.

880. NYT, 27 July 1947, p. 1.

881. Jain, J. P., *A Documentary Study of the Warsaw Pact.*

882. Plato, *Timaeus*, chaps. 21–3, 35–8; Plato, *Republic*, Bk VIII, chaps. 545–6; Adams, J., *The Nuptial Number of Plato*, p. 77; Santillana, G., *The Origins of Scientific Thought*, p. 110; Baigent, Campion, Harvey, op. cit., pp. 115–35.

883. Berosus, *Babyloniaca*, Bk I, chap. 2. Bouché Ledere claimed that Cancer was the horoscope (ascendant) in the Egyptian horoscope of the universe, based on the beginning of the Egyptian year in the summer. See Ptolemy, Tetrabiblos, Loeb edition, note p. 197.

884. Julius Firmicus Maternus, *Mathesis*, Bk III, 1:1–2, 9.

885. Gadbury, John, *Collectio Genitarum*, pp. 1–3.

886. ibid., p. 3.

887. Lilly, op. cit., p. 93.

888. ibid., p. 113.

889. Sepharial, *The World Horoscope*, pp. 25–35.

890. KCA, p. 6991.

891. KCA, p. 7425.

892. T, 27 June 1945, p. 4.

893. *Washington Post*, 25 October 1945, pp. 1, 7.

894. ibid.; NYT, 25 October 1945, p. 1, gives 4.50 p.m.

895. Ussher, James, *The Annals of the World, etc.*, p. 1.

896. ibid., introductory Epistle to the Reader.

897. Carter, Charles, in AQ, Vol. 21, p. 111.

898. Zain, C. C., *Astrological Lore of all ages*, see Campion, Baigent, Harvey, op. cit., p. 474.

899. Baigent, Campion, Harvey, op. cit., pp. 474–5.

900. McIntosh, Christopher, *Eliphas Levi and the French Occult Revival*, pp. 208–11.

901. Dixon, Jeanne, *My Life and Prophecies*, p. 180; see also Wolden, A., *After Nostradamus*, p. 116.

902. Sturgess, Jon, *The Piscean Age and the Aquarian Age*, p. 12.

902a. An antidate to the general mythology concerning the eclipse was provided by the sceptical comments of Ronald Davidson in *AQ*, Vol. 35, no. 2, Vol. 36, no. 3.

903. Stubbs, William, *Constitutional History of England*, Vol. 1, pp. 159–61.

904. See Kemp, Chester, *Journal of Astrological Studies*, no. 1, Fall 1970.

905. Campion, N., *Historical Horoscopes for the United Kingdom*.

906. Blair, Peter Hunter, *Roman Britain and Early England*.

907. Hunt, William, and Poole, Reginald, *Political History of England*, Vol. 1, p. 356. Edgar was hailed as 'king of the Saxons, Mercians and Northumbrians'.

908. ibid., Vol. 2, p. 8.

909. Official information given at site of the battle.

910. Stenton, F. M., *Anglo-Saxon England*, p. 587.

911. Anon., *The History of the Late Revolution in England*, p. 267; see also Clarke, I. W., *The Life of William III, Late King of England and Prince of Orange*, p. 188.

912. Article 1 of the Act of Union between England and Scotland, *Acts of the Parliament of Scotland*, Vol. XI, 1702–7 (29-19-121) p. 201.

913. Privy Council Register, 9 May 1708.

914. George III, Acts 39–40, Chap. 67, Article 1.

915. T, 2 January 1801, p. 3; see also Campion, N., 'A New Chart for the British Monarchy', *Transit*, no. 47, November 1984.

916. Russell, James, in AJ, Vol. III, June 1961; see also T, 6, 7 December 1921, letter to James Russell from Northern Ireland Parliament, copy in possession of the author.

917. Vernadsky, George, *A History of Russia*, Vol. 5, pp. 1–3.

918. Vernadsky, George, and Karpovich, Michael, *A History of Russia*, Vol. 3, p. 330.

919. Kluchovsky, V., *History of Russia*, Vol. 3, p. 61.

920. Browder and Kerensky, op. cit., Vol. 1, chap. 1:23, p. 47.

921. Baigent, Campion, Harvey, op. cit., p. 442.

922. Trotsky, L., *The History of the Russian Revolution*, p. 270. This time was also produced by Rupert Glendow in the 1960s, using Trotsky as the source.

923. Reed, John, *Ten Days That Shook The World*, p. 114. New Zealand astrologer Dennis Frank argues that this legitimization signifies the true birth of the Communist regime, although he does not accept the time of 2.30 a.m. I will be publishing his evidence in the UK in due course.

924. ibid., p. 105.

925. Pipes, op. cit., p. 283, citing Lenin's 'Memorandum on the National Question', 30 December 1922.

926. Carr, op. cit., Vol. 1, p. 401.

927. Pipes, op. cit.; Carr, op. cit., p. 413.

928. ibid.

929. Grant, Ernest A., and Kraum, Ralph, *Astrological Americana*, p. 7.

930. Dodson, Carolyn R., *Horoscopes of the U.S. States and Cities*.

931. Doane, Doris, *Accurate World Horoscopes*, citing C. C. Zain.

931a. Effrein, Laurie, *Common Sense: America's Roots Revisited*.

931b. Clement Hay cited in Grant and Kraum, op. cit., p. 8.

932. Serroti, B., *America's Rising Sign*.

934. Quoted by Vivian Robson, *British Journal of Astrology*, August–October 1932.

935. Penfield, Marc, *Horoscopes of the Western Hemisphere*, p. 14.

936. Armistead, Julian, 'The Second of July', in NCGR Journal, Winter 1985–86, Vol. 4, no. 2, and Winter 1986–87.

937. Baigent, Michael, 'Ebenezer Sibly and the Declaration of Independence, 1776', in AJ, Vol. XXVI, no. 1, Winter 1983–84. *NCGR Journal* Vol. 1, no. 1, Spring 1985.

938. Barry Lynes, *Astroeconomics*, p. 4.

939. Lyne, Barry, *The Next Twenty Years*, 1982 edn, p. 144.

940. See for example, Brogan, Hugh, letter to the *Guardian*, 4 July 1986, p. 16; Becker, Carl, *The Declaration of Independence*, chap. 1; Jensen, Merril, *The Founding of a Nation*, chap. XXV, pp. 687–704; Commager, Henry Steele, and Nevins, Allan, *A Pocket History of the United States*, p. 84.

941. The *Pennsylvania Gazette*, no. 2480, 3 July 1776, cited by Armistead, op. cit.

942. Journals of Congress, Containing the Proceedings from 1 January 1776 to 1 January 1777, p. 239, cited by Armistead, op. cit.

943. Butterfield, Friedlander and Kline, *The Book of Abigail and John: Selected Letters of the Adams Family*, 1762–1784, p. 139, cited by Armistead, op. cit.

944. ibid., p. 142.

945. Ryden (ed.), *Letters to and from Caesar Rodney, 1756–1784*, editor's footnote to Rodney's letter of 4 July 1776.

946. *Dictionary of American Biography*.

947. Smith, Page, *John Adams*, cited by Armistead. (After this passage was written, Armistead developed doubts concerning the 4.00 p.m. chart for historical reasons, and placed greater emphasis on the 12.00 noon chart.)

948. Butterfield *et al.*, op. cit., p. 139, cited by Armistead, op. cit.

949. Becker, op. cit., p. 5.

950. Brogan, op. cit.

951. Ford, Paul Leicester, *The Writings of Thomas Jefferson*, Vol. 1; see also p. 28, note 6.

952. Letter from Elbridge Gerry to General Warren dated 5 July 1776, quoted in Ford, Worthington Chauncey (ed.), *Journals of the Continental Congress*, 1774–1789, Vol. V, p. 516, note 1.

953. See for example Channing, Edward, *A History of the United States*, Vol. III, pp. 204–5; Jensen, op. cit., chap. XXV, pp. 687–704.

954. Hall, Manley Palmer, 'Our National Horoscope' in Grant and Kraum, op. cit., p. 83, originally published in *Wynn's Astrology Magazine*, Vol. 16, no. 3, January 1941.

956. Baigent, op. cit. For biographical details on Sibly see Timson, D., 'Ebenezer Sibly, Freemason Extraordinary' in *Transactions of the Lodge of Research*, no. 2429, Leicester, 1964–65, pp. 62f; Ward, Eric, 'Ebenezer Sibly. A Man of Parts', in *Transactions of the Quatuor Coronati Lodge* — Ars Quatuor Coronatorum, Vol. 71, no. 2076, London 1958, p. 481. Both works cited by Baigent.

957. Sibly, Ebenezer, *New and Complete Illustration of the Occult Sciences*, Vol. II, illustration facing p. 1054.

958. Robson, Vivian, op. cit.

959. Channing, op. cit., p. 205.

960. *Pennsylvania Evening Post*, Tuesday 7/9 July 1776, cited by Armistead, op. cit.

961. Langer, op. cit., pp. 473, 562.

962. Jung, *Collected Works*, Vol. 10.

963. The Centiloquy of Claudius Ptolemy in the *Tetrabiblos*, trans. Ashmand, Aphorism 1.

964. ibid., Aphorism VIII.

965. Carter, op. cit., p. vii.

966. See for example, Leo, Alan, 'Individual Horoscopes and National Destiny' in MA, Vol. 8, no. 7, July 1911, p. 282.

967. Carter, op. cit., p. vii.

968. Cicero, *De Diviniatione*, II: xlvii.

969. Addey, John, *Astrology Reborn*, p. 12.

970. Manilius, op. cit., Bk 4:585–807.

971. ibid., Bk 4:803–17.

972. Ptolemy, *Tetrabiblos*, II:3, see also I:18.

973. Al Biruni, *The Book of Instruction in the Elements of the Art of Astrology*, pp. 236–40, 357, 365, 392.

974. Lilly, op. cit., pp. 73–99.

975. Raphael, op. cit., pp. 74–9.

976. H. S. Green, op. cit., pp. 73–5.

977. Sepharial, *The World Horoscope*, p. 35.

978. Carter, op. cit., pp. 100–1.
979. Cheiro, *The Book of World Prophecies*.
980. Alice Bailey, *The Destiny of the Nations*, p. 67.
981. Vivian Robson, 'The World Horoscope', BJA, Vol. 26, no. 1, Oct. 1932, p. 4.
982. E. H. Bailey, 'The Universal Horoscope', BJA, Vol. 27, no. 6, March 1934, p. 272.
983. Alan Leo writing in MA, Vol. 8 (new series), no. 7, July 1911, p. 272.
984. Bessie Leo writing in MA, Vol. 36, no. 11, November 1925, p. 322.
985. Ussher, op. cit., Epistle to the Reader.
986. North, J. D., *Horoscopes and History*, p. 167.
987. Lightfoot, John, *A Few and New Observations, etc.*, p. 4.
988. Daniel, Glynn, *The Idea of Prehistory*, pp. 18–19.
989. Pingreee, David, *The Thousands of Abu Ma'shar*, pp. 34, 38.
990. Fagan, Cyril, *Zodiacs Old and New*, pp. 12–14.
991. Pingree, op. cit., p. 38; Pingree, David, and Kennedy, E. S., *The Astrological History of Masha'Allah*, p. 75. Abu Ma'shar and Masha'Allah also speculated on a date of 3360 BC for the deluge. See Pingree and Kennedy, op. cit., pp. 77–8.
992. Ussher, op. cit., p. 3.
993. North, op. cit., pp. 167–9.
994. Carter, M. W., and Moghissi, A. A., 'Three Decades of Nuclear Testing' in *Health Physics*, Vol. 33, pp. 55–71, July 1977; Springer, D. L., and Kinnaman, R. L., 'Seismic Source Summary for US Underground Nuclear Explosions, 1961–1970', in *Bulletin for the Seismological Society of America*, Vol. 61, pp. 1073–98, August 1971; Bolt, Bruce, *Nuclear Explosions and Earthquakes*; see also KCA and the SIPRI Year Books for annual records.
995. Lawrence, David, *Men and Atoms*.
996. Bolt, op. cit.; Carter and Moghissi, op. cit.
997. Harding, Michael, in ISCWA *Bulletin of Mundane Astrology*, no. 9, p. 10, July 1984.
998. *Parnell's History of the Twentieth Century*.
999. G, 5 August 1985, p. 15.
1000. Anniversary report on BBC London Regional News, 2 October 1984.
1001. Baigent, Campion, Harvey, op. cit., p. 205.
1002. See *The Illustrated History of Air Flight*.
1003. KCA, p. 15791.

1004. KCA, p. 18033.

1005. KCA, p. 18099.

1006. KCA, p. 23497.

1007. KCA, p. 23498.

1008. Kennedy and Pingree, op. cit., pp. 44–6, 95–6.

1009. North, J. D., op. cit., pp. 163–73.

1010. Originally published in Butler, J., *A Brief (but true) Account of the Certain Year, Moneth, Day and Minute of the Birth of Jesus Christ* (1671). The chart is the version taken from Sibley op. cit., p. 892; see also *Astrologers' Magazine*, Vol. X, no. 12, 1890; MA., Vol. 8, no. 7, July 1911.

1011. Addey, John, *Selected Writings*.

1012. Baigent, Campion, Harvey, op. cit., Appendix III.

1013. Herschel's account published in *Philosophical Transactions*, 1781, quoted in Ley, *Watchers of the Skies*, p. 399. Another source claimed that the planet was discovered at 10.30 p.m. LMT 'according to Herschel's diary', but it seems that the author in fact took the midway point between 10.00 and 11.00 p.m.

1014. Ley, op. cit., p. 411.

1015. See editorial by Michael Harding in *Transit*, no. 42, p. 1, August 1983.

1016. Ley, op. cit., pp. 425–6, quoting verbatim account in article by Clyde Tombaugh, published as 'Reminiscences of the Discovery of Pluto' in *Sky and Telescope*, March 1960.

1017. Patrick Moore, 'The Naming of Pluto', in *Sky and Telescope*, November 1984, citing primary sources. See also AQ, Vol. 58, no. 4, Winter 1984/5, p. 227.

1018. Account quoted in Chiron Ephemeris, published by *CAO Times*, p. 4.

1019. See *Bulletin of Mundane Astrology*, no. 16, July 1987.

1020. Smith, Paul (ed.), *Letters of Delegates to Congress 1774–1789*, facsimile of letter on p. 380.

1021. Ford, Worthington Chauncey, op. cit., Vol. 5, 510–18.

1022. Letter from Paul Smith, Director of Manuscript Division, Library of Congress, to Ron Howland, 6 May 1987, citing Smith (ed.), op. cit., 4: 164–5, 364–5, 379, 381–3, copy in possession of author.

1023. ibid.

1024. See Campion, *Documentary Sources for Book of World Horoscopes*.

1025. Ford, op. cit., Vol. 5, p. 515.

1026. ibid., p. 515, note 1, New York, voted in favour of the Declaration on 9 July (see Ford, *Writings of Thomas Jefferson*, p. 18).

1027. Hunt, Gaillard, *History of the United States*.

1028. Allen, Herbert S., *Patriot in Purple*, p. 228.

1029. Penfield, op. cit., p. 14.

1030. Hunt, op. cit.

1031. Clark, Jonas, *Opening of the War of the Revolution*.

1032. Grant and Kraum, op. cit., pp. 21–3, citing *Americana Encyclopaedia*.

1033. Grant and Kraum, op. cit., p. 23, citing 'Freedom's City' by Burke Davis in the *Raleigh News and Observer*, 26 May 1946.

1034. Grant and Kraum, op. cit., p. 21.

1035. ibid., p. 30.

1036. ibid., p. 31.

1036a. Shelagh Kendal, 'An American Anniversary', in *Prediction*, October 1987, pp. x–xii.

1037. ibid., p. 32.

1037a. *Daily Mail*, 17 September 1987, p. 10.

1038. *New York Daily Gazette*, 1 May 1789.

1039. *New York Daily Advertiser*, 1 May 1789.

1040. *BBC Summary of World Broadcasts*, Part IV, no. 438, 16 September 1960.

1041. NYT, 9 March 1958, pp. 19:2.

1042. NYT, 27 December 1961, p. 1:7.

1043. President Truman's appointments book, photocopy by Ron Howland in the author's possession.

1044. Clause 310a of the National Security Act, photocopy by Ron Howland in the author's possession.

1045. *The MacMillan Dictionary of Astronomy*.

NOTE ON SOURCE MATERIAL
AND LIBRARIES

Initial research for this book was undertaken at the British Library Main Reading Room, Great Russell Street, London WC1, which, as a copyright library has one of the most extensive collections of books in the country. The Official Publications Library at the same address contains records of all British Government activities, although certain official documents were also inspected at the Public Record office, Chancery Lane, London WC2. The major part of the research focused on press reports for which the Press Library at the Royal Institute of International Affairs, 10 St James' Square, London SW14 4LE, and the British Library Newspaper Division, Colindale Avenue, London NW9 5HE, were essential.

The *Summary of World Broadcasts* published by the BBC from monitoring foreign radio has also proved invaluable, and may be contacted via the BBC Data Inquiry Service, 4 Cavendish Square, London W1A 1AA, Room 3, The Langham, Portland Place, London W1 1AA, or The Written Archives Officer, BBC Written Archives Centre, Caversham Park, Reading, RG4 8TZ (0234-472742).

Specialist data was acquired from a number of sources. For example, data concerning nuclear energy was obtained from the Library and Information Centre, United Kingdom Atomic Energy Authority, 11 Charles II St, London SW14 4QP (01-930 5454).

SELECT BIBLIOGRAPHY

OFFICIAL PUBLICATIONS

United Kingdom

Hansard (Parliamentary Reports, Official Reports), Fifth Series, House of Commons, 1922, Vol. 151, 152.

Correspondence Respecting Affairs in Egypt, 1922, Cmnd 1592 (Parliamentary Accounts and Papers, 1922, Vol. XXIII, 25).

Exchange of Notes regarding Relations between the United Kingdom of Great Britain and Northern Ireland and the State of Kuwait, Kuwait, 19 June 1961, 1960–61, Cmnd 1409, Vol. XXXIV.

Agreement between Her Majesty's Government in the United Kingdom of Great Britain and Northern Ireland and the Government of the Maldive Islands (with exchange of letters), Colombo, 26 July 1965, 1964–65, Cmnd 2749, Vol. XXXIV, p. 409.

Exchange of Letters. Termination of United Kingdom Responsibility for the External Relations of Tonga, 19 May 1970, BS/14/806, 1970–71. Cmnd viii, 1135.

Great Britain

Privy Council Register, 1708.

George III, Acts, 39–40.

Scotland

Acts of Parliament of Scotland, Vol. XI, 1702–1707.

France

Collection Générale Des Loix, Proclamations, Instructions, Et Autre Actes Du Pouvoir Executif, Paris 1792.

Overture de la Convention National, Bordeaux, 1792. Journal Officiel de la Convention National: La Convention National 1792, Paris 1792.

United States
Journals of Congress, Containing the Proceedings from 1 January 1776 to 1 January 1777, Published by Order of Congress, Vol. II, York-Town, Pennsylvania, 1778.

NEWSPAPERS

Birmingham Post (UK)
La Bourse Egyptienne (Egypt)
Christian Science Monitor, London Edition (UK)
Combat (France)
Daily Express (UK)
Daily Herald (UK)
Daily Mail (UK)
Daily Telegraph (UK)
Dawn
Egyptian Gazette (Egypt)
Egyptian Mail (Egypt)
Le Figaro (France)
Financial Times (UK)
Guardian, formerly *Manchester Guardian* (UK)
The Hindu (India)
International Herald Tribune (USA)
Irish Times (Eire)
Le Monde (France)
The Nationalist (Tanganyika)
New York Herald Tribune (European Edition)
New York Times (USA)
Observer (UK)
Rand Daily Mail (South Africa)
San Francisco Chronicle (USA)
The Scotsman (UK)
Le Soir (France)
La Stampa (Italy)
Straits Times (Malaysia)
Sunday News (Tanganyika)
Sunday Telegraph (UK)
Sunday Times (Malaysia)
Sunday Times (Singapore)

Sunday Times (UK)
The Times (UK)
Times of Ceylon (Sri Lanka)
Washington Post (USA)

PERIODICAL REFERENCE WORKS

Observer Foreign News Service
BBC Daily Digest of World Broadcasts, renamed as *BBC Summary of World Broadcasts*
Keesing's Contemporary Archives
Whittaker's Almanack
Statesman's Year Book

ASTROLOGICAL JOURNALS

Astrology, pub. Astrological Lodge of London
Astrological Journal, pub. the Astrological Association
British Journal of Astrology
Bulletin of Mundane Astrology, pub. Institute for the Study of Cycles in World Affairs (ISCWA Bulletin)
CAO Times, New York
Journal of Astrological Studies, pub. International Society for Astrological Research
Modern Astrology
NCGR Journal, pub. National Council for Geocosmic Research
Transit, pub. the Astrological Association

ARTICLES AND BOOKS

Abdullah, Mohammed Morry, *The United Arab Emirates: A Modern History*, London 1978.
Addey, John, *Selected Writings* (London, 1974).
——, *Astrology Reborn* (London, 1978).
Al Biruni, *The Book of Introduction in the Elements of the Art of Astrology* (Ghaznahm, 1029), trans. R. Ramsay Wright (London, 1934).
Allen, Herbert S., *Patriot in Purple* (New York, 1965).
Anon., *The History of the Late Revolution in England* (London, 1689).
Astraude, Le Duc, *Les Petits États D'Europe* 3rd edn, (Nice, 1938).
——, *La Principauté de Monaco* (Nice, 1932).

Atkin, Ronald, *Revolution: Mexico 1910–1920* (London, 1969).

Baigent, M., 'Ebenezer Sibly and the Signing of the Declaration of Independence' in *The Astrological Journal*, Vol. XXVI, no. 1, Winter 1983–4; *NCGR Journal*, Vol. 4, no. 1, Spring 1985.

Baigent, M., Campion, N. and Harvey, C., *Mundane Astrology: An Introduction to the Astrology of Nations and Organizations* (Wellingborough, 1984).

Bailey, Alice, *The Destiny of the Nations* (New York and London) 1949

Bailey, E. H., 'The Universal Horoscope', in *The British Journal of Astrology*, Vol. 27, no. 6, March 1934, p. 107.

Bancroft, Hubert Howe, *Collected Works* (San Francisco, 1887).

Bar-Zohar, Michael, *Ben Gurion*, trans. Peretz Kidron (London, 1978).

Barbault, André, *La Prevision Astrologique* (Paris, 1986).

Becker, Carl, *The Declaration of Independence* (New York, 1966).

Bethell, Lord, *The War Hitler Won, September 1939* (London, 1979).

Bevan, Andrew, 'The National Chart of Norway', in *CAO Times* Vol. 6, no. 1, 1984.

Bilmaris, Alfred, *A History of Latvia* (Westport, Ct., 1951).

Bizzaro, Salvatore, *Historical Dictionary of Chile* (Princeton, 1972).

Blair, Peter Hunter, *Roman Britain and Early England* (London, 1963).

Blake, Robert, *The Conservative Party from Peel to Churchill* (London 1970).

Boak, Arthur E. and Sinnigen, William, *A History of Rome to AD 565* (London, 1973).

Bolt, Bruce, *Nuclear Explosions and Earthquakes* (San Francisco, 1976).

Bowder, R., Kerensky, A., *The Russian Provisional Government 1917: Documents* (Stanford, 1961).

Briggs, Donald C. and Alisky, Marvin, *Historical Dictionary of Mexico* (Princeton, 1976).

Brissaud, André, *The Nazi Secret Service* (London, 1974).

Bulgarian Academy of Science (ed.), *Information Bulgaria* (Oxford, 1985).

Butterfield, Friedlander Kline (ed.), *The Book of Abigail and John; Selected Letters of the Adams Family 1762–1784* (Harvard, 1963).

Campion, N., *British Foreign Policy with Particular Reference to the Strategic Importance of Malaysia and Singapore in the Period Immediately Following Independence (1961–1963)*, unpublished thesis in the University of London, 1976.

_____, *An Introduction to the History of Astrology* (London, 1982).

_____, 'Roman Astrology' in *Astrology*, Vol. 58, no. 1, Spring 1984.

_____, 'A New Chart for the British Monarchy?', *Transit*, no. 47, November 1984.

_____, *Historical and Chronological Analysis for Malaya 1957–1963, Malaysia 1963–1974*, unpublished research, ISCWA, 1985.

_____, *Political, Economic and Social Analysis and Chronology for France: The Fifth Republic, 5 October 1958 to 1974*, unpublished research, ISCWA, 1985.

_____, *Political, Economic and Social Analysis and Chronology for France: The Fourth Republic, 1946–1958*, unpublished research, ISCWA, 1985.

_____, *Political Analysis and Chronology for Germany: The Third Reich, 1933–1945*, unpublished research, ISCWA, 1985.

_____, *Documentary Sources for the Book of World Horoscopes* (Bristol, 1987).

Carr, E. H., *The Bolshevik Revolution*, 3 vols. (Middlesex, 1966).

Carter, Charles, *An Introduction to Political Astrology* (London, 1951).

Carter, M. W. and Moghissi, A. A., 'Three Decades of Modern Testing' in *Health Physics* Vol. 33, pp. 55–71, July 1971.

Channing, Edward, *A History of the United States*, 6 vols. (New York, 1977).

Cheiro, *The Book of World Prophecies* (London, 1925).

Cicero, *De Diviniatione*, trans. W. A. Falconer (London, 1979).

Clark, Jonas, *Opening of the War of the Revolution, 19 April 1775* (Boston, 1875).

Clarke, C. M. H., *A History of Australia*, 2 vols. (Melbourne, 1975).

Clarke, I. W., *The Life of William III, Late King of England and Prince of Orange* (London, 1703).

Cole, G. D. H., *British Working Class Politics 1832–1914* (London, 1965).

Collier, Richard, *1940: The World In Flames* (London, 1979).

Cooper, Matthew, and Lucas, James, *Hitler's Elite* (London, 1975).

Daniel, Glynn, *The Idea of Prehistory* (Middlesex, 1962).

Davies, Norman, *God's Playground: A History of Poland*, 2 vols., (Oxford, 1981).

Deacon, Richard, *John Dee* (London, 1968).

Delpar, Helen (ed.), *Encyclopaedia of Latin America* (London, 1974).

Dio Cassius, *Roman History* 9 vols., trans. E. Cary, (Cambridge Mass., 1933).

Dixon, Jeanne, *My Life and Prophecies* (London, 1969).

Dmytryshyn, Basil, *U.S.S.R.: A Concise History* (New York, 1965).

Doane, Doris Chase, *Accurate World Horoscopes* (Tempe, Az., 1984).

Dodson, Carolyn R., *Horoscopes of the U.S. States and Cities* (San Diego, 1980).

Dunn, D., Elwood, Holsoe, and Svend, E., *Historical Dictionary of Liberia* (London, 1985).

Efrein, Laurie, *Common Sense: America's Roots Revisited* (New York, 1987).

Fagan, Cyril, *Zodiacs Old and New* (London, 1951).

Feiling, Keith, *History of the Tory Party, 1670–1714* (Oxford, 1924).

_____, *The Second Tory Party, 1714–1832*

Fest, Joachim, *Hitler* (London, 1974).

Forbes, Archibald, *William of Germany: A Succinct Biography* (London, 1888).

Ford, Paul Leicester, *The Writings of Thomas Jefferson*, 10 vols. (New York, 1893).

Ford, S. Harrison, *Czechoslovakia in European History* (London, 1965).

Ford, Worthington Chauncey (ed.), *Journals of the Continental Congress*, 1774–1789.

Fullard, Harold; Treharne, R. F. (ed.), *Muir's Historical Atlas*, 6th edn (London, 1963).

Gadbury, John, *Collectio Genitarum* (London, 1662).

Gauquelin, Michel and Françoise, *Birth and Planetary Data Gathered Since 1949*, Series A, Vol. 5, *Actors and Politicians* (Paris, 1970).

Gersa, Louis, *Woodrow Wilson and the Rebirth of Poland* (New Haven, 1953).

Gjerset, Knut, *History of Iceland* (London, 1922).

Glaise-Horstenau, E. Von, *The Collapse of the Austro-Hungarian Empire* (London, 1950).

Gleadow, Rupert, *The Origin of the Zodiac* (London, 1968).

Goering, Herman, *Germany Reborn* (Berlin, 1934).

Grant, Ernest A., Kraum, Ralph, *Astrological Americana* (Tempe, Az., 1949).

Graves, Robert, *The Greek Myths*, 2 vols. (London, 1962).

Green, H. S., *Mundane Astrology* (London, *c.* 1900).

Hall, Manley Palmer, 'Our National Horoscope' in Grant and Kraum, *Astrological Americana*.

_____, *The Story of Astrology* (Los Angeles, 1933).

Halliday, Fred, Molyneux, Maxine, *The Ethiopian Revolution* (London, 1972).

Hibbert, Christopher, *The French Revolution* (Middlesex, 1980).